CW00925703

The Cambridge Companion to

THE AGE OF NERO

The age of Nero has appealed to the popular imagination more than any other period of Roman history. This volume provides a lively and accessible guide to the various representations and interpretations of Emperor Nero as well as to the rich literary, philosophical, and artistic achievements of his eventful reign. The major achievements of the period in the fields of literature, governance, architecture, and art are freshly described and analyzed, and special attention is paid to the reception of Nero in the Roman and Christian eras of the first centuries CE and beyond. Written by an international team of leading experts, the chapters provide students and non-specialists with clear and comprehensive accounts of the most important trends in the study of Neronian Rome. They also offer numerous original insights into the period, and open new areas of study for scholars to pursue.

Shadi Bartsch is the Helen A. Regenstein Distinguished Service Professor in Classics at the University of Chicago. Her work focuses on the literature and philosophy of the Neronian period in Rome. She is also the inaugural director of the Stevanovich Institute on the Formation of Knowledge, an initiative to study the cultural and historical roots of different forms of knowledge, and she held a Guggenheim Fellowship in 2007–8. Her most recent books are *The Mirror of the Self* (2006) and *Persius: A Study in Food, Philosophy, and the Figural* (2015).

Kirk Freudenburg is Brooks and Suzanne Ragen Professor of Classics at Yale University. His major publications include *The Walking Muse: Horace on the Theory of Satire* (1993), *Satires of Rome: Threatening Poses from Lucilius to Juvenal* (Cambridge, 2001), (edited) *The Cambridge Companion to Roman Satire* (Cambridge, 2005), and (edited) *Oxford Readings in Classical Studies: Horace's Satires and Epistles* (2009).

Cedric Littlewood is an associate professor in the Department of Greek and Roman Studies at the University of Victoria, British Columbia. He is the author of *Self-Representation and Illusion in Senecan Tragedy* (2004).

The Cambridge Companion to

THE AGE OF NERO

Edited by

Shadi Bartsch

University of Chicago, Illinois

Kirk Freudenburg

Yale University, Connecticut

Cedric Littlewood

University of Victoria, British Columbia

CAMBRIDGE
UNIVERSITY PRESS

University Printing House, Cambridge CB2 8BS, United Kingdom

One Liberty Plaza, 20th Floor, New York, NY 10006, USA

477 Williamstown Road, Port Melbourne, VIC 3207, Australia

314–321, 3rd Floor, Plot 3, Splendor Forum, Jasola District Centre, New Delhi – 110025, India

79 Anson Road, #06–04/06, Singapore 079906

Cambridge University Press is part of the University of Cambridge.

It furthers the University's mission by disseminating knowledge in the pursuit of education, learning, and research at the highest international levels of excellence.

www.cambridge.org
Information on this title: www.cambridge.org/9781107052208
DOI: 10.1017/9781107280489

First published 2017

Printed in the United Kingdom by TJ International Ltd. Padstow Cornwall

A catalogue record for this publication is available from the British Library.

Library of Congress Cataloging-in-Publication Data
NAMES: Bartsch, Shadi, 1966– editor. | Freudenburg, Kirk, 1961– editor. | Littlewood, C. A. J. (Cedric A. J.), editor.
TITLE: The Cambridge companion to the age of Nero / edited by Shadi Bartsch, University of Chicago; Kirk Freudenburg, Yale University, Connecticut; Cedric Littlewood, University of Victoria, British Columbia.
OTHER TITLES: Age of Nero
DESCRIPTION: Cambridge ; New York, NY : Cambridge University Press, 2018. | Includes bibliographical references and index.
IDENTIFIERS: LCCN 2017024676 | ISBN 9781107052208
SUBJECTS: LCSH: Nero, Emperor of Rome, 37–68. | Rome – History – Nero, 54–68. | Rome – Intellectual life. | Latin literature – History and criticism. | Art, Roman. | Architecture, Roman – History.
CLASSIFICATION: LCC DG285 .C35 2018 | DDC 937/.07–dc23
LC record available at https://lccn.loc.gov/2017024676

ISBN 978-1-107-05220-8 Hardback
ISBN 978-1-107-66923-9 Paperback

Contents

Illustrations

Contributors

ANTHONY A. BARRETT
Department of Classics, Near Eastern, and Religious Studies
University of British Columbia

SHADI BARTSCH
Department of Classics
University of Chicago

CATHARINE EDWARDS
Department of History, Classics and Archaeology
Birkbeck, University of London

KIRK FREUDENBURG
Department of Classics
Yale University

DONATIEN GRAU
Guest Curator, Getty Museum

ERIK GUNDERSON
Department of Classics
University of Toronto

J. ALBERT HARRILL
Department of History
Ohio State University

DANIEL HOOLEY
Department of Classical Studies
University of Missouri-Columbia

EUGENIO LA ROCCA
Scienze dell'Antichità
Universita di Roma "La Sapienza"

MATTHEW LEIGH
Faculty of Classics
St Anne's College, Oxford University

CEDRIC LITTLEWOOD
Department of Greek and Roman Studies
University of Victoria

CARLOS F. NOREÑA
Department of History
University of California, Berkeley

JOSIAH OSGOOD
Department of Classics
Georgetown University

JOHN POLLINI
Departments of History and Art History
University of Southern California

ELENA RUSSO
Department of German and Romance Languages and Literatures
Johns Hopkins University

PETER STACEY
Department of History
University of California, Los Angeles

CHIARA TORRE
Dipartimento di Studi Letterari, Filologici e Linguistici
Università degli Studi di Milano

ERIC VARNER
Department of Art History
Emory University

CAROLINE VOUT
Faculty of Classics
Christ's College, Cambridge University

GARETH WILLIAMS
Department of Classics
Columbia University

MARTIN M. WINKLER
Department of Modern and Classical Languages
George Mason University

Acknowledgments

The editors would like to acknowledge the helpful report received from our anonymous reviewer at Cambridge University Press as well as thank the contributors for their patience during an unusually long process of fruition. True to form, Nero defeated our expectations in refusing to let us, like Seneca, retire from dancing attendance upon him for as long as possible. We hope the outcome will be of appropriately dramatic interest.

We extend thanks as well to our copy-editor at Cambridge University Press and to our editor, Michael Sharp, and editorial assistant, Emma Collison, for their assistance with this volume.

Timeline of Events

BCE

49	Julius Caesar crosses the Rubicon and invades Italy.
48	Caesar defeats Pompey at the battle of Pharsalus. Pompey is murdered in Egypt.
47	Caesar is appointed dictator for ten years.
44	Caesar is murdered on the Ides of March by Brutus, Cassius, and their conspirators. The Senate recognizes Octavian as his heir, but Mark Antony refuses to cooperate.
43	Octavian and the consuls of 43 defeat Mark Antony at Mutina, but both consuls are killed. Octavian is made consul and establishes the second triumvirate, an alliance with Mark Antony and the wealthy Lepidus. They kill their enemies.
42	Caesar is deified. Octavian and Antony at Philippi defeat Brutus and Cassius, who commit suicide.
38	Octavian marries Livia Drusilla (b. 58), mother of Tiberius and of Nero Claudius Drusus, with whom she was pregnant when divorced by Tiberius Claudius Nero.
32	Hostilities lead to the collapse of the triumvirate/Mark Antony divorces Octavia.
31	The Battle of Actium occurs on September 2, with Octavian and Agrippa triumphant over Mark Antony and Cleopatra.
30	Mark Antony and Cleopatra commit suicide.
29	The Forum of Caesar is constructed in Rome
27	Octavian "transfers the state to the Roman people" and takes the name Augustus. The first Pantheon is built in Rome and dedicated by Marcus Agrippa.
19	The Arch of Augustus is built in Rome to commemorate victory over the Parthians.
17	Augustus adopts Agrippa's and Julia's two sons, Gaius and Lucius, as his own sons.

11	Tiberius marries Julia, Augustus' daughter.
9	Augustus' *Ara Pacis* is dedicated in Rome.
6	Tiberius retires to Rhodes.
4	Seneca and Yeshua (Jesus) are both born.
2	Augustus inaugurates the Temple of Mars Ultor in Rome to commemorate his victory at the Battle of Philippi in 42 BCE. Tiberius and Julia divorce; Julia is exiled.
CE	
2	Tiberius returns to Rome.
4	Gaius dies. Augustus adopts Tiberius, and Tiberius adopts his nephew Germanicus.
14	Augustus dies at the age of seventy-six. Tiberius succeeds him. Agrippa Postumus is executed.
26	Tiberius retires to Capri. Sejanus is left in charge of the administration of the empire.
30	Yeshua (Jesus) is crucified.
31	Sejanus is executed for conspiracy against Tiberius.
32 or 36	Saul of Tarsus has a conversion on the road to Damascus and becomes Paul, the follower of Christos.
34	The poet Persius is born.
37	Tiberius dies; Caligula ascends the throne. Nero is born on December 15 to Cn. Domitius Ahenobarbus and Agrippina the Younger, sister of Caligula.
39	Caligula exiles Nero's mother, Agrippina the Younger. Messalina bears Caligula's uncle, Claudius, a daughter (Octavia). Lucan at Corduba is born in Spain.
41	Caligula is murdered on January 24, and Claudius ascends the throne. Seneca is banished from Rome on a charge of adultery (and spends his time writing the three *Consolations*). Messalina bears Claudius a son (Britannicus). Claudius allows the return of Agrippina the Younger.
48	Messalina is put to death for promiscuity and conspiring against Claudius.
49	Claudius marries his niece Agrippina the Younger. Seneca is brought back from exile to be tutor to Nero.
50	Emperor Claudius adopts Nero (Agrippina's son). Nero is now Nero Claudius Caesar Drusus Germanicus. Claudius names Nero as his successor, and Nero marries Claudius' daughter, Octavia.
50–1	Paul meets with the Jerusalem church over whether Gentile converts have to be circumcised. Paul claims that Peter, James, and John accepted his mission to the Gentiles at this meeting.

51 Nero is proclaimed an adult in 51 at the age of fourteen. He is appointed proconsul, addresses the Senate, appears in public with Claudius, and shows up in coinage.

54 Claudius dies (possibly poisoned by Agrippina). Nero becomes emperor at age sixteen, taking the name Nero Claudius Caesar Augustus Germanicus. Seneca and Burrus, the prefect of the guard, are his tutors. Coinage shows Nero and his mother Agrippina together, unusual in the Roman world. Agrippina scandalously tries to sit down next to Nero while he meets with an Armenian envoy, but Seneca stops her. Sometime this year or next Seneca publishes the *Apocolocyntosis*, and in this year or the next, Seneca writes the *de Clementia*, addressed to Nero.

55 Nero murders his brother Britannicus on February 12, one day before his official entry into adulthood.

56 Tacitus (d. after 117 CE) is born; he will write the *Annales* about half a century after Nero's death.

57 Paul is arrested in Jerusalem and held for two years. Upon his release, he exercises his right to be judged in Rome.

58 War breaks out with Parthia.

59 Nero murders his mother Agrippina, who was becoming increasingly intrusive. Seneca writes a letter for him explaining his actions to the Senate. The Stoic Thrasea Paetus walks out of the meeting.

60 Nero establishes the quinquennial Neronia, a festival of music, oratory, and poetry. Lucan praises him in a panegyric. Boudica, a queen in Britannia, leads a revolt, but is defeated in 61. Paul arrives in Rome and is rearrested for two years.

62 Nero marries his mistress Poppaea Sabina, divorcing (and murdering) Octavia. Prefect of the guard Burrus dies. Seneca asks for permission to retire from public affairs (and probably starts writing the *Epistulae Morales*). The satirist Persius dies from a stomach ailment.

63 The Parthian king Tiridates lays his crown before an image of Nero, signifying he is a subject of Rome. Thrasea Paetus stops attending meetings of the Senate at all.

64 The great fire of Rome breaks out on the night of July 18, and burns over five days, destroying or damaging ten of the fourteen Roman districts. The fire is followed by the persecution of the Christians. Nero creates a new urban development plan and starts building the Domus Aurea. On its grounds is the Colossus of Nero. Nero sings for a public audience in Naples, his first public performance.

64–8	According to the Acts of Paul, Nero condemns Paul to death by decapitation at some point in this four-year period. It is unclear what Paul's actual fate was.
65	Work begins on the Domus Aurea and the Colossus of Nero (modified to the Colossus Solis after Nero's death by Vespasian). The Circus Maximus in Rome is rebuilt to hold 250,000.
	The Pisonian Conspiracy to assassinate Nero fails. Seneca (despite his probable innocence) is forced to commit suicide, as are writers Petronius and Lucan. The quinquennial Neronia is held again, and Nero sings.
	A pregnant Poppaea dies after being fatally kicked in the stomach by Nero.
66	The first Jewish–Roman war breaks out, which ends in 73 with Roman victory. Thrasea Paetus is forced to commit suicide, as is another Stoic, Barena Soranus (probably in the same year). Helvidius Priscus is exiled.
	A spectacle of Tiridates' investment as king of Armenia is staged in Rome.
67	Nero participates in the Olympic Games at Olympia, racing a chariot and singing and acting. He wins all the prizes.
	Nero marries Statilia Messalina.
	Nero goes on an extended tour of Greece with many singing performances. He tries to dig a canal through the isthmus of Corinth, but the project fails.
68	Vindex leads a revolt; Galba's troops in Spain hail Galba as emperor. Nero is forced to commit suicide on June 9 (the end of the Julio-Claudian dynasty). Year of the four emperors begins (Galba, Otto, Vittelius, Vespasian).
69	Vespasian is proclaimed emperor. Suetonius is born (d. after 122 CE), whose *Lives of the 12 Caesars* will come out more than half a century after Nero's death.
72	Vespasian begins construction of the Colosseum in Rome, partly to cover up the Domus Aurea.
80	Titus officially opens the Colosseum in Rome with a 100-day gladiator spectacular.

Abbreviations

AE	L'Année Epigraphique (1888–)
CCSL	Corpus Christianorum, series Latina (1953–)
CIL	Corpus Inscriptionum Latinarum (1863–)
EA	Epigraphica Anatolia
IG	Inscriptiones Graecae (1873–)
ILS	H. Dessau, Inscriptiones Latinae Selectae (1892–1916)
NOAB	B. M. Metzger and R. E. Murphy, The New Oxford Annotated Bible with the Apocrypha: An Ecumenical Study Bible (1994)
NYRB	New York Review of Books
OBC	J. Barton and J. Muddimann, The Oxford Bible Commentary (2001)
OCB	B. M. Metzger and M. D. Coogan Oxford Companion to the Bible (1993)
OCD	S. Hornblower and A. Spawforth Oxford Classical Dictionary (3rd edition 1966)
ODWR	J. Bowker, The Oxford Dictionary of World Religions (1997)
OLD	A. Souter, J. M. Wylie, and P. G. W. Glare et al. Oxford Latin Dictionary (1982)
PIR[2]	E. Groag and A. Stein et al. Prosopographia Imperii Romani Saeculi I, II, III (2nd edition 1933–)
RE	A. Pauly, G. Wissowa, and W. Kroll, Real-Encyclop ädie der klassischen Altertumswissenschaft (1893–)
RIC[2]	C. H. V. Sutherland and R. A. G. Carson, Roman Imperial Coinage (2nd edition 1984)
SEG	Supplementum Epigraphicum Graecum
SNTSMS	Society for New Testament Studies Monograph Series
SVF	H. von Arnim, Stoicorum Veterum Fragmenta (1903–)

Julio-Claudian Family Tree

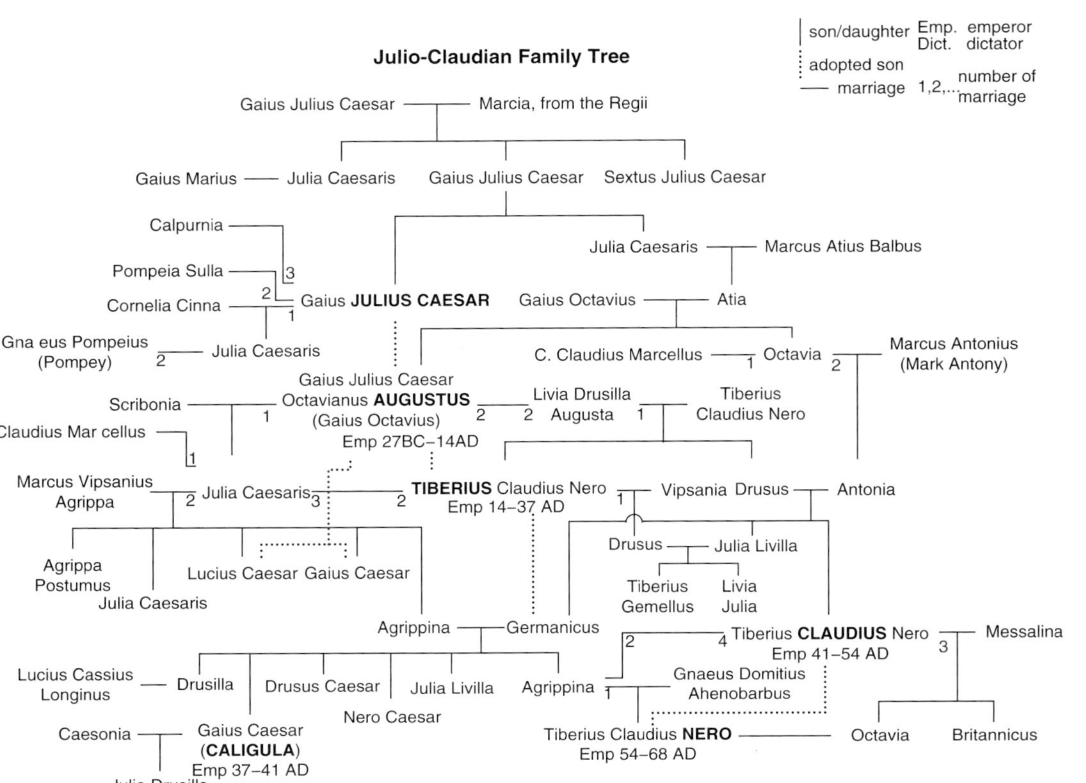

Map of the Roman Empire in 69 CE. Created by Ancient World Mapping Center

Introduction: Angles on an Emperor

Shadi Bartsch, Kirk Freudenburg, and Cedric Littlewood

For the ancient historians who write about Nero, the man and his "age" are synonymous. As if anticipating Carlyle's famous formulation about world history being "but the biography of great men," and with no Herbert Spencer to tell them otherwise, Nero's ancient chroniclers write the "age" of Nero as the biography of the man himself, the outsized performer who torched the city of Rome and brought the Julio-Claudian dynasty crashing down. Put differently, and perhaps more correctly, when Nero's ancient chroniclers wrote their histories and biographies, they were not setting out to write his "age." They did not think in terms of ages *per se*, but only of the larger-than-life Roman men who happened to initiate ages upon their rise, and to conclude them upon their fall. For "the big three" of Roman imperial history (Tacitus, Suetonius, and Dio), "big men" are the drivers of history, and there was never a bigger man to spin history with than Nero.

To help us understand the implosion of the Julio-Claudian dynasty and the imperial crisis of 69 CE, Nero's ancient historians have precious little to say about social, political, and economic structures. They do not think in these terms, and they have neither the methods nor the vocabulary to tell us what we moderns would like to know. As we peer back from our own present to the deep past, looking from this side of numerous paradigmatic "turns" (cultural, linguistic, spatial, performative, quantitative, and so on), we want to know what can be regarded as "factual," or at least "reasonably surmisable," about the workings of the Roman world under Nero, only to be treated to stories about palace intrigue, million-dollar mushrooms, asses'-milk baths, humans lit as torches, and torch-lit orgies. We find history put to us as brilliantly salacious entertainment: a performance of outrage that is also a bid for moral authority, performed by men who are themselves politically active and well placed (both Tacitus and Dio were Roman senators, and Suetonius was handpicked by Hadrian to hold multiple top-level posts in his administration), writing to men of similar cultural wherewithal and rank. History for the imperial "big three" has to do with uncovering and censuring the moral rot of their script's main players – their lack of moderation and megalomania. It is satire by other means, tragically tinged. Told the way the ancients tell it, Roman imperial history is tragic, not because historians look to tragedy for models (though they certainly do that), but because of what they take history's purpose to be, and because of where they choose to shine the genre's spotlight: on bigger-than-life protagonists feasting in their palaces, on their desires, their family intrigues, their delusions, and their cruelties.

Given the way that Nero has been passed down to us, it is no wonder that "the age" of Nero Claudius Caesar (37–68 CE) has appealed to the popular imagination more than any other period in ancient Roman history. It has been the object of repeated scholarly reevaluations, many of them focusing directly on the compelling figure of the emperor himself. The potent admixture of the historical and the imaginative in his reception, to include his immediate reception in the age that he came to define, has given us a deeply complex figure: a radical innovator who conformed to the traditions of Augustus; a leader among brilliantly talented poets who himself wrote laughably bad poems; a military bungler who pulled off a long-sought peace accord with the leaders of Parthia and Armenia; a self-delusional fool who was also a crafty propagandist. Abounding in such incongruities, the fourteen years of Nero's rule have been approached with strikingly different emphases: as a golden age that went sour and a time of marked Christian persecution; an era of architectural innovation capped by the glory (or monstrosity) of the Domus Aurea; a time of rapprochement between the Romans and Greeks of the eastern empire, and, of course, the death throes of the Julio-Claudian dynasty, whose policies the Flavians would react against in turn.

It is because he has been passed down to us as too many outrageous versions of the same man that Nero remains imaginable as something other than what all, and what little, the ancients made of him. He does not take to being sewn together merely as the sum of his parts because we have been left with far too many parts to work with, and because many of them do not take to being sewn into human form. But it is from this mass of contradictions and monstrous assertions and open ends that new ways of thinking about Nero and his age must emerge and new versions of the man be conceived. This Cambridge Companion proposes to offer a comprehensive overview of the period that pays special attention not only to the monsters that Nero was made into, by the ancients and many others since, but to the processes and the cultural stakes of these constructions. This Companion looks not only to the historical debates that the age of Nero has spurred, but also to the many ways in which Nero was received and interpreted in the Roman and Christian eras of the first centuries CE and beyond. It treats the refulgence of the plastic and literary arts in the Neronian period, and it offers fresh interpretations of the relations of the main authors of the day (Seneca, Petronius, Persius, Lucan) to the age in which they lived.

The historical facts behind the many Neros that have come down to us are looked for by many of the essays of this volume, and good headway is made in the posing of new plausibilities based on fresh critical reassessments of the information we have. That said, no single, generally accepted version of Nero and his age emerges from this effort. The coeditors of this volume thought it best not to try to make that happen because not only would such a result be hard to pull off, it would risk sending the wrong message, since it would make the Nero so attained (the one offered as historically plausible by consensus) seem the point of this project, as well as somehow more real and historically significant than the monsters into which he was made. Whatever such a Nero would look like, he could be nowhere near as compelling and/or historically significant as the Neros he gave rise to.

A common thread of many of the essays in this Companion concerns Nero the performer. His ancient chroniclers make Nero's failure to separate stage acting from ruling his signature delusion. But here (to give just one instance of where modern critical methods invite new reckonings of the same old information) we have a place where "the performative turn" in recent humanities and social sciences scholarship has added vast new dimensions to what an emperor's public playacting might be taken to entail and mean – as self-work, and as the assertion of a certain kind of political identity. No longer do we go looking for "the real man," *Nero ipse*, behind the mask (only to find him hollow inside). Instead, we look to the performances he put on as a means of centering and defining himself, in acts of posing (so as to become) a self of a certain kind. The use of such performances as a means of political self-realization and getting things done is by no means unique to Nero. Rather, it is the openness with which he staged himself as this, then that, then again as something else that made his self-performance unique among Rome's emperor actors. Taken this way, rather than as mere delusion, Nero's playacting has much to tell us about what kind of emperor he strove to appear, and what kind of performances the audiences he played to in Rome, and beyond (though clearly not all of them), could be relied on to crave and applaud.

Nero's theatricality trends through many, if not most, of the chapters of this volume because it has to do not only with his passion for the theater, but with the whole way he ruled: the palaces he built, the parties he hosted, the literature he gave rise to, the rituals he staged, and so on. This is but one area among many where this *Companion to the Age of Nero* produces new approaches to key questions, by studying them from multiple angles, and taking up with them across multiple chapters. Other areas where a number of chapters converge to produce new insights into Nero and his age concern the complicated relationship between Seneca and Nero, as well as, more generally, the complications that go with "doing philosophy" in any imperial court. This volume reassesses Nero's work as a builder, looking at the development of imperial architecture, and of the emperor's image prior to, during, and after his age. Several chapters assess the "Augustan" expectations to which Nero played, and the ways in which writers of his age take up with and redeploy some of the most troubling features of the Augustan poets whom they emulate. In addition, two of this volume's chapters provide a skeptical reassessment of Nero's treatment of the Jews and/or those Jews who followed the sect of Christos, much of which has to do with how Nero's theatricality was amplified through the desires and hatreds of later generations.

Matthew Leigh opens this volume with the problem of Nero's self-stylization as an Artist Emperor, his fatal confusion of the role of an actor with the role of a ruler. The historians tell stories of a young man whose passions for performance, and all things softly refined and Greek, could not be kept in check. The consequences for the real world over which he ruled were "tragic" in a metaphorical sense, but Nero dealt with them as if he were performing a series of demanding roles on a tragic stage: *Orestes matricida, Hercules furens*, and so on. One is right to be suspicious of this "crazed actor" of the historians as a fact of history. And yet Leigh insists that there is solid substance behind the stories, as evinced by the matter-of-fact-ness of certain descriptions of Nero's daily regimes of diet and vocal training, and by the existence of coins promoting Nero as a lyre-player. Leigh points out that the emperor's youthful enthusiasms for horses, painting, music, and acting, while unproblematic in themselves, became a source of scandal when these passions became overheated and all-consuming. Both Augustus and Nero (perhaps reprising his great-great-grandfather's last act) ended their lives by calling attention to the theatricality of the roles they had played as emperors. But what for Augustus was stylized rule, for Nero was rule both via and as style – performance devoid of substance.

In his chapter, Josiah Osgood looks at one of the main interest groups that senatorial historians, such as Tacitus and Dio, tend to feature as chief among the suffering victims of the Neronian age: the members of the Roman Senate. Osgood examines what it meant to be a senator under Nero, in an age when the powers of the Senate had long since become secondary and circumscribed, and yet were still, in some respects, very real. He reminds us that Nero was himself a man drawn from the Senate's own order who regularly sought out senators' advice and approval. He ascended to the throne in 54 CE riding a wave of enthusiasm as the *Wunderkind* who would restore dignity to the institution that Claudius had relentlessly persecuted. The evidence suggests that there were many good years of cooperation between the emperor and the Senate before Nero began to feel threatened by certain members of their order. Many of the vices that later moralizing historians scold Nero for engaging in were in fact accepted modes of luxurious living among senators. Thus, rather than directly affronting the Senate and its *mores* with his parties, playacting, and poetry salons, Nero may in fact have been reaching out to the Senate as one of its own, playing to the Senate on the Senate's own terms: a bid for *gratia* and cohesion after the debacles of Claudius and Caligula. It was only late in his career that this symbiosis was spoiled and a new climate of suspicion and rivalry took hold. But, in the end, it was not the Senate that brought Nero down. Despite impressions of risk-taking and outright senatorial defiance that senatorial writers have left for us, the Senate was very slow to condemn him and desert one of its own.

Carlos Noreña looks at the way the empire was governed under Nero, and to do that he must first clear away a number of basic confusions about what "government" was under the emperors, and what role Nero himself may have had in running things in distant parts of the Roman world. Here again the ancient historians tend to paint cartoon pictures of an autocratic Nero doing whatever he pleased by deciding and decreeing. In fact, "government" under the emperors was a highly complex system that did not take to being worked that way. Rather than a monolith of institutions, offices, and laws used as devices for carrying out the emperor's will, Rome's imperial government is better thought of as a set of evolving political arrangements worked out between the emperor, his imperial agents, and distant others whose interests were all being taken into account and promoted at the same time. Rome's imperial government, in other words, was "a system for the management of interests." For his part, Nero was heavily managed, and his policies much worked upon, by these interests through his advisory *concilium*, the Senate, the knights, civil servants, local elites, and even his own freed slaves. Seen for the complex interests that they protect and promote, many of Nero's fiscal policies, vilified by historians, make good economic and political sense, and even the conspiracies of his last years can be seen as a shakeup and a re-composition of the emperor's inner circle made necessary by the emergence of new configurations of power. In the end, a new provincial elite emerged that "Nero" (the set of existing political and economic arrangements that operated under that name) was too slow to accommodate.

Anthony Barrett examines the interactions that took place between Nero and another group within his court, but not officially within his *concilium*: the women of his family (Agrippina, Domitia Lepida, Octavia), and certain other women who took his fancy (Poppaea Sabina, Antonia, Acte). Nero, he shows, had a long history of craving and developing the company of strong women, all of whom (excepting Acte) he would eventually tire of and destroy. The most famous of these women is Agrippina, who seems to have boldly inserted herself into the running of things early in his career, only to be rendered irrelevant not long after his accession, having split with Seneca and Burrus, whose careers she had done much to rescue and promote. Agrippina, Barrett makes clear, was not out of line for aggressively promoting the interests of her son, but for promoting herself as virtual co-regent with him, invested with powers of her own that she was determined to wield as she pleased. The other main example of the same type is Poppaea Sabina, Nero's second wife. Despite telling stories of her traveling with herds of asses to supply milk for her daily bath, the ancient sources (esp. Josephus) demonstrate that Poppaea was a woman who wielded very real unofficial powers that came with being who she was, as well as the emperor's wife. As her efforts taken on behalf of her friends from Judaea show, Poppaea could get demolition projects canceled and prisoners released. For the ancient historians who tell of Poppaea's scheming and relentless ambition, such women were functions of the bad emperors who failed to assert their Roman male authority over them and keep them under control. But the fact that Nero was wont to welcome such women into his world, and to leave them free to develop and show off their powers in public, puts him solidly in the respectable traditions of Augustus (Livia) and Germanicus (the Elder Agrippina). Rather than a sign of weakness, Nero's association with such women might be taken to mean that he was not afraid of them and that he saw clear advantages to showing himself in their company.

Cedric Littlewood begins a series of essays on literature with a general discussion of the crucial role Neronian literature plays in establishing certain Augustan texts and authors as canonical. Especially in the high genres of epic and tragedy, the poetic reception of Augustan literature is characterized by inversion, contrast-imitation, and a determination to outrage decorum by saying what may not be said. But what exactly may not be said? Precisely the same material accommodates critiques of Augustan myths and ideals or, alternatively, a narrative of decline in which post-Augustan culture is portrayed as degenerate. A Neronian determination to remember the violence of pre-Augustan poems, for example, in Persius' reintroduction into satire of an "epodic" voice or in Lucan's allusions to the *Georgics*, is a pointed reversal of literary history and a challenge to Augustan reconciliations. The lament for lost grandeur, prominent in texts such as Petronius' *Satyrica*, is an ancient commonplace. The loss of political liberty is often advanced as a cause of literary decline, but, we should note, often by deeply unreliable narrators.

Much of the dissonance in post-Augustan literature is created not by inverting models of smooth perfection, but by exposing and amplifying inherited tensions. Through selective reminiscence, and often jarring juxtaposition, dialogs between Augustan authors are revisited by their successors. Seneca's *Medea* combines Virgilian and Horatian texts in a meditation on the sublimity of limitless power that is as much a fulfillment of Augustan imperial ambition as its tragic demise.

Gareth Williams begins his study of Lucan's *Civil War* with a reminder of the now lost or fragmentary historical epics that might have provided its author with models. From the Augustan age alone we know that Rabirius wrote an epic on the war between Octavian and Antony, and that Sextilius Ena and Cornelius Severus wrote civil war poems. The Elder Seneca compares their treatments of the death of Cicero. In a twenty-three line fragment of Albinovanus Pedo's poem on Germanicus' expedition in the North Sea in 16 CE, Williams detects the high declamatory pitch and artificiality that will characterize post-Augustan and especially Lucan's epic.

Lucan's *Civil War* is a poem of "chaotic contradictoriness" whose fragmented form mirrors its subject. Fractures in Lucan's authorial voice – now turning away from its subject and throwing up digressions to prevent the narrative of Rome's dissolution, now driven on by burning energy – parallel the characterization of the poem's opposing leaders. It is a conflict unresolved in the space of Lucan's poem, at least as it survives to us. The account of the elusive source of the Nile in Book 10 speaks perhaps to Nero's own ambitions (an expedition was launched ca. 61 CE), but more generally to all fantasies of global domination. If Nature is mysterious, so too are the gods who are invoked but never appear in Lucan's poem, as if to place the crime of the war and the shattering of the world beyond providence and understanding.

Kirk Freudenburg, in his chapter, "Petronius, Realism, Nero," explores the connections between the grandiose self-stylization and competitive playacting of the characters of the *Satyrica*, and the extreme aestheticization of politics in Neronian Rome. The playacting of Petronius' characters, and the confusions of art and reality, Freudenburg argues, "have less to do with their 'not getting' how things happen in the real world than with their 'getting' the ways of the late Neronian world all too well." The experience of Encolpius at Trimalchio's dinner, uncertain what is scripted, accidental, and improvised, is our own as readers of Nero's Rome. Nero singing while Rome burned, as if to the accompaniment of a play he had written, is the reverse image of Petronius making his own constrained and scripted death appear a mere accident. Tacitus' account of Petronius' final fiction both parodies and surpasses Seneca's more labored attempt to stage an image of his life. The *Satyrica* offers a series of painted windows into Roman reality. The "call of nature" (and what could be more natural than that?) that forces an intermission in the performance (*Sat.* 41–6) is revealed as a literary echo of Horace, *Satires* 2.8 and an opportunity for Trimalchio, on his return, to display his medical learning. Time and again Petronius plays a trick in order to show us how the trick is done. In this respect, Freudenburg sees a comical resemblance between the illusions of the *Satyrica* and the fakery of Nero's Rome in which Nero's actor-emperor flippantly exposes the codes of his own manufacture.

In "'Ain't Sayin': Persius in Neroland," Dan Hooley examines *nefas* (the unspeakable) in a satiric context. At the end of his programmatic first satire, Persius buries what may not be said in a hole, either sowing the seeds of free speech or consigning them to the grave. His close associate Thrasea Paetus, whose death ends what we have of Tacitus' *Annals*, once left a Senate meeting because "he could not say what he would, and would not say what he could" (Dio 61.15). Throughout his essay, Hooley looks in these apparently unpolitical satires for the words that cannot be spoken, for the implicit contrast between Persius' life under the guidance of his Stoic teacher, Cornutus, and Nero's life under the guidance of his Stoic teacher, Seneca. Nero's insincere speech of thanks to Seneca from *Annals* 14.55–6 is shockingly juxtaposed with Persius' gratitude to Cornutus, a gratitude that remains unspeakable (*non enarrabile*, 5.29) in a world whose rhetoric is bankrupt. The Roman Socrates cum Alcibiades of *Satires* 4 offers an unflattering portrait of Seneca and Nero, but not so as to place Persius' relationship with his own Socratic teacher beyond criticism. In Neroland, who doesn't have the ears of an ass? Simply naming Midas/Nero would be too easy a satire. "You want me to say that Midas has asses' ears, and worse?" writes Hooley's Persius. "I know it, and I want *you* to think about that and where *you* fit into this fallen world that I'm showing."

Seneca's works are treated in the next trio of essays. Chiara Torre argues for a more complex contextualization of Senecan drama in the art and culture of the Neronian age than it has previously received. Torre critiques the tendency to read the tragedies as *tragédies à clef*. Instead, she would have us pay attention to other less analyzed features. For one, she emphasizes the importance of the tragedies' continuing themes as echoed in the prose works, such as the relationship between monarchy and tyrannical power, the role of fate in the kingdom, and the role of the advisor figure. These themes, she suggests, are parallel across the poetry and the prose in their relentless movement from a more positive to a more negative view of power.

Torre's chapter also examines Senecan drama within a number of possible interpretive contexts related directly to their cultural milieu: as Augustanism "refigured" in order to reverse the optimistic stance of that earlier literature and represent the emperor as a sort of mad god; as a parallel to Fourth-style wall painting, in which domestic scenes are featured publicly and mythological innovation is striking; and as a reflection, metrically, of the heightened interest in music and pantomime under Nero. Examinations in this style, as she persuasively argues, help us fully understand the multidimensional nature of the theatricality marking the Neronian age.

Shadi Bartsch discusses philosophical, particularly Stoic, engagement in and disengagement from the state. Senators such as Thrasea Paetus could articulate political dissent in Stoic terms, but the philosophy was not opposed to monarchy. Although Stoics believed that "only the wise man is king" (*SVF* 3.369–700), there are many Stoic treatises on (actual) kingship from the third century BCE. Seneca's *de Clementia* exaggerates Stoic acceptance of monarchy as a possible form of government in the metaphor of the king as the mind of the body politic. This ideology for the new regime, Bartsch argues, stands in sharp contrast to the political writings of Cicero, for whom the Senate was the guardian, protector, and defender of the republic. Seneca echoes Cicero's language, but appropriates it for imperial praise.

Seneca quotes the opinion of Zeno, Stoicism's founder, that the wise man will enter public life if nothing stands in the way (*Dial.* 8.3.20). It is a crucial qualification that Seneca, who asked Nero's permission to retire from public life in 62 CE, exploits. He argues that because there is in practice no state worthy of a wise man's participation, "leisure begins to be necessary for all of us" (*Dial.* 8.8.1–3). Bartsch closes her essay with a discussion of Seneca implicitly defending himself against the charge of inconstancy, of abandoning the course he had set earlier in life. "Besides the wise man, no one plays one role; the rest of us wear many masks" (*Ep.* 120.22).

Continuing several of the themes of Bartsch's essay, Catharine Edwards confronts the contradictions between Seneca's philosophical prose and his life as an imperial courtier in "Seneca and the Quest for Glory in Nero's Golden Age." Whether to select public service or private retreat; whether to care for the soul or for one's reputation; whether glory ultimately comes from literary achievement, philosophical teaching, or political preeminence – all these questions emerge in sharp relief from Seneca's complicated legacy. In the end, as Edwards points out, Seneca touts the value of philosophy as the locus of true distinction, and the opinion, not of society at large, but of a few select men – and one's conscience. *Virtus* is within. Similarly so for writing: philosophy will trump literary achievement as a route to fame.

And yet, this affirmation aside, Seneca's claims are ultimately not so simple. For one, his view that philosophy is superior to other exploits partly rests on the posthumous glory it bestows on the philosopher; yet glory is one of the indifferents that the Stoic philosopher is supposed to scorn. Another interesting contradiction inherent in the *Letters* is Seneca's concern therein to deliberately echo earlier literary sources in making his arguments. As such he betrays, Edwards suggests, "an ambition to create a new kind of literary masterwork." His particular interest in Ovidian intertext suggests that behind the sanguine philosopher, yet another Senecan persona might be lurking unacknowledged: that of the exiled poet, who, like Ovid, "even on the very edge of the Roman empire, insisted on goading the emperor – and championing the superior power of literature."

In Part IV, this volume turns to material culture and the monuments of Neronian Rome. Caroline Vout observes in Neronian art a similarly knowing display of artifice, a confusion of the real and imaginary similar to what Freudenburg observed in Petronius'

Satyrica. Nero's gilding of a statue of the young Alexander by Lysippus reveals not just an obsession with gold and an homage to the Greek world-conqueror, but a particular aesthetic preference. Pliny wrote of Lysippus that, "whereas his predecessors had made men as they really were, he made them as they seemed to be" (*HN* 34.65). Differently but relatedly, a reflection in sculpted marble of a painted Priapus in Pompeii's house of the Vettii collapses "the space from street to garden, and between fresco and sculpture, art and life." The immersive, illusionistic paintings of the tragic figures of Pentheus and Dirce show the same taste for playing mythological scenes "for real" in the amphitheater and on the tragic stage.

Nero's building projects exemplify for historians of following ages the ruinous excess of a tyrant. Even his portraits show the face of unrestrained indulgence. Many modern scholars agree, but Vout argues that the swollen features on Nero's coinage show rather an ambition to appear larger than life. The numismatic record does not betray the emperor's gluttonous lifestyle, but is shaped by the same aesthetic impulse to exceed previous models that characterizes the emulative poetics of Seneca or Lucan. As these poets surpass and deform classic Augustan texts, Neronian portraiture pushes "visual prototypes to the point where the only move left is bursting."

In investigating the artistic and architectural achievements of Nero, Eugenio La Rocca shows that many of the most prominent stylistic innovations of the age, achievements generally taken to mark Nero as a stylistic maverick, are actually further developments and refinements of stylistic trends and traditions set in motion by Nero's Julio-Claudian ancestors. For example, in assimilating his image to that of Sol/Apollo, largely via suggestion rather than forthright assertion, Nero is doing something that Augustus had done, and thus he is conforming to the *mos maiorum* established by his ancestor. Many of the stylistic innovations of the Domus Aurea, La Rocca shows, can be read in the same way, and he indicates that, despite whatever Tacitus, Suetonius, and Dio urge to the contrary, there is no reason to think that Romans were universally critical of Nero's remaking of Rome's center in the aftermath of the fire of 64 CE. Here too such large-scale remaking of Rome's urban spaces for the public good (hostile historians would have us believe that the Domus Aurea was a pleasure palace, strictly private) had a most respectable precedent in the transformation of the Campus Martius by Augustus and Agrippa. In the end, Nero's reputation as a stylistic trendsetter has less to do with bold innovation than it has to do with the way he unleashed the full potentials of stylistic trends that were already available and ready to exploit.

John Pollini returns to the opportunity Nero exploited of remaking Rome's urban space, the Great Fire of 64, and asks anew whether the Christians were innocent scapegoats. Did they in fact play a role in that conflagration? The essay lays out the context for the Christians in Rome during Nero's era, and reminds us of the new and disturbing group whom Nero chose to blame for much of Rome's destruction. Pollini's first concern is to reexamine the traditional claim that it was Nero who "played the lyre while Rome burned." As he reveals, this accusation seems overdetermined: it comes from the elite classes who hated the emperor and had reason to claim he burned down a good part of the city to selfishly build his Domus Aurea. But the traditional account contains troubling inconsistencies: why, for example, would Nero not then start the fire at the site of the future building project? And what if his cronies apparently seen setting new fires were in fact trying to battle the blaze that had already started?

Pollini turns his gaze instead to another group scapegoated in the literature on the Great Fire: the followers of the Jew Christus (or Chrestus). Among the two camps of the Christ-ians, it was not so much the Christians of the Jerusalem Church, but the followers of Paul of Tarsus who were dangerously targeting the conversion of Romans (rather than fellow Jews) and as such had good reason to incite anxiety. As Pollini shows, the reputation of the Christians in Rome was rife with charges of *superstitio* and apocalyptic thought. Is it possible that enthusiasm for the final conflagration described later in Revelation actually did drive this group to help along the flames? Perhaps the Christians were not *only* a scapegoat, and perhaps the fact that Nero not only blamed them for the fire, but also punished them accordingly by turning them into living torches for the amphitheater, is significant: he had them exit life by the very means that characterized what he blamed them for. This essay offers a different perspective on Harrill's study, the latter suggesting that much of Paul's treatment of persecution in the age of Nero was a later construct.

The reconstructed Rome that followed Nero's death has traditionally been described as a "Flavian aftermath" that sought to overturn Nero's artistic and architectural extravagance – for example, the Domus Aurea was torn down and partially replaced by the Colosseum. In his essay, La Rocca offered a corrective to this view, and Eric Varner, in "Negotiating Nero's Memory and Monuments in Flavian Rome," argues in some detail that the Flavian interventions in Nero's Rome were actually a careful recalibration of the Neronian visual program. Such "recalibration" can even be seen as a trait of Flavian statuary: while the repurposed statues of Nero were given the faces of the new regime, readable traces remained of the original image that let viewers see the shift in the political landscape. Likewise, if the Flavians sought to reshape Nero's *Urbs Nova* as their own *Roma Resurge(n)s* ("Rome Rising Again," as promoted in the coinage) after the civil wars of 68–9, nonetheless their additions to the civic landscape often pointed back to Nero's Rome rather than erased it altogether. As Varner points out, even if the Flavian Colosseum was a construction for the public's enjoyment, and not that of a single individual, the area of the Domus Aurea on which the Colosseum was constructed may have been one of the most publicly accessible parts of Nero's residence. The other great Flavian project, the Templum Pacis, or Temple of Peace, was a new building but was used to house Nero's works of art – a major part of its attraction. Even Nero's unfinished Colossus was finished and dedicated in 75 by Vespasian. As Varner concludes, "Notwithstanding the Flavian recalibration of Nero's legacy, it would seem his memory never ceased to resonate at Rome."

How this memory is repurposed, and what can be credibly taken as "known" about Nero and his age from ancient accounts that are overwhelmingly hostile and late, are the subjects of the next sequence of essays, covering the reception of Nero from Flavian historiography to Hollywood. Donatien Grau finds evidence for a consistently negative representation of Nero soon after his death in the *Naturalis Historia* of the Elder Pliny. Here criticism takes the form not of explicit political commentary, but of brief mentions and asides casually tossed in that leave readers to conclude for themselves that Nero was depraved and out of control. Using a similar technique, both Statius and Martial offer incidental glimpses of Nero that add up to a consistent picture. But given what is made of Nero by later writers working in a full range of generic types (satire, histories, biographies, letters), it is surprising how little overt and/or sustained criticism of Nero is found in the works of the Flavian writers who wrote in the immediate aftermath of his reign. It is only with the "big three" of the second and early third centuries, Tacitus, Suetonius, and Dio, that the Julio-Claudians (excepting Augustus) came in for the full rhetorical workup that featured a demented tyrant, tragically outsized and flawed, as the last self-immolating act of a decadent line. Taking us into the rhetorical workshops of these writers, Grau shows how the portrait of Nero becomes less complex and more exaggerated over time. The moral purposes to which these histories and biographies were put help explain why the Nero these writers portray is so outsized and easy to read.

Turning to Christian sources, Albert Harrill argues that Paul's letter to the Romans, rather than the book of Acts, is the best primary source for early Christianity in Rome. The book of Acts presents Paul in retrospect as the greatest hero of a unified church, who proceeds to a martyrdom modeled on Jesus' death in Luke's gospel. The letter to the Romans addresses itself to a diverse and not yet centralized group of tiny Christian communities. Paul wrote to them as a man known to most only by reputation. He took care to mention by name a large number of the local leaders whom he hoped to win over to his own gospel. His calls to reconcile "the strong" and "the weak" (Rom. 14:1–15:13) refer to the strong and weak *in faith*, not to ethnic groups in conflict at this particular time and place. Specifically Roman, however, is Paul's patterning of an alternative Christian imperium in his address to the people at the world's political center. The letter explicitly advises Rome's Christian communities to obey imperial authorities, a commonplace in the Diaspora synagogue, and shows no evidence of a Neronian persecution. The two authentically Pauline "prison letters" (the biblical books of Philippians and Philemon) do not anticipate a martyrdom or necessarily indicate imprisonment in Rome. Paul's travails in Rome, Harrill contends, are a later construction, one that appropriated the anti-Neronian invective found in authors such as Tacitus and Suetonius, and combined it with an apocalyptic Antichrist tradition.

Nero's memory lingered on also in political thought, well into the Renaissance. Peter Stacey starts his essay on "The Image of Nero in Renaissance Political Thought" with a letter of accusation written by Petrarch to the long-dead Seneca demanding that he account for his conduct under Nero. Using the very criteria Seneca himself had set up for judging one's actions in moral terms, he hoists Seneca on his own Stoic petard. Since Seneca knew that a philosopher did not belong in politics when the political situation was beyond help, why did he linger at Nero's court, becoming an apologist for matricide and tyranny? Only for glory, Petrarch concludes.

The question resonated in Renaissance investigations of the relationship between politics and philosophy. Seneca's exalted account of the benefits of autocratic rule in the early *de Clementia* presented a noble justification for the civic princes of the Italian cities, but the picture he painted of Nero (or at least, of tyrants like Nero) in the *de ira*, together with the historical testimony of Suetonius and the portrayal of Seneca in the *Octavia*, offered a different and problematic image of Nero. To become the "right" kind of Nero is precisely why it was recommended that both kings and courtiers examine their conscience. Ironically, Petrarch himself was later accused of consorting with tyrants – like the very Seneca he had criticized. His defense was that his political associations left him free for the serious business of philosophy: unlike Seneca, he could enjoy liberty and monarchy together.

Elena Russo's essay pits two Enlightenment thinkers against each other precisely on whether tyrants such as Nero could have existed – and could still. It is a case of Voltaire versus Diderot, the former intent on playing down any possibility that such a monster as Nero could appear in history, the latter assimilating himself, through his historical writing, to Seneca, and suggesting that he himself had dealt with Neronian types in his experiences as an Enlightenment *philosophe*. Voltaire had defended both Tsar Peter *and* the Roman emperors as the victims of writers who swooped down upon the "cadavers of reputation" to dig out every foul rumor. And not only Voltaire, but indeed most of his fellow-*philosophes* also felt that decorum, at the very least, should require the rejection of some of the more hair-raising accounts in Tacitus and Suetonius. Diderot, however, took pains in his last work, the *Essai sur les règnes de Claude et de Néron et sur les moeurs et les écrits de Sénèque pour servir d'instruction à la lecture de ce philosophe* (ECN), to represent Nero in the worst light possible and to defend Seneca, the philosopher-courtier, against his modern-day critics. His identification with Seneca is so strong that the ECN reads as "a tortured reflection on the present" and a statement of Diderot's own anxieties about being a philosopher in the world of politics. In particular, Russo suggests, Diderot saw reflections of his twenty-year-long experience with Catherine the Great in Seneca's experience with Nero: both philosopher-courtiers at first generously treated, but ultimately ignored and finally even hated by the royal figures they had tried to advise. Exploring "the tangled knot of hope, idealism, dependency, exploitation, disenchantment and shame that bound the philosopher to the tyrant," Diderot's work was not only personal, but also showed that when a Nero arose in history, the answer could be only tyrannicide.

As a foil to Diderot's bleak view, Martin Winkler brings us amusingly into the present with "Nero in Hollywood," a jaunty trip through some of Hollywood's most memorable Neros. Nero, amusing? But yes. Somehow the tyrant's deranged evil and debauchery translate on the big screen into figures so excessive as to be ludicrous. Often he is entirely under the thumb of his dangerously sexy (second) wife, Poppaea, as in DeMille's *The Sign of the Cross* and LeRoy's *Quo*

Vadis, whence he emerges as a sort of pouty fat infant throwing regular tantrums. His very speech smacks of comic evil excess, his new Rome "springing from the loins of fire" (lest we forget his own loins were afire) while he proclaims, *qua artiste*, "I seek because I must be greater than man, for only then will I be the supreme artist" (*Quo Vadis*). And of course there are orgies. Already in DeMille's 1914 production we find "an astonishing lesbian seduction scene of a pagan dancer attempting, unsuccessfully of course, to undermine the virtue of the Christian heroine" 1932! It seems Nero brings out perversions even in film directors! – as in Victor Saville's *The Silver Chalice* (1954): peacock, boar, dormice, oysters, pheasant, ortolans, and grasshoppers (not mentioned in any Roman sources we know as part of Nero's diet). What could be missing here but a cartoon Nero – although, as Winkler shows us, there were in fact many cartoon Neros, perhaps the most amusing one being the emperor featured in Friz Freleng's *Roman Legion-Hare* (1955), where Bugs Bunny manages to turn the tables and send the Colosseum lions after Nero and Yosemite Sam instead. In the end, however, it's Winkler – and we – who have the last laugh, with his ending line summing up more than a century of cinematic Neros: *Vice cannot wither him, nor movies stale / his infamous variety*.

After this last laugh, then what? Not a backward-looking glance at this volume's contents in order to offer a summation or to put the refracted pieces of Nero back together again, but a leap out of "Companion" mode altogether. What if we read Nero's final words, "What an artist dies in me," as a meditation on the nature of power rather than artistry? Erik Gunderson argues that the confrontation in Christopher Nolan's *The Dark Knight* (2008) between Batman and the Joker (one of those men who, as Alfred puts it, "just want to watch the world burn"), offers a more recent cinematic meditation on masked power that resonates with the self-conscious playacting of Nero's rule. Gunderson considers what is at stake, both for Nero's ancient historians, and for us, in undertaking to strip Nero of his mask and to expose him as a fake. He shows how we establish our own dignity by exposing him as an actor and acting appalled at his act. He lays bare the power advantage gained by critics who undertake to divulge this as the big secret of his deluded age. In the actor scolded by historians, Gunderson finds not an emperor who has lost touch with reality, but an insider who speaks the truth about Roman power by performing his awareness of Rome's one biggest (unutterable) secret: that Caesars are "made" rather than just "are." This Joker-Nero parades his way through life as an actor, not to hide the truth, but to tell it. From antiquity on he is vilified for clownishly stripping the veil from the sanctity of power – for, in essence, not having had the decency to pretend, the way other emperors had done.

The question of imperial authenticity was a delicate and crucial one after the Senate had voted to depose Nero Caesar by declaring him a public enemy (Suet. *Nero* 49), and after first Galba and then more successfully Vespasian had then taken the family name of Caesar as an indispensable part of being emperor of Rome. This crisis of power's legitimate foundation at the end of the Julio-Claudian dynasty recalls the aftermath of Caligula's assassination, when some senators proposed that the memory of the Caesars be abolished. Not by coincidence does Suetonius remember Caligula as a man who so loved theater that he could not restrain himself from singing along with a tragic actor, a man who took advantage of the freedom – we should say rather the license (*licentia*) – of an all-night festival to appear for the first time on stage (Suet. *Cal.* 54). In closing, one might say: Nero's fascination with masquerade eclipses even Caligula's in the historical record because the change of dynasty after his death requires it.

Part I

Nero's World

1: Nero the Performer

Matthew Leigh

When Nero succeeded his adoptive father, Claudius, as emperor in 54 CE, he was not yet seventeen years old. His early influences were various. Suetonius claims that his child-minders had included a barber and a dancer (Suet. *Nero* 6.3), while, at the time of his ascension to the throne, he remained the pupil of Lucius Annaeus Seneca, the distinguished philosopher, rhetorician, and tragedian whom his mother Agrippina had brought back from exile on Corsica in order to guide him. The liberal education Nero received included no little exposure to the arts, and he soon demonstrated an aptitude and enthusiasm for such activities as sculpture, painting, poetic composition, song, the playing of the lyre, and horsemanship (Tac. *Ann.* 13. 3.7; Suet. *Nero* 20.1, 22.1). Little of this was in itself a cause for scandal. His newly acquired skills as a rider allowed Nero to emulate his putative Trojan ancestor, Ascanius, and lead a successful performance in the circus of the equestrian exercise known as the Game of Troy (Tac. *Ann.* 11.11; Suet. *Nero* 7; Verg. *Aen.* 5.545–603). Though Quintilian urges that the orator should study music simply in order to understand how to move the emotions and regards playing the lyre as something that even chaste girls should spurn (Quint. *Inst.* 1. 10. 31), Nero's near-contemporary, the future emperor Titus, also demonstrated skill as a singer and a lyre-player (Suet. *Tit.* 3), and it seems unlikely that either would have been allowed to follow such a path had it been seen as inherently morally corrupting. Yet from these apparently respectable beginnings something extraordinary and bizarre developed, and, by the end of his reign, Nero was not so much the ruler of the Roman world as a full-time performance artist. This chapter will examine the evidence for this process; will set out the different ways in which Nero's antics are interpreted by the principal ancient witnesses to his reign; and will consider what more modern treatments regard as being at issue in such conduct or in accusations thereof.

So much of Nero's career as a performer is indeed so exceptional that many will be tempted to regard what Tacitus, Suetonius, and Dio report as wholesale malicious invention. Yet any absolute refusal to believe would surely be unjustified. It is quite true that the fall of a Roman emperor is characteristically followed by the condemnation of his memory: the new monarch typically promises to eschew the excesses of his predecessor's reign and it is open season for writers to claim what they wish about the former ruler and his court.[1] When, for instance, we learn that Nero killed his second wife, Poppaea, by kicking her in the stomach when she was pregnant with his child, it will be important to recall that an identical crime against his sister is attributed by Herodotus to the demented Persian monarch, Cambyses (Suet. *Nero* 35.2; Dio 62.28.1; Hdt. 3.32.4). Yet it is hard to dismiss all the evidence in this way.

One of the earliest historians of Nero's reign, Cluvius Rufus, was present at the 65 CE celebration of the festival called the Neronia and actually announced to the audience that the ruler would sing *Niobe* (Suet. *Nero* 21.2); he took on the same role during the emperor's tour of Greece in 66–7 CE (Dio 63.14.3). Many will have seen Cluvius do just this. Another contemporary witness to Nero's reign was C. Plinius Secundus. Though only seven fragments survive of his thirty-one-book history of the Roman people under the later Julio-Claudian emperors, and only four of these concern Nero, much else can be extracted from the thirty-seven books of the same writer's *Natural History*, which were composed at most a decade after Nero's death and which survive in their entirety. Pliny's outright hostility to Nero emerges repeatedly (see, e.g., Plin. *HN* 2.92, 4.10, 7.45–6, 30.14–15), but some details are buried so deep in otherwise very dry disquisitions that their inclusion can scarcely be attributed to the desire to denigrate the fallen monarch. When we are told that Nero ate chives in order to benefit his singing voice (Plin. *HN* 19.108) or that he treated bruises and sprains suffered when driving his chariot with a solution of powdered boar's dung (Plin. *HN* 28.238), what Pliny is really interested in are the chives and the dung. All this has the ring of truth to it. No less valuable is the evidence of numismatics. Suetonius reports that the emperor struck coins depicting himself in the flowing robes of a lyre-player (Suet. *Nero* 25.2–3), and coins of this sort from the years 62 to 68 CE have indeed been found, though there is some question over whether the figure presented is Nero himself or the god Apollo, to whom he habitually

[1] See Elsner and Masters 1994: 4.

assimilated himself (*RIC* nos. 73–82, 121–3, 205–12, 380–1, 414–17, 451–5; Tac. *Ann.* 14.14.2; Suet. *Nero* 53; see La Rocca, Chapter 4 this volume).

Lying on his deathbed in August 14 CE, the emperor Augustus asked his gathered friends whether he had played the mime of life well (Suet. *Aug.* 99.1). He was surely aware that every aspect of being a monarch was a form of performance and that his public appearances were a means to fashion an image of himself for his watching subjects. Recent scholarship emphasizes the degree to which Seneca's work on kingship addressed to the young Nero, the *de Clementia*, reflects this view and puts words into the new emperor's mouth as a form of script for him to perform.[2] Here the theater provides an analogy that covers the life of the emperor as a whole; but the central position of spectacular entertainment in the ruler's interaction with his subjects endowed such experiences with a special significance all their own. It was clearly important to Augustus to show that he shared many of the pleasures of the people and he was careful, when attending the Circus, actually to watch the contests and not, like Julius Caesar, to catch up on his paperwork (Suet. *Aug.* 45.1). Boxing was a particular passion (Suet. *Aug.* 45.2). Yet Augustus also took various measures to impose order on athletic, gladiatorial, and theatrical performances (Suet. *Aug.* 44.1–3, 45.3–4) and was careful not to attend contests conducted in the Greek manner (Suet. *Aug.* 45.2). In the speech to the Senate composed for him by Seneca that marked his acceptance of power, Nero promised to rule according to the model of Augustus (Suet. *Nero* 10.1). Like him he therefore acted early to curtail some forms of theatrical license (Tac. *Ann.* 13.24.1, 13.28.1–2; Suet. *Nero* 16.2), but also displayed the virtue of affability or *comitas* through his provision of public performances of various sorts (Suet. *Nero* 10.1–12.4).[3] Suetonius includes all these actions among the inoffensive or positively laudable features of Nero's reign and sets them in contrast to the abuses that he will go on to describe (Suet. *Nero* 19.3), but such a division is rather too clean-cut, and already Nero was going beyond just performing the role of the affable disciplinarian and pursuing enthusiasms fit to make Augustus shudder.

In 59 CE, Nero murdered his mother and then held major games – the Ludi Maximi – in celebration of the salvation of the empire. He also began to give more public expression to his enthusiasms for charioteering and for song. Judging the former to be the lesser of two evils, his

[2] See Star 2012: 119, 125–6, 139. [3] See Manning 1975: 169–72.

guardians, Burrus and Seneca, allowed him to drive his chariot in an enclosed space in the Vatican valley and before a select audience (Tac. *Ann.* 14.14.5). The size of the audience soon increased and the crowd gladly egged him on (Tac. *Ann.* 14.14.5). By the end of the same year, Nero had also sung in public for the first time. At the games called the Juvenalia, which marked the shaving of his first beard, members of the nobility took to the boards and Nero himself topped the bill: strumming his lyre and watched over by his voice coaches, he performed an *Attis* and a *Bacchae* in a voice that Suetonius and Dio describe as weak and dark (Suet. *Nero* 20.1; Dio 61.20.2) but which it later became customary to call heavenly (Tac. *Ann.* 14.15.9, 16.22.1; Suet. *Nero* 21.1; Philostr. *Vit. Ap.* 5.7). The cohorts of soldiers, centurions, and tribunes were all on hand to watch, as was Burrus, whom Tacitus describes as "grieving and applauding" (Tac. *Ann.* 14.15.7). The same writer claims that it was at this performance that Nero first gathered together the band of Roman knights who led the formal rhythmic applause that became a feature of his performances (Tac. *Ann.* 14.15.8, 16.4.4, 16.5.1, Suet. *Nero* 20.3, 25.1; Dio 61.20.3–4; 63.8.3; Philostr. *Vit. Ap.* 5.7). This, Suetonius claims, was a practice that the emperor imported from Alexandria (Suet. *Nero* 20.3).

The Juvenalia were followed in 60 CE by the Neronia or Quinquennial Games. This was a self-consciously Greek performance (Tac. *Ann.* 14.20.1, 14.21.4, 14.21.5; Suet. *Nero* 12.3) and involved musical, gymnastic, and equestrian contests as well as a prize for eloquence, which Nero won unopposed. Oil was distributed to knights and senators in order to encourage them to indulge in some wrestling (Suet. *Nero* 12.3, cf. Tac. *Ann.* 14.47.3). In 64 CE, Nero came one step closer to completely public performance when he took to the stage in the city of Naples. Whereas the Juvenalia had been held in the palace or gardens, now he gathered the townsmen to listen to him perform over a number of days (Tac. *Ann.* 15.33; Suet. *Nero* 20.2–3). Nero had by now begun to quote to his friends the Greek proverb that there was no respect for an art that lay hidden (Suet. *Nero* 20.1) and the very Greekness of the city made it an appropriate setting for this first public appearance (Tac. *Ann.* 15.33.2). In 65 CE, such delights were finally exposed to the Roman people at large. The second staging of the Quinquennial Games was brought forward a year and here Nero both recited one of his own poems from the stage (Tac. *Ann.* 16.4.2; Dio 62.29.1) and entered the contest for lyre-players as if on a par with the other contestants and genuinely uncertain of the verdict of the judges (Tac. *Ann.* 16.4.2–4).

A recurrent theme in all Nero's performances at Naples and at Rome is his unabashed embrace of all things Greek. Here we may look back to Suetonius' statement that the emperor Augustus had avoided attendance at Greek-style contests. If Nero now had a model, it would appear to have been the first-century BCE monarch of Alexandria known as Ptolemy Auletes or Ptolemy the Piper. The last of the Ptolemies was also, in the view of Strabo, the worst of his line (Strab. 17.1.13); his epithet derived from his habit of accompanying choruses on his flute and competing in musical contests held in the palace at Alexandria (Strab. 17.1.11). The last of the Julio-Claudians appears to have found him an eminently attractive model and the two are coupled together in a passage from Plutarch's moral works (Plut. *Mor.* 56 F). Already in 64 CE, Nero had planned to travel to the Roman province of Achaia in the Greek mainland, and this dream was finally realized in 66–7 CE.[4] The cities in which the great musical contests were held had for a while made it their practice to send Nero the prize for players of the lyre and, when the ambassadors of one such city visited Rome, he invited them to dinner, accepted their invitation to treat the guests to a performance, and responded to their applause with the statement that only the Greeks knew how to listen and only they were worthy of his pursuits (Suet. *Nero* 22.3). Now all the great festivals were brought into one twelve-month period; an unprecedented musical contest was held at the Olympic games; and Nero was able to treat audiences at each and every one to the display of his talents (Suet. *Nero* 23.1). The same fiction of open competition seen at the second performance of the Quinquennial Games was maintained and the same reverence shown for the judges (Suet. *Nero* 23.2–24.1; Dio 63.9.2). At Olympia, Nero competed in the hazardous ten-horse chariot race, fell out, and suffered serious injury, but still was awarded the crown (Suet. *Nero* 24.2; Dio. 63.14.1). When finally he returned to Italy, Nero was officially a *Periodonikes*, that is to say the winner of the Grand Slam, and carried with him 1,808 first prizes (Dio 63.8.3, 63.10.1, 63.20.5, 63.21.1).[5] In token of his affection, he granted freedom to the province of Achaia (Suet. *Nero* 24.2).

It can be little surprise if his Greek experience rather turned Nero's head. When in 68 CE, the Gallic rebellion of Vindex was announced, the emperor was in Naples and absorbed in watching the wrestlers in the

[4] See Champlin 2003: 53–61. [5] On Nero's Greek performances, see Kennell 1988.

palaestra (Suet. *Nero* 40.4; Dio 63.26.1). When finally he wrote to the Senate, it was to apologize for a sore throat, as if he was unable to perform to a suitable standard (Suet. *Nero* 41.1; Dio 63.26.1–2), and, even when he made his way back to Rome, he showed more interest in a new form of water-organ than in the war (Suet. *Nero* 41.2; Dio 63.26.4). What hurt most about the rebellion was a letter from Vindex to the Senate mocking his qualities as a lyre-player (Suet. *Nero* 41.1; Dio 63.22.4–6). Nero's preparations for his campaign consisted of organizing a train of wagons for his props and dressing a legion of concubines as Amazons (Suet. *Nero* 44.1). He planned to celebrate his victory with paeans of his own composition, a performance on the water-organ, and by dancing the part of the dying Turnus (Suet. *Nero* 44.2, 54). When instead defeat seemed inevitable, Nero proposed to retreat to Alexandria and to support himself as a professional musician (Dio 63.27.2). His last words were the notorious: "What an artist dies in me!" (Suet. *Nero* 49.1; Dio 63.29.2).

Such in outline is the career of Nero the performance artist. We will not vouch for the truth of each and every allegation, least of all those from the final year of his life when the clash between imperial duty and artistic fantasy is described in ever more colorful terms, but nor is there any reason to dismiss this as a fiction spun from whole cloth. What then do these episodes mean both to the ancient witnesses on whom we depend and to modern scholars of Nero's reign?

A recurrent motif in narratives of Nero's reign is that of the confusion of roles and responsibilities.[6] When Augustus spoke of playing the mime of life, he surely felt that his part within the performance had been that of the statesman and the ruler. Nero, by contrast, appears to have put his obligations as ruler of the Roman world second to the imperatives of his art. This is surely what is at issue when we are told that Nero justified his failure to come to Rome to respond to the rebellion of Vindex on the grounds that he was suffering from a sore throat. Professional actors and singers must do all that they can to train and to improve their vocal performance. To this end Nero slept with a lead plate over his breast, ate chives, foreswore apples, and induced himself to vomit (Plin. *HN* 19.108, 34.166; Suet. *Nero* 20.1). He also employed professional voice-trainers or *phonasci* and demonstrated strict obedience to their commands (Suet. *Nero* 25.3; Tac. *Ann.* 14.15.6). In order to protect his voice, he therefore avoided any addresses to the troops and relied on the services of an intermediary (Suet. *Nero* 25.3). Some insight

[6] See, e.g., Edwards 1994: 89–91; Champlin 2003: 81.

into what is so wrong with such conduct is offered by Quintilian, whose *Institutio Oratoria* was published in the reign of Domitian and sets out the author's principles for the education of the ideal public man of Rome. Vocal training *per se* is embraced and there is no little common ground between the orator and the *phonascus* (Quint. *Inst.* 11.3.19–20). The difference is that the public man has far too much to do to be able to set aside fixed times in which to go for a walk, nor can he deliberately take time out to rest his voice because he has so many trials in which to speak (Quint. *Inst.* 11.3.22). The principles of diet are also significantly different: the *phonascus* aims at the production of a soft and tender voice, the statesman at one that is strong and durable (Quint. *Inst.* 11.3.23). The latter must often speak in a harsh and excited manner, must work through the night and breathe in the soot of the lamp, and even put up with sweat-soaked garments (ibid.). The voice of the *phonascus* is like the body of the athlete, carefully fashioned in the gymnasium for a specific event but unable to adapt to the rigors of a military campaign; the orator, by contrast, must be able to bear sun and wind and storm and never abandon his client (Quint. *Inst.* 11.3.24). The implications of these distinctions should be clear and their relevance to Nero evident: to the statesman or the emperor, the condition of his voice is significant inasmuch as it permits him to fulfill the responsibilities of public life; to the *phonascus*, by contrast, the voice is everything; the message delivered is of no relevance compared to the grace and tunefulness of the delivery itself. An emperor unable to address the troops for fear of straining his vocal chords or reluctant to speak to the Senate at the height of a national crisis because suffering from a sore throat has lost contact with what should be the substance of his role.

This emphasis on the inability to distinguish form from substance may be related to the recurrent suggestion that Nero the performer gradually loses his ability to distinguish myth or fiction from reality.[7] For Suetonius, one cannot properly know Nero unless one knows his family (Suet. *Nero* 1. 2). The biographer therefore describes the virtues and the vices of various members of the *gens Domitia* beginning with an account conflating Cn. Domitius (cos. 122 BCE) and Cn. Domitius (cos. 96 BCE). It was in fact the latter who as consul defeated the Allobroges and the Arverni and who, according to Suetonius, "rode through the province on an elephant accompanied by a crowd of soldiers as if amidst the solemnities of a triumph" (Suet. *Nero* 2.1). There is in this an element of playacting, and the unearned or bogus triumph becomes

[7] On this topic, see especially Bartsch 1994.

a feature of his descendant's reign be it after the diplomatic successes of Corbulo in 54 CE, on Nero's return to Naples after the murder of Agrippina in 59 CE (Tac. *Ann.* 14.13.2–3), at the coming of Tiridates to Rome in 63 CE (Suet. *Nero* 13; Dio 63.1.1, 63.4.3), or finally on his return from Greece in 68 CE when he entered in the city on the same chariot that Augustus himself once rode in triumph (Suet. *Nero* 25.1; Dio 63.20.3).[8] The same zeal for role-playing is also apparent in Nero's plans to lead a regiment called the "phalanx of Alexander" on campaign to the Caspian gates (Suet. *Nero* 19.2) and in his notorious performance of a song on the *Sack of Troy* as he saw Rome burn in 64 CE (Tac. *Ann.* 15.39.3; Suet. *Nero* 38.2; Dio 62.18.1). Game and reality merge most strikingly in one detail of Nero's stage performances. The very fact that Nero played the matricides Orestes and Alcmeon or the incest-stained patricide Oedipus (Suet. *Nero* 39.2; Dio 63.9.4) appears to have invited identification with the more scandalous aspects of his own family life. This can only have been heightened by his decision to wear a mask depicting his own features for certain male roles and those of the dead Poppaea for any female characters that he played (Dio 63.9.5).[9] When Suetonius and Dio describe the end of Nero's life, the conflation of tragedy and lived experience is a central motif: at Nero's last public performance he ends a work titled *Oedipus in Exile* with the line "My wife, my mother, and my father drive me to my death" (Suet. *Nero* 46.3; cf. Dio 63.28.5); and after a career of playing matricides and exiles, he is finally obliged to play himself (Dio 63.28.4).[10]

Suetonius is a biographer, not a historian, and the shape he imposes on Nero the actor is one dictated by the logic of life-writing. If it is not Cn. Domitius and his mimic triumph, it is Domitius (cos. 16 BCE) with his youthful prowess as a charioteer, the sums expended on his shows, and even his readiness to put Roman knights and matrons on the stage (Suet. *Nero* 4). Nero cannot escape the toils of heredity and is just the most extreme manifestation of those vices innate to every member of his clan. Dio, by contrast, makes no effort to trace Nero's more distant ancestry and puts all the emphasis on the machinations of Agrippina to secure the throne for her son. Yet both he and Suetonius put great emphasis on how Nero's great escape from reality is finally foiled as reality itself takes on the qualities of tragedy. They both fashion his life in such a way as to suggest that no such flight is possible and that Nero must pay in tragic fashion for crimes that themselves are all too real.

[8] Details in Edwards 1993: 136. [9] Cf. Bartsch 1994: 46–9.
[10] See Bartsch 1994: 42–3 and Edwards 1994: 93.

At the height of his excesses of every sort, Nero is reported to have boasted that none of his predecessors had known how much they were allowed to do (Suet. *Nero* 37.3). These words may readily be applied to Nero's own emergence as an artist. For the early years of his reign are marked by the adolescent emperor's initial acceptance of, then struggle against, his mother, Agrippina, and his guardians, Seneca and Burrus. Tacitus opens Book 14 of the *Annals* with Poppaea's schemes to bring about the death of Agrippina and thus facilitate Nero's abandonment of Octavia. She mocks him as a ward subjected to the commands of others and as one who lacks not just power to command, but freedom itself (Tac. *Ann.* 14.1.1; cf. Dio 61.4.5). Such raillery clearly had its sting. It is therefore striking that Tacitus places his account of Nero's first displays as a charioteer and a singer immediately after the death of Agrippina (Tac. *Ann.* 14.14–16), emphasizes that permission to ride his chariot was given in the hope of holding back public performance as a singer, and finally describes Burrus obliged outwardly to applaud Nero's singing while inwardly he deplores what he sees. For all that these tensions are a key part of Nero's individual biography, they also reflect those broader institutional problems most clearly addressed in Seneca's *de Clementia*: the success or failure of a monarchical system of power depends almost entirely on the principles and proclivities of the ruler; those around the emperor can only influence him, and the schoolmasterly chiding of a Seneca and a Burrus is likely to yield to the more indulgent, if vicious, promptings of a Tigellinus.

The distress Nero's performances provoked in the likes of Burrus and Seneca was clearly shared by others. Tacitus refers to the shock of those visiting Rome from the country towns of Italy and the distant provinces (Tac. *Ann.* 16.5.1). The high-minded Stoic Thrasea Paetus declined to join in the orchestrated cheerleading of the Augustiani (Dio 61.20.3–4), had no interest in hearing Nero play his lyre, and refused to sacrifice to the divine voice (Tac. *Ann.* 16.28.5; Dio 62.26.3–4). The tribune of the praetorian cohort, Subrius Flavus, joined the 65 CE Pisonian conspiracy against Nero, but had no illusions about Piso himself: it would scarcely diminish the disgrace to the city were a lyre-player replaced by one accustomed to sing in tragic costume (Tac. *Ann.* 15.65.2). If Nero could be dispatched in favor of Piso, then Piso himself could be seen off and power handed to Seneca instead (Tac. *Ann.* 15.65.1). Confronted by Nero with the evidence for his participation in the conspiracy, Flavus replied that he had done so out of loathing for the ruler; while Nero deserved to be loved, nobody was more loyal to him; when, however, he slew his mother and his wife, and became a charioteer, an actor and an incendiarist, then Flavus began to hate him (Tac. *Ann.* 15.67.2; Dio 62.24.2). It says something about Nero's artistic and athletic performances that they should be placed on a level with the crimes of murder and of arson. What was at issue was in part Nero's neglect of his proper duties in the name of art (Suet. *Nero* 23.1), but more urgently the unabashed violation of decorum implicit in the roles he undertook.[11] When in 65 CE, the Senate offered Nero the prizes for song and oratory at the Quinquennial Games without a contest (Tac. *Ann.* 16. 4.1), it was perhaps for fear of what his performance might involve. The shock value of an emperor playing the parts of Orestes, Alcmeon, Oedipus, Thyestes, Hercules mad, Antigone, Melanippe, and even Canace in labor should not be underestimated (Suet. *Nero* 21.3; Juv. 8. 220–30; Dio 63.9.4).

Nor was Nero content just to bring disgrace on himself. From the Juvenalia of 59 CE onward, he also induced members of the senatorial and equestrian orders to perform (Tac. *Ann.* 14.14.5–6; 14.15 2–3; 14.20.4–5; Suet. *Nero* 11.1, 12 1, 37.2–3; Dio 61.9.1; 61.17.3–5; 61 19. 1–20.5, 62.15.4).[12] Here we encounter a deeply problematic phenomenon and one where modern scholars have questioned the biases of the ancient sources.[13] Like Augustus before him, Nero was keen to be seen to share the pleasures of the common people (Tac. *Ann.* 15.44.7, 15.53.1; Suet. *Nero* 53; Dio 61.5.2, 61.18.1–2, 61.20.2). What makes Nero distinctive is his readiness to win the favor of the *plebs* precisely by bringing disgrace on those traditionally accustomed to look down on them (Tac. *Ann.* 14.15.2–3, 16.4.4; Dio 61.17.3). Cassius Dio – a Roman senator and proudly protective of the dignity of his order – pictures the Roman audience at the Juvenalia gawping at the disgrace of the surviving members of the grand senatorial families, while visiting Macedonians, Greeks, Sicilians, Epirotes, and Asians point out the descendants of their former conquerors as they shame themselves on stage (Dio 61.17.4–5). Tacitus – another senator and painfully conscious of the dignity that the Senate of old had lost – chooses not to name the participants for fear of bringing disgrace to their ancestors (Tac. *Ann.* 14.14.5). Yet for all their indignation, neither Dio nor Tacitus provides any strong evidence that those who participated in Nero's shows did so reluctantly or felt stained by the experience. In a highly controversial account of what she dubs "voluntarism" and of the various attempts of other emperors to enforce more decorous conduct, Carlin Barton even

[11] See Edwards 1997b for the *infamia* associated with acting.

[12] Noted in Manning 1975: 173.

[13] As have Barton 1993; Champlin 2003.

argues that the chance to appear on stage or in the amphitheater allowed elite Romans access to the sort of public acclaim that they could no longer achieve through more traditional means such as the celebration of a triumph.[14]

By the time of his departure from Italy in 66 CE, Nero appears to have become quite open in the expression of his hatred for the Senate (Suet. *Nero* 37.3; Dio 63.15.1–2). Though the applause of the *plebs* had offered some respite from the censoriousness of the upper orders (Plin. *Pan.* 46. 4), the only audience truly able to appreciate his talents was to be found in Greece (Suet. *Nero* 22.3).[15] So much we have already seen. What, though, did Nero's Grand Tour mean to him and how was it received by his hosts? To appreciate what went on, it is appropriate to think about what festivals such as the Olympic, the Pythian, the Isthmian, and the Nemean Games stood for in the wider Greek world. Crucial here is their status as truly Panhellenic festivals. Competitors came not just from the mainland, but from the furthest reaches of the Greek colonization area. They had already distinguished themselves in more local competitions and might also have demonstrated their prowess in lower-level games such as the Theban Iolaia. To be crowned at any one of the great festivals was a mark of enormous distinction for the winner within his home community and for the community within the Greek world as a whole. All this is evident from victory odes back to Pindar and Bacchylides. When Nero came to compete, the external forms were maintained, but neither he nor his hosts can have been unaware of what was missing. The tone had been set by those Greek communities that sent him the crown for lyre-playing without him having to compete. Like Agamemnon awarded first prize in the spear-throwing at the funeral games of Patroclos without ever taking a throw, Nero was the prisoner of his position: inasmuch as he cannot be allowed to lose, the monarch is also denied the chance truly to deserve to win (Hom. *Il.* 23.884–97). Wherever Nero was declared victorious, he proclaimed the glory that he brought to Rome and to the inhabited world that belonged to him (Dio 63.14.4). Returning in triumph, he entered Naples, Antium, and Rome through a breach in the city walls (Suet. *Nero* 25.1; Dio 63.20. 1–2). This too mimicked the honor paid to a Greek athlete returning in triumph to his home community (Plut. *Mor.* 639E). The problem with all this is easy to spot: when Pindar celebrates the winning of just one crown by a wrestler of Croton, a runner from Cyrene, or a boxer

[14] Discussed in Barton 1993. [15] Manning 1975.

from Aegina, what matters is that that single community has asserted itself over the rest of the Greek world. Now Nero claimed to have brought honor on the entire inhabited world and, by this logic, he was obliged to wreck the walls of any city he entered. For all that a triumph was celebrated as he rode into Rome, he had neither emulated true conquerors of Greece such as Mummius and Flamininus (Dio 63.8.2) nor had he acquired the glory of an authentic Pindaric honorand. What the Greeks made of this debasement of their common cultural heritage is unclear. The people of Achaia were surely glad to be granted their freedom, but the records of the 211th Olympiad were deliberately left blank (Paus. 7.17.3–4, 10.36.9).

When Nero took to the stage, this was not the time to leave your seat: women gave birth in the theater; audience members feigned death in order to escape or slipped down the walls by ropes; the future emperor Vespasian risked death when unwittingly he nodded off (Tac. *Ann.* 16.5.5; Suet. *Nero* 23.2, *Vesp.* 4; Dio 63.15.3, 66.11.2). Or so we are told. So outrageous was all that the actor-emperor undoubtedly did that it is not always easy to know where the truth stops and imaginative elaboration begins. What I have attempted to do in this discussion is first to set out the lineaments of Nero's career as a performer, then to consider what this meant to his biographers and to the historians of his reign, to his mentors, to the Senate, to the knights and the Roman people, to the Greeks, and perhaps most importantly, also to Nero himself. In doing so I have put more trust in the ancient sources for Nero's reign than would many, but I have also identified instances where political culture, literary form, and personal bias significantly impact the narrative, and where modern scholarship has read against the grain and interpreted key phenomena in strikingly different terms.

Since Nero the performance artist is so singular a figure, it is perhaps appropriate to allow him the final word on this issue. For though the end of Nero's life is figured by our sources as a gradual retreat from reality into the fictions he performed, perhaps he can also be credited with a degree of realism. Kingship had given him the opportunity to perform to a far grander audience than otherwise he could have enjoyed, and deference had granted him prizes to which he had no proper claim. Yet when he spoke of exile in Alexandria where "my little craft will sustain me," perhaps Nero began to appreciate what that "weak and dark" voice might have done for him had he never been king.

Further Reading

For general studies of Nero and his reign, see Warmington (1969), Griffin (1984), Elsner and Masters (1994), and Champlin (2003). On theater and theatricality, see Bartsch (1994), Edwards (1994, 1997b), and Star (2012). See also Manning (1975) on acting and Nero's conception of the principate and Kennell (1988) on Nero's tour of Greece. On the values and moral anxieties of the Roman elite, see Barton (1993) and Edwards (1993).

2: Nero and the Senate*

Josiah Osgood

A Roman emperor could not rule without the Senate. This body of around 600 wealthy men traced its origins back to Rome's legendary founder, King Romulus, in the mid-eighth century BCE, and thus powerfully symbolized continuity while also masking political change – above all, the de facto establishment of dynastic monarchy by Augustus. The Senate legitimized emperors by voting them their formal powers and titles (including the name "Augustus"). The Senate supplied honors that glorified the emperor and his family, including triumphal parades, statues, and arches. At critical moments, such as the death of a favored heir or the suppression of a conspiracy, the Senate could help to rally support behind the emperor. Emperors relied on senators to do the actual work of governing too. Senators commanded the emperor's armies, administered most of the empire's provinces, held important administrative roles in the city of Rome itself, and advised the emperor on policy at semi-official council meetings.[1]

Because of senators' political importance, the emperor needed to cultivate good relations with them. Until late in his long life, Augustus regularly attended Senate meetings and sought out senators' views on important matters.[2] He secured privileges for senators, such as front-row seating at games (although he also placed new restrictions on them). For a time, Augustus' successor, Tiberius, showed similar respect. But after withdrawing to the island of Capri in 26 CE, he never appeared in the Senate again, communicating instead by letter. There were other ways, though, to gain support, such as social

* I am grateful to the editors of this volume and also to Andrew Meshnick for helpful suggestions on earlier versions of this chapter. Also, I owe a large debt to the work of the scholars mentioned in the "Further Reading."

[1] Note that equestrians (wealthy individuals who did not join the Senate) did hold some key administrative posts, such as the prefecture of the Praetorian Guard charged with the emperor's security.

[2] On the relations of Augustus and his successors with the Senate, see Talbert 1996.

interactions. Augustus, for example, gambled with senators, and Tiberius drank with them.[3]

Yet, in the absence of a clear law of succession (on hereditary lines or otherwise), an emperor could feel threatened by powerful senators. Of Nero's predecessors, this was most true of Claudius.[4] Shut out of public view by his family because of illness, Claudius unexpectedly came to power in 41 at the age of fifty. The following year, he was challenged by a provincial governor; Claudius responded with a grim witch-hunt and he kept on suppressing conspiracies, or alleged conspiracies, until his death in 54. His persecution of senators and disregard of justice are motifs of Seneca's satire *Apocolocyntosis*, probably written later that year. A great moment in the work is a seething denunciation given by the divine Augustus of his successor. Claudius may look as if he could not hurt a fly, Augustus claims, but he "killed people as easily as a dog sits" (10.3).

The standard account of Nero holds that with the help of his former tutor, Seneca, the new emperor successfully turned around relations with the Senate upon his accession in 54. Not until 62 was a senator convicted of treason, and only in the aftermath of the failed Pisonian conspiracy of 65 did relations really break down. This interpretation goes back at least to Tacitus, himself a senator who wrote in the early second century an annalistic history of Rome from the death of Augustus (now referred to as the *Annals*), and it has proven hard to overturn its main outlines, given the absence of any other similarly detailed source. I shall not try to overturn it here, but use it, along with other accounts of Nero (especially those of Suetonius and Dio), to suggest that the Senate was not purely the victim of his increasing whims.[5] Nero's extreme aestheticism appealed to at least some senators, and aesthetic pursuits offered them a way to handle one another.

2.1 Senate Meetings and Rose Dinners

It is important first to understand better who senators were and what being a senator entailed.[6] Membership in the body required a fortune of one million sesterces. Sons of senators were automatically considered

[3] Recent research has drawn attention to the important role of the emperor's court in mediating relations with senators, e.g., Winterling 2009 and Potter and Talbert 2011. All dates hereafter are CE unless indicated otherwise.

[4] Levick 1990: 53–79 and Osgood 2011: 29–46, 147–67.

[5] Note that Dio's account is reconstructed by means of later summaries of his *History*.

[6] See further Talbert 1984, 1996 and Eck 1991.

eligible to join at the appropriate age, while other wealthy young men had to apply to the emperor first. In practice, old senatorial families failed to keep the Senate's ranks full, and the early emperors welcomed recruits from the towns of Italy and (in far fewer numbers) the western provinces (chiefly Spain and southern Gaul). After Nero, there would be significantly more provincial senators, including from the East.[7]

Upon joining, senators were supposed to attend two set meetings a month – although some were excused during holiday months – along with any other sessions called. Meetings could be dull. The Senate no longer got to create foreign policy, as it had in the Republic. It was likelier to discuss more mundane problems such as the periodic flooding of the Tiber River. Moreover, given the emperor's control of membership and his de facto ability to appoint directly the most senior magistrates (the consuls) along with other important administrative posts, those who spoke during the debate tended to say what they thought the emperor would want to hear.

Probably most exciting (when not too nerve-racking) were the criminal trials the Senate held of its own members. Tacitus suggests that these still furnished scope for an orator's talent.[8] The accusations could be startling, such as that against Senator Octavius Sagitta in 58. According to Tacitus' account (*Ann.* 13.44), Sagitta paid a married woman, Pontia, to sleep with him and leave her husband. While she refused to marry Octavius, they were reunited for a night of lovemaking, during which he stabbed her to death and also wounded her slave attendant. A loyal ex-slave of Octavius tried to take the blame, but Pontia's wounded maid recovered sufficiently to disclose the truth. The Senate found Octavius guilty of murder and exiled him.

If the Senate was not what it was in Cicero's day, many still found it irresistible. In Rome's steep hierarchy, membership in the Senate was the brightest pinnacle. Most lustrous were the top offices available only to senators – the overseas governorships and the consulships. The consuls who opened the year gave their name to that year in the Roman dating system, thereby winning virtual immortality. While it was not supposed to be, senators also materially profited from their status. Fortunes could be harvested in the provinces (by accepting bribes from provincials, for example, in exchange for favorable rulings), and while a senator was prosecutable for embezzlement on his return, one powerful enough could fend off the charges, as Eprius Marcellus did in

[7] On the origin of senators Eck 1991: 104–13 gives a good overview.
[8] See especially *Dial.* 41.

57. A superb orator, Eprius would take the lead in accusing Senator Thrasea Paetus of treason in 66 and was rewarded with a staggering five million sesterces by the Senate. Prosecutions were lucrative and appealed especially to new recruits like Eprius, born into a relatively humble family from the Italian town of Capua.

Danger does not seem to have diminished the glitter of the Senate. Everywhere one looks signs appear of its members' exclusivity. Senatorial families tried to intermarry, and so women – who in Roman law held their property separately from their husbands – are an important part of the story. Perfectly typical was the marriage of Rubellius Plautus, of a relatively new family but whose mother was a granddaughter of Tiberius; Plautus' wife, Antistia, was the daughter of the consul of 55, an ambitious governor of Germany. A notable exception was aristocratic conspirator Calpurnius Piso, who married "a lowborn woman whose only recommendation was her physical beauty" (Tac. *Ann.* 15.59.5). Families like the Calpurnii and Antistii paraded their lineage, another sign of exclusivity.[9] Junia Lepida, wife of distinguished jurist Cassius Longinus, by her second name (Lepida) paid tribute to her mother's family, illustrious patrician Aemilii Lepidi. Nero's critic Thrasea Paetus took "Paetus" from his wife's father, Caecina Paetus, a one-time consul who joined the failed rebellion against Claudius in 42. Nero's second wife, Poppaea, was born to the undistinguished Titus Ollius and should have been called Ollia, but simply usurped the name of her far more distinguished maternal grandfather, Poppaeus Sabinus.

Like other aristocracies, the senatorial class, female and male members alike, further reinforced its exclusivity by a busy round of socializing. This was concentrated in Rome, where these elites maintained great houses with enormous slave staffs. Burial grounds for slaves reveal job titles redolent of luxury: waiters and musicians and dressers and jewelers and many more.[10] Even Nero's mistress, former slave girl Acte, could afford her own eunuch, while the high-ranking Senator Pedanius Secundus, originally from Barcelona in Spain, was discovered to have a slave staff of 400 after one of them killed him – all were subsequently put to death in an episode that shocked the ordinary folk of Rome and provoked a debate in the Senate.[11] Vestinus Atticus (consul in 65) had a "matching set" of handsome slaves, and really these were the complement to fabulous tableware and furniture, like the 500 matching tables of citron wood with legs of ivory allegedly used by Seneca, or the so-called myrrhine cups, probably made of rare iridescent fluorspar.

[9] Flower 1996: 256–60. [10] Treggiari 1973 and Hasegawa 2005. [11] Tac. *Ann.* 14.42–5.

As he faced suicide, Petronius proudly broke one such cup so that Nero could not lay his hands on it. When not in Rome, senators often migrated to the hedonistic Bay of Naples, with its villas, oyster beds, and yachts. This was a striking setting for many episodes of the Neronian period, including most spectacularly the murder of Agrippina, after a late-night party flowing with wine.

Certainly some senators conspicuously eschewed such flamboyant luxury, like the Stoic Rubellius Plautus, who was happy to move with Antistia to estates in Asia after Nero asked him to leave Rome. But the fact was that among senatorial men and women there was a cult of beauty even before Nero appeared on the scene. In *Apocolocyntosis* Seneca called Junia Lepida's handsome sister Junia Calvina "the most fun girl of all" (8.2) while Tacitus thought she was "forward" (*Ann.* 12.4.1). Another Junia, Junia Silana, a woman of good looks as well as lineage, had been married to Gaius Silius, the most handsome senator in Rome, until Claudius' wife, Messalina, lured him away; according to Tacitus, Agrippina subsequently blocked Silana from marrying a young noble, eager not to see him scoop up Silana's immense fortune (*Ann.* 13.19–22).

Silana's fate was exile, but still Nero with his love of luxury gave a fresh impetus to the revels of the senatorial class. They were likelier to meet the emperor at a party than at Senate meetings (to which Nero often sent letters, as he was allowed to). Suetonius writes of millions being spent at a time to entertain Nero with dinners featuring silk turbans and roses (*Nero* 27.3). Nero in turn would entertain, inviting young poets who would help him with his compositions. Light verse and song was a staple at senatorial parties. Nero hailed the future emperor Nerva as the "the Tibullus of our time" for his erotic poetry (Mart. 8.70). Nero himself composed satirical poems about fellow senators such as Afranius Quintianus, a man "notorious for effeminacy" as Tacitus writes (*Ann.* 15.49.4). Yet when another senator, Antistius Sosianus, shared his own satirical poems about Nero at a dinner at the house of Ostorius Scapula in 62, he would pay a steep price.[12] At private parties, it turned out, as much as at Senate meetings, senators had to watch what they said.

2.2 Clemency: Nero's First Performance

We will return to Antistius, but first must circle back to 54 and the aftermath of Claudius' death. In a speech said to have been written by

12 Sullivan 1985: 19–48 discusses the prominence of senators in Nero's poetic circle and the (unexpectedly) dangerous turn literary gatherings took in 62.

Seneca, the sixteen-year-old Nero appeared before the Senate and promised to repudiate Claudian-style witch-hunts and to share power with the Senate and its presiding consuls. The Senate voted to have the speech inscribed on a silver tablet and read out at the start of each year. It also revived a traditional ban on lawyers being paid for their work – another jab at Claudius, who other than eating loved nothing more than legal hearings. Of course, there were ways around the ban – an exchange of other types of favors, for example – and so in many ways the gesture was symbolic.

In practice, Nero's speech did almost nothing to change the role the Senate played, but he continued keenly to parade his regard for the body. He refused, for example, the Senate's vote of gold and silver statues to him – these would be more appropriate for a divinity – as well as the vote to shift the start of the year to December, the month of his birth. These refusals exemplified the imperial virtue of *civilitas* – an emperor's comporting himself like a citizen, rather than an absolute monarch.[13] *Clementia* – an emperor's clemency toward political offenders – was its complement.[14] Both were associated with Augustus and were desired in his successors, as is made especially clear in Suetonius' imperial biographies, which regularly assess how well emperors upheld these virtues. As Suetonius shows, emperors, including Nero in his early days, tried visibly to demonstrate these virtues. Presented with the warrant for an execution of a man, Nero exclaimed: "How I wish I didn't know how to write!" (Suet. *Nero* 10.2). Seneca included the same story in his highly topical *On Clemency* of 56, specifying that it was two bandits Nero had to condemn (2.1.1–3). Of more immediate interest to senators was Nero's decision to restore to Plautius Lateranus membership in the Senate, taken away years earlier because of alleged adultery with Claudius' wife, Messalina. This act of clemency was underscored by frequent speeches by Nero on the virtue, again said to have been ghosted by Seneca.

One can guess that the theatrically minded Nero enjoyed such magnificent gestures. When complaints poured into the Senate about the collection of indirect taxes such as tolls, with a flourish Nero proposed abandoning them all (cooler heads soon prevailed). Ultimately, though, Nero had ambitions other than being a new mature Augustus. Already in *Apocolocyntosis* he is associated with beauty, poetry, and music (4.1). And unsympathetic as the later sources are, they confirm that the only doctrine Nero really lived by was aestheticism. His public performances as singer

[13] Wallace-Hadrill 1982. [14] Dowling 2006 and Braund 2009: 30–44.

are the most notorious evidence for this, but more casual details are equally telling, for instance a fascination with textiles and women's clothing. Dio writes that Nero received senators "in a short flowered tunic, with a scarf of muslin around his neck" (63[62].13.3). Tacitus pictures Nero selecting clothing from a gallery in the imperial palace and sending it to his mother along with jewelry – while she would try to appeal to Nero "all decked out" (*Ann.* 13.13.4, 14.2.1). The highborn Calvia Crispinilla emerges late in Nero's reign as a wardrobe mistress, a key member of the imperial entourage during the sixteen-month tour of Greece.

Calvia later married a former consul, and her status helps to make clear why Nero's quest for sensation really is a part of the seemingly staid subject of "Nero and the Senate." Suetonius puts his finger on something real and important when he assigns to Nero the almost Freudian view that "no person was chaste or in any part of his body pure . . . most concealed their vices, cleverly veiling them" (*Nero* 29). Nero's real soulmates were members of the senatorial class, not just Calvia and Vestinus Atticus with his "matched" slaves, but Otho, "almost feminine in the elegance of his appearance," with his constant depilation, his close-fitting wig, the perfumes he and Nero shared (Suet. *Oth.* 12.1). Otho's mirror became notorious, and it seems there were plenty more to go around in Nero's circle. When Poppaea looked in hers one day and was unpleased with what she saw, "she prayed to die before she was past her prime" (Dio 62.28.1). Five hundred asses traveled with her, to provide milk to bathe in that would keep up her complexion. Otho teased Nero for his parsimony, Poppaea for his marriage to dull old Claudius' daughter Octavia. It was not an accident that Nero's so-called arbiter of elegance was the high-ranking Gaius Petronius (perhaps to be identified with the consul of 62). Nobody did luxury quite so well as senators.

Tacitus and Dio alike have to acknowledge that at least some senators were happy enough not just to attend to Nero's performances, but to take part in them – even if others felt compelled, or at least (later) claimed they did. Well before Nero was born, legislation had been passed under Augustus and Tiberius banning senators from performance, showing that the propensity was already there.[15] Lucan entered his poetry into the Neronia, Cluvius Rufus (later to write a history of Nero) served as Nero's herald on more than one occasion, and the conspirator Piso and even Thrasea Paetus are said to have performed in

[15] Levick 1983a.

tragedies. Was the highborn octogenarian Aelia Catella really *forced* to dance a pantomime at Nero's Juvenalia, as the history of Dio implies (62[61].19.2)?

That was the question Nero raised, almost deliberately it seems. Clearly he wholeheartedly won over some in the Senate, like Otho (until he and Nero quarreled over Poppaea) or another future emperor, Vitellius, both of whom joined Nero on his nighttime prowls through the City where hidden pleasures were to be uncovered in taverns and cruising grounds like the Milvian Bridge. The less adventurous could still be swayed by Nero's control of patronage. Those who wished for a consulship or governorship, or who assured entry into the Senate for a friend or relative, or even simply an invitation to dine at the palace – which could help ensure a consulship later – would support Nero. If Nero enacted *clementia* in his early years, the Senate for its part enacted loyalty, to the point of what Tacitus calls more than once "sycophancy" (*adulatio; Ann.* 13.8.1, 14.12.1, etc.). When good news arrived from the eastern frontier in 54 CE, the Senate voted thanksgivings, parades, and a statue of Nero to stand next to one of Mars. When the letter came from Nero in 59 CE reporting the death of Agrippina, her plot against Nero, and her many earlier crimes, the Senate voted more thanksgivings, games, and another statue of Nero.

Thus even in the face of Nero's matricide most senators were eager to continue affirming their ties with him. The bigger challenge came three years later when Antistius Sosianus was denounced to the Senate for his slanderous poems about Nero – directly raising the question of loyalty. The prosecutor was Cossutianus Capito, condemned by his peers for embezzlement in 57 but now restored to membership in the Senate through the intervention of his father-in-law, the new Praetorian prefect Tigellinus, whom Tacitus sees along with Poppaea as the evil genius of the second half of Nero's reign. While Ostorius Scapula, at whose house Antistius shared his poems, testified that he had heard nothing, other witnesses contradicted him, and the Senate was ready to vote the death penalty. Then Thrasea Paetus stood up and, while denouncing Antistius, cleverly pleaded for a mitigated sentence of banishment, in keeping with the clemency of the modern age. He brought the Senate over to his view. On learning of the Senate's decision, Nero wrote back indicating his displeasure with the senators' leniency. That was the part *he* was supposed to play, and now thanks to Thrasea the Senate had usurped it. While Nero retained plenty of support in the Senate, his clemency was exposed as limited. In later years, relations with the

Senate were to follow a new script. A climate of suspicion and rivalry, including artistic rivalry, developed.

2.3 "I cannot be a slave to a lyre-player."

"I began to hate you after you were found to be the murderer of your mother and wife, a charioteer, actor, and arsonist." Tacitus quotes these blunt words of a Praetorian officer, assuring readers that they are authentic (*Ann.* 15.67.2). Piercing through the endless flatteries and doublespeak of Senate and emperor, they are well-suited to a soldier, but at least some senators likely could share the sentiment. Nero's chariot racing at the Juvenalian Games, the Neronia of 60 CE, the emperor's shocking debut as a lyre-player at Naples in 64, and the Great Fire that destroyed much of Rome: after all this, some senators quietly might have wondered literally what would be left of their City. And then there was the break with clemency in 62, the same year that effectively saw Seneca withdraw from politics.

Certainly one senator was willing to express displeasure, and that was Thrasea. Already in 59, while his fellow senators fell over one another to show support to Nero after Agrippina's murder, Thrasea simply walked out of the Senate house. Without saying a word, he had found a way to communicate his disgust at what was happening. The action may have been spontaneous, but Thrasea turned it into a kind of policy of absenteeism. Later in 59, he refused to join in the applause at the Juvenalian Games led by the large wavy-haired fan club Nero had organized along Alexandrian lines who cheered on the emperor's "divine voice." Ultimately, Thrasea would cease attending the Senate altogether for a period of three years. Decades later, a young senatorial friend of Thrasea, Junius Rusticus, wrote a memoir of Thrasea that seems to inform the later tradition concerning him that we find in Tacitus and Dio.[16] From these two authors a picture emerges of a man convinced of his own ultimate doom, and so unwilling to demean himself with any more flattery. Others, though, including the young Rusticus – on the brink of a political career – would need to decide their own path of action for themselves. This was the dilemma that haunted Tacitus, and his portrayal of Thrasea captures it perfectly.

Thrasea had his circle of friends and in 62 managed to sway the Senate to a more humane judgment of the libelous Antistius, but so far as

[16] See especially Tac. *Ann.* 16.21–35, *Agr.* 2.1; Suet. *Dom.* 10.2–3; Dio 62[61].15.

we can tell he made no effort to remove Nero from power. The first major conspiracy, in 65, came from elsewhere, bringing in members of the Senate as well as some equestrians – and also officers of the Praetorian Guard. As was true in earlier conspiracies, including the successful plot to assassinate Julius Caesar on the Ides of March 44 BCE that served as an inspiration in 65, there was a range of motives for the senators involved, many of them frankly personal. Afranius Quintianus, for example, was smarting over Nero's abusive verses, and even Lucan is said to have acted because of Nero's jealous attempts to suppress his talent.[17] The plan was to kill Nero at the Circus during the festival of Ceres in April in an ambush and replace him with Calpurnius Piso, an aristocrat who attracted enthusiasm for his eloquence, generosity, and good looks. Piso himself sang in costume, and his villa on the Bay of Naples had captivated even Nero with its baths and banquets. That he should be intended as Nero's replacement raises the nagging question here of whether it was less "Neronianism" than simply Nero himself who stirred the conspirators' hostility.

In any event, it was a moment of revenge for the large slave households. A freedman of the senatorial conspirator Scaevinus named Malichus reported suspicious doings to one of Nero's freedman. Scaevinus was taken into custody, and gradually the whole plot unraveled, as more and more conspirators were seized and then informed on one another. Some were implicated on dubious if not outright false grounds, including Seneca and Vestinus, the man of the "matched" slaves who had enjoyed a bantering friendship with Nero until he married Statilia Messalina, on whom Nero had his eye. Before it was all over, Piso was urged to take action anyway, but he refused, and took his own life as would Seneca and Vestinus. In the inquisition that continued, Nero took the chance to settle some other scores, banishing Seneca's friend Novius Priscus, for example, and Poppaea's former husband. Rewards were given to those who showed loyalty, including praetor designate Cocceius Nerva, future emperor of Rome. The Senate also heaped on thanksgivings and celebrations. Tacitus (*Ann.* 15.74.3) cannot resist a moment of dark humor that he discovered in the Senate record: consul designate Anicius Cerialis zealously proposed immediate construction of a temple of Divine Nero – an honor normally reserved to emperors *after* their deaths.

Essentially Nero had reverted to the Claudian pattern of government. The last pages of Tacitus' *Annals* – which breaks off, midsentence,

[17] Tac. *Ann.* 15.49.3–4 (15.48–73 is the major account of the conspiracy).

in the year 66 – are replete with persecutions the emperor initiated in collusion with friendly prosecutors and carried through by a compliant Senate. Nero wrote to the body of his suspicions concerning the ancient blind jurist Cassius Longinus, his wife, Junia Lepida, and their young nephew Silanus; the men were banished. In 65, Antistius Vetus, his mother-in-law, Sextia, and his daughter Antistia, the wife of Rubellius Plautus (himself murdered several years earlier) were caught in the net and died in a mutual suicide pact. Thrasea's absenteeism caught up with him this year too. The loathsome Cossutianus Capito, with several scores to settle now, joined Eprius Marcellus in the prosecution, and denounced him for disloyalty: Thrasea did not even make sacrifices to protect the Divine Voice!

With the loss of Tacitus, it is hard to say much about a second major conspiracy, "contrived by Vinicius at Beneventum and uncovered there" as Suetonius writes (*Nero* 36.1). Other evidence suggests that this was in 66, as Nero was heading for his Grand Tour of Greece, and the Vinicius was actually Annius Vinicianus, son of a conspirator against Claudius in 42 and the son-in-law of Nero's greatest general, Domitius Corbulo, who spent virtually the whole reign in command of operations in Armenia. Annius, not yet of senatorial age, served with Corbulo until 65 when he was sent to Rome with Tiridates of Armenia and may have found the scene unfolding there too much.

2.4 "I HATE YOU, CAESAR, FOR BEING A SENATOR."

Our sources suggest that as Nero made his long-desired visit to Greece, relations with the Senate virtually ended. A figure of hideous fascination is the court jester, Vatinius, a deformed cripple from a family of shoemakers. Nero took particular pleasure whenever Vatinius teased, "I hate you, Caesar, for being a senator" (Dio 63[62].15.1). The reality, though, was that the Senate kept on meeting, and members kept on agreeing to serve as consuls; Nero's last appointment was Silius Italicus, who later burnished his reputation by writing epic poetry, but was never able totally to bury rumors that he was an informer.[18] More than widespread alienation in the Senate caused by the Grand Tour itself (or the preceding prosecutions), what doomed Nero was his summoning to Greece of several senatorial governors, including Domitius Corbulo, who were killed or forced to commit suicide.[19]

[18] Plin. *Ep.* 3.7. [19] On Corbulo's importance, see Vervaet 2002.

Commanders felt endangered, and – equally important – Nero's actions helped alienate some key powerbases across the empire.[20] Nero's failure to acquire very much military prestige (as even Claudius did, with his conquest of Britain) made him a less plausible *imperator* in the eyes of officers. And a shortfall of money, arising not just from personal extravagance, but from the rebuilding of Rome after the Great Fire and the long eastern war, led to increased exactions throughout the provinces and to delays in soldiers' pay and discharges.

Senator Julius Vindex, from a great family of Aquitaine and governing in Gaul, was inspired by (or at least relied on) suffering there to raise a revolt in March 68.[21] He issued edicts that insulted Nero; circulating widely, they undermined Nero's legitimacy. Vindex also wrote to other governors, including several times to Galba, the governor of Spain whose distinguished patrician ancestry made him a likelier successor to replace Nero than Vindex himself. Galba's troops took the step of proclaiming Galba *imperator* in early April, but he refused the title (as well as the name Caesar) and called himself "general of the Roman Senate and people."[22] This was to assert that armies were not to make emperors, even as it also cleverly allowed Galba an out if a more plausible contender emerged. Otho, banished to a governorship of Portugal years earlier by Nero after their quarrel over Poppaea, declared his support for Galba. The Senate declared Galba a public enemy, but then the governor of Africa, Clodius Macer, revolted, joined by wardrobe mistress Calvia Crispinilla – further destabilizing Nero's position, since Africa supplied the city of Rome with much of its grain.[23] And although the governor of Upper Germany with its large concentration of legions, Verginius Rufus, put down Vindex' revolt – in circumstances the truth of which was later, understandably, buried – Verginius declared that he would not assume power himself, but would follow the Senate's lead, persisting in this view even after Nero's suicide. His soldiers swore the oath of loyalty to Galba after the Senate recognized Galba.

Nero was back from Greece and in Naples when he learned of Vindex' rising. A remarkably vivid account of his actions from this point on is given by Suetonius (*Nero* 40–9), likely deriving from the history of Nero's old herald Cluvius Rufus.[24] According to it, despite the news from Gaul, Nero stayed for eight further days in Naples, enjoying

[20] Griffin 1984: 197–207, 221–34 and Drinkwater 2013: 169–70.
[21] Brunt 1990: 9–32 is a key discussion. [22] Plut. *Galb.* 5.2; Suet. *Galb.* 10.1.
[23] For a different view on Macer and Crispinilla, see Morgan 2000.
[24] This is suggested, in part, by the close overlap with Dio 63.26–29.2; see Champlin 2003: 49–51.

athletic contests; even when back in Rome, he did not personally address the Senate about the crisis, but called a few men to his house and after a quick consultation "spent the remainder of the day exhibiting some water-organs of a new and previously unknown type." Only when word came of Galba's revolt did he decide to take action, though we are told that his primary concern was "to choose wagons that would transport his instruments for the stage, to give his concubines . . . masculine haircuts, and to outfit them with Amazonian battle-axes and shields." This masks the seriousness of Nero's preparations, which can be seen from other evidence.[25] But as further troubling reports came into Rome, key supporters abandoned him, beginning with his household staff (including personal bodyguards) and the Praetorians. The Senate acted last, declaring Nero a public enemy. When word reached Nero, hiding in the outskirts of Rome, he stabbed himself, helped by one of the four freedmen who had stayed loyal to him.

The fall of Nero makes for a good case study in where power lay in the Roman empire.[26] If united, an army commander and his troops could pose a serious threat to the emperor (and after more than one commander rebelled, there could be a contagious effect). In Rome itself, it was also soldiers who mattered (the Praetorians), as well as the emperor's household staff. The Senate was not guiding events, even if commanders appealed to its authority. Still, at least a handful of senators were key figures in bringing down Nero. Nero's total obsession with performance and aestheticism may have offended them, but probably more decisive was the growing difficulty of doing their job as governors. Back in Italy, many in the Senate, prone to boredom, awash in money, and deeply vain, were happy enough with rose dinners, wigs and gowns, even singing on the stage. While as emperor he was able to go to brutal extremes, Nero's cult of beauty owed quite a bit to the senatorial milieu out of which he emerged.

Further Reading

Nothing can beat Tacitus' account of Nero in books 13–16 in the *Annals*; Woodman 2004 gives a faithful translation into English. Griffin 1984 and Rudich 1993 are two penetrating accounts of Nero relevant for this topic, the latter especially powerful in its recreation of Nero's critic Thrasea Paetus. For the larger context, Talbert 1996 gives

[25] E.g., Tac. *Hist.* 1.6.2, with Champlin 2003: 3.

[26] Drinkwater 2013.

a useful overview of the early imperial Senate; Hopkins 1983: 120–200 (a chapter coauthored with G. Burton) and many works of Syme portray the senatorial class as a whole, including his late masterpiece, Syme 1986. On the essential Claudian background, see Levick 1990 and Osgood 2011.

3: Nero's Imperial Administration

Carlos F. Noreña

In a curious passage at the end of his biography of Nero, Suetonius reports that Vologases, the king of the Parthians, responded to the death of the emperor by sending envoys to the Roman Senate in order to make the solemn request that Nero's memory be honored (*Nero* 57). This brief notice provides a useful way into the larger problem of empire and government under Nero. For it underlines that ancient empires were not really about planting flags in conquered territories or drawing colors on maps. Instead, they were about the creation and maintenance of institutional frameworks and interpersonal relationships through which the disparate interests of a handful of key actors could be brought into a functional equilibrium of social power. Ancient empires, that is to say, were less about territoriality and more about the arrangements that perpetuated the dominance of the few widely scattered haves over the far-flung masses of have-nots.

On this understanding of empire, what we rather loosely call "government" was nothing more and nothing less than the management of a whole constellation of potentially divergent interests, from the center to the peripheries and beyond. The story of Vologases' envoys, who sought to preserve the standing of a deceased emperor who had authored an arrangement favorable to the Parthian royal house (as we will see), provides us with a fleeting glimpse of this management-of-interests in process. It was from a thousand such arrangements that the Roman empire, as a particular configuration of power, was not just governed, but continuously made and remade. The aim of this chapter is to explore the nature of imperial government, understood as the management of interests by means of both formal institutions and individual actors, during the reign of the emperor Nero (54–68 CE).

The ancient tradition on the empire under Nero, and on Nero as an imperial administrator, leaves the impression of a worsening moral decay at the center that came to contaminate the whole imperial system. This picture does not bear close scrutiny. In the first place, given the size and complexity of the Roman empire, there was only so much damage that any emperor, however "bad," could do. Indeed, because the administrative apparatus of the Roman empire was for the most part cumbersome, sluggish, and subdivided into many moving (and disconnected) parts, the overall structure of imperial government was largely insulated from the particular impulses of this or that emperor, or the short-term developments that occurred during this or that reign. So in order to put Nero's reign into proper perspective – to highlight what was typical and what was distinctive about it – it will be necessary first to review the basic features of Roman imperial government in the early empire. The discussion will then turn to the Neronian period proper. The bulk of this chapter will examine imperial government under Nero as a system for the management of interests, and will address standard topics such as fiscal and monetary policy, frontier defense, and provincial administration. The conclusion will then shift to imperial government as a system for maintaining the power of the monarchic regime itself – not the empire as a whole, in other words, but the Neronian court in particular. What should emerge by the end of this chapter is a sketch of the relationship between empire, government, institutions, political authority, and social power during the late Julio-Claudian period.

3.1 ROMAN IMPERIAL GOVERNMENT IN THE EARLY EMPIRE

The aggressive and continuous conquests of the Roman state in the last two centuries BCE, under the Republic, more or less came to an end in the last decade of the reign of the first emperor, Augustus (27 BCE–14 CE). By this time Rome had built an empire that stretched from one end of the Mediterranean to the other, with several extensions into the sea's continental hinterlands. Imperial expansion slowed considerably over the course of the first century CE. The annexation of the entire perimeter of the Mediterranean was finally completed, mainly through the absorption of several former "client" kingdoms. There was also one large-scale invasion, of Britain, under the emperor Claudius (41–54). During the Julio-Claudian period, this increasingly stable, tributary empire measured just under 2.5 million square miles, and held within its borders something like 50 million inhabitants (Figure 3.1).

In the management of this gigantic realm, ultimate decision-making authority rested with the emperor, whose executive supremacy

3.1 Map of the Roman Empire in 69 CE. Ancient World Mapping Centre © 2016 (awmc.unc.edu). Used by permission.

was formally granted by statute (and confirmed by the learned opinion of the jurists). But he could not rule alone. In practice, the emperor depended on an array of institutions and individual actors in order to govern the territories and peoples under his control. An inner circle of advisors, the *consilium*, formed a quasi-formal body available for consultation on all matters, while a secretarial staff helped to manage fiscal matters and the emperor's voluminous written correspondence. The Senate, which remained the institutional embodiment of the empire's political elite, was a vital organ of imperial administration. As a corporate body, the Senate exercised important diplomatic and legislative functions, the latter through the passage of binding decrees (*senatus consulta*). Individual senators of high rank not only governed most of the empire's provinces, where they administered justice and sought to maintain order, but also served as commanders of the legions. Members of the equestrian order, which sat just below the senatorial order in social prestige, filled out the ranks of an expanding, proto-bureaucratic civil service. Its portfolio was largely financial, with particular concentrations in the collection of indirect taxes, especially customs dues (*portoria*), and in the management of the emperor's own estates. In these capacities, equestrians were often assisted by the emperor's slaves and freedmen, the *familia Caesaris*. Finally, some of the mundane, day-to-day tasks of provincial administration were performed by soldiers, seconded from military service for this purpose.

The total number of Roman administrators was small relative to the size and population of the empire. At any one time during the first century CE, there were fewer than 300 high-ranking, salaried officials dispersed throughout the empire's thirty or so provinces, and something on the order of 10,000 administrative personnel in all – roughly one official or lower-level functionary for every 5,000 subjects.

To keep the empire running, this thin spread of state agents operated in part by means of coercion, and in part by forging a degree of consensus between rulers and subjects. Coercion depended on the application (or threat) of armed force. This was provided by the state's 350,000 legionary and auxiliary soldiers, stationed in bases concentrated along the empire's northern and eastern frontiers, but available for service elsewhere, either in mobile detachments or in garrisons in the larger cities. Their internal policing duties included the suppression of local uprisings and the meting out of judicial punishments, both of which helped to keep subjects in line. The Roman empire could not, however, rely on coercion alone. Imperial officials also worked to generate normative buy-in to the ideological claims of the Roman state. Advertised benefits of imperial rule included the provision of peace and prosperity, the promise of a government that was responsive to subjects and fair in its adjudication of disputes and dispensation of justice, and the provision of monetary gifts to cities, civic benefactions (especially public buildings), and assistance with infrastructural projects such as roads and aqueducts.

Even when the instruments of coercion and consensus were operating effectively, the central state and its institutional representatives needed help in the day-to-day running of the empire. They got it from the wealthy, landed, urban-based upper classes that controlled the cities and towns of the Roman world. Indeed, these local elites were the linchpins of the whole system of government in the early Roman empire. For it was the local elites who oversaw the collection of the empire's direct taxes, on land (*tributum soli*) and on persons (*tributum capitis*), which not only paid for the armies that enabled imperial coercion, but also underwrote the imperial patronage that helped to induce consensus in Roman rule. And as the primary exponents of Roman culture in the provinces, they catalyzed the "Romanization" of the emperor's subjects, and that, too, reinforced the ideological hegemony of the Roman imperial state. In (implicit) exchange for these critical services, the local elites of the Roman world came to be incorporated into the wider social and political networks of the imperial power, which naturally increased their status within their own communities. This form of collaboration between central state and local elites reached its apogee in the golden age of the Antonine empire (second century CE), but it had its roots in the Julio-Claudian period. In thinking about the haves of the Roman world, we should imagine a spectrum that ran from the reigning emperor, at the apex, down to the ruling classes of the empire's thousands of urban settlements, large and small. In material, political, and ideological terms, the Roman empire belonged to them, and they were the ones who ran it.[1]

3.2 Imperial Administration and the Calibration of Interests

Nero assumed the throne, in October 54, with the bold declaration that he would rule in the manner of Augustus, with reference to the administration

[1] Hopkins 2009 offers a concise account of the structure and political economy of the early Roman empire.

of justice, the division of responsibilities between emperor and Senate, the collection of taxes and fines, and the dispensation of largesse (Tac. *Ann.* 13.4–5; Suet. *Nero* 10). This pronouncement on imperial governance may be read as an expression of Nero's distributional politics, addressing administrative structures, on the one hand, and the allocation of material resources, on the other. Since material resources – especially money and taxes – were the lifeblood of the state, we begin with the latter.

Fiscal policy under Nero was characterized by a confounding mix of dramatic proposals, radical initiatives, and a series of modest and prudent measures. One rather astonishing tax scheme was proposed near the beginning of the reign; another was actually implemented near the end. In the year 58, Nero floated the possibility of canceling all indirect taxes (*vectigalia*), aiming, by this measure, "to give the human race a fantastic gift" (Tac. *Ann.* 13.50). According to Tacitus, the senators applauded Nero's generosity, but warned the emperor that the loss of these revenues, especially the *portoria*, would be disastrous for the state's finances. So the idea was scotched. More drastic was the awarding of "freedom" to the Greeks, which Nero formally granted during his provincial tour of Achaia in 67. An honorific decree from Akraiphia in central Greece records the grant's central provision (*IG* 7.2713 = *ILS* 8794):

> For you, men of Greece, it is an unexpected gift which, even
> though nothing from my generous nature is unhoped for,
> I grant to you, as great a gift as you would be unable to request.
> All Greeks inhabiting Achaia and what is now known as the
> Peloponnesos receive freedom from taxation! A thing which
> none of you ever possessed in your most fortunate of times, for
> you were subject to others or to yourselves.
>
> (trans. Sherk)

As a result of this measure, then, an entire province was to be free both from Roman governors and from the burden of paying the *tributum*. The grant was spectacular but short-lived, repealed by the emperor Vespasian in the early 70s. To these fiscally adventurous projects one might add the public burning of debts to the *aerarium*, or state treasury (Tac. *Ann.* 13.23), and the proposal that tenants pay one full year's worth of rent not to their landlords, but rather to the *fiscus*, or imperial purse (Suet. *Nero* 44).

The hostile literary tradition on Nero can make it difficult to assess his fiscal and financial programs.[2] Dio, for example, writing in the first

[2] Contrast, for example, Griffin 1984: 197–207, who argues for "grievous financial difficulty" and the need to "exact money and seize treasure from Italy and the provinces" (197), with Rathbone

half of the third century CE, reports that Nero – represented throughout the narrative as a wastrel – imposed a raft of burdensome new taxes at the beginning of his reign (61.5), and that he appropriated vast sums from individuals and communities following the fire of 64 (62.18). But there is no good evidence for either of Dio's claims. Nor, upon closer examination, are Nero's better-attested schemes and measures quite so preposterous. The proposal to cancel all indirect taxes was never actually realized, and was probably intended from the beginning to promote the image of the magnanimous ruler. The loss of public revenues from the "freeing" of Achaia was balanced by the transfer of Sardinia's tribute from the imperial purse to the public treasury (Paus. 7.17.3). And several canonically "good" emperors, such as Augustus, Vespasian, and Hadrian, also publicly burned debts owed to the treasury.

A series of more mundane initiatives gives a better picture of fiscal policy under Nero. In 58, for example, the emperor instituted a set of incremental reforms concerning the activities of the tax-farmers (*publicani*) who contracted with the Roman state to collect several of the indirect taxes. Nero's edict mandated the publication of the regulations by which the farming of taxes was organized; declared that judicial cases against the tax-farmers should take precedence over all other cases; and repealed a pair of illegal surcharges, in the amounts of 2 percent and 2.5 percent, respectively, that the tax-farmers had concocted in order to increase their gains (Tac. *Ann.* 13.51). The thrust of these reforms was to reign in the tax-farmers, and to give some leverage back to provincial communities in the perpetual tug-of-war between central and local agents in the competition over resources. A key provision of the edict was designed to make the organization of the tax-farming operation as a whole more transparent. Documentary evidence for its implementation comes from the so-called customs law of Asia, a censorial regulation (*lex censoria*) from the year 62 that enumerated a series of regulations, going all the way back to 75 BCE, concerning the farming of customs dues in (and perhaps around) the province of Asia (*EA* 14 [1989] = *AE* 1989.681 = *SEG* 39.1180). Indeed, the inscribing of this law in Ephesos, an important commercial hub in the Roman East, shows that local communities were invested in the publicization of imperial administrative policy, presumably in order to hold imperial agents accountable for their actions. The fact that a board of three consulars was established to oversee the collection of indirect taxes, reported by Tacitus

2008, suggesting that the record of Neronian finance has been distorted by the systematic denigration of Nero's reign under Vespasian and his successors.

(*Ann.* 15.18) and confirmed by this very text (ll. 3–4), is another indication of the seriousness with which the Neronian regime took the oversight of the state's fiscal apparatus.

Taxation was not just a framework for articulating the proper relationship between state and subject. It was also, of course, the principal mechanism through which the central state collected revenues, which in turn underpinned imperial expenditures. One of the ways that emperors could maximize expenditure was through manipulation of the currency. Though Nero's predecessors had tinkered with the weight and fineness of the precious-metal denominations, it was Nero who authorized the first significant changes to the weight standards of the *aureus* (gold) and *denarius* (silver). The big reductions came in 64 (which may be the context for the transfer of the main state treasury from Lugdunum, in Gaul, to Rome itself). The number of *aurei* to the pound of gold was increased from forty to forty-five, and the number of *denarii* to the pound of silver from eighty-four to ninety-six. In addition, the silver content of the *denarius* was reduced by about 10 percent. These devaluations may indicate a sophisticated effort to bring the *aureus* and *denarius* into better harmony with the market prices of gold and silver, respectively, but they were probably intended simply to increase the money supply and the short-term spending power of the imperial state.[3]

The major ongoing expense of the Roman state was the army, which consumed anywhere from one-half to three-quarters of the annual imperial "budget." And the Roman imperial army was very active during Nero's reign, deployed to consolidate territorial expansion in Britain, to confront the Parthians for control over Armenia, and to suppress a major Jewish revolt. Each episode bears on the theme of imperial government as a system for the management of interests, so let us consider each in turn.

The initial conquest of Britain had taken place in 43, during the reign of Claudius, but the native inhabitants of the new province were not yet resigned to the Roman occupation when Nero came to power more than a decade later. Part of their resentment was symbolic in nature – the Temple of Claudius at Colchester, it seems, was a particularly irritating sign of alien domination (Tac. *Ann.* 14.31) – but the outbreak of an armed uprising in 60 was driven by material considerations (*Ann.* 14.31–2; Dio 62.2). When Prasugatus, the king of

[3] Market correction in gold and silver prices: Lo Cascio 1981: 80. Increase in money supply: Griffin 1984: 198; Duncan-Jones 1994: 221, n. 35. Mixture of "administrative and aesthetic" reasons: Rathbone 1996: 319.

the Iceni (a tribal group in eastern Britain), bequeathed part of his kingdom to Nero, a number of Roman officials took advantage of the opportunity to fleece his subjects. Two singled out in the sources for their rapacity are Decianus Catus, an equestrian financial official (*procurator*) in Britain, and Seneca, alleged to have called in a massive loan at just this moment. From this episode comes one of Rome's most memorable enemies, Queen Boudicca, the widow of Prasugatus and de facto leader of the Iceni. Dio gives her a speech that highlights the fiscal component of the Roman occupation (62.3.2–3):

> Have we not been robbed entirely of most of our possessions, and those the greatest, while for those that remain we pay taxes? Besides pasturing and tilling for them all our other possessions, do we not pay a yearly tribute for our very bodies? How much better it would be to have been sold to masters once for all than, possessing empty titles of freedom, to have to ransom ourselves every year! How much better to have been slain and to have perished than to go about with a tax on our heads!
>
> (trans. Cary)

The rebels under Boudicca managed to defeat a small Roman contingent and even to sack three large Roman settlements (Colchester, London, and St. Albans), but the uprising was ultimately extinguished by Suetonius Paulinus, the commander of the legions in Britain (*legatus Augusti*) and one of the literary archetypes of the "good" Roman general operating under a "bad" emperor (Tac. *Ann.* 14.33–8; Dio 62.8–12).[4]

Another such figure was Domitius Corbulo, charged with overseeing Roman operations on the eastern frontier. The big challenge here was to retain Roman hegemony, against increasing pressure from the Parthian empire, in the region of Armenia.[5] At issue was control over the Armenian throne. When Tiridates, brother of the Parthian king Vologases, refused to receive his crown from a Roman official – and to acknowledge, by this gesture, Roman suzerainty – Corbulo was authorized to invade Armenia. In the campaign that ensued (58–9), Corbulo captured the strategic strongholds of Artaxata and Tigranocerta and drove Tiridates from the region (Tac. *Ann.* 13.34–41, 14.23–26; Dio 62.19–20). Further fighting ensued several years later when Nero himself rejected Tiridates' belated offer to be crowned by a Roman.

[4] Clear account of the revolt of the Iceni in Mattingly 2007: 101–13. [5] Braund 2013.

Following a Parthian victory over a smaller Roman force (62), Corbulo once again invaded Armenia with a massive army (64), a move that impelled Vologases to acquiesce in Rome's renewed insistence on authorizing Tiridates' kingship (Tac. *Ann.* 15.1–18, 24–31). The subsequent coronation of Tiridates in Rome was one of the great "set pieces" in the spectacle that was Neronian government. Suetonius paints a vivid picture of the scene (*Nero* 13):

> Armed cohorts stood around the temples in the Forum and Nero himself was seated in a curule chair on the rostra, dressed in the robes of a triumphant general and surrounded by military standards and flags. When Tiridates approached up the sloping platform, Nero first let him fall at his feet but then raised him up with his right hand and kissed him. Next, while the king made the speech of a suppliant, Nero removed from his head the turban and replaced it with a diadem. (trans. Edwards, modified)[6]

This arrangement suited both sides. The Parthians got their man onto the Armenian throne, but the Romans could nevertheless assert their hegemony in the region. They marked the occasion by closing the Temple of Janus in Rome (66), symbolizing peace through their realm (Suet. *Nero* 13).

The Jewish revolt that broke out that same year, narrated in great detail by one of its protagonists, Josephus (*The Jewish War*), shattered the illusion of a *pax Romana*.[7] Once again, it was misconduct by a provincial official – in this case, Gessius Florus, the provincial governor of Judaea – that was the proximate cause of the uprising. He not only seized seventeen talents of gold from the Temple in Jerusalem, but also sat idly by as the non-Jewish inhabitants of Caesarea attacked the Jewish community there. When the governor of the neighboring (and heavily militarized) province of Syria failed to suppress what had quickly become a large-scale rebellion against Roman authority, Nero sent the battle-tested Vespasian, the future emperor, to assume command of the war (67). Nero himself would not live to see the ultimate Roman victory over the Jews, which came after seven years of hard fighting, an

[6] "produxit quo opportunissime potuit, dispositis circa Fori templa armatis cohortibus, curuli residens apud rostra triumphantis habitu inter signa militaria atque vexilla. Et primo per devexum pulpitum subeuntem admisit ad genua adlevatumque dextra exosculatus est, dein precanti tiara deducta diadema inposuit, verba supplicis."

[7] Goodman 1987.

epic siege (at Masada), much loss of life, and the destruction of the Temple in Jerusalem.

The cases of Catus in Britain and Florus in Judaea exemplify the challenges the imperial regime faced in maintaining the always delicate balance between center and periphery in the distribution of resources. But local antipathy toward provincial officials did not always explode into armed rebellion. One reason is that the Roman state had established an institutional mechanism, the court for official misconduct (*repetundae*), for checking the personal ambitions (and avarice) of provincial governors and other central administrators. Tacitus reports no fewer than eleven trials for various forms of official delinquency under Nero in the provinces of Sardinia (*Ann.* 13.30), Crete (13.30), Asia (13.33), Cilicia (13.33), Lycia (13.33), Africa (13.52, two cases), Cyrene (14.18, two cases), Mauretania (14.28), and Bithynia (14.46). This is the highest number of attested trials for any emperor between Augustus and Trajan (98–117), which may suggest that Neronian administrators were especially rapacious, or that the Neronian court for official misconduct was especially active (or both).[8] Prosecution of imperial officials was normally initiated by provincial councils (*koina/concilia*). Prominent provincials could also get caught up in this web of legal recrimination. One such case involved Claudius Timarchus, a local magnate from Crete, who had boasted that it was in his power to determine whether a provincial governor in Crete, following his term, would be formally honored by the council – the structural alternative to a prosecution. Timarchus' conviction was followed by a decree that provincial councils could no longer vote formal thanks to provincial governors (*Ann.* 15.20–2), a decision that removed at least one incentive to collusion between greedy governors and unscrupulous provincial elites.

Roman government in the Neronian age was not just an elaborate tool for the self-enrichment of imperial officials. The central state also provided some tangible benefits to provincial populations, especially in the financing and execution of infrastructural projects. The best known such project under Nero was the attempt to cut a canal through the isthmus at Corinth (Suet. *Nero* 19; Dio 62.16), but there were smaller-scale initiatives, too, such as the reinforcement of the Rhine embankment (Tac. *Ann.* 13.53) or the upgrading of the facilities along the highways in Thrace (*CIL* 3.6123 = *ILS* 231). And sometimes there were simple monetary gifts to favored collectivities, such as the judges at the Olympic Games, who received 1,000,000 sesterces from the

[8] Brunt [1961] 1990, with App. 1 (90–4) for the list of known trials between Augustus and Trajan.

emperor (Dio 62.14, also recording the gift of 400,000 sesterces to the Pythian oracle at Delphi), or the people of Lugdunum, recipients of 4,000,000 sesterces following some unspecified disaster there (Tac. *Ann.* 16.13), possibly a fire (cf. Sen. *Ep.* 91.14). When Nero incorporated the previously independent kingdoms of Pontus and the Cottian Alps into the Roman empire (Suet. *Nero* 18), then, it was not all doom and gloom for the subject populations of those territories.

3.3 Government, Court, and Social Power

Nero's promise to rule on the Augustan model implied a positive working relationship with the Roman political elite, and an equitable sharing of the decision-making authority that structured imperial governance. Coming to the throne at the age of sixteen, and with limited administrative experience, Nero initially relied on a small inner circle of trusted advisors. Prominent in literary accounts of the Neronian court in its first phase are Sextus Afranius Burrus, an equestrian from Gallia Narbonensis who served as prefect of the Praetorian Guard in Rome; and Lucius Annaeus Seneca, also of equestrian rank, from Hispania Tarraconensis, a prolific writer, rhetorician, and philosopher who rose to become a senior advisor to the young emperor. It is the putative influence of these allegedly sober and virtuous advisors, especially the philosopher Seneca, that explains the late-antique tradition of the so-called *quinquennium Neronis* (Aur. Vict. *De Caes.* 5.1–4, attributing the judgment to the emperor Trajan), a period of five years of exemplary rule, normally dated from Nero's accession in 54 to the murder of his mother, Agrippina, in 59. But the ideal of responsible and stable government enshrined in the fantasy of the *quinquennium Neronis* would not last forever.

The problem was that Roman imperial government was always in part a complex system for the perpetuation of the emperor's own power and authority. That made the whole edifice of government potentially unstable, as other members of the imperial family, or high-ranking officials within the system, might want the imperial throne for themselves. This ambition was partly a matter of such men hoping to gain preferred access to the material wealth of empire. After all, not everyone in the Roman empire could confiscate "half of North Africa" by the execution of a handful of large landowners, as Nero was said to have done (Plin. *HN* 18.7.35). But it was also a matter of maximizing honor and social prestige. Competition for the throne among those close to the center of power is a structural feature of monarchy, of course, and explains much of the internal violence of Nero's reign. The murder of potential rivals from within the imperial family itself, such as Nero's stepbrother Britannicus (Tac. *Ann.* 13.15–17; Suet. *Nero* 33; Dio 61.7), and the proliferation of treason trials (*maiestas*) in the 60s, in which enemies (real or perceived) were eliminated, are just the most obvious illustrations of a tendency that is always latent within any monarchic regime.[9] But this form of competition and violence also articulates the theme of imperial government in interesting ways, as shown in three interrelated episodes from the latter part of Nero's reign.

The first is the Pisonian conspiracy of 65 (Tac. *Ann.* 15.48–74; Suet. *Nero* 36; Dio 62.24–7). According to Tacitus, who provides a very full account of this failed coup, a number of disgruntled elites sought to assassinate the "tyrant" Nero and replace him with Gaius Calpurnius Piso, scion of a distinguished noble family. When the plot was betrayed, Nero's retribution was vicious. Among those purged in the immediate aftermath – including many against whom very little hard evidence was adduced – were Faenius Rufus, who had been serving as one of the two Praetorian prefects, Seneca, the poet Lucan, and Piso himself. Others destroyed in a second wave of reprisals included the novelist Petronius (surely to be identified as Nero's "director of taste," *arbiter elegantiae*) and the Stoic philosophers Borea Soranus and Thrasea Paetus. In taking his vengeance, Nero relied heavily on his other Praetorian prefect, Ofonius Tigellinus, who in 62 had replaced Burrus (possibly murdered: Suet. *Nero* 35 and Dio 62.13, but cf. Tac. *Ann.* 14.51), and who was rewarded for his brutality with a triumphal statue in the Forum (Tac. *Ann.* 15.72). The whole episode illuminates the fluid composition of an emperor's inner circle, and the ways in which the changing attitudes and perceptions of the emperor himself could be exploited by high-ranking officials in the furthering of their own interests.

A second conspiracy, led by Annius Vinicianus (Suet. *Nero* 36), was uncovered in 66. In the retaliations that followed, the most prominent victim was Vinicianus' father-in-law, Corbulo, whose execution should be seen not as punishment for his alleged role in the plot, but rather as the permanent eradication of a legionary commander who had become too powerful in his own right. This was a common problem in large, premodern empires, in which *generalissimos* on distant frontiers posed a constant threat to the monarch at the center. It is true that other legionary commanders achieved great fame under Nero – the martial

[9] On *maiestas* trials and factional politics under Nero, see Rutledge 2001: 111–21, 150–5.

exploits recorded in an honorific inscription for Tiberius Plautius (*CIL* 14.3608 = *ILS* 986), for example, which include victories over several seminomadic tribal groups north of the Danube in the 60s, are impressive enough – but Corbulo's defeat of the Parthians, and his formal status as commander of the entire eastern frontier, elevated him far above his peers. In fact, he was seen by many as a preferable alternative to Nero (Dio 62.19). His execution reveals just how dangerous was the intersection between imperial government and court politics in the Neronian age. The implicit threat posed by a figure like Corbulo was surely exacerbated by the deficit of military glory that Nero could claim on his own behalf. The suppression of Boudicca in Britain and the crowning of Tiridates in Rome were not enough. In this important regard, Nero did not really live up to the Augustan model.

It was a third effort to supplant the emperor that brought the Neronian age to an end once and for all. This was the rebellion initiated by a provincial governor in Gaul, Gaius Julius Vindex (Suet. *Nero* 40 ff., *Galba* 9–12, 16; Dio 63.22 ff.).[10] A second-generation senator of native Gallic descent, Vindex did not have the necessary social credentials to make a credible bid for the imperial throne. Instead, he persuaded Servius Sulpicius Galba, a senator of distinguished lineage then serving as governor of Hispania Tarraconensis, to offer himself as a "liberator of humanity" (Suet. *Galb.* 9). Galba successfully navigated the maze of imperial politics to become emperor, but had reigned for only three months when he was assassinated by the Praetorians in Rome in January 69 (Tac. *Hist.* 1.41). Vindex did not last even that long, committing suicide after his defeat by Verginius Rufus, the commander of the legions on the upper Rhine frontier (Dio 63.24). But Vindex had nevertheless triggered a fast-moving series of events that left Nero without any support, political or military, and that ended with the emperor's suicide in June 68 (Suet. *Nero* 49; Dio 63.29). So it was this representative of the new provincial elite of the Roman West – this typical product of empire – that launched the larger movement that would bring down Nero and exterminate the Julio-Claudian dynasty. It is perhaps worth noting in conclusion that Nero was said to have oppressed the Gauls with taxes (Dio 63.22). If we view Roman imperial government as a system for the management of interests, as this chapter has suggested, then this could well be seen as Nero's fatal miscalculation.

[10] Brunt (1961) 1990: 9–32.

Further Reading

Lavan 2013 and Drinkwater 2013 offer complementary studies of the subject examined in this chapter, the first providing a general sketch of government in the early Roman empire (which can be supplemented by the more detailed treatment of Eck 2000), the second focused more on the "job" of Nero himself. For a systematic overview of Nero's reign, with sober and sensible discussion of governance and imperial administration, Griffin 1984 remains a standard account. Cottier et al. 2008 is a critical edition, with translation, commentary, and analysis, of the "customs law of Asia"; for Nero's fiscal policy in particular, Rathbone 2008 is essential. For general studies of treason trials and conspiracy narratives in the early Roman empire, setting the Neronian episodes in context, see Rutledge 2001 (treason) and Pagan 2004 (conspiracy).

4: Nero's Women

Anthony A. Barrett

When the Roman state made its celebrated transition from republic to empire under Augustus, the private household of the princeps underwent a no less dramatic transformation. Perhaps inevitably, the *domus* of the princeps became an idealized microcosm of the larger constitutional entity over which he presided, and as that entity became more overtly monarchical than republican, its ruler more emperor than princeps, so the *domus* assumed the characteristics of an *aula*, or court. The imperial *domus* still reflected the hierarchy and structure of its republican predecessor, and two key components of the republican institution, wives and freedmen, came to enjoy unprecedented opportunities.

Striking the correct balance between monarch and republican official was a major challenge for each successive emperor. The women of the imperial household, especially the wives, found themselves in equally unfamiliar territory. And while each princeps had before him the magisterial example of Augustus, the wives could find guidance in the precedent of Augustus' wife, Livia, who proved that disqualification for public office was no barrier to prestige, and indeed to practical influence, provided that influence was deftly exercised. The women of the immediately post-Augustan court, in a period of intense political experimentation and evolution, merit special study in their efforts to exploit the Livian model to their own advantage. Never was this process more intense than under Nero, where they functioned under a ruler who grew increasingly autocratic and sought his inspiration from the Hellenized east. The practical effect of this process should not be exaggerated. The literary sources focus on the influence, usually malign, of powerful women on the "policies" of the emperor and are especially riled by the notion that women were the ones pulling the strings. But feminine influence and effect rarely extended beyond the confines of internal court intrigue. The workings of the empire depended mainly on the officials, often unrecorded, or, if recorded, little more than names, responsible for the smooth operation of military and civil administration. In the case of Nero, as of several other emperors, the fate of his regime was in the end dependent not on intrigues within the court, but on the decisions taken by military commanders in the provinces.

Apart from the political significance of female activity within Nero's court, a separate and disturbing phenomenon came into play, psychological rather constitutional, one that created a uniquely dangerous situation for the prominent women in his ambit. Those women were, with a single exception (noted at the end of this chapter), individuals with distinguished backgrounds and strong personalities to match. At the outset, this merely reflected circumstances; as time went on, it seems to have reflected Nero's personal predilections. In the Tacitean view of things, it is Claudius who stands out as an emperor under the thumb of powerful wives. But in fact, the imperial termagant was a more marked feature of the principate of Nero, who seems to have craved female domination and yet to have simultaneously resented it. His relationship with the women of his court was a psychologically complex one, of initial subservience, followed by antipathy, followed almost invariably by brutal violence. This interplay between the constitutional and the psychological makes the study of Neronian women particularly fascinating.[1]

The earliest influences on the young Nero were decidedly feminine. He can hardly have retained much of a lasting impression of his father, Gnaeus Domitius Ahenobarbus, a man lacking drive and ambition and who, in any case, died when his son was barely three (Suet. *Nero* 6.3).[2] By contrast, his mother, Agrippina (the Younger), had been raised to harbor a sense of personal destiny: her father was Germanicus, the immensely popular grandson of Livia, while her mother, Agrippina (the Elder), was the proud granddaughter of Augustus, and a woman obsessed with the rightful place of her offspring in the grand scheme of Rome's future. Nero's mother fell heir to this family pride and sense of providence, and created a role for herself as a ruthless version of Livia, devoting much of her energies, as had Livia, to forwarding the imperial prospects of her son, and, thereby, of herself.[3]

1 "Psychological" throughout this chapter is employed in an everyday, nonprofessional sense.
2 Sen. *Contr.* 9.4.18. Nero's conspicuous efforts after he became emperor to honor his father (Tac. *Ann.* 13.10.1, Suet. *Nero* 9.1) were almost certainly less a reflection of filial affection than a public gesture to distance himself from his adoptive father, Claudius (and perhaps from his mother too).
3 Recent studies have been far more skeptical of the ancient sources: Barrett 1996; Griffin 2000; Späth 2000; Keegan 2004, 2007; Ginsburg 2005; Elbern 2011.

There was a brief hiatus in Nero's maternal supervision between late 39 CE and 41 CE, when Agrippina was exiled for an ill-defined involvement in a conspiracy against her own brother Caligula, who had succeeded Tiberius in 37. But the dominant influence remained female. Nero was committed to the charge of a strong-willed and morally ruthless aunt, Domitia Lepida, sister of his father, niece of Augustus and mother of the notorious Messalina. He thus passed under the care of a woman who matched his mother's lack of scruples and penchant for scheming: Tacitus describes both of them as "immoral, disreputable and violent" (*Ann.* 12.64.5). But for all her formidable persona, Domitia Lepida apparently treated the infant Nero with kindness and affection.

Agrippina was reunited with her son in 41 CE, when she was recalled from exile after the assassination of Caligula. Following the cataclysmic fall of Messalina in 48, she married Claudius and lost no time in strengthening Nero's position, engineering his adoption by her new husband, as well as his betrothal, then, in 53 CE, marriage, to Claudius' daughter (by Messalina) Octavia (Tac. *Ann.* 12.58.1; Suet. *Nero* 7.2). History has recorded little of the personality of Octavia, and since the marriage was an arranged one, designed to reinforce the priority of Nero's claim in the succession to Claudius, the choice of her as his first bride tells us nothing about his own psychological makeup. We do know that he very quickly tired of her and within two years had started to find her distasteful; she, for her part, simply learned to suffer in silence (Tac. *Ann.* 13.12.2, 16.7; Suet. *Nero* 35.1).

In 54 CE, Claudius died and Nero's accession followed with an almost mechanical efficiency. The investment of political energy devoted to securing this end brought rich dividends to Agrippina. Building on foundations laid under Claudius, she pushed the boundaries of what was deemed politically acceptable for a woman to unprecedented and, in the end, politically unacceptable limits. Astonishingly, she seems to have sought nothing less than a de facto and even perhaps a quasi-constitutional co-supremacy. Nero claimed after her murder in a letter to the Senate that she had aspired to *sharing* the government (*consortium imperii*), and his words would have struck a responsive chord (Tac. *Ann.* 14.11.1).

Agrippina's period of political ascendancy was short-lived, but it was no less remarkable for that. Its most obvious manifestation was in her public persona. Under Claudius, she had in CE 50 received the title of Augusta, the first wife of a living emperor to do so (Tac. *Ann.* 12.26.1; Dio 60.33.2a). This in itself was striking enough. But even more remarkable were the series of gold and silver coins issued by the official Roman

4.1 Denarius, Nero, and Agrippina, 54 CE. Photo Andreas Pangerl www.romancoins.info.

mint. One should resist the temptation to read complex and sophisticated messages in the coin types adopted in ancient Rome, not least because we are totally in the dark about the process by which their types were chosen and who made the selection. But there can surely be little doubt that coins from the official mint depicting the head of the emperor and his wife must at the very least reflect the wishes of the court. These issues bear Claudius on the obverse (front), and Agrippina on the reverse (*RIC*[2] *Claudius* 80–1) and constitute a quasi-official statement about the role Agrippina was clearly seeking, not only as Claudius' wife, but also as his junior partner in the management of the principate. With Nero's accession, Agrippina felt emboldened to go even further, and numismatic innovation was pushed to the extreme. Agrippina's image now appeared together with Nero's on the obverse of gold and silver issues, beginning immediately after his accession in late 54 CE. This was a stunning innovation, since she became the first woman to share with the princeps the obverse of a coin minted in Rome. Nero and his mother are depicted face to face, the legend identifying Agrippina as the Augusta, wife of the deified Claudius and mother of Caesar (Nero's own legend is on the reverse of the coin) (*RIC*[2] *Nero* 1–3) (Figure 4.1). This comes dangerously close to symbolically proclaiming a co-regency.[4] The impact that these types would have had on the public

[4] After the beginning of 55 CE, coins continue to show the emperor and his mother on the obverse, but now overlapping, with Nero's head superimposed on that of his mother (*RIC*[2] *Nero* 6–7). This need not necessarily indicate, as often assumed, a demotion of Agrippina's status.

4.2 Relief depicting Nero and Agrippina. Sebasteion, Sevgi Gönül Gallery, Aphrodisias. NYU – Aphrodisias Excavations.

can perhaps be gauged by the fact that while the likeness of the revered Livia may have inspired the representation of abstractions like Iustitia, Salus, or Pietas on official Tiberian coinage, she never once appeared in any official issue of Tiberius (or of Augustus) as herself.

This same boldness seems to be reflected in sculptural representations. It is presumably in this period that a relief from the Sebasteion at Aphrodisias was sculpted, depicting a youthful Nero being crowned with a laurel wreath by a female figure bearing the likeness of Agrippina. Whether this was meant to be Agrippina herself, or a personification, perhaps of Roma, whose features have been assimilated to those of Agrippina, is uncertain, but there is no doubt that it would have been a powerful statement, well away from Rome itself, of Agrippina's power and status (Figure 4.2).[5]

The depiction of Agrippina on Neronian coins and sculpture was a symbolic display of her power. But she aspired to the reality of power, not just to its trappings. Tacitus speaks generally of the widely held impression that at the outset of Nero's reign Agrippina was in control of the government. This is, of course, typical of Tacitus' technique of using a putative general public reaction to events to imply a reality (*Ann.* 13.6.2). That said, he also provides a concrete example of her participation in state affairs. He notes, for example, that senators were summoned to meetings on the Palatine (his use of the imperfect *vocabantur* suggests repeated practice) so that Agrippina could gain access to the chamber by a rear entrance and follow the proceedings concealed behind a heavy curtain (*Ann.* 13.5.2). Nero later claimed that it was only with difficulty that she was restrained from bursting into the chamber itself, which indicates that she did not actively participate in the deliberations (Tac. *Ann.* 14.11.2).[6] Indeed, the most arresting aspect of the whole arrangement was Nero's apparent willingness to accede to his mother's strikingly irregular demand.

The most celebrated instance of Agrippina's determination to insert herself into the very center of state activities was in what might be characterized as "foreign relations." Dio reports in very general terms that early in her son's reign she received various embassies and sent letters to peoples, governors, and kings (Dio 61.3.2). There was a concrete demonstration of her self-perception in this sphere before the end of 54, when a delegation arrived from Armenia. The context of the visit was a major crisis in relations between Rome and Parthia, and the delegation's arrival prompted widespread interest. This afforded an excellent opportunity for a public statement about her status that Agrippina was determined to exploit. It seems that no role had been planned for her in welcoming the ambassadors. This did not deter her. As Nero sat on the raised tribunal to hear the speakers put their case, he was presented with the spectacle of his mother approaching the company, with the intention of joining him on the dais. The awkwardness of the situation was resolved by the inspired intervention of Seneca (Burrus

[5] Smith 1987: 127–32, pls. 24–6. Scherrer 2008 argues that Agrippina here represents Concordia. Rose 1997: 47 points out that Agrippina's dominant position of the pair has no known parallel before the time of Caracalla.

[6] Only the *epitomator* of Dio, John of Antioch (fr. 90 M v. 102–5), suggests that she actually entered the chamber.

too, according to Dio), who advised Nero to descend and honor his mother by greeting her (Tac. *Ann.* 13.5.3; Dio 61.3.3–4), thus curtailing her public performance while allowing her to save face. This event illustrates perfectly the great difficulty the ambitious Julio-Claudian woman faced in maintaining a delicate balance between political obscurity and a too overt public presence, and how even a shrewd individual like Agrippina could seriously misjudge what was attainable.

The Armenian incident would have caught the public attention. But the most remarkable foray by Agrippina into the heart of the Roman state was behind the scenes, in the sensitive area of *militaria*. Romans regarded the profession of arms as a strictly male prerogative, especially during the Julio-Claudian period, and any female intrusion was viewed with the utmost suspicion. This was another boundary that Agrippina had challenged during Claudius' reign, when the rebellious British ruler Caratacus was brought, after capture, to Rome. He paid respect not only to the emperor, but also to Agrippina, seated on a nearby tribunal. Tacitus observed the novelty of a woman sitting before Roman standards and suggested that she was claiming a share in the empire won by her forefathers (clearly Augustus, Drusus the Elder, and Germanicus) (*Ann.* 12.37.5).

In the military sphere also Agrippina sought the reality, not just the symbolism, of power. In 59 CE, when tensions arose between her and her son, she was obliged to face charges of tampering with the Praetorian Guard, and after her death, Nero reported to the Senate that she had actually made the Guard swear allegiance to her (Tac. *Ann.* 13.21.7, 14.11.1). These assertions no doubt played on the standard paranoia about women and the military. But in this case the suspicions were actually well grounded. Agrippina had started the process before Nero's accession, when she extended her sphere of influence to embrace the Praetorian Guard. She made sure in 51 CE that the commander would be loyal to her through the appointment of her own candidate, Sextus Afranius Burrus, as sole prefect (Tac. *Ann.* 12.42.1). But she went much further, and set about imposing her authority over officers at the rank of tribune and centurion. Her approach was inspired. It seems that the most hostile were removed on what Tacitus calls "fictitious" grounds; but a widespread purge would have risked raising alarm and Agrippina used the subtle device of promotions, whereby men of dubious loyalty could be promoted to the senior centurionates of the legions, posted far away from Rome (*Ann.* 12. 41.5). By ensuring that her own men occupied the middle and upper positions in the Guard (in addition to the command), she could maintain an indirect hold on the rank and file.

The effects of Agrippina's control over entry into the guard lasted throughout Nero's reign. When in 55 CE she was suspected by her son of fomenting trouble, Tacitus observes, one of the emperor's concerns was her close rapport with the tribunes and centurions of the Guard (*Ann.* 13.18.3). In 59, Nero tried to enlist the Praetorians in Agrippina's murder and was given the disheartening news by Burrus that they could not be counted on because of their loyalty to her (Tac. *Ann.* 14.7.5). As late as 65, during the Pisonian conspiracy, it was his old loyalty to Agrippina that brought the prefect Faenius Rufus under suspicion, and the tribune Subrius Flavus listed the murder of Agrippina first among the crimes that drove him to conspiracy (Tac. *Ann.* 15.50.4, 67.3). She had clearly done her work well.

The initial phase of Nero's reign was a triumphant one for Agrippina. But one apparent victory over a hated enemy should, in fact, have given her serious pause for thought: the fall of Nero's aunt Domitia Lepida, the formidable lady who had looked after him in his infancy. In 54, Lepida was accused of magical practices against Agrippina. More seriously, she was charged with planning sedition, using the slaves on her estate in Calabria (Tac. *Ann.* 12.65.1). Nero, who owed so much to her kindness (possibly the source of much of Agrippina's resentment), denounced her publicly, and she was condemned to death (Suet. *Nero* 7.1). Her fate would be chillingly ominous.

The first year of Nero's reign saw Agrippina engaged in a bitter rivalry with her former protégé and reputed lover, Seneca, who had forged an alliance with the prefect Burrus. What caused the rift between Agrippina and the two men whose careers she had more or less created is not known. It may have been fueled by a kind of survival instinct if they came to feel that her blatant lust for power would bring her down, along with those close to her. The actual process by which Agrippina lost her power and influence and ceded it to Seneca and Burrus is far from clear, and the topic has attracted much scholarly interest.[7] In reality, the causes may well have been as much personal as political. At the time of his accession Nero was only sixteen years old. His far more mature and experienced predecessor, Tiberius, had found it difficult to deal with his own debt to his far more diplomatic and tactful mother, Livia. Thus the deep personal nexus binding mother and son that had served Nero so well was ironically almost bound to transform itself into resentment and to result ultimately in her shattering downfall. Tensions were evident by

[7] See, in particular, Griffin 2000: 38–40, 60–1, 97–9; Barrett 1996: 157–60; Ginsburg 2005: 37–42; Champlin 2003: 84–8.

as early as the beginning of 55 CE, when Nero, no doubt encouraged by Agrippina's enemies, started to fear that his mother was plotting against him (Tac. *Ann.* 13.19–22). She successfully repudiated the allegations, but her position seems to have been permanently compromised. From late 55 to 59 CE, she essentially disappeared from the literary record and her influence over events at the heart of government ended. Her remarkable constitutional experiment had failed.

The sources record only one activity in Rome, Agrippina's seduction of Nero in a desperate attempt to cling on to power. Ancient opinion was divided on who initiated the supposed liaison, but perhaps even more disturbing than the actual charge of incest is the allegation, recorded in Suetonius and Dio, that Nero had a mistress who bore a striking resemblance to Agrippina; Dio adds the detail that after sex he would joke that he had slept with his mother (Tac. *Ann.* 14.2; Suet. *Nero* 28.2; Dio 61.11.3–4). This claim of a "substitute" woman will be made again later about Nero in a different context (described later in this chapter). The apparently different accounts may, of course, just be doublets, but the pattern may also be evidence of a strange behavioral aberration. It seems to be a perverted device to enable Nero to maintain his intense bond with a dominating woman while at the same time feeling that he was liberated from her control.

Given Agrippina's absence from the political scene, it is all the more remarkable that by 59 CE Nero had decided to eliminate her. Whether he did so from political or from complex private and psychological motives there is no way of telling. His decision led to one of the most celebrated incidents of antiquity, his notorious collapsing boat.[8] When this supposedly proved unfit for purpose, he sent his trusted thugs to dispatch her.[9]

Nero was now free of his powerful mother, but psychologically he was still in awe of her. It was claimed by some that he went to her villa to inspect the corpse and was amazed at how beautiful it was, still apparently experiencing a compelling bond but now no longer subservient and in fact able to enjoy a controlling role (Tac. *Ann.* 14.9.1; Suet. *Nero* 34.4, Dio 61.14.2). Her murder was followed by that of another female relative, Nero's aunt Domitia, sister of, and to be distinguished from, the

[8] On the general topography of this famous incident, Barrett 1996: 284–7; Keppie 2011.

[9] Agrippina was apparently struck in the abdomen, and reputedly offered up her womb to the assailants (*Octavia* 369–72; Tac. *Ann.* 14.8.6; Dio 61.13.5). See the interesting observations of O'Gorman 2000: 141 and Edwards 2007: 200. On Tacitus' intentions in the account of Agrippina's death, see Piecha 2003; Baltussen 2002 stresses the influence of tragedy and rhetoric on the description of her last hours.

previously executed Domitia Lepida. Domitia seems in fact to have replaced that sister in Nero's affections, and remained affectionate until her very last days, but she discovered, as had her sister and her sister-in-law Agrippina, that Nero's youthful fondness in the end brought no protection. Even though by 59 CE she was close to death from old age, Nero poisoned her with an excess of laxative, supposedly to get his hands on her estates near Baiae and Ravenna (Suet. *Nero* 34.5, Dio 61.17.1–2).

The earlier death of Domitia's sister, Domitia Lepida, might be ascribed to the animosity of Agrippina. The same argument cannot be made about Agrippina or Domitia herself, and these deaths, and other subsequent ones of women close to Nero, present a disturbing pattern. Unlike, say, Tiberius, who escaped his domineering mother by avoiding her presence, Nero liberated himself from his close female ties through death and violence. It might be argued that this simply reflects a callous disregard for human life, and for women's lives in particular. But the situation is clearly more complex. A number of prominent Roman women, either through their husbands or in their own right, represented threats to Nero. But he went out of his way to spare their lives. During the Pisonian conspiracy of 65 CE, for instance, Acilia was denounced by her son Lucan, but escaped punishment (Tac. *Ann.* 15. 71.12). Paulina, wife of Seneca, had even started to commit suicide along with her husband when Nero reputedly intervened and ordered her resuscitation (Tac. *Ann.* 15.64.1). In the aftermath of the conspiracy, a number of prominent Stoics were put to death, including, most notably, Thrasea Paetus and his son-in-law Helvidius Priscus. But Thrasea's wife, Arria, who was prepared to follow her husband into death, was spared by Nero, as was her daughter, Helvidius' wife, Fannia (Tac. *Ann.* 16.34.3). When Nero executed his perceived rival Rubellius Plautus in 62 CE, he spared his wife, Antistia Politta (she voluntarily committed suicide [*Ann.* 16.10–11]). Clearly it was not politically dangerous women who suffered from the violent side of Nero's personality, but women with whom he had formed a close *personal* and *emotional* bond.

The death of Agrippina unfettered Nero from his mother's domination, and he might have been expected to avoid placing himself again in a similar situation. To the contrary, he made every effort to acquire a wife seemingly shaped in the same very mold as his mother. Poppaea Sabina, born about 31 CE, was reputedly the most beautiful woman of her day, already twice married when she became Nero's lover (Tac. *Ann.* 13.45.2). Nero faced an obstacle to any plan to marry her in that he had a wife, the popular Octavia. She had borne no children, and by the code of the Roman upper classes divorce would have occasioned neither surprise nor scandal. A divorce did in fact come about, on the grounds that she was barren (Tac. *Ann.* 14.60.1). But Nero went much further. A case of adultery was manufactured. Octavia was initially banished to Pandateria, then, finally, put to death, in her twentieth year, according to Tacitus.[10] That punishment was extraordinary, without parallel under the Julio-Claudians, where exile was the normal penalty for the reputedly errant imperial woman. Exceptions like Messalina or Agrippina the Elder were women whose overtly dangerous conduct may have left little alternative to more severe measures. Nero's excessive response lies surely not so much in politics, as in his own peculiar psychological makeup.

Poppaea is generally depicted in the sources as the epitome of wild and frivolous excess, with a traveling herd of asses supplying milk for her daily bath, and with her own brand of celebrity perfume (Dio 62.28.1, Plin. *HN* 11.238, 28.183, Juv. 6.461–4). But in actuality, she seems to have been a woman of considerable drive and ability.[11] Tacitus concedes that she was highly intelligent and an engaging conversationalist, indeed that she had everything going for her, except decency (*Ann.* 13.45.2: *cuncta alia fuere praeter honestum animum*). She also carried much weight in the court, and, although this is not generally appreciated, was no less enthusiastic than Agrippina in expanding the boundaries of female power and influence.[12] Again, we have this expressed in general terms. Tacitus speaks of her controlling her husband (*Ann.* 14.60.1: *mariti potens*) and Dio reports that she was fawned upon because it was recognized that she "had power" (62.13.4: ἴσχυε). These are broad characterizations. But Tacitus also provides a concrete glimpse of her power in action. When during the Pisonian conspiracy a Praetorian tribune submitted a confidential report on the conduct of Seneca, he delivered it to Nero in the presence of Tigellinus, the sinister prefect of the Guard, as might be expected, but also of Poppaea (*Ann.* 15.61.4). Tacitus describes these two as constituting Nero's closest advisors (*intimum consiliorum*). Whether they were part of the formal *concilium principis* that traditionally advised the princeps on matters of state is not made clear, and it perhaps is not important in this context; on this occasion, the centrality of Poppaea's role, however defined, is not in doubt.

[10] Tac. *Ann.* 14.64.1. The information looks suspicious. Octavia was older than Britannicus (born February 13, 41) and must have been older than twenty in 62 CE, the year of her death.

[11] She was also popular, at least in her hometown of Pompeii, to judge from a graffito found there (Buren [1953]).

[12] Holztrattner 1995 argues that Poppaea played a major role in Nero's court.

The most detailed accounts of Poppaea's political interventions appear in Josephus, who was witness to her keen interest and active involvement in matters relating to the administration of Judea, and was clearly impressed by her, going so far as to call her θεοσεβής (devout).[13] When, during the procuratorship of Festus (about 60–2), a deputation came to Rome to protest the demolition of a wall in Jerusalem, on the grounds that it would expose part of the Temple to public view, Poppaea intervened on their behalf and Nero ruled in their favor. Josephus comments that he did so specifically to please her (*Ant.* 20.195). Later Josephus made personal contact with Poppaea. In around 64 CE, he visited Rome to speak for certain Jewish priests imprisoned under a previous procurator, Felix (52–ca. 60). He gained an entrée to Poppaea through a mutual acquaintance, a popular Jewish actor, and was able to secure their release, receiving generous personal gifts from her in the process (*Vit.* 16). Later Josephus informs us that Gessius Florus (procurator ca. 64–6), whom he considered horrendously wicked, owed his appointment to his wife Cleopatra's friendship with Poppaea (*Ant.* 20. 252).

All of this suggests a powerful and ambitious woman, and it is striking that Tacitus uses very similar language to characterize both her and Agrippina. He observes of the latter that when she married Claudius, she imposed *adductum et quasi virile servitium* "strict despotism with a masculine character," being a woman void of sexual impropriety except when it could add to her power (*Ann.* 12.7.3: *nihil domi impudicum, nisi dominationi expediret*). He similarly says of Poppaea that she was not a woman subject to her emotions, but used her sexuality to her practical advantage (*Ann.* 13.45.3: *neque adfectui suo aut alieno obnoxia, unde utilitas ostenderetur, illuc libidinem transferebat*).

Poppaea had relatively little time to test the limits of her potential. In 65 CE, she died. She was accorded divine status, and a splendid shrine was built in her honor.[14] Two aspects of her death, as reported, follow a by now familiar pattern. There are suggestions that she died violently: kicked in the stomach, according to Tacitus and Suetonius, or jumped on, according to Dio (*Ann.* 16.6.1; *Nero* 35.3; Dio 62.27.4). These versions, which presumably go back to a single source, follow a familiar sequence of thralldom to a powerful woman and a brutal response to it. How reliable they are is disputed, but it certainly must be

[13] On the meaning of that term, see Smallwood 1959; Williams 1988. For epigraphic evidence of Poppaea's interest in Judaism, see Benke 2011.

[14] Tac. *Ann.* 16.21.2; Dio 63.26.3; the shrine may have been built in Naples (see Kragelund [2010]).

conceded that the conduct they describe, of subservience accompanied by violence, is not at all out of character.[15]

There is another familiar theme. Dio relates that Nero missed Poppaea so much after her death that he found a mistress who looked like her, and later even castrated a freed slave boy, Sporus, who resembled her, and married him, giving him the name Sabina. Dio also reports that Nero would put on passages of tragedy where all the female masks represented the likeness of Poppaea, so that she could take part in the performance, even though dead (Dio 62.28.2, 63. 9.5,13.1, cf. Suet. *Nero* 28). As happened with his mother, it seems that a "substitute" was called on to fulfill Nero's emotional attachment without the angst of actual personal bondage.

This pattern of violence toward women close to Nero would apparently be repeated not long after Poppaea's death. Nero reputedly sought to marry Antonia, the oldest daughter of Claudius, and technically Nero's half-sister, as Octavia had been. She rejected him. Suetonius reports that because of this Nero had her put to death, and as an excuse implicated her in the Pisonian conspiracy (Suet. *Nero* 35.4).[16] There is some evidence that Nero's third and final wife, Statilia Messalina, matched the profile of other women in his life. She seems to have been an ambitious woman, several times married, and sought later as wife by Otho (Suet. *Otho* 10.2). According to the scholiast on Juvenal (6.434), she was wealthy, beautiful, intelligent, and an eloquent speaker. But the loss of Tacitus' *Annals* for the later years of Nero's reign means that we simply know too little about Statilia's activities to evaluate her role in Nero's life properly. Her good fortune in the post-Neronian period suggests that she probably did not ally herself too closely to his cause.

We can with more confidence say that the closing phase of the reign did highlight Nero's one successful female relationship. Interestingly, social mores obligated him on this occasion to be the *dominant* partner in this affair, which may account in large part for its success. Casual sexual relations between master and freedwoman were not uncommon in ancient Rome, but the love affair that began very early in Nero's reign between Nero and Acte, a former imperial slave from Asia, proved a major force in his life. Suetonius even claims that Nero was prepared

[15] F. A. Mayer 1982 doubts the stories, noting that kicking a pregnant wife suggests the stereotype of the vicious tyrant.

[16] Dio 61.1.2 [in epitome] simply notes that Nero put Britannicus' sisters (plural) to death. Pliny the Elder claims, according to Tacitus, that Piso planned to marry Antonia after the murder of Nero, an assertion that leaves Tacitus (and Syme 1958: 192) unconvinced (*Ann.* 15.53.4–5).

to marry her, and bribed some former consuls to attest to her royal blood (*Nero* 28.1). Seneca and Burrus actively encouraged the affair, to counter the influence of Agrippina (Tac. *Ann.* 14.2). Acte outlived Nero and prospered; inscriptions testify to many slaves and property at Puteoli and Velitrae (*PIR*[2] C 1067). But it would be a mistake to dismiss her as a lowborn woman on the make. She remained loyal to her imperial lover right to the end. His wife Statilia Messalina is conspicuously absent from the scene during Nero's final days, but Suetonius records that Acte stood by him, and, along with his old nurses Egloge and Alexandria, buried his ashes in the family mausoleum of the Domitii on the Pincian Hill (*Nero* 50).

The reign of Nero was remarkable for the roles that strong-willed imperial women tried to carve out for themselves in the political life of the state. It was no less remarkable for the dramatic personal repercussion these ambitions would provoke for many of them. Future reigns would see no shortage of prominent and able women, individuals like Plotina or Julia Domna or Julia Maesa. But events in the Neronian period cast a long shadow, and ambitious women of the imperial court would henceforth be reluctant to challenge constitutional restraints. That particular revolution essentially died, along with Nero, not long after its birth.

Further Reading

For a general treatment of women in the classical world, see Fantham et al., eds. 1995; chapter 11 focuses on the Julio-Claudian period. On imperial women and their representation in public imagery, see Wood 1999. On Agrippina, the main studies are Barrett 1996, Eck 1993, Ginsburg 2005, and Späth 2000. Holztrattner 1995 focuses on the fate of Poppaea Sabina. On Livia as the first of the new genre of "imperial wife," see Barrett 2002 and Bartman 1999.

Part II

Neronian Literature

5: Post-Augustan Revisionism

Cedric Littlewood

> "From this time writers will struggle self-consciously not to be post-classical, mere imitators falling away from the high point of creativity and confidence reached during the Augustan age."[1]

Neronian literature[2] plays a crucial role in establishing Augustan literature as the primary literary point of reference not only for itself, but for later Latin literature. Horace is for Persius, "the nearly compulsive center of regard."[3] Even discussions of Persius' engagement with Old Comedy or iambic verse turn inexorably to discussions of Persius' engagement with Horace's construction of literary history.[4] Yet Tiberian author Velleius Paterculus could, a generation earlier, omit Horace from the canon of Roman poets.[5] In this chapter, I shall consider to what extent Neronian literature represented itself as having fallen away from an Augustan high point. The writing of literary history is bound up with the writing of political history, and I shall consider also to what extent Neronian literary emulation accommodates a narrative of political decline from an Augustan ideal.

5.1 Anti-*Aeneids*

The great epic of Nero's age, Lucan's *De bello civili*, is commonly read in opposition to the great epic of Augustus' age.[6] Where Virgil charted the

[1] Fantham 1996: 1.

[2] Some Neronian authors are more uncontestably Neronian than others. Persius and Lucan are comparatively unproblematic, even if two-thirds of Lucan's *De bello civili* were published after his own death in 65 CE and probably also after Nero's in 67 CE. Seneca's tragedies surely date from Nero's lifetime, if not all from his reign – see Marshall 2014: 37–40. More dispute a Neronian date for Petronius *Satyrica* than for the pastoral poems of Calpurnius Siculus, though both are widely accepted hypotheses. On the *Satyrica* see Prag and Redpath 2009: 5–10. On Calpurnius Siculus see Mayer 2006: 454–6.

[3] Hooley 1997: 19. [4] McNelis 2012.

[5] For the particular point, see Mayer 1982: 308 and the entire article for the argument that the Augustan canon is in large part a Neronian creation.

[6] For recent discussion, see Casali 2011.

beginning of a journey that would lead to Rome's eternal mastery of the world, Lucan sings of her final and lasting destruction and the relapse of the world into chaos. The opposition is underlined by engagement with rather than simple difference from the Virgilian predecessor. The civil war between Caesar and Pompey is the particular civil war that Anchises vainly urged his descendant to avoid (Verg. *Aen.* 6.828–35). Lucan's project, formulated in his first lines as an evisceration of the body politic (1.1–3), recalls the literary father's metaphor. Lucan's opening question, *quis furor, o cives, quae tanta licentia ferri?* ("What madness was this, O citizens? What this excessive freedom with the sword?" 1.8), is born of Ascanius' words to the Trojan women, burning their own ships when the long and dangerous journey was all but achieved: *"quis furor iste novus? quo nunc, quo tenditis," inquit / "heu miserae cives?"* ("What strange madness is this?" he cried. "Where, oh where is this leading you, you unhappy women of Troy?" Verg. *Aen.* 5.670–1).[7] A mad impulse to self-destruction, happily strange and new in Rome's prehistory, would become foundational when "Rome's first walls were drenched with a brother's blood" (Luc. 1.95) and traditional in the history that followed – or at least as the late Republic and early Empire constructed that history.[8] However gleefully Lucan violates Virgilian piety and insists that his epic poem is unspeakable (*nefas*), the wounds of civil war and the verses with which they are drawn are traditional. Hardie (1990) has argued convincingly that Lucan's "anti-*Aeneid*" is anticipated by the Theban narrative of Ovid's *Metamorphoses* (3.1–4.603). Neronian literature cannot claim an antagonistic aesthetic as the distinctive and peculiar spirit of its age, for what author is more Augustan than Ovid?

In a famous passage at the end of *De bello civili* 1, a Roman woman, possessed by Apollo and condemned to retrace in prophetic vision the cycle of civil war, asks in vain to see something new (1.693–4). A headless body lying on the shore is recognized simultaneously as Pompey and as a textual corpus, as a line of Virgil now disfigured (Luc. 1.685–6 cf. *Aen.* 2.557).[9] The horror of recognition and of repetition arguably tropes an anxiety of influence, in which a self-consciously secondary or "silver" age is unable to escape the canonical

7 Translations for Lucan, Virgil, and Persius from Braund 1992, West 1990, and Rudd 1973, respectively.

8 On this, the Virgilian reminiscence, and *furor Romanus*, see Hershkowitz 1998: 198–218.

9 Hinds 1998: 8–10 with bibliography and Masters 1992: 143 on the matron as a poet figure. On the metaphor of textual bodies broken and reconstituted in Lucan and Seneca, respectively, see Dinter 2012a: 27–9 and passim with bibliography and Segal 1986: 215. On "the appropriation and mutilation of . . . inherited literary models," see Peirano 2013: 99 on Seneca the Elder.

models of a previous age. But such a representation of the relationship between the Neronian and Augustan texts can obscure the extent to which all Latin literary culture, not least the *Aeneid*, always was self-consciously secondary. The *Aeneid* aspired to a destiny beyond the limits of Troy's fatal pattern, as an epic to surpass Homer (so Prop. 2.34.66), yet perpetuated that pattern by repetition.[10] When the Sibyl foresaw another Simois, another Achilles, another war over a foreign bride, Aeneas replied that this was nothing new, that he had been through it all before (*Aen.* 6.86–105).[11]

"The imprisonment of form," one might say, "binds the allusions to the past into an imprisonment of events." But this quotation I take not from a commentary on the *Aeneid*, but from Boyle's commentary on Seneca's *Troades* (1994: 26). *Troades* is rightly read as an anti-*Aeneid*: the ghost of Hector who cannot hold out to Andromache any hope of escape (*Tro.* 438–60) is a negation of his Virgilian predecessor who awakened Aeneas to a new destiny (*Aen.* 268–97).[12] But at the same time the tragedy of Troy's constraining doom is a prominent motif already present in the *Aeneid*.[13] The inversions or negations of Virgil that Seneca and Lucan offer are achieved by reading to some extent partially or against the grain, but they are nevertheless readings of the original. The *Aeneid* is too fine a text for the direction of its grain to be simply traced, and for many, Lucan's poem stands in opposition less to the *Aeneid* than to a particular Augustan reception of the *Aeneid*.[14]

The prologue of Seneca's *Thyestes* (*Thy.* 1–121) is clearly influenced by the summoning of Allecto (*Aen.* 7.286–571). Clearly also the Tantalid palace that Seneca's Fury overwhelms (*Thy.* 641–64) recalls in distorted form the temple-palace of King Latinus (*Aen.* 7.170–91), which in its anachronistically Roman detail recalls that of Augustus on the Palatine Hill.[15] Tarrant (1985: 19) writes: "(I)t is hard not to infer that Seneca too is making an implicit commentary on contemporary Rome, and that his evocation of Vergil bitterly points up the gap between Augustan ideals and the imperial realities of his own time."

10 On the threat of repetition, see Quint 1993: 50–96 and Hardie 1992 on Augustan poetry more widely.

11 For Seneca (*Ep.* 79.6) alluding to this passage of Virgil in discussion (and illustration) of literary imitation, see Trinacty 2014: 11.

12 Zissos 2008 more fully on *Troades* and Putnam 1995 on *Troades* among other Senecan tragedies.

13 On tragic memories as obstructive of imperial destiny in the *Aeneid*, see Panoussi 2009: 145–73.

14 E.g., Maes 2005 and Thomas 2001, who sees the *Aeneid* recalled by Horace in the *Carmen Saeculare* but with its nuance changed and thus "converted ... into a piece of Augustan propaganda" (71).

15 For bibliography and commentary on Latinus' palace, see Horsfall 1999: 146–50.

From precisely the same evidence Schiesaro (2003: 35) makes an argument for continuity: "By pointing directly at *Aeneid* 7 and acknowledging Virgil's archetypal role as a poet of *furor*, Seneca reconstructs a meaningful sequence of literary history and invokes a powerful model for his own nefarious endeavours." Political and literary continuity then run in parallel: far from expressing how far contemporary Rome has fallen from an ideal Augustan past, Seneca uses Virgil damagingly against the idealization of that past to strip away its illusions.[16] If Seneca's text represents "a challenge to . . . repressive decorum" (Schiesaro 2003: 36), it is a challenge to an entire system, to the reverence demanded by a whole dynasty of Roman god-emperors (97). The tragic city holds up a dark mirror to Rome,[17] but to what Rome specifically? To Augustan Rome? To a particular idealization of Augustan Rome? To Neronian Rome? To Rome under the Caesars?

The historical record has not been kind to Nero, representing him as an unwitting parodist of Augustus or a degenerate conclusion to a glorious line. Such a record predisposes us to one reading of the intertextual dynamics of Seneca's tragedies and Lucan's epic. Tacitus himself can be read as practicing such intertextuality in the *Annals*, recalling Augustan texts to mark a contrast with post-Augustan Rome.[18] But ancient sources offer more than a uniform rhetoric of decline from Augustan perfection. Velleius Paterculus represented Tiberius, not Augustus, as the pattern for his successors and the high point of Roman history (2.131.1–2). Describing the gratitude a philosopher owes his ruler for the enjoyment of leisurely retirement (*Ep.* 73.10–11), Seneca found contemporary relevance in the figure of Virgil's Tityrus, grateful to the god of his own world for an idyllic life (*Ecl.* 10–11). Elsewhere Seneca goes further, contrasting the poor illusion of clemency offered by Augustus' "exhausted cruelty" with Nero's realization of the ideal (*Cl.* 1.11.1–2).[19] As for the transition from Republic to Empire and the institution of the principate, as interesting as Seneca's and Lucan's differences of opinion is the fact that the historiographical narrative remains a live issue: Seneca interrogates Cato (*Ep.* 14.12–13); Lucan famously writes that to read his civil

[16] So also Narducci 1979: 35 on Lucan's relationship with Virgil.

[17] On the tragic city, usually but not necessarily Thebes, as Rome's "other," see Braund 2006 as a development of Zeitlin 1990 on the relationship between Athens and Thebes.

[18] See, e.g., Bloomer 1997: 176–95 on a deluded longing for classicism generally and on a particular reminiscence of Livy and Virgil: "Tacitus has clouded both classical models; the classical subtext creates an expectation of order restored that the *Annals* never produces" (1997: 188).

[19] See also Whitton 2013: 164–5 on Nero outshining Augustus just as S. *Apoc.* 4.2 (probably of similar date to *Cl.*) surpasses V. *Ecl.* 4.57.

war is to refight it, to take the past as something still to come (*venientia fata / non transmissa*, 7.212–13). The restoration of the Republic may not have been a live issue in Neronian Rome, the praise of Cato or Brutus and Cassius an increasingly clichéd attitude of political dissent rather than a serious constitutional statement. But the memorialization of the Republic, the construction of rupture between Republic and Empire and the writing of a narrative between them, was.[20] When Pompey dies at *De bello civili* 8.613–18, he veils his face and closes his eyes and his lips. In this silence, the narrator, addressing posterity, invents his last thoughts and epitaph. The remaining 250 lines of the book are taken up with a long, restless sequence of the funerals and memorials he had, might have had, and should have had. What is at stake here is not just Pompey's reputation, but the memory of the Republic he represented. How should it be remembered – and is remembrance an immortalizing act or a closural gesture which, by enacting a death, confirms it?

Readers of Lucan's poem are jarred at its opening by the juxtaposition of Hesperia as a wasteland, barely inhabited (1.24–32), with an encomium of Nero (1.33–66). Even setting aside later references to freedom lost for all time on the plains of Pharsalus (7.640), one cannot sensibly reconcile a Rome simultaneously graced by divinity and ruined. The poem is divided against itself, and nowhere is this more apparent than in the voice of the narrator, possessed alternately by Caesar's criminal energy and by Pompeian hesitation. Masters elevates the poetics of division and fracture to a fundamental structuring principle of the work.[21] If this single text defies consistency, coherence, and closure within itself, and with them any simple narrative of political history, how much more so the dialogs between texts. The intertextual relationships between Lucan or Seneca and Virgil are implicated in the construction of historical and political narratives. The harsh juxtaposition of the encomium of Nero with a wasteland is a condensation of an opposition in *Georgics* 1 which begins with the catasterism of Augustus and ends with the ruin of civil war.[22] Virgil is constructed and reconstructed by his successors' selective reminiscence. When Quintilian ends his survey of classic Roman epic with praise of that potentially greatest of poets, Germanicus Augustus (Domitian), he finds in Virgil a voice with which to praise a Caesar

[20] See Gowing 2005: 67–101 with bibliography.

[21] Masters 1992: 214–15 and passim and cf. Bartsch 1997: 131–49.

[22] See Casali 2011: 89–92 on the influence of *Georgics* 1.24–39 and 505–13. Intertextual density is one aspect also of Persius' poetics of condensation (see Cucchiarelli 2005: 68), a contemporary who characterizes himself as "clever at the harsh juxtaposition" (*iunctura callidus acri*, 5.14).

(*Ecl.* 8.13 quoted at *Inst.* 10.1.92). But, as Lucan's different recollection shows, Virgil has other voices. Neronian authors to a large degree created the Augustan classics by obsessive imitation, but they did not always create them as docile as Quintilian here chooses to recall. What Augustan closure the *Aeneid* offers to the anxiety of the *Georgics* and to the wounds of civil war is open to debate, as for that matter is the anxiety of the *Georgics*.[23] Lucan and Seneca participate in that debate by exposing dissonance within each classic text, and also by choosing to remember the pre-Augustan texts of those who would become Augustan authors. By drawing inspiration from the *Georgics* at the beginning of the *De bello civili*, Lucan refights more civil wars than one.

5.2 Genre and the Poetics of Emulation

A challenge to any attempt to construct a relationship between the Age of Nero and the Age of Augustus from the intertextual dynamic of literary texts is the issue of genre. Genre has "a determining power over the kinds of things the poet says."[24] While of course poets choose genres in which to write and shape them through their writing, where few texts survive, accidents of survival distort constructions of literary history. Senecan drama may rightly be characterized as "Virgil's tragic future" (Putnam 1992), but if Roman tragedy survived for us not through Seneca, but through Ovid's *Medea* and Varius Rufus' *Thyestes*, would we be so inclined to construct the history of Julio-Claudian Rome as a descent into tragic madness?[25] Senecan tragedy's rivalry with the past is typically characterized as a pursuit of criminal excess. Fury's determination to reenact and surpass the Thracian crime, familiar to her readers from Ovid's *Metamorphoses*, may be taken as representative: *Thracium fiat nefas / maiore numero* ("let the Thracian outrage be performed with greater numbers," *Thy.* 56–7).[26] But are such "poetics of *nefas*" the poetics of Neronian Rome or the poetics merely of high poetry? Horace, from the perspective of lyric, associated Virgil's voyage on the high seas of epic with audacity and the pursuit of forbidden wrong (*C.* 1.3.21–6).

[23] For less anxious *Georgics*, see Morgan 1999.

[24] Roman 2014: 22 for the quote and further discussion.

[25] No tragedies are more highly praised than these in Quintilian's review of Latin literature (10.1.98).

[26] See Schiesaro 2003: 221–8 on intertextuality and "the author's staged counterparts – a group of obsessed, determined criminals" (224).

Some ancient authors do work to interpret the pursuit of crime as more than a marker of genre.[27] By presenting Nero's reign in the style of a Senecan tragedy, *Octavia* made tragedy as Seneca practiced it the genre proper to the realities of his age.[28] Allusion to Seneca in Tacitus' *Annals* likewise "upholds a mimetic relationship between Julio-Claudian history and Senecan tragedy."[29] Others, including Seneca himself in epistolary mode, offer an entirely different intertextual dynamic for his literary moment. The maddened and murderous author-surrogates of Lucanian epic[30] and Senecan tragedy do not subscribe to the argument of his *Epistles* 79.5–9 that the wise strive to equal, not surpass their predecessors. Writers are likened in *Epistles* 84 to bees flitting from flower to flower to distill literary honey (3–5) or to a chorus blended harmoniously from many voices (9).[31] Seneca advises Lucilius to take the literary impress of the past and to resemble it as a son does his father (*Ep.* 84.8).[32] Contrast Andromache looking at the body of Astyanax, smashed to a degree that far eclipses any descriptions of the mutilation of the bodies of Hector or Priam, and commenting of this *deforme corpus* (see note 9 of this chapter), *sic quoque est similis patri* ("Even in this he is like his father," *Tro.* 1117). Such irony is barely tolerable and difficult to interpret except through the character's mad obsession with the past and through a pathology of emulation in the epic-tragic continuum of high poetry.[33] The line may recall Procne's words to Itys, *a quam / es similis patri* (Ov. *Met.* 6.621–2). Running parallel to the physiognomic reminiscences that condemn Itys to death are intra- and intertextual reminiscences. The cannibal feast in which Itys will be devoured recalls the incestuous rape of Philomela that it avenges, but also the Medea tragedies of Euripides and probably Ovid himself.[34] The homologous acts of

27 Compare on Horace, Davis 1991: 101 for whom "*pius* . . . is not so much a moral as a literary badge of competence" with, e.g., Oliensis 1998: 107, "Horatian lyric matches the aesthetics of containment with an ethics of contentment that would seem to leave little room for imperial ambitions."

28 On Nero as a character out of Senecan tragedy, see Buckley 2013b.

29 Ker 2009: 143 for the quote and 140–5 for discussion and bibliography.

30 On Erichtho as an image of Lucan's creative self, see O'Higgins 1988: 217–26.

31 Cf. Boyle 1997: 112 on the re-composition of Hippolytus' body at the end of *Phaedra* as "an attempt by Seneca to put together the separated fragments of the dismembered *oeuvre* of Euripides . . . into a new, harmonious whole." Trinacty 2014: 1–25 relates the apian imagery of *Epistles* 84 to the generic diversity of Senecan tragedy: "tragedy is an amalgam of different genres" (18).

32 On "self-actualization through the act of writing" in this letter, as the mind crafts a literary corpus that is the image of itself, see Graver 2014: 287 and passim.

33 See Fantham 1982: 374 and Boyle 1994: 227–8 on Seneca as characteristically post-Augustan but also Ovidian in this scene.

34 See Feldherr 2010: 203 with bibliography.

cannibalism and incest serve as tragic metaphors for the digestion and conception of new textual bodies.[35]

Significant in discussions of historicized aesthetics are parallels across genres. Rimell (2002) argues that a "rotten recycling of Philomela's myth" (159) appears also at the end of Petronius' *Satyrica*, where the devouring and regurgitating of bodies "violently debunks the very notion of a classic text, with all its connotations of permanence, unchangeability and metaphysicality" (199). *Nefas* characterizes Neronian verse satire no less than high poetry. At the opening of his first satire, Persius questions whether it is right (*fas*) for him to speak (1.8–9) and toward its end he characterizes his words as a *nefas*:

> me muttire nefas? nec clam nec cum scrobe? nusquam?
> hic tamen infodiam. vidi vidi ipse libelle:
> auriculas asini quis non habet?
>
> "Wrong for me to mumble a word? Not even in secret? Not into a ditch? Nowhere? But here I'll dig a little hole to bury it. I've seen the truth, my little book, I've seen it: Everyone has asses' ears!"
>
> (Pers. 1.119–21)

He represents himself also as pissing on sacred ground (1.112–14), and in so doing as following, in his own way, in the footsteps of Lucilius and Horace (1.116–19). Forbidden speech thus defines the satiric genre as a whole, but in particular its expression at the historical moment when all the world had asses' ears. The allusion to the myth of Midas and his barber entrusting his secret to a hole in the ground has to some suggested "the powerful inhibition of speaking out the truth about Nero, his court, and the Roman society that tolerates them."[36] The material is ready to hand to turn Midas and his botched golden world, Midas who dared believe that Apollo's songs could be surpassed,[37] into a counterfeit of the Augustan ideal. It is the aesthetic tyranny of this emperor, arguably, that Persius represents himself as outraging with his satire.

Another line of argument originates from Persius' engagement with Horace. Persius' image of sacrilege is Horatian to the extent that it is taken from *Ars Poetica* 470–2, but the mad poet who there defiles the ashes of his forefathers is a negative model whose disregard for the rules

35 Cf. Schiesaro 2003: 85–95 making the same point, but of Seneca's recycling of Ovid in *Thyestes*.
36 Reckford 2009: 151.
37 See Ov. *Met.* 11.155. The audacity is initially Pan's but repeated in Midas' judgment.

of art Horace condemns.[38] If, as Reckford (2009: 144–50) argues, the persona of the naughty child runs through Persius' satires, Horace is the most important of his father figures in defining the terms of his rebellion.[39] Literary rivalry may be conducted more heroically in other genres, but pissing on one's father's grave can be seen as a satiric version of a parricidal intertextual dynamic.[40] Critics have noted that Medea's killing of her children on stage is an aesthetic offense as well as a moral crime, for *Ars Poetica* 185 specifically prohibits such a scene.[41] However different in register this act is from the satirist's sacrilege, it is equally a violation of Horatian decorum.

Such community across genres and the elevation of Horace to a position of poetic authority – an authority to rebel against – can support an argument that the poetics of *nefas* are as much Neronian as they are the poetics of high poetry. Even if they are pervasive, however, their interpretation remains contested. What and whom does the radicalism and isolation of Persius' dissent rebuke? Freudenburg (2001: 125–30) moves from images of neo-Callimachean polish[42] to a neo-Augustan project too easily convinced of its own smooth perfection as one take on Neronian culture, a perspective "configuring our Neronian imaginations" (130) in one very contestable way. Persius' deviations from Horace, his disruption of his predecessor's balancing act, can be read as critique, as representing such balance as spineless compromise. His reintroduction into satire of an "epodic" voice, with its "strong expressionistic tones of aggression, of death, of sex, and magic," a voice Horace had carefully excluded from the genre, is a pointed reversal of the trajectory of Horace's – and Rome's – literary history.[43] Roman (2014: 279) ends a discussion of Persius, "The savagery of satire has been redirected in various ways: diffused outward towards social convention in general, and turned inward, towards the flaws in our own thoughts, desires, and motives. As in Horatian satire, the poet is still deemed a dangerous figure – but to whom?" To the extent that flawed thoughts, desires, and motives are a textual

[38] On Persius *Satires* 1 and Horace, *Ars Poetica*, see Hooley 1997: 26–63.

[39] On literary father figures, cf. Schlegel 2000 on Horace, *Satires* 1.4 and 1.6.

[40] See, e.g., Trinacty 2014: 38 for analogy between Laius, Oedipus' father, and Virgil, Seneca's father figure. Longinus speaks of Plato "breaking a lance" (διαδορατιζόμενος) in (metaphorical) battle with Homer (13.4). Bloom 1973 characterizes poetic anxiety of influence in heroic terms because his study is born of a reading of *Paradise Lost*.

[41] Mowbray 2012: 400 on this aspect of a Senecan poetics of *nefas*.

[42] Sullivan 1985: 74–114.

[43] Barchiesi and Cucchiarelli 2005: 217–18, quotation from 217. See Oliensis 1998: 68–103 on the *Epodes* as presenting both a poetics of *impotentia* and a "desiccating, invidious energy . . . that is unleashed above all in times of civil war" (78), which Horace then eradicates in the decorous triumph of the *Odes*.

inheritance, the poet is a danger to, among others, Horace and the Augustan tradition.[44]

5.3 Lost Sublimity?

Petronius' comic novel, *Satyrica*, obsessively remembers the figures and situations of a Roman literary and rhetorical education. Its most important characters are incapable of thought or action except in such terms. Trapped on the boat of an enemy, Eumolpus warns his friends, "You have to imagine we've got into the Cyclops cave" (*fingite . . . nos antrum Cyclopis intrasse* 101.7). Other strategies include dyeing themselves to resemble Ethiopians, for surely Eumolpus as a literary man will have the necessary ink (102.13). If the device works on the theatrical stage, why would it not work it in reality?[45] Surely the *iter salutis* ("path to safety," *Sat.* 102.13 and *Aen.* 2.387–8) lies this way? Much of the novel's humor depends on the deformation or frustration of ink-born fictions of this kind by the gross and unaccommodating "reality" constructed by forms of comedy and satire. No text returns more commonly as farce than the *Aeneid*. In Trimalchio's house, Encolpius and his companions find themselves "trapped in a new kind of labyrinth" (*novi generis labyrintho inclusi*, 73.1). This labyrinth, patterned on the underworld to which Aeneas descended,[46] is new only in the degradation of its model. For Conte (1996) and others, the relationship between the Virgilian pattern and the Petronian copy models a longing for a lost sublimity. The separation between the two is expressed in terms of the generic difference between high and low art, but commonly also historicized: "In its mythomaniac excesses the character of Encolpius is to some extent the embodiment of current imperial culture" – a world of pantomime and its "degraded and banalized *tragôidia*," and "the corruption of the *grande ingenium* (that is, of the literary conquests which the world of Virgil and Horace had achieved)."[47]

The surviving fragments of the *Satyrica* begin with a lament on the ruin of education (*Sat.* 1–2) and end in Croton, a city in a state of terminal cultural decline (*Sat.* 116.6–9).[48] Such a "rhetoric of decline"

[44] Persius, *Satires* 4 ends with the image of bankruptcy (4.51–2). For Hooley 1997: 122–53, these lines come as the culmination of a poem marking Persius' alienation from "the valorized landscapes of Vergil" (152), but also his rejection of "the easier consolations of self-contented virtue . . . proposed by Horace" (146). See further Freudenburg 2001: 151–72.

[45] Panayotakis 1995: 147. [46] Bodel 1994.

[47] Conte 1996: 186. Cf. Connors 1998: 5 on the vulgarities of the *Satyrica* as "far from Augustus' grandeur, but not so different perhaps from Nero's performance in the role of emperor."

[48] See Malamud 2009: 282–3 on Croton "at the end of its historical cycle" (282).

can be paralleled in other texts from the time of Tiberius to that of Trajan. The date of Longinus' "*On the Sublime*" is unknown and contested, but one of the arguments for dating it to the first century CE is that the decline of oratory described in its chapter 44 might be the product of the same world, very broadly defined, that produced the Elder Seneca's *Controversiae* 1 pr. 6–11, Petronius' *Satyrica*, Quintilian's lost work, *De causis corruptae eloquentiae*, and Tacitus' *Dialogus* 28–35.[49] A common theme in these narratives of decline is that declamation's fictions are fantastic and poorly equip their practitioners for public life. The theme may be related to and developed into a more pervasive blurring of reality in which imperial tyranny is represented as corrupting public life into mere political theater.[50] Political liberty is the indispensable foundation of great oratory and literature (Longinus, 44.2–5). Roman rhetoric reached its acme in the time of Cicero (Sen. *Con.* 1. 6–7). It should be noted, however, that Longinus "canvasses and then dismisses as hackneyed the political interpretation of his interlocutor,"[51] and that the narrators of Petronius' *Satyrica* are dangerously unreliable. One should tread carefully when interpreting their declamation about declamation that begins the *Satyrica*,[52] and question the opinions of characters who elsewhere reveal themselves to be either flatterers or genuinely incompetent judges of art.[53]

In the realm of poetry, Eumolpus insists that writers fill themselves with Virgil, Horace, and other great writers if they wish to achieve a sublime epic, but this lecture on literary imitation is compromised by the preceding scene of Giton imitating Corax's farts.[54] Eumolpus follows his theorizing with the recital of a civil war poem (*Sat.* 119–24), whose composition we probably read about in a scene where his animal bellowing and failure to complete his work remind commentators of (respectively) the mad poet from the end of Horace's *Ars Poetica* and Lucan.[55] That this Horatian persona has currency across genres in marking a deviation from Augustan poetics is clear, but the spirit of that deviation far less so, and need not be uniform. Petronius' Eumolpus

[49] Brink 1989 on Quintilian and Segal 1959 on Longinus, and Van den Berg 2014: 31–5 on the date of the *Dialogus*.

[50] Bartsch 1994: 1–35 for the general point and 197–9 for particular application to Trimalchio and Nero.

[51] Van den Berg 2014: 297 on Longinus 44.2, and see further 2014: 294–303 on Tacitus dismantling any simple opposition of Republican freedom to Imperial tyranny in the *Dialogus*.

[52] Gunderson 2003b: 9–12.

[53] Schmeling 2011: 10–12.

[54] They are in fact old farts, literary imitations before ever Giton copies them. See Courtney 2001: 180–1.

[55] Connors 1998: 144–5 on *Sat.* 115.

is a bungler, but such a characterization hardly fits the persona of Persius' satirist.

5.4 Augustan Prophecies Fulfilled

For Calpurnius Siculus, as for the anonymous author of the *Einsiedeln Eclogues*, pastoral poetry is the genre of Virgil rather than Theocritus. When, for example, Ornytus reads to Corydon of a golden age reborn under the leadership of a Julian youth (Calp. *Ecl.* 1.42–5), it is a literary imitation and a fulfillment of the promise of the miraculous Virgilian child (Verg. *Ecl.* 4). The cruelty of Claudius, whose reign could be represented as usurping Julian rule and as maintained "by what amounted to a continuous civil war" (Wiseman 1982: 67), had come to an end. By allusion to the texts from an earlier age of civil war, Neronian authors like Calpurnius Siculus constructed a parallel history for their own.[56] While Virgil's Sicilian Muses had in *Eclogues* 4 to adapt their genre and their woods to a slightly higher theme (*paulo maiora canamus* Verg. *Ecl.* 4.1), Calpurnius' poem is carved so high up on the tree that the humble shepherd Corydon cannot see it (Calp. *Ecl.* 1.24–27). It revises not just Virgilian pastoral, but the *Georgics*.[57] At the end of *Georgics* 1, Virgil described the baleful comet that marked the death of Julius Caesar and ensured that Philippi would once again see civil war.[58] The accession of Calpurnius' Trojan prince is explicitly different, attended not by another Philippi, but by a comet shining serene in an untainted sky (Calp. *Ecl.* 1.50–1, 77–83). Whether looking beyond its boundaries to more elevated poetic registers (Verg. *Ecl.* 4, 6), beset by greater darkness and the affairs of the city (Verg. *Ecl.* 1.83, 2), or expressing rupture and the loss of poetic memory (Verg. *Ecl.* 9), Virgilian pastoral is a fragile, vulnerable genre. More accurately, it is a poetic mode for the expression of fragility and vulnerability: the idyll exists only to be destroyed or exceeded. As Nero's glory exceeds that of his predecessors so the fragility of Virgilian pastoral is intensified.[59] Virgil's Tityrus journeyed to a Rome that he discovered surpassed his local town as a dog does a puppy (Verg. *Ecl.* 1.22), but the poem closes with an

[56] Cf. Paschalis 1982 and Groß 2013 on Lucan's reminiscences of Horace, especially 76–81 on *Epodes* 7 and 16.

[57] On this poem as programmatically defining Calpurnius' relationship with Virgil, see Slater 1994.

[58] Geo. 1.487–90. It was an enduring poetic fiction that Pharsalus and Philippi were fought on the same ground.

[59] Cf. Schiesaro 2006: 427–49 on pastoral anxieties in Senecan drama.

account of the gifts the countryside has to offer (Verg. *Ecl.* 1.80–1). When Calpurnius' Corydon returns to the countryside from the imperial spectacle on view in Rome, it is with a realization of the comparative poverty of his own existence that robs him of any joy in its simplicity (Calp. *Ecl.* 7.1–6, 40–2, 55–82). The idyll of Virgil's Tityrus existed only through the grace of Rome's divine ruler, but within that idyll he was free to play whatever songs he pleased (*et ipsum / ludere quae vellem calamo permisit agresti*, Verg. *Ecl.* 1.9–10). This is not true of his Calpurnian successors. The grand song Ornytus reads to Corydon in the first *Eclogue* and destined for august ears is given them for singing by the god himself (1.92–4). Nero's glory leaves no room for any other kind of poetry, and the pastoral idyll is overrun.[60]

Virgilian prophecies are recalled and surpassed also at the close of the first Argonautic Ode of Seneca's *Medea* (364–79) and the description of a world in which every boundary is removed. Recent commentators have noted allusions to the first *Eclogue* and the frightening miracle of an empire in which East meets West (*Ecl.* 1.59–63), to the first *Georgic* and Octavian's anticipated divine mastery over *ultima Thule* (*Geo.* 1.30), and to the first book of the *Aeneid* and Jupiter's promise of limitless empire (*Aen.* 1.278–85).[61] To all of these beginnings *Medea* is the final chapter. Vengeance, that of outraged nature and Medea herself, will challenge these claims of global domination. Crucially, Medea is not just an image of the elemental feminine that man crosses at his peril,[62] but the agent of that transgression. "This Medea is both the realization of imperial power and its undoing" (Rimell 2012: 224). Qualifications of excessive ambition are expressed in part by a synthesis of Virgilian and Horatian texts. *Odes* 1.3 and its representation of Virgilian aspiration as transgressive is an important influence on Seneca's lyric. The dialog between the Augustan texts thus continues through their influence on Seneca. In the sublimity of power without limits *Medea* is as much the fulfillment of Augustan imperial fantasy as its demise.

Further Reading

On Columella's Neronian critique of Virgil's *Georgics*, Doody 2007. On Calpurnius Siculus, Garthwaite and Martin 2009. On Lucan and

[60] Cf. Champlin 2003: 208–9 on the city of Rome absorbed by (or welcomed into the radiance of) the Domus Aurea. Even in the latter more benevolent formulation boundaries are overrun.

[61] Rimell 2012: 219–23; Trinacty 2014: 161–4. [62] Fyfe 1983: 87–9.

Ovid, Wheeler 2002 and Keith 2011. On ancient reception of Lucan, Malamud 1995. On tragic Seneca and Ovid, Hinds 2011. On Neronian literary culture, Dinter 2012b. On Petronius, Horace, and the rhetoric of consumption, Gowers 1993. For particular authors, see also the chapters in this volume.

6: Lucan's *Civil War* in Nero's Rome

Gareth Williams

Of the fifteen literary works attested for Marcus Annaeus Lucanus (39–65 CE), nephew of the younger Seneca, the ten extant books of his civil war epic on the events of 49–48 BCE – central to the poem is Julius Caesar's defeat of Gnaeus Pompeius Magnus at Pharsalus in 48 – are all that remains (some few fragments apart) of what was evidently an extraordinary output for one still so young at the time of his death. The familiar storyline has it that initially cordial relations with Nero turned to acrimony, allegedly because of the jealousy that Lucan's precocious literary talents aroused in the emperor; thereafter, Lucan's apparently enthusiastic participation in the anti-Neronian Pisonian conspiracy of 65 CE led ultimately to his forced suicide in that year. This storyline relies on a range of sources extending from Tacitus' *Annals* and Dio's epitomized Books 61 and 62 to the lives composed by Suetonius and by one Vacca, who is otherwise unknown; the Suetonian life was written some half-century after Lucan's death, but the Vacca life may well date to the fifth century or later.[1] In *Silvae* 2.7, Statius movingly pays tribute to Lucan in a posthumous birthday poem (itself a new kind of birthday commemoration)[2] addressed to his widow, Polla Argentaria: extravagantly praising him in the voice of the Muse Calliope as a genius surpassing the Homeric and Apollonian streams of epic and even rivaling Orpheus, Calliope's own son (43–53), Statius briskly surveys Lucan's poems on Troy's fall (his Iliacon, 55–6), on the Underworld (his *Catachthonion*, 57), in praise of Nero (58, presumably the *laudatio* delivered at the quinquennial Neronia festival of 60 CE), on Orpheus (59), on the fire of Rome in 64 CE (*De* incendio urbis, possibly of dangerous provocation to Nero: 60–1),[3] and to

[1] On the available sources, Fantham 2011: 4–5; for Vacca and the Suetonian life in particular, Hosius 1913: 332–6.

[2] Newlands 2011a: 224–5 and 2011b: 43; further on *Siluae* 2.7, Malamud 1995.

[3] On this provocation, Ahl 1971.

his wife (*Allocutio Pollae*, 62–3);[4] but the list reaches its climax in the eight lines Statius devotes to the masterpiece that was Lucan's *De bello civili* or *Pharsalia* (64–72), a work usually conjectured to have been started in or around 61 CE, its first three books published around 63.[5]

In lines 64–9, Statius' Calliope succinctly characterizes the three main protagonists of the epic, Julius Caesar, Cato, and Pompey:

> Thereafter, more noble of spirit in early manhood, you will thunder forth Philippi white with Italian bones, /and Pharsalian wars, where amidst arms the thunderbolt of the divine leader [sc. Caesar] . . . *** [and you will thunder forth] Cato, relentless in his devotion to freedom, and Magnus, the people's favorite.[6]

In the broad brushstrokes of this sketch, Statius nicely aligns Lucan's thundering poetics (*detonabis*) with the lightning bolt (*fulmen*) that is fundamental to Caesar's characterization in *De bello civili* itself;[7] and the possible ambiguities of *grauem* (Cato so admirably relentless in one way, so Stoically intransigent in another) and *gratum popularitate* (Pompey so committed to the Republican cause in one way, so craving popular favor in another) also capture major tension points in the Lucanian original. These complexities in the anatomy of *De bello civili* will be explored more deeply in due course, but first the poem's place in the tradition of historical epic at Rome.

6.1 Before Lucan

The remains are few, but to judge by the many surviving attestations of mythological epics in the Augustan era,[8] the form lost nothing of its older appeal in the early empire. So too historical epic: while Lucan was writing in a tradition that extended back to the *Bellum Punicum* of Gnaeus Naevius (ca. 27–201 BCE) and the *Annales* of Ennius (235–169 BCE), that "father of Roman epic"[9] who arguably exerted

[4] On these works, Fantham 2011: 8–11 with Rose 1966 and Ahl 1971 and 1976: 333–53; fragments in Courtney 1993: 352–6. For *De incendio urbis* and *Allocutio Pollae* as poetic works, not prose, Ahl 1971, esp. 2–5, and 1976, esp. 335–8.

[5] *De bello civili* is the title in most MSS, and *Bellum ciuile* is found in Suetonius and Vacca. Lucan arguably refers to the poem as *Pharsalia* (*Pharsalia nostra/ uiuet*, 9.985–6; on this phrase see later in this chapter); further, Ahl 1976: 326–32 with Fantham 1992: 1 n. 1.

[6] "mox coepta generosior iuuenta/ albos ossibus Italis Philippos/ et Pharsalica bella *detonabis*, quo *fulmen ducis* inter arma diui . . . /* * * *libertate grauem pia* Catonem/et *gratum popularitate* Magnum." For a one-line lacuna posited after 67, Newlands 2011a: 54 and 239 *ad loc.*

[7] See later in this chapter.

[8] Bramble 1982a: 483–4; Duret 1983: 1488–9.

[9] Fantham 1992: 5.

a direct influence on *De bello civili*,[10] he also had influential Augustan models to hand. Beyond the survival of names alone, some few fragments survive of Rabirius "of mighty voice" (Ovid, *Letters from Pontus* 4.16.5), author of an epic on the war between Octavian and Antony[11] – a work probably to be distinguished from the so-called *Carmen de bello Actiaco*, fragments of which were recovered from a Herculaneum papyrus and attributed by their first editor to Rabirius.[12] Sextilius Ena too wrote a civil war poem, a single verse of which is preserved by the elder Seneca (*Suasoriae* 6.27), on Cicero's death: *deflendus Cicero est Latiaeque silentia linguae*.[13] A good verse, Seneca intimates, but outdone by the superior one that it inspired in Cornelius Severus, who is hailed by the exiled Ovid as "the mightiest bard of mighty kings" (*Letters from Pontus* 4.2.1). Beyond Ovid's allusion to a work on *reges* (cf. *Letters from Pontus* 4.16.9), a *Res Romanae* and a *Bellum Siculum* (on the war of 38–36 BCE against Sextus Pompeius) are also reported of Severus. Probably from the *Res Romanae*[14] is the twenty-five-line fragment on Cicero's death preserved in Seneca (*Suasoriae* 6.26)[15] that contains the verse inspired by Sextilius Ena: *conticuit Latiae tristis facundia linguae* (11). The paradoxical quality of the line typifies the declamatory influence that gives artificial flavor to the fragment more broadly, as if the work of an author who prioritizes point over description, the in-moment effect over cross-moment development.

Similar tendencies are visible in the twenty-three-line fragment, also preserved by Seneca (*Suasoriae* 1.15), of Albinovanus Pedo's poem on Germanicus' disastrous expedition in the North Sea in 16 CE.[16] The fragment, which graphically pictures the anguish of voyagers lost at night in waters unknown and threatening, is presented by Seneca under the declamation-theme of "Alexander debates whether to sail the Ocean" (cf. *Suasoriae* 1.1–4); hence it suitably echoes various declamatory commonplaces associated with human transgression (e.g., 20–1: "The gods call us back, and forbid mortal eyes to know the limit of things") and with Alexander's fabled thirst for distant conquest. In poetic texture, the fragment shows many points of contact with Virgil's *Eclogues* and *Georgics* as well as the *Aeneid*.[17] But despite this reassuring, classicizing presence, Pedo bears the mark of a thoroughly "modern" poet, outdoing the declaimers ranged alongside him in Seneca's *Suasoriae* 1 ("None of them could match

[10] Conveniently on this controversy, von Albrecht 1999: 233–5.
[11] Courtney 1993: 332–3; Hollis 2007: 382–8. [12] Courtney 1993: 334–40; Hollis 2007: 385.
[13] Courtney 1993: 329; Hollis 2007: 338–9. [14] Hollis 2007: 348.
[15] Fr. 13 Courtney 1993: 325–7; fr. 219 Hollis 2007: 345–7, 358–67.
[16] Courtney 1993: 315–19; fr. 228 Hollis 2007: 373–81.
[17] Bramble 1982a: 489–90 and 490, n. 1.

Pedo's verve . . .," 1.15). In the earlier part of the fragment, objective reality vies with the sailors' nervous projection of what lies beneath the murky waters (e.g., 6–7: "Ocean, home beneath its sluggish waters to terrible monsters, savage beasts and sea-dogs everywhere . . ."). Fantasy here supplants myth: we see through the sailors' eyes and into their imaginings, the pressure building through the exaggerated construction of a close-to-surreal vision until direct speech dramatically intervenes and a sailor declaims against the mission (16–23). In sum, the high declamatory pitch and artificiality of the Pedo fragment signal a poetic mode in transition: the two Senecan quotations from Severus and Pedo anticipate – or, perhaps better, bear witness to the shaping of – the stylistic world of post-Augustan epic, and especially of Lucan. The latter may have given extreme, idiosyncratic, and even unique expression to inherited tendencies; but he was no stylistic solipsist writing in wholly uncharted territory.[18]

6.2 The War on Epic Form

The boldness of Lucan's approach is perhaps nowhere more evident than in his treatment of the traditional epic gods. In Petronius' *Satyricon*, the poetaster Eumolpus launches into a sample rendition of his own *Bellum ciuile* (§§119–24), so applying the tenets of his prescription for the genre in §118:

> Look at the vast theme of the civil war: whoever takes that on will sink under the burden unless he's immersed in literature. Historical events are not to be dealt with in verse; historians are far better at that task. Rather, the free spirit is to be hurled headlong into windings of plot, the activities of the gods, and a catapult-barrage of mythological material. The outcome should seem like the prophecies of an inspired soul, not the faithful testimony of a statement scrupulously made before witnesses.[19]

Modern critics are divided as to whether Eumolpus' ensuing sample of civil war epic in 295 verses is to be read as a parody of the form, as an

[18] Bramble 1982a: 487; Hollis 2007: 347.

[19] "Ecce belli civilis ingens opus quisquis attigerit nisi plenus litteris, sub onere labetur. Non enim res gestae versibus comprehendendae sunt, quod longe melius historici faciunt, sed per ambages deorumque ministeria et fabulosum sententiarum tormentum praecipitandus est liber spiritus, ut potius furentis animi vaticinatio appareat quam religiosae orationis sub testibus fides."

exuberant tribute to it in Virgilian mold, or as a more measured model (as Eumolpus sees it) of "correct" composition.[20] But if we accept that Eumolpus implicitly – if none too subtly – targets Lucan's *De bello civili* in §118, the pro-Caesarian accent of the Petronian treatment perhaps countering the opposite Lucanian tendency, his jab at historical epic as unpoetic anticipates a familiar charge against Lucan in later antiquity.[21] Especially stinging is Eumolpus' call for divine participation in the proceedings – an emphasis that pointedly draws attention to the *almost* complete absence (the qualification will matter below) of the gods in Lucan's epic. Despite the dearth of surviving historical epic, it is surely reasonable to suppose[22] that divine involvement was more conventional than exceptional, not least because Lucan's non-conformity on so many other fronts might imply a heterodox approach on the divine front as well. If we accept as much, beyond his credentials as a "prosaic" epicist, for Quintilian "more suitable for imitation by orators than by poets" (*Institutes of oratory* 10.1.90),[23] Lucan works aggressively against the generic code by dismantling the divine machinery as part of his construction of a full-blown anti-epic of sorts – a *tour de force* that explodes the myth of Rome propagated by the *Aeneid* in particular.

Of course, Lucan's epic defies simplistic labeling as an anti-*Aeneid*, not least because significant aspects of Lucan's pessimism and anti-providential skepticism are relatable to the complex political, moral, and philosophical tensions that already go unresolved in the *Aeneid*.[24] At both the macro-conceptual and episodic levels, however, clear Lucanian reminiscences and reversals appear,[25] with Ovid's *Metamorphoses* arguably invoked in *De bello civili* as an allusive presence by which Lucan further challenges, even subverts, staple features and emphases of the *Aeneid*.[26] So, e.g., whereas the *Aeneid* plots a course that progresses westward from Troy to Italy and forward in time to the making of Rome, Lucan stirs painful memory of Pompey's flight eastward from Italy to Pharsalus and then to Egypt, Caesar relentlessly pursuing him in the violence of Rome's *un*making. The positive Virgilian teleology that shapes Rome's past as a prefiguration of the Julio-Claudian future thus gives way in Lucan to a retrogressive slide

[20] See, e.g., Luck 1972; George 1974; Beck 1979; Connors 1998: 100–46; Courtney 2001: 181–4, 186–9; Schmeling 2011: 453–4.

[21] Sanford 1931: esp. 235–6. [22] With Feeney 1991: 269.

[23] See Bonner 1966 = 2010; Morford 1967, esp. 1–12.

[24] See Narducci 2002: x–xi after 1979: 35–9.

[25] Thompson and Bruère 1968 = 2010; now Casali 2011.

[26] On the important imprint of the *Metamorphoses* in *De bello civili*, see esp. Wheeler 2002 and 366–7, n. 16 for further bibliography, and now Roche 2009: 25–7.

into chaos, with the focus on Caesarian enslavement via the demise of Republican *libertas* rather than on any optimistic dawning of Imperial renewal (cf. Lucan in apostrophe at 7.426–7, exclaiming that "the fatal day of Pharsalus reversed your [sc. Rome's] destiny": ***retro*** *tua fata tulit . . . / Emathiae funesta dies*). In this undoing, the Virgilian one man (cf. *arma* ***uirum****que cano, Aeneid* 1.1) is replaced by two combatants vying to be that one,[27] their struggle suitably tinged with gladiatorial color;[28] the Virgilian *arma* of Trojan Aeneas and his Italian foes give way to the perversity of kin fighting kin, Roman vs. Roman, in Lucan's *cognatas . . . acies* ("related battle-lines," 1.4); and whereas Virgil introduces Aeneas as "a man outstanding for his dutifulness" (*insignem pietate uirum*, 1.10), *pietas* collapses into its opposite in the clash of impious arms at Lucan's Pharsalus (7.196: ***impia*** *concurrunt Pompei et Caesaris arma*). If the war-strewn second half of the *Aeneid* constitutes Virgil's "greater task" (*maius opus moueo*, 7.45), Lucan pitches his own task as still more immense and literally measureless (*immensum . . . aperitur opus*, 1.68; *immensus* from the negative prefix *in-* + *metior* "measure"). Hence the meaningful hyperbole of "the war worse than civil" (*Bella . . . plus quam ciuilia*) that Lucan declares as his theme in his epic's very first words, where *bella* is no mere poetic plural for singular: if his choice of *bella* already outdoes Virgil's synecdochic *arma* ("Virgil gives part, Lucan the whole"),[29] the plural form also signals that war in Lucan can never be a singular event, limited and with clear *telos*; it is inevitably extended and pluralized in the ongoing struggle between Caesar and *libertas* (cf. 7.695–6).

6.3 Straining for Silence

Whereas Virgil narrates the *fata* of Roman destiny (cf. *Aeneid* 1.257–8, 8.731), Lucan sings of *nefas*, of what is not to be uttered (*ne-* + *fas*): "[I sing of . . .] the contest waged with all the forces of the shattered world, to the common guilt (*in commune* ***nefas***)" (1.5–6). The unspeakable civil war resists Lucanian narration; and yet the ineffable cannot *not* be told.[30] So, just before the climax of Pharsalus, Lucan resists at 7.552–6:

> Turn away from this part of the war, my mind, and leave it to darkness.

[27] Hardie 1993: 7, 11.

[28] On this "poetics of the amphitheater" (Hardie 2013: 235), e.g., Ahl 1976: 84–115; Masters 1992: 35, 109–10; Leigh 1997, esp. 234–91.

[29] Martindale 1993: 48.

[30] For the approach, Feeney 1991, esp. 174–9; Masters 1992, esp. 7–10, 205–15.

> Let no age learn from my poetic telling of such great evils
> how much license is granted to civil war.
> Rather let our tears be shed in vain, these complaints vainly uttered:
> whatever your deeds in this battle-line, Rome, *I shall not tell of them.*[31]

Tacebo ("I shall not tell," 556): yet Lucan immediately breaks his pledge, as if powerless to derail the train of history and to resist the telling of what is ironically cast as Caesar's *own* act of silencing. Addressing the exiled Senate in Epirus, P. Cornelius Lentulus (himself of the patriciate that Caesar is eviscerating: cf. 7.597–8) struggles to preserve senatorial dignity and relevance even as "Caesar has in his control the sorrowing buildings, the empty houses, the silenced laws (*leges . . .* ***silentes***) and the courts closed by a bleak vacation" (5.30–2). Systems of narrative delay put off the telling, and improvised textual boundaries that repeatedly show Caesar in transgression try to impede his progress; so, e.g., the Rubicon, so small at 1.185 and 213, is suddenly swollen by winter at 1.217–19, as if rising against the invader in hopeless resistance to the force of (un)nature that he is. Lucan even tries to impose a form of textual silence through narrative excision: Caesar's actions receive but fleeting description (less than forty-three lines by Paul Roche's count) in the whole of 1.183–695, and just at the moment when Caesar's "measureless strength convinced him to dare greater enterprise" (1.466–7, again with the telling epithet *immensus*), Lucan reverts to events at Rome, as if stalling until Caesar's rage for war *forces* Lucan's reversion to his invasion narrative at 2.439 (*Caesar in arma furens . . .*).[32]

History thus takes its relentless course, but even after these initial delay tactics the epic remains full of discontinuity and diversion: lurid and, for some critics, grimly ridiculous descriptive set-pieces of necromancy in Book 6, say, or wounds bizarrely dealt and received in, e.g., the naval battle at Massilia in Book 3 (516–762),[33] his contortions in sentence structure, the highs and lows of his variable pitch (now hyperbolical, now "scientific,"[34] now banal[35]), his cultivation of arresting epigram and paradox (e.g., *in bellum fugitur*, 1.504), his interest more in

[31] "hanc fuge, mens, partem belli tenebrisque relinque,/ nullaque tantorum discat me uate malorum,/ quam multum bellis liceat ciuilibus, aetas./ a potius pereant lacrimae pereantque querellae:/ quidquid in hac acie gessisti, Roma, tacebo."

[32] Roche 2009: 13. [33] Now Jolivet 2013.

[34] See Fantham 1992: 17–19 ("Lucan as a poet of natural science").

[35] See at the level of diction and meter Bramble 1982b: 541–2; Fantham 1992: 34–41; Roche 2009: 51–3.

the interpretation than in the telling of events that often need elucidation from more conventional sources: through all of these features and more, Lucan's compositional mode reflects in its disturbed hyperactivity, its war on epic form, the chaotic contradictoriness that *is* his civil war. His markedly frequent use of apostrophe in particular (e.g., "It is an outrage [*nefas*], you gods . . . !" 4.791–2; 6.301–5, 9.982–6, etc.) gives his authorial voice a highly obtrusive, subjective presence in the epic, not just guiding our moral interpretation of events by investing the poem with a judgmental conscience,[36] but also providing a last line of resistance to Caesar even as he storms through the narrative. So when, after Pharsalus, Caesar pursues Pompey to Egypt and, Alexander-like,[37] he tours the site of Troy in Book 9, he wanders unknowingly (cf. *inscius*, 9.974) amidst the ruins, only for a local guide to tell him not to tread upon Hector's shade (*Phryx incola manes/ Hectoreos calcare* ***uetat***, 9.976–7); if we detect in the hint of defiance in *uetat* Lucan's sub-presence in the guide,[38] and if the Troy episode as a whole functions as an allegory of the ruin that Caesar inflicts on Rome,[39] apostrophe enables Lucan directly to match himself against Caesar, and even to assert his own powers of (self-)memorialization over those of the all-conqueror, 9.980–6:

How great and holy is the poet's task! From death you snatch all,
and on mortals you bestow immortal life.
Be not jealous, Caesar, of their sacred glory;
for if it be right for the Latin Muses to promise anything,
as long as Smyrna's priest-poet [sc. Homer] remains honored,
generations to come will read you and me; our Pharsalia will live on,
and no age will consign us to darkness.[40]

"Generations to come will read you and me; our Pharsalia will live on, and no age will consign us to darkness" (9.985–6): through this conjoining of "you and me," this sharing of "our Pharsalia" and the fusion of their destinies in the first-person plural verb, Lucan here speaks out as a preserver of memory who is empowered even to control the Caesarian legacy[41] – a form of empowerment exerted far more widely in *De bello civili* if Lucan is seen to offer a deliberate counter-narrative that

36 Now D'Alessandro Behr 2007.

37 Zwierlein 1986: 464–9 = 2010, 416–20 with Morford 1967: 13–19.

38 Green 1991: 251–2 = 2010: 179–80.

39 Hardie 1993: 17, 107.

40 "o sacer et magnus uatum labor! omnia fato/eripis et populis donas mortalibus aeuum./ inuidia sacrae, Caesar, ne tangere famae;/ nam, siquid Latiis fas est promittere Musis,/ quantum Zmyrnaei durabunt uatis honores,/ uenturi me teque legent; Pharsalia nostra/ uiuet, et a nullo tenebris damnabimur aeuo."

41 Further, Gowing 2005: 90–2.

"exposes" the partiality of Caesar's own version of events in his *Commentarii de bello ciuili*.[42]

6.4 CAESAR, POMPEY, AND CATO

A potent corollary of this antagonism between poet and protagonist, Lucan and Caesar, is to find civil war actively waged within the text: the word goes to war[43] as language struggles with its own meaning (e.g., "unspeakable crime will be called virtue," 1.667–8) and turns upon itself when, in a significant programmatic moment, Roman standards face each other and javelin confronts javelin at 1.6–7. This fracturing of language is symptomatic not just of the disunity of the larger narrative, but also of disintegration within the body politic – a fragmentation objectified in horrific scenes of bodily mutilation (e.g., 7.617–30, at Pharsalus),[44] and summed up in the vision of Pompey's severed head at 8.663–73 (cf. 711), with Rome as *caput mundi* (cf. 2.136, 655; 9.123–4) in one sense symbolically decapitated (via Pompey's demise), in another sense subservient to a new head (cf. *caput* of Caesar, 5.686).[45] In turn, the contrary forces that fracture Lucan's authorial voice – the will not to sing of a *nefas* that *will* be sung – are also felt in the contrasting characterizations of Caesar and Pompey. The former strides forth as a restless and ruthless man of action, "his vigorous energies (*uirtus*) not knowing how to stand in one place" (1.144–5; cf. "headlong in everything," 2.656), intense and indomitable (1.146), quick to take up arms and to seize opportunity; for all his transgressive villainy, his redeeming features (e.g., his capacity for clemency at 4.363–4) extend to a charisma, even a sublimity,[46] which (as in the case of Sallust's Catiline, say, or Seneca's Atreus in the *Thyestes*) fascinates even as it repels. In contrast to this streak of lightning (cf. 1.151–7), Lucan's Pompey is likened to a venerable oak that stands by its weight alone, now that its roots have lost their resilience (1.136–43)[47] – an oak still worshiped (1.143), but ominously vulnerable to Caesar's bolt. Pompey is cast as aging (1.129–30), Caesar as youthful, even though the latter was only six

[42] On this Lucanian "countermemory," Gowing 2005: 83–4 with Henderson 1987: 132–3 = 2010: 451–2; Feeney 1991: 274; Masters 1992: 17–18, 23. On the transmission of *De bello civili* as Lucan's title, p. 94 and n. 5.

[43] Henderson 1987 = 2010.

[44] Most 1992; Quint 1993: 140–7; now Dinter 2012a, esp. 9–49.

[45] On *caput*, Dinter 2012a: 19–21.

[46] Now Day 2013, esp. 106–78; yet Day's Pompey exhibits a form of counter-sublimity of his own in his grandeur amidst/despite ruin.

[47] On these two key similes, Rosner-Siegel 1983 = 2010.

years younger. Whereas Caesar moves the action, Pompey postpones it, avoiding conflict by fleeing from Rome (cf. 1.519–22, 2.392–3) and then Italy (2.680–736), and succumbing to "the allurements of delay" (*blandae ... morae*, 5.732–3) before dispatching his beloved Cornelia to the safety of Lesbos. This Cunctator is a Magnus in name only, the shadow of his *own* great name (cf. *stat magni nominis umbra*, 1.135),[48] at least until his shade finds release in death ("nor did that handful of dust imprison his mighty ghost [***tantam*** ... ***umbram***]," 9.2), he undergoes catasterism, and his soul subsequently descends to reside in the breasts of Brutus and Cato (9.3–18). At Pharsalus, however, Magnus is no match for the all-powerful Caesar (cf. *omnia Caesar erat*, 3.108): he is harried into arms against his better judgment (7.85–123), seemingly "slow and cowardly" (7.52) in the eyes of troops seized by a frenzy for rash action.

It is fitting that at the poem's outset (1.33–66) Lucan claims inspiration for his epic from Nero, hailed as *Caesar* at 1.41; for if *De bello civili* is Pompeian in one way, a Lucanian effort to delay the telling of *nefas*, it is also positively Caesarian in its transgressive energy and ruthless path to victory at Pharsalus in Book 7. For Jamie Masters, these different sides, Pompeian and Caesarian, oppose each other in a war that Lucan engages with himself with no decisive outcome;[49] and even Caesar's victory over Pompey may be undercut late in the epic. When in Book 10 we find him in Egypt, seduced by Cleopatra's charms, he proves to be more vulnerable and defensive (cf. 10.449–64), surviving one assassination plot only to be shown desperately fighting off another Egyptian threat before the text expires. The great mover now shows a new appetite for delay and for luxury:[50] ensconced at Alexandria, he draws out a night of feasting (10.172–4) in order to converse with Acoreus, that wily Egyptian priest, on the secrets of the Nile, only to be led by Acoreus on a circuitous tour of theories of the river's summer flooding and then a meandering description of its course (10.194–331). Acoreus' serpentine account is ultimately more cryptic than illuminating, all but declaring that the Nile's mysteries will remain beyond discovery, not least by Caesar himself; the Nile frustrated Alexander and Cambyses (10.272, 280), and so (we infer) it will frustrate the latest *tyrannus* (cf. 269) with designs on teasing out its secrets – not just Caesar, we might suspect, but also Nero, who launched his own expedition to the Nile ca. 61 CE.[51] Here at last in Lucan's Egypt, Caesar's rampaging

[48] Feeney 1986 = 2010. [49] Masters 1992.

[50] Possibly with Neronian overtones, Perutelli 2000: 157.

[51] On these and other implications of the Acoreus episode, Barrenechea 2010; Manolaraki 2011 and 2013, esp. 80–117; Tracy 2011, esp. 35–8, and now 2014.

progress though *De bello ciuili* collides with limit and containment, as if the Nile defies conquest, a Rubicon (cf. 1.185) that will *not* be crossed. And if Caesar finally meets his match in Acoreus (that cipher for Lucan?),[52] in this post-Pharsalus phase of the epic M. Porcius Cato (95–46 BCE), Lucan's third main protagonist, also comes into his own, as if the continuing essence of Republican opposition to Caesar.[53]

Cato importantly complicates the characterization of Lucan's Pompey in particular, first taking sides with Pompey in Book 2 not least to check the latter's autocratic tendencies (2.320–3). That equal hater of Pompey and Caesar alike when the outcome of their war was uncertain (cf. 9.21), Cato is cast firmly as a *Pompeianus* (9.24) only after Pompey's demise; and for all his overt praises in the tribute that he delivers at 9.190–214, Cato also treads a fine line between generosity and candor: did Pompey serve the state, or seek to dominate it? Cato's resolute Stoicism may itself be flawed (as we shall see), but, on the positive side, it usefully exposes the inadequacies and/or excesses of both Pompey and Caesar. Whether or not we accept that Pompey is cast as a Stoic "progressive" who gradually advances toward wisdom before his death,[54] Caesar is "an unphilosophically passionate conception,"[55] one who shatters the Stoic order by instigating chaos at all levels, moral, civic, and in nature (cf. 2.2–4: "and prescient nature overturns the laws and ordinances of the world with portent-filled disorder, and proclaimed the unspeakable [sc. civil war]").[56] Against this force of disorder stands Cato, so staunch in his defense of *libertas* after Pompey's death (9.23–30), so committed to self-sacrifice in order to atone, as if in *deuotio*, for his nation's sins (cf. 2.314–19), and so resilient in enduring nature's torture (contrast Caesar's disruptions of nature) as he leads his men across the snake-infested Libyan desert in Book 9 by the example of his *dura uirtus* (9.445). But for all his god-like virtue (cf. 1.128), this Cato remains a controversial figure in modern scholarship. From one perspective, in choosing participation in the civil war over inaction (2.289–97), this embodiment of Republican *libertas* stands as an exemplar of action despite paralysis and futility, offering for Shadi Bartsch's fully engaged reader of Lucan the lesson that "our best option, however flawed it might be, is to believe in an impossible future."[57] Alternatively, Cato has

[52] Manolaraki 2011: 157 and 2013: 83–6.
[53] On Lucan's Cato, Johnson 1987: 35–66; Fantham 1992: 29–30; Bartsch 1997 and 2005: 500–1; now Seo 2011 and 2013: 66–93; Tipping 2011.
[54] Marti 1945; but for brief but strong rebuttal, Lintott 1971: 504–5 = 2010: 267–8.
[55] Bramble 1982b: 536.
[56] On this cosmic fragmentation, Lapidge 1979 = 2010 with Bramble 1982b: 537–9, 554–7.
[57] 2005: 499 after 1997.

been viewed as a grotesque caricature of Stoic over-perfectionism (cf. 2.380–91), obsessive, arrogant, and priggish, Lucan's treatment of him "a mockery of misdirected philosophical virtue."[58]

Yet on either reading, positive or negative, Cato's Stoicism is surely betrayed in *De bello civili* by the absence of any beneficent providence within the Stoic framework of Lucan's world, where fortune seemingly predominates instead. Early in Book 2, the Stoic determinism that guarantees the chain of causes for all eternity (2.7–11) vies with a non-Stoic (Epicurean) vision of randomness (2.12–15) in explanation of the disaster that is about to befall Rome.[59] Right or wrong, the non-teleological possibility constantly hovers in *De bello civili* as another *nefas* of sorts, a seemingly unsayable, unthinkable challenge to Cato's faith in destiny; and the gods merely add to the uncertainty. "It will be a reproach to the gods," Cato declares somewhat sanctimoniously at 2.288, "to have made even me guilty." But where are they? They are not completely absent (cf. 2.1: "And now the gods' anger was revealed"), but why their almost total removal? As we have seen,[60] generic constraint offers no good explanation, given that the gods appear to have been no strangers to historical epic; nor are they omitted because of any Lucanian crisis of belief, given that there is no absence of belief in the gods within the poem.[61] The gods' absence is surely better viewed[62] as a form of denied presence, their inscrutability placing their motivations and actions beyond representation. By this device, their absence speaks volumes: "[Lucan] has not abandoned the gods, they have abandoned him."[63]

6.5 End of Story?

In this poem of contradiction, how is the pessimism that pervades this godless battle-scape to be reconciled with his notorious praise of Nero at 1.33–66?[64] If that praise is taken at face value, or at least as something more than a stereotypical gesture delivered without conviction, one solution is offered by Vacca's report that Lucan published the first three books of *De bello civili* separately from the rest of the epic; his glowing tones in this early phase only later gave way to the disenchantment[65] that

[58] Masters 1999: 402; cf. Johnson 1987, esp. 37–8, 72, 109 (Cato "parodic of dead Stoicism").
[59] Feeney 1991: 279–80. Further on Lucanian *fatum/fortuna*, Friedrich 1938 = 2010 with Dick 1967; Sklenář 1999; Long 2007.
[60] See p. 97. [61] Feeney 1991: 274. [62] With Feeney 1991: 269–85.
[63] Feeney 1991: 285. [64] Now Roche 2009: 7–10 and 129–46 with 129–30 for bibliography.
[65] See on this approach Fantham 1992: 13–14.

is all but blatant at 7.444–5: "Of all the peoples who endure tyranny, our lot is the worst, because we are ashamed [*pudet*, emphatically in the present] of our slavery." Then 7.455–9:

Yet we have revenge for this disaster,
as much as gods can rightfully give to mortals:
civil war will make [Caesarian] divinities the equal of the gods above,
and Rome will honor the dead with thunderbolts, rays and stars,
and in the temples of the gods she will swear by [mere] ghosts (*umbras*).[66]

In retrospect, these lines deliver their own damning indictment of Lucan's effusive portrayal of Nero as a Jupiter or an Apollo in waiting (1. 45–50), or as any god he would want to be (1.50–2; the case for pure parody is not completely closed). The Vacca-based theory eases the glaring incompatibility between the two passages, 1.33–66 and 7.455–9, but it too runs into obvious difficulties that begin with its reliance on convenient but unproven biographical reconstruction, and with the fact that Books 1–3 are themselves by no means unexceptionally or uniformly laudatory.[67] Yet there is another way: if the two passages are set dynamically against each other, the two deliver competing versions of "truth" in yet another manifestation of Lucan's fractured voice, both Pompeian and Caesarian, pro- and anti-imperial; and/or they play an open-ended game of self-canceling speech, *fari* in contention with *nefas*, with Lucan's potentially sincere praises always compromised on each rereading that is hijacked by the anti-voice in Book 7.[68]

This latest example of open-endedness contributes yet further to the self-absorbed exercise in contradiction and paradox that is Lucan's *De bello civili*. It is commonly accepted that the poem as it survives is incomplete, and that, had Lucan lived, he would have extended it to one of several plausible end-points, such as Cato's suicide at Utica (in modern Tunisia) after the Republican defeat at Thapsus in 46 BCE.[69] The opposite argument that the poem is complete in its extant form[70] has gained limited traction. But even if the case for completeness is dismissed, the correlation that it posits between the extant epic's abruptness of ending and the intrinsic messiness and endlessness of civil war still usefully illuminates *De bello civili*: in the open-endedness of its tensions at

[66] "cladis tamen huius habemus/ uindictam, quantam terris dare numina fas est:/ bella pares superis facient ciuilia diuos,/ fulminibus manes radiisque ornabit et astris/ inque deum templis iurabit Roma per umbras."

[67] Roche 2009: 6–7. [68] Further, Hinds 1998: 87–8.

[69] Now Stover 2008 for the post-Thapsus position, with 571, n. 2 for bibliography on this and other theories.

[70] Now Tracy 2011 after Haffter 1957 and Masters 1992: 216–59.

every step of the way, and in the dissonance of its fractured Pompeian/Caesarian voice(s), Lucanian civil war *inevitably* resists comfortable closure. If the text as we have it is taken to be incomplete, any putative ending, we might reasonably suppose, would have been determinedly inconclusive – a predictable *finis sine fine*, and perhaps an all too fitting denouement for an epic that sheds its own perturbing light on the still unfolding story of the age of Nero.

Further Reading

Fine Anglophone commentaries on Lucan are offered by Roche 2009 on Book 1, Fantham 1992 on Book 2, Asso 2010 on Book 4, and R. Mayer 1981 on Book 8. Seminal essays on Lucan include Lapidge 1979, Bramble 1982b, Feeney 1986, and Henderson 1987; Bramble 1982b apart, all of these are reproduced in Tesoriero 2010, while state-of-the-art essays are now assembled in Asso 2011. Important book-length treatments of Lucan in English from various angles of approach are Ahl 1976, Johnson 1987, Masters 1992, Bartsch 1997, Leigh 1997, and now D'Alessandro Behr 2007, Dinter 2012a, Day 2013 and Tracy 2014.

7: Petronius, Realism, Nero*

Kirk Freudenburg

In the scholarship on Petronius' *Satyrica* Nero is everywhere. In the novel itself, he is nowhere: never taken up as a topic, never named, pilloried, or praised in the novel's off-hand and salty talk, a fair amount of which concerns small-town politics, not the politics of Rome. As a picaresque parody of higher forms such as romance and mythological epic, the novel "takes place" in a Neverland that is unspecified. And yet the *Satyrica*'s world is highly ascribable in ways that the forms parodied are not, curiously attuned as it is to Roman (especially south Italian "Greco-Roman") cultural realities of the mid-to-late first century CE.[1] Numerous parallels have been detected linking the Priapic novel's starring upstart, Trimalchio (hereafter T), to Nero. Some of these parallels, such as T's vainglorious dedication of his first shave in a golden box (§29), are so exotic and rhyme so powerfully with things said to have been done by Nero (Suet. *Nero* 12.4) that to fail to take note of them would be to shortchange the little evidence we have for making sense of T as a vainglorious performer, and his performance as a product of and reflection on, its age. The parallels are there to be hit upon.[2] The real question is what to do with them. For some, they have been taken to constitute the political/satirical meat of the *Satyrica*'s main meal: a way of scoffing at Nero's outlandish showmanship by way of a comic stand-in.[3]

This way of reducing things has its obvious enticements, and yet the novel gives us plenty of reason to be more circumspect, especially

* For their help in assessing earlier drafts and providing helpful criticisms, I would like to thank Gareth Schmeling, a master of all things Petronian, and my two coeditors, Shadi Bartsch and Cedric Littlewood. All undercooked assertions that remain I am glad to claim as my own.

1 On the question of "when was the *Satyrica* written," see Prag and Repath 2009: 7–9.

2 For the main parallels, see Rose 1971: 81–6 and Vout 2009: 101–2.

3 A particularly strong example is Walsh 1970: 139: "The comic detail of Nero's appearance and habits is incorporated to cause merriment to contemporaries close to the court. I conclude that Nero could hardly have been present at a recitation of the *Cena*." The idea is no longer evident in Walsh 1996.

given the way it shares out the penchant for vainglorious self-stylization among a number of characters who are every bit as prone as T to putting on imperial airs of one kind or another, some of which parallel behaviors ascribed to Nero, others the behaviors of his associates (esp. Seneca), or of earlier emperors (e.g., Claudius), the poets he admired (Lucan), and so on.[4] We recall, for example, that it is not T, but T's bookkeeper who disdains wearing once-laundered clothes (§30), the way Nero is said to have done (Suet. *Nero* 31), and it is the nymphomaniacal Quartilla who caps off a multi-day orgy of her own proud design with a mock wedding, complete with torches, marriage bed, wedding veil, and drunken partiers as witnesses to the "bride's" deflowering (§19–26, cf. the "wedding orgy" of Tac. *Ann.* 15.37). And so on. All of which suggests that T's "Neronian" posturing, his playing at having hit upon and mastered the hottest trends of his age, is not unique to T. It is what everyone is playing at in the *Satyrica*, such that to find in T Nero done up in a fun house mirror is to miss the larger and infinitely more complex potentials of the novel to engage with its culture and to satirize.

As Conte has expertly shown, the protagonists of the *Satyrica* are "mythomaniac" dreamers who happily confuse their sketchy and battered circumstances with those of epic heroes and the lovers of romance.[5] They have, in essence, spent far too many hours in front of late first-century television, ruining their minds on tales of pirate abductions, shipwrecks, and forlorn suicides, and it is precisely their failure to know this about themselves that marks them as delusional, narratologically unreliable, and satirizable.[6] This same failure to respect the vast distance that separates their own "low" from the "high" that fuels their imaginations can be taken to apply to the imperial airs the characters of the *Satyrica* so often put on. In the end, this penchant of theirs for grandiose self-stylization does not have to be about Petronius, the hidden author, secretly poking fun at Nero by way of an idiot Trimalchio. The problem is not, I suggest, that T is trying to keep up with Nero; it's that everyone is trying to keep up with Nero. In Petronius, we have a world where, in any given triclinium, bathhouse, or backwater art gallery, one might be dragooned by some local

4 On Eumolpus as a hypocritical and vainglorious stand-in for Seneca, see Sullivan 1968: 193–213. For a more circumspect and nuanced version of the idea, see Rudich 1997: 221–4. For a recent, thorough, and nuanced study of Senecan parody in Petronius, see Star 2012.

5 Conte 1996.

6 A symbiotic relationship can be observed between finding the author who "hides" and naming/proving the *Satyrica* a satire: to find that "hidden author" always finds one locating the "satiric point" of the work as well. Put differently, to name the work a "satire" is to give it an "author," i.e., someone with social/critical and "real-world" points to make.

arbiter elegantiae into playing audience to his or her latest Neronian stylizations, whether of food, poetry, or sex (or some clever mixture thereof). It is a world where everyone who is anyone is trying to style themselves imperial by stepping to the strangely provocative tunes played at the world's center by Nero, his freedmen, and his friends. It is a "star-struck" world where no one can distinguish the real from the fake because Neronian fakery is the new real. And that may be the bigger satiric payoff to take from the novel's many allusions to Neronian pretense and imperial show.

What we see of that fakery in Petronius is at several removes from its stylish source, played badly by locals who misconstrue, garble, and don't know when to stop. Quartilla turns pleasure into torture, doing to sex what T does to food (and Eumolpus to poetry). And certain features of her party management, such as her penchant for puns that trick and surprise, for pretend rituals, for droning musical accompaniment, dress up, playacting, and going on and on to all hours of the night, bear a strong resemblance not only to the antics of T, but (as mentioned earlier) to some of the more notorious features of the parties Nero was said to have thrown. But this is a problematic observation, because the most notorious of Nero's orgies, the one that Tacitus, by innuendo, connects to the fire of 64 (*Ann.* 15.37–8), is said to have been artfully designed not by Nero, but by Tigellinus, head of the Praetorian Guard, and the very man who, Tacitus says (*Ann.* 16.18), had it in for Petronius and arranged for him to be put to death because he was jealous of his skills as a rival stylist of indulgence and vicious living – skills that gave him influence over Nero.

Little can be said about Tigellinus as a designer of parties other than that his designs were outrageous enough to be taken for scandal and artfully overblown by censorious historians. But it is clear that, whatever these parties were, everyone was watching them and talking about them. The stories subsequently told about them suggest that Nero's parties were highly scripted, designed to make Nero "show" in a certain way, and to obligate his guests to him by folding them into his *gratia*, dazzling them with sensual surprises, putting them on the inside, pampering them, and making them part of the empire's most innovative and sought-after show. As Nero's go-to man on all things stylistic (his so-called Overseer of Elegance, *arbiter elegantiae*), Petronius had ideas about what constituted stylish entertainments. He was, for a time, highly favored by Nero: in essence, his "Maecenas," a very powerful thing to be. Tigellinus saw him as a rival, so he arranged for his execution. To modern ways of thinking this all seems rather ridiculous and unlikely: that one man should snuff out another over matters of elegance and stylization. But in a world where a refined and highly innovative style, generously lavished, generates *gratia* and powerful enthusiasm for the emperor's cause among those who are lavished upon (i.e., given the extreme aestheticization of politics under Nero, amounting to a "rule by style"), it makes perfect sense to think that Tigellinus should have killed Petronius to eliminate him as a rival in the arts of elegance. Theirs was not a catfight over how best to fold the emperor's dinner napkins. It was a struggle for power.

In the aftermath of the fire of 64, Nero rounded up Christians to torture and heap with blame. Tacitus tells us that among the "utterly recherché/exquisite punishments" (*quaesitissimis poenis*) that Nero hit upon to dispatch the Christians, he had them nailed to crosses and lit as lamps to provide lighting for his gardens at night (*Ann.* 15.44). The sarcastic turn of phrase Tacitus has reprised from Sallust at a moment of high censorial dudgeon.[7] It invites us, in the blink of an eye, to see the torture of the Christians from Nero's own point of view: as a stylistic stroke, an innovation of high (decadent) design. Taken as such, the punishment Tacitus describes *qua* stylistic stroke has all the markings of a mocking pun, in that to kill Christians in this way finds Nero making torches of those whom he had accused of torching the city – or perhaps a mocking reference to the lamp-lighting rituals of the Sabbath that Romans found so odd,[8] or as a literalizing play upon some fiery or phosphorescent aspect of their rites of the Christians' own self-styling, e.g., as "lights/lamps of the world" (Ev. Matt. 5:14–16), "a light to those in darkness" (Ep. Rom. 2.19), bearing a message that spreads like an irrepressible fire (Act. Ap. 2), and so on.[9] A similar punning design can be detected in the execution of an outspoken satirist by Tigellinus, later recalled by Juvenal near the end of his first satire (verses 155–7). There Juvenal says that in dispatching the offending free-speaker, Tigellinus had the man's trachea pierced (presumably by his own writing pen), and that he then had him lit on fire. By being killed in this way, the man was literalized into the "flaming satirist" he claimed to be (cf. the satirist's "flaming passion" *animo flagrante* in v. 152), and as the fire heated his

[7] Outside of two uses in Tacitus (*Ann.* 2.53 and 15.44), the unwieldy five-syllable superlative occurs elsewhere in classical Latin only at Sall. *Hist.* fr. 2.70 line 13, where it describes the excessively luxurious banquets (*epulae quaesitissimae*) put on to celebrate Metellus' triumphant return from Spain in 71 BCE.

[8] For Roman mockery of the Jewish custom of lighting lamps during daylight hours (the *ritus lucernarum*) to prepare for the Sabbath, see Kissel *ad* Pers. 5.180–2.

[9] On *crematio* (being burned alive) as a punishment suited to the crime of arson, see Kyle 1998: 53, esp. n. 129.

frame, you could see smoke shooting from his pen/throat. Death by paronomasia.[10] I call attention to these cruel doings not to suggest that Petronius "alludes to" the puns of Nero/Tigellinus by having his party throwers, Quartilla and Trimalchio, engage in punning wordplay, but to point out that puns tend to crop up in descriptions of the Neronian age in ways that cannot be tracked in any other age, as the stuff of trickery, one-upmanship, and self-stylization.

Tacitus tells us at *Annals* 16.19 that when Petronius was ordered to commit suicide, he set out to kill himself in a way that would make his death seem natural rather than forced (*ut quamquam coacta mors fortuitae similis esset*). A play-actor to the end, Petronius fakes his own death, playing it as a death by chance.[11] After writing out a list of pornographic novelties indulged in by Nero and Tigellinus, Petronius broke his signet ring so that no one could fake being him after his death. He then passed peacefully away. The tale is impossible to credit as "the basic facts" of Petronius' demise. Yet what stands out from Tacitus' highly crafted account is the dying man's determination to "play" his death in a certain way, as if adhering (to the bitter end) to specific principles of style. In contrast to Nero's Christian torches and Tigellinus' seething satirist, Petronius wanted his demise, no matter how scripted (by himself) and forced (by Nero) it actually was, to be seen as natural, taken in stride, and unforced. He wanted to hide his art, thus to make it look like the way of things, all the while it was not; a clever piece of realistic and highly parodic fiction.[12] He died as he wrote.

But the most famous example among several under Nero of a scripted death parading, or in this case attempting to parade, as a stroke of chance concerns not Petronius, but Nero's mother, Agrippina, whose attempted murder by way of a collapsing ship was crafted to look like an accident (*quasi casu evenisset*, Tac. *Ann.* 14.8.8). The historians' creative accounts of the debacle (Tac. *Ann.* 14.3–8; Suet. *Nero* 34) suggest that the ruse failed because of faulty mechanics (the main prop's failure to fail), and because the lead actress refused to die the death scripted for her. Realizing that she was trapped in a play that required her to die, Agrippina chose to improvise a new ending for herself, one that found her not in the role of an accident victim, but that of a tragic heroine

[10] On executions staged as various kinds of fictional plays in Rome, see Coleman 1990.

[11] Highet 1941: 194: "His suicide was as carefully arranged as that of any Stoic: its very nonchalance was meant to be significant."

[12] On the death of Petronius as a parody of the death of Seneca, see esp. Star 2012: 12, n. 32. As "deliberate rejection of the Platonic/Stoic tradition," see Edwards 2007: 176–8. On the rhetorical, parodic, and dramatic aspects of Tacitus' account of Petronius' suicide, see esp. Schmeling 2011: xv–xvii (with full bibliography *ad loc.*).

struck down by a mad, matricidal son: "'Strike my belly,' she cried, presenting her womb to the centurion as he drew his sword" (Tac. *Ann.* 14.8.8).[13] As with so much that historians tell us about the cruel schemes of Nero, Anicetus' collapsing ship begs to be taken as apocryphal, a contraption of the historians' own clever design.[14] And yet there is a strong tendency among historians, satirists, and other writers who tell of Nero's outrages to craft him both as an actor and as a maker of elaborate contraptions, stages, and scenes (see La Rocca, Chapter 13 in this volume).[15] As an actor, they find him out in his attempts to "play upon" disaster as if it were scripted, and as a maker of illusions, they expose the scripted-ness of his ostensibly non-scripted schemes. The most famous example of the former concerns Nero's playing his own song of Troy's demise as he watched Rome burn from atop Maecenas' tower on the Esquiline Hill, as if singing the accompaniment to a play that he wrote, with the whole of Rome serving as his (utterly realistically) burning stage. Tacitus says that, in rebuilding the city after the fire, Nero's architects, Severus and Celer, "attempted to create what nature had denied" (*Ann.* 15.42) by building a sprawling fantasy house with artificial lakes, fields, and woods where once houses, tenements, and temples had stood. At tremendous expense, a remote, naturalistic backdrop is erected within the city's walls. To the historians who write about it, the fire of 64 seems to have been scripted: a "disaster" parading as real. As they do with Agrippina's shipwreck, they expose the fire as a play written by Nero (the *Incendium*) to give the impression of a chance disaster, but badly performed and much too easily taken as script: art that fails to stay hidden.

One final example of a random disaster turned to art by Nero before returning to the *Satyrica*. In this case, the events described stand a decent chance of not being apocryphal because they make sense as good politics. At *Annals* 15.34, Tacitus describes the collapse of a theater at Naples in the immediate aftermath of a performance by Nero, his first as a performer before a public audience after ten years of holding back,

[13] On Nero's scripting a role for Agrippina to die in, and Agrippina's last-minute self-assertion in breaking free from that script, see Bartsch 1994: 20–2; cf. Edwards 2007: 201.

[14] Suet. *Nero* 39 quotes five examples of anonymous lampoons that Nero suspiciously neglected to care about and/or investigate. Three of the quoted poems taunt Nero as a matricide, but none makes mention of a collapsing ship. Beyond these lampoons, the earliest references to the accident (Martial *Ep.* 4.63 and Seneca *Octavia* 310–57, dating to 87–8 CE) come nearly thirty years after the fact (March 59 CE). Martial makes no reference to a collapsing ship. For discrepancies in ancient accounts of Agrippina's demise, see Dawson 1968: 255.

[15] On the extreme confusion of dramatic representation and reality in the age of Nero, see esp. Bartsch 1994: 1–62. On the theatrics of T, see Rosati 1999.

limiting himself to invited audiences in private.[16] The theater was empty, so no one was hurt. Tacitus says that most regarded the theater's collapse as a sinister omen: a sign of divine anger, or so Tacitus implies, at Nero's public singing.[17] But Tacitus adds that Nero himself took the disaster as a sign of divine favor, and that he subsequently composed songs celebrating the event and thanking the gods for their divine favor. Once again, then, we have yet another story told by a historian about a collapsing stage that finds Nero playing upon a disaster, as if to render chance into the gods' own well-crafted, Nero-centric design. Thus the theater's collapse, a portent from the gods telling Nero to stop singing, is taken by Nero as a reason to sing.

The dinner party thrown by T abounds in accidents and chance intrusions that are not part of his carefully designed script: plates fall, bowels become irritable, acrobats crash, and so on. And many of these events, like the collapse of the theater in Naples, become occasions for songs, many of which are strangely, often delusionally matched to the events they purport to sing.[18] With great consistency the accidents that befall T's party are artfully rendered by him by being folded into the show, leaving his guests to wonder whether these "accidents" had anything accidental about them at all. When a silver plate falls to the floor in §34, a servant stoops to pick it up. T jumps in with orders to have the boy's ears boxed, not because he dropped the plate, but because he picked it up. He demands that the plate be tossed down again so that it can be swept away with the trash, a magnificent show of devil-may-care wastefulness that puts T's lavishness on bright display. Perhaps the best known of these disasters played up by T for his own self-glorification is the acrobat's fall in §54–5.[19] Many have pointed out that Nero had his own encounter with a falling acrobat when a scripted fall (the acrobat was playing Icarus) failed to deploy as a fake: Nero ended up being spattered by the acrobat's very real blood (Suet. *Nero* 12). When the narrator, Encolpius, describes the acrobat falling on T's arm, he does so as a much more seasoned and skeptical narrator than he was at the beginning of the meal when the silver plate was swept away.

[16] On the significance of this performance in the aftermath of ten years of relative "forbearance," see Bartsch 1994: 3–4.

[17] Tacitus makes no mention of the more obvious reason for the theater's collapse: the devastating earthquake of the previous year (February 5, 63 CE) that flattened countless buildings in the region and severely damaged and/or weakened many others.

[18] On how the poems of Petronius are tied into the narrative structure of the *Satyrica*, see esp. Connors 1998.

[19] On the problem of the accident's prearrangement, see Setaioli 2011: 110–11, listing basic bibliography in n. 109.

He says that T was hunched over his arm, groaning, "as if" his arm had been injured (*bracchium tamquam laesum*). For his part, the boy who fell on T was by this point crawling around begging the guests for mercy, a bit of playacting that Encolpius had already seen and been taken in by. He suspects that the guests are being duped again, the way they were when the cook had "forgotten" to gut the pig. Even as he thinks this thought to himself, he sees T working the disaster for all its worth, giving it a plot and meaning and putting himself at the center of attention. The slave who wraps T's wounded arm is given a beating for daring to use a white bandage rather than a purple one, and the fallen acrobat, rather than being punished, is tossed his freedom by T lest it should be said that a man as great as he had been wounded by a mere slave. Applause follows (as if marking the end of a highly emotional scene on stage). T orders his writing materials to be brought in, whereupon he recites for all posterity a three-line *carpe diem* epigram on the fickle ways of fortune.[20] Thus, what Encolpius suspects is a scripted "disaster" T's poem renders into a stroke of chance. The play-acted is memorialized as the random.

The beauty of this last example is that we cannot know whether T planned the acrobat's fall or merely made the most of a "real" accident by playing it up as part of his show. Encolpius cannot tell, and neither can we. I put scare quotes around the word "real" here because, of course, none of what happens in the novel is real: it is all made up, a comic fiction, to be marveled at for seeming so real. Nearly seventy years ago, Auerbach lauded the *Satyrica* as the pinnacle of ancient realism. For him, it was especially the freedmen's tales that opened a window, albeit narrowly confined to the comic and low, into the scrabbling lives and petty obsessions of Rome's lower classes on the make.[21] It is precisely by way of the work's many unexpected, low, and incidental details that it produces the "effects" of reality that invite readers to relish in the realism it portrays.[22] But, as we have just seen in the vignette of the falling acrobat, at the same time as "the accident" begs to be taken as real, the *Satyrica* shows a high level of awareness of its ability to trick us by seeming so real. It thematizes the difficulties of distinguishing the scripted and real-looking from the random, as well as the fungibility of these terms in the hands of clever manipulators.

[20] See Rosati 1999: 102 on T's "tendency to record with scrupulous solemnity, and to comment in verse, the events which happen in his own little world."

[21] Auerbach 1953: 24–49.

[22] On the role of everyday objects in conjuring the effects of reality, see Feeney 2012: 31 (citing Barthes 1968).

The problem is especially marked by T's prestidigitational razzle-dazzle in rendering the scripted as happenstance, and chance happenings as art; party tricks that bear a weird, comical resemblance to high Neronian political art. The exploding wild boar of §40 is perhaps the best ecphrastic symbol of T's feast, and of the *Satyrica* more generally. Take it for what it looks to be, as Encolpius did, and the joke is on you: this is no roasted boar, but a Trojan Horse, stuffed with live birds that explode from it when the slave actor slices into it (a ruse altered for re-performance in §49). Pork turns out to be poultry in disguise, an elaborate, exploding contraption parading as something old-fashioned and straightforward. Like the boar that is the meal's main course, the novel itself tricks us into thinking that things are just what they look to be, Roman "nature" and happenstance put down on paper, and a window into real life. And yet it is all an elaborate fiction.

Consider, for example, the way in which the novel includes something as low and undeniably "natural" as T's excusing himself to go to the bathroom in §41. Here we have a realistic detail, a banal instance of just the way things really are that one does not normally find in scripted feasts: without exception, heroes of epic and romance have bladders and bowels of steel. It is precisely this sort of low and random detail that gets us thinking that here, for once, we have a window into the routines of daily life; that we are flies on the wall of a first-century Roman triclinium, observing the habits of Rome's lesser peoples, overhearing the tales they were wont to tell, the jokes they traded, the insults they leveled, and the funny ways they talked. Near the end of the freedmen's banter that T's exit gives rise to, one of the freedmen (Norbanus) turns to the rhetoric professor (Agamemnon) and says, "you're not a man of our stripe, and so you think it's funny the way we poor people talk," and that gets us thinking about ourselves as readers of the text who happen to be doing the same thing, drinking in its "realistic" pleasures in precisely these same terms. The metaliterary aside puts us in mind of the fact that the offhand banter we are relishing in is not random after all. It has been scripted for our entertainment, highly crafted as comic art.

In its own way, the freedmen's banter that sounds so true to life is a version of T's exploding pig: something that looks utterly ordinary, but is highly crafted, brilliant art parading as nature. Until sliced into, it hides that art. As seasoned consumers of multiple literary feasts, Petronius' Roman readers know that the "casual" exit of T that allows his humbler and funnier guests to have their say has a literary precedent in the eighth satire of Horace's second book, where the host's departure from the room to rescue the meal allows the jokesters, Vibidius and Balatro, to take center stage and entertain the other guests with their improvisational riffs on reality (*ridetur fictis rerum*, v. 83).[23] Seasoned readers have seen this before. As natural and random as it seems, nothing could be more scripted than T's bathroom break and the funny talk that ensues. When T finally returns to the dining room after relieving himself, he takes the opportunity to describe to his guests the many troubles of his ailing bowels. He then goes on to cast aspersions on his doctors, to give a new-fangled recipe for an effective laxative, and to bring his guests into the know about how to keep *anathymiasis* from getting to the brain. And thus, once again, a "random" incident (a bathroom break) is played upon by T and worked up as show, as an incidental "call of nature" becomes a mechanism for the display of "Doctor Trimalchio, Physician Genius!"[24]

We cannot really be sure what's going on inside T's insides so as to distinguish "nature's calling" from a trick played on us. He has no insides. All that he can ever be is what Petronius has us see of him. As with those pillows purporting to be stuffed with purple wool and gushed over for their extravagance by a guest in-the-know at §38, we cannot really get inside them.[25] To believe that they are really stuffed with purple, that Romans really did do such absurdly decadent things (Arrowsmith, Bacon, Highet, et al.), that freedmen really did talk the way Petronius has them talk (Auerbach), or, for that matter, that Nero really did play a lyre to his own tune while Rome burned (Tacitus, Suetonius, et al.), finds us sitting in Encolpius' seat, dazzled by the idea that this might really be true, and much too easily taken in by the performer's (Petronius') show.

Although it is highly evocative of everyday life, Petronius' *Satyrica* defies us to take any of its evocations of the everyday as living specimens of the real.[26] Its main characters are too far-fetched and outrageous to be

[23] On the literary affiliation of Petronius' *Cena* to the *Cena Nasidieni* (Hor. *S*.2.8), see Schmeling 2011: 222, with basic bibliography *ad loc*.

[24] Schmeling suggests *ad* 47.4 that T's digestional philosophy may parody a corresponding philosophy espoused by Claudius (many have seen this). But he adds that the parallel connecting T to Claudius may also be taken to show "T. imitating (and thus associating himself with) accepted imperial manners." In other words, a fake world (Petronius') that is made to seem real reflecting on a real world (Nero's) that offers itself as a fake.

[25] Schmeling 2003: 186: "Because of the thick literary texture of the *Satyrica*, it is difficult to penetrate it or peer into it, even though it casts so much light on life in the Roman world."

[26] In the end, as Rimell 2002 has so well shown (see esp. pp. 123–39), there is no rising above "the tricky theatricality and literary complexity" of the *Satyrica* so as to gain a distant, knowing perspective from which to sneer. We are not extractable from our reading of (and wallowing in) the *Satyrica*, since whatever we take to be the low, Bakhtinian (dialogic) "real" is just as fake as

considered features of the everyday, and the same can be said of the props they interact with and the behaviors they engage in. All are ridiculous, the products of magnificent comic invention, and yet all are strangely evocative of things commonly taken for real in the Neronian age. Whatever its form, realist satire gets us to see the everyday differently. It does this by giving special attention to some feature of the ordinary so as to have it stand out on its own, marking it as isolable as such: something to be regarded as alien and odd rather than taken for granted as run-of-the-mill. It is the work of the realist comic artist not to invent *ex nihilo*, but to pounce on things already there in the everyday: to mark them as "pounce-on-able," to overblow and defamiliarize them, all the while keeping them recognizable as versions of things, persons, and behaviors that one might encounter on any given day, or perhaps on an especially bad day.[27]

Petronius' *Satyrica* is loaded with material and behavioral *realia* that have been "pounced on" by an especially creative comic imagination. The work's *realia* are rendered (not presented but represented) in artfully iridescent ways that make them not only gaudier and more ridiculous than anything known in the everyday, but ultimately unknowable as "the facts" of life under Nero. And yet they remain highly ascribable to Nero's age all the same. My point in this chapter has been to insist that the novel's illusionistic and utterly new form (as a fiction of the everyday that calls attention to its own powers of realistic deception) is itself a product of its time: not just specific to Neronian culture, but an uncannily appropriate way of reflecting on it. Put simply, if the characters of this novel tend to "play out" their lives as if from a script, unaware of the crucial distinctions that separate life from literature, a dining hall from a stage, low from high, and so on, such delusional behavior may, in the end, have less to do with their "not getting" how things happen in the real world than with their "getting" the ways of the late Neronian world all too well. To feature them competing in party design, seeking to dazzle and win affection with their illusions, and playacting their way from one disaster to the next, I suggest, finds Petronius pouncing on things well known in late Neronian Rome – all rather prominent features of Nero's own playacting, but long since folded into the daily routines of performers in every bedazzled

the "unreal" (monologic) sublime. Or, as T might have said (adapting the sentiments of §52) "it's all so real that you'd swear it was fake."

[27] On comic writers acting as "anthropologists of our humdrum everyday lives," letting us see things that we take for granted as strange, see Critchley 2002: 65–6. Beard 2014 (see esp. pp. 196–200) draws heavily on Critchley in her analysis of Roman jokebooks and "humor."

backwater of the Roman world. The same might be said of the peculiar habit of the *Satyrica*'s self-promoting fools to play upon moments of high emotion by bursting into song. Routinely that habit is explained as a generic feature of Menippean satire– a category the *Satyrica* can be made to fit only by special pleading, putting unduly heavy emphasis on the fact that it mixes prose with verse.[28] But this is perhaps to take the work's satiric contents for its form, for it is to ignore the strangely perfect connection that that particular form, with its easy flow from prose to verse, has to the stagey, category-defying ways of Nero himself. The old generic "prosimetric" code, a sign for designating a specific kind of fictional practice, picks up a surprising new ability to satirize, and to refer to things utterly real in the world, just by being "done yet again" in the age of Nero.

For their part, the second- and third-century chroniclers of the age of Nero pounce on the overt theatricalization of public life under Nero, isolating it as the hallmark of his vainglorious rule. To explain the historical phenomenon, they give any number of variations on "the great maniacs of first-century Roman history" theme: Nero was a pampered and passionate enthusiast, they say, who gradually lost the ability to distinguish between theatrical fiction and reality; he was mad for all things theatrical, delusionally so, and that's why he acted the way he did. And yet, when viewed from a broader, comparative-sociological perspective, Nero's imposition of theatrical fictions upon others, in fact upon the whole of Rome, can be appreciated for the political work it achieved, serving purposes that went far beyond any irrepressible desire that Nero may have had to act in public, or to be applauded and loved, or to treat Rome as his personal stage. As Stephen Greenblatt famously pointed out in his study of public life in the society dominated by Henry VIII and Cardinal Wolsey, the point of imposing one's fictions upon others is to lock them into roles they must play, and to show them who controls whom: "The point is not that anyone is deceived by the charade, but that everyone is forced either to participate in it or watch it silently."[29] Those who refuse to participate, or have the temerity to fall asleep (Vespasian), or walk out mid-act (Thrasea Paetus), break the political genre's cardinal rule by marking the play as a play (meta-theater), a farce not to be tolerated.[30] Like it or not, they are acting as

[28] On the vexed question of the genre of the *Satyrica*, see Schmeling 2011: xxx–xxxviii.

[29] Greenblatt 1980: 13.

[30] On Vespasian and Thrasea Paetus as put-upon individuals, "actors in the audience," who deviated from their assigned roles, see Bartsch 1994: 6–7.

well, and yet they are breaking free of the roles they were assigned by the imposer in chief, choosing instead to act the part of "sincerity."

To put a particularly Roman spin on this, like players in the "lead following" roles of a mime play (*secundae partes*), those who were imposed upon by Nero were expected to pick up on the lead actor's improvisations and to play their assigned roles straight. They were not allowed to switch parts or to improvise for themselves. Only Nero could do that. Rather, they were to demonstrate that they were trapped in a play not of their own making. That's what the charade's imposition was all about – all of which sounds uncannily like a night of fine dining with Trimalchio. But, as Erik Gunderson points out in Chapter 21 of this volume, this had always been the unspoken way of things in imperial Rome. The emperor's role had always been highly contrived as an act, one that forced others to pick up on the lead actor's cues and play along. What separates Nero from those who preceded him on the same stage, and in the same act, was not his theatricality per se, but his failure to observe the genre's one most important rule: that the inherited role, that of august emperor, had to be played straight, as a classic, *as if it were not a role.* The politics of that role had always been highly aestheticized in Rome, but when it came to playing the next Augustus down the line, the rules of generic propriety demanded that the role's staginess had to be downplayed, not called attention to and played to the hilt. Hewing to a different aesthetic, Nero governed (i.e., played emperor) as he sang: as a self-aware, late-arriving Callimachean, oddly stuck in a role much too grand for any Callimachean to play. In a genre that required him to be Ennius, Nero played at being Ovid, flippantly exposing the codes of his own manufacture.[31]

Further Reading

A full and up-to-date bibliography covering all aspects of the *Satyrica* can be found in Schmeling 2011. Schmeling's commentary has valuable discussions of mimesis, realism, and realist satire dispersed throughout. See also the online bibliography of C. Panayotakis in the *Oxford Bibliographies* series, which has a separate heading for books and articles on the "Social, Historical, and Cultural Context" of the *Satyrica.* On the question of Nero's presence in the *Satyrica*, see esp. Vout 2009, and Courtney 2001: 8–11.

[31] On Ovid as an exposer of the conventions of the elegiac genre, see esp. Barchiesi 2001, chapter 2: "Narrativity and Convention in the *Heroides.*"

On the playacting of Nero, see Bartsch 1994. For playacting and the staging of theatrical scenes in the *Satyrica*, see Panayotakis 1995. For the specific theatrical qualities of Neronian death scenes, see Edwards 2007. For connections linking Roman mime and theatrical mimesis to the culinary mimesis of Trimalchio, esp. to his fictionalizing of food to make it seem "natural," see Cucchiarelli 1999. The best large-scale treatment of the realism of the *Satyrica* and its highly problematic relation to things real in the world is Rimell 2002. On the subject of realist satire more generally, see Matz 2010, who is heavily indebted to Wood 2004.

8: "Ain't Sayin'": Persius in Neroland

Daniel Hooley

8.1 The Prince and the Poet

When in early December 34 CE Aules Persius Flaccus was born on his ancestral estate near the Etruscan settlement of Volaterrae, nestled at the base of wooded hills roughly midway between modern Siena and Pisa, Rome's leading man and Augustus' successor Tiberius had just over two years to live. He would be succeeded by Gaius Caesar Germanicus, "Caligula," in 37, the year of Nero's birth to Iulia Agrippina and the unpleasant Gn. Domitius Ahenobarbus. During Caligula's short and violent reign, Agrippina would be exiled in 39 for her association with a conspiracy against her brother the emperor, and Domitius, as Nero was then called, would be left with his aunt Domitia Lepida, who, according to Suetonius, chose as his tutors "a dancer and a barber."[1] Agrippina would return to Rome after Caligula's assassination in 41, and in 49, soon after Messalina's disgrace and fall (and some necessary legal rigmarole), marry her uncle Claudius, thus setting the course of Nero's rise to power. Meanwhile, in quite another sort of household, the young Persius would spend his early years under the supervision of teachers provided by his widowed mother, Fulvia Sisennia. Subsequently, sent to Rome roundabout the year 46 in order to complete his education, initially studying under the *grammaticus* Remmius Palaemon and the *rhetor* Verginius Flavus, he would arrive well in time to watch the last, remarkable act of the Julio-Claudian succession drama play out.

Persius was uncomfortably close to that drama. Both boys, three years apart in age, would have at least some occasion to encounter one another, especially after Persius at the age of sixteen moved to more advanced studies in philosophy under the guidance of well-known Stoic scholar and tragedian Annaeus Cornutus. Soon he would come to know another student of Cornutus, the precocious Lucan, who enthused over

[1] Suetonius, *Nero* 6. See Dinter 2012b: 44–5.

Persius' poetry, would join in the literary "circle" sponsored by Nero; bandy verses with the emperor, and, in the end, come to a catastrophic falling out. Cornutus too was familiar enough to Nero to have insulted him memorably.[2] Probus' *Vita* tells us that Persius also met Lucan's uncle and Nero's own teacher, Stoic philosopher and writer of tragedies L. Annaeus Seneca, but was disappointed with the philosopher's *ingenium,* probably meaning his character. Persius also became acquainted with Servilius Nonianus, historian and likely source of Tacitus' histories; Claudius Agathinus, physician, medical theorist, and teacher; and Petronius Aristocrates, sometimes offered as a (less plausible) candidate for authorship of the *Satyrica* – the latter two both were philosophical enthusiasts with whom Persius was much taken. Of similar stamp was the Stoic Thrasea Paetus, author of a life of Cato, who along with Cornutus was Persius' most significant associate: "for nearly ten years he was especially attached to Thrasea Paetus, so much so that he travelled with him at times; he was related to Thrasea's wife, the younger Arria" (*Vita*). Persius composed a poem in praise of Arria's mother, the famous Stoic suicide under Claudius. The connection was strong, and of this group Thrasea especially, a man of very public profile and action, is our best indicator of Persius' own politics.[3]

In the 40s and early 50s, Domitius was still in school himself, then (in 49 and after) tutored by Seneca, who had been recalled from his own exile by Agrippina for the purpose. As Agrippina and perhaps Claudius contrived his advancement over Claudius' own son Britannicus and it became apparent that the elder boy would eventually succeed to power, Agrippina depended on Seneca to prepare Domitius for his anticipated responsibilities. Seneca took that job seriously. Whether or not Seneca, who had lost his only child, ever thought Domitius a kind of adoptive son,[4] their close relationship would ultimately steer Nero (as he was called after his official adoption by Claudius in 50) away from his natural mother's influence in the mid-50s. In 54, after Claudius' death and Nero's succession, Seneca wrote Nero's early speeches, winced his way through the persecution of Nero's young wife Octavia and the murder of Britannicus, and worked hard to counter Agrippina's ambitions. At the end of a long series of morally compromising blinks and

[2] Dio 62.29.3.

[3] Niall Rudd's introductory essay to his translation of Horace and Persius (Rudd 1997) neatly situates Persius among his influencing contemporaries and argues, "in an autocracy anything that offends a dictator is a political act, and some passages of Persius could certainly have given offence" (16).

[4] Cp. Cicero who plays father figure to his sometime student Caelius, *Pro Caelio* 16. 38ff.

slips, he would be complicit in the matricide of 59. Seneca took Nero's part, maybe hoping for a better outcome than could ever reasonably have been expected, and Nero too *his* part, holding this father figure at court despite Seneca's appeals to withdraw after Burrus' death when any hope of influencing the emperor in more salutary directions had gone. Tacitus represents Nero's response to Seneca's plea for release in 62 in language heavy with impertinence and insincerity:

> "My first gift from you [for you taught me well] is that I can extemporize my reply to your prepared speech. . . . You supported my childhood and youth with whatever the situation demanded: wisdom, advice, philosophy. Your gifts to me will endure as long as my life does. . . . [Those less deserving have been enriched], and I'm ashamed that you, my dearest friend, are not the richest of men. . . . If youth's slippery paths lead me astray, why not, strong in support, more zealously rule my manhood? . . ." Then he embraced and kissed him. (*Ann.* 14.55–6)[5]

There is in this fashioned speech, its mockery notwithstanding, something of what might still have mattered to Nero: the real memory of shared alliance against other forces, the Stoic's urgent impulse to make Nero better, to further the cause of the moral case (he had written *de Clementia* and other pieces in an overt attempt to influence Nero's character).[6] Nero, despite his drift in other directions, did not want this old Stoic master to walk away. The two were bound inextricably, in fact: for as much as Seneca had made the young emperor Nero, Nero had made Seneca. Recalled from exile *for* Nero, the Stoic sage became in Nero's court the Seneca we know: compromised fashioner of noble ideas, hypocritical apologist for the simple life (Nero had made him vastly rich), flawed imitation of Socrates.[7]

For Persius, also orphaned, also in search of a paternal stay, a path in life, and a kind of control that would become obsessive if always

[5] "quod meditatae orationi tuae statim occurram id primum tui muneris, habeo . . . quod praesens condicio poscebat, ratione consilio praeceptis pueritiam, dein iuventam meam fovisti. et tua quidem erga me munera, dum vita suppetet, aeterna erunt: . . . unde etiam mihi rubori est quod praecipuus caritate nondum omnis fortuna antecellis . . . quin, si qua in parte lubricum adulescentiae nostrae declinat, revocas ornatumque robur subsidio impensius regis? . . ." his adicit complexum et oscula.

[6] Dinter 2012b: 44–5.

[7] Griffin's 1976 chapter relevant to charges of hypocrisy over his wealth, "Seneca *Praedives*," 286–314, leaves room for differing conclusions. Seneca's own response to the criticisms of Publius Suillius Rufus (Tacitus *Ann.* 13.42.4) can be found in his *De Vita Beata*.

elusive in his verse, father-Cornutus played his part as well. Teaching, fostering, guiding, even dictating what we would ultimately hear from Persius. Not the travel poem in the spirit of Lucilius and Horace, not the brief verse on the elder Arria, not the *praetexta*, not even all of Persius' satire, for some was cut to fit *Cornutus*' sense of an ending. Everything then extant outside of Persius' small book of choliambics and hexameter satires was destroyed on Cornutus' counsel after the poet's death in 62. Yet within what remains is recorded a fierce struggle of words and ideas that most certainly cannot be contained by the Stoic lessons Cornutus propounded; Persius too could speak a little darkly.

> Now urged on by my muse,
> I give you my heart to explore, and it delights me to show you
> how great a part of my soul is yours, dear friend.
> Tap here; you know how to distinguish carefully
> what sounds solid from the deceptions of rhetoric's
> painted tongue. I might even ask for the proverbial hundred
> tongues
> so that I could set out in the purest language how much of *you*
> I have worked into the folds of my heart, and so that my words
> might unseal all that lies unspeakable and secret inside me.
> (5.21–9)[8]

Persius' *dulcis amice* sounds uncomfortably like Tacitus' Nero's insincere *praecipuus caritate*, and there is more than a little resemblance in the two expressions of gratitude and allegiance. Both allude to rhetoric as manipulable expression. Both strain, however (in-)sincerely, to express something latent in their shared pasts. We don't know how much Nero might have felt real affection and gratitude in the words he actually did speak to Seneca, nor can we quite discern the full registers of Persius' confession here. In the end, he frankly tells Cornutus that he cannot say it adequately himself, only point to "all that lies unspeakable and secret inside me," that ineffable, hidden truth.[9] Certainly epic's

[8] "tibi nunc hortante Camena/ excutienda damus praecordia, quantaque nostrae/ pars tua sit, Cornute, animae, tibi, dulcis amice,/ ostendisse iuuat. pulsa, dinoscere cautus/ quid solidum crepet et pictae tectoria linguae./ hic ego centenas ausim deposcere fauces,/ ut quantum mihi te sinuoso in pectore fixi/ voce traham pura, totumque hoc verba resignent/ quod latet arcana non enarrabile fibra."

[9] Cp. (thanks to Cedric Littlewood for this) Vergil, *Aen.* 8.624–5: *tum levis ocreas electro auroque recocto, / hastamque et clipei non enarrabile textum* ([then Aeneas gazed upon] the polished greaves of refined electrum and gold / and the spear and the indescribable fabric of the shield). Persius neatly trades out these polished exteriors for his own satiric decoctions and inward "indescribables." Bartsch 2015c: 184–7, is very good on the implosion of conflicted imagery of this passage.

hundred mouths can't say it, nor will rhetoric's embroidery or even the "purest language" (*voce pura*), which only potentially might draw out the truth from its secret places.[10] It is not likely that the truth Persius means to not-say is anything as overtly disingenuous as Nero's speech in Tacitus. But it must also be that it was complicated – complicated by the glaring example of Stoic mentorship going wrong on the Palatine and by Persius' own disturbing, satiric depiction, in Satire 4, of the tortuously degraded student/teacher pair, Alcibiades and Socrates. The characters of that poem projected on satire's screen reflect mercilessly all ways in Neronian Rome; if they are seen to imply Nero and Seneca, they cannot spare, either, the principals of Satire 5's "Socratic embrace."[11] Nor does Persius demonstrate his mentor's Stoic equilibrium in the remainder of Satire 5, themed by the Stoic paradox that "only the wise man is free"; rather he descends into the hopeless maelstrom of human ambition, addiction, and desire – concluding it all with a centurion's scoff.[12] Persius' only means of "saying more" is to give it up: "here, you try. Tap here, you diagnose this, find out what's in me." That trope is medical and one of many in the same vein in Persius, diagnosis of the sick society and self.[13] It is a meta-poetic gesture as well; the reader, Cornutus or his larger audience, is *meant* to (try to/dare to) make out the unsaid at the heart of Persius' verse. Explicitly, however, there is silence (*non enarrabile*). Persius' language of devotion, with all its disturbing qualifications, has opened the space, the possibility for (likely painful) mutual understanding, one that remains unspoken, relegated to the silences of the listening mind.

8.2 Satire and Silence

What can and cannot be said anchors the poetry of Persius. You see it in the close of the programmatic first satire (1.119–23).

> Can't I just mumble it? Not alone? Not into a ditch? Not
> anywhere?
> Yet in this poem, I'll dig a hole to speak into. I've seen it,
> my little book! Who doesn't have the ears of an ass?

[10] Homer, *Il.* 2.489; the ten mouths there first squared by Hostius, in his *Bellum Histricum* according to Macrobius, *Sat.* 6.3.6.

[11] Sat. 5. 36–7: *teneros tu suscipis annos / Socratico, Cornute, sinu*. Littlewood's essential piece on Satire 4 (2002) gets there first (82, note 100).

[12] Another satiric cackle? See Sat. 1. 11–12 and below. Hooley 1997: 119–21. Also Bartsch 2015c: 178–212, on the disintegration of the speaker's Stoic control.

[13] See Bartsch 2012: 228–30 and especially 2015 for Persius' food imagery and Stoic medical implications. Also Bramble 1974: 26–66.

> This is my secret, my bit of a joke; but I wouldn't trade it
> for any old *Iliad* of yours.[14]

The *Iliad* reference makes this on the face of it an aesthetic point;[15] the first satire has been all about the rotten literary sensibility of contemporary Rome. The ass's ears reference is aesthetic as well, since Midas, first recipient of those ears, got them for preferring the music of Pan to that of Apollo.[16] Here, effectively then, "everyone's got Midas' bad taste"; true enough from Persius' perspective though not much to hang all the passion of the first satire on. Or is it?[17] That dirty little secret in the context of Nero's Rome barely disguises comment on the boss-artist himself; Rome's aesthetic decadence plays in tune with the Nero/Apollo Seneca had marked from the beginning.[18] Saying that one cannot "say" this satiric secret but into a hole is a declaration of lost *libertas*, and it comes after the satirist has canvassed the manners of satiric expression in Lucilius and Horace. Each *could*, in his way, utter some kind of truth about things and people around him. Persius says he cannot do so, except in the paradoxical secrecy of a poem read by no one (*quis leget haec? . . . nemo hercule*; "who will read these things? No one!") – but would eventually be published and read by nearly everyone.[19]

The image of the "hole" employed here has been neatly parsed by Andrea Cucchiarelli, who considers the figure a pivotal link between the satirist's silence and his words. Persius claims aphasia, yet plants the "seeds of free speech."[20] The programmatic image, original to Persius, might too resonate in other ways: *scrobis*, whose primary meaning here must be "hole" since the sense of the fable depends on it, can signify "grave" as well, the implication being that Persius casts his words into this *scrobis* for disposal. The anti-climactic "who doesn't have ass's ears?" is thus presented as the dead end of a too-old joke: "This is where we bury old rubbish like this." Yet its very fabular quality and generic moralizing color might let us see the phrase as some kind of verbal

[14] "me muttire nefas? ne clam? nec cum scrobe? nusquam?/ hic tamen infodiam. vidi, vidi ipse, libelle:/ auriculas asini quis non habet? hoc ego opertum,/ hoc ridere meum, tam nil, nulla tibi vendo/ Iliade."

[15] The undistinguished *Ilias Latina* dates mostly likely from Nero's reign; Lucan wrote an *Iliacon* and Nero a *Troica*.

[16] Hygenus, *Fabulae*, 191 and Ovid, *Met.*, XI 172–93.

[17] The *Vita*'s claim that Persius' line ran *auriculas asini Mida Rex habet*, "King Midas has ass's ears," emended to its present state by Cornutus, has been much discussed and usually dismissed. See Sullivan 1978.

[18] *Apocolocyntosis* 4.15.

[19] Midas' secret is revealed by the singing reeds rooted in the buried truth. The *Vita* tells us that the book sold very well upon its release. See Cucchiarelli 2005: 65–77.

[20] Cucchiarelli 2005: 67 and note 8.

enactment of satire. Resolving the aposiopesis opened at line 7, *nam Romae quis non – a, si fas dicere*, "for at Rome – ah, if only it were permitted to say it . . .," as he does here, effectively contains the whole poem. Its simplicity and naiveté make it an emblem of primitive or childish satire, name-calling, and somehow atavistic – satire before even the lashing Lucilius or the winking Horace. Is Persius laying not only his censored words but this image of his craft in its grave and so harking back to the very opening of the satire (no audience, for satire is dead)? Certainly, as he explicitly says, Lucilian and Horatian satire *are* dead and gone, and Persius seems to construct himself here as heir to a moribund art form; no one can speak the satiric truth and no one any longer listens.[21] As Cedric Littlewood puts it, "This dying world, with no recessed landscape for poetic renewal, is distinctive of Persius' isolationist stance and the presentation of his satire as a hopeless and misguided departure from the sanctuary of a silent self."[22]

Why this despairing satirist would choose to write on through his self-scripted dead end is a natural question, for this first satire is full of lively satirizing and he surely did write on. One might hazard that he writes *for* this silence of the grave. Persius seems to contend that for all its words, satire *means* this disconnect between writer and reader, means silence. Poetry in these satires does seem to fail at the expressive and receptive ends. Satire 1 is obsessed with images of blocked or corrupted communication; the stopped-up ear (1.107: *sed quid opus teneras mordaci radere vero / auriculas*, "but why scour out tender ears with biting truth?";[23] 126: *inde vaporata lector mihi ferveat aure*, "let my reader's ears bubble" [with the acid of old comedy]); or the ear imaged as gluttonous mouth (23–4: *tun, vetule, auriculis alienis colligis escas, / auriculis* (or is that *articulis*?[24]) *quibus et dicas cute perditus "ohe"?*, "what are you doing, old man, collecting tasties for other men's ears, ears that will stuff the skin to bursting?"); or the silent, waggling mime-ears of mockery (58–9: *o, Iane, a tergo quem nulla ciconia pinsit / ne manus auriculas imitari mobilis albas*, "Janus, no stork pecking you from behind, no deft hand miming a white donkey's ears.").

[21] The ironically colored lines at 1.36–40 figure the poet and poetry as dead: ashes, bones, and tomb. Reckford 1998, especially 346–8, discusses the broken, flawed, and dying body in the self-reflexive Satire 3; the satirist too is broken.

[22] Littlewood 2002: 77, thinking of Persius' imagery of sterility and death in Sat. 4, and contrasting alternative, life-giving landscapes in Horace and Vergil.

[23] Bartsch 2012: 222, and 2015: 145–6 for the cleansing, biting truth of satire and philosophy. The connection between Stoic teaching and Persius' language also pursued on 220–4 and by Cucchiarelli 2005: 71–5.

[24] A crux. Clausen accepts Madvig's reading of *articulis* for the second *auriculis* here; the referent for *quibus* is also disputed. Among other discussions, Bramble 1974: 79–87.

Just as the satirist's audience is imaged as variously dysfunctional ears, the satirist's words too fail; memorably in the verbal and literary stuttering of the late-sleeping student, an image of an earlier Persius maybe, in the opening of Satire 3 (7–8, 11–14). In Satire 1 too the emphasis falls on the satirist's not saying or not finding a way to say. *Tunc tunc – ignoscit (nolo / quid faciam?) sed cum petulanti splene – cacchino*, "then, then, pardon me (I don't know, what shall I do?), but when my spleen's gone wild, I have to laugh" (11–12). Or guffaw, howl, burst out something (precisely) inarticulate. *Scribimus inclusi*, "shut in we write" (13), represents the tight paradox of writing that goes nowhere; followed immediately by an alienating description of *what* is written (13–14): "[Someone writes] something metrical, another something not, /a big thing for the puffed up lung to belch out" (*numeros ille, hic pede liber, / grande aliquid quod pulmo animae praelargus anhelet*). *Aliquid* here specifies what *non enarrabile* does in Satire 5, the failure of language. Or language de-/re-natured, or as in the most notorious passage of the first satire (17–21):

> You sit up on the high seat with your throat
> well gargled, then all louche, eye orgasmic,
> you'll see huge Rituses moaning, trembling
> shamelessly when the poetry enters their backsides
> and pricks their inmost parts.[25]

Tossed into *satura*'s jumble (*haec sartago loquendi*, "this frypan of speech" [80]) next are *escas*, "tasty treats for greedy ears" (22), and immediately after that *fermentum*, "bubbled-up froth," or *caprificus*, the nuisance wild fig (24–5), both emerging in a spectacular concentration of imagery, from the poet's liver. Or *rancidulum quiddam*, "something gone off, rotten" in 33, or *istud dedecus*, "that unseemly thing." In 104 it is merely "something lame swimming in the lips' spit and drool," *summa delumbe saliva / hoc natat in labris*. On into Satire 5 (5ff.), it might be *robusti carminis offas*, "gobbets of coarse song," or *nebulas Helicone*, "mists from Helicon," or *nescio quid grave*, "something solemn," "popped" childishly from puffed out cheeks. Images like this can be expected when satire attacks others' poetry as Persius does in Satire 1, and in the Choliambics too where he figures contemporary verse as the imitative cawing of crows and magpies. But Persius does not spare his own satiric words.

[25] "sede leges celsa, liquido cum plasmate guttur/ mobile conlueris, patranti fractus ocello/ tunc neque more probo videas nec voce serena/ ingentis trepidare Titos, cum carmina lumbum/ intrant et tremulo scalpuntur ubi intima versu."

At best they are *quid . . . aptius* (45), "something all right," or in 107 (above) imaged as vinegar when his interlocutor asks what might be the point of irritating all those tender ears with biting truth. That image is taken up again in 126ff., where he claims that only those who like "a well-cleaned ear" will approve of his verse. For those who don't, satire is shit and piss: "*hic*," *inquis*, "*veto quisquam faxit oletum . . . extra meiite*," "'I forbid anyone to shit here,' you say, 'Piss elsewhere'" (112–14). There is too Persius' most evocative if vague image for his satire, *aliquid decoctius*, "something more cooked down" (125) or digested – take that satire one way or the other – and under this analysis his most precise image (121–2), *hoc ego opertum*, "this secret, this hidden thing" / *hoc ridere meum*, "this joke, this laugh of mine."[26] The apposition is epexegetic, the secret thing, this mystery of what the word has become in Nero's Rome is the satirist's dark joke.

All of the figurations of the world's and satire's word amount to this frustrated laugh, an inarticulate expression of disgust at what the satirist sees and hears before him in the new, muddled Rome (*turbida Roma*, 5). *Quid dia poemata narrent?*, "what does divine poetry have to say?" (31). The answer to that is the extended, degraded catalogue of poetic instances in Satire 1 to which the satirist's answer is the inarticulate cackle (*cacchino* 12), a satirically noisier version of the silent sneer of Persius' older friend Thrasea Paetus. In 59, after the matricide, when the Senate heard a letter Seneca composed denouncing Agrippina and praising her murderer, Thrasea, as Dio presents it, "at once rose from his seat and without a word left the chamber, inasmuch as he could not say what he would, and would not say what he could" (61.15).[27] Tacitus tells us that Thrasea's attitude was echoed at Nero's Juvenalia, at which: *parum spectabilem operam praebuerat . . .* "[Thrasea] had been too little in evidence." The recalcitrance would mount (*Ann.* 16.21): "When divine honors were voted to Poppea at her death, Thrasea was intentionally not in attendance and was not present at her funeral" [. . .(*et cum deum honores Poppaeae decernuntur sponte absens, funeri non interfuerat*)

Thrasea abandoned senatorial duties for three years as well, as his enemy Cossutianus Capito reminded Nero in 66 (*Ann.* 16.22):

> At the year's beginning Thrasea avoided the oath ratifying the emperor's *acta*; he was not present at the official vows, though he was a member of the priestly council; he never

[26] For *decoctius*, see Gowers 1994 and Bartsch 2015c: 70–4; for "digested," see Kirk Freudenburg *per litteras*.

[27] Tacitus' version is at *Ann.* 14.12.

> sacrificed for the health or divine voice of the emperor; once a regular and tireless member of the senate ... he has not entered the Curia in three years.[28]

As Dio's formulation makes clear, speech and silence (denial, recusancy), the latter often more expressive than the former, stand in taut opposition. Tacitus has Cossutianus neatly include a reference to Nero's *caelestis vox* as if to highlight the silent *non serviam*. But by this point, after the Pisonian conspiracy, abstention and silent reserve had become dangerous signals of outright opposition. Cossutianus' indictment would lead to the death – by compliant senatorial *decree* – of Thrasea, and to the death or banishment of friends and relatives. It is a poignant accident of transmission, and not the least fitting coda to the entire work, that Tacitus' *Annales* themselves break off, stop telling, in the middle of his description of Thrasea's lingering and painful death (*post lentitudine exitus gravis cruciatus adferente* ... *Ann.* 16. 35). Even earlier, say in 59, the choices available to a powerless senatorial class in the face of hostile autocracy increasingly showing itself to be more rather than less of a piece with Nero's predecessors Claudius and Caligula, were few.[29] Thrasea's speaking silence was one. Arguably it is Persius' too. For all the cackling noise of the six satires, its shocked and shocking language does not mention Nero. Words fail.

8.3 Nero

A Stoic silence then, *anachoresis*, a literal retreat *into* these satires, away from naming the evil out there? Stoicism did in fact offer a kind of escape into a personal discipline permitting a degree of control and personal autonomy.[30] While many Stoics hedged, were either complicit or quietist, with even the few intractables like Thrasea making intermittent accommodation,[31] the discipline itself did become for many –

[28] "principio anni vitare Thraseam sollemne ius iurandum; nuncupationibus votorum non adesse, quamvis quindecimvirali sacerdotio praeditum; numquam pro salute principis aut caelesti voce immolavisse; adsiduum olim et indefessum, ... triennio non introisse curiam ..."

[29] See Tacitus *Agr.* 45 for the historian's aggrieved description of the Senate's – and his own – powerlessness and silence before a murderous imperial autocracy. Kirk Freudenburg points out to me that Pliny the Elder in his early years under Nero wrote a treatise "On Ambiguous Speech" (or "Uncertain Language") because the slavishness of the age made free speech impossible: Pliny Secundus *Ep.* 3.5.5.

[30] For Persius' Stoicism, see Bartsch 2012: 218–35 and 2015 passim; Martin 1939; Cucchiarelli 2005; Reckford 2009; Nichols 2013: 267–9.

[31] Thrasea reconciled for a time with Nero before the final break. Generally, on Stoic political involvement, Griffin 1984: 171–7.

like Seneca, who wrote furiously on Stoic themes especially when his situation in the court became precarious – a place to go, a way out of the madhouse. Thus, maybe, Persius' much discussed inward turn, the attention to the self one sees everywhere in his satire, yet so difficult and rare "out there": *ut nemo in sese temptat descendere, nemo,* "Look, how nobody, but nobody attempts the climb down into oneself" (4.23). But Persius may make a slightly different case.[32] Stoic discipline in these satires fights its way through – his language is "hard" – struggles for control, even for sense, as his readers well know. It often fails.[33] After his most extended and serious Stoic diatribe (Satire 5), Persius imagines this response (5.189–91).

> If you say these things among varicose centurions,
> Big Pulfenius will burst out laughing and give you
> a clipped half-penny for a hundred Greek philosophers.[34]

Persius writes a philosophically colored satire that inscribes its own receptive failure. He is never so sure as Seneca about Stoicism's efficacy in the world; he cannot trust the expressed word "out there." But Persius is equally sure to point out that *where* it fails does matter – in Pulfenius' and Nero's world. Maybe too much ink and quibble has been spent attempting to make out Persius as merely the scholarly introvert mostly concerned with the state of his own soul, staying prudently out of the political fray.[35] Widely noted and implicitly deplored is the want of overt political frankness; we might have hoped for a little more of Thrasea, direct satire of the regime and its principals. It is clear that Persius had no interest in being *that* kind of satirist.[36] In fact, being the kind of satirist he was constitutes an indictment, call it satire, of the naïveté of our hopes for the truth-to-power martyr, the writer looking into the dark heart of Nero and telling us outright what he sees, naming *Him*. The real, perilous, weirdly complicated world isn't quite like that, we should know. Persius acknowledges the desiderated *parrhesia* and deflects it, so building our desires into his meaning: "You want me to say that Nero has ass' ears, and worse? I know it, and I want *you* to think

32 See Henderson 1999: 228–48. 33 Bartsch 2015c: 178–212, describes this well.

34 "dixeris haec inter varicosos centuriones,/ continuo crassum ridet Pulfenius ingens/ et centum Graecos curto centusse licetur."

35 Among others: Griffin 1984 works hard to demonstrate that imputations of hostility to Nero in the *Satires* are not conclusive (156–7). Reckford 2009 is reluctant to identify direct political criticism in the poet: "[h]e was . . . a small-d dissident" (127). Sullivan 1985 is more sanguine in identifying passages that point critically toward Nero, and Rudich 1993 is certain that Persius, largely from the company he kept, was an opponent of the regime.

36 Cucchiarelli 2005: 75–7.

about that and where *you* fit into this fallen world I'm showing." Nero's fallen world, then, still uncertain for some by 62 when Persius died and not yet the slaughterhouse it would become a few years later, is what we see in the satires, even as we see Persius looking inward and outward at the same moment – that is the trick of these satires. Yet more poignantly, Persius shows us himself – sampling the nauseating aesthetics of the first satire and the self-interested prayers of the second; playing the flawed, struggling ephebe of the third, the not quite finished student of the fifth, and end-of-the-line satirist of the sixth wondering about his legacy. What, given the unfolding character of Nero in 59–62 when the satires were being composed, does the writer see, think, see, hear? How does it *feel*? Persius' *Satires* are one possible and persuasive representation of all of that.

Is the unspeakable Nero *in/out* there? In the putting-on-fat patron, *largitor ingeni*, enfigured in that crass belly of the Prologue?[37] Is (the post-Juvenalia/Neronia of 60) Nero there, in the degraded recitation scene of Satire 1.13–21; or the coterie, literary chitchat of 30–8; in the mix of technical incompetence and flattery of 63–106; in the neo-Callimachean mannerisms of 93–102, said to be Nero's styling if not as the scholiast alleges actual quotation of the emperor's verse;[38] in 128, "one vulgar enough to call a blind man squinty," quoting the title of Nero's squib against Clodius Pollio;[39] in the reference to tyrants' savage cruelty and its due punishments in 3.35–8? Intriguingly, are both Nero and Seneca there in Satire 4, Seneca as degraded Socrates, Nero as obscenely preening Alcibiades?[40] Is the actor Nero there in the *Thyestes* (overdone potboilers) reference of 5.8?[41] Does the parody of imperial flattery in Satire 6.43–7, the case of Caligula, hit rather close to home? Persius' reception history gives us most all we need to know about that: viz., the fact that people have been asking just these questions for centuries. Persius has led us *this* far down the road pointing to the source of the calamity that is the Rome he lives in and satirizes. More important, certainly, he shows how – Satires 2, 3, 5, and 6 are the keynotes – *one* Stoic lives in and with that calamity: angry, fumblingly, partly made (Satire 3), cocksure and half-sure (Satire 5) that the creed he

[37] Freudenburg 2001: 144.

[38] Sullivan 1985: 100–4. Nero had by 60 performed *Attis* and begun his *Troica*; line 93 mentions derisively *Berecyntius Attis*. See too Freudenburg 2001: 170–1.

[39] Suetonius, Domitian, 1.1. . . . *Clodium Pollionem praetorium virum, in quem est poema Neronis quod inscribitur "Luscio,"* . . . Sullivan 1985: 103. Bramble 1974: 140, discusses options.

[40] Freudenburg 2001: 190–1 for a brief recounting of both sides of the longstanding question.

[41] Dio 63.22, where Vindex accuses Nero of frequently playing the part. Early enough for Persius to note the interest? Seneca's *Thyestes* probably dates from 62 or after.

espouses will be enough to bring him or anyone the "freedom" we all want.[42] Yet hasn't the perennial fight over Neronian Persius always centered on his intentions? Did Persius intend to satirize Nero along with his Rome? What did he *mean to say*? Like his fellow Stoic traveler Thrasea, Persius isn't saying. He declares in fact that he *can't* quite tell us *quod . . . latet non enarrabile* (5.29), "what lies hidden and unexplained." "Here, you sort it out."[43]

Further Reading

The best general book on Persius is Reckford 2009. Among earlier book-length studies, Dessen 1968 (1996) and Morford 1984 are excellent. Bramble 1974 remains a classic source for Persius' language and imagery, and Gowers 1993 does much with Persius' food images in particular. Hooley 1997 considers Persius' engagement with Horatian language and sensibility, and Bartsch 2015c, in the finest recent study, offers an enlightening reappraisal of his Stoicism and use of metaphor. Among collections by various hands Braund and Osgood 2012 on Persius and Juvenal is very good and provides a range of up-to-date chapters. Plaza 2009 contains, Oxford-Readings style, a selection of important shorter pieces.

For Persius as he appears in his Neronian context, see Griffin 1984 and the still-rewarding Sullivan 1985. Buckley and Dinter 2013 represent the near-current state of things with some excellent essays on various aspects of the period. For Persius' reception, see Frost 1968, Morford 1984, and the newer essays in Braund and Osgood 2012. The standard commentary is now Kissel 1990, in German. A good English commentary is Harvey 1981, with solid information in the translation-commentaries of Barr and Lee 1987 and Jenkinson 1980.

[42] Henderson 1999: 242–8.

[43] I am grateful to all three editors of this volume who have offered me especially helpful suggestions, nearly all of which I have (mostly silently) incorporated.

Part III

Neronian Seneca

9: Senecan Drama and the Age of Nero

Chiara Torre

9.1 Tragedies in an Iron Mask

The year 65 CE brought a conspiracy to finally rid Rome of its actor-singer emperor. The details of the so-called Pisonian plot to kill Nero are related by Tacitus (*Ann.* 15.48–74), who emphasizes the general confusion and cowardice of the perpetrators; among them, only a few – the tribune Subrius Flavus, the centurion Sulpicius Aper, and the freedwoman Epicharis – bore death nobly when the plot was revealed. Another resolute figure was Seneca, who did not participate in the plan, but was ordered to kill himself after being falsely implicated. Seneca was rumored to be the plotters' best hope for the new regime: they planned first to have the *princeps* killed by Gaius Calpurnius Piso, a leading statesman, and then to get rid of Piso himself (*Ann.* 15.65). The Empire would be handed over to Seneca, who (they felt) was widely recognized as preeminent in virtue. As one of the supporters of the plot, Subrius Flavus, said of Piso, it would not have made much difference in terms of infamy (*dedecus*) to replace a cithara player with a tragedy performer. Indeed, Tacitus points out, just as Nero used to sing to the lyre, Piso would sing in tragic dress (*ut Nero cithara, ita Piso tragico ornatu canebat*).

Flavus' witticism depicts the transition of power from Nero to Piso as a simple change of performative mode. Flavus mentions two types of performance: *citharoedia* and tragic song, modes of performance that were similar but not identical. Both were very much in fashion at the time. The coup's conspirers looked to Seneca to play a more dignified role. Yet all of the performers, including Nero, met tragic ends. It is as if Neronian theatricality in some way affected the staging of imperial power as well.[1]

[1] In general, on Neronian theatricality, see Bartsch 1994; Edwards 1994; Erasmo 2004: 52–140; Littlewood 2015.

One reason why Nero's era has so often been taken as theatrical is that Tacitus has famously larded into his description of it the themes and trappings of tragedy (see Grau, Chapter 16 in this volume). Set against such a background, Piso, and even more so Seneca, feature as performing characters interacting with a performing prince. Such a theatricalization of imperial power emerges clearly also in the ps. Senecan *Octavia*, probably composed during the Flavian era. In the play Nero is transformed into a tragic tyrant while Seneca is turned into a tragic failed advisor-figure (*satelles*). As Littlewood rightly argues, "there is a particular irony in reading Seneca himself caught in Tacitus and the ps. Senecan *Octavia* in tragedies of his own making."[2] However, focusing on this representative strategy also has a disturbing and dangerous side effect that has distorted the reception of Seneca's tragedies. Given that not only the *Annals* but also the *Octavia* associate Nero's performing power with tragedy – and given, of course, Nero's many performances on stage – Seneca's own plays have been caught in a sort of hermeneutical "iron mask" that has determined that they should always be about Nero.

One can see a striking parallel between the fate of the Domus Aurea's set designer, the painter Famulus, and the reception of Senecan tragedy. The Domus eventually turned into a jail for Famulus (see La Rocca, Chapter 13 in this volume). In like manner, the pervasive theatricality that characterizes both Nero's conceptualization of his own political role and modern readings of the Neronian age has forced Seneca's tragedy into a narrow interpretative space. This chapter endeavors to break free of that space as a means of gaining a fresh perspective on the Neronian character of Seneca's dramatic production. My aim will be to consider how Seneca's plays relate to aspects of Neronian culture other than the theatricality of imperial power; that is, I will examine the possibility of looking at the plays without reading Nero's grotesque masks[3] into the tragedies' characters.

Significantly, art historians face a similar methodological challenge. The study of Neronian wall painting must deal with a crucial hermeneutical problem: how to disentangle the developments of the genre, in particular the Fourth style, which is characteristic of the second half of the first century CE, from the influence exerted by imperial patronage. Indeed, the theatricality of Nero's performing power seems to be inextricably bound with the iconographic revival of the *scaenae frons* (the architectural backdrop of the stage) and other theatrical motifs

[2] Littlewood 2015: 166. [3] For Nero's tragic roles and masks, see Suet. *Nero* 21.3.

in contemporary wall paintings. By looking at perspective not only as a stylistic device, but rather as an organizational principle arranging shapes and objects within a space and defining the relationship between the image and its beholders, art historians have been able to find new ways to explore the theatricality of Neronian wall painting.[4] Similarly in literary studies, we need to find new ways to synchronize two different systems of meaning; that is, Nero's performing power and Seneca's theatricality. And we need to break free of the vicious circle wherein Seneca's tragedies are read against the background of Neronian literary taste at the same time as they are regarded as having a major impact on that taste.

Tellingly, the most recent studies dealing with the chronology of Seneca's tragedies ascribe most of them to the reign of Claudius, or, at the latest, to the early stages of Nero's reign and Seneca's career as a politician (*Agamemnon, Phaedra*, and *Oedipus* may be dated to the period of the exile, or else right before/after; *Troades, Medea*, and *Hercules Furens* should be dated around 54 CE, but again they might also be earlier). Only the *Thyestes* and *Phoenissae* seem to belong to a later period and were probably composed during the years of retirement.[5] Needless to say, we cannot draw any reliable conclusions from a highly hypothetical chronology. And yet the large chronological span seems to suggest that Seneca's tragedies must not be regarded as a product only of the Neronian age.

In what follows I shall examine the ideological and aesthetic connections that link Seneca's tragedies to the politics of the *age* of Nero and imperial power more generally rather than to Nero's own biography (§§2–3); the strategies whereby spatiality, narrative, and perception are negotiated both in Neronian art and in Seneca's plays (§§4–5); and the way in which Seneca's tragedies interact with other dramatic genres of their age (§6).

9.2 Tragedy and Politics in the Looking Glass: Beyond Nero . . .

The first issue to be tackled concerns the Narcissus complex affecting Seneca's modern readership. Often Seneca's tragedies are interpreted as a mirror that distorts the idealized reflection on Nero's power that one finds in the *de Clementia*, a Senecan treatise addressed to the young

[4] Lorenz 2013. [5] Marshall 2014.

emperor at the beginning of his reign. Following in the footsteps of seventeenth- and eighteenth-century theater, twentieth-century interpreters have tried to read Seneca's plays as *tragédies à clef.* Such an approach, however, is strongly marked by a positivistic-biographical bias, and it has proved ineffective in matters of chronology. Allusions to contemporary persons and/or events cannot be ruled out, but they are always highly speculative, and in the end there is no way to verify that conventional statements against tyrants, voiced by characters of myth, have anything to do with Nero himself.[6] In fact, Nero tolerated the restaging of plays that might be taken to allude to him.[7] It was when authors were suspected of alluding maliciously to tyranny in particular that they were forced to go underground. That said, there is no evidence that Seneca's tragedies were withheld from circulation, or that he circulated them only among close friends.

Seneca's tragedies contain certain anachronisms that could be taken to look forward to his own Neronian era, especially when it comes to their reference to uniquely Roman customs.[8] Yet such anachronisms are compatible with Roman dramatic tradition, both comic and tragic, that had quintessentially Greek features reshaped to fit Roman practice. Such references to contemporary Roman realities need not be read politically. Some examples of such anachronisms: in *Troades*, Hecuba deems Priam blessed since he was spared the humiliation of the *Argolicus* (Argive, hence Greek!) *triumphus* (*Tro.* 148–56; a 'Greek triumph' is mentioned also in *Phoe.* 577–8). Of course, the triumph was a Roman institution, not a Greek one. Similarly, Theseus displays his grief for Hippolytus' death by giving his son a Roman (imperial) funeral (*Phae.* 1244–80).[9] Further anachronistic details can be detected in the outlines of royal luxury (*Thy.* 454–7) and in female coiffure (*Tro.* 884–5). Some of these details match with analogous anachronisms found in mythological scenes of contemporary panel paintings.[10] Moreover, a hint at Claudius' 43 CE expedition to Britain can be traced in *Medea*'s second choral ode (364–79), while other plays seem to allude to the canal newly cut through the isthmus of Corinth, an endeavor the emperor actively promoted and emphasized.[11]

[6] Malaspina 2003: 294–6, 312. [7] Suet. *Nero* 46.3; see Bartsch 1994, p. 88.

[8] Tarrant 1995: 215–30.

[9] On this imperial and dynastic reading of Hippolytus' funeral rites, see Degl'Innocenti Pierini 2008: 251–75.

[10] Varner 2000: 121–3.

[11] Plin. *HN* 4.10. Repeated references to the Isthmus are made in Seneca's tragedies (*Ag.* 562; *HF* 332f., 1163; *Med.* 35; *Phae.* 1024; *Thy.* 124–5, 181–2, 629–32). Notably, in *HF* 332f. the Isthmus is kept under control by Mount Citheron, which is in turn the "figure" of the tyrant Lycus (Rosati 2002: 231–2).

Finally in the *Thyestes* we can trace a few historical and geographical details that possibly pertain to Nero's activities in the east of the Empire.[12] The scene in which Atreus crowns his brother Thyestes (*Thy.* 544), recalled later by the Chorus (*Thy.* 599–606), might hint at the Parthian King Vologaeses, who set the diadem of Armenia round the head of his brother Tiridates (61 CE) during a short-lived truce between the two. Similarly, the fierce Alani (*feri Alani*) fleeing across the frozen Danube (*Thy.* 629–30) probably recall the kindred Rhozolani, a Sarmatian tribe who had diplomatic and military contacts with the Romans during the 60s. Finally, the mention of the so-called Caspian Ridge (the Caucasian Gate) could refer to recent Sarmatian incursions from the northeast. At times, anachronisms may disclose the autobiographical purposes of the author. In the *Thyestes*' second ode (393–7), the nostalgia for a life away from the *Quirites* can easily be read as a farewell to Seneca's old life at Nero's court.

The nexus between politics and tragedy can be explored more fruitfully by comparing Seneca's plays with his prose works to illuminate his political thought.[13] Granted, topics traditionally belonging to the realm of the "political" (e.g., discussions of the different forms of government, critique of constitutions, analysis of foreign politics, etc.) are absent both in Seneca's tragedies and in his philosophical works, including the *de Clementia*. "Seneca says far more about the men than about the system," as Griffin points out.[14] His political vision of the Empire cannot be separated from his moral vision of the *princeps*. However, tragic myths, typically revolving around questions of tyranny and power, granted Seneca the opportunity to enlarge on ethical and political issues. *Hercules Furens* offers one of the most significant examples. After returning from Hades, Theseus gives a speech in which he draws a distinction between the good king and the tyrant (*HF* 738–47). Although his words resonate with topics common in Hellenistic political discourse, the general framework is quite different. Theseus is sustained by a strong faith in divine justice. From his theological perspective not even the tyrant can escape divine punishment. The *Thyestes*, on the contrary, teaches us a lesson in *Realpolitik*. In the dialog between Atreus and his attendant (*Thy.* 203–335), we are told that the source of kingly power lies in deeds alone, a statement fully in tune with Roman practices of imperial power. This is to learn a lesson on *Realpolitik*, rather than simply seeing Atreus as Nero.

[12] Nisbet 2008. [13] For this political reading, see Malaspina 2003. [14] Griffin 1976: 210.

From this view, a classification of the poetic material according to recurring political themes proves particularly useful. Such themes include: the relationship between monarchy and tyrannical power; alternatives to power; the role of fate in the kingdom; the function of attendants and advisors. These categories show that the tragedies, in spite of their traditional and mythological character, delve into the same questions of political ethics that Seneca addresses in his prose work. Each tragedy, moreover, tackles the subject in its own distinctive way. Thus, if we look at the tragic corpus in its entirety, we detect the same spectrum of approaches that we find in Seneca's philosophical writings. At one end of the spectrum we find the optimistic stance of *Hercules Furens*, characterized by a strong faith in the superior order, an approach resembling that of the *de Clementia*, Seneca's most significant reflection on power, and written when he was actively involved in imperial politics. At the opposite end of the spectrum we find a remarkably pessimistic stance toward supreme power in the *Thyestes*, where power and tyranny overlap, and seclusion from both politics and human society at large is regarded as the only viable option. The other six plays are situated between these two poles.[15] Seen from this perspective, Seneca's tragedies provide some of the earliest and most complex reflections on the nature of the principate *qua* institution.

Last, the political contents of Seneca's tragedies have to be assessed from an aesthetic standpoint. The plays – and the *Thyestes* is particularly relevant here – could easily be regarded as reflections on the aesthetics of tyranny, revolving around the core theme of passions.[16] Exceptional passions are not only the ethical hallmark of Seneca's "tyrant" characters; they are the source of their sublime "poetics" as well. Their crimes, constituting the *fabula* of the tragedies themselves, exceed anything tried before (*maius solito*). From this perspective, the words through which Atreus, Juno, and Medea express their *furor* are not just poetic, but rather poietic, constitutive of an aesthetic previously unexplored.

9.3 . . . Back to Augustus

Taken this way, the *Thyestes* suggests a meta-theatrical connection between the (theatricalized) political power of tyranny and the demiurgic power of poetry. Though it is tempting to see this aestheticization of tyranny as an expression of political opposition, it is best taken as

[15] Malaspina 2003: 300–1. [16] On the aesthetics of tyranny, see Schiesaro 2003.

a version of the "Augustanism reconfigured" that characterizes Seneca's theater and, more generally, the literary production of the Neronian age.[17] In *Troades*, for example, large portions of Virgil's epic discourse are fragmented into the body of the play. For his part, Seneca adopts a reversed teleological perspective, going backward from Rome to the destruction of Troy, thus exposing the contradictions of Virgil's teleology. In the *Thyestes*, Fury speaks in the voice of the Virgilian Allecto, thus drawing on Virgil's epic as the source of her tragic *nefas*.[18] In *Medea*, the sublime character of the heroine's boundless powers resonates with the depiction of the conquest of the world by the human race, which in turn appears as both the fulfillment and the demise of an Augustan imperial fantasy.[19] At the end of *Phaedra* (1109–14), the messenger plays the role of an herald, proclaiming the death of the illustrious heir to the imperial throne in an official capacity. This speech leads the audience to meditate on the troubles of Julio-Claudian dynastic succession, starting from Augustus' painful search for an heir.[20]

Two further examples from the *Thyestes* show to what extent Neronian and Augustan readings sustain each other. The killing of Thyestes' sons follows the patterns of a Dionysiac ritual.[21] It is presented as a sacrifice in which Atreus is at once both executor and recipient. Already under Augustus, who was himself both *sacerdos* and *divus*, Dionysus was regarded as an attractive symbol of regenerative power. Atreus manipulates this symbol, exposing it to a range of diffracted and conflicting perspectives. His sacrifice stages the essence of imperial power as a form of ritualized violence. In this respect the sacrifice presupposes the new theomorphic image of the emperor that became popular during the first century CE. During the second half of his reign, Nero himself pushed his divine associations to new limits, leading to a change in the perception of the *princeps* in Rome.[22]

The second example involves the setting of the *Thyestes*. In designing it, Seneca acknowledges the foundational role of Augustan, and in particular Virgilian, poetry in defining how the space of power articulates itself within a set of fluid relationships, both topographic and symbolic, linking the city and the *palatium*. The description of the Domus Pelopia (*Thy*. 641–82) given by the messenger occupies a central position in the play, adding dramatic unity to the tragedy. The whole setting is structured in separate frames, just as the play itself. There is the

[17] Littlewood, Chapter 5 in this volume. [18] Schiesaro 2003: 187–208.
[19] See Littlewood, Chapter 5 in this volume. [20] Degl'Innocenti Pierini 2008: 251–75.
[21] Schiesaro 2003: 97–98.
[22] Cadario 2011 and Bergmann 2013 deal with this topic through an analysis of Nero's different portraits types.

palace (641–8), with its conspicuous and capacious throne room, big enough for the entire population; within the palace, we find a secret maze, symbolizing the tragic plot and inhabited by infernal presences. A sinister forest grows there, dominated by a gigantic oak and surrounded by a gloomy spring (649–79). Finally, the forest contains the cave where Atreus carries out his *nefas* (679 f.).This merger of a *locus horridus* (featuring abruptness and larger-than-life dimensions) with a Dionysian space (ominous natural revelations) follows a pattern found in contemporary landscape painting.[23]

The cave at the heart of Atreus' inner palace raises questions about the use of Augustan poetry as a source of poetic inspiration.[24] The multilayered structure of the Domus Pelopia is replete with Virgilian references: the infernal imagery from *Aeneid* 6, Latinus' palace (*Aen.* 7.170–91), the temple of Apollo (*Aen.* 6.9–13), Cacus' cave (*Aen.* 8.241–305).[25] Such references invite the reader/viewer to see in the Domus Pelopia an image of Rome's imperial palace. It has also been hypothesized[26] that the tragic palace hints at the future Domus Aurea. More to the point, however, are similarities between the *Thyestes*' gloomy palace and the structure of Nero's imperial villa in Subiaco. The villa was built on the shore of several artificial lakes created by damming the upper stream of the River Anio. The villa included a series of narrow wings, nestled between high cliffs and following the water's high differentials. The uppermost two-story wing, overlooking the River Anio, featured a gigantic recess, with its own apse, nestled between two large jutting structures, covered by a groined vault. On the lower level was a series of connected rooms, decorated by false doors and deep recesses.

The description of the Domus Pelopia might also hint at the Domus Transitoria, situated on the Palatine and constructed prior to the Domus Aurea. The Domus Transitoria seems to have featured the same spatial articulation on different levels as the Subiaco villa. On the grounds of the former Vigna Barberini, recent excavations have discovered a circular-shaped structure formed by a pillar, several fan-style arches, and a room that may have had a linchpin and a rotating mechanism. It is perhaps possible to identify this structure if not with the *cenatio rotunda*, Nero's rotating dining room traditionally located in a wing of the Domus Aurea on the Oppian Hill, at least with its precursor in the

[23] Aygon 2004: 364–5. [24] Schiesaro 2006: 441–9.

[25] Petrone 1986–7: 137f.; Smolenaars 1998; Rosati 2002; Riemer 2007.

[26] Tarrant 1985: 183, on v. 642.

Domus Transitoria.[27] In this case we would have a point of comparison, both symbolic and material, for one of the most striking images of the *Thyestes*; namely, Seneca's depiction of the world's end (virtually caused by the *Thyestea cena*) as a swirling collapse of the constellations, each breaking away one by one from the celestial vault under the centrifugal force caused by the world's crazy spinning.

Here again, one must take into account the symbolic construction of the space of power through time, starting from the Augustan age. The text shows many clues pointing in this direction. First, the Fury orders Tantalus to decorate the gates of his palace with laurel garlands (*Thy.* 54–5), thus echoing a custom initiated under Augustus.[28] Second, the many references to solar and circus imageries that characterize the Domus Pelopia (*Thy.* 123, 409–10, 659–62) are not exclusive to Nero, who reintroduced the "solar" conceptualizations of the Circus Maximus and of the Palatine that Augustus had promoted (see La Rocca, Chapter 13 in this volume).[29] After 64 CE, Nero became ever more identified with the sun. The image of the celestial charioteer suggested links with Nero's own athletic pursuits.[30] Whereas the *Thyestes* emphasizes the Neronian image of *Sol* as a charioteer, *Medea* (probably composed at the beginning of Nero's reign) purposely challenges that association: at the play's opening Medea asks to ride in her familial, solar chariot and set Corinth on fire (32ff.). But at the end of the play she is carried away into a sky devoid of gods by a chariot of serpents, chthonian creatures, possibly resonating with Ovid's *Metamorphoses*.[31] The chariot of the sun in which Euripides had her fly away has disappeared from the scene.

9.4 Space and Narrative

Seneca's scenic space can be viewed as an exemplary, condensed system of signs and symbols.[32] On the stage, the space of Senecan tragedies is endowed with semantic significance and from the first act onward it

[27] Further excavations and researches are required to verify this interesting hypothesis, which has been formulated by Tomei 2011: 131 and Villedieu 2011.

[28] Monteleone 1991: 218. See, e.g., Aug. *R.G.* 34; Ov. *fast.* 4.953; *met.* 1.562–3; Mart. 8.1.1 *laurigeros ... penates* (for Domitian's palace).

[29] For the "Cirque du Soleil" and its relationship with the *Palatium*, see Barchiesi 2008.

[30] Cadario 2011: 176–7, 185–8 on Nero's *loricata* statue coming from the theater of *Caere* as well as the lost purple *velarium*, spread over the theater of Pompey during festivities for Tiridates' coronation ceremony in 66 CE.

[31] For resonances with Ovid and the poetic tradition in Seneca's tragedy, see Trinacty 2014: 124–6.

[32] Segal 1986; Rosati 2002; Schmidt 2014: 539–41.

congests the dramatic atmosphere, foreshadowing the final tragic disaster. Besides the *Thyestes, Phaedra* provides an excellent case in point. At the beginning of the play, Hippolytus praises the Attic woodlands surrounding Athens, and in so doing he directs the audience's attention to the offstage world. Such a move serves to offer an alternative to the stage-space, that is, to the palace. The prince himself leaves the palace in a hurry, as if he did not want to belong there. Hippolytus then exits the scene, and the stage is occupied by the overwhelming presence of Phaedra. Through her *furor* the woman defines the stage/palace as the source of the ill-omened fate that will destroy her stepson. The structuring of the relationship between stage and off-stage shows that the world of the prince and that of his stepmother are irreconcilable.

The characterization of dramatic figures by placement in their own particular landscapes has a counterpart in changes in contemporary wall painting (the Fourth Pompeian style) and in particular the revival of the model of the *scaenae frons*.[33] On one hand, the Fourth style continues a well-established tradition: the *scaenae frons* already appears in late Republican and early imperial iconography, and its use is attested also in the Second style. On the other hand, the Fourth style innovates, reducing the dimensions of scenography in private contexts and populating the scenes with mythological figures. Such a difference perhaps reflects changes in the modes of consuming dramatic literature, resulting from a new emphasis placed on the text rather than on its public mass performance. Seneca's tragedies also testify to this new trend. In addition, one further conceptual change needs to be taken into account. The *scaenarum frontes* of the Second style, devoid as they are of any human presence, led to a theatricalization of domestic rituals by providing an ideal background for dramatizing the roles played by the people inhabiting the relevant private spaces. That is, these domestic scenes devoid of characters inevitably drawn in actual people to play domestic roles against the backdrops and become actors in the scenes. If, on the contrary, the painted scenes are already populated with characters, there is no theatricalization of the homeowner's "performance of domestic life." The frescoes decorating Neronian houses, featuring dramatic scenes complete with characters, can be read as shows offered by the hosts. In contrast to the Second style, the world of theater represents an alternative to the world of the *domus* and to everyday life, as spectators are cut off from the painted stage, which is now an autonomous and

[33] On the model of the *scaenae frons*, see Leach 2004: 93–122 and Elsner 2004: 2 with further bibliography.

exclusive space. Viewers are not invited to play their part, but rather to imagine the development of the *fabula* in their minds.

Finally, in the Fourth style, the proliferation of *scaenae frontes* creates the capacity for double illusion. In the way in which it opens narratives to the imagination and closes them to external access (engaged participation), the Fourth style *frons scaenae* establishes a sophisticated, yet quite ambiguous relationship between spatial organization and mythological contents,[34] which bears some resemblances to the structure of Senecan tragedies as a whole. We may think here, for example, of the multiplication of various frameworks of action at different levels, and the winding relationship between the different levels of drama. Second, the function of the chorus in Senecan drama is no longer mimetic, but semantic, producing a *fabula altera*, i.e., an alternative to the staged plot, thus multiplying narrative perspectives.[35] Third, imagination plays a major role. In all of the tragedies, regardless of how they were consumed, the stage is created by the words of the poet while the audience must use its imagination to visualize the scenes. Traditional messenger speeches thus become full-fledged scenes – another parallel with Neronian wall painting, which features a proliferation of autonomous scenes.

It has to be stressed that the analogy between Seneca's tragedies and the painted stages in contemporary wall painting does not involve Nero's imperial palaces, where the *scaenae frons* is present but devoid of human figures; as in the Domus Transitoria, where a series of rooms decorated with polychrome marbles was built around a fountain in the shape of a stage. In this case, the tyrant himself takes center stage.

9.5 COLORS AND ICONOGRAPHY

Senecan tragedies share several features with other masterpieces of the Neronian period – an eagerness "to be more than"; a high degree of rhetoricization in style and content; a language characterized by paradox and hyperbole; an emphasis on the word's ability to construct reality; and an emphasis on the body and its (political, poetic, cosmological, etc.) imagery. Several of these features lend themselves to a comparison with contemporary artistic tendencies, particularly with an overriding interest in grotesque narratives and baroque forms:[36] gruesome details, red tones (especially blood-red and fire), stark contrasts between light

[34] Lorenz 2007: 676–7. [35] Mazzoli 2014: 569–74. [36] Varner 2000.

and darkness, overemphatic gestures and bodily postures. Parallels between single scenes from Seneca's tragedies and contemporary paintings/reliefs have a long history in scholarship.[37] But a comprehensive analysis of the relationship between the tragedies and Neronian art has yet to be written. In particular, a new model for an integrated reading of parallel iconographies is needed. One of the key issues here concerns the criteria by which artists or commissioners selected the scenes to be translated into images, in pictures that offered a "pregnant moment" that required viewers to complete the story in their own imaginations.[38]

But in order to reach this integrated method of reading we must resist the temptation to determine "who came first?" Given the loss of so much Roman and Hellenistic literature, it is almost always impossible to establish whether Seneca builds on previous traditions or boldly invents.[39] A fresco in Pompei, for instance, shows blind Oedipus standing in front of Jocasta (R III 4.2), just as happens in Seneca (*Oed.* 998 ss.). For his part, Sophocles had Oedipus blind himself with the buckle of Jocasta, who has already hanged herself. A similar parallel is found in a wall painting from Palermo (H 1467) that has Oedipus meeting the messenger with Jocasta nowhere in sight. A fresco from the Domus Aurea (RPGR 209, 4) shows the same sequence of scenes that is followed in Seneca's *Phaedra*: Hippolytus off hunting, Hippolytus and the nurse discussing the nature of love, Phaedra love-sick. The parallel has led art historians to reinterpret the central scene, which had previously been read as the revelation of Phaedra's love through the nurse (as Euripides has it). In Seneca, Phaedra reveals her love to Hippolytus directly, while the nurse is given a more "philosophical" role (*Phae.* 435–579). By way of the Senecan parallel, the central scene of the fresco becomes the pivotal part of a narrative that is framed as a sort of rhetorical debate for and against (*disputatio in utramque partem*), in which Phaedra (the choice of love) and Hippolytus (the choice of chastity) are contrasted as irreconcilable.

9.6 TRAGEDIES IN THEIR OWN TIME

Still to be addressed is the question of how Seneca's tragedies relate to other dramatic genres of the Neronian era.[40] Sources testify to a rich and

37 See, among others, Croisille 1982.

38 As Varner 2000: 127 pointed out, in Senecan theater, such a "pregnant moment" demands strong viewer involvement in the events represented.

39 The following examples are taken from Croisille 1982: 78–100, 162–86.

40 Kelly 1979. See also Zanobi 2008.

varied generic landscape, where the term "tragedy" could be taken to mean many things:[41] *tragoedia cantata* was a short concert or "lyric" production; *tragoedia saltata*, a pantomime ballet; *citharoedia*, a solo performance consisting in a tragic aria accompanied by the lyre. Seneca's plays, however, attest to the survival of full-length literary tragedy, in spite of the loss of professional playwrights and the extravagances of the late Republican stage. Rhetorical declamations played a major role in the persistence of tragedy. In this respect, literary tragedy stands starkly against other forms of contemporary mass spectacle that were characterized by a rather loose structure.[42] However, Seneca's tragedies are also affected by the generic enrichment that characterizes literary production in the Neronian era. For instance, the refined metrical structure of the choral parts – and of some monodies as well – points to a keen interest in musical component.[43] Such an interest in turn reflects the proliferation of public musical performances during the Neronian age; performances directly promoted by the emperor through the creation of schools open to the public.[44] Moreover, some specific features of Seneca's tragedies are better read against the backdrop of pantomime: the "running commentaries," for instance – that is, the detailed description of a character's emotions, actions, or looks – introspective monologs and narrative set-pieces, as well as the extensive naming of body parts and facial expressions, all resonate strongly with pantomime.[45] The connection is not surprising per se. Petronius' *Satyricon* has distinctively mimic overtones, and according to ancient sources, Lucan too composed librettos for pantomime (*salticae fabulae*). Furthermore, the reading of the *Apocolocyntosis* as a Menippean reworking of a libretto that was originally written for a mime to be staged at Nero's court fits this context very well.[46]

Finally, we cannot rule out the hypothesis that Seneca's tragedies were excerpted to become *tragoediae cantatae* or *citharoediae*, or that they were modified into *tragoediae saltatae* designed for a broader audience. Graffiti from Pompei featuring lines from Seneca's tragedies seem to point in this direction.[47]

This brings us back to the generically overlapping figures with which we began: Nero the cithara player, Piso the singing *tragoedus*, and Seneca the dramatist. Future research that aims to assess the role of

[41] On Nero's artistic career, see, e.g., Edwards 1994; Champlin 2003: 69–108; Fantham 2013: 20–5 and Leigh, Chapter 1 in this volume.

[42] On the fall and rise of Roman literary tragedy, see Goldberg 1996.

[43] For Seneca's competence as a musicologist in the Neronian milieu, see Wille 1967: 338–50; Luque-Moreno 1997; and Mazzoli 2014: 565–7.

[44] Rea 2011: 210.

[45] Zanobi 2008.

[46] Fantham 1988–9: 160. See also Zanobi 2008: 66–73.

[47] Cugusi 2008: 59–62.

Senecan tragedies in the Neronian age will look for new elements of cultural mediation in order to gain a sense of perspective as well as to highlight mutual interconnections. This is the only way to grasp the multidimensional character of the theatricality that stamps the Neronian age.

Further Reading

For a useful introduction to Neronian literary culture and the place of Seneca's plays in it, see Buckley and Dinter 2013 (especially 6–12). A convenient overview of current research on Senecan tragedy, dealing with single plays and their sources, language and style, topics, date, and reception is found in part 3 of Damschen and Heil 2014. Perceptive surveys on Senecan tragedy as a whole, placing it in its various contemporary contexts, include Liebermann 2014 and Trinacty 2014. On the role of Seneca in the political tradition of Roman tragedy, see also Davis 2015. Edwards 1994 should still be referred to on the role of acting as a central metaphor in the ancient representation of Nero as well as of his relationship with Seneca. An in-depth investigation of Senecan theatricality is offered by Littlewood 2015. Much research remains to be done in the area where Senecan tragedies and Neronian art could overlap: besides Croisille 1982 and Varner 2000, a comprehensive analysis of this relationship is still to be written. Newly opened perspectives on Fourth-style wall paintings (see La Rocca and Vout, Chapters 13 and 12, respectively, in this volume) may prove useful in revisiting this topic.

10: Philosophers and the State under Nero

Shadi Bartsch

10.1 The Greek Influence

In Plato's *Republic*, Socrates famously suggested that governance by a sequence of philosopher-kings would be the ideal form of governance for a *polis*. On this view, just as the rational part of the soul should rule over the appetitive and spirited parts, so too the king himself would embody the rational element of the polis and rule over the other classes (*Rep.* 431a–444e).[1] Of course, this ideal was of dubious applicability to the real world; *inter alia*, the philosophical training of Plato's kings had little direct application to the demands of governance and consisted largely of knowledge of the Forms. Indeed, Plato's own voyages to Sicily to give the tyrant Dionysius II of Syracuse training in philosophical thought ended only in failure and expulsion (*Ep.* 7). Still, the prospect that ethical philosophy might find a place for itself in politics even without philosophical kings, and that the teachings of a wise individual might guide the otherwise self-indulgent impulses of an autocrat, has had a tenacious hold on thinkers throughout political history: not for nothing has Mark Lilla dubbed the hope that drew Plato to a tyrant's realm "the lure of Syracuse."[2] As Socrates' fate might suggest, it is a lure with dangerous liabilities for the active philosopher: his theories may bolster the regimes of vicious autocrats,[3] he may end up betraying his own principles, or he himself may fall prey to those he professes to guide.

Following Plato, the Hellenistic philosophers and the Roman inheritors of their thought offered further theories on the nature of an

[1] The *Statesman* asks the question omitted here: what is political expertise? On Plato's lack of interest in *euboulia* in the *Republic*, see Schofield 1999: 3–4. The later *Laws* seem to represent a second-best alternative, the rule of law.

[2] In the *NYRB*, September 20, 2001.

[3] A critique often lobbed at Heidegger, Schmidt, Strauss, and other anti-democratic thinkers.

ideal state and the role of philosophers in that state. If Plato's student Aristotle was willing to tutor Alexander the Great until he took power, Epicurus, by contrast, preached the tranquil pleasures of a life lived in peaceful anonymity and detachment from politics (represented by the phrase *lathe biosas*, "live in obscurity").[4] Cicero, Plutarch, and others criticized this point of view, but whether Epicurus' Roman followers were quite so quiescent is up for debate.[5] As Don Fowler points out, some justifications for political action existed, and we know of a fairly large roster of Roman Epicureans who manifestly did participate in government during both the Republic and the early Empire – for example, L. Manlius Torquatus (who like Cato killed himself in the war against Caesar), or Caesar's assassin Cassius. Some ended up in exile under Nero. Here again we see the pressure of the Roman elite standards for the noble life on abstract theorizing about an existence aside from the political realm (cf. Armstrong 2011). It is not surprising that Cicero's Scipio emphasizes that his own thought, unlike Plato's, has to do with the real world (*Rep.* 2.51).

The Stoics, by contrast to the Epicureans, seem to have openly called for the wise man's participation in government even if that government did not match the ideals set out in their own utopian treatises. Zeno's (lost) *Republic*, in sharp contrast to Plato's, abolished class hierarchies by extending citizenship only to the wise in the first place: this ideal city would have no non-rational representation.[6] Chrysippus penned *On the Republic*, likely offering an analysis of Zeno's work.[7] According to Dio Chrysostom, all of the three main figures in early Stoicism, the founder Zeno, Cleanthes, and Chrysippus, held that participating in (actual) public life is in accordance with nature (*Or.* 47.2). Diogenes Laertius attributes similar sentiments to Chrysippus in the first book of the latter's *Peri bion*, since by participating the wise man "will check vice and encourage virtue" (7.121). In Nero's own day, Seneca

[4] On Epicurean distance from politics, see Cicero's comments at *Att.* 14.20.5, *Fam.* 7.12, *Leg.* 1.39; Diogenes Laertius 10.119. Plutarch devotes an essay to the topic of *lathe biosas*. On Epicureans at Rome, see, e.g., Benferhat 2005 and Erler 2009.

[5] For a good discussion of Lucretius' Epicurean poem *De Rerum Natura* as political commentary, see Fowler 1989.

[6] On the Stoic *Politeia* (*Republic*) of Chrysippus, the landmark study is Schofield 1991. As Schofield shows, the Stoics emphasized mutual obligation between humans even outside the framework of the *polis*. Despite the sexual communism they shared with Plato's *Republic*, they proposed a "good eros," a kind of friendship with benefits inspired by beauty.

[7] On the content of Zeno's *Republic*, see Schofield 1999: 51–68. On Zeno's *Republic* as a response to Plato, see Doyne 1992: 183–7. Both remark on the possibility of Cynic as well as Platonic influence. See also Plut. *Stoic Self-Cont.* 1033de, 1034b.

repeats that Zeno taught that the wise man will enter public life if nothing stands in the way (e.g., *Dial.* 8.2; of course, what might be sufficient hindrance poses its own subjective problem).[8] Monarchy was not a sufficient negative condition to abstain, and indeed, there are many Stoic treatises *On Kingship* from the third century, written by Cleanthes, Persaeus, Sphaerus, and others.[9] Centuries later, a famous Senecan quotation would condemn Brutus' murder of Julius Caesar as not being "*ex institutione Stoica*" (not in accordance with Stoic thought): in killing the dictator, Brutus had not treated "monarchy" with the philosophical respect it deserved, "even though a state reaches its best condition under the rule of a just king" (*Ben.* 2.20).[10]

Plutarch and others mocked the Greek Stoics for not putting their money where their mouth was (*Moralia* 1033b–1034a): according to his account, Chrysippus urged the wise man to become a courtier while avoiding politics himself. Certainly the Stoic paradox that "Only the wise man is king" (*SVF* 3.694–700) emphasized the self, not the state, as the object of control. Be this as it may, we have repeated evidence for actual political participation by Stoics from the start;[11] many Hellenistic Stoic philosophers played a role in practical politics, and in the first century BCE, members of the school served several times as ambassadors to Rome.[12] In the early Empire, Augustus himself sent his quondam teacher, the Stoic Athenodorus, back to his native Tarsus to govern (Strabo 24.675). By Nero's age, there was plenty of precedent for Stoics in government, whether republic or monarchy.

8 Cf. Cic *Fin.* 3.20.62–8, where the Stoic Cato speaks for both himself and Chrysippus in saying that the wise man would wish to assist in the running of the republic. For exceptions to political participation, see Arius Didymus *SVF* 3.690 and discussions of the appropriate *persona* for politics in Cic. *Off.* 1.71–3, 107–21. See further later in this chapter for Seneca and Epictetus on role-playing.

9 Dawson 1992: 196 points out that there were more such treaties by the Peripatetics; he is skeptical that we can take Stoic metaphors about kingship as representing an affinity with monarchy. See discussion in Dawson 1992: 196–8, 200–3; Schofield 1991: 84–90; Braund 2009: 64–6. Musonius fr. 8 assumes the existence of a monarch, and tells him to behave well.

10 See Griffin 1976: 205–6 for the possibility that the Stoics preferred a mixed constitution to monarchy.

11 Persaeus (307/6–243) BCE, and Sphaerus both served monarchs (in Persaeus' case, Antigonus II Gonatas, in whose service he died defending Corinth (*SVF* 1.439–44), while Sphaerus seems to have advised both Cleomenes of Sparta and Ptolemy IV Philopator respectively (*SVF* 1.624, DL 7.177).

12 Diogenes the Stoic was chosen with Carneades the Academic and Critolaus the Peripatetic to go as an ambassador to Rome on Athens' behalf in 155 BCE; Posidonius likewise served as an ambassador to Rome from Rhodes in 87–86 BCE.

10.2 Philosophers under Nero

Stoicism and Epicureanism were particularly influential among the Roman elite classes in the late Republic and early Empire; we hear far less about prominent followers of the Academy, of Aristotle, or of the Cynics. As P. A. Brunt (1975) definitively documented, the circulation of general Stoic ideas was widespread even among those whose priorities were not philosophical, such ideas often meshing comfortably with Roman mores about masculine self-control and elite political involvement. But Roman Stoics in the imperial period held varying interpretations of the conditions under which participation in government was to be accepted or abjured, and even during the Neronian years, a broad gamut of behaviors can be found. The two extremes of this range might be represented by Nero's tutor and political advisor Lucius Annaeus Seneca on one hand, a man whose vast wealth and implication in Nero's crimes have cast a pall on his philosophical legacy; and on the other hand, by members of the Roman upper classes in the (by now largely *pro forma*) Roman Senate who chose to represent themselves as Stoics in rebuffing Nero and paying the price. While few scholars now argue for the presence of a principled "Stoic resistance" fueled by philosophical objection to Nero's rule, it is clear that the traditional Roman elite objection to the figure of the *rex* found additional articulation in some anti-Neronian senators via the high-minded values of philosophy and the striking example set by the Stoic Cato the Younger, who committed suicide rather than accept Julius Caesar's mercy.[13]

The most famous figure among the Stoics who seceded from government under Nero, Thrasea Paetus, started off amenable enough to Nero's rule; he was appointed consul in November–December 56, and an honorific priesthood followed. But the situation deteriorated after Thrasea spoke against a routine motion in the Senate in 58 CE – in Tacitus' claim, as a show of independence from servility (*Ann.* 13.49). Later, worse still, he walked out of a senatorial meeting when motions were proposed to congratulate Nero on his "safe escape" from Agrippina, the mother he had ordered murdered.[14] Why walk out at this point? The historian Dio tells us that "he could not say what he

[13] Cf. Wirszubski 1950: 138; Syme 1958: 558; Brunt 1975: 23, n. 91, all in agreement that Stoicism fortified Thrasea but was not the source of his actions.

[14] Tacitus mentions Thrasea's "air of moral disapproval" as a source of Nero's irritation (*Ann.* 16.21–2, Suet. *Nero* 37.1). Cf. Tigellinus' comments to Nero about "Stoicorum adrogantia" in *Ann.* 14.57. On Tacitus' attitude toward Thrasea and the other Stoics under Nero, see Turpin 2008: 379–89.

would, and would not say what he could" (62.15.2–3); Brunt comments that "Thrasea's conduct marked Nero as a tyrant" (1975: 27).[15] In 62 CE, Thrasea twice pushed his peers to vote against Nero's will (once on a serious *maiestas* charge). In 63 or 64, he withdrew from attending the Senate altogether (*Ann.* 16.22.1), an action that spoke of the "hindering circumstances" of which the early Stoics had already written. It was probably also in this period that he wrote his *Life of Cato* in praise of that martyr to the Republican cause. Eventually he was brought to trial on trumped-up charges in 66 and ordered to commit suicide. Thrasea had the veins of his arms opened in the company of his friends, calling the shedding of his blood a libation to "Jupiter the Liberator" and thus, like Socrates and the Stoics themselves, identifying his death as a transition to a state that held no fear. As such, he stood not only for liberty, but also for a Stoic refusal to yield to force – and reenacted the example of Cato, but now as an *exemplum* of the fate of the philosopher in the non-ideal republic.[16]

Among the Neronian Stoics, Thrasea was not alone. In the same year, the elderly Stoic Barea Soranus was also condemned to death on a charge of intrigue with the provincials apparently dating back to his proconsulship of Asia in 61/2 (*Ann.* 16.23), and Thrasea's son-in-law Helvidius Priscus was exiled for declaring his sympathy with Julius Caesar's assassins.[17] Epictetus imagines the dialog with Vespasian that spurred Helvidius' second banishment under that emperor:

> "I must say what I think right." "But if you do, I shall put you to death." "When then did I tell you that I am immortal? You will do your part, and I will do mine: it is your part to kill; it is mine to die, but not in fear: yours to banish me; mine to depart without sorrow."
>
> (*Disc.*, 1.2.19–21, tr. W. A. Oldfather)

Thrasea's action had said as much. At least two other Stoics, Paconius Agrippinus and Curtius Montanus, were exiled on libel charges. In addition, L. Annaeus Cornutus, an active teacher of Stoicism at Rome (the Stoic poet Persius was one of his students), was banished

[15] For Epictetus' treatment of passive resistance, see *Disc.* 1.29.

[16] Tacitus, *Ann.* 13.49, 14.12, 48, 15.20–2, 16.21–35, *Hist.* 2.91, 4.5; Pliny the Younger, *Ep.* 3.16.10, 6.29.1–2, 8.22.3; Dio Cassius 61.15, 62.26; Juvenal, 5.36 with scholia. On the persecution of the Stoics, see MacMullen 1966: 46–83; Griffin 1984: 171–7. On family traditions of dissent and Flavian crack-down, see Penwill 2003. On *exempla* in Stoicism, cf. Seneca *Ep.* 6.5 and Turpin 2008.

[17] The informer Eprius Marcellus called him "a Thrasea in revolt" (*Ann.* 16.28), possibly implying a more active role than simple secession.

for criticizing Nero's projected history of the Romans in epic verse (Dio 62.29) while the philosopher C. Musonius Rufus elicited Nero's suspicion as an active teacher of Stoicism and was banished to the island of Gyarus in 65 CE on false charges of participating in the Pisonian conspiracy (*Ann.* 25.72, Dio 62.27.4; one of his pupils was the philosopher Epictetus, himself later banished). It was Musonius' friendship with Rubellius Plautus, a Stoic Nero murdered in 62 CE for allegedly plotting against him from exile, that was the underlying cause of Nero's hostility. There was one prominent Stoic who genuinely did plot against Nero – the poet Lucan; despite allegations, Seneca himself probably did not.[18] Interestingly, Musonius returned to Rome in 68 CE and soon joined an embassy on behalf of Vitellius to the victorious soldiers of Vespasian, telling them that peace was preferable to war. Here is the philosopher in politics *par excellence*, but unsurprisingly, he was ineffectual in the attempt (Tac. *Hist.* 1.81).

10.3 Senecan Compromises

Although philosopher, dramatist, and statesman L. Annaeus Seneca was not part of the senatorial opposition that raised Nero's dander, it is he who looms largest on the Neronian landscape. He is a figure whose actions were deeply contested already in antiquity:[19] his service to a tyrant, his complicity in Nero's crimes, his huge wealth, his apparent usury in Britain, have all been seen as deeply incompatible with the Stoic ideals of self-governance, indifference to worldly goods, and participation in the state "if nothing hinders."[20] Perhaps for these reasons, Seneca fascinatingly obscures his own role in Neronian politics, choosing to write either philosophical exhortations (the prose works) or tragedies on mythological figures, with the result that, as Ronald Syme has remarked, "Without the testimony of Tacitus, Seneca the statesman could hardly exist" (1958: 52). Only the evidence of the *Apocolocyntosis* and the *de Clementia* pull back the curtain on the eventual royal advisor recalled from exile in 49 CE to be Nero's tutor; both are early works

[18] As Griffin points out (1984: 171), other Roman senators and *equites* were exiled or put to death at the same time – but this does not rule out Stoic affiliation as a factor in Nero's distaste.

[19] Dio calls Seneca a hypocrite at 61.10.2–6; so did his enemies (Tac. *Ann.* 13.42). Griffin (2008: 54–7) examines the question of how much Seneca actively tried to amass wealth rather than just coming by it.

[20] An early example picked at random: Seneca writes that "External things are of slight importance, and can have no great influence in either direction. Prosperity does not exalt the wise man, nor does adversity cast him down; for he has always endeavored to rely entirely upon himself, to derive all of his joy from himself" (*Dial.* 12.5.1, tr. J. W. Basore).

from near the beginning of Nero's reign. Thereafter, the absence of almost any reference to current events or to Seneca's difficult position is striking: the man who theorizes on the correct conditions for the philosopher's participation in government never speaks of his own.[21] If Plato's ruler, as reason embodied, played the leading role in Plato's idealizing *Republic*, Nero, by contrast, has only a bit part in Seneca's writings on the logos-infused Stoic soul, and if Seneca avows in *Ep.* 95.52 that the state is part of the rational cosmos, there is by that date no question of Nero's nonparticipation in that ideal.

As mentioned, the *de Clementia* of 55–6 CE lets us see, if through a glass darkly, the world of the imperial advisor *cum* philosopher: a Seneca who set Roman republican ideals aside to praise the ruler as a *rex*[22] and who was willing to modify aspects of Stoic theory to emphasize Nero's absolute power over his subjects – in theory, to sway him to clemency rather than cruelty. Given Nero's god-like position (writes Seneca), he must care for the safety of all, uphold the social order, lower himself to observe the laws, and even remember that he belongs to the state, and not vice versa (*Cl.* 1.1.1, already after the murder of Nero's stepbrother Britannicus). The adulatory stance on kingship in the *de Clementia* exaggerates the Stoic acceptance of good monarchy as a possible form of government, and in casting the *rex* as the mind of the political corpus and the people as his body, Seneca chooses a flattering metaphor neither Stoic nor Platonic (*Cl.* 1.3.5–4.3).[23] Naming *clementia* as the main characteristic of the *vir sapiens* embodied in Nero,[24] Seneca innovates in making this trait a Stoic virtue – either nodding to the fact that *clementia* had been a traditional part of Julio-Claudian rhetoric, or anticipating and trying to avert Nero's future abuses.[25] In this work, the ruler's wisdom *de facto* supersedes that of

[21] On this topic, see Edwards, Chapter 11 in this volume. Not even the burning of Lyons (*Ep.* 90.1–2) provokes comment on Rome's own conflagration.

[22] He uses the word interchangeably with *princeps*, establishing the analogy while never addressing Nero as *rex* directly.

[23] The metaphor occurs in the Aesopian fable "The Belly and the Members." Dawson 1992: 235–43 addresses what happens to Stoic utopian thought in the Roman Republic.

[24] Schofield 2015: 75, writes: "What Greek Stoicism did talk about was pity (*eleos*), forgiveness (*sungnômê*), and forbearance (*epieikeia*; Stob. *Ecl.* 2.95.24–96.9; D. L. 7.123). Their view was that none of these dispositions was properly rational. All of them prompt remission of penalties prescribed by the rationality of the law, and the wise person will therefore not forgive or show pity or be prone to ask for a reduction of the punishment that is due." For a discussion of the difficulties in Seneca's treatment of Neronian *clementia*, see Star 2012: 130–9.

[25] In squaring his position with the Stoic view in book 2, Seneca casts pity as a fault, while mercy is a sort of reasoned avoidance of emotion that simply offers remittance of punishment when rationally appropriate (*Cl.* 2.5.4–6.3). On the conflicts between the two books of the *de Clementia*, see Griffin 1992: 151–8 and Braund 2009: 30–44. On the (attempted) shaping of the psychology of the emperor in the *De Clementia*, see Star 2012: 117–28.

the law, and there is no murmur here of abolishing hierarchies to create a community of the wise.[26] Ironically, while Seneca mentions the fact that the Stoics had traditionally been seen as too unbending to offer useful advice to a ruler (*Cl.* 2.5.2), he himself is no such model of rigidity in the *de Clementia*. We have here, in Miriam Griffin's words, "an ideology for a new regime" (1992: 129–71).

We might profitably contrast some of Cicero's political thought, a century earlier. Cicero likewise finds kingship an acceptable form of government under certain conditions, but he emphasizes the rule of law over the wisdom of an individual leader: the just republic consists of "a group of people agreeing with respect to justice and sharing in advantage."[27] Accordingly, he emphasizes that no republic can exist if there is disagreement as to justice, or a cruel and self-interested man as ruler, for under tyranny agreement on justice collapses (*Rep.* 3.43). As Malcolm Schofield summarizes (1999: 189), "A degree of political liberty is essential to a true *res publica.*" Cicero's position offers an argument for the traditional aristocracy that he naturally thinks is the best form of government: in his words, it is no absolute ruler, nor the people themselves, but the Roman Senate that is the "*rei publicae custodem, praesidem, propugnatorem*" – "the guardian, protector, and defender of the republic" (*Sest.* 137). This is worth pointing out not only because the Senate becomes the supreme moral arbiter of the Republic, but also because Seneca echoes this highly charged, superlative language when he turns to extol Nero. For example, in his essays *On Anger* and *On Clemency*, Seneca calls Nero the *praeses* (protector) of the laws and the healer of the people (*Dial.* 3.6.3) or their *custos* (guardian; *Cl.* 1.13.1); in the *Consolation to Polybius*, written to Polybius from Seneca's exile under Claudius, it was Nero's predecessor Claudius who conveniently took on the noble role of a god-like protector of all, safeguarding (*custodiatur*) the Empire by benefits rather than by weapons (*Dial.* 11.12.3).

But Seneca does not just usurp Republican political language for imperial praise. He uses the same language for his descriptions of Stoic ideology as well, highlighting (we might say) his readiness to find greatness on both sides of a stark divide. In the *Letters*, it is generally God that is the guardian (e.g., *Ep.* 4.2), as in the *Natural Questions* (*HN* 1. *praef.* 3), and in *De Vita Beata*, it is again God or the gods who are the

[26] Schofield 1999: 84–92 has a good discussion of the use of Stoic and Platonic elements in monarchical theory in the empire.

[27] Cicero accepts the kingships of early Rome as possibilities for good government.

praesides of the world, censors of word and deed (*Dial.* 7.20.5). Here the good Stoic steps up as the *propugnator* (defender) of his country (*Dial.* 7.15.4; in the *Consolation to Helvia* too, the Stoic philosopher merits this language of guardianship and care (*Dial.* 12.5.3). And abstract Stoic virtue can play this role, as in Seneca's work on reciprocating benefits (*Ben.* 3.33).[28] In other words, Seneca, whether hopefully or hypocritically, will put now the emperor, now the Stoic god (or Stoic philosopher) in charge of the welfare of the state – but in any case, not Cicero's Senate.

Given this situation, we will not be surprised to find Seneca originally arguing *for* Stoic political involvement – who could be more involved than Nero's own advisor? – at least until his later writings and his retirement in 62 CE.[29] In *On tranquillity*, for example, while admitting that setbacks in politics will send him home smarting, he lauds participating in government, not in order to win honors, but to help one's fellow men, and points out that he is following the advice of Zeno, Cleanthes, and Chrysippus, even if none of them actually took up political office (*Dial.* 9.1.10). Elsewhere he reminds us not to be womanishly vulnerable, for sensitivity to insult or weariness makes us "pass up necessary public and private duties, even beneficial ones" (*Dial.* 2.19.2). As he remarks, the happy life cannot come *from* participation in politics, but nonetheless, virtue may be exercised there as in seclusion: "Virtue you will find in the temple, in the forum, in the senate-house, standing before the city walls, stained and dusty, with calloused hands" (*Dial.* 7.7.3). Of course, this position may be variously nuanced depending on context; for example, Seneca can advise Paulinus to retire to focus on wisdom after he has already devoted many years to public service (*Dial.* 10.18.1–19); here and elsewhere, as Miriam Griffin points out, Seneca redefines the concept of leisure and retirement to mean devotion to the practice of philosophy (1992: 318).

Tacitus tells us that Seneca asked Nero for permission to retire after his ally in controlling Nero, Praetorian prefect Afranius Burrus, died in 62 CE. Nero refused out of a concern for appearances, but Seneca seems to have withdrawn nonetheless (Tac. *Ann.* 14.53–6). Perhaps unsurprisingly, then, Seneca is less willing to endorse the active life in his later writings, while fully aware of the difficulty involved in explaining this

[28] As much recent scholarship had noted, the idea of the *custos* or guardian figure occurs in the *Letters* to describe the imaginary viewer under whose gaze one is to regulate one's behavior and ideals (usually a republican hero). On the imaginary watcher, see Bartsch 2006: 183–229, with additional bibliography.

[29] The question is addressed with individual attention to each essay by Griffin 1992: 315–66.

about-face. Indeed, he publicly offers a rebuttal to Lucilius' reproach that the teachings of his school – Stoicism – forbid men to live a life devoid of political participation (*Ep.* 8.1). Likewise, while the dating of the *De Otio* is uncertain, it is striking that we are told here that no state exists that would justify the wise man's participation:[30]

> Such a state will always be lacking to the scrupulous searcher. I ask, in what state should the wise man participate? That of the Athenians, in which Socrates was condemned, and from which Aristotle fled to avoid condemnation? . . . Will the wise man, then, participate in the government of Carthage, in which faction is constant and "freedom" is hostile to all the best men . . . ? But if that state which we have imagined cannot be found anywhere, leisure begins to be necessary for all of us, because the one thing that could have been preferred to leisure does not exist. (*Dial.* 8.8.1–3)

In the *Letters*, which date to the last years of his life, Seneca's position on participation is reliably negative. In *Letters* 19, 20, and 22, Lucilius is advised to give up both his procuratorship and his business duties, which are merely fool's gold, "showy and depraved pursuits" ("*istis occupationibus speciosis et malis*," *Ep.* 22.1). In *Letter* 98, he is told to reject office even if obligated to take part: "The elder Sextius refused the honors of office; he was born with an obligation to take part in public affairs, and yet would not accept the broad stripe even when the deified Julius offered it to him" (tr. R. M. Gunmere). Such participation would again have been for show, *speciosa* (*Ep.* 98.13) – perhaps here with a hint at the philosopher's visible presence as part of the emperor's own show. In fact, the philosopher will be grateful to the ruler who has let him retire to study, for by choosing apolitical contemplation, the *sapiens* will serve the larger republic. A wise philosopher can set an example even in isolation (*Dial.* 9.3.6).[31]

But once at court, retirement is not so simple. We saw earlier that nonparticipation in the Senate could be construed as an act of philosophical condemnation, and even Lucilius is warned to keep a low profile in retirement rather than join those philosophers, "contemptuous of

[30] It is impossible to be sure of the relative dating of many of the essays; I generally follow Griffin 1992: 395–411 (an appendix on the chronology of the prose works). The date of *De Otio* is not known, but it seems reasonable to assume it was written when *otium* became, in fact, an immediate issue for Seneca.

[31] "The call to *otium* in the *Letters*, though accompanied by conditions, cautions, and justifications, is a categorical imperative" (Griffin 1992: 334).

magistrates, kings, and those who administer the republic," who comment by seceding (*Ep.* 73.1). Other statements that Seneca lets slip suggest that he knew the risk of being assimilated to the other Stoics who had withdrawn. In *Letter* 22, he emphasizes to Lucilius that the latter must be careful to retire at the *right time*. Seneca can disguise the meaning of this by stressing that it should be after much participation in government already (22.6; cf. his comments to Paulinus, cited earlier in this chapter); what remains unspoken is "if it is too dangerous to stay" and "when you can do so without imperial rage."

10.4 ROLE-PLAYING UNDER NERO

Seneca faced an additional difficulty in justifying his change of emphasis in favor of retirement in the later works. For the Stoics, the notion of playing one's correct role in life well and consistently right to the end was a philosophical principle and a means of articulating the rationale for one's own choices and actions in life – such as, for example, the decision to stay or go, to be complicit (while perhaps doing some good), or to retire (with the defense of helping the cosmopolitan city, rather than the real one). On Cicero's report (in turn based on the lost work of the Stoic Panaetius), a human lifespan consisted in the correct performance of four related roles: our role as rational agents, our distinctive qualities and talents, the status we were born into, and the active choices we make when there is such opportunity (*Off.* 1.107–21).[32] It was appropriate for *Cato* to choose suicide (Cic. *Off.* 1.112, Sen. *Dial.* 2.2.2) because he was Cato; and as Brunt writes of Thrasea Paetus, the question of whether he should appear in the Senate to answer the charges against him was (according to Tacitus) a question of "what course it was fitting ('*deceret*') for him to take" (1975, 15, citing Tac. *Ann.* 16.26.5). Helvidius is likewise said to have been inspired in his attitude by the stance of his friend Paconius Agrippinus, who refused to enter Nero's festival; these decisions might be small things, but they contribute to the loss of one's role. For Helvidius, his role – even at the cost of death – was to be the red thread that bordered the toga, not the humdrum threads that made up the rest of it (Epict. 1.2.12–18). As Epictetus put it, people differ in

[32] On the four-personae theory, see Brunt 1975; Gill 1988 (stressing the rational element over the "individual" aspect); and Gill 2009. The influence of the idea of the appropriate role is also found in Musonius and Epictetus; on the latter, cf. Long 2002: 233–44. This is not the place to discuss the importance of *prohaeresis* in Epictetus' thought. On picking the life that suits one's nature, see also Sen., *Dial.* 9.6.2–3, 7.2; cf. Tacitus' remarks on Helvidius Priscus, *Hist.* 4.5.

the prices at which they sell themselves; for a Helvidius or a Cato, there was no price high enough.[33] Whoever you are, whatever skills you have, "your function is to play the assigned role well, but the choice of the role is another's" (*Ench.* 17). Your abilities dictate what is "moral" for you to do.

Seneca knew well that one's correct role, or *persona*, in life might depend on a number of factors. So did he feel, at least initially, that it was an appropriate role for him to work with the Neronian court? Like the other Stoics, he endorsed the view that we must pick the correct choice of occupation for our nature (*Dial.* 9.6–7.2). And, like Epictetus, he felt it necessary to fulfill your role *well*, that is, with constancy. "Consider it a great thing, to play the role of one man," he exhorts Lucilius in *Letter* 120.22. The letter is late: as we know, by this time Seneca had already put on a new mask by retiring. But he is willing to concede that "besides the wise man, no one plays one role; the rest of us wear many masks" (*Ep.* 120.22). Did his audience find this concession shocking? His interlocutor in *De otio* seems confused:

> What are you saying, Seneca? Are you abandoning your role?[34] Surely you Stoics say: "Right up to the last boundary of life, we will not cease to work for the common good, to help individuals, and to give aid even to our enemies with an aged hand."
>
> (*Dial.* 8.1.4)

In rebutting him, Seneca quotes Zeno's line, "The wise man will enter politics unless something prevents him." He then continues: "If the state is too corrupt to be helped, if it is taken over by evils, the wise man will not struggle in vain, nor spend himself with no gain in sight" (*Dial.* 8.3.3). Stoic doctrine is thus pliable enough to justify subjective judgments even on the constancy of the role one is playing.[35] Here, Seneca, who has repeatedly said he himself is no wise man, obviously means to justify his decision to retreat from the battleground where he had previously thought it fruitful to ply his skills

[33] This stance explains the apparently ridiculous comment of Epictetus that he would commit suicide if ordered to cut off his philosopher's beard (*Disc.* 1.2.29): it would be a violation of his commitment to his chosen persona and his chosen value system. It would also show an attempt to disguise his identity qua philosopher. Epictetus speaks of roles at *Disc.* 1.2.5–11, 1.2.30, 3.23.1–8, 2.10.1–2, 7–12; for discussion, see Long 2002: 236–7.

[34] For *partes* in this sense in Seneca, see *Ben.* 1.2.4, 2.17.6, 2.18.1, *Ep.* 14.13, 80.7, etc. But it could also mean "party," in the metaphorical sense of the Stoics as a political "party."

[35] On a split consciousness as characteristic of Seneca's writing in particular, see Gunderson 2015: 152–3.

But disavowals aside, Seneca knew he had long ago arrogated for himself the role, if not of the philosopher-king, at least of the wise counselor, a Plato to his own Dionysius. And at the end he likewise knew he had miscalculated his ability to play that role. Where once he said, "The wise man may even do what he disapproves of, if the end justifies the means" (Haase fragment 9), near the end of his life he finally admits that all his compromising was in vain; he had found the right path "too late, and tired out by error" (*Ep.* 8.3).[36] Despite his hope to leave behind an "*imago vitae suae*" at the moment of his suicide – the image of the philosopher of the moral essays – for his later audiences Seneca would always bear the stain that Plato successfully eluded: that of fruitless complicity with a tyrant.

FURTHER READING

On the early Stoic "Republics," see Dawson 1992 and Schofield 1991 and 1999; for the Epicurean stance at Rome, Benferhat 2005. On the wide scope of Stoic thought at Rome in the late Republic and early Empire, see Brunt 1975. Political role-playing under Nero is addressed both by Roller 2001 and by Bartsch 1994, 2006, and 2015b. On Seneca's representation of his self, see Bartsch 2015b. The standard and most detailed account of Seneca's life is still that of Griffin 2nd ed. 1992, though Romm's readable study speculating on the ties between the philosopher's works and his life is also recommended.

[36] Epictetus, on the other hand, stresses the virtues of quietism much more and concentrates on the uselessness of all worldly goods and ambition throughout the *Discourses*.

11: Seneca and the Quest for Glory in Nero's Golden Age

Catharine Edwards

Seneca, one of the most prolific and wide-ranging Roman authors, exercised extraordinary power and influence as tutor and then advisor to the emperor Nero. His father, Seneca the Elder, was merely an equestrian of Spanish origin. Seneca himself, though educated in Rome, embarked on a senatorial career relatively late (in his mid-thirties) in the last years of Tiberius' reign. Having narrowly avoided execution under Caligula, he fell afoul of Caligula's successor, Claudius, in 41 CE and spent eight years in exile on Corsica. But, favored by the emperor's new wife, Agrippina, "on account of the brilliance of his studies" ("ob claritudinem studiorum eius," Tac. *Ann.* 12. 8. 2), Seneca was recalled in 49 CE to serve as tutor to her son, who became emperor in 54. Soon promoted to the consulship, Seneca was for years very close to Nero, even writing his speeches, if we believe Tacitus (*Ann.* 13. 11. 2).[1]

Though many of his works cannot be securely dated, his satire on the apotheosis of the emperor Claudius, the *Apocolocyntosis*, evidently dates from the early years of Nero's reign, as does *On Clemency*, offering advice on the exercise of benign (and thus secure) rule to the young emperor.[2] Other works too probably belong to the Neronian period, including *On Benefits, On Leisure*, and *On Providence*.[3] Of his tragedies, the gruesomely violent *Thyestes* is most likely to be Neronian (as is the *Phoenissae*).[4] The *Epistulae morales*, or *Letters* (along with the *Natural Questions*) were composed after Seneca's withdrawal from the imperial court in 62 CE; he died in 65.[5]

[1] For the details, see Griffin 1992. [2] Leach 2008; Braund 2009.
[3] On the dating of Seneca's works in general, see Griffin 1992: 395–411.
[4] Fitch 1981; Nisbet 2008.
[5] On *Q Nat.* Hine 2006; Williams 2012. On the complementary relationship between the Letters and *Q Nat.* Williams 2014.

The wide range of Seneca's literary achievement was already remarked on by his near contemporary Quintilian (*Inst.* 10.1. 125–31). In recent years Seneca's multifaceted career has come in for renewed attention, notably in the collections of essays edited by Volk and Williams 2006; Colish and Wildberger 2014; Damschen and Heil 2014; Bartsch and Schiesaro 2015; and Gunderson 2015. For Habinek 2000, 2014, Seneca's career exemplifies the new possibilities offered by cultural mastery as a source of political legitimacy in imperial Rome, highlighting the key role education played in the replication of the Roman elite. Some, it seems, even spoke of Seneca as a possible replacement for Nero, citing the *claritudo*, "brilliance" of his virtues (*Ann.* 15.65).

Seneca's life has seemed to many (most recently Emily Wilson in her 2014 biography) to be fraught with paradox and contradiction.[6] Much of his work is devoted to the contention that only virtue and reason have value, that wealth, power, and public acclaim are matters of indifference. Yet he is reported to have amassed a vast fortune, through sometimes dubious means. For many years he occupied a position of virtually unparalleled influence in the imperial court, complicit to some degree in a tyrannical regime. And in his writing Seneca often seems preoccupied with his own posthumous reputation.[7] Seneca's *Letters*, written in his last years, reflect intermittently on the question of whether the would-be wise man should pursue a career of public service, the traditional route to distinction in Roman culture. What kind of glory might a philosopher legitimately seek? Virtue, the *Letters* suggest, may often be better cultivated in private. Yet such virtue, perhaps as manifest in a great literary achievement, may ultimately eclipse the ephemeral glory even of the sun emperor in his golden palace.

Organized in twenty books, Seneca's 124 letters (more were known in antiquity – Aulus Gellius quotes from the now lost Book 22, *NA* 12.2.3) constitute an ambitious and many-layered philosophical – and literary – project. Varying significantly in length, tone, and content, the *Letters* offer an extended series of lessons in how to live one's life better, according to a distinctively Stoic model. Seneca's addressee is exhorted to scrutinize his own thoughts and actions minutely, in a process of ceaseless self-improvement.[8] Earlier letters, apparently simpler, give advice on asserting control over oneself through

[6] E. Wilson 2014. See also Griffin 1992: esp. chapter 9; Romm 2014; and Bartsch, Chapter 10 in this volume.

[7] E. Wilson 2014: 3.

[8] Veyne 2003; Edwards 2008; Bartsch and Wray 2009.

mental exercises, spurred on by edifying quotations from Epicurus and vignettes of inspirational fortitude on the part of both philosophers and statesmen. Later letters pursue increasingly complex issues in Stoic ethics. From the outset, time, in particular the right use of time, is a pressing concern. The letters articulate a range of strategies to enable the would-be philosopher to overcome challenges to his self-possession, above all the fear of death.[9] Like Cicero's letters to Atticus, Seneca's letters have a single addressee, Lucilius (to whom *On Providence* and *Natural Questions* are also dedicated). Yet, while suggesting the *Letters* are addressed as much to himself as to Lucilius (27.1), Seneca clearly envisages a much broader audience (8.6, 21, 64).[10]

For those in search of Seneca's thoughts on his role in Nero's government, the *Letters* can seem a disappointment. Much of Seneca's life was spent in Rome, but the empire's capital is barely mentioned in the *Letters*.[11] *Letter* 91 explores what consolation may be offered to a friend whose hometown, Lyons, has been devastated by fire. This fire apparently struck in the late summer of 64 CE (according to Tac. *Ann.* 16.13.3), thus postdating the terrible fire of Rome (whose ravages are described in *Ann.* 15.38–41). Yet Seneca makes no mention of the earlier disaster, reported by Tacitus to have reduced a large part of the city to smoldering ruin – thus offering Nero a splendid opportunity for palace building.

Nero's shadowy presence may intermittently be sensed in this work, however.[12] The *Letters*' obsessive return to the question of how to live with pain and how to overcome the fear of death probably reflects not only the relatively advanced age of their author (whose life had apparently been dogged by ill health), but also the all-too-likely prospect of a violent death at the hands of the emperor's emissaries; an emperor who had killed his mother would hardly baulk at murdering his tutor. Tacitus, indeed, describes the arrival of the imperial order in 65 CE and Seneca's ensuing suicide, protracted and painful (*Ann.* 15.60–4).[13]

"The wise man will never provoke the anger of those in power," advises Seneca (14.7). In the concluding sections of *Letter* 47, the topic of relations between rulers and their subjects is touched on, through the telling analogy of master and slave; masters, like rulers, are too ready to

[9] Ker 2009. [10] References are to the *Letters* unless otherwise specified.

[11] See Henderson 2004; Edwards forthcoming.

[12] Habinek emphasizes the "double game" of the letters; Seneca steers clear of the emperor while making it obvious how and why he does so (2014: 14–15). Cf. Veyne 2003, esp. chapter 3.

[13] Edwards 2007: 109–12; Ker 2009.

forget their own strength and the weakness of others. In *Letter* 73 Seneca argues at some length that the philosopher above all is grateful to the ruler (here termed *rex*, "king," as in Seneca's earlier *On Clemency*), who, by ensuring the state is secure and peaceful, makes possible a life of philosophical leisure.[14] It is wrong, he asserts, to think of philosophers as stubborn and rebellious (73.1). Seneca seems to be distancing himself from any equation of Stoic philosophy to opposition to the emperor.[15] "Just as a man honours and reveres his teachers, through whose help he has left behind earlier wanderings, so too he regards those under whose protection he is able to put his philosophy into practice" (73.4). Given Nero's treatment of his own teacher and his increasingly errant behavior, it is tempting to see irony in this analogy.

In pursuit of virtue, the would-be wise man, if suitably gifted, might be expected, according to Stoic orthodoxy (as Shadi Bartsch highlights in the preceding chapter of this volume) to undertake a career of public service, the traditional Roman route to distinction;[16] retirement following such a career was also justifiable (*Brev. vit.* 18). But since the Stoics had always conceded that, in a corrupt state, it was better to withdraw from public life (*De otio* 3.3), withdrawal itself could be construed as criticism of the regime. Seneca warns that it may be prudent to cloak such principled withdrawal under the pretext of ill health (68.3–6). He comments earlier in the *Letters*:

> Although people may often have thought that I withdrew (*secessisse*) because of being fed up with state business and regretting my unfortunate and thankless position, still in the retreat to which fear (*timor*) and exhaustion (*lassitudo*) have thrust me, ambition (*ambitio*) is sometimes rekindled. (56.9)

It would be unwise, however, to read any of Seneca's first-person comments as a straightforward reflection of his own experiences; this example serves to illustrate the general claim that even in seclusion, the would-be philosopher is still prey to mental disturbances such as anxiety – and ambition, too.

Yet the distinction a political career offered, as traditionally conceived, is, Seneca implies, devoid of true significance. The rituals and structures of Roman public life surface intermittently in the letters, but Seneca insistently reworks them, translating them into the mind of the

[14] On this letter, see Habinek 2014, Trinacty 2014: 51–3. For the resonance with Seneca's *De beneficiis*, see Griffin 2013: chapter 8.

[15] Seneca's nuanced exploration of this is discussed by Bartsch in Chapter 10 of this volume.

[16] On this issue, see Griffin 1992: 129–71, 315–66.

would-be philosopher. The would-be philosopher should strive for *potestas,* "power," not over others, but over himself; the domain of true *libertas* is not politics or law, but philosophy (75.16–18).[17] Conquering the fear of death is a greater achievement than conquering Carthage (24.10). Contrasting his own letters with those Cicero wrote to Atticus, perpetually fretting about the ins and outs of elections, Seneca advises his own addressee, "see for how many things you are a candidate and vote for none of them" (118.2).

Philosophy, he asserts, offers an alternative and more authentic sphere of achievement, quite distinct from the sordid world of public office. Seneca contends, moreover, that the pursuit of philosophy will bring Lucilius true fame and distinction: *studia te clarum et nobilem efficient* (21.4). *Claritas* (or *claritudo*), "brilliance," is a critical term here. The *Letters* in particular may be seen as redefining the ideal of *gloria*, traditionally conceived as public recognition for achievement and something central to Roman political life. According to Cicero, such *gloria*, provided it depends on the opinion of good men, rather than merely that of the multitude, confers a kind of immortality (*Tusc.* 1.110).[18] Seneca reworks both the notion of "virtue," *virtus* (a term whose connotations were often military for earlier Romans), and the attendant notion of *gloria*, introducing what Newman terms "a new 'interior' relationship" between them.[19] On this view, the intrinsic value of doing the right thing, such as dying for one's country, is not diminished, even if the deed is forgotten (76.29). Moreover, *virtus* is to be shown not primarily on the battlefield, but in the struggle to correct one's own disposition toward "indifferents" (82.12). One can show *virtus* even lying on a sickbed (78.21).[20]

But although *virtus* is interior, if the wise man is not presented with challenges of some kind to overcome, his *virtus* will remain invisible both to himself and to others. The heroic virtue-revealing acts of Cato and of Socrates (often invoked in the *Letters*) play a critical role in spurring others to virtue. The wise man must seek to set an example to others; he has a social responsibility. "The essence of glory for the *sapiens* is providing *exempla*."[21] What he looks for is not praise, but imitation. In *Letter* 102, Seneca distinguishes at length between *fama*, mere popularity, *gloria*, the praise of a virtuous act by others, and, much more precious, *claritas*, the intrinsic brilliance of a truly virtuous act.

[17] Edwards [1997] 2008; Bartsch 2009.

[18] Cf. *Tusc.* 3. 3–4 and Hardie 2012: 19–26, 316–17.

[19] Newman 2008: 319–20. On gladiatorial imagery and an "amphitheatre of textual virtue" (87), see Gunderson 2015: 76–87.

[20] On the interiorization of virtue, see also Roller 2001: 64–126.

[21] Newman 2008: 323–4.

Claritas does not depend on externally expressed praise, but on the desire to move others to virtue through example.[22] The memory of great men enables the value of their good deeds to live on (102.30).

Elsewhere Seneca attacks false glory, that is, when an individual seeks popularity for himself rather than recognition for his virtuous deeds, expressing disapproval of those philosophers who practice their profession for self-advancement, *ambitio*; the applause of the ignorant is valueless (52.9). *Studia*, philosophy, had brought Seneca himself power, influence, and social distinction in Roman public life, as Tacitus underlines (*Ann.* 12.8.2). It is perhaps in his tragedies, particularly the *Thyestes*, where Seneca allows the conflict between desire for earthly power, for fame, for riches, on one hand, and, on the other, the desire for inner peace to play out most explicitly. Atreus craves eternal notoriety (192–3); his brother Thyestes recognizes the value of the peace and tranquility afforded by a life of poverty (446–70), yet ultimately cannot resist Atreus' (deceptive) offer to share the bright light (*clarus nitor*) of kingship (414). He returns to Argos, to an unspeakable fate at his brother's hands. Yet this tension also runs through many of Seneca's prose works. Seneca's wry acknowledgment of the strong pull exerted by worldly achievement, by fame, gives drama to his exhortations to turn toward the pursuit of virtue.

For texts, as well as deeds, might offer inspiration to virtue. Seneca conceives his *Letters* as bringing benefit to others long into the future. The *Letters* offer *exempla* vividly conveyed, ethical instruction, and freshly wrought reconceptions of central philosophical questions. Though Seneca sometimes writes dismissively of the more technical aspects of philosophy, he is himself well recognized as an innovative philosophical thinker.[23] Seneca exploits to the full the insistently personal form of the letter; the literary texture of his work, his often virtuosic style, and his arresting use of imagery are intrinsic to the articulation of his philosophical thought.[24] Seneca himself insists the *Letters* are put together without excessive polish; their style is "unlaboured and plain," *inlaboratus et facilis* (75.1). Though in philosophy, too, there is a place for *ingenium*, "literary talent," his words, he asserts, are intended not to give pleasure, but to help (75.4–5). A recherché style should be seen as

[22] Newman 2008: 327–8.

[23] Underlining his originality, particularly in relation to conceptions of the will, Inwood terms his work "a rare example of first-order Latin philosophy" (2005: 20–1). See also Asmis 2015.

[24] Inwood 2005: 31–3; Roby 2014. On Seneca's use of imagery, see Armisen-Marchetti 2008; Bartsch 2008. On his style more generally, see notably Traina 1987.

morally dubious (114).[25] But his reproof to Lucilius for excessive concern with literary polish also makes clear how much the right style matters (115.1–2). *Letter* 75's insistence on the unimportance of words (75.7) is surely disingenuous; the letters are crafted with extreme care.[26] Seneca was celebrated in his own time not just as a philosopher, but as a brilliant writer (even if Caligula, for one, found his style affected).[27]

The notion that one might as a writer successfully pursue lasting *fama* was central to Roman literary culture.[28] Neronian Rome witnessed a remarkable burgeoning of literary talent; whatever Nero's own abilities, he is reported to have presided over a ferment of competitive poetry writing.[29] As Gowers comments: "Neronian literature, more than that of any other period in Rome, demands to be read in the shadow, or rather the glare, of its ruler."[30] Seneca himself was inevitably implicated in the literary rivalries of the imperial court. His enemies asserted that, as well as monopolizing all the recognition due to oratory, he was writing poetry more often, now that Nero had developed a love of it; for too long nothing in the state was considered distinguished, *clarum*, they alleged, unless it was thought to be Seneca's creation (Tac. *Ann.* 14.52). Petronius, Seneca's younger contemporary, seems to parody the moralizing style of the *Letters* in his *Satyricon*; epigrams attributed to Seneca offer a pointed response.[31]

The *Letters* themselves, it can be argued, bear significant traces of this deeply competitive literary culture. Seneca's addressee, Lucilius, is presented as a man of acclaimed literary talents. Seneca repeatedly refers to Lucilius' literary works, commenting, for instance: "you have become a public figure through the strength of your literary talent, the elegance of your writings and your friendships with distinguished men" ("in medium te protulit ingenii vigor, scriptorum elegantia, clarae et nobiles amicitiae," 19.3–4). *Letter* 46 is entirely devoted to praise of Lucilius' writing, as Seneca describes his own excitement at reading a new piece; it shows true *ingenium*, "literary talent." Later in the series, *Letter* 79 opens with a request for Lucilius' report on the natural features of Sicily, particularly the volcano Aetna.[32] Seneca here characterizes

[25] Graver 1998. [26] See notably the analysis of Henderson 2004. [27] Suet. *Calig.* 53.
[28] Hardie 2012.
[29] For Nero's poetry writing, see Tac. *Ann.* 14. 16. 1; Suet. *Nero* 10. 2, 52; Sullivan 1985; Baldwin 2005.
[30] Gowers 1994: 131.
[31] Sullivan 1985: 174–5 argues the *cena Trimalchionis* episode of the *Satyricon* engages particularly with *Letter* 47.
[32] An inquiry that resonates with the concerns of *Natural Questions*, composed around the same time (Williams 2014).

Lucilius' devotion to writing poetry as a vice, *morbus*. Nothing can dissuade Lucilius from indulging his urge to write a poem on Aetna; it is a subject no serious poet could overlook. Virgil had covered it fully, but that did not deter Ovid, Seneca notes.[33] Of course the only impediment to Lucilius outdoing Virgil and Ovid may be his own modesty, his reverence for earlier masters, *tanta tibi priorum reverentia* (79.8). But Seneca also perhaps hints at the risk involved in literary aspiration; Lucilius' Aetna, *Aetna tua*, might collapse, fall flat, he warns, blurring the distinction between the volcano itself and the poem (79.10). When it comes to philosophy as opposed to literature, however, such concerns are unnecessary. Here, competition is not an issue; whatever the different personal qualities of those who have attained wisdom, in *virtus* they are all equal (79.9). Philosophical achievement is thus apparently uncoupled from ambition, which drives the desire to stand out for literary achievement.

True *gloria*, Seneca argues, is that which follows virtue; it is virtue's shadow (79.13).[34] The following sections of the letter make clear that such glory, in the sense of recognition by good men, may sometimes be manifest only in the distant future; individuals of outstanding virtue have often gone unrecognized in their own lifetimes. Seneca's examples here include Greek philosophers (Democritus, Socrates), as well as Roman statesmen (Rutilius, Cato). The writings of Epicurus' companion Metrodorus make plain that, while the two of them might remain obscure in their own lifetime, those who followed in their footsteps would win renown (79.15). As a route to lasting fame, philosophy, Seneca seems to argue, trumps literary achievement.

Seneca's insistence on the intrinsic value of virtue for itself seems in tension with his assertion of the fame its leading exponents will attain among future generations.[35] The terms in which this claim is made deserve scrutiny. In commenting on the prospect of future glory, Seneca observes: "even if envy has imposed silence on all your contemporaries" ("etiam si omnibus tecum viventibus silentium livor indixerit," 79.17). The word *livor* occurs only here in the *Letters*. This striking term is one Roman poets repeatedly used to defy their critics and rivals. Ovid, for instance, in *Amores* 1.15, dismisses the carping of *livor edax*, "biting envy"; his commitment to poetry is what will win him "lasting fame,"

[33] Presumably an allusion to *Aeneid* 3. 570–87 and *Metamorphoses* 15. 340–55. Schönegg, in his discussion of this letter 1999: 179–94, lists further examples at 184. See also Trinacty 2014: 9–12 on the treatment of literary *aemulatio* here.

[34] Cf. Cic. *Tusc.* 3. 3–4.

[35] Newman's attempt to resolve this in 2008: 321 is not ultimately convincing.

fama perennis (1.15.6), just as Virgil's work will be celebrated as long as Rome rules the world (1.15.25–6). Ovid's later *Metamorphoses* deploys this trope in a much more disturbing context. The supremely talented human weaver Arachne has been challenged to a competition by the goddess Athena. Having described in detail the brilliant tapestry created by Arachne, which depicts scenes of metamorphosis – and the gods' cruelty to humans (and is often read as figuring for Ovid's own poem), the poet comments: "neither Pallas nor envy could find anything to criticise in that work" (*Met.* 6.129–30).[36] Enraged (by being outdone? by what Arachne's tapestry shows?), Athena transforms the creator of this subversive masterpiece into a spider. For readers of Seneca's time, aware that Ovid himself was condemned to languish at the empire's edge by the divine rage of Augustus, the parallels between weaver and poet, between deity and emperor, must have been irresistible.[37] Might this confrontation between an outspoken and brilliantly talented human artist and a powerful and capricious deity have had an echo in relations between Seneca and Nero, who, himself undoubtedly prone to *livor*, resenting both the content of his tutor's advice and the superior *claritas* of his talents, would shortly give the order for Seneca's death?

The Rome of Virgil and Ovid was already celebrated as golden in Augustus' day, the metaphorical refulgence a transcendent manifestation of the newly restored temple roofs, shining golden on the Capitoline Hill; Augustus' own home, by contrast, was conspicuously frugal.[38] Nero, disdaining such domestic simplicity, had constructed for himself in the wake of the fire of 64 CE a new palace, the Golden House, Domus Aurea, the most conspicuous symptom of a new and more material golden age.[39] Even before this, as coins attest, Nero was identifying himself with the chariot-driving sun god Apollo.[40] Luxurious building looms large among the vices of his age castigated by Seneca, who excoriates at length colored marbles and elaborate water features (*Letters* 86, 122). In *Letter* 115, Seneca returns to criticism of those who think wealth is the greatest good; we should admire rather the true *splendor* of virtue (115.3), to which the gleam of shining riches, *divitiarum radiantium splendor*, is liable to blind us (115.6–7). Poets, he contends, should be held to account for celebrating (in words he takes

36 On this episode and its meta-poetic significance, see Johnson 2008: 74–95.

37 See Fredrick 2003: 223–7 for a discussion of the legacy of Ovid's treatment of Arachne in the time of Domitian.

38 *Capitolia ... aurea nunc* (Virg. *Aen.* 8. 347–8); *nunc aurea Roma est* (Ovid *Ars* 3. 113). On the resonance of golden imagery in Augustan Rome, see Barker 1996.

39 See La Rocca, Chapter 13 in this volume.

40 Champlin 2003: 112–44, 209.

from Ovid *Metamorphoses* 2.1–2), "The Sun-god's palace, high with lofty pillars, bright (*clara*) with flashing gold" or (quoting another passage from the same book of the *Metamorphoses*) the sun's chariot, also forged from gold. Also reprehensible are those who celebrate an era by terming it "a golden age," *saeculum aureum* (115.13). Champlin persuasively reads this letter as a denunciation of Nero's solar ideology, contrasted with true light of philosophy (*Ep.* 115.6–7) – a pointed attack on the new golden age of Nero.[41]

Letters might seem a low-key, "private" genre of writing, not the obvious route to literary renown. But in *Letter* 21, consoling Lucilius, who is apparently concerned that withdrawal from public life may lead to obscurity, Seneca makes the claim that Cicero's letters did more to preserve Atticus' name than all the latter's connections with the imperial family (21.4–5). A few decades after Seneca, Pliny the Younger, publishing his own elegantly articulated letter collection, also anticipates, at least implicitly, that they will make his correspondents and those he writes about famous.[42] For Pliny, letter writing did indeed turn out to be a path to the literary *gloria* he so desired;[43] Seneca is for him an important (if not explicitly acknowledged) forerunner.[44] But in *Letter* 21, celebrated letter writers (Epicurus, as well as Cicero) are not the only precedents Seneca invokes; he also quotes (at 21.5) Virgil's apostrophe in the *Aeneid* to Nisus and Euryalus, the young Trojan heroes killed in battle against the Latins, promising them, if his own poem has any power, undying fame, so long as rites are still celebrated on the Capitoline (*Aen.* 9.446–9). Virgil (followed by Ovid and Horace) is the author cited most often in the collection.[45] Cicero's letters to Atticus are also flecked with quotations from literary works (particularly Homer), but in Seneca's letters, the engagement with poetry is a more strategic one.[46]

Despite the recognition now accorded their literary qualities, the specifically literary ambition of Seneca's letters is not always fully appreciated.[47] Following the first three books, comprised mainly of shorter letters, *Letter* 33 marks a turning point.[48] Here Seneca advises Lucilius that he will no longer be offering easily digestible morsels of Epicurus (a feature marking most of the earlier letters). Rather, Lucilius'

[41] Champlin 2003: 127–9. [42] Cf., e.g., 3. 16 and 3. 11.
[43] Fitzgerald 2007: 191–2, noting esp. *Ep.* 9. 11. Cf. Hardie 2012: 315–21.
[44] Marchesi 2008: 14–15.
[45] Mazzoli 1970. On Seneca's engagement with Virgil in Letters 53–7, see Berno 2006.
[46] On Cicero's use of quotations, see White 2010: 101–9.
[47] Among the exceptions, Schönegg 1999.
[48] Suggestively analyzed by M. Wilson 2001: 179–84.

impressive philosophical progress has equipped him to engage with written texts and with Stoic philosophy itself as integrated wholes. Aesthetic unity is also important (33.5).[49] Earlier in this letter, which counsels against taking tags from larger works, Seneca nevertheless includes a short quotation from Ovid's *Metamorphoses*, "It's a poor man's trait to count his livestock" (33.4; *Met.* 11.824). Commentators have struggled to see a larger significance in this four-word phrase, taken from the clumsy courtship speech of Polyphemus (*Met.* 13.824). Seneca quotes thirty times (though, as we have seen, not always with approval) from Ovid's epic, a poem to which Lucilius is said to be particularly partial.[50] The programmatic opening lines of Ovid's poem (1.1–4), in which he declares his intention to tell of forms changed into new bodies, are perhaps relevant to Seneca's philosophical project; both works, though in different ways, are profoundly concerned with subjectivity, with transformation.[51] Ovid's project does not conceal its towering literary ambition. Seneca's epistolary project is, it might be argued, no less ambitious in its scope.

Seneca asserts in this letter that the elements of Stoic philosophy should be seen as *perpetua* (33.7). This term, invoked by Ovid in the opening lines of the *Metamorphoses*, his *perpetuum . . . carmen,* is one itself associated with lasting literary glory.[52] *Letter* 33 ends making a grand claim to novelty, both philosophical and literary. Seneca advises that one must not follow the lead of others unquestioningly. "Shall I not follow in the footsteps of earlier generations? Indeed I shall use the old road, but if I find one that is shorter and more level, I shall lay a new one" (33.11). This imagery engages with similar claims by earlier Roman (and Greek) writers, notably Lucretius. In terms of philosophy, Seneca's assertion diverges from that of Lucretius with respect to Epicurus; Lucretius promises, when it comes to doctrine, to follow faithfully in Epicurus' footsteps (*DRN* 3.3–4).[53] As a Stoic, Seneca aims to add something new rather than be content with established doctrines.[54] But with regard to literary form, Seneca's promise echoes Lucretius' insistence on the pioneering nature of his poetic project: "I traverse the pathless tracts of the Muses, untrodden yet by any other" (*DRN* 1.926–7).[55]

[49] Graver 1998: 627. [50] *Q Nat.* 4a. 2. 2; cf. Mazzoli 1970: 240; Setaioli 2000: 178–9.

[51] For the attainment of Stoic perfection as a kind of transformation, see, with verbal echoes of *Met.* 1. 1: *quaedam processu priorem exuunt formam et in nouam transeunt*, 118. 17.

[52] An explicit preoccupation of Seneca's Letter 21, discussed previously. On *perpetuum . . . carmen*, see Barchiesi 2005 *ad* Ovid *Met.* 1. 4.

[53] As Setaioli observes 2000: 210.

[54] Maso 1999: 99. Cf. Nussbaum 1994: 345–53; Asmis 2015.

[55] Kenney 1970 reads Lucretius' untraversed path as a Callimachean motif. This imagery is also deployed by, e.g., Horace *Ep.* 1. 19. 21–4.

Seneca's concern with literary *aemulatio* is especially evident in *Letters* 73–9.[56] *Letter* 73, one of the few in the collection to reflect explicitly on the relationship between philosophers and rulers (as noted earlier), underlines the debt of gratitude the philosopher owes to the ruler who makes his life of contemplative leisure possible. Seneca (at 73.10–11) quotes Virgil's first *Eclogue*: "O Meliboeus, a god made for us this leisure. For to me he shall always be a god" (*Ecl.* 1.6–7). If the shepherd is grateful for the chance to play his rustic reed (*Ecl.* 1.9–10), how much more grateful, asks Seneca, must the philosopher be for the opportunity to pursue a life of true virtue? Is Seneca here casting himself as Virgil to Nero's Augustus? A few lines later, the dominant Virgilian text is rather the *Aeneid*. The words *itur ad astra*, "this is the way to the stars," put in the mouth of the philosopher Sextius (73.15), are taken from Apollo's address to Aeneas' son (*Aeneid* 9.641). Often in the *Letters*, the would-be philosopher, striving toward virtue, takes on the mantle of the epic hero, laboring on his mission to found a city he will never himself see. One with the right mental preparation is put off by nothing; even when he knows his fellow citizens will soon forget his bravery, he spurs himself on to face suffering with the words of Aeneas to the Sibyl (76.33, citing *Aeneid* 6.103–5). At 77.12, the would-be wise man reminds himself, with the Sibyl's words, of the inexorable nature of fate (*Aeneid* 6.376). At 78.15, Seneca advises that, wracked with the suffering of illness, one should repeat to oneself the words of Aeneas, "perhaps one day the memory of this sorrow will bring pleasure" (*Aeneid* 1.203). While *Letter* 79, explicitly pitting Ovid against Virgil, may advise Lucilius to shift his sights from literary *aemulatio* with its attendant anxieties to the serenity of philosophy, the finely wrought literary texture of the *Letters*, their creative engagement with Virgil and Ovid, betrays Seneca's own ambition to create a new kind of literary masterwork.

Seneca's *Letters* constitute a vastly ambitious philosophical project, a self-help guide to becoming the perfect Stoic, transcending worldly concerns. Forswearing ambition, Seneca had conspicuously withdrawn from the Roman political scene. Yet, even while they celebrate the superiority of true philosophical *claritas* to the illusory gleam of worldly achievement, the *Letters* also manifest a literary competitiveness, intrinsic to Roman elite culture but given a particular inflection at the court of the would-be emperor of the arts, Nero. Seneca dazzles with his intense

[56] Suggestively discussed by Trinacty 2014: 9–12, 51–9, who contrasts Seneca's use of *Eclogue* 1 at 73. 10–11, with treatments at *Ben.* 4.6.4–5 and *Thyestes*.

imagery, his gripping analogies, with his reworking of Cicero, Virgil, and Ovid; the world of Roman politics is interiorized, the philosopher becomes an epic hero on his journey of self-generated metamorphosis. If *Letter* 73 figures the philosopher as a deferential Virgilian shepherd, secure, he hopes, in his contemplative *otium*, the trajectory of Seneca's career, the circumstances of his end, suggest a more compelling resemblance to the heroic survivor of Troy's fall or ultimately, perhaps rather, to the exiled poet, who, even on the very edge of the Roman Empire, insisted on goading the emperor – and championing the superior power of literature.

Further Reading

Miriam Griffin's 1992 treatment of Seneca's relationship to Nero is both accessible and scholarly, while the briefer but more recent biography of Emily Wilson 2014 is also engaging and perceptive. Margaret Graver and A. A. Long 2015 offer a modern translation of all the letters, accompanied by an informative introduction and notes. Fitch 2008 brings together a number of often cited essays, several of which focus on the *Letters*, while Henderson 2004 offers a powerful, if sometimes elliptical, analysis of their literary and political articulation. Bartsch and Schiesaro 2015 includes numerous essays engaging with aspects of the *Letters*.

Part IV

Nero's Monumental Rome

12: Art and the Decadent City

Caroline Vout

12.1 All that Glitters . . .

If Augustus found Rome a city of brick and left it a city of marble,[1] Nero added gold dust. Each of the Julio-Claudians did his bit to maintain and improve Augustus' cityscape, aware that Rome was now an imperial capital and his impact on it an index of his abilities as emperor. Nero was no exception, erecting a bathhouse, gymnasium, and temporary amphitheater on the Campus Martius before the fire of 64 CE, and after it, ensuring that a stronger, safer, more ordered city rose from its ashes.[2] According to Tacitus, this new Rome enjoyed a "decor" or beauty befitting its status, with avenues flanked by buildings as radical in their design as they were rich in materials.[3] But not everyone was convinced: as with Hausmann's Paris, many preferred the appearance of the old city. Without the jumble of high-rise *insulae* and narrow, meandering streets, the sun, and the emperor, shone *too* brightly.[4]

After Nero's enforced suicide in 68 CE, the heat generated by his building and by his art more broadly grew more intense. The ensuing civil war made Vespasian's inauguration the following year all the more momentous, and his and his immediate successors' investment in the idea of a "*Roma resurgens*," Rome resurrected, made Nero's demise all the more spectacular. If this need for restoration was to convince, then the city had to have been on its last legs; either that, or to have strayed so far from its roots as to have become an alien or anti-Rome, closer to Alexandria than to the Rome of Augustus, Servius Tullius, and

[1] Suet. *Aug.* 28.3.

[2] Beste and von Hesberg 2013. On Augustan building, Zanker (1987) 1988, Favro 1996, and Haselberger 2007.

[3] Tac. *Ann.* 15.43: "These reforms, welcomed for their utility, also brought 'decor' to the new city."

[4] Tac. *Ann.* 15.43: "There were those, however, who believed that the old form had been more salubrious, since the narrow streets and high buildings were not penetrated by the rays of the sun. But now the open space, unprotected by any shade, glowed with a more intense heat."

Romulus.[5] As Vespasian and his sons made their mark on the landscape by erecting their own buildings, most famously the Colosseum, Nero's projects were rebranded and his statues defaced.[6] It is in this light that we must read the ancient literary sources about his reign, almost all of them, including Tacitus, posthumous. Suetonius sums up this negative feeling when at about the same time he concludes, "In nothing was he [Nero] more ruinous than in his building."[7] In keeping the empire in his family, Vespasian established a new Flavian dynasty, the trajectory of which demanded that the Julio-Claudian regime had a beginning, middle, and, crucially, an end, with Nero as tipping point. Everything about the Neronian city came to signal decadence.

This rhetoric weighs heavy even today: for every bit of Neronian art to survive from antiquity, there is a damning anecdote about Nero's extravagance. These anecdotes prove particularly difficult to navigate where the remains of his Domus Aurea are concerned, a private palace so extensive as to turn Rome into a house, and this house into the equivalent of several cities, complete with fields (or so Suetonius would have us believe).[8] But they infect all of his visual culture, making all of it evidence of the conspicuous consumption that comes of tyranny.[9] Even Nero's portraiture is seen as proof of his incontinence, the busts produced after his mother's death in 59 CE, and fortunate enough to escape destruction after his demise, widely recognized as capturing the bloated features of a megalomaniac.[10] When, at the end of the nineteenth century, Oscar Wilde sought to make a statement as a decadent and a dandy, it is unsurprising that he should have imitated the curls of these very portraits.[11]

What is "Neronian" about Nero's portraits once put back into a Rome prior to 68 CE, or about the wall paintings of the Domus Aurea, or of other buildings in Italy, many of them never subject to his direct patronage? Scholars are divided on how to tackle this issue: some of them prefer to stay with(in) the rhetoric and to examine how ancient authors manipulated his building to contribute to his construction as

[5] On the idea of Nero as the enemy of Rome and his city as alien, see Woodman 1998: 168–88.

[6] Davies 2000 and Varner 2004: 46–85.

[7] Suet. *Nero* 31.1.

[8] Suet. *Nero* 31.1 and 39.2. And symptomatic of the problems of navigation, e.g., Hales 2003: 74: "The Domus Aurea was presented as decimating the city faster than the most determined B-movie monster. . . . Nero's power as Roman emperor eclipsed the city. . . . Although the palace certainly did encroach on once public territory, the threat to Rome was principally rhetorical rather than physical. . . . On the other hand, the Domus Aurea would have seemed a hugely innovative project."

[9] In the same league as his gilding of Pompey's theater (Plin. *HN* 33.54; Dio 62.6.1–2) or having his mules shod in silver and those of his second wife in gold (Suet. *Nero* 30.3; Plin. *HN* 33.140).

[10] See, e.g., Kleiner 1992: 139.

[11] Sherard 1916: 45.

a tyrant;[12] others work hard to liberate his monuments and rediscover their primary aesthetic.[13] Either his art is fashioned *ex post facto*, or is deemed, in compensation almost, so innovative in execution and design as to count as a *creatio ex nihilo.* Architectural historians speak of a "revolution in architectural technology and taste" and a new "semantics of form" to acclaim a golden age scripted from his accession.[14]

This chapter charts a different course, stressing neither the novelty of Nero's image making nor the impact of his character or condemnation, but Neronian art's inbuilt inclination toward exaggeration and deconstruction. When Nero came to power in 54 CE at the age of sixteen, the world had witnessed some eighty years of imperial representation, by which point the dead Julius Caesar, Augustus, his wife, Livia, Claudius, and Caligula's sister Drusilla had all been deified. This stairway to heaven, or slippery slope, begged bolder iconographies to invigorate what was quickly becoming a formula. Nero's extraordinary youth demanded its explosion. If the weak and feeble Claudius could be given the body of Jupiter, and even the first Princeps Augustus be commemorated by a colossal, bare-breasted statue in the theater at Arles,[15] what tricks were left for Nero's artists? Not being a man like other men was already a complex status to manage. What to do when the emperor in question was a boy? Beyond the palace, wealthy Romans, increasing numbers of freedmen among them, were themselves after new things to do with a visual language inherited from Greece and from elites close to the court. There was only so much continuity even a copying culture like Rome could take. As we are about to discover – by turning first to Nero's portraiture and then, briefly by way of the Domus Aurea, to Roman painting more broadly – the art of the period had its own reasons, Nero's reputation for despotism aside, for finding its peculiar "wow factor" in self-indulgence.

Gilding the Lily

Not that this will lead us to ignore the ancient literature. Pliny the Elder, who lived through Nero's reign, describes in a work dedicated to Vespasian's son, Titus, how Nero had been so delighted (*delectatus*) by

[12] Elsner 1994.
[13] At the most extreme, Ball 2003, which omits ancient authors from its index.
[14] Boethius and Ward Perkins 1970: 211 and Beste and von Hesberg 2013: 329.
[15] E.g., Claudius, 42–3 CE: Vatican, inv. 243 and Augustus, variously dated, from the late first century BCE to the beginning of the first century CE, Arles, Musée départemental Arles Antique, inv. P.215. On the latter, see La Rocca 2013: cat. no. IX. 2.

a statue of Alexander the Great made by Alexander's most famous sculptor, Lysippus, that he had ordered it to be gilded – a further example of his obsession with gold functioning as an index of his extravagance.[16] But there is more to the story, for the increase in the object's monetary value so damaged its aesthetic value that the gilding had to be removed, leaving it pricier still, even with the scars (*cicatricibus*) left by his intervention. The statue was also, significantly, of Alexander as a youth. It is surely no accident that it was a representation of the *young* dynast that this adolescent emperor was passionate to graffiti.

There are many ways of reading this passage. All art collecting changes the object in question, and paying homage to Alexander's image was simply *de rigueur* at this point in Rome's imperium: at the end of the Republic, Pompey's portrait had already borrowed the central lock of hair or cowlick characteristic of Alexander, and Suetonius and other sources conjure Julius Caesar, Augustus, and Caligula all visiting his gold-encased corpse in Alexandria. Caligula goes so far as to plunder his breastplate, as respect for a leader of the past debases and elevates that leader and transmutes into unhealthy obsession with monarchical government.[17] There is a real sense in which all the moves vis-à-vis this icon have been made by the time Nero comes along – except for putting a premium on redundancy and on the damage inflicted by adherence.[18] Pliny's word *cicatricibus* is as Roman as it is graphic: it is as though the scars Nero inflicted personalize both image and referent, turning Alexander into a Republican hero like Marcus Sergius, who was wounded twenty-three times in the Second Punic War, his body so broken that only his spirit remained.[19] And ironically, they increase Alexander's greatness, evoking perhaps his own near fatal wounding.[20] By refusing to respect Lysippus' ideal form, they make his statue more articulate.

Not that Lysippus himself was a great respecter of tradition: as Pliny goes on to note, he "is said to have contributed greatly to sculpture by representing the details of the hair and by making his heads smaller than the old sculptors used to do, and his bodies more slender and firm, to make his statues seem taller . . . He used commonly to say that whereas his predecessors had made men as they really were, he made them as they

[16] Plin. *HN* 34.63 and on the statue in the context of Nero's art collection, Moormann 1995: 308.

[17] Spencer 2009.

[18] Augustus is reputed to have broken off a piece of Alexander's nose as he bent to kiss his corpse (Dio 51.16.5), but this is more about the corruptibility of all human flesh.

[19] Plin. *HN* 7.104.

[20] Alex. *Anab.* 6.10.1. And on Alexander's proclivity for wounds more broadly, Sternberg 2006: 109–10.

seemed to be."[21] There is something apt in Nero's enthusiasm for this sculptor, an artist who understands that the artfulness of art lies neither in seamless tradition nor a straightforward relationship to the real (mimetic or deceptive), but in its illusionary honesty. All of the art in this chapter shares this frankness about its artifice, a refusal to cite existing tropes without being self-conscious about this citation. Sometimes, as with Nero's portraiture, this results in a nigh-on rejection of the classicism that had defined the Julio-Claudians since Augustus, at other times, as with wall painting, in a celebration and magnification of *trompe l'oeil* techniques so as to make mistakes of the kind that the artist Zeuxis made when he sought to pull back the painted curtain of his rival Parrhasius impossible,[22] or, through clever use of scale and perspective, in what we might call a "theorization" of representation that threatens to collapse the distinction with the real world entirely.[23] This visual culture turns out to be as formative of Nero's reputation as his subsequent reputation is formative of interpretations of him, the period, and its artworks.

Nero's Portraits

Nero's portraiture is a marked departure from the portrait types of his imperial predecessors. After Agrippina's assassination in 59 CE, his image makers turned their backs on the brushed-forward hairstyles preferred by previous Julio-Claudians in favor of a more obviously styled style with a row of parallel curls worn wreath-like across the forehead.[24] By 64 CE, this exuberance had spread to his facial features, giving a doughy quality that revels in the softness of the sculpted form (Figures 12.1 and 12.2). This portrait type not only flies in the face of the "ageless perfection of Augustan classicism"[25] as represented by the Primaporta statue[26] and by the heads of Gaius and Lucius Caesar, Tiberius, and Caligula, but also of the more "veristic" features of Claudius, which blurred this classicism with the more drawn looks of Rome's Republican senators.[27] Nero's realism is different from this and from its possible origins in Hellenistic sculpture or Italic works – less a sunken or "lived-in" face marked by experience, than a face puffed by ambition and good living. One scholar, led, in part, by the emphasis in ancient texts on the gluttony of Nero and of tyrants more widely, describes the effect as follows: "the emperor ostentatiously

[21] Plin. *HN* 34.65. [22] Plin. *HN* 35.65. [23] Lorenz 2013.
[24] Welch 2002:135 describes this decision as a "rottura," a "breach" or "breakdown."
[25] Kleiner 1992: 162. [26] After 20 BCE, Vatican Museums, inv. 2290.
[27] On "verism," see Pollini 2012: 39–68, with bibliography.

12.1 Portrait of Nero, 55–9 CE, Museo Nazionale, Cagliari, inv. 6122 (Photo: DAIR 66.1946).

confessed to a life of indulgence as visually expressed through fatness, a double chin, and small eyes sunk into the surrounding flesh."[28]

Ancient society, however, is less interested in the fatness (and relative slimness) of male or female bodies than we might at first imagine, especially given our own culture's obsessions.[29] Indeed, I would go so far as to say that the "fatness" of Nero's mature portrait, if that is what it was for those confronted with it in the 60s CE, is less a statement about his lifestyle than about his art's style, his features swollen as the Farnese Hercules' muscles are swollen,[30] similarly pushing their visual prototypes to inflated levels where the only additional move left is bursting. In a sense, Nero had to look like this: as Virgil's Anchises predicted (in comparing Rome with Greece, but perhaps too with reference to Augustan imagery): "others will mould the breathing bronze in softer ways and will bring living faces from the marble."[31] When Nero had come to power in 54, a classic Julio-Claudian mask served him well, its forward fringe and broad cranium making him look like the biological son he was not, and the logical conclusion to a story of imperial succession that had been predestined from the beginning. But after 59, the story had to change. Coins showing Nero and his mother's profiles opposite or

[28] Bergmann 2013: 336. Also Bradley 2011: 31 and 33.

[29] Here I am at odds with Bradley 2011. Although "tryphé" or overindulgence was a mark of the tyrant, there is far less indication in Greek or Roman art or text that weight was an issue.

[30] Naples, National Archaeological Museum, inv. 6001.

[31] Verg. *Aen.* 6.847–8.

12.2 Portrait of Nero, 64–8 CE, Worcester Art Museum, inv. no. 1915.23 (Photo: Museum).

cheek to cheek were explicit about her being "his ticket to ride"; after her murder, Nero had no alternative but to assert his independence.[32] Augustus' portrait types had set the precedent of only minor aging, suspending his imperial body in a semi-divine state as his human body labored into its seventies. Growing old was not yet suffered by the imperial image. But, for Nero, growing *up* became imperative: and he achieves it both by his portraiture, which eventually makes him seem so much larger than life, and by his penchant for the colossal, most famously embodied by the bronze he commissioned for the vestibule of his Domus Aurea in 64–8 CE.[33] Scholars are split over whether it ever depicted Nero, but at more than thirty meters in height, the statue, which rivaled Lysippus' Tarentine Zeus (by then in Rome) and the Colossus of Rhodes (by then collapsed), is further evidence of Neronian distention.

[32] From 54 CE, Mattingly 1923: 200, nos. 1 and 2 and from 55 CE, 201, nos. 7 and 8.
[33] Note also the colossal canvas of Nero in the Horti Maiani, an "insanity of the age" (Plin. *HN* 35.51).

Nero's love of "going large" swallows the sugarcoating of previous imagery, pushing the age-old equation between marble and flesh and man and god[34] to its limit. In so doing, it accentuates the "making" in image making, whether that is in the machinery needed to construct a colossus, the "increased plasticity and textural contrast" of his portraits,[35] or the artifice of his and his mother's sculpted hairstyles,[36] which suggest hours with the curling tongs. These curls underline that there is nothing natural about any of this. As is the case with images of Louis XIV,[37] the emphasis is on constructed-ness, as the emperor and his court consciously perform the imperial role in ways that draw attention to its cultivation. This, in turn, draws attention to the artifice of all imperial portraits and appearances, exposing the "habitus" (the systems of styles, bodily skills)[38] unexamined within them, and short-circuiting the charges of delusion leveled at Caligula. Nero's portraits may look more realistic than those of Augustus and his heirs, but like Lysippus' statues, their power is in their seeming.

Roman Painting

If we want to think about Neronian art more broadly, we could do worse than return to his Domus Aurea, a site that gives its name to the "Grotesque" (after the decoration of its cave-like rooms or "grottoes" that were back-filled in later imperial building activity and rediscovered underground in the Renaissance). This decoration is, on the surface, the complete antithesis of the engorged aesthetic of Nero's sculpture – attenuated, airy, unrealistic.[39] But it is no less monstrous than the colossal, its figurative elements tapering into vegetation or ornament to produce chimeric creatures that hover between the real and the imaginary, the physical and insubstantial, the symbolic and inane. "With the grotesque, representation was simultaneously invoked and discredited,"[40] interrogated as it was in Nero's portraits by putting air-brushing under the microscope. The palace's painter, Famulus, is both "florid" and "dignified and old-school" (*grauis ac seuerus*), notorious for a Minerva who invariably meets every viewer's gaze.[41]

[34] He also adopts more attributes in later years including the radiate crown of divine Augustus as both an honorific emblem and a solar attribute, linking him with Sol-Apollo: Bergmann 1998.

[35] Kleiner 1992: 139. [36] Wood 1999: 297. [37] Burke 1992.

[38] On "habitus," see Bourdieu 1977.

[39] Although note that the "tryphé" of note 29 can mean "daintiness" as well as "luxury."

[40] Harpham 1982: 178. Not that Nero's artists invented grotesques (Vitr. 7.5.3–4).

[41] Plin. *HN* 35.120.

12.3 Central octagonal of vault mosaic showing Odysseus and the Cyclops, room 13, Domus Aurea, Rome, 64–8 CE (Photo: DAIR 70.2074).

Similarly knowing is the octagonal mosaic medallion high in the vault of the palace's nymphaeum, which depicts Odysseus handing a cup of wine to Polyphemus (Figure 12.3), a subject rendered in three dimensions in the main niche of Claudius' dining grotto at Baiae on the Bay of Naples.[42] Not only do the colored glass tesserae give the protagonists a strangely plastic quality that has them resemble (and dissemble as) a bronze sculptural group, but the conceit of looking up to see into the giant's cave further disorientates, as though everything is topsy-turvy and the viewer as inebriated as the Cyclops. Where does the boundary between the respectful and the ridiculous or the inventive and the decadent lie? As with postmodern irony, where citation is less about

[42] Lavagne 1970; Dunbabin 1999: 241; and Carey 2002. Pumice-stone stalactites made the vault look more cave-like.

commitment to particular pasts than about questioning commitment and sincerity,[43] so Nero's art knows too much, forcing its audience to doubt their perception and place in the universe. In a world as "kitsch" as this, it takes the Golden House to make him feel human.[44]

Nero no more equals Neronian art than Augustus equals imperial art. Beyond the confines of the palace and the tentacles of his patronage and paranoia, wall painting as far afield as Campania showcased similar sublimations and spatial effects, revisiting and amplifying earlier fashions for illusionistic art to create what one art historian has recently called a "pervasive form of virtuality."[45] Proof of this more pervasive phenomenon is found in the dining rooms around a colonnaded garden in a (semi-)public building in Moregine, a suburb south of Pompeii, in which scholars have been keen to see portraits of Nero, his mother, and his second wife, Poppaea.[46] We will return to these identifications presently, but first their visual context, on three red walls of "triclinium A" (Figures 12.4 and 12.5). The figures in question occupy the center of each, framed by trompe-l'oeil architecture: the male carries a lyre, and the two females, on the east and west walls, respectively, a mask and shepherd's crook, and stylus and writing tablet. Flanking them, further out still within separate frames, are six smaller females, two per wall, all positioned on green and gold pedestals, and again laden with attributes. Are they statues? Despite their bases and miniature size, their animate posturing challenges this.

Certainly, the three central figures are Apollo and the Muses, Thalia (comedy) and Calliope (epic poetry). But almost more interesting than the frescoes' content is the way in which they play with perspective, refusing to give guidance on how to respond: Apollo is suspended and anxious, his attention caught by something to his right, Thalia strides forward, contouring the "air" behind her as though it were earth and turning her head to look left, and Calliope pauses as though in self-contemplation. Whose gaze do we follow? And how does this gaze compare to the stare of the smaller figures anchored on their pedestals? Around them, the architectural detail is also multi-perspectival. Do the tiny framed landscapes above the central figures

[43] Colebrook 2004.

[44] On the house's completion, Nero is supposed to have said that he could now live like a human (Suet. *Nero* 31.2). Compare Cicero's criticism of Chrysogonus for believing that his lavish house and lifestyle made him alone human (Cic. *Rosc. Am.* 46.135).

[45] Lorenz 2013: 378. Also 369.

[46] E.g., Mastroroberto 2003 and 2007; Mattusch 2008: 244–7; and Beard 2008: 50. Torelli 2003 dismisses the Neronian identifications on various grounds including chronology, preferring a date prior to the earthquake of 62 or 63 CE, as early as the mid-50s CE.

12.4 North wall of Triclinium A, Moregine, showing Apollo and the Muses Clio and Euterpe, Fourth style, first century CE (Photo: SAP 85182).

12.5 East wall of Triclinium A, Moregine, showing the Muses Urania, Thalia, and Melpomene, Fourth style, first century CE (Photo: SAP 85183).

hang in front, or are they part of the coffered canopy that we can peek up into? Shiny silver vessels sit on sections of balustrade, some of them positioned like urns on a mantle-piece, and others tipped slightly so as to offer a glimpse inside. Yet more metal objects and masks compete for attention with griffin-acroteria, trees, garlands, and birds, some of them perched at precarious angles, their placement so unpredictable as to tease us to try to find them. Only latterly do we note that one of them is a gorgoneion: should we be looking at all?

In the adjacent dining room, where the background is black, not red, the painted architecture is heavier, and the central figures on each of the walls firmly grounded on "marble" thresholds of palatial doorways. In Apollo's place is a female figure, her colossal size accentuated by a little girl who stoops in attendance. The Dioscuri assume this position on the other walls, one of them (on the east) clothed, and the other nude as though of stone, far more sculptural in appearance than the figures on pedestals in the previous triclinium. Is the female their sister Helen, or is she a goddess, as her size might dictate? Is she more or less godlike than them, more of less of a cult statue than her brother to the west? Usually summoned in moments of crisis, and usually identical, are the Dioscuri present because of Helen's kidnap, or because of a crisis in representation? Their refusal to resemble each other flouts artistic expectation.[47]

Faced with visual fields as destabilizing as these, it is unsurprising that scholars have searched for something concrete to grip onto: hence seeing Nero in Apollo. This is the only one of the identifications worth pondering, the fleshiness of the figure's cheeks and rounded chin finding possible resonance in Nero's portraiture, and the overall composition in the image of a laureate Apollo with a lyre on the reverse of coins of Nero issued ca. 62 CE.[48] Upon Nero's accession, Seneca was already likening him, his looks, and his singing to the god of culture and prophecy.[49] The "is it, isn't it?" question adds to the fascination/frustration of Triclinium A's decoration and gets to the heart of image making at this period. Only Apollo's maleness marks him out as special. A focus on him or anything else has been replaced by distraction, as all of the figures, those on the pedestals included, appear less to be looking than listening, and urging their audience to listen also, in pursuit of unseen inspiration. "Far from being mere personifications of the arts, they [the Muses] are rather the expression of the capacity, granted to man alone, for self-reflection and taking a place in history."[50] Dining within this decor affords a bigger boon than an audience with Nero; it realizes art's transportive potential.

Similar games of iconography, scale, and viewpoint define other decorative schemes of the Neronian period or slightly later, such as the frescoes of Pompeii's House of the Vettii.[51] From the moment visitors spied the painted ithyphallic Priapus high up on the west wall of the entrance, the eye was led across the atrium to a marble version of the same

[47] Hermary 1986. [48] Sutherland 1984: 158 and plate 18.

[49] Sen. *Apoc.* 4.1.22–3 and supra, note 34. [50] Walde 2006: 322.

[51] Pompeii VI.15.1: Clarke 1991: 208–35 and Severy-Hoven 2012. These frescoes postdate the earthquake of 62 CE and could be as late as the 70s CE.

figure in the peristyle, its giant phallus drilled so as to spit water into the basin of a fountain. The visual quotation counters the aggressive erections of both of them to attract and repel, collapsing the space from street to garden, and between fresco and sculpture, art and life, turning the house's interior into a quasi-canvas, and animating the god of the painting. In the process, viewers are attuned not just to "seeing," but to "ways of seeing," and their visit transformed into an ekphrasis. The experience inside the house does not disappoint; panels showing everyday sexual activity and edifying mythology populate a number of independent visual programs, many of these panels framed, as at Moregine, by complex architectural settings, containing masks, jugs, and garlands. Compared to earlier paintings of the same story,[52] the painting of Dirce from entertainment room *n* is especially pornographic, the vulnerability and femininity of her body accented by necklaces (or ropes?) around her arms, neck, and torso, and by the paleness of her skin against her bronzed aggressors who press the bull to trample her (Figure 12.6). On the neighboring wall, Pentheus' suffering increases hers, asking viewers to weigh the transgressive actions that have led to these punishments, while opposite her, baby Hercules reveals his divinity by strangling the snakes sent by Hera.[53] The effect is beyond narrative – epiphany. Viewers are put in the witness box to ponder their own hubris and piety.

The discomfort that comes of looking at Dirce or Pentheus' suffering, and the propensity of all of these paintings to do more than describe, but to immerse, and turn narrative into event, develop out of what has been described as an "increasing taste for realism on the stage," when "dramatic scenes that had hitherto been acted out in the theater as mere make-believe could now be actually recreated and played out 'for real'" in the amphitheater.[54] As was the case with Nero's portraits, the power of these dramatic performances lies in them looking like flesh: only gullible spectators at Nero's games thought that the bull in the reenactment of the Pasiphae story was actually penetrating a living girl (though their naïveté shows the extent to which the real and imaginary had become confused).[55] But the more real, the more beyond the frame or unfiltered, until the "good taste" usually associated with connoisseurship was corrupted. Seneca, writing in the late Claudian or Neronian period, transfers Medea's murder of her children from the wings where

[52] E.g., the version from the House of the Grand Duke, Pompeii (VII.4.56), ca. 20–40 CE: Naples, National Archaeological Museum, inv. 9042.

[53] Apollod. Bibliotheca 2.4.8, which includes an alternative account of the snakes' origin.

[54] Coleman 1990: 68.

[55] Suet. *Nero* 12.2. Also relevant here is Petr. *Sat.* 29.1 and Zeitlin 1971: esp. 681–4.

12.6 South wall of room *n* in the House of the Vettii, Pompeii, showing the punishment of Dirce, 62–79 CE (Photo: Alinari).

it had been in Euripides' play onto the stage in front of her husband,[56] and Lucan, forced into suicide by Nero at the age of twenty-five, composes an epic on the conflict between Caesar and Pompey that revels not in the "beautiful death" of Homer's heroes, but in mutilation and self-destruction.[57] Every act of artistic reinterpretation does damage to the source, but, like Nero's statue of Alexander, these find value in dissolution.

Qualis Artifex Pereo[58]

It is common practice to make Nero's patronage, and the Domus Aurea in particular, "an important influence on the decorative fashions of its

[56] See Boyle 2014.

[57] For the concept of the beautiful death, see Vernant [1982] 1991 and as an introduction to Lucan's self-annihilatory imperative, see Bartsch 1997, Dinter 2012a, and Vout, forthcoming. Also relevant here is Gowers 1994 on the thematics of "boiling down" or "over-cooking" in Neronian literature and culture.

[58] Suet. *Nero* 49.1: "What an artist the world loses!"

time, including in middle-class homes" such as the House of the Vettii.[59] But this is to ignore that the style of painting described earlier was already under way in the Claudian period,[60] and but the apogee of an interest in perspective in art that went right back to the Republic.[61] Whereas pre-Claudian perspective impressed viewers by deploying illusionistic windows, doors, and colonnades to make walls recede and dark rooms feel more open or expansive, later examples like those in this chapter confounded viewers either by evading classification or by invading their territory in unsettling ways, turning the wall into "a kind of baroque stage-set" with figures that pressed the issue of commensurability between their world and reality.[62] Neronian art is born of this evolution, and chimes with what was happening in Latin literature, where Tragedy and Epic grabbed their audiences by the throat to question the conviction of their characters. How unseemly would Medea's behavior or Dirce's punishment have to be before they stopped watching? How cruel Caesar's civil war to resent his Julio-Claudian legacy? Rome had long been an empire but, as it expanded under Augustus and its chain of emperors extended, the line between experience and imagination, the mundane and the impossible, became so blurred as to require analysis.

Nero, his art, and his reputation for acting, singing, and aspiring to change nature are as much shaped by this requirement as they are influential on it.[63] How much bigger could Nero's portraiture or palace get and still be understood as belonging to the Roman emperor? His final words, "What an artist the world loses!," are indicative not only of his knowingness, but the knowingness of the period as a whole. It is arguably this self-awareness or heightened sensibility that amounted to "a new semantics of form" and also perhaps to a "revolution in architectural technology" as builders as well as emperors pushed at the limits of what was humanly possible. The emperor had to be master of these experiments and, as an image himself, to inhabit a world as unworldly as the Moregine frescoes, yet a marble flesh as absurdly convincing as the

[59] Pappalardo 2009: 174. Note too de Caro, who wants the influence to go the other way and Villa A at Oplontis near Pompeii to have influenced the Domus Aurea: de Caro 1996: 24.

[60] This style is known as "Fourth style" after Mau's division of Roman painting, and now identified as beginning in the 40s and 50s CE: see Torelli, supra, n. 42 and Strocka 2007: 320: "The Fourth Style under Claudius gives the impression of a fresh new kind of invention, superabundant but delicate in ornamental details. . . . The Neronian Fourth style heightens illusionism."

[61] Stinson 2011 on what Mau classified as "second style" painting.

[62] Ling 2014: 371, and Perrin 2002: 393, who claims that the relationship between the representational and real is now dreamlike.

[63] Useful here is Bartsch 1994.

body of the playacting Pasiphae. The extremity of this position makes the Neronian city a decadent city well before Flavian ascendancy.

Further Reading

The art chapters of the 2013 *Blackwell Companion to the Neronian Age* provide a wealth of material and bibliography within new frameworks. In addition to La Rocca's contribution on the Domus Aurea in Chapter 13 of this volume, I highlight only Meyboom and Moormann 2013, and, on its grotesques, Perrin 1982. Elsner 1994 and Purcell 1987 are important for understanding how the ancient literary discourse of building, and its intersection with issues of identity and "luxuria," impact the Domus' place in the construction of Neronian decadence. The perceived "fatness" of Nero's portraiture and the strange hairstyle of its later types with their rows of curls (see also Suet. *Nero* 51) have long fascinated. See Bergmann 1998 and Vout 2013.

Ling 1991 still provides the fullest history in English of Roman painting based on the "four styles" of German scholar August Mau (1840–1909). New discoveries from areas outside of Vesuvius' reach nuance Mau's dating somewhat: see Strocka 2007. Underrated on Neronian painting in particular is Perrin 2002, and it and Lorenz 2013 are particularly important for the approach taken in this chapter.

13: Staging Nero: Public Imagery and the Domus Aurea

Eugenio La Rocca

Nero understood that the best outlet for his boundless enthusiasm for the arts was in stagecraft and in the grandiose use of theatrical forms that were congenial to his tastes. The masterwork of Neronian stagecraft was the emperor's private imperial house, the Domus Aurea, designed as it was to amaze with surprises and sudden changes of vista. Such effects were achieved by introducing into Rome's heavily populated urban center certain architectural elements that had previously belonged only to rustic and maritime villas, and by fusing those schemes with structures drawn from the world of theatrical production.

Paradoxically, then, even Nero's home represents such a fusing of elements. For the most part, judging from portrait sculptures and coins of the period, as well as from the sparse remains of other kinds of figurative evidence (very little of which can be dated with certainty), the arts of the Neronian age are not characterized by grand innovations, but as novel developments of the traditions established by Nero's Julio-Claudian ancestors (for the chronological development of the portrait sculptures of Nero into four distinct types, see the Appendix to this volume). In fact, some of the more grandly theatrical aspects of Nero's personal character might be explained in terms of the larger tastes and trends of the period. In what follows, I will explore the ways in which these received tastes and trends came together in bold new forms during Nero's reign, in highly theatrical articulations that put Nero on public display as a bearer of light, a rising sun, and the herald of a new golden age.

13.1 A Golden Sun on the Rise

Following a Greek precedent redeployed by Augustus, the sun was conflated with the god Apollo. The resulting solar Apollo was then exploited as a symbol of the emperor's capacity to wield the reins of the empire, and thus to steer the arrival of a new golden age. In literature, the comparison between a newly enthroned Nero and Apollo/Sol appears already in Seneca's *Apocolocyntosis*, the small satiric work written shortly after the death of Claudius. But the turn toward a more complete assimilation of Nero/Sol came about much later. In 63 CE, the twenty-six-year-old emperor contracted an important accord with Vologaeses, the king of the Parthians, concerning the fate of Armenia. As a result of the accord, Tiridates (Vologaeses' brother) agreed to lay the symbols of his kingly rule over Armenia at the feet of an image of Nero and, as if a vassal, to receive them back from the hands of the emperor himself. To confirm the pact, a magnificent spectacle celebrating Armenia's pacification was staged in Rhandeia in Mesopotamia. On one side, squadrons of Armenian cavalry were lined up wearing their tribal uniforms, and on the other side were Roman legions arranged in columns with military insignia and images of the gods. Between them was a raised platform that supported a curule seat, and on the seat was a statue (an *effigies*, according to Tacitus; not one, but several *eikones*, according to Dio) of Nero. Tiridates approached the statue(s) and, after the customary victims were sacrificed, he lifted the diadem from his own head and put it at the feet of the image (*Ann.* 15.29).

Though it was not an actual military victory, the political settlement was celebrated as a triumph in Rome. By decree of the Senate, trophies were erected in Rome and a triumphal arch on the Capitoline. The figurative program of the Capitoline arch can be inferred from coins of the period, which show a single arch with columns protruding at the corners of the piles, with a statue of Mars(?) inserted in a niche on one of the short sides and Nero riding a four-horse chariot on top, situated between a winged victory and a female personification with a cornucopia (Fortuna?) (Figure 13.1).[1] Remains ostensibly belonging to the arch were found during excavations conducted in the area of today's Via del Tempio di Giove. Foundations that may correspond to the slab on which the arch was constructed have also been discovered, along with one of the figured plinths that held the protruding columns. On it were represented female figures, some with wings (certainly Victories) and others without (one of which is well known from a drawing attributed to Fra Giocondo). Behind them one can see the *porticus Triumphi* (Figure 13.2). Numismatic evidence suggests that the side walls inside the arch were decorated with Victories and trophies. Halfway up were dancers whose classical design dates back to the fifth century BCE. Under Augustus they had been used to represent the

[1] On Nero's arch on the Capitoline, see Kleiner 1985 and La Rocca 1992.

13.1 Nero's sestertius of 63 CE ca. Detail of reverse with the Arch of Nero.

sacred dances before the Palladium, a symbol of Rome's eternity. Also attributable to the arch is a depiction of prisoners on the *ferculum* (a triumphal parade float) sitting amid a panoply of arms (Figure 13.3). Unlike the other remains, this fragment was discovered not on the Capitoline, but in the Campus Martius. But the style and iconography make clear that it belongs either to the Arch of Nero, or at least to a Neronian monument dedicated to mark the celebrations of 63 CE (the base of one of the trophies?).

13.2 The Colossus of Sol/Nero, and the Solar Spectacle of 66 CE

Up to this point, Nero's "solar" associations are in keeping with tradition. But beginning in 63 CE, coins were minted at Rome on which

13.2 Column plinth with female figures and Victories, probably from the Arch of Nero on the Capitoline Hill. Rome, Capitoline Museums.

Nero appears with a radiate crown on his head, whether as a portrait (Figure 13.4) or in full figure wearing a toga, sometimes accompanied by his wife (it is unclear whether she is Poppaea Sabina, dead in 65 CE, or Statilia Messalina). The issue of these coins underscores the parallelism between the activities of Augustus and those of Nero – just as with other coins issued for the same occasion showing a closed Temple of Janus and the *Ara Pacis*, both of these explicit references to a new and fertile age of peace and prosperity.

Already at the beginning of his principate Nero had declared his desire to live up to the policies prescribed by Augustus and to follow in his tracks. But there proved to be one big difference between the two: no emperor in Rome, not even Augustus, had dared to wear a radiate

13.3 Fragment of relief with Parthian warrior, probably from the arch of Nero on the Capitoline Hill. Rome, Museo Nazionale Romano.

13.4 Nero's dupondius of 63 CE ca. Obverse: Head of Nero (type 4) with *corona radiata*.

crown. The minting of coins, and perhaps also the raising of statues that featured a radiate image of Nero, must have caused quite a stir in conservative circles. In Rome, where members of the Senate were in theory *primi inter pares*, emperors wisely chose not to go too far in taking on iconographic formulae that would render them godlike. Such "theomorphism" was left to the realms of literature and incised jewelry, genres well suited to honorific and encomiastic representation. Coins showing a radiate Nero likely raised eyebrows. But their daring seems understated when compared to that of the colossal gilded bronze statue Nero installed in the vestibule of his Domus Aurea.[2] The work of Zenodoros, the statue stood between 100 and 120 feet high (between 29.5 and 35.4 meters). It depicted Sol, but it seems to have worn the specific facial features of Nero. The overall design is known from gems (Figure 13.5). Atop the head were seven rays, each one twenty-two feet in length (*Notitia Urbis regionum* XIV 12). It is unknown whether the work was completed while Nero was still alive or in 75 CE during the principate of Vespasian (Dio 66.15.1: at some point, the Colossus was supposed, certainly wrongly, to bear the facial features of Titus). It seems that Hadrian, when he moved the statue toward the Colosseum from its

13.5 Gem. The Colossus in the Flavian age (from a plaster cast). Berlin, Pergamon Museum.

[2] On the Colossus of Nero, see Bergmann 1994. The position of Ensoli 2000 entails a significant reassessment of the statue's size that is, in my opinion, not entirely in keeping with the sources.

13.6 Multiplum of Gordianus III. Reverse: the Colosseum with the Colossus at left and the Meta Sudans at right.

original spot in order to make room for the Temple of Venus and Rome (as on coins issued in the age of Gordian III, Figure 13.6), may have reworked the statue's head in order to erase any resemblance to Nero (*Hist. Aug.*, Hadr., 19, 12 s). Commodus subsequently had the statue's head replaced with a likeness of his own, and by changing the statue's attributes he transformed it from Sol into Hercules (Dio, 73, 22, 3; Herodian., 1, 15, 9; *Hist. Aug.*, Comm. 17, 9 s).

The statue's original version seems to have been ambiguous, in that it could be taken to represent Sol, and not Nero himself. The statue's dedication suggests their assimilation without flatly asserting it. In like manner, on the reverse side of coins that can be dated to just before the emperor's trip to Greece, an image appears of a citharode (a singer who accompanies himself on his *cithar*, a stringed wooden instrument) who resembles Nero, but who, because of his hairstyle, probably represents Apollo himself. And yet even this image poses a further puzzle in that in 67–8 CE, upon his return from his triumphal traverse across the stages and stadia of Greece, statues were dedicated to Nero showing him wearing the clothing of a citharode (Suet. *Nero* 25.2).

Precedents for likening the emperor to Apollo/Sol are known from the age of Augustus.[3] In Nero's case, the symbolic assimilation to Sol may have had a specific motivation in and around the fateful year of 63 CE, a motivation that can be inferred from the grand spectacle that

[3] On Nero's political and cultural references to the age of Augustus, see Picard 1962.

concluded the treaty of peace with the Parthians and Armenians in 66 CE (Dio 63.4).[4] Tiridates finally arrived in Rome to receive his royal crown from the hands of Nero himself. The main ceremony, after having once been "postponed because of overcast skies" (*propter nubilum distulisset*, Suet. *Nero* 13.1), took place in the forum, where it was arranged for Nero and Tiridates to enter at dawn, just as the sun was rising, so that the day's first light might illuminate the togas of the Romans who, as in a theater, were arranged by rank and clad in white. The arms of the soldiers who were milling about also gave off a brilliant glare. Wearing triumphal garb, Nero came in from the east, directly in front of the rising sun. He was followed by Tiridates. The emperor then mounted the rostra and sat down on the *sella curulis*. As Tiridates approached him, Nero's face and luxuriant garb were struck by the sun as it rose in the sky. Followed by his delegation, the Armenian leader passed through two lines of troops that were drawn up facing one another. When he reached the rostra, he turned to Nero and said: "I have come before you, who are my god, adoring you as I adore Mithras. And I will accept the lot that you assign to me. You are my fate and my destiny." Then the king, mounting the rostra, took a seat at the foot of Nero's *sella curulis*. Nero raised him with his right hand and kissed him. Nero then removed Tiridates' tiara, the symbol of a king's authority in the East, and put on his head a diadem, the symbol of a king's power according to traditions of the West, thus declaring him the king of Armenia.

For those who followed the religion of Zoroaster, the sun was the eye of Mithras, and Mithras was associated with, if not identified as, the sun. It is for this reason that Tiridates in his rhetoric likened Nero to the sun. And that must have been how Romans interpreted the ceremony as well, especially since the second part of the spectacle took place in the Theater of Pompey, which had been gilded for the occasion. The theater was overhung by an awning of purple on which was depicted a gigantic figure of Nero as the sun riding his chariot in the sky surrounded by stars resplendent with gold. On this occasion, the emperor's assimilation to Apollo/Sol was flaunted, much more so than it was on the Colossus. To be sure, this happened in a theatrical milieu, during a celebration that was ephemeral in its effects. Still, a basic motivation for Nero's identification with Sol may lie with the conventions of Mithras worship in the East. The homage Tiridates paid to Nero was itself fully in keeping with Parthian practice, and yet the times were not ready for an assimilation that went beyond the allusive and symbolic, extending to cult.

[4] On Nero as Sol, see Bergmann 1998.

13.3 The Fire of 64, and Nero's "Golden House"

In 64 CE, the same year in which Nero celebrated the tenth year of his reign, a disaster took place that would forever change the face of Rome. Fourteen days before the calends of August (the first day of every month in the Roman calendar) on the night between July 18 and 19, a large part of the city's center was destroyed by fire. The fire started near the Circus Maximus, in the area that touches the Palatine and Caelian Hills. It laid waste to the Palatine itself as it headed toward the Oppian and Esquiline Hills. Two-thirds of the city's urban space fell prey to the flames. Historical sources disagree on whether blame for the disaster should be pinned on Nero (see John Pollini, Chapter 14 in this volume).[5] Certainly if the fire was not caused by him, it granted him one of his wishes, one that he did not keep well hidden: a desire to refashion the center of the city by setting within the urban fabric a new and gigantic imperial house.

The ambitious project had an important precedent in the Domus Transitoria, the so-called House of Passage, which Suetonius tells us was part of a plan to enlarge the residences of the Palatine toward the Esquiline Hill so as to include the Gardens of Maecenas and other *horti* (gardens) that were by that time imperial property (Suet. *Nero* 31.1). But before 64, Nero had to content himself with the available spaces, which were few in this densely populated part of the city. The sheer bulk of the building activities that were successively pursued on the Palatine from the time of Augustus on makes it difficult to isolate with absolute certainty which works were completed under the direction of Nero. In fact it is Claudius, not Nero, who is to be credited with building the grand peristyle that rests atop the huge covered gallery or *cryptoporticus*. The peristyle features a fountain-basin that marks the very center of the Domus Tiberiana (n. 4 on Figure 13.7). On the other hand, the so-called Baths of Livia located under the triclinium of the Domus Flavia (n. 5 on Figure 13.7) belong to Nero. The structure's principal feature is a nymphaeum made to resemble a theater façade, with a stage (*pulpitum*) and backdrop (*scaena*). From the central door of the backdrop a waterfall cascaded down a series of steps. From there the water fed a series of small fountains beneath the front of the stage. Opposite the stage was a small shrine (*aedicula*) held up by ten porphyry columns, with a basin beneath the anterior side. Here the

[5] On the fire of 64, see Giardina 2007; Dando-Collins 2010; and Panella 2011.

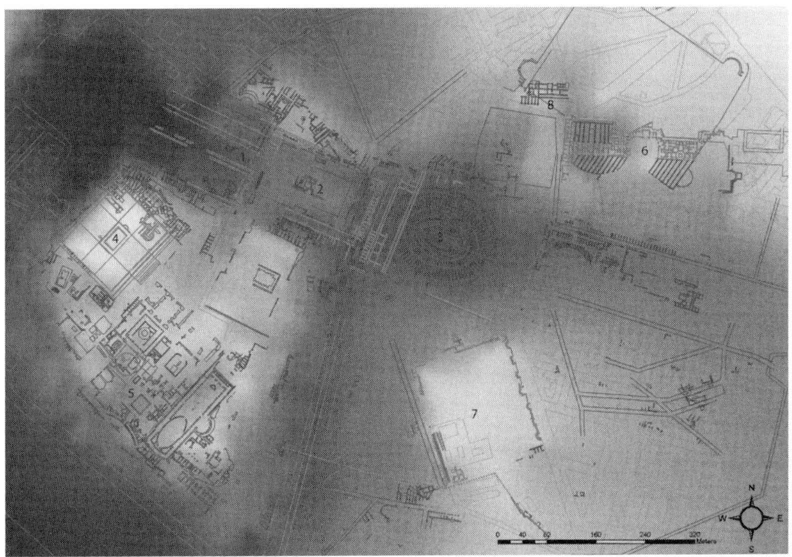

13.7 Plan of the Golden House (in orange) superimposed on a plan of the valley of the Colosseum and surrounding areas: 1. The main entrance to the Domus Aurea from the Forum Romanum; 2. The hall of the Colossus; 3. The lake; 4–5. Claudian or Neronian buildings on the Palatine; 6. The pavilion of the Colle Oppio; 7. The temple of Claudius with gardens on the Caelian Hill; 8. Neronian or Flavian buildings under the northwest corner of the Trajan's thermae.

emperor, likely reclining in a small apse at the base, could delight in his surroundings on hot summer days, as if shaded within a cave that was aglow and shimmering with precious marbles, inlaid with jewels and glass baubles, surrounded by stuccoes and paintings heavy with precious gold. Frescoes of the fourth "Pompeian" style still survive under the surrounding vaults. They feature lacy threads of vegetal motifs, among which are cut panels with Homeric and Dionysiac scenes (Figure 13.9). The whole of it seems attributable to Nero and to his taste for luxury and gold, but good arguments can be made for a Claudian provenance as well.[6]

The new imperial dwelling had the huge advantage of being drawn up *ex novo* atop the ruins of preexisting structures, and thus of not having to be laid out according to what was already there (Tac. *Ann.* 15.38–43, Suet.

[6] Guze 2008 includes a splendid series of late eighteenth-century watercolor etchings by Vincenzo Brenna, Franciszek Smuglewicz, and Marco Gregorio Carloni depicting the frescoes of the Domus Aurea.

13.8 Virtual reconstruction of the Domus Aurea seen from the south (Katalexilux Project 2011): 1. The main entrance to the Domus Aurea from the Forum Romanum; 2. The hall of the Colossus; 3. The lake; 4. Neronian buildings on the Palatine; 5. The pavilion of the Colle Oppio; 6. The temple of Claudius with gardens on the Caelian Hill; 7. Neronian or Flavian buildings under the northwest corner of the Trajan's thermae.

13.9 Rome, so-called Domus Transitoria on the Palatine Hill. Painted decoration from the vault.

Nero 31). The project, attributed to builders Severus and Celer, was extremely ambitious. Nero wanted to redesign the entire city, which lacked an urban plan to match its political importance. Since the great Gallic fire of 390 BCE, Rome had grown without any real regular plan: the streets were narrow and dark, the buildings lofty and built without the least attention to the risks of fire that were endemic. Even Augustus, despite his aggressive efforts in the Campus Martius, did not have the courage to lay a hand on the chaotic jumble of overcrowded tenements at the city's center, buildings that lacked even the most basic provisions for good hygiene. Instead, he preferred to build in narrowly circumscribed areas.

In the aftermath of the Great Fire, Nero wanted to see that the city's various needs were met, but at the same time he wanted to construct a luxurious home for himself and to transform Rome into a city that matched the grandeur of the great metropolises of the Greek East, all products of unified urban designs. Certainly Nero had in mind the splendors of Augustus' Campus Martius as well. Already before the fire Nero had exposed plans to remake the city by building an imposing bath complex. These baths had a Greek-style *gymnasium* attached on the south side that was built along with the baths in 60 CE, dedicated in 61, then destroyed by a fire the next year when it was struck by lightning.

We need not believe that the people of Rome rejected the imperial residence Nero conceived. Sources hostile to Nero would have us accept this, as would Martial, who pounds home the idea of public displeasure by vaunting the munificence of the Flavian emperors who dismantled great sections of Nero's palace in order to make space for public buildings, and the Flavian Amphitheater (Mart. *de Spect.* 2). On the contrary, as with all of Nero's other activities on behalf of the people, the palace would have resembled the Campus Martius in being a space available to all, open for common enjoyment.

We should imagine the Domus Aurea as a cluster of buildings of different sizes spread out between the Palatine and Esquiline, all within a vast park that had gardens made to resemble the countryside, with vines, agricultural and pastoral zones, lakeside vistas, groves, and forests (Figures 13.7 and 13.8). Nero wanted to create an enormous suburban villa in the heart of Rome: a place for aristocratic leisure (*otium*), which usually took place in rural environments, but was now situated inside the city itself. The basic logic was similar to that of the kingly palaces (*basileiai*) of Alexandria and Pergamum, but inflected by a regard for aristocratic Roman traditions of the late Republic. Later Hadrian seems to have overturned Nero's overly daring idea by conveniently constructing his own palace with its immense park far from Rome.

Recent excavations of the Domus Aurea have helped give substance to the descriptions of the structure in ancient sources. The *domus* had a main street leading up to it, corresponding to a stretch of the Via Sacra that was surrounded by porticoes and multipurpose rooms (n. 1 on Figure 13.8). The enormous vestibule was equivalent in size to the terrace on which the Temple of Venus and Rome sits (n. 2 on Figure 13.8). In the vestibule stood the famous colossal statue of Sol (see earlier in this chapter) that, because of the statue's later proximity to the Flavian Amphitheater, gave the Colosseum its name (Figure 13.5). In the valley where the Colosseum now stands there was a large rectangular lake surrounded by porticoes and terraces (n. 3 in Figure 13.8). A grandiose nymphaeum that functioned as a terrace on the Caelian Hill stood just below the Temple of Divine Claudius, which, under Nero, was in the process of being constructed, and later completed by Vespasian (n. 6 of Figure 13.8 and Figure 13.10). On the Oppian Hill stood the building that is usually called the Domus Aurea, but that is actually only one component of a vast complex of buildings that stood above the lake, like one of the great aristocratic villas that overlooked a lake or the waters of the sea (n. 6 of Figure 13.7 and Figure 13.11).

13.10 Virtual reconstruction of the east side of the nymphaeum-substruction of the temple of Divus Claudius on the Caelian Hill.

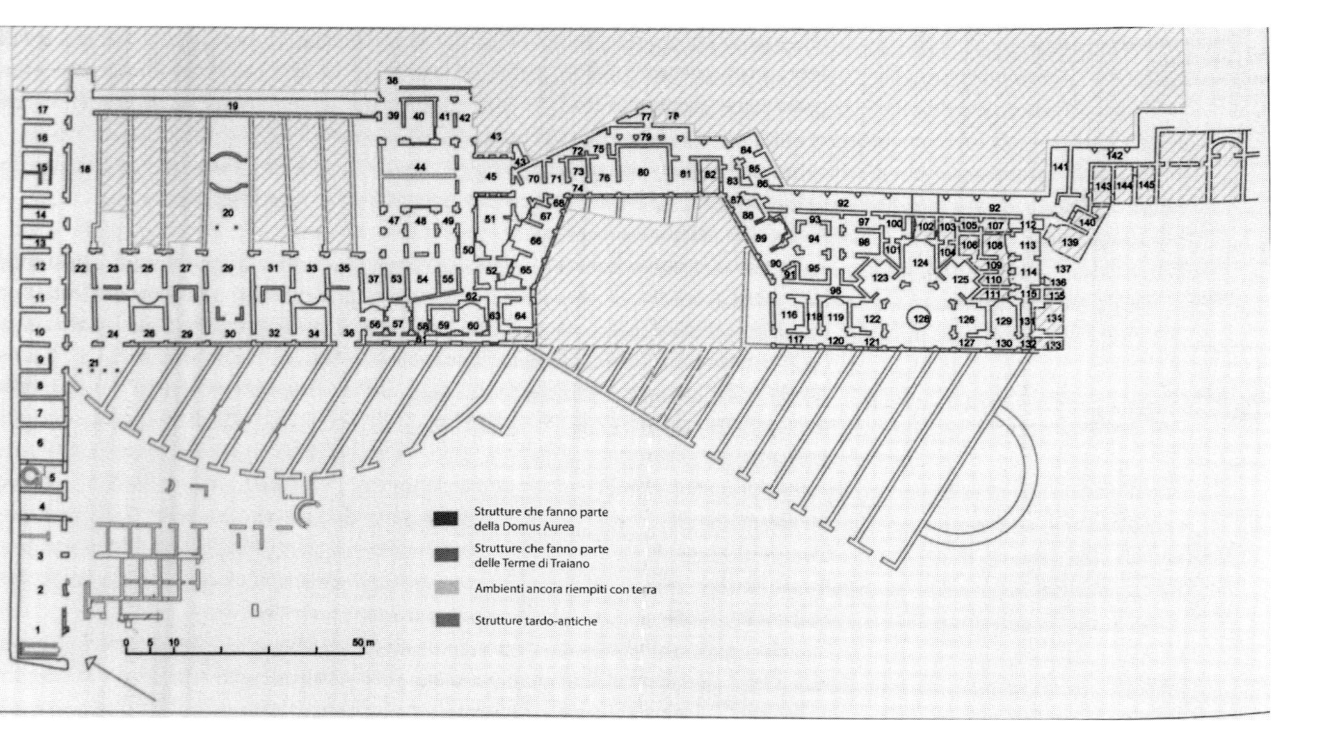

13.11 Plan of the Neronian building on the slopes of the Colle Oppio.

13.12 Pompeii, Casa di Marco Lucrezio Frontone. Fresco painting: landscape with a villa, from the north wall of the tablinum.

The pavilion of the Domus Aurea on the Oppian Hill resembles seaside villas such as those that appear in domestic wall paintings of the third and fourth styles in Pompeii (Figure 13.12). The Oppian structures became famous for the fourth-style paintings discovered there during the Renaissance, giving impetus to a taste for "the grotesque" (from *grotto*, the term commonly used to define the subterranean rooms of the building, buried as it was beneath the baths of Trajan). Undoubtedly by the time of the Domus Aurea the potentials intrinsic to the fourth style of painting, already adopted during the reign of Claudius, were in the process of becoming more pronounced. The fourth style replaces the cold and extremely refined geometric partitioning of walls in the third style, which trends toward both a vertical partition (base, main section, upper section) and a horizontal one (panels of mixed sizes, but in perfect proportion to one another). On these "third-style" surfaces, themselves devoid of spatial depth, were inserted, by way of refined contrast, abstract decorations that give the illusion of thin architectural elements nearly devoid of three-dimensionality. In this style, the exquisite decorative elements avoid the illusion of perspective, which is confined exclusively to the figured panels and to the vignettes that are framed centrally between the separate panels.[7] It is in reaction to this decorative scheme that a "fourth" style develops that preserves its geometric partition, but trades its two-dimensionality for a plethora of fragile architectural elements that are rendered with a greater plasticity and that cover the base, the upper section, and also the

[7] On the four painting styles, see further Vout, Chapter 12 in this volume.

spaces between the main panels in the middle section – like little windows opening onto theatrical dreamscapes. Finally, amid this sumptuous proliferation of decorative motifs, set within the architectural elements, and at the center of monochrome panels, are figures rendered in motion.

In the Age of Nero, particularly in the Domus Aurea, this fourth style evolved toward a more expansive "theatricality" of its forms. The walls come to resemble actual theater stages set atop very high bases with backdrops several levels high. Inserted into the architectural partitions are figures resembling stage actors: mythological characters recite from stages and from among columns, or at times they stand on balconies or floors amid the grandiose flights of "flimsy" architectural fancy. Likewise in the Pavilion on the Oppian Hill are pictorial decorations in the soffits that produce extraordinary effects: a play of fake curtains, finely woven, and of ribbons and lace decorated with floral and faunal designs. These are spaced out with geometrical precision so as to leave regular spaces in the center and at the sides for panels painted with figurative designs (Figure 13.13). The fantastical elements of this decorative system are exceptional, but even here the "newness" one sees in the Neronian design is limited: as I proposed previously, the soffit paintings discovered in the "Baths of Livia" should be connected to building completed under Claudius.

There is nothing particularly new in the "fourth style" decorative schemes of the Domus Aurea described earlier in relation to the artistic conventions of the Age of Claudius. There is perhaps an updating/revision – but even here one would need a more certain chronology of the available evidence – in the use of a pictorial technique that, in modern terms, we might define as "impressionistic" and "blotted" (*a macchia*). As in an impressionistic painting, the effect is "optical" in the sense that the whole is best perceived not from close up, but from a certain distance, because only at that distance does the desired contrast of colors and of shadows and light come together into a coherent whole. The difference from the third style, which was more precise in its details, is obvious. The rapid-stroke *a macchia* technique dominates in the rusticizing landscapes of the Domus Aurea to the extent that it might be attributed to Famulus (or Fabullus), one of the few Roman painters actually named by ancient sources.[8] Always dressed in a toga, Famulus painted only a few hours per day. Pliny refers to the Domus Aurea as the "prison-house of his art" (*carcer eius artis*, Plin. *HN* 35.120), apparently because the vast size of the project prevented Famulus from working

[8] On the painter Fabullus (or Famulus), see Dacos 1968; Meyboom 1984 and 1995.

13.13 Rome, Neronian building on the slopes of the Colle Oppio. Vault fresco painting, from room 119.

anywhere else. According to Pliny, his style of painting was dignified and severe and, at the same time, florid and watery. Pliny's contrast between a limited set of colors and a full palette of colors offers little help in understanding Famulus' style, but one might suppose that, despite his use of many colors, these colors were of complementary tones, or that they were harmoniously fused in such a way that the overall effect was not brightly splashed with color. Perhaps, as happened with the late paintings of Titian, an impressionistic technique, dictated less by the rapidity of the work's execution than by the possibilities intrinsic to the process, along with its own methods of mixing and combining colors, came to be used in the service of a new artistic vision.

Outside Rome, stylistic influences (whether in painting, architectural design, or statuary) that are specifically attributable to Nero are severely limited, but provide further evidence of Nero's interest in sustaining the figurative programs of the Augustan age to the very end of his reign. To conclude, the knowledge gained from the archaeological discoveries of the past twenty years, primarily in Rome, and much less so in other parts of the Empire, have vastly improved our understanding of Nero's political activities as a builder. It is by now obvious why the emperor could say with a certain air of impudence that he was (with the construction of his Domus Aurea) "at last beginning to be housed like a human being." A human being, one should add, who wanted to seem a bit too godlike, and who paid a tragic price for his lack of moderation.

Further Reading

For general studies of the Age of Nero, see Warmington 1969; Griffin 1984; and Champlin 2003; Giardina 2011; Panetta 2011; and Bergmann 2013. On the myth of Nero, see Di Branco 1996; Champlin 1998; and Pucci 2011. On Nero the artist, see Sande 1996; Champlin 2003a; Malitz 2004; Kissel 2006; Meier 2008; and Rea 2011. On the portraiture of Nero, see Hiesinger 1975; Zanker 1979; Bergmann and Zanker 1981; Maggi 1986; Born and Stemmer 1996; Geominy 1997; Schneider 2002; and Cadario 2011.

On Nero's building activity in Rome (excluding the Domus Transitoria and Domus Aurea), see Tamm 1970; Filippi 2010; Viscogliosi 2011a; and von Hesberg 2011. On the Domus Aurea, see Fabbrini 1983; Perrin 1987; Gros 1999; Ball 2003; Beste 2011b; Carandini, Bruno, and Fraioli 2011; Panella 2011a; and Viscogliosi 2011b. On the Domus Transitoria, see Bastet 1971; Beste 2011a; and Tomei 2011. On the Fourth style, and the frescoes of the Domus Aurea, see Dacos 1969; Strocka 1994; and Iacopi 1999.

Optimo Magistro Erich Gruen

14: Burning Rome, Burning Christians*

John Pollini

In the year 64 during the Principate of Nero, in the night between July 18 and 19, a fire broke out in Rome that within nine days destroyed or badly damaged a substantial part of the City, leaving many dead or homeless. Rumors circulated that the fire had been set by Nero, who, it was claimed, sought to divert blame from himself by holding responsible a new sect of aggressively proselytizing Jews, known as Christians. Most recent scholarship has rejected the popular view of Nero as an arsonist "who fiddled while Rome burned."[1] Largely ignored, however, has been the question of whether the Christians, generally regarded as innocent scapegoats of Nero, might in fact have played some role in the fire. This chapter considers the problematic nature of Christianity and Roman attitudes toward Christians in the first century CE and suggests based on this evidence that Christian involvement is not out of the question.

14.1 Nero and the Fire

Of the few surviving ancient accounts of the Great Fire of 64, the most detailed is that of Tacitus (*Ann.* 15.38–44), who wrote in the early second century. Most sources contemporary with Nero say nothing

* Too late to be incorporated and discussed *in extenso* in my essay is a new article by B.D. Shaw, "The Myth of the Neronian Persecution," *JRS* 105 (2015) 73–100. I do not agree with Shaw's major premise that it is most unlikely that Christians were specifically targeted as arsonists, but that they instead suffered punishment – or rather "persecution" – for their faith. Tacitus notes that Christians were punished for arson, but carefully and skillfully leads us to deduce that the real culprit was indeed Nero. In my opinion, the reason that other elite post-Neronian authors omit reference to early "Christianized Jews" in connection with the conflagration is that they were intent upon laying the blame for it at the feet of the tyrannical Nero, rather than the new heretical Jewish sect.

[1] See, e.g., Warmington 1969, especially 123–4; Griffin 1984: 133; Wiedemann 1996: 250–1; Dyson 2010: 164–5; Panella 2011b: 85–6. Cf. Champlin 2003: 178–209, especially 191, who is of the opinion that Nero intentionally set the fire to create a new Rome.

about the fire, and it is not mentioned in Juvenal, Martial, or Josephus. Pliny the Elder (*HN* 17.1.5), who hated Nero, merely alludes to "Nero's conflagration" (*Neronis principis incendia*). The opinions of Nero's detractors appear to have convinced later authors like Suetonius and Dio of Nero's culpability. In order to appear objective, Tacitus does not state categorically that Nero was guilty of arson. However, Tacitus leads his reader in that direction by means of innuendo, arrangement of selective facts and suppositions, and at times the presentation of only partial information.

Tacitus begins his narrative by expressing uncertainty as to whether the fire started by chance or by the treachery of Nero (*forte an dolo principis*), since both theories, as he tells us, had their supporters (*nam utrumque auctores prodidere*). At the beginning of his account, Tacitus notes that the fire broke out in the Circus Maximus in the area between the Palatine and Caelian Hills, where shops, jam-packed with flammable goods, were located. Although not generally noted, the fire may have actually started in one of the low-class eating houses or cook shops (*popinae*) along the side of the Circus Maximus, since Suetonius (*Ner.* 16) comments that among the measures Nero took after the fire to help prevent future conflagrations was an ordinance outlawing in such establishments the sale of anything cooked, except for pulse and vegetables.[2] Winds swept the fire along the length of the Circus Maximus both to the northwest toward the Tiber and due east toward the Caelian Hill (Figure 14.1). After spreading up the southwestern slope of the Palatine and over the Caelian, the blaze snaked around to the east and north sides of the Palatine, where it consumed much of the imperial estates that Nero had joined to his own home, the Domus Transitoria, as well as a number of the old aristocratic houses on the northeast slope of the Palatine. Only the House of Augustus, it seems, escaped the conflagration (Figure 14.2). Although the fire was extinguished on the sixth day at the foot of the Esquiline Hill, it broke out again on the "Aemilian estates of Tigellinus" (*praediis Tigellini Aemilianis*) (Tac. *Ann.* 15.40). This was perhaps a suburban villa that once belonged to the old noble Aemilian family in the Campus Martius overlooking the Tiber River, but that now belonged to Tigellinus, Nero's infamous Praetorian commander (Figure 14.3).[3] By the ninth day, Tacitus relates, perhaps with some exaggeration (*Ann.* 15.41), that when the blaze was finally

[2] Although Dio (62.14) reports this ordinance under the year 62, it would seem more likely to date after the fire of 64. There may also have been concerns about foods like fatty meats that required higher temperatures to cook and therefore necessitated greater flames.

[3] Cf. Panella 2011b: 82, 89.

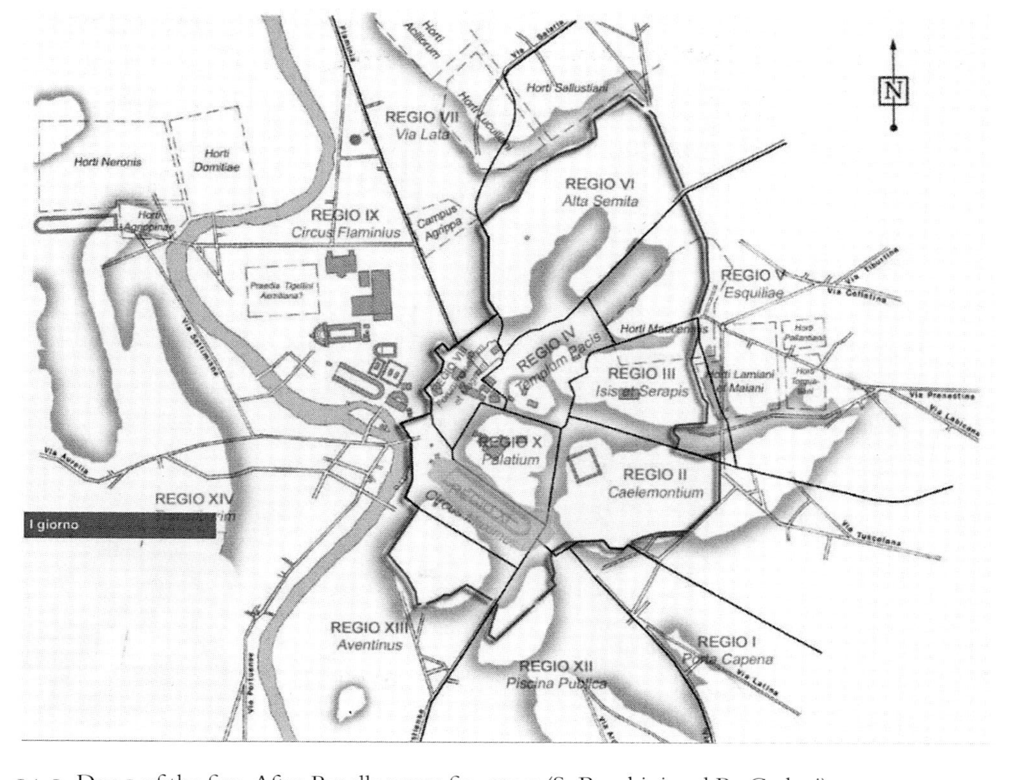

14.1 Day 1 of the fire. After Panella 2011: fig. 10a.1 (S. Borghini and R. Carlani).

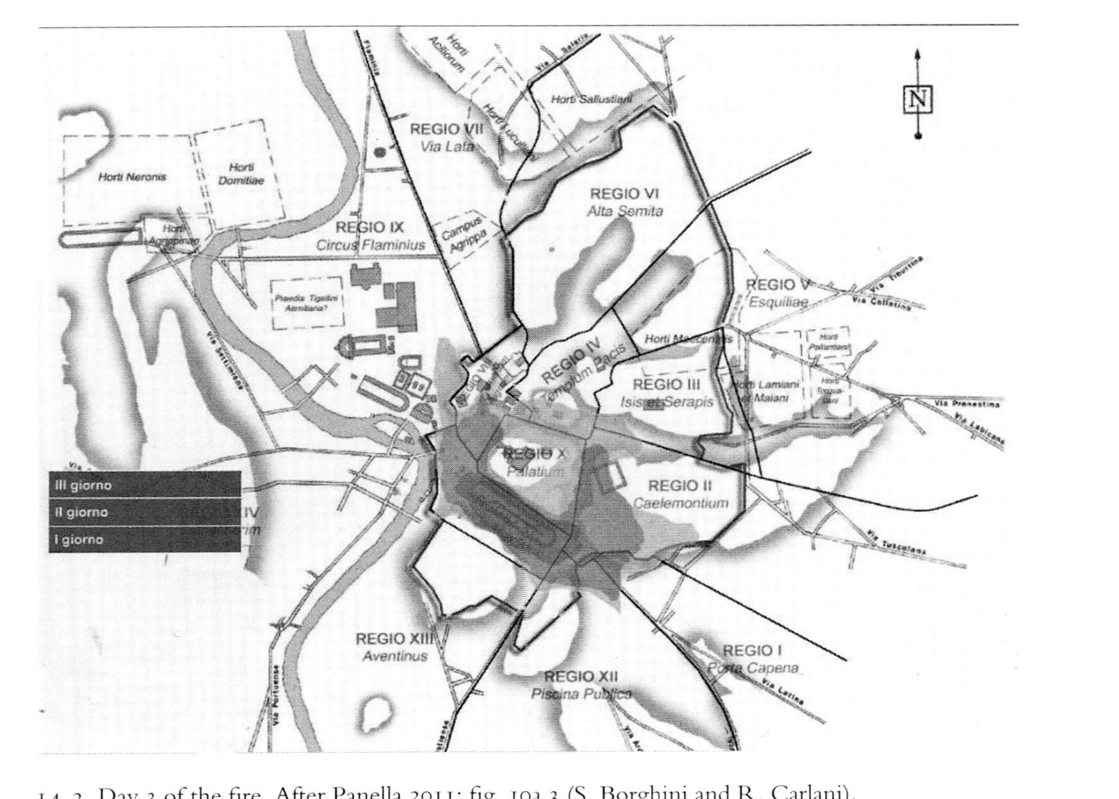

14.2 Day 3 of the fire. After Panella 2011: fig. 101.3 (S. Borghini and R. Carlani).

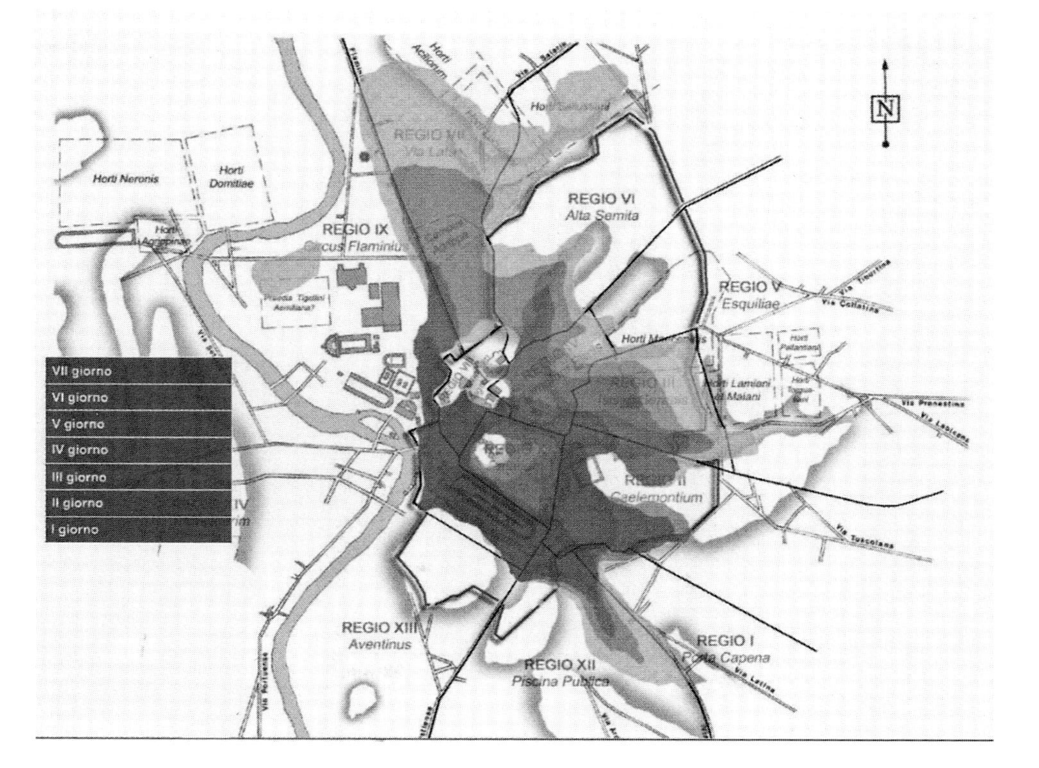

14.3 Day 7 of the fire. After Panella 2011: fig. 10a.4 (S. Borghini and R. Carlani).

extinguished, only four of the fourteen Augustan *regiones* remained intact, while three were leveled and the other seven greatly damaged (Figure 14.4). This account has been more or less confirmed by the archaeological evidence.[4]

Tacitus introduces into his narrative of the horror and devastation of the conflagration an interesting piece of information; namely, that a large number of unnamed individuals threatened anyone trying to extinguish the fire, while others openly threw firebrands "shouting out that they were authorized – whether to carry out their looting more freely or whether by order" (*Ann.* 15.38).[5] The latter phrase "or whether by order" (*sive iussu*) is clearly intended to raise suspicion that such a directive had come from above, ultimately from Nero himself. Yet, as Tacitus goes on to state, Nero at that time was at Antium (modern Anzio) and returned to Rome only when his own palatial residence, the Domus Transitoria,[6] was threatened by the fire. Tacitean innuendo, however, would lead us to believe that Nero had already given the order to set Rome ablaze and that his absence from Rome was to serve as an alibi. Why else would a "large number" of people have been preventing some of the urban population from putting out the flames, while setting more fires themselves? But anyone knowledgeable about the early days of urban firefighting or even contemporary forest or wild fire-fighting methods knows that to prevent fires from spreading, fire walls are created by controlled burning of areas in advance of the main conflagration.[7] Suetonius (*Nero* 38) notes that stone granaries in the area of the Esquiline were demolished with war machines (*bellicis machinis*) and then burned, though he gives no hint that these were preventative fire-fighting measures. These actions are perceived instead as part of Nero's plan to gain land on the Esquiline for the main wing of his future Domus Aurea, one of the reasons he allegedly started the fire in the first place. That many individuals were involved in this endeavor indicates that Rome's substantial fire-fighting force, the "Night

[4] Excavations, especially in more recent years, have brought to light various pieces of evidence for the fire of 64, allowing more reliable topographical plans for its progressive spread. See, e.g., Santangeli Valenzani and Volpe 1986; Carandini and Papi (eds.) 1999, especially 3–14; Carandini 2010. See also Panella 2011: 84, with figs. 1–9 showing the sequential advancement of the fire.

[5] See also Dio 62.16.3–7.

[6] This huge domus ("home") was called "transitoria" because it "crossed over" the valley, where the later Colosseum was built, thus joining imperial residences on the Palatine with those of the Esquiline.

[7] For example, when fire broke out after the San Francisco earthquake of 1906, firemen created such a fire wall, even using dynamite to blow up buildings. I thank the San Francisco Fire Department for this information.

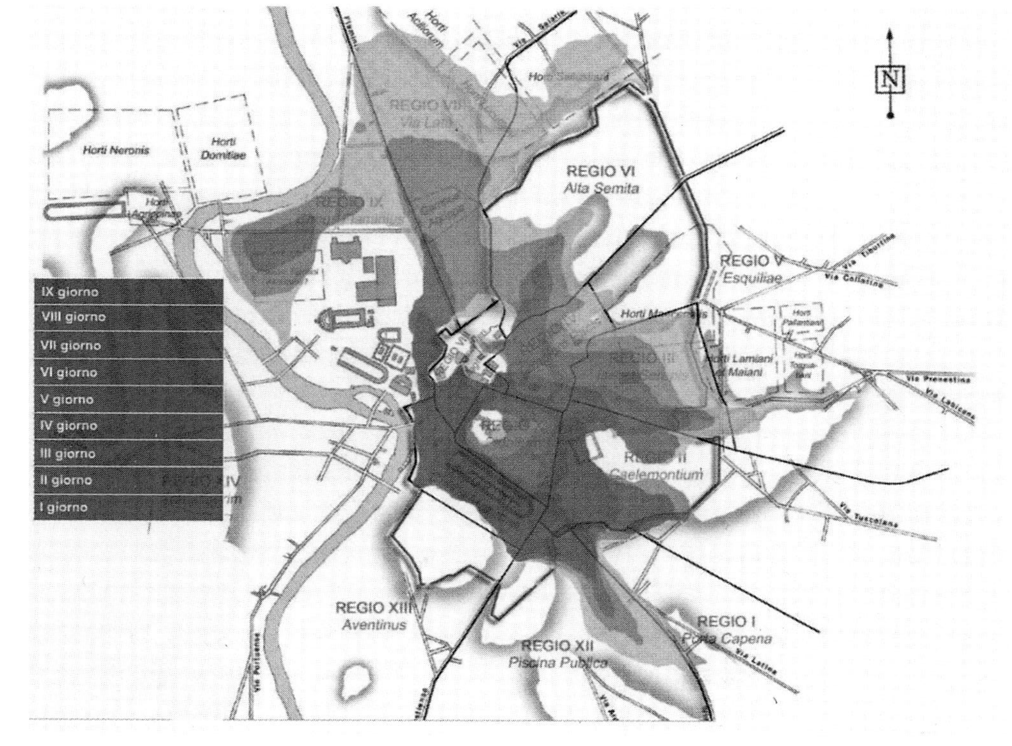

14.4 Day 9 of the fire. After Panella 2011: fig. 10a.6 (S. Borghini and R. Carlani).

Watch," or *Vigiles Urbani*,[8] had sprung into action, creating fire walls as part of its fire-fighting operations. Dio, in fact, states specifically (62.17.1) that among those setting fires were soldiers and the *vigiles* (here, the "fire brigade"), but he too puts a negative spin on it by suggesting that their motive may have been plunder, rather than extinguishing the flames. Tacitus clearly knew why such fires would have been set, for later on in another context, he states (*Ann.* 15.40), "Then, on the sixth day, the fire was extinguished at the foot of the Esquiline after buildings had been demolished over a vast area so that an area like an open clearing would oppose the continuing violence [of the flames]."

Tacitus recounts (*Ann.* 15.39) that many viewed with suspicion Nero's efforts to alleviate suffering after the fire. Nero's relief program included opening to the homeless Agrippa's structures in the Campus Martius and his own gardens (*horti*), as well as putting up makeshift shelters. He also ordered foodstuffs to be brought from Ostia and other nearby municipalities and lowered the cost of grain. Tacitus would have us believe that Nero's only motive for these positive actions was to divert attention from the suspicion that he was to blame for the conflagration, since Tacitus goes on to speak of rumors that during the blaze Nero sang of the destruction of Troy from a stage in his home (*scaena domestica*). Suetonius and Dio have slightly different versions of this story. Suetonius (*Nero* 38.2) indicates that Nero, dressed in stage costume, sang of the Sack of Ilium from the "Tower of Maecenas,"[9] while Dio (62.18) speaks of Nero's singing of the capture of Troy in the garb of a lyre-player on the "palace roof," which apparently escaped the flames in the section of Nero's Domus Transitoria on the Esquiline Hill. This part of his villa had once belonged to the suburban estate of Maecenas, who willed it to his friend and benefactor Augustus. From such a high vantage point, Nero would have been able to see what needed to be done to fight the fire. It would have been hardly surprising, in any case, if Nero – artist and author of the *Troica* (Juv. 8.220–1) – had been moved to reference the conflagration of Troy, as had Publius Scipio Aemilianus when seeing Carthage in flames in 146 BCE (Polyb. 38.22; App. *Punica* 132).

Suetonius (*Nero* 38.1) maintains that Nero "set the City ablaze because of his disgust with the unsightliness of its antiquated buildings and the narrow and winding streets." According to Tacitus (*Ann.*

[8] About 7,000 men: Strabo 5.3.7; Suet. *Aug.* 25, 30; Dio 62.17.

[9] For the "Tower of Maecenas," its location, and the topography of the Esquiline, see Häuber 2013: 213 with no. 155, 440 (see map 3: location of the tower under and to the right of the "L" of FAGUTAL; map 4: yellow tower), 873–4.

15.40), Nero wanted to re-found Rome, naming it after himself (i.e., as Neropolis: Suet. *Nero* 55). No hard evidence, however, is produced for this claim other than the fact that he undertook a large-scale urban-building program after the fire had caused massive damage. Other leaders of Rome did likewise both before and after Nero. If he were really responsible for the fire as a means of improving the urban landscape, he would have logically started the blaze in the Subura, the slums behind the Forum of Augustus, which were apparently not badly damaged in the conflagration. Ironically, this area may in part have been shielded by the Forum of Augustus, with its roughly 100 foot high retaining wall of fire-resistant peperino stone (*lapis Gabinus*), which was designed to contain fires from spreading from the Subura. Even Nero's new planned constructions in fire-resistant Gabinian and Alban stone and novel types of flat-roofed structures to help fight future fires (Tac. *Ann.* 15.3; Suet. *Nero* 16) came under attack for no credible reason other than that their author was Nero.

Following the destruction of much of his Domus Transitoria, Nero undertook the construction of his even larger estate, the Domus Aurea ("Golden House"), which would cost an outrageous sum of money (see La Rocca, Chapter 13 in this volume). The project was highly criticized not only because of the new taxes levied for this extravaganza, but also because Nero was in reality creating for his own pleasure a sprawling country landscape villa of enormous proportions (ca. 300–350 acres) in the very heart of the City.[10] Highlighting the vastness of this enterprise, Martial (*Spect.* 2.4) speaks of Nero's house taking up the whole City, while Suetonius (*Nero* 39) reports a popular lampoon that Rome was becoming a house and that Romans should migrate to Veii (ca. 16 km northwest of Rome), if Nero's abode did not engulf that town too. The largely destroyed properties of the nobility in and around the northeastern slopes of the Palatine, along the so-called Via Nova, were bought up by Nero to increase the size of his new palatial residence. Suetonius' statement (*Nero* 38.2) that "... the houses of the leaders of old were burned, still adorned with spoils of enemies ..." is undoubtedly a reference to some of these properties. To give further credence to Nero's culpability for the fire, Suetonius comments (*Nero* 38.1) that "his [Nero's] chamberlains (*cubicularii*) were caught with tow and torches on the estates of a number of those of consular rank." However, these *cubicularii* may in

[10] For both these estates, see in general Ball 2003; Dyson 2010: 165–9; and the various essays in Tomei and Rea 2011, especially 76–176. The total size of the Domus Aurea is difficult to determine. For the estimation of 300–350 acres, I follow Ward-Perkins in Boëthius and Ward-Perkins 1970: 214.

reality have been sent to convey orders by Nero to create fire walls to stop the spread of the conflagration.

Having lost their estates, the resentful Roman nobility, many of whom already detested Nero, would have understandably been motivated to circulate the rumor that he had set the fire to acquire more land for his new palatial ambitions. Some of these aristocrats might also have been involved in the so-called Pisonian conspiracy against Nero in 65, though Tacitus does not suggest this.[11] He does note (*Ann.* 15.67), however, that when Subrius Flavus, one of Nero's Praetorian tribunes who joined the Pisonian conspiracy, was caught and examined, he reproached Nero for burning Rome, calling him an *incendiarius*. According to Tacitus (*Ann.* 15.50), Subrius Flavus had considered assassinating Nero on the night of the fire, but feared being captured; the absence of any outcome here makes it difficult to know Subrius' intent.

If Nero had sought by means of the conflagration to make available a vast tract of land for a new residence, why would he have started it on the opposite side of the Palatine from where the new great domestic wing of the Domus Aurea was built? Most of this land, especially on the slopes of the Esquiline, was already part of his Domus Transitoria. Moreover, because of the difficulty in controlling fires, it would not have made sense to start a fire anywhere near the Circus Maximus, a fire hazard itself because of its wooden superstructure, which ran all along the Palatine Hill. Located here on the western slope of the Palatine were all of the imperial estates, including the House of Augustus and several important temples, all embellished with great works of art. As it was, the fire consumed much of the property on the Palatine that Nero had already annexed to create his Domus Transitoria. Many of the City's other splendid and famous temples were also destroyed, along with their irreplaceable artistic treasures (Suet. *Nero* 38; Tac. *Ann.* 15.41) – far too great a visual and religious heritage for a self-proclaimed lover of art like Nero to send up in flames! If the agency ascribed to Nero in the fire is problematic, then where else do the voices from this era suggest we look?

14.2 Christians and Christianities

It would appear that our earliest Roman source for Christians living in Rome and fomenting discord is Suetonius (*Claud.* 25.4).[12] He recounts

[11] For the Pisonian conspiracy, see Griffin 1984: 166–70.

[12] As J. Albert Harrill has discussed in the present collection of essays, the earliest Christian congregations were in Rome at least since the 40s.

that probably around the year 49, not long before Nero came to power,[13] Claudius had expelled "Jews" from the City because they were constantly making disturbances at the instigation of Chrestus (*Iudaeos impulsore Chresto assidue tumultuantis Roma expulit*).[14] Though there has been much scholarly debate about who is meant by "Chrestus," this is most likely a reference to Christ.[15] There are at least three possibilities for the spelling as Chrestus rather than Christus: 1) a manuscript error in spelling, 2) confusion or mispronunciation of the name of Christus,[16] or 3) an alternate spelling of Christus, since the ancients were not as fixated on orthography as are moderns.[17] In fact, Tertullian states (*Apol.* 3.5) that *Christianus* was sometimes mispronounced as *Chrestianus*. What is undoubtedly meant by the phrase *impulsore Chresto* is that Christ was ultimately the inspiration and driving force behind those followers who were now spreading his message in Rome.[18] Since Christ himself never wrote, these followers of Christ, who at this early date could be called Jewish Christians or Christianized Jews, were going about interpreting what they thought Jesus' message was. But lacking any one accepted version of his message, these early Christian proselytizers were, in effect, creating different but related forms of Christianity, or more accurately, Christianities.[19] With the Christian take-over of the Empire beginning in the fourth century, a number of these Chrisitianities would come to be regarded as heresies by the so-called Orthodox Church (*Cod. Theod.* 16.5).

From what little we know about the historical Jesus, it would appear that he saw himself as a reformer of Judaism who wished to unite Jews and bring them back to the path of righteousness, as reflected in the gospels. For example, Matthew (10:5–6) states, "These twelve [disciples] Jesus sent out with the following instructions: 'Go nowhere among the Gentiles, and enter no town of the Samaritans, but go rather to the lost sheep of the house of Israel')." In Matt. 15:24 Jesus says to his

[13] Orosius (7.6.15) also places the expulsion in this year, a time that appears to be confirmed by Acts 18.2: On this point, see Gruen 2002: 38.

[14] Cf., however, Gruen 2002: 36–41 for a more complex interpretation. See also Harrill, Chapter 17 in this volume.

[15] That this Chrestus was some otherwise unknown troublemaker, as some have suggested, with a name similar to Christus, would be, in my opinion, too much of a coincidence and implausible in this context. See further Engberg 2007: 99–104.

[16] Gruen 2002: 38–9; Engberg 2007: 100–1.

[17] For confusion of the names Chrestus/Christus, see Engberg 2007: 99–102, especially with n. 226. Tacitus (*Ann.* 15.44) is the first Roman source to refer to Christians as *Christiani* and to the author of that name (*auctor nominis*) as *Christus*. Incidentally, the proper name Chrestus is the Latin transliteration of the Greek *chrēstos*, literally meaning "good man," which of course is not the same as Christus, which in Greek (*christos*) means "the anointed."

[18] Cf. Engberg 2007: 99–104 *et passim*.

[19] See in general White 1988.

disciples, "I was sent only to the lost sheep of the house of Israel." These passages make clear that he did not see himself as the founder of some new religion that was to be spread to all peoples of the Roman Empire.[20] That appears to have been essentially the idea of Saul of Tarsus (St. Paul), who went on to found mainstream Christianity, or what can be called Pauline Christianity.[21] To make this new brand of Christianity more acceptable to non-Jews, Paul did not require a convert to observe all the traditional Jewish religious restrictions and requirements (especially its dietary prohibitions and circumcision) that non-Jews found so unpalatable and repugnant. This revolutionary change, however, went against the Torah-based form of Christianity of the so-called Jerusalem Church, headed by the apostles James (the brother of Jesus) and Peter (Gal. 2).[22] However, it was Paul's version that won out in the end, becoming mainstream Christianity. Paul's overly dramatic, miraculous story about a blinding light that caused him to fall off his horse and his vision of Jesus on the road to Damascus (Acts 9:1–9; Cor. 15:9; Gal. 1:11–17) was undoubtedly invented to give Paul apostolic authority, since he was not a disciple of Jesus, nor did he even know him.[23] It is only at the very end of Matthew (28:18–20) and of Luke (24:47) that the resurrected Jesus appears to his followers to tell them that they were now to go forth to preach and convert the gentiles of all nations. This new and very specific directive is found only in the gospels of Matthew and of Luke, aside from of course Acts (esp. 14–15), which follows Paul's theology. The story in Matthew and Luke is like the "longer ending" of the resurrection story found in the earlier gospel of Mark 16:9–20, but which lacks Jesus' mandate to convert gentiles.[24] This directive was probably an invented interpolation, added later on to promote Paul's version of Christianity.

[20] See further White 1988: 7–24 with additional bibliography.

[21] For the invention of Pauline Christianity, see Maccoby 1986, which is highly controversial, but has some interesting insights.

[22] For the Jerusalem Church and Paul's split from it, see Maccoby 1986: 119–55.

[23] The aspect of the blinding light was probably inspired by the Jewish myth of Moses and the "Burning Bush" (Exodus 3:1–4:17). For an interesting interpretation of Paul's story, see Maccoby 1986: 85–109. Cf. also the miraculous story of the archangel Gabriel's revelation of the Qur'an to Muhammad. For a discussion of the Islamic story and tradition, see Peters 1994: 147–52, 206 *et passim*.

[24] As scholars have acknowledged, the later gospels of Matthew and Luke derive from Mark. In addition, it has likewise been pointed out that the style of the language of the "longer ending" is very different from the rest of Mark, which originally had an unsatisfactory "shorter ending" (16:8) that lacks the reappearance of *redivivus* Jesus to his followers. Christian mythographers of a later period clearly conflated elements from Acts and other gospels to create a longer and more satisfying ending to the resurrection story. See *NOAB*: 74 with commentary on 16:8 and 9–20. For Mark being the oldest of the synoptic gospels, on which Matthew and Luke are closely based, with John being the last of four to be written, see *OBC*: 886, and 1001–27.

Whether Torah-based or not, all forms of Christianity were regarded by mainstream or orthodox Jews as blasphemy and heresy.[25] Even the notion of "converting" a Jew to another religion or a heretical form of Judaism was punishable by death under Jewish religious law (Deuteronomy 13:8–10). Conflict, which often resulted in physical violence, was inevitable for those who subscribed to a religion whose fundamental belief system rested on universal monotheistic notions of a singular "God" and a singular "Truth" for all peoples. When Paul turned up at the Yahweh Temple in Jerusalem, for example, he was seized by fellow Jews, who beat and threatened to kill him. He was saved only by soldiers of the Roman cohort in Jerusalem, who protected him because he revealed to the commander that he was a Roman citizen.[26] Conversely, St. Stephen, the first of the so-called Christian martyrs, was not a Roman citizen, for which reason, according to Christian tradition, he was stoned to death by Jews (Acts 7:58–60) in accordance with Jewish law.[27] It is a mistaken notion that only Rome could carry out the death penalty in such religious matters.[28]

With Christianity rejected as a heresy by most traditional Jews, aggressive Christian proselytizers like Paul were forced to begin targeting more receptive non-Jews, including Roman citizens. Unlike monotheism, ancient polytheistic religions themselves (that is, as cults) make no pronouncements about the validity of other peoples' gods, for which reason polytheists could freely adopt or adapt foreign cults or aspects of them, without the necessity of giving up their own traditional gods. Novel and/or exotic religions, especially mystery cults, that promised a better life to come in the hereafter were particularly attractive, particularly among the credulous lower classes, whose existence was often grim and who saw little justice in life. Being "weak in mind" (*imbecilli*), according to Cicero (*Div.* 2.81),[29] such people were all the more susceptible to *superstitio*, while Columella (*Rust.* 1.8.6; 11.1.22), writing at the end of the first century CE, speaks of *vana superstitio* ("false superstition") that seduces *rudes animos* ("ignorant minds") to *flagitia* ("vices"). Both *superstitio* and *flagitia* were specifically associated with Christianity in Pliny the Younger's famous letter to Trajan (*Ep.* 10.96.2,

25 See especially Henrichs 1970: 22–3.

26 See, e.g., Maccoby 1986: 156–71; Wilson 1997: 16, 35, 83, 127–8, 175–6, 187–8, 190–1, 202, 209–12.

27 *OCB*: 714 s.v. "Stephen."

28 This is also often and incorrectly stated in the case of the trial of Jesus, based on John 18:31, which was undoubtedly an invented part of his story. For the Jews' right to employ the death penalty in matters of religious (non-political) transgressions, see Smallwood 1981: 148–50.

29 See also Cic. *Div.* 2.125, 148.

8–9), while those Christians who could be characterized as being *rudes animi* were the very people (townspeople, villagers, and rustics) whom Pliny reports (*Ep.* 10.96.9) were being infected by the "contagion of this wretched superstition" (*superstitionis istius contagio*).

The problem with Christianity, as with Judaism (and Islam later on), was that it allowed for belief in only one God, whereas it considered the gods of other peoples false or "demonic" and their worship "idolatrous" (e.g., 1 Corinthians 10:20).[30] It is little wonder, then, that Christians were commonly reviled by polytheists for their "impiety" (*asebeia*) and "atheism" (*atheotes*), in the sense that they denied the existence of the gods of other peoples.[31] Blasphemous insults and flagrant disrespect of the religious beliefs of others, moreover, posed a threat to the *pax deorum* ("peace of the gods"), the divine equilibrium Romans sought to maintain through religious devotion and sacrifice for the well-being of the state. Any acts that resulted in the disruption of the *pax deorum*, which by association threatened the stability of the Roman state, were considered *insania* ("insanity") and *amentia* ("madness"), especially with regard to the frenzied behavior of fanatics.[32] In fact, *amentia* is the very term Pliny the Younger (*Ep.* 10.96.4) used in referring to the Christian *superstitio*. It was undoubtedly Paul's blasphemy against the goddess Artemis/Diana that caused a near riot in Ephesus, when a mass of polytheists, as we are told in the book of Acts (19:34), rushed to the city's theater and chanted in unison for two hours "great is the goddess of the Ephesians."[33] According to the Acts (19:26), the Ephesians said that Paul was preaching to them that "gods made by human hands are not gods at all." In short, Paul was also reviling the Ephesians as "idol-worshipers." To polytheists, Christians like Paul were preaching hatred of whatever did not conform to their narrow religious view of the world – a message that earned them the enmity of not only mainstream Jews but also the wider polytheistic populations of the Empire.

[30] Christianity inherited this form of religious bigotry from Judaism: So King David, who declared "all gods of [other] nations are demons": See Septuagint 95:5, translated into Greek, πάντες οἱ θεοὶ τῶν ἐθνῶν δαιμόνια, from the Hebrew, which calls them "idols." Cf. also Psalms 96:5 for the gods as idols.

[31] See MacMullen 1984: 15, 128 n. 12 (for the various ancient sources). See further Pollini 2008: 193 with additional references.

[32] See Horace (*Sat.* 2.3.79), for example, who equates *superstitio* with *morbus mentis* ("mental disorder"). For *superstitio* being a manifestation of an insane mind, see Janssen 1997: 137–8, 158. Also in the case of the Jews and fanatical religious behavior, see Pollini 2012: 375–6.

[33] The Christian story that the silversmiths were behind the protest because they feared the loss of business is totally specious, since Ephesus was a major pilgrimage site and the number of potential converts to Christianity at this time would have been negligible.

Unlike Christians, Jews generally kept largely to themselves (see Tac. *Hist.* 5.5.4) and, accordingly, were not on some specific aggressive mission to convert others to their religion.[34] Because of the antiquity of their religious beliefs, they were exempted from direct participation in the imperial cult. Instead, they expressed their loyalty to Rome by offering prayers and sacrifice to their god for the safety of the emperor, which, in effect, was equated with the safety of the state.[35] It should be remembered that in antiquity there was no meaningful division between the state and religion, so that when people pledged loyalty to Rome during the Empire, it could only be done through sacrifice to the *Genius* of the Emperor and gods of Rome, an act that was not a problem for the polytheistic peoples of the Empire.[36] Because of their irreconcilable differences with traditional Judaism, Christians eventually no longer considered themselves even Jewish Christians. Consequently, as non-Jews, they could no longer enjoy certain privileges, exemptions, and concessions that Rome made only to the Jews.[37] The loyalty of the Christians became suspect, and their aggressive proselytizing, especially among Roman citizens, became a concern to the Roman state as Christianity spread, since Roman citizens were expected to continue to revere the Roman gods, even if they added foreign gods to their pantheon. For those who became exclusive Christian monotheists,[38] tensions and problems were inevitable. Early on, Christianized Jews preaching in Jewish communities had caused civil discord and disruption of the peace, and later on, the same things occurred when they proselytized among non-Jews. Christian communities sometimes expected converts to become exclusively monotheistic and to avoid polytheists and even their families who worshiped the gods. This could lead to familial discord, especially because all aspects of Roman life revolved around worship of the gods, including domestic cults.[39]

[34] Whether or not Jews were proselytizing in the Roman period has been greatly debated. Although some Jews might have done so, it was certainly not a specific mission of Judaism, for the very reason that they stuck to themselves and were even endogamous. On the lack of any Jewish proselytizing mission, see especially Gruen 2002: 30–1, 46–7, with n. 206.

[35] Smallwood 1981: 147–8; Gruen 2002: 44.

[36] Sacrifices were also performed before conducting all official and legal business. See also Barnes 2010: 111.

[37] For these privileges, see, e.g., Smallwood 1981: 147–52.

[38] Since there were many different forms of Christianity, some may have accepted aspects of Christianity, even worshiping Christ among their other gods.

[39] For discord of a sexual nature, see also Justin Martyr, 2 *Apol.* 2; North 2000: 75; Barnes 2010: 20. Christians were redefining the notion of the traditional Roman family by creating their own communities, in which they called one another "brother" and "sister." As Janssen 1979: 158 notes, they were encouraging people to isolate themselves from the surrounding world and to

As their numbers increased over time, especially after the Emperor Gallienus legalized Christianity in 260,[40] more and more problems arose with Christians, especially among competing Christian sects or factions, as well as the more fanatic trouble-makers and aggressive proselytizers among them. But long before the post-Gallienic period, most Christians had initially refused to serve in the Roman army or to assume civic responsibilities.[41] Because such antisocial and anti-Roman behavior went against Roman mores and values (the *mos maiorum*),[42] as well as the religious beliefs of other peoples, Christians were accused of hatred of the human race (*odium generis humani*, Tac. *Ann.* 15.38–44).[43] Their hostile attitude toward the gods and traditional Roman values became of great concern to Roman authorities.[44] Rumors had also begun to circulate about strange and obnoxious Christian cult practices (Tac. *Ann.* 15.44), some of which the Romans clearly misunderstood, while others they did not. In the early days, many Christianities had their own interpretation of what it meant to be "Christian." Some more orthodox Christian writers, for example, condemned sects like the Christian Carpocratians for their bizarre rites and libertine sexual habits (Clem. *Al. Strom.* 3.2.10).[45]

Nevertheless, as we know from Trajan's correspondence with the Pliny the Younger (*Ep.* 10.97), who was the governor of Bithynia-Pontus in the early second century, Christians were not to be sought out and arrested, but "if they are brought to trial and proven guilty, they must be punished" (*si deferantur, arguantur, puniendi sunt*). Those most likely to be arrested and convicted were the ringleaders and trouble-makers, who were aggressively proselytizing and promoting civic unrest and discord, while Christians who minded their own business and practiced a harmless form of Christianity in private were left alone. Those falsely accused of being a Christian (usually by neighbors with grudges) could, of course, be exonerated simply by offering wine and incense to the *Genius* or *Tyche* of the Emperor and/or the gods.[46] Nor were all Christians who confessed to being Christian systematically

transform themselves into members of a new *nomen*, the *nomen Christianum* (not the *nomen Romanum*), a tightly knit social unit held together by their own idea of *fides* and *pietas*.

[40] It is often said that toleration of Christianity first came about with the so-called Edict of Milan in 313. However, the "Edict of Milan" was neither an edict nor issued by Constantine in Milan in 313. See recently Barnes 2010: 97–8 with n. 4, 113–14, and, for the legalization of Christianity by Gallienus, 97–105.

[41] See, e.g., Wilken 1984: 117–25.

[42] On this point, see especially Barnes 1968: 50.

[43] See further below.

[44] See Janssen 1979, especially 158.

[45] See also Justin Martyr (1 *Apol.* 26.7) on the unacceptable behavior of other Christian groups. See further Wilken 1984: 19–21.

[46] Barnes 1968: 44 *et passim*; Wilken 1984: 24–30.

executed,[47] except very briefly under Nero because of the charge of arson. In short and contrary to popular belief, Christians were not systematically "persecuted" and martyred over the three centuries of Roman hegemony and on the rare occasions that they were actually executed, it was for a brief period of time.[48] Those who did perish tended to be recalcitrant clergy and/or those with fanatical tendencies, or the credulous who believed they were going to a better place. Therefore, it is largely a myth that there were three centuries of continuous Roman "persecution" of Christians. This notion was perpetuated by Christian religious propagandists in order to spread Christianity by creating the impression that these innocent Christians were willing to sacrifice their lives for the "Truth" of the Christian message – hence the erroneous claim that the seed of the Church was the blood of the martyrs (Tert. *Apol.* 50).[49] In fact, many of those said to be martyrs were fictitious.[50] Instructive, too, is the case of Ignatius, the bishop of Antioch, who appears to have had a great desire to become a martyr.[51] While en route to Rome for his trial during the Trajanic period, Ignatius was allowed by his Roman guard to meet with local Christians, to preach to them, and even to write letters to various Christian congregations along the way. None of these Christians were arrested and thrown into prison and/or executed. Christians – like Paul – who were punished were those who had caused civic disturbances, usually as a result of their aggressive proselytizing mission and blasphemy against the gods.

The fomenting of discord by Christianized Jews, who preached in Jewish communities that which orthodox Jews considered blasphemy and heresy, was undoubtedly the reason that Jews – Christianized or not[52] – were expelled from Rome under Claudius, as Suetonius noted. This action would also be consistent with what we

[47] See, e.g., Barnes 2010: 55–7 (for Dionysius of Alexandria going into exile), 77–82 (for Cyprian, Bishop of Carthage, going into exile under Decius, returning, and later being executed under Valerian). Other Christians were imprisoned for a while; sometimes only clergy were executed (as in the case of Cyprian). Much depended on time, place, circumstances, social status, and especially the changing attitudes of individual emperors.

[48] Even the so-called Great Persecution, technically dated from 303 to 313, was not Empire-wide, being only piecemeal and for the most part for short periods of time. For example, in the West, Christian executions took place over a three-year period (303–6). In propagandistic Christian hagiographies, the number of "martyrs" was generally exaggerated: See Barnes 2010: 97–150, especially 111–15, 126, 139–40, and for a summary, 293–4, 296–7.

[49] See in general Stark 1996: 163–89, especially 178–84 and more recently Barnes 2010, especially 106, 155; Moss 2013.

[50] See especially Barnes 2010. [51] See Stark 1996: 180–81.

[52] At this time, moreover, it should be remembered that the Roman state would not have distinguished between Jews and Christians, precisely because Christianized Jews, who were relatively few in number, were regarded as members of an heretical sect of Judaism.

know from Christian sources about the Christianized Jew Paul being beaten by Jewish authorities and driven out of Jewish communities throughout the Empire (2 Corinthians 11:25).[53] There has, nevertheless, been much scholarly debate about the nature of the expulsion from Rome – including whether there was one or possibly two banishments – and about exactly who the expelled "Jews" were. This controversy is partly due to the statement of Dio (60.6.6) that because of the great numbers of Jews resident in Rome and Claudius' reluctance to cause a tumult among them, he "did not expel them, but ordered them, while practicing the way of life of their fathers, not to have meetings." As has been rightly argued, Dio was probably referring to another incident that occurred earlier, at the beginning of Claudius' Principate in the year 41.[54] Suetonius' comment about expelling "Jews" later on in 49 did not mean that Claudius was expelling *all* Jews, which, as Dio noted, would have been impossible, especially since a number of them were Roman citizens. Suetonius' comment was most likely a generalization, as in the case of the expulsion of members of other problematic groups, like astrologers, philosophers, and Egyptians.[55] Moreover, identifying the troublemakers – whether proselytizing Christianized Jews or reactive orthodox Jews – would probably not have been particularly difficult at a formal inquest, since there were bound to have been informers and opponents who would have blamed one another.[56] As a result, all those who could be identified would have been expelled from Rome. Although Claudius was not interested in sectarian Jewish theosophical disputes, he did take seriously his responsibility for maintaining peace and order in the City.

14.3 The Christians and the Fire of 64 CE

As for the Christians and the fire of 64, interestingly no ancient source other than Tacitus (*Ann.* 38.44) connects them with this great conflagration. Dio, for example, does not speak of the Christians at all at the time of Nero, and Suetonius, who does mention them, does not associate them in any way with the conflagration, perhaps because neither Dio nor Suetonius wanted to deflect blame from Nero. This may also explain why later Christian writers, who selectively followed earlier sources,

[53] For St. Paul and the Christian communities of Rome, see Harrill (above n. 12).

[54] See, e.g., Smallwood 1981: 210–16, and more recently Engberg 2007: 92–6. For Jews in Rome, see Gruen 2002: 15–53 and cf. 36–41 on this issue.

[55] See Harrill (above n. 12).

[56] Cf. the somewhat analogous case, in which the Jews of Corinth hauled Paul before Gallio, the governor of Achaia (Greece), for his heretical teachings: Acts 18:12. See also Barnes 1968: 33.

generally do not mention Nero's blaming the Christians for the fire,[57] since that might raise questions about their possible involvement in causing the conflagration and divert attention from their being punished supposedly only for being Christians.[58] The fifth-century Christian author Orosius, who is not always reliable, goes further, asserting (7.7.10) that not only was Nero the first to "persecute" Christians for their religious beliefs, but also that he did this throughout the Empire, despite no evidence to support any such Empire-wide persecution. We know only that Christians were punished in the City of Rome on the charge of arson.

There was also another aspect to the case against the Christians. Suetonius (*Nero* 16) notes that during Nero's rule numerous abuses were dealt with severely and that among those punished were Christians, "a class of people who practiced a new and nefarious superstition" (*genus hominum superstitionis novae ac maleficae*). Tacitus, for his part, characterizes this new cult as a "destructive superstition" (*exitiabilis superstitio, Ann.* 15.44). The Romans generally regarded Christianity, like Judaism, as *superstitio*[59] in part because Christians were prone to go beyond proper religious behavior by, as noted earlier, professing their hatred of the gods of Rome and of the religious beliefs of other peoples, as well as not recognizing the ultimate authority of the Emperor, but rather only that of their god. In addition, Christians preached the second coming of Christ, which would mean the destruction of Rome,[60] and promoted zealotry and fanaticism among adherents.[61] They also were considered to practice magic.[62] In short, Christianity was regarded as a perversion

[57] The first Christian source to mention the Christians being blamed and punished by Nero for the fire is Severus Sulpicius (early fifth century), who in his *Chronica* (2.29.9) clearly follows Tacitus. On this matter and the suspicion – unfounded, in my opinion – that the passage in Tacitus is a Christian interpolation, see Walter 1957: 173–4; Barnes 1968: 35. This is also argued in a popular book on the fire by Dando-Collins 2010: 9–16, 106–10, with Egyptians being substituted for Christians in the putative interpolation! The earliest Christian source for Nero's punishment of Christians (without mention of the fire) is Melito (mid-second cent.) in Eusbius *HE* 4.26.9. See Barnes 1968: 34–5.

[58] See also Melito (*ap. Eus. Hist. Eccl.* 4.26.9); Tertullian (*Apol.* 5.3); Lactantius (*De mort. pers.* 2.6); Orosius 7.7.4.

[59] Cicero is one of the earliest sources for Judaism as being a *barbara superstitio* (*pro Flacco* 67). See further Gruen (2002) 42–4.

[60] Such predictions about the destruction of Rome were characteristic of what Romans regarded as *superstitio*, as we know, for example, in the case of the German prophet-priestess Veleda (Tac. *Hist.* 4.61). For these *vates superstitiosi* ("superstitious-minded prophets/preachers"), see further Janssen 1979: 135, 152.

[61] Regarding Christian *superstitio*, see especially the excellent article by Janssen 1979. Cf. also Wilken 1984: 48–50, 60–7 *et passim*.

[62] Christ himself was also regarded as a magician by some because of the miracles his follower claimed he performed. See, e.g., Celsus's charge preserved in Origen (*C. Cels.* 1.38, 68). See also

of religion and was eventually deemed illegal formally by imperial rescript by the time of Trajan.[63]

Little did the Romans realize in these early days how great and real a danger Christianity would ultimately pose to the polytheistic peoples of the Empire, beginning with Constantine's embrace of Christianity in the fourth century. It was only after the defeat in 324 of Licinius, the polytheistic Emperor of the East, that Constantine publicly declared that he was a Christian. However, it was probably not long after 324 that Constantine began to outlaw officially forms of polytheistic religion, especially blood sacrifices, which were at the core of institutionalized polytheistic religion.[64] This marked the beginning of the first assault on traditional polytheistic religions throughout the Empire. Constantine and his successors – except, of course, for Julian – gave the Church increasing power and help over time in implementing an intolerant and dogmatic ideology in an attempt to eradicate polytheism and to Christianize the Empire.[65] From the time of Constantine on, Christians began not only to persecute polytheists, non-orthodox Christians ("heretics"), "apostates," Jews, and Samaritans, as evidenced in the *Codex Theodosianus* (16.5–10), but also to destroy and desecrate a great deal of the religious and material culture of the polytheistic peoples of the Empire.[66]

Given the fundamental nature of Christianity, how is the punishment of Christians following the fire to be understood? Were they generally viewed as in some way a cause of the conflagration or were they merely scapegoats for Nero? Tacitus provides information about perceived Christian culpability for the fire and Roman animosity toward the Christians. He indicates (*Ann.* 15.44) that they were blamed and

Smith 1978. In addition, transubstantiation (1 Corinthians 11:23–5) could be interpreted as an act of magic. In Christian theology regarding the Eucharist, transubstantiation – the changing of the substance of the bread and wine into the substance of the body and blood of Christ – is considered not as symbolic but literal. See *ODWR*: 324 s.v. "Eucharist," 988 s.v. "transubstantiation." To change one substance into another in this fashion is fundamentally an act of magic, and the practice of magic under Rome was illegal: MacMullen 1966: 124–7; *OCD*: 908–11 s.v. "magic," especially 910 for Roman law with further bibliography. Transubstantiation/communion could also lead to the misperception of cannibalistic practices: Wilken 1984: 17–18; McGowan 1994.

63 And it remained so, at least on the books, until Gallienus decriminalized it in 260: See Barnes 1968: 36–48.

64 In the period from 342 to 356 Constantine's son Constantius II issued a series of laws (*Cod. Theod.* 16.10.3–6) that reiterated his father's edict, outlawing polytheistic religion and animal sacrifice in particular. At this time, it is also decreed that temples be closed and any access to them in the cities be forbidden (16.10.4). Also, the penalty for those polytheists who do not comply is for the first time specified as death, with their property remitted to imperial fiscus, that is, the personal treasury of the emperor (16.10.4, 6). Also discussed in Pollini, in progress.

65 See especially MacMullen 1984. Also Pollini (in progress).

66 See Sauer 2003; Pollini 2007, 2008, 2013; Kristensen 2013. Also Pollini, in progress.

cruelly punished not so much for arson as for their hatred of the human race (*haud perinde in crimine incendii quam odio humani generis convicti*).[67] He also speaks of Christians as loathed for their vices (*flagitia*)[68] and of Judaea as the home of this evil (*originem eius mali*). Following the fire, some Christians were burned alive, which was a well-known penalty for arson, since the Romans tended to make the punishment fit the crime whenever possible.[69] Although St. Peter is said to have perished in Rome under Nero, there is no hard evidence for this. Had he actually died there, he would probably have been burned alive and his charred remains either thrown into a common burial pit or dumped in the Tiber like most criminals. This, of course, is at variance with the unreliable Christian tradition that has him crucified upside down and buried under St. Peter's Basilica.[70] His burial in Rome, supposedly like that of Paul, who was probably executed and buried in Spain after being acquitted in Rome,[71] was undoubtedly intended to imbue the City of Rome with sanctity (Peter and Paul became the patron saints of Rome), in order to make it the most holy city of the West, as Jerusalem was for the East. Being burned alive for arson was a punishment still employed under Christian emperors, as the *Codex Justinianus* makes clear (*Digest* 49.9.9). When Nero blamed Christians for the great fire of Rome, his charge of arson would have been viewed by the Roman populace as credible, for even if Christians had not set Rome ablaze by their own hands or helped rekindle it after it had died down, they

67 In a lecture titled "Tacitus and the Defamation of the Jews" at UCLA (6/17/08), Erich Gruen suggested that the phrase *odio humani generis* could also read "because of the hatred of the human race" [toward the Christians]. This may be a stretch because the common charges of "misanthropy" (*misanthropeia*) and *amixia*, among others, brought against Jews for their anti-social opinions and behavior toward non-Jews applied equally to Christians: See Pollini 2012: 375–6. Tacitus (*Hist.* 5.5.2) also charged Jews with a similar hatred of mankind (*adversus omnes alios hostile odium*). Therefore, if Tacitus meant the human race's hatred toward Christians, he probably would have said *odio humani generis adversus eos*.

68 As already discussed above.

69 See Juvenal (8.235), Martial (10.25.5), and Seneca (Ep. 14.5).

70 On the lack of any hard evidence for the death of Peter in Rome, see Moss 2013: 134–8. With regard to Peter's alleged crucifixion in Rome, see Barnes 2010, who carefully and critically reviews the sources and mistaken scholarship, which has followed late second-century Christian sources for the traditional fiction of Peter's being crucified head-down. If he did perish by crucifixion, he would most likely have been bound to a pole or some sort of cross, dressed in a special tunic smeared with a flammable substance, such as is mentioned by Seneca (*Ep.* 14.5), that would have been set ablaze: 5–9, 26–31, 331–42; for the archaeological finds, including the putative bones of Peter in the so-called aedicular shrine of St. Peter, constructed ca. 150 to 170 under the high altar of St. Peter's Basilica, see Barnes 2010: 26–7 with n. 60, 397–413.

71 Paul's "martyrdom" in Rome appears to be another Christian fabrication of the late second century, when the tradition of "martyr stories" begins to come into vogue. For a review of the various sources, see further Barnes 2010: 31–5.

deserved to be punished because their blasphemy had angered the gods, who did not protect Rome against the conflagration.

Another important factor in Nero's blaming Christians was likely to have been his wife Poppaea, who is referred to by Josephus (*AJ* 20.195) as a "god-fearer (θεοσεβὴς) . . . [who] pleaded on behalf of the Jews."[72] But rather than being a convert to Judaism, Poppaea, like certain other non-Jewish intellectuals, was probably interested in Jewish philosophy and would therefore have been sympathetic to the Jewish point of view, especially regarding Christians, who were hated by mainstream Jews. She would undoubtedly have had ties to the leadership of the Jewish quarter of Rome and would have been a strong advocate for them.[73] Poppaea probably learned from them of the heretical sect of Jews (i.e., Christianized Jews) who was stirring up trouble not only in Rome but throughout the Empire, so who better to blame than the Christians? By planting in Nero's mind the idea of Christian involvement in the fire, Poppaea would have been instrumental not only in bringing down the wrath of Rome on these Christianized Jewish heretics, but also in providing an alternative to rumors of Nero's alleged culpability. In short, she was blaming the Christians because of what her Jewish sources said or implied. This hypothesis would be in keeping with late Christian writers, who say that the Jews denounced the Christians for the fire.[74]

It is also not out of the question that more fanatically inclined Christians may in fact have played an active role in the conflagration. Tacitus tells us (*Ann.* 15.44) that those Christians who were apprehended confessed. Although he does not state to what they confessed, it is reasonable to conclude that under torture they probably would have admitted that they were guilty of arson – whether that was really true or not – and implicated others. Tacitus' claim (*Ann.* 15.44) that a great many Christians were convicted (*eorum multitudo ingens*) is undoubtedly an exaggeration, since at the time of Nero there could not have been a large number of them in Rome,[75] especially so soon after Claudius' expulsion. A few Christian extremists may have interpreted the Great Fire of 64 as the beginning of the predicted fiery apocalypse and the second coming of Christ, which Christians of that time believed was imminent, rather than something that would take place at some distant

[72] See further *RE* 22.1 (1953) 85–91, especially 87–8 s.v. "Poppaea Sabina"(R. Hanslik); Hanslik 1963: 92–108, especially 99–100. For Poppaea, see also *OCD*: 1221 s.v. "Poppaea Sabina."

[73] See, e.g., Hanslik 1963: 99–100; Henrichs 1970: 23–4.

[74] See Momigliano 1934: 726.

[75] Furneaux 1907: 375, 575, in his commentary on *multitudo ingens*, is certainly correct in stating that this is rhetorical. See also Clarke 1996: 870; Stark 1996: 179–80.

time in the future.[76] Some might even have felt that it was their duty as Christians to hasten this day of judgment and so helped to spread the flames or at least refused to do anything to extinguish them.

The Christian message of a fiery apocalyptic end and of eternal damnation for "idol-worshipers," as well as for those who did not accept Christ, was not a new idea. It had a long history in the apocalyptic literature of Hellenistic Judaism and in the Jewish Sibylline Oracles, which Alexandrian Jews had modeled on the oracular sayings of the Greeks and which the Christians later further adapted.[77] Dozens of books of Christian revelations were found along with Gnostic gospels in the 1945 Nag Hammadi finds in Upper Egypt.[78] The most infamous vision of this fire-and-brimstone myth, of course, is captured in the Book of Revelation, probably written in the late autumn of 68 C.E. by a malcontent Christianized Jew, possibly by the name of John, not to be confused with the Apostle John.[79] The Book of Revelation reads like the rants of a lunatic, in which Nero is cast as the Antichrist who will return from death (13:3), and the eternally detested Rome will in the end be destroyed with the second coming of Christ (17:6, 18:24, 19:2). With such predictions of the destruction of Rome, little wonder that Christianity was thought to be a *superstitio* and the product of a *mens insana* ("insane mind"), going beyond proper *religio* and causing disruption in the fabric of society.[80] The invention of such a fiery apocalypse was intended to terrify and at the same time reassure believers – whether Jews or Christians – of their righteousness and to give them hope that their suffering on earth would be rewarded with their final triumph over the "wicked idolaters" of the world – strong motives perhaps for some

[76] For the imminence of the apocalypse in Paul's thinking, see e.g., 1 Thessalonians 4:15-17 (dated ca. 51); for a number of early Christian followers, as well as for some Jews, see, e.g., Hopkins 1999: 87 et passim. For the apocalyptic tradition in the Jesus movement, see Meeks 1983: 171–80; White 1988, especially 12–13. This impending destruction was also in the prophecies of the Jews (e.g., Malachi 4.1). For the apocalyptic literature of the Jews and Christians, see *OCB*: 34–41 s.v. "Apocalyptic Literature."

[77] The original Sibylline Oracles were widely circulated in the Greek and Roman world long before the Jews appropriated them. For the Sibylline Oracles in general, see Parke 1988. For the appropriation and revision of the Sibylline Oracles in Jewish tradition, see Gruen 1998: 268–91. In *Sib. Or.* 3.63-74, Nero appears to be equated with the wicked Beliar. See further Collins 1974: 80–7; Gruen 1998: 271, 285–6. The view of an imminent end of the world ("the Second Coming") was also held by the fiercely monotheistic Qumran sectarians: Hopkins 1999: 51.

[78] Pagels 2012: 40, 74, 99–101, 145, 167, 202 n. 28.

[79] See especially Barnes 2010: 36–40. Cf. Pagels 2012. For the role of the imperial cult in the creation of the Book of Revelation, see Friesen 2001. For a succinct commentary, see *OBC*: 1287–1306, but for a comprehensive and exegetical treatment of its text and its reception from antiquity to the present, see Stevens 2014.

[80] For the relation of *superstitio* and *insania*, see above. For the possibility of Christians being put to death for merely disturbing the peace, see Barnes 1968: 49.

unhinged Christian fanatic(s) to resort to arson. In the end, however, whether a few Christians helped to spread the fire, especially after it had died down, should remain an open question. What is far more certain is that many Romans of that time would have believed that the Christians were guilty of arson or at least indirectly responsible for the Great Fire because of their denigration of the traditional gods, leading to the disruption of the *pax deorum* and consequently the loss of divine goodwill and protection, resulting in the fiery holocaust of 64.

Further Reading

For Nero and the fire of 64, see especially Momigliano 1934, Warmington 1969, Griffin 1984, Wiedemann 1996, Panella 2011b, and cf. Champlin 2003. For the topography of Rome with regard to the archaeological evidence for Nero's building activities, see Ball 2003, Carandini and Papi 1999, Carandini 2010, Tomei and Rea (eds.) 2011 and La Roca Chapter 13 of this volume.

For Christianity, see Meeks 1983, MacMullen 1984, Clarke 1996, Engberg 2007, and especially Wilken 1995 and Hopkins 1999 for how the Romans saw them. See also Harrill's bibliography in Chapter 17 of this volume. For Christianity as a *superstitio*: Janssen 1979 and Wilken 1995. For the Christian apocalyptic tradition: Barnes 1968; Pagels 2012, and Stevens 2014. For the myth of Christians' being systematically persecuted by the Romans, see Stark 1996, Barnes 2010, and Moss 2013. For the destructive nature of Christianity, see Sauer 2003, Pollini 2007, 2008, 2013, and Kristensen 2013. The best late antique source for Christians persecuting polytheists and others is the *Codex Theodosianus* (to be used with caution), especially 16.10 (polytheists), 16.5 (heretics), 16.7 ("apostates"), 16.8 (Jews and others).

For the Jews under Roman rule, see Smallwood 1981, Gruen 1998, 2002, and Pollini 2012: 369–411. For a detailed study of Roman religion, see Beard, North, and Price 1998; for a more concise survey: North 2000. For the Sibylline Oracles in general, see Parke 1988.

15: Nero's Memory in Flavian Rome

Eric Varner

The Flavian period (that is, the reign of Vespasian, Titus, and Domitian, 69–96 CE) is often characterized as a violent reaction to the excesses of Nero's principate and, in the visual arts, as a wholesale repudiation of Nero's artistic legacy. In particular, the Colosseum and Templum Pacis are positioned as vehement interventions in the urban landscape that corrected the reckless excess of the Domus Aurea. Authors like Packer and Darwall-Smith frame the Flavian architectural program as a "restoration of public order" and a "monumentalization of the emperor's piety," and characterize the new emperors Vespasian and Titus as "constitutional fathers of the country building for the common good."[1] For Frederick, Flavian buildings typically "overwhelm and erase" those of Nero.[2] Nevertheless, in Rome, the "Flavian aftermath" is not so much an antithesis of Nero's artistic and architectural extravagance, but rather a careful recalibration of the Neronian visual program. While it is true that some of Nero's monuments were destroyed or obliterated, Flavian works of art and architecture also consciously reposition and expropriate much of Nero's impressive artistic output.[3]

Nero was the first of Rome's "bad" emperors whose memory was officially condemned as an immediate result of the Senate's declaration of the emperor as an enemy of the Roman state (*hostis*; Suet. *Nero* 49.2).[4] Prior to Nero, the Senate had officially condemned the memories of Sejanus (Dio 58.12.2), Livilla (Tac. *Ann.* 6.2), and Messalina (Tac. *Ann.* 11.38.3), and Caligula was subjected to tacit sanctions that were not,

[1] Darwall-Smith 1996: 252–62; Packer 2003, 176–7. [2] Frederick 2003, 206.

[3] On Nero's artistic and aesthetic program, see C. Vout and E. La Rocca, Chapters 12 and 13 in this volume. For Flavian Rome and the memory of Nero, see Flower 2006, 228–32.

[4] *Se hostem a senatu judicatum et quaeri ut puniatur more maiorum* (he had been condemned as an enemy of the Roman state by the Senate and they sought that he be punished according the custom of the ancestors).

however, officially endorsed by the Senate at Claudius's direct behest (Suet. *Claud.* 11.3; Dio 60.4.5; Packer 2003, 176–7, 6). Actions taken against Nero's memory included the erasure of the emperor's name in some inscriptions, the countermarking of coins, as well as the destruction, reconfiguration, and removal of Nero's portraits.

These sanctions against Nero and his wife Poppaea were certainly enforced during the eight-month principate of Galba, but were clearly rescinded under Otho, who returned the portraits of Nero and Poppaea to public view (Suet. *Otho* 7; Tac. *Hist.* 1.7).[5] Both Otho and Vitellius exploited the positive side of Nero's legacy: in his portraits, Otho deliberately evokes Nero's later portraits with their elaborate and artificial waved coiffures, and he was not averse to being called Otho Nero, while Vitellius made sacrifices to Nero's departed spirit, allowed his songs to be performed in public, and generally followed a policy of *imitatio Neronis* (Suet. *Otho* 7.1; Suet. *Vit.* 11.2; Dio 64.7.3).[6] Ultimately, it fell to Vespasian to reinforce the sanctions.

15.1 Flavian Portraits: Obliteration and Expropriation

The tension between canceclation and defamation that informed all memory sanctions (popularly known as *damnatio memoriae*) in ancient Rome was especially fraught for the Flavian emperors in their response to Nero's posthumous legacy.[7] While Nero had lost the support of the army and much of the senatorial elite by the end of his principate, he remained astonishingly popular with much of the populace after his death. The emperor's cremated remains were actually interred in a magnificent porphyry sarcophagus surmounted by a Luna marble (modern Carrara) altar and surrounded by an enclosure of Thasian marble that was added to the funerary complex belonging to his father's family, the Domitii Ahenobarbi, at the summit of the Pincio.[8] The tomb complex would have been a commanding presence in the Flavian cityscape overlooking the Via Flaminia as visitors to the city entered from the north, effectively producing a Neronian punctuation mark to the Mausoleum of Augustus across the Via Flaminia to the west. Suetonius notes that the complex of the Domitii was visible from the Campus Martius (*quod*

[5] See also Paus *Otho* 3.1; Hekster 2015, 10. [6] Carré 1999; Rosso 2008: 46.

[7] On the tensions that result from "remembering to forget," see Hedrick 2000: 89–130; for the ambiguous responses to Nero's memory during the Flavian period, see, in particular, Rosso 2008.

[8] Suet. *Nero* 50; Marigliani 2012: 296–8.

15.1 Tomb of the Domitii, Pirro Ligorio, *Effigies Antiquae Romae* 1561 (1773 edition by Carlo Losi), Atlanta, Emory University, Rose Manuscript Archives and Rare Book Library and the Michael C. Carlos Museum.

prospicitur e campo) (Figure 15.1).[9] Nero's posthumous admirers decorated the tomb with flowers during the spring and summer and placed his togate images on the Rostra in the Roman Forum (Suet. *Nero* 57). Significantly, Nero's continued popularity also spawned a number of posthumous

[9] Locchi 2012: 104; for the alternative theory that the tomb was on the southern edge of the hill, toward the Quirinal, see Colini 1977; Locchi 2012: 107.

imposters into the second century CE who have aptly been termed *Nero-messiahs* (Suet. *Nero* 49, 57.2; Tac. *Hist.* 2.8.1; Dio 64.9.3, 66.19.3).[10] Dio Chrysostom, in an oration delivered ca. 88 when he was in exile under Domitian, claimed that many people still believed Nero was alive (*Orations* 21). Indeed, the myth of Nero *redivivus* proved enduring in Jewish and early Christian apocalyptic literature.[11]

A small number of Nero's portraits do appear to have been destroyed or intentionally mutilated as a result of the memory sanctions. Portraits from Cos and Cagliari have been defaced, with severe damage to the eyes, noses, mouths, and chins.[12] The Cagliari portrait, which is thought to have been acquired on the mainland, has suffered the additional indignity of having VICTO (to the vanquished) scratched on its right breast in an ironic inversion of victory invocations. Three other substantially damaged portraits in Vicenza, Syracuse, and Vienne may owe their fragmentary and compromised formats to acts of intentional destruction.[13] Nero's glyptic (carved or engraved) images were also mutilated, as in an amethyst from Xanten where facing portraits of Nero and Poppaea have been attacked.[14] In the Xanten amethyst, the features of the emperor and empress are defaced, with the forepart of their profiles chiseled off. Poppaea's profile has been similarly mutilated in a sardonyx cameo in a private collection in Bonn.[15] The use of amethyst for early imperial portrait gems is rare, so its employment in the Xanten example, together with other Neronian gems, suggests a Neronian predilection for the stone.[16]

A bronze replica of Nero's fourth and final portrait type, in use between 64 and 68, now in a private collection, seems to have been violently attacked and decapitated from its statue body and then buried.[17] Corrosion evidence to the breaks at the back of the head confirm the antiquity of the damage to the head. A number of other portraits, including two from a cryptoporticus associated with the Temple of Apollo on the Palatine, appear to have been warehoused following Nero's

[10] Klauck 2001, 685–6; De Jong and Hekster, 2008, 85; Maier 2013, 386.

[11] Klauck 2001; Maier 2013.

[12] Cos, Museum, inv. 4510; Varner 2004, 49–50, 114, 171, 186, 237, cat. 2.2; Cagliari, Museo Nazionale, inv. 6122; Varner 2004, 49–50, 114, 237, cat. 2.1, figure 42.

[13] Vicenza, Museo Civico, inv. EI-19; Varner (2004) 50, cat. 2.4; Syracuse, Museo Nazionale, inv. 6383; Varner (2004) cat. 2.2, figure 43; Vienne, Musée Archéologique; h. 0.195 m; Varner (2004) cat. 2.5; figure 44.

[14] Xanten, Grave 10, Viktorstrasse 21, no. 10.4; Platz-Horster (2001).

[15] Megow, 1987, 260–1, no. B 28, pl. 34.14–16.

[16] For other Neronian amethysts, see, e.g., Spier (2010) 54, no. 30; Vollenweider and Avisseau-Broustet (2003) 114–15, no. 128; Platz-Horster (2001) 63–4, figure 4.

[17] Born and Stemmer 1997.

15.2 Nero, Rome, Museo Nazionale Romano, Palazzo Massimo alle Terme, inv. 616, photo E. Varner.

demise (Figures 15.2 and 15.3).[18] These likenesses, replicas of Nero's second and third portrait types, were removed from their statues, stored in the cryptoporticus, and presumably replaced with new portrait heads. A bronze bust from a cycle of Julio-Claudian portraits displayed at a residence in the Campus Martius was stored in an underground room of the house, together with the other Julio-Claudian likenesses that included Augustus and Gaius Caesar.[19] The house may have belonged to T. Sextius Africanus, *Consul Suffectus* in 59 CE, and all of the Julio-Claudian portraits may have been removed from view and stored during the political upheavals of 68–9 CE.[20]

The destruction and removal of Nero's likenesses, however, was a fairly limited phenomenon and is paralleled in the epigraphical record by

[18] Museo Nazionale Romano, Palazzo Massimo alle Terme, inv. 616; C. Gasparri and R. Paris, eds. 2013, 107, no. 58 (S. Gianetti); Museo Palatino, inv. 618 Gasparri and Tomei, eds., 2014, 237, no. 55 (L. Di Franco).

[19] On the hiding of Roman statuary, see Ambrogi 2011.

[20] *CIL* 6.31684; Richardson 1992, 135 ("Domus T. Sextius Africanus"); Eck 1995.

15.3 Nero, Rome, Museo Palatino, inv. 618, photo E. Varner.

the erasure of his name in inscriptions.[21] Rather, the overwhelmingly preferred response to Nero's representations seems to have been recycling. Indeed, the sheer number of portraits of all three Flavian emperors, Vespasian, Titus, and Domitian, that have been sculpturally redacted from preexisting likeness of Nero (at least forty-six) reveal both the profound power of the original Neronian images and the conscious choice made to reclaim them through reconfiguration.[22] At least sixteen portraits of Vespasian's main, older type and his more youthful secondary type have been re-carved from portraits of Nero. In many cases, Vespasian's more veristically rendered and emphatically older facial features cancel almost all trace of the Neronian original and signal a radical stylistic break from both of Nero's prevailing portrait modes, the youthful and idealized Julio-Claudian images from the first five years of the principate, or the more emphatically modeled and monarchic representations introduced in 59. Nevertheless, legible remnants of the reworked portraits' Neronian

[21] Eck 2002.

[22] See Varner 2004, 240–54, cat. nos. 2.15–59; Prusac 2011, nos. 134–7, 55–110.

15.4 Nero/Vespasian, Rome, Museo Nazionale Romano, Palazzo Massimo alle Terme, inv. 53, photo E. Varner.

iterations are almost always preserved so that astute viewers can read the transformation that has ensued: namely, Vespasian has subsumed Nero's image and all of its inherent potency. For example, while a portrait in the Palazzo Massimo presents Vespasian's realistically rendered facial features, the longer, more elaborately styled hair from Nero's third portrait type is still clearly visible at the back of the head and behind the ears (Figure 15.4).[23] More portraits of Nero have been re-carved than for any other emperor, and their reconfiguration held powerful political, as well as aesthetic implications. The readable traces of the original image allowed visually astute viewers to assess the shift in the political landscape and the regime change from the Julio-Claudians to the Flavians. Portraits that remained in their original contexts would have made the political readings that much more apprehensible to viewers. The new hybrid images merged the realistically aged facial features of Vespasian with the remnants of Nero's likeness.

[23] Rome, Museo Nazionale Romano, Palazzo Massimo alle Terme, inv. 53, h. 0.35 m; Gasparri and Paris, eds., 2013, 167, no. 108 (G. Scarpati).

15.5 Nero/Titus, Rome, Galleria Borghese, inv. 748, photo E. Varner.

The same is also true for portraits of Vespasian's sons, Titus and Domitian, that have been refashioned from likenesses of Nero. At least ten surviving representations of Titus have been reconfigured from images of Nero, including a re-carved head in the Villa Borghese (Figure 15.5).[24] As with the recut portraits of Vespasian, clear traces of the Neronian original are evident in the carefully ordered locks over the forehead, which are oriented as in Nero's third type and the full receding lower lip. Nero's glyptic portraits were also reworked; in an onyx cameo in Florence Titus reprises Nero's role as Jupiter, replete with *aegis*, eagle-topped scepter and oak-leaf crown (*corona civica*).[25] Nero's longer waved coiffure has been left in evidence over most of the top and back of the head, creating a kind of hybrid Nero-Titus configuration, so that once again the transformative history of the gem is plain to see for informed viewers. The Neronian inflections of Domitian's recut images can be even more heightened because of formal similarities between Domitian's hairstyles and those of Nero's final two portrait types. As the youngest of the Flavians, Domitian adapts the innovative and transgressive aspects of Nero's last two hairstyles (see La Rocca in

[24] Sala del Ermafrodito 171, inv. 748; Moreno and Viacava 2003, 212–13, no. 195.
[25] Florence, Museo Archeologico, inv. 14546; A. Giuliano (1989) 246–7, no. 178; Megow (1993).

15.6 Domitian, Rome, Palazzo dei Conservatori, inv. 1156, photo E. Varner.

the Appendix to this volume, with Figures A.3 and A.4) in his first portrait type introduced at the outset of his father's principate, and returns to them again in his third and final portrait type, created to mark his accession in 81) (Figures 15.6 and 15.7).[26]

Domitian also coopted Nero's glyptic legacy. A sardonyx cameo in Minden with Domitian's third portrait type has been recrafted from a preexisting likeness of Nero's second type.[27] Clear traces of the original Neronian coiffure are still evident over the forehead, in front of the ears, and on the nape of the neck. The overall mass of the head and neck, as well as the size of the oak-leaf crown (*corona civica*) are no longer commensurate in scale with the reduced size of the face, reinforcing the fact that this is a recycled image. With the exception of the Florentine cameo of Titus recut from Nero, large-scale portrait gems that had been so prevalent under the Julio-Claudian emperors are essentially nonexistent under Vespasian and Titus, but their production noticeably resumes under Domitian, as he sought to leverage their power and potential.

[26] Fittschen and Zanker 1985, 36–7, no. 33, pls. 35, 37.

[27] Domschatz; Megow 1987, 218–20, no. A 107, pl. 36.4; Varner 2004, 60–1, 249, no. 2.45, figure 69.

15.7 Nero/Domitian, Naples, Museo Nazionale Archeologico, inv. 6061, photo E. Varner.

Nero's portraits could also be recuperated through retrospective recycling, as confirmed by a portrait of the first emperor Augustus in the Vatican, which has been recut from a replica of Nero's third portrait type (see Figure 15.8).[28] The waved arrangement of the hair on the top of the head is still clearly visible from the Neronian likeness, as is the reverse direction of locks over the outer corner of the right eye. The portrait has also retained some of the fullness of Nero's physiognomy. The portrait is unusual for its headgear, which is the *corona spicea* made up of wheat stalks. This crown is more usually associated with female deities like Ceres or imperial women, such as Nero's great grandmothers, Livia and Antonia Minor, or his mother, Agrippina Minor.[29] Nero is, in fact, the first emperor to feature the crown in his sculpted portraits (see La Rocca, Chapter 13 and the Appendix in this volume).

[28] Sala dei Busti 274, inv. 715; h. 0.33 m.; Spaeth 1996, 23, fig. 9; Spinola 1999, 128, no. 124; Varner 2004, 11, n. 63, 61–2, fig. 72a–b.

[29] Spaeth 1996, 171, no. 1.20; 172, nos. 1.16, 1.21; 173, nos. 1.23–6 (Livia); 173, nos. 2.1–2 (Antonia Minor); 174, nos. 6.4, 6.6–9 (Agrippina Minor).

15.8 Nero/Augustus, Rome, Musei Vaticani, Sala dei Busti 274, inv. 715, photo E. Varner.

In the male imperial sphere, the crown is associated with the Arval Brethren. The Vatican head is thought to have come from La Magliana, the site of the Arvals' main sanctuary of the Dea Dia. Nero features prominently in the lists of the Arvals, which record numerous sacrifices in his honor or at his behest, and the portrait's re-carving may have rehabilitated the image of his great-great grandfather Augustus, who had revived the Arval Brethren. A second portrait of Nero from the Arvals' sanctuary was reconstituted as Titus or Domitian.[30] The reconfiguration of the two Neronian likenesses at the site may have been part of a Flavian attempt to reclaim the Arvals during their interventions at the sanctuary, and their repurposing stands in contrast to the inscribed records of the Arvals where Nero's name is not erased.[31] Nero's images could also

[30] Museo Nazionale Romano, Terme di Diocleziano, Chiostro Piccolo, inv. 587757, h. 0.24 m; Friggeri, Cianetti, Caruso 2014, 72, no. 2 (C. Evers).

[31] See Flower (2006) 223–8; For the Flavian interventions at the sanctuary, see Friggeri, Cianetti, and Caruso, eds. 2014, 62–3 (Caruso).

be retrospectively refashioned as Claudius, as evidenced by a portrait now in Baltimore.[32]

Two cuirassed portraits of Nero re-carved as images of Titus in Olympia and Domitian in Rome[33] (see Figure 15.9) suggest that both emperors were also willing to coopt new and innovative marine imagery introduced onto breastplates during Nero's principate. In both statues, the cuirasses feature Nereids, dolphins, and sea creatures, introduced by Neronian artists into the repertoire of cuirass decoration in order to celebrate Nero's dominance over land and sea, imagery now coopted by the new Flavian rulers. At least five other statues including works in Rome, Bologna, Durres, Narona, and the Louvre, have nearly identical marine decoration on their cuirasses comprising dolphins and Nereids on hippocamps, suggesting that they also originally belonged to portraits of Nero as well.

In all of the reused portraits and cuirasses, as well as Domitian's direct adaptation of Neronian hairstyles, there is an implicit *imitatio* Neronis that is at odds with notions of repudiation and denigration embedded in the memory sanctions. According to Suetonius, the similarities between Nero and Titus were strong enough that during Vespasian's principate it was widely thought that Titus would be another Nero (*denique propalam alium Neronem et opinabatur et praedicabant*; Suet. *Titus* 7.1.). The two are also compared and contrasted in other ways. For Pliny, Nero is *hostis generis humani* (the declared enemy of the human race), while Suetonius describes Titus as the *amor ac deliciae generis humani* (the love and delight of the human race). Suetonius may well have Pliny's formulation in mind, as well as Martial's formulation of Titus as *deliciae populi* (Pliny, *HN* 7.8.46; Suet. *Titus* 1; Mart. *Lib. Spec.* 2.12). Suetonius also seems to contrast the two for their building and construction habits; Nero could not be more financially wasteful (*damnosior*) for his building, especially the two imperial residences, the Domus Transitoria and the Domus Aurea, while Titus is not to be outdone for the munificence associated with his buildings, like the Colosseum and his Baths.[34] Titus's Baths, however, also seem to have been coopted from Nero as they appear to have been originally constructed as baths for the Esquiline wing of the Domus Aurea, which were then adapted by Titus and dedicated, together with the Colosseum in 80

[32] Walters Art Museum, inv. 23.118; Varner 2004, 63, 240, no. 2.13.

[33] Olympia, Museum no. 144; K. Stemmer (1978) 33–4, no. III 5, pl. 18. 1; L. Sperti (1990) 10, figure 32; E. R. Varner (2004) 56, 57, 72, 247, no. 2.3. Rome, Musei Vaticani, Braccio Nuovo 126, inv. 2213; h. 2.45 m.; E. R. Varner (2004) 57–8, 70, n. 206, 72, 125, figure 59.

[34] *Nero* 31.1: *non in alia re tamen damnosior quam in aedificando* (not in any other thing, however, was he more wastefully extravagant than in building). *Titus* 7.3: *et tamen nemine ante se munificentia minor* (and his munificence was not less than any of his predecessors).

15.9 Nero/Titus or Domitian, Museo Nazionale Romano, Chiostro Piccolo, inv. 587757, photo E. Varner.

CE.[35] Titus's Baths share a number of design similarities with Nero's Baths in the Campus Martius. Their alignment with the Esquiline wing of the

35 Caruso (1999); Ball 2003, 249–53.

Domus Aurea, rather than to the Colosseum, together with the apparent speed with which they were built (approximately one year), strongly suggest that the Baths of Titus, are, in fact, Neronian, expropriated in much the same way as the portraits.

15.2 Flavian Rome: Reclaiming Neropolis

Even one of Nero's most virulent historical detractors, Tacitus, begrudgingly admits the remarkable beauty of the rebuilt city (*tanta resurgentis urbis pulchritudine*) following the Great Fire of 64 CE, which had destroyed nearly two-thirds of the city (*Ann.* 14.51). The Flavians sought to reshape Nero's *Urbs Nova* as their own Roma Resurge(n)s (as promoted in the coinage) after the civil wars of 68–9 and the devastation inflicted on the city during the conflict with Vitellius that included the total destruction of the Temple of Jupiter Optimus Maximus Capitolinus.[36] The Colosseum remains a primary *locus* of Flavian efforts to purge the city of Nero's architectural excesses and reclaim it for the public benefit. In the second epigram from the *Liber Spectacularum*, Martial famously contrasts the venerable mass of the new amphitheater with the hateful atria of a ferocious king (*Spect.* 2.3, 2.5–6). The epigram ends with Rome being restored to herself and the luxuries of the master now belonging to the people (*Spect.* 2.11–12).[37] Thus the Colosseum translates the private pleasure park of Nero into a public arena for spectacle. The Colosseum, however, navigates Nero's cultural legacy in a much more complex fashion. The Domus Aurea was assuredly not a private residence with highly restricted access, but like all elite Roman residences a very publicly visible architectural backdrop for its owner.[38]

Indeed, the area of the Domus Aurea on which the Colosseum was eventually constructed may have been one of the most publicly accessible parts of Nero's residence. Here, the artificial lake Suetonius described as being as large as a sea was surrounded by a colonnade whose excavated architecture suggests extensive commercial activity in the form of numerous shops. The Colosseum is also noteworthy for the quality and refinement of its architectural details and decoration, and it is surely a direct response to Nero's opulent amphitheater in the Campus

[36] *Roma resurgens* on Vespasian's coins cf. Bravi 2009 177; Carradice and Buttrey 2007: 67, nos. 109–10, 73, nos. 194–5, 85, no. 382; see also Rosso 2008, 58–61.

[37] See Coleman 2006, 14–36.

[38] Champlin 1998; Davies 2000; Welch 2002; Rutledge 2012.

Martius, which was likely destroyed in the fire of 64 and not yet rebuilt at the time of Nero's suicide in 68.[39] The Colosseum in effect relocates Nero's spectacular amphitheater from the Campus Martius, the site of other entertainment complexes like the theaters of Pompey, Balbus, and Marcellus, to the valley between the Palatine, Caelian, and Esquiline Hills where Nero's artificial lake (*stagnum*) had been a central landscape feature of the Domus Aurea. The dedicatory inscription of the Colosseum, in both its original version under Vespasian, and slightly modified form under Titus, refers to the structure as the Amphitheatrum Novum in direct contradistinction to what would have been the older, Neronian amphitheater, now destroyed.[40]

During much of the Flavian period and into the reign of Trajan, the Domus Aurea was staged as a dilapidated ruin, despoiled of its precious materials, its rooms given over to humble utilitarian uses like slaves' barracks or gladiators' quarters, its opulent architecture now thoroughly upstaged by the Colosseum.[41] The Domus Aurea seems to have been purposefully abandoned by the Flavians and Vespasian is said to have preferred the Horti Sallustiani as an imperial residence.[42] Martial characterizes Nero's residence in famously negative terms, its odious halls of a ferocious king shining and taking up the whole of the city (*Ep.* 2.3). *Invidosus*, the word used to describe the Domus Aurea as odious, can also mean enviable, which highlights the tensions inherent in the Flavians' engagement with Nero's monumental legacy. For Tacitus, the Domus Aurea is "that hateful residence extracted from the spoils of the citizens," suggesting a kind of victory monument from a civil conflict, which implicitly contrasts it with the Flavian Amphitheater, whose inscription says that it was constructed *ex manubiis*, from legitimate foreign conquests. Furthermore, the inappropriateness of the architecture and decoration of the Domus Aurea and its lack of decorum confirm Nero as a *princeps malus*.[43]

Vespasian intervened in other aspects of the Domus Aurea. Although Suetonius claims that Vespasian completed construction of the Temple of Divus Claudius, which Nero had neglected, it seems far more likely that he only rededicated the monument (Suet. *Claud.* 45,

[39] D. Palombini, 1993; Von Hesberg 2011, 111; Beste and von Hesberg 2013, 318.

[40] *IMP CAES VESPASIANVS AVG/AMPHITHATRVM NOVVM/EX MANIBUS FIERI IVSSIT*; Alföldy 1995; Noreña 2003: 36; Welch 2002: 133; Rosso 2008: 58–9, figure 3. Alföldy, G. 2002. "*Amphitheatrum Novum* l'innaugurazione," in R. Rea, ed. *La Rota Colisei. La Valle del Collosseo attraverso I secoli* 14–35. Milan.

[41] Ball 2003, 94, on the late revisions to the pentagonal court.

[42] Dio. 65.10.5. See Scheithauer 2000, 129–32, for the perceived Flavian policy of distancing themselves from Nero's building projects.

[43] Scheithauer 2000: 116.

Vesp. 9.1).[44] Within the overall context of Nero's two residential projects, the Domus Transitoria and the Domus Aurea, the large temple with its massive nymphaeum (at fifty meters in length the largest fountain ever constructed in Rome) would have functioned as a spectacular villa monument to Nero's divine father, much like other villa memorials.[45] With the destruction of the artificial lake and surrounding gardens, the Temple was effectively dissociated from Nero's residences and Vespasian's rededication of it acted to effectively recuperate a divine imperial ancestor for the Flavians, again like the retrospectively recycled portraits or the restoration coins of Titus. The Flavians also seem to have reclaimed the Curiae Veteres, a venerable structure associated both with Romulus and Augustus at the northeast corner of the Palatine. Nero had significantly altered the precinct, but the substantial Flavian architectural interventions seem to have restored it to more of its original format.[46]

Like the Colosseum, with its *ex manubiis* inscription, the Templum Pacis has been read as another victory monument, celebrating the cessation of civil war as well as the foreign victory over Judaea (see Figure A.4 in the Appendix). It is also a monumental response to integral aspects of the Domus Aurea, intended to instantiate an architectural dialectic between Templum and Domus. In particular, the Templum Pacis became the locus for display of works collected by Nero for the Domus Aurea, and its water features and garden elements reprised landscape features of Nero's residence.[47]

Dedicated in 75 CE, the Templum Pacis was constructed on the site of the republican indoor market, or *macellum*, whose earlier layout dictated the square shape of the Templum Pacis.[48] Nero's construction of the new Macellum Magnum on the Caelian made elimination of the old Macellum possible. Tabernacles with triangular pediments lined the back walls of the colonnade, and these were presumably designed to showcase works of sculpture retrieved from the Domus Aurea. Sculpture may also have been displayed amidst the plantings and water features that filled the open area of the Templum.[49] What struck visitors to the Templum was the vast quantity and quality of the works of art on display there. Pliny the Elder lists the Templum Pacis among the most beautiful of works of architecture (*pulcherrima operum*) in the city of

44 For the Temple's likely completion under Nero, see von Hesberg 2011, 110 and Beste and von Hesberg 2013, 317.

45 On villa monuments, see Bodel 1997.

46 Panella and Ferrandes 2013.

47 Meneghini, Corsaro, and Pinna Caboni 2009, 190.

48 De Ruyt 1983, 160–3; Noreña 2003, 26; Packer 2003, 170.

49 Packer 2003, 171, 181.

Rome, together with the Circus Maximus as reconstructed by Julius Caesar and the Forum of Augustus (*HN* 36.101–2), and astute readers would recall the great masterpieces of sculpture (*operibus*) Pliny listed earlier in book 34 which had been collected by Nero and later transferred by Vespasian to the very same Templum Pacis (*HN* 34.84). For Josephus, the Templum Pacis contained all of the greatest works of art that people formerly had to travel the world to see (*BJ* 7). Because of its comprehensive display of art, the Templum Pacis is a paramount achievement of Vespasian's architectural legacy, made possible, however, by Nero, who had largely curated the collection by transferring the monuments to Rome.[50] Ancient authors consistently condemn Nero for his rapacious collecting habit, while Vespasian receives maximum praise for putting Nero's collection on view in the new Templum Pacis.[51] The list of known works on display at the Templum is impressive. According to ancient authors, the Templum showcased sculptures and paintings by Myron, Pheidas, Leochares, Polyclitus, Apelles, and Timanthus.[52] Statue bases found at the site also confirm sculptures by Praxiteles (or Pasiteles), Cephisodotus, and Parthenokles.[53]

Because of its extensive landscaping, the Templum Pacis has also been described as "imperialist botanical gardens."[54] The plantings on display appear to have come from all over the world, and there is archeo-botanical evidence for the *rosa gallica*.[55] Nevertheless, the landscape elements of the Templum can also be read as a response to the gardens of the Domus Aurea, especially those surrounding the artificial lake that appear to have had the most public access. While it is true that the Templum Pacis does delineate a clear distinction between the notional aspects of *templum* and *domus* intended to denigrate Nero, his Domus Aurea and the art displayed within it, the architectural format of the Templum, a large portico containing garden elements and showcasing works of painting and sculpture, recalls the peristyle gardens of elite residences, essentially erasing and restaging Nero's Domus Aurea. The Templum also recalls its two great museum portico predecessors,

[50] On the Templum as the culmination of Vespasian's architectural program, see Henderson 2003: 229–3; Pliny describes the monument in *HN* 36.101–2.

[51] Noreña 2003, 28; Miles 2008, 255–9.

[52] Sculptures included the Venus of Paphos, Pliny *HN* 36.27; a bronze cow by Myron, a bronze bull by Pheidias or Lysippus, Procopius *de Bello Gothico* 8.21.12–14; a Ganymede by Leochares: *Anth. Pal.* 12.221; Pliny *HN* 34.79; *IG* 16.1523, Juv. 9.22–6 and scholia; a Pythocles by Polyclitus: M. Guarducci *Epigrafia Greca* 3 (1974) 419–21; Noreña 2003, 28–9; etc. Paintings included Cheimon, wrestling victor at Olympia in 488 BCE by Naukydes: Paus. 6.9.3; Aulus Gellius 3.21.9, 16.8.2; HA *Tyr. Trig.* 31.10; a painting by Timanthes of Cynthus (or Sikyon) representing a hero and admired for its depiction of the human figure: Pliny *HN* 35.74.

[53] La Rocca 2001, 197–9, figures 19a–c. [54] Pollard 2009. [55] Corsaro 2014, 325.

the Portico of the Theater of Pompey and the Portico of Octavia. Vespasian, then, repositions Nero's collection in a new monumental display environment created to celebrate the peace he has secured throughout the empire via the new dynasty's military victories. Nero's collection ostensibly had an aesthetic rationale, but was reviled by his critics for its allegedly "private" character, imprisoned, like the work of his painter, Famulus, in the Domus Aurea (*HN* 35.120). By redeploying it in the Templum Pacis, Vespasian effectively endows Nero's hated collection with new imperialist implications that transform it into a positive civic asset adorning one of the great architectural marvels of the Flavian capital.

The Templum Pacis, however, was not capable of containing all of Nero's assembled collection of masterpieces. Many other works were dispersed to other locations, including the Portico of Octavia, where the famous Eros of Thespiae by Praxiteles was on display. The Eros was an especially contested work of art. Verres had apparently acquired the statue, but it was eventually returned to Thespiae. Caligula brought it again to Rome and Claudius subsequently had it returned to the Thespians (Cicero, *Verr.* 4.2.4). Nero brings the work once again back to Rome, where Pliny sees it in the Portico of Octavia. Unlike Claudius, Vespasian fails to repatriate the statue.

Pliny indicates in his narrative table of contents for the *Historia Naturalis* that the extensive list of the most important bronze sculptures in book 34 consists of 366 statues and he later says that Nero brought all of the most famous of them to Rome through violent means (*HN* 1.34; 34.49–84). The number of sculptures must have been staggering, and apparently included Attalid Gaul groups associated with Isogonus Pryomachus, Stratonicus, and Antignous, and the "Boy Strangling a Goose" by Boethius. Pliny claims that all of these works were displayed in the sitting rooms (*sellaria*) of the Domus Aurea. The use of the unusual word *sellaria* was probably intended to imply intimate, personal spaces, and Suetonius also uses it to describe the rooms at the Villa Iovis on Capri where Tiberius had his notorious sexual escapades with the *spintriae* (Suet. *Tib.* 43.1). It seems unlikely, however, that display of the collected masterpieces was exclusively confined to the Domus Aurea or if it was, many of the sculptures were surely exhibited in more publicly accessible parts of the Domus Aurea and its gardens. The Vatican Laocoon, for instance, was displayed in the Gardens of Maecenas, which had already been annexed into Nero's residence as part of the earlier Domus Transitoria project intended to link the Palatine with the gardens, like those of Maecenas, that Nero had inherited on the

Esquiline (Suet. *Nero* 311; Tac. *Ann.* 15.39.1).[56] None of the works Pliny enumerated was repatriated by Vespasian, but rather redeployed and re-curated in new Flavian venues like the Templum Pacis and other purportedly public locations. Nero's collection was clearly both eclectic and encyclopedic in its scope, as underscored by Pliny's descriptions, and it must have been crucial for emerging imperialist and aesthetic conceptions of Rome as a compendium and repository of the world's art and treasure.[57] As the Flavians sought to reclaim Nero's *Urbs Nova*, dispersing his vast collection of paintings and sculpture was no longer a viable option.

The Templum Pacis stood just outside the Roman Forum and the Via Sacra, which Nero had broadened and realigned with the vestibule of the Domus Aurea. The vestibule was designed to contain one of Nero's most impressive and ambitious artistic projects, the Colossus.[58] Apparently not yet completed at the time of Nero's suicide in 68 CE, the monumental project was expropriated and redirected by Vespasian. Commissioned from the sculptor Zenodorus, the Colossus is described by Pliny as the most impressive of the colossal statues in the Mediterranean, surpassing even the famed Colossus of Rhodes (*NH* 34.42). Initially intended as a standing representation of Sol-Helios with facial features derived from Nero's last portrait type, the Colossus was finally dedicated by Vespasian in 75, the same year as the Templum Pacis, and Dio notes that the statue was thought by some to have resembled Titus, rather than Nero (66.15.1).[59] The dedicatory inscription would have claimed Vespasian as its patron, rather than Nero. Eventually, this area of the city comprising the Velia, valley of the Colosseum and the northeastern slope of the Palatine would form a powerful nexus of monuments dedicated by Vespasian, Titus, and Domitian: the Colosseum, Meta Sudans, the Flavian-inflected Colossus, Templum Pacis, Arch of Titus, and the rebuilt Curiae Veteres. Nevertheless, the Colossus was never fully dissociated from the memory of Nero and continued to be known as the Colossus of Nero, despite its cooption by the Flavians. Its profound significance within the urban landscape of the city and its evocations of Rome's *aeternitas* would continue. Hadrian employed the architect Decrianus to transport the

[56] On the findspot of the Vatican Laocoon, see Volpe and Parisi (2009) and Ambrogi (2011) 511, n. 1.

[57] Carey (2003); Rutledge (2012).

[58] For the Colossus, see La Rocca, Chapter 13 in this volume.

[59] For the intended appearance of the Colossus under Nero, see Bergmann 1997, 189–201; Smith 2000.

Colossus from its location on the Velia to its final position near the Colosseum in order to clear land for his Temple of Venus and Roma, and Commodus apparently remodeled the Colossus into an image of Hercules with facial features resembling himself.[60] In the early fourth century, Maxentius appears to have rededicated the Colossus to his deified son Romulus, and the statue was a crucial element of Constantine's monumental engagement with the city and the design and placement of his arch.[61]

Domitian not only incorporated artistic echoes of Nero in his self-presentation in portraiture, but he became a "bad emperor" like Nero before him. Domitian's building projects, however, did not suffer the same level of opprobrium as Nero's. Domitian's Domus Augustana is a more restrained and contained version of Nero's residences, carefully confined to the southeast corner of the Palatine. Like the coiffure of his third portrait type, which clearly revived the more elaborate hairstyles of Nero's later types, his Stadium in the Campus Martius may be the architectural successor of Nero's Gymnasium, which was dedicated in 60 in conjunction with the establishment of the first quinquennial Neronian games.[62] Domitian's own quinquennial games can be read as a revival or reconfiguration of their Neronian predecessors. Although there were sporadic attempts to suppress the memory of Nero, all three of the Flavian emperors were forced to confront and recalibrate Nero's monumental legacy in architecture and portraiture, as well as his performative politics.

Nero's memory continued to resonate long after the collapse of the Flavian dynasty. Nero's images would continue to be repurposed well beyond the Flavian period, with Neronian images refashioned as Trajan, and others to Antinous, Gallienus, and Julian.[63] Hadrian's more elaborate coiffures, with their ringlets and his introduction of the beard, find clear precedents in Nero's last portrait types. Hadrian's deep interest in Greek culture and *paideia* also has strong Neronian echoes, as do his geopolitical engagements throughout the empire.[64] Nero's image would also be resuscitated for the contorniate medallions distributed at the Circus Maximus in Rome in the late fourth and early fifth centuries, and his portrait occurs frequently on the medallions, second only to

60 *HA Comm.* 17.5; Dio 72 (73) 22.3; Herod. 1.15.9. 61 Marlowe (2006).

62 Dio 61 (62) 21; Suet. *Nero* 12.3; G. Ghini 1995.

63 Varner 2004, 254–5, cat nos. 2.60–3; for the cameo of Nero recut to Julian in Florence, see Megow 2011, 212–13, no. 8, figure 35.

64 Braund 2013.

Trajan.[65] A late Roman onyx cameo in Paris, dated to the later fifth or early sixth century, faithfully revives Neronian imagery and depicts him on a *quadriga*, wearing a radiate crown, the trabeated toga, and holding a *mappa* with the legend NERUN AΓOUCTE (Neron agouste).[66]

Notwithstanding the Flavian recalibration of Nero's legacy, it would seem his memory never ceased to resonate in Rome.

Further Reading

Nero's complicated historical and monumental legacy began to be seriously reappraised in English by Elsner 1994. Subsequent significant contributions followed with Champlin 1998 and Davies 2000 on the Golden House, Albertson 2001 on the Colossus, and Bergmann 2013 on Nero's portraits. The 2011 exhibition in Rome "Nerone," and its catalog edited by Tomei and Rea also provided an important arena for reassessments of Nero's cultural impact. Rosso 2008 is fundamental for Nero and the Flavians. The reconfiguration of Nero's portraits under the Flavians and later emperors are analyzed by Jucker 1981, Bergmann and Zanker 1981, Pollini 1984, Varner 2004, and Vout 2008.

[65] Alföldy and Alföldy (1976–90–90) 36–79, nos. 128–233.

[66] Bibliothèque Nationale, Cabinet des Médailles; Vollenweider and Avisseau-Broustet 2003, 118, no. 133.

Part V

The Neros of Reception

16: Nero: The Making of the Historical Narrative

Donatien Grau

Nero is an essential – and controversial – figure whenever he makes an appearance in history, poetry, or politics. These different genres treated him in different ways, creating a many-faceted picture of this hard-to-understand emperor. It's worth our while, then, to look closely at the approaches of the various ancient accounts Nero provoked. The extant texts are enough for us to trace the development of how he was represented, starting with early material provided by Pliny the Elder in his *Natural History* (in the mid-first century) and ending with the three main sources, Tacitus, Suetonius, and Dio, all writing from fifty to a hundred years later.

16.1 Pliny the Elder

Pliny was not a fan of Nero's. On the contrary, all that we know from Pliny's life and social class to his prodigious rise under Vespasian must have contributed to making him an open enemy of the Neronian regime that preceded Vespasian.[1] Although Pliny's historical works have not survived, the references scattered through his *Natural History* seem designed to participate in the destruction of Nero's image – even though Nero's actual statue had been long since been toppled. The genre of Pliny's work, a "scientific" encyclopedia in which narrative serves to illustrate, entertain, and introduce variations, is not particularly appropriate for long digressions on the former enemy of the new government. Given the opportunity, however, Pliny does not hesitate to evoke a few details of small or greater significance. We do not know if these details represent the truth or a twist on reality – or even if they are outright lies – and so they have spurred different modern

[1] Serbat 1986.

interpretations. Nonetheless, Pliny's anecdotal material fulfills at least three functions, scanty as it is: it manages to instruct as it narrates; it entertains and provides relief for the learned reader who might be at times weary of the dryness of Pliny's physiological materials; and, last but not least, it demonstrates a scientific and political intention in its approach.

The figure of Nero supplies Pliny's text with an underlying network of references to his reign.[2] First, there are brief mentions of the emperor that build a particular, overwhelmingly negative image of his character. These are numerous in the *Natural History*, but take a form that is allusive enough not to saturate the encyclopedia and make it openly polemical and political. In his scientific persona, Pliny the analyst is reporting apparent facts, and in this context, such facts seem so straightforward as to rule out alternative readings. For example, in book 8 (dedicated to terrestrial animals), Pliny relates an edifying anecdote:

> Metellus Scipio counts it among the charges against Cato that Babylonian coverlets were already then sold for 800,000 sesterces, which lately cost the Emperor Nero 4,000,000. (*HN* 8.196, tr. H. Rackham)[3]

On the surface, this looks like a bare fact without any intervention by the author, who is only relating economic details. But under this lies a biting, even if implicit criticism. The emperor is accused of one of the greatest sins to which a citizen might bear witness in Rome: *luxuria*.[4] Four million sesterces, or the equivalent of a year in wages for an entire legion, paid for a piece of cloth. To make matters worse, this piece of cloth comes from the Orient, a region old-fashioned Romans were obsessed with, and which they hated and despised. The author paints an even grimmer picture by evoking Cato the Elder, the Censor, a model of restraint and frugality, accused here of *luxuria* for having paid a sum far less than what the infamous Nero had really dispensed. The contrast is striking: in a few lines, Pliny has indicted the former princeps of frivolity, incompetence, and Hellenistic decadence. He has done so while giving the impression of only narrating a quick anecdote, a detail of the depraved days that had just come to an end.

[2] Schubert 1998: 312–24.

[3] "Metellus Scipio tricliniaria Babylonica sestertium octingentis milibus venisse iam tunc ponit in Catonis criminibus, quae Neroni principi quadragiens sestertio nuper stetere."

[4] R. F. Martin 1991: 303–5.

In another significant example, Pliny mentions the emperor's initiation into the mysteries of the Parthian religion (Persian Mazdaism). In doing so, he implicitly accuses Nero of cultural treason and collusion with an age-old enemy, the two of them – Persians and treason – overlapping in the end and thus preparing his fall. In book 30, dedicated to Magic and Pharmacopea, Pliny mentions the huge pull occult practices had for Nero, whose "passion for the lyre and tragic song was no greater than his passion for magic" (HN 30.14, trans. W. H. S. Jones):

> Tiridates the Magus had come to him bringing a retinue for the Armenian triumph over himself, thereby laying a heavy burden on the provinces. He had refused to travel by sea, for the Magi hold it sin to spit into the sea or wrong that element by other necessary functions of mortal creatures. He had brought Magi with him, had initiated Nero into their banquets; yet, the man giving him a kingdom was unable to acquire from him the magic art. (*HN* 30.16–17, trans. W. H. S. Jones)[5]

This rather elaborate passage has elicited a great deal of commentary. Before even asking whether Nero was in fact initiated into Oriental cults,[6] we should note the recurrence of the word "Magus," which appears twice, and even a third time in the form of the derived adjective "magic." Clearly, Pliny is eager to emphasize the esoteric character of the temptation the emperor experiences, a temptation outside the bounds of his city, his legitimate rule, and his traditional religion. Beyond the strong lexical presence of the witchcraft theme, one should observe how this passage is carefully arranged in the Latin, with a liveliness characterized by the absence of conjunctions (*asyndeton*). The encyclopedist's narrative hints at a voice that disapproves of the Neronian principate's constant drift from the norm. And if Nero chooses to abandon the gods of the Empire, the implication is that the gods of the Empire will abandon him in turn, as they indeed seem to do in 68 CE.

With this passage, Pliny also gives us an example of the rewriting of history. Magus is none other than the king of Armenia, who came to

[5] "Magus ad eum Tiridates venerat Armeniacum de se triumphum adferens et ideo provinciis gravis. navigare noluerat, quoniam expuere in maria aliisque mortalium necessitatibus violare naturam eam fas non putant. Magos secum adduxerat, magicis etiam cenis eum initiaverat; non tamen, cum regnum ei daret, hanc ab eo artem accipere valuit."

[6] Picard 1962: 223–8.

Rome to offer his submission in 66 CE. In reality, he is a sovereign first and, second (perhaps) a sorcerer. But Pliny uses the image of the Orient to reverse these polarities: the official character of the visit, "a success of Nero's foreign policy" (to use Eugen Cizek's phrase),[7] is completely erased and gives way to an edited and partisan view of the meeting. Far from a foreign triumph, it becomes the symbol for the whims of a fallen emperor, who strives without cease to transgress his appropriate role in government, society, and the world. Pliny the Elder delicately suggests what he does not say but nevertheless exposes, and "historical truth," however much of it he may have known, contributes little. As Nicole Méthy emphasizes,[8] "the text is arguably not so much a document about the last Julio-Claudian as a document of the thought and method of Pliny the Elder himself." The Magus element is not attested elsewhere and has been considered most likely a fiction, but its insertion into a "scientific study" such as the *Natural History* helps to suspend the reader's disbelief.

The case is sometimes made that the anecdotal material about Nero in our sources from Pliny on is in fact genuine. This argument runs: "But people must have known![9] It could not have been possible to write brazen lies!" Nevertheless, in the interest of being skeptical: such narratives often have to do with the arcana of the Empire, not public material known to all. Second, those who actually did have close knowledge of the reign of Nero must have belonged to his court and, as a result, had to keep their mouths shut, not open, under the subsequent generations. Finally, nothing prevented a writer from creativity with the official version produced under a new regime. On the contrary: as soon as Nero died, the path was open to a nearly total reconstruction of a former figure of power.

16.2 Suetonius, Tacitus, Dio: The Sources of the Neronian Tradition

Pliny's narrative is fragmentary. If we know of Nero's more depraved acts, it is thanks to the detailed narratives written by the three main historians of the period: Tacitus, in books 13 to 16 of the *Annales*; Suetonius, in his *Life of Nero*; and Dio Cassius, in books 51 to 53 of his *Roman History*. But their views of the Neronian period raise a certain number of questions about structure, objectivity, and the modern

[7] Cizek 1972: 332. [8] Méthy 2000: 399.
[9] On the question of reception, a good example is given by Syme 1958: 203–16.

division between history (facts) and rhetoric (interpretation and persuasion), divisions these ancient authors do not necessarily respect.

There was in Roman antiquity a very narrow view of what makes history: it is a collection of moralizing tales that must serve as lessons for the future (Luc. *Hist. conscr.* 40.5–6). The genre of annals or biography is invested with a pedagogical purpose. By purging Nero of any element that would have caused him to look too complex politically (and therefore not coherent enough for a straightforward message), the Roman historians served their own cause:[10] they used him to create a protreptic, that is, an exhortation that was as much moral[11] (to do with Roman self-control) as political (encouraging moderation in government).[12] For that reason, Tacitus, Suetonius, and Dio were writing the "most oratorical" form of literature (Cic. *Leg.* 1.5) and made abundant use of the devices of rhetoric, whose correct usage, in the traditional Platonic perspective, was to lay the foundations for an ideal ruler – if not truthfully, at least morally.

While simplifying the emperor's political position and univocally emphasizing his personal character, especially its vices, Suetonius and Tacitus – more than Dio, whose work survives only in fragmentary excerpts – stage the deeds of a cruel character indeed. Both historians present great scenes that have fed our knowledge of the past: the accounts of the deaths of Britannicus (Tac. *Ann.* 13.15–17; Suet. *Nero* 33.3–7), of Agrippina (Suet. *Nero* 34; Tac. *Ann.* 14.1–13), and of Seneca (Tac. *Ann.* 15.60–4; Suet. *Nero* 35.5) have lived on through history as well as art history. Both historians described the fire of Rome, with the scene of Nero playing the lyre in front of the burning city (Tac. *Ann.* 15.39; Suet. *Nero* 38), as well as the persecution of the Christians, turned into living torches (Tac. *Ann.* 15.44; Suet. *Nero* 16): so many moments of grand tragedy in the historical world! Their historicity may have been contested, but they nonetheless fed the perception of the Neronian world as a universe of the extreme occupied by an emperor beyond all norms.

Many of these accounts, especially those in Tacitus, are set up like the scenes of a play unfolding – even beyond the characterization of the figure of Nero as a tragic character. But the authors do not merely aim at articulating Nero's character: they give it an immediate reality. In many scenes, he is not actually physically there, but seems like a specter present

[10] For a similar device, cf. Ginsburg 2005: 69–75. [11] Drexler 1939: 121–54.

[12] On the question of the political function of history, cf. the fundamental and illuminating article of Syme 1956.

in his very absence. For example, he is not present at Seneca's death, which itself had an extraordinary longevity in the history of art and literature;[13] nor is he at Agrippina's death. During the Pisonian conspiracy, he did not turn up at any of the executions – though he does personally interrogate the freedwoman Epicharis. Those absences render even more effective the few scenes in which he is present. At Britannicus' death, when the young prince falls down poisoned, the emperor is present, and does not react at all – claiming that it was just a fit of epilepsy (Tac. *Ann.* 13.16). At the time of Agrippina's assassination, he is absent, but the whole show takes place according to his commands. Even when Agrippina orders her assassin to "strike the belly," she points to the womb that had produced Nero so long ago (Tac. *Ann.* 14.4–8). And after her death (in Suetonius' account), Nero inspects his mother's corpse and her anatomy with great interest (Suet. *Nero* 34.4).

Above all, the issue of the presence of the sovereign takes shape around the topic of spectacle and the outbreak of spectacle into the world. It takes shape, first of all, through his vocation as a charioteer, then as a singer and an actor. It also takes shape in the hybridization of politics and play: in Tacitus, a famous sentence tells of the rumor that the princeps had sung about the fall of Troy during the fire of his city – of the city:

> [T]he report had spread that, at the very moment when Rome was aflame, he had mounted his private stage, and, typifying the ills of the present by the calamities of the past, had sung the destruction of Troy. (Tac. *Ann.* 15.39, trans. J. Jackson)[14]

The annalist also dedicates a passage to Nero's desire to be taken seriously on the stage (Tac. *Ann.* 16.4.). The historical record makes frequent reference to the emperor's theatrical ambitions,[15] as well as his passion for song and poetry (Suet. *Nero* 23–5). The way in which imperial presence gets theatricalized is visible in the fire of Rome as well as in the persecution of Christians: each time, the real world becomes a stage set. It is a fact that clearly shows through in his last words as reported by Suetonius: "Qualis artifex pereo!" ("How great an

[13] Ker 2009: 15–38.

[14] "pervaserat rumor ipso tempore flagrantis urbis inisse eum domesticam scaenam et cecinisse Troianum excidium."

[15] For instance, on the *Nero* by Pseudo-Lucian, see Whitmarsh 1999.

artist dies in me!" Suet. *Nero* 49.1), which were often repeated thereafter.[16]

Those scenes are like the brush strokes adding up to a fresco of Nero's times – for Tacitus more than for Suetonius or Dio. And they plainly serve to tie the figure of the emperor to a presence that is always evil – whether dead or alive.

16.3 Approaches

Two positions are possible vis-à-vis those representations of the end of the Julio-Claudian dynasty: acceptance or refusal, trust or mistrust. For a positivist, trustworthiness is a history writer's obligation and constraint. It is possible, however, while acknowledging the weight of facts, without really challenging them, to examine their interstices, their descriptions, the interventions of the authors, and the moments of emphasis, which testify abundantly that history in Rome is not solely a matter of truth. It is also the construction of an active and present memory, one that is therefore highly political.

Paradoxically, the debate around truth in Roman studies has triggered completely opposite reactions. Ancient authors proclaimed their own objectivity and their desire to say truthfully and plainly what had actually taken place:[17] they had to be impartial. Facing those statements of neutrality, one group of scholars has trusted those assertions. In a well-known passage of his monograph on Tacitus, Ronald Syme underscored, precisely about Nero, that:

> Not much need be said about the personality of Nero, no item where the credit and veracity of Cornelius Tacitus can be seriously impugned. He wrote of times within the reach of memory or of reliable testimony. What has been transmitted by Suetonius or by Dio shows a remarkable concordance – save that Tacitus omits the grosser enormities and suspends judgment where those authors are cheerfully or ignorantly asseverative. The concordance has been ascribed to the influence of a single dominant source, used by all three. A better explanation serves: the portrayal of Nero corresponds in large measure with the facts.[18]

[16] On the theatricality of Nero's rule, see Bartsch 1994.
[17] Marincola 1997: 158–74.
[18] Syme 1956: 437.

The same point was made for Suetonius: the impact of rhetoric on his work could be only peripheral, and since he held an office at Hadrian's court, he would have had access to first-rate sources, notably imperial archives. His use of these made him an incomparable biographer, lavish in anecdotes that are unequaled for their pungency as well as their historicity.

Finally, Dio has his devotees too. They point out his unique information regarding some events, presumably from texts now lost. For instance, even in the shortened form of the epitome, he gives a very detailed description of the emperor's stay in Greece in 67 which extends over more than half of book 62 – twelve paragraphs out of twenty-one (Dio 62.8.2–20.1). This constitutes an essential source for the "tour." It may also have seemed relevant that Dio, because he wrote in Greek and belonged to Greek culture, would have had direct access to sources unavailable to other authors. Just so, without Suetonius or Tacitus in the first place, no narrative would be possible. It is therefore impossible to write history while disregarding the ancient historians; their evidence cannot be put aside.

Still, some elements do lead us to underscore the rhetorical character of the historical writings of the "three greats" as well as their propagandistic purpose. It has been possible to prove that facts reported by Tacitus cannot have taken place – or, at least, cannot have taken place in the way Tacitus has described them. In particular, his accounts of the crimes of Nero are not reliable. For example, René Martin[19] has studied the famous scene of the death of Britannicus (Tac. *Ann.* 13.15–17). Following the analysis proposed earlier by Charles Roux in 1962, he has demonstrated that Nero cannot have used the methods described in the *Annales* to poison his adoptive brother. In fact, no poison was known to the Romans that could have caused immediate death without a massive dose. That flaw in Tacitus' narration, while very striking, is not the only one. A great deal is at stake with that fissure in "credit" – to use Ronald Syme's word. If Tacitus, at a given moment in his account, privileges virtuosity of style over veracity in his accusations, we can call into question either the quality of his sources (including the tradition to which he had access, the same tradition that Syme claims guarantees his authority) or his own objectivity.

There is a further consideration: Tacitus engages in a veritable critique of historiography about his sources for Nero's beginnings:

[19] R. Martin 1999.

> According to Fabius Rusticus, letters patent to Caecina Tuscus, investing him with the charge of the praetorian cohorts, were actually written, but by the intervention of Seneca, the position was saved for Burrus. Pliny and Cluvius refer to no suspicion of the prefect's loyalty; and Fabius tends to overpraise Seneca, by whose friendship he flourished. For myself, where the sources are unanimous, I shall follow them: if their versions disagree, I shall record them under the names of their sponsors. (*Ann.* 13.20, trans. J. Jackson)[20]

Given such a declaration of candidness, it seems difficult to question the objectivity of Tacitus' gaze on the history of the Neronian era. In that case, the culprit for the most fiercely and falsely hostile passages on the previous emperor would no longer be Tacitus, but his sources, which are few and fragmented in the period immediately following Nero's principate.[21]

In reality, the facts presented in the narrative of the reign by Tacitus, Suetonius, and Dio are on the whole similar: Seneca and Burrus as his aides; the deaths of Britannicus, Agrippina, and Octavia; the conspiracy of Piso; the fire of Rome; the establishment of the Neronia; wars; the end. All these facts are related by the three authors, but the inflections, causalities, and dynamics display no agreement. For these are the areas in which our authors may intervene freely in their interpretation and their increasingly negative readings of Nero's character.

16.4 Tacitus' Fabrication

Tacitus' great contribution consists in linking history to a double interpretation of Nero's character. On one side, he poetically transforms him into a character of tragedy; on the other, he shapes him to political ends as the model of the tyrant. Indeed, the writer clearly turns Nero into a character on the tragic scene of a dying dynasty.[22] In this regard, Tacitus fits with the patterns of Senecan aesthetics, such as they were at work in the Octavia. The princeps has taken the initiative in a double

[20] "Fabius Rusticus auctor est scriptos esse ad Caecinam Tuscum codicillos, mandata ei praetoriarum cohortium cura, sed ope Senecae dignationem Burro retentam. Plinius et Cluvius nihil dubitatum de fide praefecti referunt. sane Fabius inclinat ad laudes Senecae, cuius amicitia floruit. nos consensum auctorum secuturi, quae diversa prodiderint, sub nominibus ipsorum trademus."

[21] Cizek 1972: 9–13. [22] Galtier 1999.

"accursed crime":[23] fratricide, then matricide,[24] which are both, as it were, the foundational act of Nero's "tragedy." They represent the original stain, which simultaneously testifies to his nature as an evil force and provide an opening to a world of suffering.

The all-consuming passion of the emperor for the theater is a theme in Suetonius, Tacitus, and Dio: the performance of the princeps on the stage is like the *mise en abyme* of a play within a play. At this moment we see the man show his mask – even though he is just a man, not an actor. He represents here a transgression of convention: he who, as emperor, is above other men, finds himself below them, as actor. He who is master over the bodies of others makes an exhibition of his own for public consumption.[25] Nero provides a particularly evident proof of tragic irony when performing in Naples: he literally makes a show of himself; he makes a gift of what is truly himself, that is to say the tragic meaning of his fate.[26]

Even if Nero is mostly overcome by "fear,"[27] he also demonstrates the tragic quality called furor,[28] exposed in book 15 when the conspiracy of Piso is crushed.[29] And the historian, becoming a moralist, bemoans the casualties at Rome that occupy much of book 16: "As it is, this slave-like patience and the profusion of blood wasted at home weary the mind and oppress it with melancholy" (Tac. *Ann.* 16.16; trans. J. Jackson).[30] Those casualties are caused by the free hand given to a tragic character, who knows no limit: only a character haunted by tragic furor could have been the origin of such violence. In addition (another characteristic feature of the genre), Nero has a difficult relation to the world of the divine: he seeks to transcend his humanity and join the gods, but he only succeeds in offending them (Tac. *Ann.* 16.13). Instead of imposing order by ruling, he becomes a force of chaos.[31] Finally, like the great tragic characters Oedipus and Orestes, he is at once terribly alone in front of Destiny and surrounded by a court and counselors[32] who deceive and fool him, playing with his fears. Nero's solitude becomes heavier and more dangerous over the course of the *Annales*. Nero, as pictured by Tacitus, is indubitably a tragic hero, but also, as a corollary, a tyrant.

[23] Dupont 1986: 165.
[24] Tac. *Ann.* 13.15–17 and 14.1–9; with the commentary by Croisille 1994: 75–93.
[25] Duncan 2006: 24. [26] Shumate 1997: 395–401. [27] Galtier 1999: 68–9.
[28] Dupont 1986: 181. [29] Devilliers 1999.
[30] "at nunc patientia servilis tantumque sanguinis domi perditum fatigant animum et maestitia restringunt."
[31] Devilliers 2007. [32] Ducos 2006.

Through his outrages, Nero is a character marked by the hubris of the statesman who exceeds the bounds of his prerogative.[33] The theme is not new when Tacitus takes it up; the word *tyrannus* is used to designate Nero in the *Octavia*. But the author of the *Annales* gives it an unequaled impetus through which it lives on through subsequent periods. Tacitus, in that moment, gives shape to some fundamental elements of a Neronian thematic whose genesis belongs to the double perspective of history and literature. Three features are characteristic of the tyrant's traditional image, and all can be found in Tacitus' depiction of the last heir of Augustus' blood. The first is of course hubris,[34] immoderation combined with the arrogance of someone who wants to do more than he may, be more than he can. Many passages of the *Annales* testify to this primordial quality. To cite only one example, the very fact that Nero attempts to get recognition for his dubious talent on stage and condemns to death those who deny he has any, is considered with supreme disgust by the historian: with that gesture, Nero attempts to distort reality, to compel the vital forces of the Roman city to lie. His excess is twofold: first, he puts himself on the stage, making an ignominious actor of himself; then, he condemns those who have kept their common sense and will not tolerate his game.

The tyrant also manifests himself by his unceasing willfulness: he has no reason or justification to do what he does, except whim. The paradigm of this willfulness is the Tacitean episode of "Dido's hoard," according to which Nero would have taken off to North Africa to seek the riches of the ancient queen of Carthage:

> Accordingly, Nero, without sufficiently weighing the credibility either of his informant or of the affair in itself, and without sending to ascertain the truth of the tale, deliberately magnified the report and dispatched men to bring in the spoils lying, he thought, ready to his hand. (Tac. *Ann.* 16.2, trans. J. Jackson)[35]

Here the *vanitas*, the "fickleness," of the emperor is highlighted and corresponds to his situational unawareness and all-powerful willfulness – even if this trait must eventually run up against real facts. His persecution of the Christians during the fire of Rome is similar. The Christians, although perhaps guilty in other cases, were not guilty in that one (says

[33] Dunkle 1971. [34] For a definition of *hubris* applying to Nero, see Griffin 2002.

[35] "Igitur Nero, non auctoris, non ipsius negotii fide satis spectata nec missis per quos nosceret an vera adferrentur, auget ultro rumorem mittitque qui velut paratam praedam adveherent."

Tacitus), and the persecution bears witness to Nero's thoughtlessness and violence.

Finally, the last touch to the portrait of Nero as tyrant consists in his *crudelitas*, or rather his *saevitia*: the first notion is basically tied to the fascination in seeing bloodshed, whereas the second, broader one assumes various forms, from a cruel thought to a government of cruelty. These forms undergird Tacitus' construction of the emperor Nero as a rhetorical image, as much as – if not more than – the historical image of Nero the emperor. In a late rhetorical text, the *Progymnasmata*, Aphthonios analyzes the knowledge of oratory in the early and late imperial world, and elaborates on the theme of the tyrant (Aphth. *Prog.* 7.3–11). In his section on blame, he presents one topos of the tyrant, the claim that his impurity contaminates the entire city: "A murderer is terrible, but a tyrant is worse. The one commits butchery on some single individual, but the other overthrows in their entirety the fortunes of the city" (trans. M. Heath).

The magnitude of the troubles he caused reveals the character of a tyrant. One need only read the last two books of the *Annales*, which detail the number of deaths the princeps ordered, to understand that the list of names illustrates a characteristic of the tyrannical ruler; the work follows the rules of rhetoric in its construction of Nero's image. Tacitus did not invent the themes on which he bases and corroborates his presentation of the character. Nor did he invent the escapades of an unequivocally ill-famed emperor. He undoubtedly owes a great deal to the authors who preceded him. But he provides us with the first available instance of an intentionally and generically historical form of writing on Nero. In addition, the *Annales* have served as a model for a great part of the subsequent historiography. For modern critiques, it is the first step toward the construction of a Neronian persona, based essentially on combining the historical elements inspired by the emperor's life and the persona of a tyrant.

16.5 SUETONIUS AND DIO

The treatment of Nero in Suetonius and Dio is not as artful as that of Tacitus, who found in Nero the main character for the last tragedy of the Julio-Claudian principate. Rather, they aim at elaborating on the theme of the tyrant. Their version is not, on the whole, different from that of Tacitus, but some nuances are lost in order to emphasize the perversion of the princeps. If the annalist acknowledged Nero's "auspicious beginning" (Tac. *Ann.* 14.4–5), Suetonius stresses the determinism shaping Nero as its object, because of his blood connection with the Domitii rather than with Augustus (Suet. *Nero* 1–5); as a proper tyrant, he is the son not of tyrants, but of intemperate individuals whose perversion forecasts that of their descendant.[36] In addition, he presents none of the features that define Roman citizens. The "deromanization" of Nero is already present in a suggestive form in Tacitus,[37] but it is fully in the open with Suetonius. Nero is fully devoid of *virtus* in all the senses of the word: he has no virility, since he prostitutes himself (Suet. *Nero* 29), and has no martial courage, since he refuses to fight (Suet. *Nero* 18). He is thus presented by the biographer as the champion of an anti-civic relation with the city.

That approach may imply cursory parallels, unobvious associations, and interpretations on the part of the author of the *Twelve Caesars*. Even Eugen Cizek, although very quick on the whole to accept the information conveyed by the *Life of Nero*, cannot deny that Suetonius sometimes offers "direct allegations" that are his alone.[38] As he puts it, they "crisscross" the biography. One should therefore differentiate between the information itself and the inflection given to it in the narrative. For instance, the account of Nero's auspicious beginning – "he declared that he would rule according to the principles of Augustus, and he let slip no opportunity for acts of generosity and mercy, or even for displaying his affability" (Suet. *Nero* 10.1, trans. J. C. Rolfe)[39] – may be read as such, a piece of knowledge about the beginnings of the princeps. It may also be viewed as a rhetorical technique on Suetonius' part, since it stands in vigorous opposition to another passage in which the flaws of the prince are exposed:

> Although at first his acts of wantonness, lust, extravagance, avarice and cruelty were gradual and secret, and might be condoned as follies of youth, and even then their nature was such that no one doubted that they were defects of his character and not due to his time of life. (Suet. *Nero* 26.1, trans. J. C. Rolfe)[40]

[36] Sansone 1986. [37] Woodman 1992. [38] Cizek 1977: 143–5.

[39] "ex Augusti praescripto imperaturum se professus, neque liberalitatis neque clementiae, ne comitatis quidem exhibendae ullam occasionem omisit."

[40] "Petulantiam, libidinem, luxuriam, avaritiam, crudelitatem sensim quidem primo et occulte et velut iuvenili errore exercuit, sed ut tunc quoque dubium nemini foret naturae illa vitia, non aetatis esse."

Such moments in Suetonius' text are clearly constructed to echo and contrast in a movement between climax and anti-climax: the announcement of auspicious beginnings conflicts with an appalling end. Beyond the organization of facts into one category or the other, it is worth pointing out that the biographer's position on the evolution of the emperor is exactly contrary to that of Seneca in his *de Clementia*: in the philosopher's view, the nature of the princeps is good and guarantees order; in the writings of the biographer, it is wicked and leads to his ruin.

Suetonius' approach does not represent the opinion of a single man. First, it echoes the contemporary reaction to Nero's death. Next (and this is not negligible) there is the influence of the equestrian order, which was Suetonius' own; they were bound to oppose an emperor who had wanted to side with the plebs.[41] Finally, one has to reckon with the taste of the ancient historians for rhetoric, which has an impact on the way the text is structured. This violent, determinist, and pessimistic rhetoric, turning Nero into a cursed figure from a family itself marked by the worst depravities, can be related to the genre of political invective as practiced in forensic oratory.[42] Suetonius clearly puts into practice Quintilian's lessons on *vituperatio* from the same era (Quint. 3.7. 19–22): the typical methods of an accuser – the description of the vice as original, the vivid representation of this vice, the presence of excess – are reproduced exactly in the text of the *Life of Nero*. Suetonius' work is the result of a hybridization between a factual account and a political and aesthetic orientation – the hybridization that is ancient history.

As for Dio, the sections of his *Roman History* that concern Nero survive only in an abridged form, the epitome. It seems Dio exaggerates even more: unlike the two other historians,[43] who recall some of the good deeds performed by the monster, this senator under Septimius Severus transforms Nero into an evil character right from the beginning. He is irrefutably wicked without any possible nuance (Dio 61.4.3), and surrounded by sycophants who sustain his baseness. Dio's evocation dramatizes at every turn the feeling of a condemned era, an era in which even Seneca – whom Tacitus presented heroically and Suetonius positively – is a wheeler-dealer who takes advantage of his influence to become wealthy at the empire's expense: a hypocrite who did nothing but lead his pupil astray (Dio 61.10).

[41] Della Corte 1967: 174. [42] On the parallel, cf. Barton 1994. [43] Heinz 1948: 146.

Further Reading

The portrayal of Nero in ancient Roman historical writing is a major issue. Tacitus and Suetonius have played a major role in shaping the notion of politics and power from antiquity to now, and their accounts (which represent the primary sources for the emperor) are difficult to question without breaking down the very history we have. Those historians who consider our sources basically accurate (e.g., Syme 1958; Cizek 1977; Gascou 1984) tend to be outnumbered by later treatments of the period.

A less trusting approach is try to carve out a space between philology and history by questioning specific aspects of what the sources tell us, and highlighting their incoherence or rhetorical transformation (e.g., Heinz 1948; R. Martin 1999). Alternatively, one can privilege the force of rhetorical thought on history, and regard these texts as architectural structures made of topoi, or attempt to analyze the structures of rhetoric in history. Or, the text can be read as itself the subject of a series of reception studies (Schubert 1998).

There are several works on the theatricality of Nero's reign and the influence of the sources in our seeing him this way (Barton 1994; Bartsch 1994; Rubiés 1994; Galtier 1999; Malitz 2004; Meier 2008; Fantham 2013).

17: Saint Paul and the Christian Communities of Nero's Rome

J. Albert Harrill

Scholars often follow church tradition to tell a familiar story about St. Paul and the Christian communities of Nero's Rome. This story links the apostle's martyrdom with the epic horror of the Great Fire of July 64.[1] In the conflagration's aftermath, so the story goes, the megalomaniac Nero became the First Persecutor of the Church when he scapegoated as the alleged arsonists local Christians, among them Paul (Saul) of Tarsus. Such legends should not be taken at face value. They built on and exploited the tales of Nero's purges to remake Paul into a martyr and the ultimate civic hero, who by the fourth century had replaced Romulus as the "second" founder of Rome.[2] Christian writers in late antiquity developed these legendary fictions largely from stock themes of anti-Neronian satire and invective that were commonplace in their Roman literary culture.[3]

The aim of this chapter is to clear out the mythology of Paul's "Neronian travails" in order to look carefully at what we can know about the earliest Christians in Rome and how later writers built on and exploited fictions about Paul and Nero. Rather than historically reliable sources, it was Roman satire and invective assailing Nero as the archetypical bad emperor (an anti-figure) that provided the chief background and themes into which later Christian authors set their fanciful narratives of Paul's martyrdom. The matrix generating the monster (tyrant) Nero in late ancient Christian culture was the widespread criticism of Nero in the Flavian era, which flourished under Trajan and then turned on Domitian as *Nero redux/redivivus*.[4] Open equations between Domitian

1 Beaujeu 1960; Barnes 1968; Benko 1984: 1–29; Hommel 1984; Keresztes 1984; Lichtenberger 1996; Gray-Fow 1998.

2 Eastman 2011.

3 Scholars tend to follow church tradition, e.g., H. H. Scullard 1982: 310. History of scholarship: Asbell 1990.

4 See Schubert 1998: 439–48.

and Nero fueled apocalyptic oracles about an eschatological adversary, which eventually fashioned Nero as the Antichrist.[5] Accounts of Paul's Neronian travails thus reveal more about how late ancient Christians *remembered* the Age of Nero than about how the earliest followers of Jesus in Rome may have lived (or died) in that so-called age.

The first section makes the case for Paul's letter to the Romans (ca. 58), as opposed to the book of Acts (ca. 95–115), as the best primary source for early Christianity in Rome and explains what little we can learn about Paul's relationship with these congregations from the letter's general, ad hoc choice of themes and its stated purpose of preparing for Paul's final journeys (Jerusalem, Rome, then Spain). An evaluation of the principal arguments in the so-called Romans Debate, which seek to find a more concrete purpose for the letter as a response to some present issue in Nero's Rome, constitutes the second section. This chapter then concludes with the reception of Nero in early Christian writings, showing how Nero became cast into Antichrist myths, and thus why so many stories of "Paul in Nero's Rome" were developed and taken as meaningful.

17.1 THE BEST PRIMARY EVIDENCE: PAUL'S EPISTLE TO THE ROMANS

Paul wrote the Epistle to the Romans in order to commend his gospel and himself to coreligionists in Rome, in advance of his intended stopover in the imperial capital on his way to a new mission in Spain (Rom. 15:23–4). Unlike his other extant letters, the apostle addressed this one to Christ-believers whom he had not converted, in a city he had never visited. Because he had not founded these congregations, Paul had no authority over them, which explains the letter's unusually elongated style and content. Paul asks rhetorical questions, quotes popular maxims and proverbs, parodies rival positions, personifies stock dramatic characters, and uses the rhetoric of antitheses and *reductio ad absurdum*. Greco-Roman popular philosophers deployed this form of protreptic discourse (an "introduction") with its schoolroom style of apostrophe, called *diatribe*, to introduce their distinctive tenets to an audience of potential students.[6]

[5] Origins of the Antichrist: Jenks 1991; Lietaert Peerbolte 1996; McGinn 2000: 45–54; Klauck 2003; Malik 2012; and Mucha 2014.

[6] Standard critical commentaries on Romans: Dunn 1988; Fitzmyer 1992; Stowers 1994; Jewett 2007. See also Stowers 1981; Aune 1991.

Romans is Paul's longest and probably last known writing. An alternative hypothesis, however, identifies Philippians (or a fragment embedded in it) as Paul's final writing, allegedly composed in Rome during his so-called Neronian imprisonment.[7] But this claim is based on slim evidence: (1) πραιτώριον, "praetorium" (Phil. 1:13, either a palace or a *cohors praetoria*), and (2) οἱ ἐκ τῆς Καίσαρος οἰκίας, "those of the emperor's household" (Phil. 4:22, the *familia Caesaris*). That these terms require Paul's presence in Rome is far from obvious.[8] Members of the *familia Caesaris*, the imperial slaves and freedmen, could be found in any major city of the Roman Empire. "Praetorium" need not necessarily refer to the Praetorian Guard because it also names the residence, even if temporary, of a provincial prefect.[9] There is, then, no basis for assigning Philippians to Paul's alleged imprisonment in Rome under Nero; the letter likely originated during some other imprisonment elsewhere (e.g., Ephesus). The Epistle to the Romans thus remains our best primary evidence for Paul and Rome.

Paul told the Roman believers that he had desired to visit their Christian communities "for many years" (Rom. 15:23). Because the epistle likely dates to ca. 58, the earliest of the congregations evidently arose sometime in the 40s.[10] If they had heard of Paul at all, the Christians in Rome likely knew him only by reputation and with some suspicion, though a few individuals apparently were acquainted with him personally (Rom. 16:3–15). This mixed response reflects first-century Christianity's diversity: it was not a single, unified movement (or a religion separate from the varieties of ancient Judaism). There was no standardized ("orthodox") faith, ecclesiastical hierarchy, or centralized institution. The tiny Christian communities in Rome were, as one scholar puts it, "fractionated" into various house-based congregations, a diversity persisting well into the second and third centuries.[11] The fractionated groups did share expressions of solidarity, but also engaged in activities of self-definition aimed at constructing boundaries between each other by means of different scriptural practices, rituals, and teachings about Jesus. In Nero's Rome, as elsewhere, to become and be a "Christian" meant strong social change: entry into a household association that called itself a new family; shunning involvement in any

[7] See Betz 2013, 2015.

[8] Kümmel 1975: 324–32; Reumann 2008: 170–3, 196; cf. Bingham 2013: 12.

[9] Mark 15:16; John 18:28; Epictetus 3.22.47; ChLA XI 505 (Egypt, ca. 85–8 CE); SB VIII 9718 (Alexandria, ca. 90–133 CE); P. Wisc. II 48 (after 154–9 CE); P. Petaus 47 and 48 (Arsinoite, 185 CE); see Mitthof 2002: 111–19. I thank Anna Maria Kaiser for these papyrological references.

[10] Lane 1998: 202. [11] Lampe 2003: 359–65.

other cult; and learning to expect hostility from outside society, including former relationships and sources of identity.[12] The earliest congregations in Rome evidently arose among the city's substantial Jewish communities concentrated in the Transtiberinum (modern Trastevere) and the Via Appia outside of the Porta Capena, where the poorest of Rome's *peregrini* (foreigners) resided. Crossing these crowded neighborhoods were the major thoroughfares on which multitudes of immigrants and other travelers flowed into Rome.[13] Paul aspired to be one of those travelers to the imperial capital.

Substituting for Paul's physical presence, the letter lauds the global fame of the Roman congregations – "your faith is proclaimed throughout the world" (Rom. 1:8) – with much hyperbole. For them, Paul writes, he will violate his rule not to evangelize "where Christ is already named" (Rom. 15:20), because the whole world is represented in Rome ("all the nations," Rom. 1:5–6). Paul's language thus participates in a particularly Roman mapping of people by their provinces and around a single imperium; Rome, not Zion, is the center.[14] Like the imperial map in the *Res Gestae* by the emperor Augustus, Paul's itinerary uses the language of reaching limits, and it deploys the particular Roman meaning of *imperium* as a sphere of duties granted to an overseas envoy (Greek, *apostolos*).[15] (This vision of an alternative imperium would serve as a foundation for later devotees honoring Paul with Roman imperial virtues.) Although not their apostle, Paul engages the Roman Christians in his mission nonetheless – because of their very geography. The letter explains his plans to stay only long enough to have "enjoyed your company for a little while," while en route to Spain, imploring them to help him out with the travel costs and to pray for him in his appointed tasks beforehand (Rom. 15:23–32).[16] Underscoring the mutual profit that Paul and the Roman believers will be to each other, the letter qualifies any potential misstatement to the contrary (Rom. 1:11–12).[17] The letter apologizes for occasionally lapsing into a bossy tone in parts, for Paul's repeated failures to come sooner, and for yet another delay due to a necessary return to Jerusalem.[18] Paul must first deliver to Jerusalem a collection of money he has raised from his Gentile congregations for the poor in the Judean churches, the crowning achievement of his

[12] Meeks 2003: 183–4.
[13] Lampe 2003: 19–66; Meeks 2003: 29. Jews in Rome, including the question of expulsions: Rutgers 1998; Gruen 2002: 38–53; Das 2003: 53–61; Das 2007: 149–201.
[14] Meeks 2013. [15] Harrill 2012: 84.
[16] Jewett 2007 argues that Paul has interest in the Romans only as financial supporters for his mission to Spain.
[17] Fitzmyer 1992: 248–9. [18] Rom. 1:10, 12:15–16, 15:22–32.

Aegean mission. After that task, the letter promises, Paul will succeed, at last, in his long-standing goal "of many years" (ἀπὸ πολλῶν ἐτῶν) to visit Rome (Rom. 15:23). In the meantime, the letter designates Paul's patron (προστάτις), Phoebe, the "minister" (διάκονος) of a house church in Cenchreae (the seaport of Corinth), as the letter's carrier and envoy (Rom. 16:1–2).

The letter thus aims to persuade the Roman congregations to join his gospel and particular circle of supporters. The letter's conclusion greets a remarkably large number of persons (Rom. 16:1–15) in comparison with other Pauline letters. Prosopographical study suggests that more than two-thirds of the names indicate low-status origins – slaves, freedmen, and other immigrants from the Greek East.[19] The greetings single out personal coworkers and leaders of house churches in a position to be Paul's advocates within the Roman congregations. This turn of epistolary greetings toward Paul's own need for local advocacy suggests that he had only a limited number of firsthand acquaintances in Rome.[20]

From these few mutual acquaintances, Paul supposed his Roman readers to be, like him, Greek-speaking urban residents and autonomous Christ-believers already familiar with Judaism. The letter's composition in Greek, its extensive quotations of the Hebrew Bible in a Septuagint version, and its peculiar techniques of biblical exegesis (known as *pesher* and *midrash*) all suggest an invited audience knowledgeable about Torah, Hellenistic-Jewish scriptural practices, dietary regulations, synagogue prayer, apocalyptic eschatology, and messianic expectations. The letter cultivates the common ground of that shared religiosity; it explicitly identifies Paul's invited audience as from τὰ ἔθνη (former pagans, "Gentiles"), most likely uncircumcised Gentile sympathizers to the God of Israel – known as Godfearers.[21] Calls to obey imperial authorities, a stock of commonplace *paraenesis* (moral exhortation) in Diaspora synagogue preaching, makes intelligible why Paul's letter explicitly advises the recipients to obey imperial authorities (Rom. 13:1–7), including doubtless the emperor Nero.[22] Paul's language, borrowed from the Diaspora synagogue, stands in sharp contrast to the (later) portrayal of Nero's persecution of the Christian communities.

[19] Lampe 2003: 153–83. [20] Gamble 1977: 91–5; Jewett 2007: 951–5.

[21] Rom. 1:5–6, 13, 11:13, 15:16, 27, 16:4; Stowers 1994; Thorsteinsson 2003: 100–22; Das 2007, 262–4.

[22] Käsemann 1961: 574–81. The alternative hypothesis of Rom. 13:1–7 as a non-Pauline interpolation is unpersuasive.

The legend of Paul's Neronian travails does not, therefore, originate with Paul's letter to the Romans.

Nor does such a negative portrayal appear where we would expect it the most – in Paul's so-called prison epistles (Ephesians, Philippians, Colossians, Philemon, with 2 Timothy). To understand the nature of these sources, we need to know that a consensus of critical biblical scholarship holds that Paul did not write all the letters attributed to him in the New Testament. Among the prison epistles, only Philippians and Philemon are considered authentic – the rest are forgeries made after Paul's death.[23] Regardless of where the historical Paul was imprisoned (Ephesus is the leading guess of most scholars today), he expects freedom soon (Phil. 1:18–19, 26) and requests a guestroom (Phlem. 22). The two authentically Pauline prison letters thus provide no evidence of an impending martyrdom or an imprisonment necessarily in Rome.

We might turn to the canonical Acts of the Apostles (ca. 100–20) to provide more data, given the importance of Paul as a major character in that book and its coherence as a narrative. Although such a proposal has the advantage of including one of the earliest and most extensive sources on Paul by later interpreters, it would also be inadequate because modern critical scholars dispute the historical reliability of Acts. Acts is not a "history" in the modern meaning of the term. Rather, its theological narrative presents Paul schematically, as the greatest hero of a "unified" church, who brings the gospel from its origins in Jerusalem to Rome, with powerful orations, spectacular miracles, and dramatic adventures as God's "chosen vessel" of salvation (Acts 9:15). Accepting the book of Acts literally as straightforward and unproblematic evidence for Paul's life is naïve.[24] In any case, the work does not provide the additional data we seek. To be sure, the book of Acts narrates a dramatic and detailed adventure of Paul's arrest in Jerusalem, his series of trials before Jewish royals and Roman magistrates, his appeal based on the legal status of being a full "Roman citizen" to move the hearing to Rome with "Caesar" (unnamed, presumably Nero) as the final judge; his transport to Rome as a prisoner for trial on capital charges before the emperor; and his final days under house arrest in a Roman apartment while awaiting the trial (Acts 21–8). The last lines imply strongly that Paul would be found guilty and executed in the near future. Yet the story ends oddly, without narrating the expected appeal

[23] Meeks and Fitzgerald 2007: xxvii–xxviii. Ehrman 2013: 171–222.

[24] Esp. Knox 1987; Hemer 1989: 1–29; Luedemann 1989; Fitzmyer 1998: 124–52; Pervo 2009: 14–18; Ehrman 2016: 312–33.

before the emperor or Paul's death.[25] Because Paul's impending martyrdom in Acts so stereotypically parallels Jesus' death as a martyrdom in Luke's gospel, the first half of the author's two-part work (called Luke-Acts), the narrative is likely an artificial literary creation.[26] Indeed, the whole account of Paul's last days is strange (Acts 28: 11–30). The Lukan "Paul" has time and interest only for the local Jewish communities and especially its leaders, not for the Roman Christian community (and certainly not with being its founder); such a community, to all intents and purposes of the plot, is nonexistent.[27] The work's open ending and the absence of the Roman churches thus render Acts largely unhelpful to our inquiry into Nero, Paul, and the Christian communities in Rome.

We thus return to Paul's letter to the Romans as our best primary source on this question. From an examination of this letter, we have learned a little about Paul's relationship with the Christian communities in Rome. First, Paul was a stranger to them. An elaborated epistolary opening and closing, together with the trick of a diatribe style to unfold themes in the letter's body, indicate a need to introduce both himself and his basic teachings. Second, Paul hoped to engage the Roman congregations in his autonomous missionary circle, separate from rival Christian communities and apostles of Messiah Jesus. Third, Paul imagines the Roman congregations to have been τὰ ἔθνη (former pagans, "Gentiles"), to whom Paul had made it his mission to speak as the apostle to τὰ ἔθνη. And, fourth, Paul adapted general synagogue paraenesis to commend himself (and his gospel) to Gentile congregations, already familiar with Jewish traditions, in the imperial capital.

17.2 The Romans Debate: Seeking an Occasion for the Letter in Neronian Rome

The general character of Romans as an introductory *logos protreptikos* ("word of exhortation") has not prevented biblical scholars from reading the letter as a response to specific circumstances in Neronian Rome. The attempts have yielded much debate. While the historical value of

[25] On the apparently odd ending of Acts, see Hemer 1989: 383–9; Fitzmyer 1998: 270–2; Pervo 2009: 688–90. Still very useful is Cadbury 1933: 319–38.

[26] See Pervo 2010: 149–56; Harrill 2012: 7–11, 70–4. Cf. Rapske 1994: 173–276, which follows Acts as a historical source.

[27] Pervo 2009: 681.

the solutions proposed in the Romans Debate varies considerably, its overall importance is immense as a testimony to the demand in critical scholarship to read Romans no longer as a timeless compendium of the Christian faith (after Philip Melanchthon's famous appraisal), but as an actual letter addressed to a particular audience on a specific occasion.

A leading solution, sometimes called a *consensus*,[28] places events, often conjectural, on a single trajectory that claims to show an escalating ethnic conflict between Christians and Jews in Rome. The trajectory begins with the so-called Edict of Claudius expelling Jews from Rome (ca. 49 CE), runs through Paul's letter (ca. 58), and culminates with the local persecution of Christians under Nero (64 CE).[29] The Edict of Claudius had expelled "the Jews" from Rome just as Suetonius describes.[30] Suetonius identifies the ringleader of the disturbances that prompted the expulsion to have been a certain *Chrestus* (ca. 49), most likely a misspelling of *Christ*, which scholars within this camp then claim means Jesus followers who must have caused tensions in their Jewish communities.[31] Pure conjecture follows to make up three modern claims: (1) in 54, when Nero became the new emperor and the Claudian Edict allegedly lapsed, the Jewish Christ-believers returned to find their former influence gone and dramatic social changes in the make-up of the local Christian communities; (2) because the synagogues in Rome must have closed down due to the expulsion of their leaders, the local communities of Jesus followers had become Gentile, more household-based, and unenthusiastic about welcoming back their Jewish brethren; (3) the resulting conflict of "the strong" (allegedly Gentile, non-Torah observant) and "the weak" (allegedly Jewish, Torah observant) members of the Christian communities led Paul to send his letter urging all the believers in Rome – "the strong" and "the weak" (Rom. 14:1–15:13) – to love and reconcile with one another.[32] The Pauline exhortations then, on this view, refer to a concrete situation in Nero's Rome.[33] The view overlooks the problem of mass expulsions of disruptive subcultures (Greeks, philosophers, astrologers,

[28] Donfried 1991a: ixix. [29] Walters 1993; Lane 1998; cf. Luedemann 1984: 164–71.

[30] Suetonius, *Life of Claudius* 25.4. Cf. Acts 18:2 and Dio 60.6.6–7 (without mention of a Chrestus). The date of 49 comes from Orosius, *Adv. Pag.* 7.6.15. Levinskaya 1996: 171–81; Riesner 1998: 157–201.

[31] Boman 2011; Trebilco 2012: 272–97; cf. Slingerland 1997: 151–245 on Suetonius referring not to Jesus Christ, but to an individual in Rome named Chrestus (a well-known imperial slave or freedman of Claudius).

[32] Standard view: Marxsen 1968: 100; Wiefel 1991; Lichtenberger 1996; Brändle and Stegemann 1998; cf. Das 2003: 49–77.

[33] Wedderburn 1988: 44–87; Walters 1993: 56–66; nuanced in Reasoner 1999: 1–44.

actors) being a trope in ancient Roman historiography that in actuality would have been very difficult to enforce and likely symbolic.[34]

A few biblical scholars then suppose that a tax revolt in Rome, which broke out in 58 when the public demanded an end to the extortions by *publicani* (freelance revenue collectors), prompted Paul's specific paraenesis on Roman imperial authorities. Because Nero responded to the revolt with an edict requiring the posting of previously secretive tax regulations and other popular reforms (see Tacitus, *Ann.* 13.50–1), Paul's admonition to pay taxes and to honor all imperial authorities (Rom 13:1–7) came at a time when public support for the emperor must have been high, during the supposedly felicitous *Quinquennium Neronis*, and when Paul's audience would have been most receptive to such an exhortation.[35] This trajectory then culminates at the end of the *Quinquennium*. The growing ethnic conflict internal to the congregations of Jesus believers caused the (Gentile) Christians to become a recognizably separated group from the Jews as a whole – and therefore an easy target for Nero to scapegoat during the Great Fire of 64, just as Tacitus describes (Tacitus, *Ann.* 15.44).

It is difficult to see how the evidence in Romans supports this reconstructed trajectory, however. Paul mentions no correspondence or news from the Christians in Rome to which he needs to respond, and he has never been there. Rather, Paul's admonitions draw on the responses he worked out in prior letters (Galatians, 1 Corinthians), addressing the specific conflicts in those particular congregations respectively, which he now generalizes toward the new goal of introducing "his gospel." The rhetoric of Romans reduces Paul's audience to tropes (e.g., the "weak" and the "strong" Christians *in faith*) probably chosen more because they exemplify the main themes of the epistle (e.g., justification by faith) than because they describe ethnicities in social conflict at Rome. Though undoubtedly Paul had enough information to convince him that his advice about behavior in Christian groups learned from his previous controversies in Corinth and Galatia would be relevant in Rome, no evidence appears in Romans of a specific conflict, despite moderns scholars' many efforts at "mirror reading."[36] To be sure, Paul could employ tropes while simultaneously addressing a concrete Neronian occasion of which he may have become aware, but this possibility does not in itself validate the leading solution in the

[34] Gruen 2002: 15–41, 2011: 348; Goodman 2007: 369–71; cf. Ripat 2011.

[35] Friedrich, Pöhlmann, and Stuhlmacher 1976; Dunn 1988, II. 757–73; Fitzmyer 1992: 661–75; Jewett 2007: 780–803.

[36] Meeks 2002: 154–7, 164, n. 3.

Romans Debate (outlined previously).[37] Particularly unexamined is the alleged endpoint of this whole trajectory, Nero's persecution of Christians in 64, as an established "fact" from which modern scholars then look backward to write their histories of Paul and the Roman Christians in the so-called Age of Nero.

The main problem concerns the anachronistic use of Roman classical sources. Suetonius and Tacitus should not be used as prior, independent witnesses to the events they describe. The earliest surviving "pagan" mention of Christians is neither one of these authors, but a letter by Pliny the Younger (*Ep.* 10.96) written during his second year governing Bithynia and Pontus (ca. 110–11). Suetonius accompanied Pliny as a member of his *cohors* (staff).[38] He first learned about the Christians while likely present during their trial proceedings. After Pliny's death in office, Suetonius also likely edited his mentor's letters from Bithynia into a corpus for wider public dissemination.[39] The dedication of at least part of his *Lives of the Caesars* dates the work sometime in 119–22, later than Pliny's letters.[40] Tacitus, likewise, had a close relationship with Pliny, each regularly exchanging drafts of his work to the other. Writing his *Annals* five to ten years after Pliny's encounter with Christians in Bithynia-Pontus, Tacitus engaged Pliny's language competitively, with clear verbal echoes present throughout that work.[41] The references in Tacitus and Suetonius tell us more about the authors' own second-century experience (with Pliny) than that of the first-century context of "Paul and Nero."[42] The myth of Paul's Neronian travails finds its origin in the reception of Nero in late ancient Christian literary culture.

17.3 Remembering the Age of Nero in Late Antiquity

Ancient Christian literary culture remembered Nero and his age in various ways. The book of Revelation (ca. 93–6) provides the earliest reception of an apocalyptic Nero representing all cosmic evil. The author's visions include a multi-headed "beast" revived from an

[37] Against a Neronian occasion for Romans: Meeks and Fitzgerald 2007: 63, with Karris 1991; Sampley 1995; Thorsteinsson 2003: 92–7; Barclay 2008: 91–4; and Krauter 2009: 55–160.

[38] Sherwin-White 1966: 659–60; Syme 1984: 1261, 1339; Bradley 1998: 7.

[39] Noreña 2007: 263; Ameling 2010: 274; among others.

[40] Power 2010: 140.

[41] Griffin 1999; Gibson and Morello 2012: 161–8, 304; Whitton 2012; among others. Cf. Power 2014.

[42] Wilken 1984: 49–50.

ineffective deathblow, who reclaims his imperial rule of the world as the agent of Satan identified by the number 666 (Rev. 13:1–18, 17:9–11). These oracles provide thinly veiled references to the legends of Nero's return in current circulation. The common Jewish numerology (*gematria*) deploys a name whose transliterated Hebrew letters in Greek spell out *Caesar Neron*.[43] The author's hatred of Rome finds particular expression in the role of the unnamed but unmistakable Domitian as *Nero redivivus*, an eschatological adversary fashioned as a bloodthirsty tyrant and a persecutor of the Christians. That the historical Domitian was not a persecutor of Christians matters more to history than to ancient apocalyptic imagination. His reign represented Roman imperial power, which was enough cause for this author's polemic.[44]

If the book of Revelation represents an apocalyptic Nero, quite a different representation appears in *The Martyrdom of Paul*, the earliest extant account of Nero as the persecutor of Paul.[45] The work became incorporated into the broader apocryphal *Acts of Paul* (ca. 190), possibly predating it by several decades. Although the *Martyrdom* attributes Nero's actions to "the Evil One," the contest between Paul and Nero is more individual than cosmic. After the enraged Nero has Paul beheaded, the apostle returns later that day to the imperial court with his head reattached to rebuke the emperor for lacking self-control and violating Roman laws. An admonished Nero obeys the postmortem Paul's commands to free the remaining prisoners. The narrative ends with the released Roman soldiers and slaves pledging their allegiance to Paul, who baptizes them and glorifies God. *The Martyrdom of Paul* thus characterizes Paul as more Roman than Nero, and better suited to rule the world. While clearly anti-Neronian in theme, the text is neither anti-Roman nor "anti-imperial." *The Correspondence of Paul and Seneca* (fourth century) also belongs in this mix. The forged Latin correspondence appropriates Seneca as Paul's friend, who decries his emperor's acts of injustice, against Roman law, on Paul and the Christians in Rome.[46] The effete, lawless Nero – a "bad emperor" – resembles the anti-Neronian character portraits in Tacitus and Suetonius.[47]

The apocryphal portrait thus received its themes and background information from anti-Neronian invective already present in wider Roman literature.[48] Authors such as Tacitus (*Ann.* 15.44) and

[43] Collins 1976: 174–90; Ehrman 2016: 540–1; Maier 2013: 388–91. Jewish apocalyptic context: Collins 1998: 234–6.

[44] Klauck 2003: 286, with further literature.

[45] Lipsius 1959: 105–77; tr. in Elliott 1993: 385–8; commentary in Rordorf 1993.

[46] Fürst 2006; tr. in Elliott 1993: 549–53; Harrill 2012: 97–103.

[47] Snyder 2013: 24–65.

[48] Sullivan 1985: 27–73; Rubiés 1994; Woodman 1998: 168–87, 2009a; Dinter 2012b; Woodman 1998: 168–87, 2009a.

Suetonius (*Nero* 16) had denigrated Nero by pointing to the specific atrocities of a "bad" emperor's megalomania – murdering his mother, raping a Vestal Virgin, committing incest, and marrying a freedman dressed up as his dead wife. These vicious acts illustrated the harmful effects of *luxuria*, which transformed Nero into an Eastern tyrant and the enemy of the *populus Romanus*. Late antique authors continued to present Nero as a monster.[49] As commonplace rhetoric, the invective emphasized the vice of Nero to show by contrast the virtues of the "good" emperor – which the Christians then appropriated to characterize the apostle Paul as besting Nero in imperial virtues.[50] In the late fourth century, John Chrysostom would compare Paul and Nero, highlighting the apostle's virtue.[51]

By condemning Nero and Domitian as ruthless tyrants, Christian apologists were aligning themselves closely to Latin intellectuals: like the Greek intellectuals of the Second Sophistic who criticized these vicious emperors, they were not opposing Rome but attempting to join Roman mainstream culture.[52] Tertullian, who likely had read the *Acts of Paul*, makes the connection explicit. His *Ad Nationes* (197 CE), *Apologeticus* (ca. after 197), and *Scorpiace* (ca. 204) were among the most widely cited sources in late antiquity for Nero's persecution.[53] Tertullian famously coined the phrase "*institutum Neronianum*,"[54] deploying Roman legal terminology. This phrase attempted to brand the persecution as yet another instance of Nero's habitual vice, rather than denoting an actual law or decree enacted under Nero against the Christians. Tertullian even instructs his readers to find more details about Nero's lurid habits of vice and sacrilege by consulting *commentarios vestros* and *vitae Caesarum*, references to either Suetonius or, more likely, the annalistic history of Tacitus.[55]

The picture of Paul's Neronian travails thus comes from late, unreliable sources. *Seven Books of History against the Pagans* (ca. 416) by Orosius, which achieved immense popularity during the Middle Ages, provides the fullest account. Orosius is a notoriously unreliable author historically.[56] Late Christian appropriation of anti-Neronian invective

49 Dio Chrysostom, *Or.* 21.9–10; Dio 41.4–10, 42.16–19; Philostratus, *VA* 4.35–8, 5.10; *Scriptores Historiae Augustae, Comm.* 21.2.

50 Nero as the stock tyrant: Griffin 1984: 100–82; Kragelund 2000; Champlin 2003: 38–44; Keitel 2010; Maier 2013; a trope including charges of arson (Johnstone 1992) and a contrast between kingship and tyranny (Dunkle 1971). Schubert 1998.

51 Mitchell 2002: 206–11. 52 Moles 1990; Madsen 2009: 125. 53 Barnes 1968: 32–5.

54 Tert. *Ad Nat.* 1.7.8–9 (CCSL I: 18); tr. Coxe 1993: 114.

55 Tert. *Apol.* 5.3–4 (CCSL I: 95); tr. Coxe 1993: 22. Tert. *Scorp.* 15.3 (CCSL II, 1097); tr. Coxe 1993: 648. Barnes 1985: 105–202; cf. Zwierlein 2009: 119–27.

56 Orosius, *Hist.* 7.7.1–10 (ed. Arnaud-Lindet 1991: 32–4), tr. Fear 2010: 333–5, an elaboration on Jerome (*Chronicle, A. Abr.* 2084) and Rufinus (*Ecclesiastical History* 2.24–5), with lines plagiarized from Suetonius (e.g., *Nero* 26). Nuffelen 2012.

merged with apocalyptic Antichrist traditions in the writings of fourth-century patristic authors, such as Eusebius and others, when the book of Revelation gained wider but still incomplete acceptance.[57] Lactantius, the accomplished Latin rhetorician and advisor to Constantine the Great, in *De Mortibus Persecutorum* (ca. 315) recounted God's punishment of each persecuting emperor from Nero to Diocletian. Despite its use in late antiquity as a history of the Roman Empire, the treatise ascribes fictional motivations for Nero that come from the circumstances of Lactantius' own day living under Diocletian, whose Great Persecution fueled the Antichrist legends of another *Nero redivivus*.[58] Arising from these ashes, a full Roman cult of Paul had developed in Rome, imperially sponsored, that restructured Rome's sacred landscape around Paul as the city's new founder. The decorative iconography of Paul's purported burial sites recalled Roman military laurels and athletic trophies, and his relics received a state feast day on the imperial calendar (July 29).[59] Late Christian authors placed Paul in Rome because in their imagination Rome became the home of the martyrs.[60] Martyrdom there came to symbolize victory over the Antichrist, which in late ancient myth and cult ensured everlasting unity between Christianity and the current imperial order. Such remembrances of "Paul in the Age of Nero" belong to this developing hagiography, not to history. Beyond that hagiography, we have little evidence for Paul in Rome.[61]

Further Reading

Two studies by Ehrman 2016 and 2013 can introduce the reader to a historical-critical assessment of Paul's letters and other early Christian writings. For more on the apostle Paul, see Knox 1987, Meeks 2003, Roetzel 2009, and Harrill 2012. On Christians (and Jews) in ancient Rome, start with Lampe 2003. Consulting Walters 1993, Donfried and Richardson 1998, Gruen 2002, and Das 2007 should further help the reader to survey the history and scholarly discussions. Donfried 1991 offers the best treatment of the Romans Debate, which must be

57 See Shoemaker (2016).

58 Eusebius, *Hist. eccl.* 26.5 (Williamson 1989: 134). Lactantius, *De mort.* 2.5–8; Creed 1984: xxxv–xxxvii, 7, 80–1. See also Sulpicius Severus, *Chron.* 2.28–30 (Senneville-Grave 1999: 288–93); Andel 1976: 40–3. Maier 2013: 391–3.

59 Eastman 2011.

60 Moss 2012: 78. Recent archaeological evidence suggests rival, late ancient commemorations of Paul's martyrdom in Philippi; see Bakirtzis and Koester 1998.

61 Shaw 2015 confirms the conclusions presented here; pace Jones 2017.

consulted alongside the excellent studies in Aune 1991 and Sampley 1995. Jewett 2007 provides the most recent and extensive commentary on Paul's Epistle to the Romans; the review in Barclay 2008 helpfully critiques its thesis. The reader can find the apocryphal and patristic sources for Paul's Neronian travails in Elliott 1993 and Meeks and Fitzgerald 2007. Barnes 1968 evaluates the evidence of Nero's so-called persecution. For the reception of Nero in late antiquity, see Eastman 2011, Malik 2012, and Meier 2013. To learn more about Roman attitudes toward Christians, start with Wilken 2003.

18: The Image of Nero in Renaissance Political Thought

Peter Stacey

Several intellectual and ideological preoccupations with the figure of Nero that begin to recur in the political and moral literature of the Renaissance were gathered up and given a pronounced conceptual shape, as well as some demonstrably enduring content, in August 1348 in a letter that Petrarch wrote to Seneca.[1] The letter is one of several addressed to various classical writers and philosophers that Petrarch placed in the final book of the *Epistulae Familiares* (*Letters to* Friends), the first of his two great epistolary collections. The central conceit of each epistle in this closing book is that Petrarch is intimately acquainted with the classical figures with whom he is corresponding, his ability to converse with them in tones of easy familiarity rendered plausible by the demonstrable degree of immersion in their writing that the style and content of his letters exhibit.

Rehearsing some accusations of classical origin and adding a few of his own to the list, Petrarch summons the Roman Stoic philosopher from "the peace of the grave" to account for his conduct under the Neronian regime.[2] The charges are laid out; witnesses are called to testify; the questioning begins.[3] Petrarch's interrogation carefully characterizes Seneca's conduct as morally reprehensible on terms drawn from the Stoic's own philosophical conscience.[4] Renaissance students of his philosophy well knew that Seneca had fervently advocated the practice of conscience, an ethical regime of self-inspection and self-interrogation that he had envisaged as a matter of "daily pleading my case at my own court"; of rendering

[1] For the text (= *Fam.* XXIV.5), see Petrarca 1933–44: IV, 231–7; for an older translation (which I cite except where stated) and notes, see Petrarca 1910: 43–68; for a modern translation, see Bernardo 1975–85: III, 322–5.

[2] Petrarca 1910: 43.

[3] For a concentrated deployment of this language, see Petrarca 1933–44: IV, 234.

[4] Petrarca 1933–44: IV, 232 (my translation).

an account for one's words and deeds before "the judge of reason"; and of delivering an interior monolog in a mental space conceptually configured as a tribunal in which one is "praised or admonished."[5] By the conclusion of Petrarch's letter, Seneca has been convicted on several counts of having persistently lapsed into inconsistency, thereby falling short of the virtue of *constantia* that he had so lauded and that Petrarch himself wishes to underline as a key intellectual and moral value.[6] But Petrarch also uses the imaginative architecture of the letter to insinuate that one of the principal examples of Seneca's repeated failure to practice what he preached is also one of its principal causes. For Seneca's political career demonstrated his inability to keep his reasoning finely tuned by the rigors of rational self-examination that he had expounded in his political and moral theory. He stands impugned, above all else, for having acted in bad conscience.

Petrarch's letter merits a more central position in the developing historiography of the fortunes of Nero in the Renaissance than it currently occupies.[7] In addition to constituting a somewhat overlooked episode in the revival of one element of classical political theory that was elaborated with Nero very much in mind – the role of conscience in government – it also broaches some general topics, ranging from the relationship between freedom and autocracy to a consideration of the relationship between politics and philosophy itself. These questions remained pressing for commentators concerned with monarchical politics from the Renaissance to the French Revolution.[8] They were recognizably still in place when Diderot attempted to rehabilitate Seneca's increasingly battered reputation in his *Essai sur les règnes de Claude et de Néron et sur la vie et les écrits de Sénèque* of 1782 by recasting him in the role of an exemplary *philosophe engagé*.[9] Traces of these concerns persist today, although they have migrated from the public sphere to modern scholarship of Seneca. From Miriam Griffin's classic work of 1976 to the recent books of James Romm and Emily Wilson,

[5] For Seneca's description of the practice of conscience as an oratorical performance in the courtroom of reason, see Sen., *Ira.* 3.36.1–38.2; *Clem.* 1.1.1–4.

[6] For inconstancy of mind (*animi levitas*) as the "root" of all of Seneca's difficulties, see Petrarca 1933–44: IV, 234.

[7] It is cited in a single footnote in William B. Gwyn's pioneering and still indispensable 1991 essay, "Cruel Nero: The Concept of the Tyrant and the Image of Nero in Western Political Thought" (Gwyn 1991: 433, n. 37). Note, however, that the letter itself has now been subjected to an extremely penetrating scrutiny in Monti 2003, an analysis to which my own interpretation is much indebted. See also Rubiés 1994; Braund 2013; Maier 2013; Squire 2013.

[8] These concerns about conscience and the politics of the letter are not raised in Monti 2003.

[9] Detailed contextualizations of Diderot's work are in Bonneville 1966; Strugnell 1973: 73–89; Conroy 1975. A recent discussion is in Andrew 2004.

the question remains, as Mary Beard frames it: "how could the true Stoic philosopher, who wrote so strenuously of the importance of virtue in politics, square his conscience with the role he had chosen to play at Nero's right hand . . . how could a man who denounced tyranny take on the job of tutor to a tyrant?"[10]

The aim of this chapter is to contextualize the early Renaissance version of this query, and to retrieve the sense of political anxiety that accompanied its formulation. In section 1 of this chapter, I examine some features of the political and intellectual landscape around Petrarch that help explain why the ghost of Nero came to haunt the pages of post-classical monarchical political thought with an insistence that called for a response at this early stage of the Renaissance. In section 2, I examine Petrarch's attempt to rise to that challenge in the letter to Seneca, and I point to some of the directions in which his arguments were subsequently taken.

18.1 The Political Culture of the Early Renaissance

Of our three major sources for Nero's reign, it is the Latin authorities – first, from the ninth century onward, Suetonius, and then, increasingly, Tacitus – rather than the Greek historian Dio, who are principally used to flesh out the historical details in the Renaissance.[11] And of the two Roman accounts, Petrarch had access only to Suetonius. Our text of books 11–16 of the *Annals* derives from a single eleventh-century manuscript retrieved from the monastery of Monte Cassino in the 1350s, probably by Zanobi da Strada, a humanist friend of Petrarch (who never read Tacitus) and of Boccaccio (who certainly did, and used it in the 1360s).[12] The codex was brought to Florence, where its contents were slowly diffused until they began to appear in printed editions of Tacitus' works in the early 1470s. Interestingly, the speeches of Seneca and Nero in the dialog between them in book 14 were excerpted and circulated in both Latin and Italian translation from the

[10] Beard 2014. On this topic, see further Bartsch, Chapter 10 in this volume.

[11] For the Renaissance reception of Tacitus' account of the Neronian years, see Salmon 1991; Rubiés 1994. For Tacitus in Renaissance political thought more generally, see Schellhase 1976; Burke 1991.

[12] For a summary of the *fortuna* of the manuscript, the *Annals*, and Tacitus in general, see Ulery 1986, esp. 92–7; for the attribution of a crucial role to Zanobi, now widely accepted, see the seminal essay republished in Billanovich 1996: 134–5; for a detailed account of Zanobi and Tacitus, see Baglio et al. 1999: 205–24.

1380s onward.[13] The relationship between philosopher and prince was now open to reinterpretation in light of the new textual material.

Shifts in the canons of humanist historical criticism also explain why the charges Petrarch leveled at Seneca would remain eminently debatable. These developments altered the basis on which Montaigne mounted his defense of Seneca's "pure and ... inflexible" virtue 200 years later (1991: 817). Here Seneca is vindicated in the face of a contemporary revival of some "deeply insulting" comments found in Dio, "whose testimony," Montaigne remarks, "I simply do not believe" (1991: 818). Dio had been reintroduced to Italy by Sicilian humanist Giovanni Aurispa in 1423; by the 1430s, his treatment of Nero's reign preserved in Xiphilinus' epitome was in the hands of Guarino Veronese.[14] Dio was translated into Italian in 1533 by a distinguished Greek scholar, Niccolò Leoniceno of Vicenza, while the *editio princeps* of Xiphilinus was produced by Parisian royal typographer Robert Estienne in 1551.[15] For Estienne's fellow-countryman, Dio was nevertheless unreliable. "In matters such as these," Montaigne pronounced, "it is more reasonable to trust the Roman historians than foreign Greek ones" (1991: 818). Montaigne's judgment is proffered in the course of an attempt to expose the weaknesses in Bodin's handling of Plutarch as a source of evidence in his *Methodus ad facilem historiarum cognitionem* of 1566. These polemics between humanists about how to place their classical materials in a reliable interpretative framework are similarly detectable in Girolamo Cardano's *Encomium Neronis* of 1562.[16] Cardano's thoughts about politics appear to have been no more – but possibly no less – coherent than his thoughts about anything else.[17] Perhaps his panegyric of Nero's virtues was not the exercise in mock encomium that some of his contemporaries took it to be. But it is unquestionably a systematic attempt to demolish the famous opening claim advanced in the *Annals* by Tacitus – "a man of the utmost ambition and improbity," Cardano warns in his opening – to have written *sine ira et studio*.[18]

13 For a full reconstruction, see Baglio 2000. The speeches are in *Ann.* 14.52–6.

14 For the recovery of Dio and its circulation, see Sabbadini 1898 (esp. 400–2). Guarino also had access to Xiphilinus' epitome; as did Venetian humanist Francesco Barbaro (d. 1454): see, respectively, Diller 1961: 319, 1963: 260.

15 For the *volgare* translation, see Gualdo 1990; for the edition of Xiphilinus, see Armstrong 1954: 29, 136.

16 For the text, see Cardano 1663; for a recent critical edition with a German translation, see Cardano 1994; for Italian editions and translation, see Cardano 1998, 2008.

17 Recent interpretations of the *Encomium* include Eberl 1999; Galimberti Biffino 2003; and Valenti 2005. Grafton 1999 supplies an intellectual biography.

18 Cardano 1663: 179. For Tacitus' claim, see *Ann.* 1.1.

In the middle of the fourteenth century, prior to the reception of either Tacitus or Dio, Petrarch holds Seneca himself, along with Suetonius, responsible for the circulation of a great deal of the imagery informing contemporary perceptions of the emperor. In so doing, he draws on some texts from the Neronian period that have so far scarcely featured at all in the relevant historiography.[19] Recalling passages in the *de Clementia*, the *Consolatio ad Polybium*, and the pseudo-Senecan tragedy *Octavia* (whose attribution to Seneca, conventional among his contemporaries, Petrarch begins to question in the letter), the humanist rounds on Seneca, juxtaposing some awkward home truths alongside these portrayals of "your Nero."[20] Seneca's texts were increasingly mined in medieval and early Renaissance literature for the purposes of political argument, but the problem, as Petrarch saw, was that the Senecan material yielded highly ambivalent depictions of Nero.

Consider *de Clementia*, in circulation since the early ninth century.[21] In its opening, Seneca invites his pupil to behold his virtuous reflection in the mirror of the text, conjuring an image of an impeccably merciful Nero into existence by the figure of impersonation and showing him in an extended act of introspection, enjoying the benefits of a spotless conscience.[22] Here the moral *persona* of Nero encapsulates the doctrines that Seneca's theory of princely government subsequently explicates. This image attracted increasing attention from the twelfth century onward, often because Seneca's incomparably exalted account of the benefits of monarchical government was repeatedly phrased as an argument about royal as much as princely power. In 1188, Gerald of Wales commended the English king, Henry II, for having "frequently in your hands the book which Seneca addressed to Nero 'On Clemency' during a recent uprising against him."[23] In 1231, Emperor Frederick II rearticulated the opening of Nero's speech in *de Clementia* virtually verbatim in the prologue of the law codes for his Sicilian kingdom.[24] As their first glossator underlined, the monarch spoke with "the words of Seneca in the first book of *de Clementia* to Nero, where he says: 'Have

[19] But see the new discussions of the Renaissance *fortuna* of *Octavia* in Braund 2013 and Manuwald 2013 (particularly chapter 1). The Enlightenment setting of Vittorio Alfieri's *Octavia* is examined in Galimberti Biffino 1999.

[20] Petrarca 1910: 50–1, 53 (modernizing the translation of "tui Neronis" from "thy Nero" in Cosenza).

[21] For the circulation of *de Clementia* from the Middle Ages into the early Renaissance, see Stacey 2007: 75–169.

[22] For further discussion of this passage, see Stacey 2007: 42–5, 2014: 141–3. I cite the translation of the text provided by Cooper and Procopé in Seneca 1995: 128–64.

[23] Gerald of Wales 2000: 87.

[24] For the citation and the context, see Stacey 2007: 75–81.

I, of all mortals found favour and been chosen to act on earth in place of the gods? I am the arbiter of life and death over peoples.'"[25] The price of picking up Seneca's political theory was the perpetuation of the historical Nero's theoretical *doppelganger*. Bodin encounters this bind in book 2 of *Six Livres de la République* (1576), observing that Seneca's account of "soveraigne authoritie" – upon which he draws repeatedly – is articulated by "Seneca speaking in the person of Nero his scholler."[26] Seneca's *princeps* bore all the crucial "marks" of sovereignty – but wherever the *de Clementia* was brought into contention, the ghost in its conceptual machinery also tended to show its face. Furthermore, every writer who played the part of princely preceptor and presented a mirror to a monarch worked in the shadow of an infamous classical relationship. This fact had its polemical uses, of course. Montaigne observes that some Calvinists had recently exploited it in an anti-royalist pamphlet "which extended and filled out the similitude it intended to establish between the rule of our poor late King Charles IX and that of Nero, by comparing the late Cardinal of Lorraine (the king's counsellor) to Seneca" (1991: 817).

One way of exorcising these spectral traces was to continue to impress upon rulers the need to embody the sovereign *persona* of Seneca's text – a fiction replete with all the necessary princely virtues of clemency, magnanimity, humaneness, and moderation specified by the theory – while using a quite different image of Nero, one now fashioned from other historical materials testifying to his horrendous qualities, to illustrate Seneca's corresponding theory of tyranny. The Senecan vision of the prince engendered a remarkably brisk dismissal of the relevance of constitutional definitions or legal procedure as criteria for assessing legitimate political rule. Everything turns on the moral character of the ruler, Seneca argues, asserting that "no one could conceive of anything more becoming to a ruler than mercy, whatever the manner of his accession to power and whatever its legal basis"; for "what distinguishes a tyrant from a king are his actions, not the name."[27] If clemency – that is, the possession of "self-control of the mind when it has the power to take vengeance," and the quality of "moderation that remits something of a deserved and due punishment" – was the crowning virtue, the defining characteristic of tyrants was cruelty.[28] Seneca's anatomy of cruelty was a resource of unparalleled depth for post-classical writers; even Aquinas – certainly no Senecan – depends heavily on it in

[25] *Constitutionum Regni Siciliarum* 1999: 4, n.(h). [26] Bodin 1962: 221.
[27] Sen. *Clem.* 1.19.1, 1.12.1. [28] *Clem.* 2.3.1–2.

the *Summa*.[29] Seneca distinguishes cruelty from a more general disposition to derive pleasure from inflicting pain by refining it into an exquisitely political vice. Like clemency, it shows up in the behavior of those wielding judicial power when they display "nothing other than grimness of mind (*atrocitas animi*) in exacting punishment" and a "lack of self-control by the mind in exacting punishment" (*Clem.* 2.4.1–3). Cruelty, then, is mercilessness; and it involves "a pursuit of retribution" and "anger at someone's misdeed," either real or perceived (*Clem.* 2.4.2). This is why the practice of conscience, first recommended in *De ira*, becomes crucial in *de Clementia*: it is self-imposed psychotherapy that impedes the prince, in the absence of any formal restraint upon his power, from degenerating into the kind of raging tyrant "who refuses to hold back even from his closest friends" (*Clem.* 1.26.4). No reader of classical history – and certainly not Petrarch – could miss the terrible irony that this was the *persona* the real Nero embodied, turning not only on his mother and his wife, but also on his mentor. Unsurprisingly, then, Nero came to illustrate an understanding of atrocious cruelty often derived from Seneca's own work.

Seneca's theory of tyranny was one of several inherited from classical antiquity that informed Renaissance political thinking, but it was an inseparable part of Seneca's monarchical argument, which began to infiltrate the turbulent ideological context of the northern Italian city-states from the late *Duecento* onward.[30] The consolidation of monarchical forms of power in communes formerly wedded to electoral and representative procedures self-consciously styled on Roman republican governmental practice was accompanied by the exploitation of some crucial ideological resources to celebrate, in Augustan tones, the rise of the so-called *signori* as the restoration of liberty, peace, and tranquility over *res publicae* racked by internal dissensions. These claims sustained political developments that often structurally guaranteed, with considerable constitutional specificity, the conferral of a degree of power into the hands of the new princely figures and their heirs that was total and absolute, its exercise entirely dependent on the arbitrary will of the ruler. In Verona, in 1277, Alberto della Scala was awarded "full, general and liberal authority and power of ruling and governing over all in all things"; in Mantua, in 1299, the new *signore* was proclaimed to "rule and govern the city ... with his undiluted, pure and free will, as shall best

[29] See especially the discussion of justice, clemency, and cruelty in Aquinas 1964-: vol. 44, 34–81 (= 2a2ae. q.157–9). The Senecan debts are discussed in Baraz 1998: 196–202.

[30] For this context, see Skinner 1978: II. 23–8, 31–5; Green 1993; Stacey 2007: 95–115.

and most usefully seem agreeable to him, with counsel or without counsel"; and in Ferrara, in the 1260s, seventeen-year-old Obizzo d'Este was reputedly entrusted "with fullest dominion," which left him wielding "more power than God eternal."[31] The Senecan theory flourished in this environment, helping to legitimate the new political orders, but it acquired the requisite conceptual purchase precisely because of the autocratic pretensions of the new rulers, which in turn raised fears about the emergence of a new Nero.

In this setting of political instability and heightened anxieties about unbridled, arbitrary government, Seneca's dramatic accounts of blood-soaked, vengeful tyranny also began to circulate.[32] After the eleventh-century *Codex Etruscus* containing the authentic Senecan plays was rediscovered by scholar and poet Lovato dei Lovati, Renaissance tragedy took off in early *trecento* Padua. Its development was profoundly inflected by the inclusion within the Senecan canon of the *Octavia*, the only *praetexta* (a Roman drama of historical subject matter) to have survived intact. Lovati's pupil Albertino Mussato pioneered the genre of neoclassical tragedy in his *Ecerinis* in 1314, digging deep into the newly available resources.[33] The debt to the *Octavia* – in which Nero is one of the *dramatis personae* – was profound. Mussato used the recent experience of the Paduan commune under the tyranny of his depraved eponymous antihero, Ezzelino III da Romano (1194–1259), as the setting for his drama, thereby implicitly warning his fellow citizens about the dangers of succumbing to the domination of another *signore*, Cangrande della Scala, whose recent politics in the Veneto were once again threatening the autonomy of their *civitas*.[34] The Neronian elements of the protagonist's career and character – whose boundless savagery is declared by the Chorus to have even outdone the "brutality of the depraved Nero" – were as conspicuous in Mussato's work as its structural and syntactical similarities to the *Octavia*.[35] Cangrande nevertheless came to power in 1328.

[31] For these citations and an illuminating discussion, see Larner 1980: 143–5, 138.

[32] For the transmission of Seneca's tragedies, the inclusion of *Octavia* within the canon, and an authoritative discussion of the relevant scholarship, see Ferri 2003: 75–82; a briefer overview is in Grund 2011: xiv–xx. For the impact of Seneca on Renaissance drama, see Braden 1985; Miola 1992; Mayer 1994; Locati 2006; S. Braund 2013.

[33] For Mussato's *Ecerinis*, see Locati 2006; Grund 2011: xx–xxiv.

[34] For Ezzelino's politics, see Larner 1980: 129–33. For Cangrande's career, see Green 1993: 338–44; for allusions to Cangrande in the text, see Locati 2006: 108–15.

[35] For the citation, see Grund 2011: 19; for the parallels, see Locati 2006: 148–57.

Elsewhere in the peninsula, monarchical encroachment on communal government was more successfully resisted. In Tuscany, Siena was one of a few republics that survived the rise of the new princes. A rarely mentioned feature of Ambrogio's Lorenzetti's famous frescoes allegorizing good and bad government in Siena's Palazzo Pubblico is the appearance of Nero in them.[36] The lower medallions on the west wall of Lorenzetti's cycle in the *Sala dei Nove* (the seat of executive government) form a band running under the *Allegory of Bad Government*. Once filled with images of ancient tyrants, only the figure of Nero remains discernible. Located directly below the enthroned figure of Tyranny, he is shown impaled upon his own sword in a creative rendition of his suicide (Suetonius talks of a dagger to the throat; Suet. *Nero* 49.3).

The Renaissance history of the history play thus commenced with the inscription of Nero into the drama of tyranny; and there he stayed for centuries. As Colin Burrow remarks of the neo-Senecan environment in which Shakespeare wrote, "the inclusion of the *Octavia* within the canon meant that Seneca gave a clear classical precedent for writing historical dramas . . . this was the underlying reason why Shakespeare could people historical plays . . . with characters who frequently sound like Seneca's heroes."[37] The same environment in which "old-fashioned Senecan ghosts stalk the stage of Shakespeare's Hamlet" also ensured the reappearance of Nero.[38] The image of the emperor rises to the lips of Hamlet himself – "Let not ever/The soul of Nero enter this firm bosom" – just as he steels himself in Act 3, at "the witching time of night," against the temptation to rage like a Senecan tyrant and "drink hot blood/ and do such bitter business as the day/Would quake to look on" (3.2.377–83).

18.2 Petrarch, Stoic Philosophy, and the Politics of Tyranny

By Shakespeare's day, the authorship not merely of the *Octavia* but of virtually every play traditionally included under the heading of "Seneca's Tragedies" was contested.[39] Matters looked very different to

[36] For an influential reading of the iconographical scheme in general, see Skinner 2002: II, 39–117. Rubinstein 1958 mentions the image of Nero at 191, n. 88.

[37] Burrow 2013: 169.

[38] Burrow 2013: 173. Braden points out that "plays on Nero eventually surface in almost every language in Europe" in the early modern period (Braden 1985: 108 – a point reiterated in S. Braund 2013: 440).

[39] Underlined in Burrow 2013: 169. For a complete analysis of the complexities of the attribution history, see Mayer 1994.

Petrarch. The view he inherits is that Seneca had written the *Octavia* as a clear denunciation of Nero's descent into tyranny. And that decision meant that Seneca had changed his tune, to say the least. Petrarch reports elsewhere that he was prompted to write to Seneca upon "re-reading the tragedy entitled the *Octavia*."[40] In the letter, he similarly mulls over the implications of "that much-discussed play."[41] With the reemergence of his tragedies, it now looked as if Seneca had penned an utterly contrasting portrait of the ruler to the more familiar characterization he had furnished at the start of Nero's principate in *de Clementia*. Petrarch's questions to the philosopher proliferate around his attempt to extract an explanation for this massively jarring disjunction in Seneca's representations. In the absence of Tacitus, Dio, or any historiographical tradition from the relevant fourth-century sources of the *quinquennium Neronis* in which to construe this problem, Petrarch is reliant on Suetonius, whose account, as Griffin underlines, differs from the later sources in offering no sharp distinction between some promising early years and unencumbered tyrannical government later, although the narrative certainly outlines a "decline in conduct, if not in character" throughout the reign.[42]

One key to unlocking the letter's philosophical character is to recognize that its recurrent image of Seneca's political career as the journey of a vessel navigating the treacherous shallows and tempestuous waters of high politics is itself a highly Senecan theme.[43] Petrarch possessed all of Seneca's surviving works, but in order to encircle the specific debts on display in the letter, we need in particular to focus our attention on the argument of *De otio*, in which Seneca had reiterated the Stoic wisdom that the wise man "will go into public life, unless something impedes," only to alter the doctrine's underlying thrust by broadening its restrictive applicability.[44] The conventional Stoic position was to counsel involvement in politics unless "the *res publica* is too corrupt to be helped, if it has been taken over by the wicked" (*De otio* 3.3). Under these conditions, in which he may have "too little authority or strength, if the *res publica* will not accept him," the *sapiens* would "not embark on a course which he knows he cannot manage," just as he would not "launch a battered ship onto the sea . . . it is possible even for one whose

40 Petrarca 1910: xi (citing the *Praefatio ad Socratem*, which opens the last book of Petrarch's letters).

41 Petrarca 1910: 50. The letter also reprises and reverses Petrarch's own, earlier judgment of Seneca's stance toward Nero in the *Octavia* in *Rerum memorandarum libri* III 44. For further analysis of this point, see Monti 2003: 224–7.

42 Griffin 1987: 83.

43 As Monti stresses, the imagery is "profondamente senecana."

44 *De otio* 3.2. For the depths of the complicated relationship between his own thought and the Roman philosopher's oeuvre, see Bobbio 1941.

resources are still intact, before experiencing any storms, to settle in safety" (*De otio* 3.3–4). But Seneca objects that the political sphere is frequently an inauspicious environment for philosophy; in public affairs, "we fluctuate . . . we depend wholly on the judgments of others"; and Zeno and the other early Stoics had anyway never been in government, instead applying themselves to the *negotia*, or affairs, of the one *res publica* that fundamentally mattered to the Stoics: the cosmic *civitas* (*De otio* 1. 2–3). Their philosophy was pursued in *otium* – at leisure – but it was, Seneca claimed, far from otiose.

Petrarch wants to know why Seneca failed to apply this kind of reasoning to his own circumstances. He is generous enough to interpret Seneca's decisions against the background of the strongly deterministic universe that Stoic metaphysics should have supplied to ground those moral choices. He understands, he says, the "hard, inexorable laws of necessity," to which the wise should submit bravely when difficult, dangerous situations are unavoidable.[45] Seneca may simply have been constrained to accept the imperial summons initially; and, on a Stoic view, his real freedom may have consisted in recognizing and obeying just these dictates of necessity. But Petrarch suspects that Seneca did have a choice about staying at the court of "the most savage ruler within the memory of man." He doubts that this part of the story can be equally sustained by the Stoic's defense that "Fate leads the willing and drags the unwilling."[46] The charge, then, is that he remained when he could and should have left. One explanation advanced for Seneca's behavior is that he wished to show his virtue by skillfully steering through choppy political waters; if so, Petrarch thinks he displayed foolishness "in so stormy a sea" rather than virtue.[47] But the allegations that follow all point to one fundamental cause to explain Seneca's error: his pursuit of "the elusive phantom of glory."[48] Petrarch here means not due recognition for properly virtuous deeds, but the vain desire for approbation among one's contemporaries – for false glory, in short, which blinded his judgment.[49] The rhetorical strategy in *de Clementia* had been to impress upon Nero the impeccably merciful *persona* in the mirror by praising him for already embodying it. But Petrarch thinks it highly implausible that the material in Seneca's hands could have ever appeared

[45] Petrarca 1910: 46.
[46] Petrarca 1910: 47 (the verse cited here – "Ducunt volentem fata, nolentem trahunt" – is in Sen. *Ep*. 107.11, where it is attributed to Cleanthes).
[47] Petrarca 1910: 45. [48] Petrarca 1910: 49.
[49] On Seneca's desire for glory, see Edwards, Chapter 11 in this volume. On his failure to retire, see Bartsch, Chapter 10 in this volume.

promising. Nero's "youth"; the "promise of better results"; a "sudden and unexpected change in life" – such justifications were only sustainable by radically misinterpreting, at very close quarters, "a few, unimportant acts" and some "murmured hypocritical phrases on duty."[50] Sarcasm is heaped upon Seneca's imagined protestations: did he really take Nero's consecration on the Capitol of his first growth of beard for a sure sign of the kind of "good and conscientious ruler" that he had so lauded in *de Clementia*?[51] Worse still, having finally recognized the true character of his "inhuman and bloodstained pupil," what kind of response was it to pen a tragedy "to avenge the burden of your yoke?"[52] The *Octavia* sprang from an indecent thirst for revenge. If it was indeed Seneca's, it was more evidence of the fluctuations in his evaluative activity that his desire for worldly glory entailed.

It may well be that the inventive literary cast Petrarch gives to his preoccupations played as much a part in the letter's subsequent circulation as their content. Humanists studied Petrarch's pioneering work in the neoclassical epistolary genre attentively. The letters to his favored classical authorities were sometimes treated as a subgenre, transmitted either singly or in groups.[53] One fifteenth-century Florentine manuscript carrying the complete series as a discrete body of work was owned by Pietro Crinito, a pupil of the brilliant classical scholar Angelo Poliziano. A university lecturer, Crinito had been taught at grammar school by Ser Paolo Sasso da Ronciglione, the schoolmaster responsible for instructing the young Niccolò Machiavelli. We find Machiavelli himself on markedly Petrarchan terrain in his famous letter of December 1513 to his friend Francesco Vettori, as he describes his evenings in his study with his books during his period of exile in the countryside outside Florence:

> Before I go in, I remove my everyday clothes, which are very muddy and soiled, and put on clothes that are fit for a royal court. Being thus properly clad, I enter the ancient courts of the men of old, in which I am received affectionately by them and partake of the food that properly belongs to me, and for which I was born. There I do not hesitate to converse

50 Petrarca 1910: 51–2. 51 Petrarca 1910: 53.

52 Petrarca 1910: 47, 50 (translation amended).

53 For some reconstruction of the manuscript tradition and the information relayed in this paragraph, see D'Alessandro 2007: 21.

> with them, and ask them why they acted as they did. . . . I have written down what has been valuable in their conversations, and have composed a little book *On Principalities*.[54]

Machiavelli's conversations with the ancients were reputed to have mattered to him so much that he was prepared to go to hell to continue them – a rumor whose currency depended on a recognition of the distance that his own political theory had traveled from the Christianized Senecan concerns about conscience, clemency, and cruelty that crowd Petrarch's thoughts. But Petrarch's extended *j'accuse* is not simply a case of moral priggery couched in the idiom of classical erudition. His hectoring, indignant tone conveys a deep uneasiness as he re-treads the steps that carried Seneca away from philosophical coherence and toward an intractable political dilemma, in part because the threat of finding himself in a not dissimilar quandary was far from remote.[55] The letter was composed in Parma during the same summer in which he had received the archdeaconate of the city, now under Visconti rule from Milan.[56]

Five years later, after accepting an invitation from his Visconti patron to settle in Milan itself, Petrarch was accused of consorting with tyrants.[57] In his *Invective Against a Man of High Rank* (1355), Petrarch set out to refute these aspersions "on another's conscience," claiming that his acceptance of benefits and honors in Milan placed no meaningful constraints on his *libertas* or his *otium*: "political deliberations and measures as well as the administration of public funds are entrusted to others . . . to me, nothing is entrusted but leisure (*otium*), silence, security and liberty . . . these are my concern and my business (*negotia*)."[58] Petrarch's point that the government leaves him free of public commitments for the serious business of leisure is part of a deeper account of the compatibility of liberty with monarchy. Even if it were true, Petrarch begins, that the Visconti were tyrants, "virtue is not infected by the proximity of vice."[59] After all, he asks – now papering over his earlier doubts – "didn't Plato live with Dionysius . . . and

54 Machiavelli 1988: 93.

55 The troubled tone is noted by Monti but explained in slightly different terms. See Monti 2003: 227–8.

56 Wilkins 1963: 454. For Petrarch in Parma, see Dotti 2006.

57 For Petrarch's report of the accusation, see Petrarca 2003: 202, 208–14 (discussed in Wilkins 1958: 8–12).

58 Petrarca 2003: 204–5 ("de aliena conscientia . . . sententiam fers"); 215. For the importance of the debate about *otium* and *negotium* to humanist political thought, see Skinner 2002: II, 216–24.

59 Petrarca 2003: 209.

Seneca with Nero?"[60] After disclaiming any direct involvement in government, Petrarch denies that his life under the Visconti is tantamount to servitude by asserting that he subjects himself to the dominion of only virtuous masters. But on his reckoning, that kind of voluntary submission to the dictates of virtue is no servitude at all.[61] It is merely what reason demands. Reprising Seneca's dualistic formulation of the condition of liberty in *De beneficiis*, Petrarch observes that "the earthly part of me must perforce be subject to the lords whose lands it inhabits," while "the better part of me is free."[62]

By his death in 1374, Petrarch had offered kings, *signori*, and their counselors in Naples, Parma, Milan, and Padua instruction in their moral and political duties in numerous *specula* and in one immensely influential *institutio regia*.[63] This literature was similarly suffused with Senecan doctrine; it introduced topics that became recurrent; and it exemplified a role that humanists continued to play as teachers and advisors of Renaissance princes. But Nero remained nightmarish for advocates of princely government because the history of his reign manifestly undermined their confidence that an education in the *studia humanitatis* necessarily mitigated the possibility of bad monarchical government. Pier Paolo Vergerio admitted as much in his seminal contribution to Renaissance pedagogy, *The Character and Studies Befitting a Free-Born Youth* (1402–3). Sardonically recalling the "merciful" Nero of *de Clementia*, he ruefully conceded that "the discipline of letters takes away neither madness nor wickedness ... Claudius was quite learned. ... Nero was particularly well-educated ... of these two, the former was notoriously deranged, and the latter was steeped in cruelty and all the vices."[64]

But from one well-defined perspective in the Italian Renaissance, the decision to descend to detailed discussions of Neronian misrule was predicated upon a set of concerns whose conceptual shape – even before one considered their content – appeared to be indicative of a fundamentally slavish fixation. For humanist theorists of self-governing constitutions, the question of Nero was subsumed within a consideration of the perils of monarchy per se. From their point of view, to be reduced to dependency on the *arbitrium* of one person alone

[60] Petrarca 2003: 209. [61] See Petrarca 2003: 211.

[62] Petrarca 2003: 211. The Senecan discussion invoked here virtually verbatim is at Sen. *Ben*. 3.20. 1–2. I have been unable to find any discussion of this debt.

[63] For this literature and its impact on the pre-Machiavellian ideology of the prince, see D'Alessandro 2007: 15–54; Stacey 2007: 119–57, 2015: 297–300.

[64] Kallendorf 2002: 37–9 (and for the restraining effects of the preceptor's conscience on the prince, see 23).

was tantamount to slavery, and it is merely an unexpected relief from the horrors of servitude, rather than a liberation from the condition itself, if one's political masters happen to be good rather than bad.[65] As Leonardo Bruni put it in his *Panegyric of the City of Florence* (1403–4), "the Caesars, the Antonines, the Tiberiuses, the Neros" were all "plagues and destroyers of the Roman Republic."[66] Elsewhere, Bruni happily acknowledged that the problem underlying Nero's cruelty was his uncontrollable rage.[67] But Nero was a generalizable – indeed pluralizable – symptom of the degradation of the Roman free state into monarchical servitude. Once we grasp this ramification of the ferociously anti-Caesarian historical critique underpinning the ideology of the Florentine republicans, we can better appreciate the drivingly political character of the anxiety that surrounded the question of Nero elsewhere. The most pressing problem for Florentine political theorists from Bruni to Machiavelli was how to prevent the *res publica* from collapsing into monarchy in the first place. Given that concern, the careers of Catiline and Julius Caesar were far more deserving of attention.

Further Reading

The historical picture of Nero in the Renaissance is still very fragmented. Fundamental points of departure for any systematic investigation are Gwyn 1991 and Rubiés 1994. Specific parts of the textual, pictorial, and archaeological history are handled in S. Braund 2013; Squire 2013; Maes 2013; and Maier 2013. For more detailed discussions of the relationship between Petrarch and Seneca, see Bobbio 1941; Monti 2003; and Stacey 2015. Depictions of Nero and his relationship with Seneca in the literature of Jacobean England are discussed in Salmon 1991. Citti 2015 usefully traces from the early modern era to the modern era the literary and pictorial traditions that convey the conflicts and contradictions in Seneca's career under Nero.

65 For the conceptualization of liberty and its absence along these lines among humanist republican theorists, see Stacey 2013: 178–81.

66 Bruni 1968: 245

67 Bruni 2001: I, 50.

19: Resurgences of Nero in the Enlightenment

Elena Russo

In chapter 10 of his *History of the Russian Empire under Peter the Great*, Voltaire could not avoid tackling the delicate affair of Peter's murder of his own son, the Tsarevich Alexei. Delicate not only because witness accounts were scarce and contradictory, and because Voltaire had been solicited to write that story by none other than Peter's daughter Empress Elizabeth, but also because, as a matter of principle, Voltaire balked at the necessity of having to deal with such extremes of brutality in the private affairs of a family, and a reigning family no less. Voltaire promised Count Shuvalov, the minister of education and Elizabeth's lover, who was pressing him to tread as lightly as possible, that he was going to make the best of a bad situation, but that he, as a historian of worldly repute, had to defer to ethics and public opinion, and was thus quite unwilling to go for a total whitewash and pass for a sycophant of the Russian court and a hired hack. The truth was, Voltaire told Shuvalov, that not a soul in Europe bought into the official story that the Tsarevich had died of natural causes.[1] Among the skeptics was one Guillaume Lamberty, a Swiss journalist whom Voltaire saw as highly credible and conscientious, who had included damning, if somewhat colorful witness accounts of the murder of Alexei in his monumental chronicle *Mémoires pour servir à l'histoire du XVIIIe siècle*.[2] "Fear not, though," Voltaire added: "I believe I may refute him successfully by

[1] Bestermann, D10141; Voltaire to Count Ivan Ivanovich Shuvalov, November 7, 1761. Electronic Enlightenment *Scholarly Edition of Correspondence*, ed. Robert McNamee et al. Vers. 3.0. University of Oxford, 2016. http://www.e-enlightenment.com/item/voltfrVF1080097_1key001cor/.

[2] Lamberty, 1724–1740. According to Lamberty (as reported by Voltaire), Alexis had been beheaded by his father with a sword, and when he was placed into the coffin for public viewing, his head was made to adhere to the body so closely that nobody realized that the two no longer belonged together. Voltaire, 1999, 855.

relying upon some manuscripts that are favorable to us, and by ignoring those that aren't."[3]

In the published version, Voltaire closed his account of the death of the Tsarevich (Alexei had died of apoplexy, following the exhaustion of a stressful trial) with a surprising aside on how much better history writing was today than in the past:

> Let us see this as an instance of how easy it was – in the days before the printing press, when manuscript histories, entrusted to the hands of a few, did not circulate broadly and were not subject, as they are today, to universal scrutiny and critique – for one man to damage the reputation of another for eternity, in the memory of all nations. One line by Tacitus or Suetonius . . . was enough to make a prince hated by the entire world, and to perpetuate his disgrace from one century to the next.[4]

Behind Peter and his ugly little family secret peeked the disreputable shadows of Caligula, Tiberius, and especially Nero's, the ultimate embodiment of the unnatural son and matricide. Unlike them, however, Peter would not have to spend eternity moping in the Tartarus: for he had found in Voltaire an impartial historian who, by separating rumor from truth, had been able to more or less save his reputation for posterity.

That was not the first time Voltaire had asked his readers to sympathize with the plight of powerful men slandered by unscrupulous historians with personal agendas: "As soon as a Roman emperor was assassinated by the praetorian guards, the vultures of literature would sweep upon the cadaver of his reputation. They would dig out all the rumors that circulated in town."[5] To be sure, Voltaire had a soft spot for autocratic rulers (especially those who read his work and promised reforms), as the fawning tone of his epistolary exchanges with Frederick II of Prussia and Empress Catherine II show. But snobbery was not the only reason why Voltaire was inclined to doubt Tacitus and Suetonius when it came to the private lives of the Caesars. His reasons were based on historical method and philosophy. In the name of common sense and probability (*vraisemblance*), Voltaire not only rejected reports of miracles and prodigies, but also those

[3] D10141, Voltaire to Shuvalov, November 7, 1761. http://dx.doi.org/10.13051/ee:doc/voltfr VF1080097alc. All translations from the French are mine.

[4] Voltaire, 1999, 857. [5] Voltaire, 1999, 857.

actions that he deemed morally improbable and incompatible with his notions of what "human nature," conceived as a normative, timeless ideal, was like. In Aristotelian parlance, we might say that there wasn't much difference between Voltaire the tragedian and Voltaire the historian: for according to him, both genres of writing had to abide by similar criteria of probability.[6] "Let us disbelieve every ancient and modern historian who tells us things that run counter to nature and to the temper of the human heart."[7]

Voltaire's philosophy of history looked askance on everything that smacked of the extraordinary, the "abominable," and the "extravagant." Excesses of cruelty, self-destructive, unreasonable behavior, especially of a sexual nature, and everything that seemed to depart from the ordinary course of human action must be imputed to the historian's gullibility or outright, malicious lying: "I don't believe Suetonius when he says that Nero wanted to kill the entire Senate: can an emperor commit useless crimes?"[8] The lives of Tiberius and Nero provided the chief evidence of Tacitus' disingenuousness and politically motivated bias against the Caesars: "I have been asking myself, when reading Tacitus and Suetonius: all those extravagant atrocities imputed to Tiberius, Caligula and Nero, can they really be true? . . . Turpitudes that abominable do not belong with human nature."[9] Voltaire's conception of an immutable human nature, scripted in a familiar, preordained grammar, could not accommodate the notion of monstrosity. His concern for what may be called cultural and social history left no space for exceptions and radical deviations from the middle of the road. In addition to those concerns, an unspecified, unspoken notion of propriety forbade the historian to cast his eye upon certain unpleasant things: "Every time I read the abominable history of Nero and his mother Agrippina, I am tempted to disbelieve it entirely. The interest of humankind urges us to conclude that all these horrors have been greatly exaggerated. They would put human nature to too much shame."[10] Voltaire was hardly alone in holding that history ought to be a tool for enlightening and edifying the reader, in a triumph-of-the-human-spirit mood. Most of his fellow *philosophes* also felt that history's decorum required that certain chapters of Tacitus' and Suetonius'

[6] The *Poetics* of course made no such claim for history, which was the realm of the particular; the historian's sole concern ought to be to relate what had happened to such and such, regardless of general notions of probability. See Aristotle, *The Poetics*, part 1, ch. 9.

[7] Voltaire, 1996, 573. [8] Voltaire, 1968, 465. [9] Voltaire, 2007, 281.

[10] Voltaire, 2007, 285.

histories of the Roman emperors be rejected as improbable or outright false, or else be omitted altogether.

Denis Diderot, however, was not one of them. The last work he published during his life, the *Essai sur les règnes de Claude et de Néron et sur les moeurs et les écrits de Sénèque pour servir d'instruction à la lecture de ce philosophe* (1782; henceforth *ECN*), a rambling, lengthy companion volume to a recent French translation of Seneca's philosophical works, contained the darkest, most explicit portrait of Nero to date.[11] A first version, published in 1778, titled *Essai sur la vie de Sénèque*, had been received with harsh criticism by the conservative press, especially by the Jesuit and Jansenist-leaning press, who had understood very well that by devoting himself to an analysis of Seneca's life and work, Diderot was suggesting that the work he and his friends had been doing was not dissimilar to that of the Roman Stoic.[12]

Four years later, Diderot gave a decidedly polemical twist to his much-augmented second version, which engaged extensively (and, we might say, exhaustively) with the modern-day critics of Seneca and of Diderot. He grafted the controversies of the day onto the century-old debate about the plight of the philosopher confronted by the evils of power – from Tacitus to Dio, to Montaigne to Justus Lipsius, to La Mothe Le Vayer to La Mettrie, all the way down to Marmontel. The book that emerges from that philological and dialogical hall of mirrors is at once a work of filial piety, a self-portrait, an angry, personal apology, and an homage to Diderot's lifelong passion for Latin, and for Tacitus in particular. It is also the settling of an old score with the recently deceased Jean-Jacques Rousseau, an old friend turned enemy, who is featured here under the guise of Suillius, the cowardly slanderer of Seneca.

All in all, *ECN* is a painfully personal book. The identification of Diderot with Seneca is intimate, obsessive, and a little crazy. Seneca is surrounded by a constellation of characters who are inevitably cast as heroes or villains – for we are not operating here on a scholarly axis of true vs. false, but on a faith-based axis of good vs. evil. Tacitus' word is presented as sacred and his testimony unassailable; Burrus is a devoted but an ineffective ally; Suillius, Suetonius, and Dio are the scum of the republic of letters. But the major counterpart of the philosopher is of course his devious, murderous depraved disciple, Nero. The book is

[11] *Les Oeuvres de Sénèque le Philosophe*, 1778–9.

[12] "You've got to agree that the enemies of our philosophers sometimes resemble astonishingly Seneca's detractors." Diderot, 1994, 1009.

organized as a trial: Seneca's case of corruption and collusion with power is judged before the court of history, with Diderot playing in turn the role of co-defendant, defense attorney (a role he embraces in close collaboration with Tacitus), and judge.

Diderot's *ECN* is thus not a work about ancient history, but a tortured reflection on the present. More precisely, it deals with Diderot's anxieties concerning the failure of enlightened ideals, and with what he perceives as the political irrelevance of philosophy in the modern world. But why Nero? We know what Seneca represents: but who or what does Nero, the ultimate embodiment of political monstrosity, stand for? For there is no doubt that Diderot's Nero is much more than a simple foil to Seneca's righteousness. He certainly serves that purpose, for in this book Nero and Seneca are functionally two sides of the same coin, but he is also a political actor in his own right, one that clearly fascinates Diderot. Can Nero represent anyone or anything in Diderot's modern Europe? Can an extreme case such as Nero – and we shall see that Diderot purposefully darkens Nero's already pretty dire features – have any paradigmatic use in the modern world?

When Diderot accepted enthusiastically his friend d'Holbach's invitation to write a preface to Seneca's collected works, and sat down to reread them, it was the summer of 1777, and he had been back from Saint Petersburg for three years. Between October 8, 1773 and March 5, 1774, Diderot had been the honored guest of Empress Catherine II. Just about every day, or at least several times a week, for the duration of his stay, Diderot and Catherine had had two- or three-hour-long private audiences that had been the object of much speculation throughout Europe. Diderot had written down a summary of those conversations for the empress, and even though he had been the one doing most of the talking, he self-effacingly and prudently called them "reveries," "rags and scraps," "a child's babble," and "the ideas of a wretched scribbler who dreams about politics holed up in his garret."[13] But it had been serious stuff: the *philosophe* and the empress had been discussing a comprehensive program of political, economic, and educational reforms for Russia. Diderot had talked extensively about the abuses of absolutism in France, and had praised Catherine for the innovative plans she had for her own country. He had queried her about the census of the

[13] Diderot, 1995a, 227 and passim.

population, the status of the nobility, the bourgeoisie and the serfs, the postal system, the production and selling of grain, tobacco, and furs, taxation, and many other questions.

In the *ECN* Diderot wrote that "Seneca was summoned to Nero's court, on account of his brilliant talents and virtues, by an ambitious woman who was eager to reconcile herself with the nation, and who, either did not know the extent of the philosopher's fortitude, or was convinced that she could break it."[14] Diderot and Catherine went way back. In March 1765, Catherine had bought Diderot's library for the lavish sum of 15,000 livres and had pledged to pay him 1,000 livres annually for his job as her "librarian." It was a tactful way of turning herself into Diderot's patron and putting an end to the *philosophe*'s chronic money troubles. That widely publicized gesture happened to take place three years after Catherine's coup against her husband, Czar Peter III, had brought her to power. Rumor had it that the czar had not died of a sudden hemorrhoidal crisis while he was in custody, as the official story went, but that he had succumbed to a combination of poison and strangulation administered by his wife's coconspirators. Barely a month after her accession, anxious to garner legitimacy, Catherine embarked on a charm offensive aimed at enlightened public opinion. Her first attempt (in September 1762) was to invite mathematician Jean Le Rond d'Alembert to become her son's tutor. D'Alembert declined because, as he told Voltaire, "I suffer from hemorrhoids, and I am afraid that it's too dangerous a condition to have in that country."[15] Voltaire however, was totally seduced and took to calling her with names like the northern star, Semiramis, and Minerva. "I am proud to say that I am a little in her good graces. I am her knight against each and everyone. I am aware that people chide her for some trifling matter about her husband, but family affairs are none of my business."[16] It had certainly been worthwhile, Voltaire added, to get rid (however unpleasantly) of an incompetent ruler (as Peter seemed to have been), if that meant doing "great things" for her people, as Catherine – "my Catherine" – was poised to do.[17]

In the early days of their interaction, Diderot had felt the same toward his benefactress. His devotion and admiration for her were such that in 1768 he was ready to put pen to paper to defend her against the

[14] Diderot, 1994, 1009. Agrippina had of course just poisoned her husband, Claudius.

[15] D10731; Jean Le Rond d'Alembert to Voltaire, September 25, 1762. http://www.e-enlightenment.com/item/voltfrVF1090242_1key001cor/.

[16] D14187, Voltaire to Marie Anne de Vichy-Chamrond, marquise Du Deffand, May 18, 1767. http://www.e-enlightenment.com/item/voltfrVF1160117_1key001cor/.

[17] D14187, Voltaire to Mme Du Deffand, ibid.

juicy memoir by Claude Carloman de Rulhières (1734–91), the former secretary of embassy of the Marquis de Breteuil (the French ambassador to Russia), who had been in Saint-Petersburg during the time of the palace revolution. In his *Anecdotes sur la Révolution de Russie en l'année 1762*, Rulhières had described a Russian state entirely at the mercy of the monarch, ruled by fear, mistrust, and subject to the whims of a few "vigorous souls" who, "placed between the alternative of a degrading slavery or audacious conspiracies, chose by necessity to become atrocious." Witnessing the current situation in Russia at the dawn of its civilization had made Rulhières give new credence to Tacitus' account of the situation in Rome at the time of its decadence.[18] The Tacitus reference stuck with Diderot, who gave the *Anecdotes* a reluctant endorsement by comparing Rulhières' work to Tacitus': "–Did he read his *Revolution of Russia* for you? –Yes. – What do you think? –That it's a historical novel, quite well written, very interesting, a patchwork of lies and facts that our grandchildren will compare to a chapter by Tacitus."[19]

In *ECN*, however, Diderot is less interested in defending Catherine than in discussing the quandary of the courtier who feels he is obliged to engage in such defenses. He includes a long discussion of Seneca's responsibility in covering up for Agrippina's murder of Claudius, and later for Nero's murder of Agrippina; for putting the best face on Nero's crimes; and for putting his pen at the service of the tyrant. Diderot describes, with bitter eloquence, the competing commitments that bedevil the philosopher-turned-courtier, caught in a rapidly worsening situation, damned if he does, damned if he doesn't: "When they become corrupt, powerful rulers take everything for granted . . .; and when we don't grovel as much as they'd like, they dare accuse us of being ungrateful. The man who accepts or solicits benefits from a corrupt court does not know the price he'll have to pay one day. When the day comes, that man will be torn between sacrificing his duty and his honor, or forsaking his obligations; between self-contempt, or hatred of his benefactor" (*ECN*, 998).

In *ECN* Diderot explored the tangled knot of hope, idealism, dependency, exploitation, disenchantment, and shame that bound the philosopher to the tyrant. That Diderot underwent all those emotions in stages, during his two-decade-long relationship with Catherine is never

[18] Rulhières, 1797, 1797. Preface, xiii.
[19] Diderot, 1989, 26. The *Satire première* was probably started in 1768 and revised over the years.

spelled out in his writings, for he never made a confession. What is clear, however, is that Diderot's work became unmistakably more radical after he returned from Russia, and that he disseminated a number of clues in *ECN* about his experience – and not very subtle ones. Indeed, *ECN* is not a subtle work, and one may flinch at the prospect of a modern-day Nero in a powdered wig, a ball gown, and an ample bosom (though the cross-dressing Nero might not himself have been displeased). Yet Diderot found the myth of Nero useful for talking about modern-day despotism and about the burning issue of what the *philosophe* (we would say the intellectual) was going to do about it. "There is no doubt that the empress of Russia is a despot," Diderot wrote in the shockingly candid *Observations sur le Nakaz*, the work he managed to send Catherine posthumously, circumventing the vigilance of Catherine's librarian and secretary, Baron Friedrich Melchior Grimm.[20] We'll get back to that.

Diderot makes the relationship between Seneca and Nero as dramatic – or melodramatic – as possible. It is obvious that Diderot's aesthetics of drama is not the same as Voltaire's, for he does not recoil from blood and gore and he likes his hero to suffer as much as possible: "The spectacle of virtue fiercely tested is beautiful. We want its trials to be as dreadful as they can be."[21] Thus, when Nero kisses Seneca in order to seal their apparent reconciliation, Tacitus' vague "to these words the emperor added embraces and kisses"[22] gains, in Diderot's translation, a visual vividness augmented by a Christ-Judas motif: "[Nero] touches with his cheek the cheek of Seneca, and kisses him" (*ECN*, 1061). A simple mention of Poppaea and Tigellinus as being "the emperor's most confidential advisors in his moments of rage" becomes: "The bloodthirsty tribunal of the prince, the intimate advisors to his furor, Poppaea and Tigellinus."[23] Although Diderot claims to follow Tacitus obediently and reverently, he rearranges Tacitus' narrative structure and chronology so as to put Seneca's actions in the most dramatic and favorable light. For instance, while Tacitus situates the narrative of Seneca's offer to resign after the death of Burrus, Diderot places it immediately after Rome's Great Fire, thus suggesting that it was not

[20] In Diderot, 1995b, 508. For the present purpose, I'll be using *despot* and *tyrant* interchangeably. "Tyranny is nothing but the exercise of despotism," Diderot ed., *Encyclopédie*, art. "Souverains," 15:424 (University of Chicago, The ARTFL Project, https://artfl-project.uchicago.edu/).

[21] Diderot, 1995c, 196. Else Marie Bukdahl et al. Paris, Hermann, 1995, 196.

[22] Tacitus, *Annals*, XIV, 56: *his adicit complexum et oscula.*

[23] Tacitus, *Annals*, XV, 61: *ubi haec a tribuno relata sunt Poppaea et Tigellino coram, quod erat saevienti principi intimum consiliorum.* "When the tribune reported this answer in the presence of Poppæa and Tigellinus, the emperor's most confidential advisers in his moments of rage..." Tacitus, 2009, 363. trans. Michael Grant (Penguin Books, 1971).

concern for his own safety that troubled Seneca, but horror for the general degradation of the events: "At last, disgusted by so many crimes and sacrileges, Seneca asked permission to retire" (*ECN*, 1058).

When it comes to his use of sources, Diderot is strategically selective. Thus, whereas he rejects Suetonius' claims when they are unfavorable to Seneca, Diderot turns to Suetonius whenever the latter's account is more damaging to Nero. Diderot follows Suetonius in making Nero, not Agrippina, the initiator of the incestuous liaison (*ECN*, 1017); like Suetonius, he also presents as a fact, not a rumor, Nero's lascivious treatment of his mother's cadaver, and preempts any skeptical reactions by grandstanding on the authority of the historian he disparages elsewhere: "Could you believe it was possible to add to the horror of this crime [matricide]? Who could ever imagine it if the historian hadn't told us? His mother just murdered, Nero hastens to satisfy his impure curiosity on her cadaver" (*ECN*, 1048). In a similar vein, Diderot follows Suetonius in placing Nero in Rome, on top of a tower in the gardens of Maecenas, watching the fire and singing about the destruction of Troy – something that Tacitus, who says that Nero was miles away at Antium, offers as a mere rumor. And finally (but the list could go on), no one had ever doubted that Tacitus was anything but sharp and malicious, yet Diderot thinks he's being too nice to Nero: "This last feeling [Nero's semblance of remorse while he embraces his mother for the last time] is too flattering to Nero and not flattering enough to Tacitus's acumen" (*ECN*, 1039).

One image in particular characterizes Nero throughout *ECN*: that of a feral animal, a tiger in his den, his teeth bared and dripping with blood. "The eyes of the tiger sparkled with ferocity" (*ECN*, 1047); "Seneca, what did you do with Nero? –I did the only thing possible. I muzzled the ferocious beast. Without me, he would have devoured [his victims] five years earlier" (*ECN*, 1012). Nero's court is "the den of a ferocious beast" (*ECN*, 1081); Nero is "a tiger turned mad" (*ECN*, 1078). In a letter written from the Hague, on his voyage back to France, Diderot had used the same image of a tiger in the wild, but this time he was referring to Catherine and her court: "I'll say to you in a whisper that our philosophers, who claim to know despotism, have only seen it through the neck of a bottle. What a difference between the tiger painted by Oudry and the tiger in the forest!"[24] The recurrent motif

[24] To Suzanne Necker, September 6, 1774, in Diderot, 1997, 1252. Oudry was a famous painter of animals and still life.

of the tiger as a relentlessly bloodthirsty creature is likely rooted in Diderot's lifelong fascination with Latin poetry: it's there that we may find several examples of the tiger as a metaphor for the cruelty of the powerful. Although Diderot professed not to hold Seneca's theater in much esteem, and did not think Seneca was the author of the plays attributed to him (yet there is much in common between Diderot's dramatic language and Seneca's!), the image of Nero as tiger might be a reminiscence of the pseudo-Senecan play *Octavia*, I. 3: "*the Tygre stoute, Then mankynd Tyrantes brutish breast.*"[25] Furthermore, as the one creature considered more bloodthirsty than a tiger was a tigress, we may conjecture that Diderot would have found in Virgil's and Lucan's depictions of "Hyrcanian tigress" a particularly apt metaphor for Catherine: Hyrcania was the ancient name of the lands south of the Caspian Sea.[26]

At the time he wrote that letter, Diderot had been working on an annotated commentary of the *Instruction de l'impératrice de Russie aux députés pour la confection des lois*, or *Nakaz*, a legal and political document Catherine had written with the purpose of making it the foundation for the new code of laws that was being devised by the Russian legislative commission convened by the empress in 1767–8 (and then dismissed because of internal dissensions). Catherine had freely plundered Montesquieu and her language had enough of a veneer of liberalism that the work was forbidden in France. However, despite promises to develop agriculture and commerce, renounce the use of torture, and make all citizens subject to the same laws, Catherine made no attempt to set legal limits to her own power. What's more, she was evasive about serfdom, which she called euphemistically "a kind of dependency," and was content to pay lip service to an unspecified need to "alleviate" the condition of serfs "within the limits of reason." She completely ignored Diderot's recommendation that she create free-for-all primary schools to provide basic reading, writing, and math skills to the children of serfs.[27]

In his commentary (*Observations sur le Nakaz*, 1774), Diderot gave her a piece of his mind, gloves almost off. Grimm had been vetting all of Diderot's manuscripts before they reached the empress, but Diderot had

[25] Seneca, 1581 [1992], 163.

[26] Dido accuses hard-hearted Aeneas of having been nursed by a Hyrcanian tigress. In Lucan's *Pharsalia*, Caesar compares Pompey to Hyrcanian tigresses who, having once lapped the blood of slaughtered animals, never cease from rage. See *Aeneid*, 4.366–7 and *Pharsalia*, 1.327–9. I am grateful to Cedric Littlewood and Kirk Freudenburg for bringing these references to my attention.

[27] Nadejda Plavinskaia, 1998, 83.

managed to slip the manuscript into a shipment of his books.[28] When Catherine read it, in November 1785 (Diderot had died in July 1784), she penned a furious letter to Grimm. The *Observations*, she said, were "sheer drivel devoid of any knowledge, prudence, foresight," written by a philosopher who "should have been placed under guardianship long ago." Grimm had no choice but to throw his former friend under the bus. He agreed that the *Observations* were the "vagaries of an imbecile," that their author owed his survival to Catherine's "imperturbable goodness," and ended his letter assuring her that she had the only extant copy. (She did not: Diderot had made four extra ones.)[29]

Diderot had come to the bitter conclusion that Catherine's allegiance to the Enlightenment was a travesty and that he had been used (much in the same way that Voltaire had been used by his beloved Frederick II): "The light of reason [*les lumières*] on those issues [the rights of the people and the abuse of authority] has gone nowadays as far as it can go. What has the result been? Nothing. Amidst the remonstrance of all the peoples who have been enlightened by the voices of magistrates and philosophers, despotism has been flourishing everywhere."[30] What had especially galled Diderot was Catherine's unwillingness to consider the possibility of a binding pact of mutual obligation between the monarch and the people. Any sovereign who refused to respond before the people for the legality of his or her actions was a despot and a tyrant, Diderot wrote on the first page of the *Nakaz*. And the people had not only the right to depose a tyrant, but also the right to put him to death, for when the nation is "under a bad ruler, the nation is at war with its sovereign."[31] Thus, it was squarely and insolently on the first page of his critical commentary of Catherine's masterpiece that Diderot argued for the legitimacy of tyrannicide.

Now we can better grasp the significance of Nero's figure in those last decades of the *ancien régime*. Nero was the ultimate example of the corrupt ruler, the emblematic case that demonstrated that tyrannicide could sometimes be necessary and acceptable. In the *History of England*, Hume had presented Nero as the one exception, the one case in which the benefits of dethroning and executing a tyrant would outweigh the "pernicious effects upon the people" of having a sovereign formally put to trial and punished. "The crimes of that bloody tyrant are so enormous, that they break through all rules," Hume wrote, and thus they

[28] See Georges Dulac, "Le discours politique de Pétersbourg," *Recherches sur Diderot et sur l'Encyclopédie*, 1, October 1986, 32–58.

[29] Quoted in "Le Discours politique de Pétersbourg," pp. 51–2.

[30] *Observations sur le Nakaz, Oeuvres*, vol. 3, 546.

[31] *Observations sur le Nakaz*, 518.

justified the "act of extraordinary jurisdiction" taken against him.[32] But Hume's message had been that, unless a king was Nero *himself*, executing a king could never be legitimate, no matter how tyrannical that king might be: just as there could never be another Nero, there should never be another tyrannicide.

But Diderot's own message, in *ECN*, in the *Observations*, and in the texts he wrote in those years for the *Histoire des deux Indes*, was just the opposite. To be sure, Diderot, like Hume, portrays Nero as an exceptionally bad case; yet, by repeatedly inviting the reader to imagine himself in Seneca's place, "under the flashing eyes of the beast, nails drawn out, fangs dripping with a mother's blood" (1081), Diderot brings Nero vividly close to the reader, in a theatrical, emotional way. But most importantly, by constantly traveling back and forth between the past and the present, between Seneca and the modern-day *philosophe*, between Nero's den, Poppaea's "boudoir," and the corrupt monarchical court of his day, Diderot puts the reader at the steps of Nero's throne and makes him disturbingly contemporary. He suggests that Nero's feral nature, far from being unique, is emblematic of the ferocity of all modern-day tyrants. A fragment composed in 1772, at the time of the *Observations*, blasts the hypocrisy of the notion of "public interest" (the same that had been summoned to support the continuance of serfdom in Russia), and then proceeds to place slave societies within the realm of the predatory carnivore: "Never can a man be the property of a sovereign, a child that of a father, a woman that of a husband, a servant that of a master, a Negro that of a colonist. . . . Greeks therefore have been ferocious animals against whom their slaves could rightly rebel. *Romans* therefore have been ferocious animals against whom their slaves could legitimately use any kind of means to free themselves. Feudal lords therefore have been ferocious animals worthy of being crushed to death by their vassals. This, and nothing else, is the real principle that absolves tyrannicide."[33]

One may doubt, however, that Diderot would have endorsed the language of Louis-Antoine de Saint-Just, when, on November 13, 1792, he pleaded to deny King Louis XVI the benefit of a trial, and asked that the king, the enemy of the nation, be dispatched as they used to do in Rome with the enemies of the Republic: "One day, the people will be astonished by the fact that in the eighteenth century things were less

[32] David Hume, 1983; 5, 1778. [33] Diderot, 2011, 121–24.

advanced than in the time of Caesar. Then, a tyrant was destroyed in the midst of the Senate with no formalities but thirty blows of a dagger and with no other law but the liberty of Rome."[34]

Further Reading

On the historiography of ancient Rome in the Enlightenment, see Vanessa de Senarclens: *Montesquieu, historien de Rome: un tournant pour la réflexion sur le statut de l'histoire au XVIIIe siècle*, Genève: Droz, 2003 and Chantal Grell: *L'Histoire entre érudition et philosophie: Étude sur la connaissance historique à l'âge des Lumières*, Paris: Presses Universitaires de France, 1993. On Tacitus in the Enlightenment (with a chapter devoted to Diderot and Tacitus), see Catherine Volpilhac-Auger: *Tacite en France, de Montesquieu à Chateaubriand*, Oxford: The Voltaire Foundation, 1993. For a recent intellectual biography of Diderot, see Gerhardt Stenger, *Diderot, Le combattant de la liberté*, Paris: Perrin, 2013. For a thorough analysis of Voltaire's courtly politics, see Jonathan Israel: *Democratic Enlightenment. Philosophy, Revolution and Human Rights, 1750–1790*, Oxford: Oxford University Press, 2011, especially part I, ch. 5. Israel also discusses at length, in the same book, the "radicalism" of Diderot.

[34] Louis-Antoine de Saint-Just, 1984, 377.

20: Nero in Hollywood

Martin M. Winkler

In 1944, classical archaeologist Ludwig Curtius reflected on the contrast between Roman history and "the popular conception of the decline of Roman culture into vice and debauchery during the later Republic and the Empire." He then commented on a particular aspect of this view: "Roman emperors have to suffer the indignities of being dressed down like schoolboys, and scandalous stories get fabricated out of Suetonius for the purpose of making Roman history comprehensible for contemporaries."[1] Rome's most infamous emperor is a case in point, especially in cinema and television. The screen can thrillingly parade villains before our very eyes. Nero is unbeatable as the most evil of all bad guys: cruel and sexually depraved, burning Rome to satisfy his megalomania, sadistically persecuting innocent Christians, and becoming the Antichrist in Christian apocalyptic writings. No other Roman can equal Nero in his "vice appeal." So he is a natural for the cinema.

20.1 In the Beginning

Nero was there from the start. As early as 1896, when the cinema was only in its second year, Auguste and Louis Lumière featured Nero in *Néron essayant des poisons sur des esclaves* (*Nero Trying Out Poisons on Slaves*). It ran for fifty-two seconds, then the standard length for one reel of film. The first *Quo Vadis?* (1901) was made in France by Ferdinand Zecca and Lucien Nonguet. In 1907–8, Georges Méliès devoted an episode of *La civilisation à travers les âges* (*Civilization across the Ages*) to *Néron et Locuste: un esclave empoisonné (an 65 de notre ère)* (*Nero and Locusta: A Poisoned Slave [Year 65 of Our Era]*). Also in 1908, André

[1] Quoted, in my translation, from Curtius 1963: 21.

Calmettes filmed Jean Racine's *Britannicus*, a tragedy about Nero's potential rival. Full-fledged historical epics appeared throughout the silent era. Most noteworthy are Enrico Guazzoni's *Agrippina* (Italy, 1911) and his gigantic (for then) *Quo Vadis?* (1912), Mario Caserini's *Nerone e Agrippina* (Italy, 1914), J. Gordon Edwards's *Nero* (United States, 1922), and an Italian-German *Quo Vadis?* (1924) starring Emil Jannings.

Nero was blamed during his lifetime and ever after for the fire that devastated Rome in the year 64. The cinema followed suit from the beginning, availing itself of the opportunity to show its viewers a spectacular catastrophe. Edwin S. Porter, best known today for *The Great Train Robbery* (1903), made the short *Nero and the Burning of Rome* in New York City for Thomas Edison five years later. The following year, Luigi Maggi and Arturo Ambrosio made *Nerone o L'incendio di Roma* (*Nero or The Burning of Rome*, Italy, 1909), a prestigious epic of about sixteen minutes' running time that became an international success. As the title of a series of American television "documentaries" has it: *You Are There*. One installment was "The Burning of Rome (July 64 A.D.)," directed in 1954 by Sidney Lumet before he became a distinguished director for the big screen.

The persecution of Christians, who were blamed for the fire to divert suspicion from Nero, had first appeared on screen in Great Britain in 1904 with the earliest of three adaptations of Wilson Barrett's stage melodrama *The Sign of the Cross* (1895). After its 1914 remake, it became indelible with Cecil B. DeMille's spectacular sound version of 1932, although the cross was not a symbol of Christianity during Nero's reign. Nero and the Christians had been filmic subjects in France with *Martyrs chrétiens* (*Christian Martyrs*, 1905) and the United States (*The Way of the Cross* or *The Story of Ancient Rome*, 1909).

Appearances of Nero on American screens are too numerous even to be surveyed, much less analyzed, in any detail here. Instead, I will provide a *summa vitiologica*, a summary statement of Nero and his time across screen history.

20.2 Witnesses for the Prosecution

That Nero could be the cinema's ultimate "bad guy" became obvious with the American release of Maggi and Ambrosio's film of 1909: *Nero, or The Fall of Rome*. That fall, at least for the western half of the Roman Empire, came only 400 years later, but here Nero was already its cause.

Why? The fall of Nero presages that of Rome because Nero was the first to sink into an abyss of depravity. American viewers had been able to encounter this message at the conclusion of Guazzoni's *Quo Vadis?* A text card follows Nero's death and precedes an apparition of Christ the Savior:

> Thus died Nero. Like fire, he brought nothing but destruction, mourning, pain and death. But from the rain of strife and blood sprang a new life: the life of Christianity, in the sign of love and peace.

During the color-and-sound era, Nero even became a star witness for Satan himself. This occurred in *The Story of Mankind* (1957), a loose adaptation of Hendrik Willem Van Loon's 1921 best seller written for his children. Producer-director Irwin Allen, the 1970s Master of Disaster (*The Poseidon Adventure, The Towering Inferno*), here perpetrated another disaster on unsuspecting cinemagoers. His film looks cheap; Allen intercuts footage from various historical epics and rarely manages to put anything on screen that is visually attractive.

The fate of mankind in the nuclear age is being decided before some supernatural court. A Mr. Scratch argues that wicked mankind should be allowed to destroy itself. The Spirit of Man presents the case for the defense. Since we are still here, the outcome is never in doubt. The two advocates adduce various historical periods and personages to bolster their cases. After ancient Egypt, the Old Testament, and classical Greece, it is time for Rome: "We mustn't forget Nero, one of my most talented disciples," avows Mr. Scratch over images of a Roman banquet-cum-orgy. He calls Nero "evil and depraved." His "debauchery and perversion surpassed even the wildest and wickedest dreams of the most deluded." Nero was "nursed on a witch's venom, twisted by endless orgies," a "madman" who "knew no end to violence, no limit to lunacy." He was an inveterate poisoner, forced many into suicide, and "had his mother clubbed to death," among other "amusements." Since the orgy is one of the tamest ever put on screen, Nero is bored. But then a soldier whispers a message into his ear, and Nero announces his "greatest triumph." To shouts of "Ave Nero!" he snatches up his lyre and leaves the hall to witness Rome burning. According to Mr. Scratch, the fire of Rome is "this madman's greatest folly." The Spirit counters that Nero was an aberration, "only a mad moment of history." Mr. Scratch, however, sees Nero as embodiment of "all the lunacy of mankind." The two then watch Nero's reaction to his towering inferno. Looking upward, he exclaims: "Burn, burn, my glorious Rome, burn up to heaven, so that – that Jupiter can see who is greater, you or I." Scratch sums it all up: "Murderer, maniac, rapist, pervert, matricide, arsonist, bigamist, and sometimes accomplished musician and singer for all social occasions." He then delivers his peroration: "This was Nero, whose depravity and lunacy could not possibly have been foisted upon mankind had mankind not been content and willing to accept it." The Spirit counters the indictment by recalling voices other than Nero's being heard that night: those of Christians in the catacombs. "New hope had come into a world where hope had been dead," the Spirit explains. Although a Christian family is hauled off by Nero's soldiers, Allen foregoes showing us their fate. He could have learned a lesson or two from the arena sequence in Mervyn LeRoy's *Quo Vadis* (1951) or, even better, from that in DeMille's *The Sign of the Cross*, which contains the most ferocious horror show in the history of Hollywood's Roman films. But then, Allen had neither time nor budget nor presumably any stock footage to include this side of Neronian Rome. Instead he moves directly on to Attila the Hun.

My discussion of this film, which does not even qualify as camp, would be superfluous were it not for its almost complete laundry list of negative clichés about Nero. Van Loon had not even mentioned Nero in his book. The dressing down of Roman emperors Curtius complained about has here reached a depressing nadir.

20.3 Megalomania and Tyranny

Before becoming emperor, Nero had been a highly promising young man. His first years in power, the *quinquennium Neronis*, may have been a kind of golden age, mentioned by, e.g., Seneca (*Apocol.* 4) and Calpurnius Siculus (*Ecl.* 1.33–88). Then it all changed. The general consensus about Nero's decline and fall into vice and madness that made him a downright incarnation of evil could be summarized by Lord Acton's well-known dictum concerning the corrupting influence of absolute power. Roman emperors of the first century provide us with instances, mainly owing to Tacitus' vivid dissections of their characters in his *Annals*.

The most noteworthy portrayals of Nero as psychopath are those by Charles Laughton in *The Sign of the Cross* and Peter Ustinov in the 1951 *Quo Vadis* The comparatively little-known Nero of Klaus Maria Brandauer in Franco Rossi's six-hour Italian television film *Quo Vadis* (1985) may exhibit the clearest features of clinical pathology, if perhaps with too heavy a dose of psychoanalysis. But the perversion of societal norms that comes with tyrannical power may best be illustrated by the ways in which some of the films show us Nero's conception of justice and his helplessness before a domineering wife; both are inseparable. Here are especially telling moments from two classic epics.

In DeMille's *The Sign of the Cross*, Nero is the embodiment of infantile cruelty. At the same time he is hopelessly under the thumb of his unscrupulous wife Poppaea, incarnated by a sexy and slinky Claudette Colbert. In one crucial scene Nero and Poppaea invoke justice in strong contrast to what anyone would understand by this word. Marcus Superbus, the film's fictional hero, is pleading for the life of his beloved, a Christian maiden and Poppaea's rival. (She [Poppaea] has adulterous designs on Marcus.) "Is Nero justice in the Roman world or merely a puppet emperor?" asks a clearly manipulative Poppaea. Various courtiers, including the villainous Praetorian prefect Tigellinus, are present, so Nero dare not lose face. "Caesar is compassionate, but he is also justice," he states. "I must remain justice, Marcus." But he suggests a way out: "If she renounces, then justice can be merciful." Poppaea makes sure that Nero remains only a perversion of unmerciful justice. A long inscription on the curved wall above Nero's throne emphasizes the point. The text is difficult to make out in its entirety; it is probably this:

> [GLORIA?] ET AVCTORITAS IMPERATORVM ROMANORVM IN AETERNVM [MANEBVNT *vel* VALEBVNT]
>
> [The Glory?] and the Authority of Roman Emperors Will in Eternity [Remain *or* Prevail]

The inscription is unhistorical. So is an earlier torture scene in the Praetorians' dungeons. Tigellinus orders two hellish and virtually subhuman minions to extract information from a young Christian boy. A wall decoration shows us a Roman eagle, symbol of power, clutching a wreath, symbol of victory, inside which there are scales, the familiar symbol of justice. But no justice is to be had. At one harrowing moment, the boy's screams on the soundtrack are accompanied by a close-up of the scales. We imagine the worst. The eagle-and-scales decoration speaks volumes: *Abandon all justice ye who enter here*. The glory and authority of Roman emperors, and with them that of the Roman world, is no longer in evidence. It is high time, we are meant to conclude, that this evil empire be overthrown by a kingdom not of this world.

The prologue of LeRoy's *Quo Vadis* makes the same case, priming viewers to adopt an attitude of righteous indignation at all the vice and sin of Neronian Rome. Over images of a victorious legion returning to Rome, the narrator tells us:

> Imperial Rome is the center of the empire, an undisputed master of the world. But with this power inevitably comes corruption. No man is sure of his life, the individual is at the mercy of the state, murder replaces justice. . . . There is no escape from the whip and the sword. That any force on earth can shake the foundations of this pyramid of power and corruption, of human misery and slavery, seems inconceivable. But thirty years before this day a miracle occurred. On a Roman cross in Judaea, a man died to make men free, to spread the gospel of love and redemption. Soon that humble cross is destined to replace the proud eagles that now top the victorious Roman standards. This is the story of that immortal conflict.

He does not fail to inform us that the immortal conflict starts "in the reign of the Antichrist known to history as the Emperor Nero."

The single most famous aspect of Nero's megalomania may be the city he envisioned after the devastating fire of 64, going so far as to propose a new name for it: *Neropolis* (Suet., *Nero* 55). This Rome included Nero's new domicile, the Golden House (Domus Aurea). In *Quo Vadis*, Nero looks at an elaborate model of his future Rome. He mentions the destruction of the city as a precondition:

> Ah, but what pulsating purity there is in fire. My new Rome shall spring from the loins of fire, a twisting, writhing, breathing flame . . . to bring this greatest of my accomplishments into being.

Roman imperial architecture usually conveys a message of absolute power. It "expresses [a] moral order by an environment which cannot be disobeyed."[2] Where architecture in totalitarian societies is concerned, we could also speak of the immoral order of such an environment. Nero's building program for Rome has become symptomatic of this.

[2] Brown 1958: 114.

20.4 Scenes from a Marriage

Nero, the man in absolute power, is almost powerless before his wife. The cinema has often turned Poppaea into a ruthless and sex-crazed adulteress.[3] LeRoy's Poppaea wears a tight-fitting and, at crucial moments, poison-green dress (see Figure 20.1). DeMille's was more alluring but no less dangerous. Claudette Colbert wears skimpy black clothing that effectively contrasts with her snow-white skin. She achieves this by her infamous baths in asses' milk, one of which we watch her take. Both Poppaeas are characterized by their pets: leopards. The lesson, at least to male viewers, is self-evident: *Beware of all powerful (and all-powerful) women in tight dresses with large felines for pets!*

DeMille's Poppaea manages to manipulate Nero with her feminine and feline wiles. While Nero, lounging on a sofa like an overfed baby (Figure 20.2), is getting a manicure, Poppaea arrives to set her revenge scheme against Marcus' Christian maiden into motion. Nero is suffering from a hangover after an orgy the night before: "A delicious debauchery." Then he burps, the naughty boy. "I'm not at all well, Poppaea." Her reaction, simultaneously soothing and superior, is like that of a mother with an upset child: "I know. You had such an exciting night." She puts a kind of cold compress on his forehead: "There now. Relax." Poppaea is clearly the one in charge. Yes, Nero is a puppet emperor.

Nero's infantilism is evident from this film's first sequence. Rome is a sea of flames. Nero, seated on a throne-like seat, declaims ("Burn, Rome, burn") and plays his lyre. When a string breaks, Nero collapses in a sulky fit. "Look at this" – he holds the lyre out to Tigellinus – "I was in excellent voice, too." Soon we see him languidly squirming on his seat in utter enervation while plotting with Tigellinus to shift the blame for the fire onto the Christians.

Like history, film history repeats itself. Our first glimpse of Nero in *Quo Vadis* shows him getting a pedicure and having his hair groomed while composing verse.[4] Beginning here, his mood swings will be unpredictable, as if this Nero had bipolar disorder. He is also easily manipulated by flattery and sycophancy. His infantile nature is on

[3] I omit soft- and hardcore exploitation films about Nero, Messalina, et al. from discussion here. *Caveat spectator!* Television "docudramas" are omitted as well; they tend to be more fictional than documentary.

[4] The music comes from the Seikilos Epitaph, a Greek melody from around 100 CE found on a stele near modern Ephesus. Film composer Miklós Rózsa took pains to base his scores on historical sources.

20.1 Publicity still of Nero (Peter Ustinov) and Poppaea (Patricia Laffan) in *Quo Vadis* (1951). Jerry Murbach Collection.

astonishing display in a scene set in his bedroom (Figure 20.3). When he is informed about Petronius' suicide, Nero throws a tantrum ("Without my permission?") while crouching on his bed in a nightshirt. His voice rises to a squeak, then breaks. After reading Petronius' last message to him, which denies Nero any artistry, we observe an even bigger attack of childish anger. Still in a crouch on his bed, Nero is flailing his arms about while ordering the deaths of all in Petronius' household. This overgrown and chubby child is being very wicked. But he is also lethal. The grotesque fascination this Nero exerts is unrivaled in screen history. His eerie megalomania had become manifest when Nero the striver was

20.2 Nero (Charles Laughton) lounging about in *The Sign of the Cross* (1932). Screenshot.

20.3 Nero (Peter Ustinov) on his bed in *Quo Vadis* (1951). Screenshot.

revealing his artistic creed: "I seek because I must exceed the stature of man in both good and evil. I seek because I must be greater than man, for only then will I be the supreme artist." He closes with a call for the absolute: "Let it be wonderful. Or let it be awful. So long as it is uncommon." The fire of Rome is next.

Imperial banquets and orgies are integral parts of Neronian decadence. Any pretext will do. In *The Sign of the Cross* of 1914, Nero orders a feast to celebrate the arrests of Christians throughout Rome. Skimpily clad dancing girls writhe to faux-exotic strains before lascivious or languidly blasé voluptuaries. This is standard fare, as it were. The most uninhibited orgy must be the one in DeMille's *The Sign of the Cross*, with an astonishing lesbian seduction scene of a pagan dancer attempting, unsuccessfully of course, to undermine the virtue of the Christian heroine. Roman culinary luxury is best attested by its satiric hyperbole in the *cena Trimalchionis* ("Trimalchio's Banquet"), the central episode of Petronius' *Satyrica*. This Roman novel has generally if not unanimously been dated to the age of Nero. The greatest cinematic homage to Trimalchio's Banquet comes in Victor Saville's *The Silver Chalice* (1954). Nero and Poppaea's huge oval dining hall sports gleaming white columns decorated with gold at their bases and capitals, an elegant contrast to the reflecting black of its granite floor. Arches between columns are filled with countless statues in a variety of poses and are topped off by yet another level of busts. The astonishing sight reminds us of the Colosseum. The fact that it was built only after Nero's death does not detract from the visual impact of this remarkable set. As slaves carry heavy trays laden with exotic food of uniformly golden color, an off-screen *maître d'* announces to Nero as much as to viewers the courses to be served:

> If it please you, Caesar: Roast peacock from the land of Egypt. Wild boar from Caesar's preserves in Dalmatia. Succulent dormice, saturated with poppy juice. Oysters, surrounded by damson plums and sprinkled with cumin and benzoin root. Sausage, stuffed with golden plovers' eggs and the breast of pheasant. Aged grasshoppers, fried in honey to a light golden brown. Eggs, made of crushed pearls colored to a golden hue and filled with yolks in which we've nestled fat little ortolans roasted to a turn.

A full-sized peacock and boar decorate their respective trays. So does a turtle. All are gilded. More trays come in. Boar and dormice are familiar to lovers of Roman literature from Petronius. Without even looking, Nero waves everything away before finally taking a taste. To him, this is drab, everyday fare. The extreme artifice of food and setting expresses the unreal nature of what Nero's extravagant court may have looked like in the modern imagination.

20.5 Comedies and Cartoons

The Nero of comedy is even more of a ne'er-grow-up than the one of melodrama. Comedies and burlesques had begun in Denmark in 1907 with *Keiser Nero paa Krigsstien* (*Emperor Nero on the War Path*). Serious and pretentious epics were ready prey for satirists. Maggi and Ambrosio's film was parodied a year later in the short *Tontolini Nerone* (*Tontolino as Nero*), the first of many comedies starring Ferdinand Guillaume as Tontolino. William Watson made fun of Edwards's epic in his short *Nero* (United States, 1925), the fourteenth installment in the "Hysterical History" comedy series.

Nero made his three-strip Technicolor debut in *Good Morning, Eve* (United States, 1934). Adam and Eve travel down in history and predictably land in "Rome A.D. 100." A full-screen Latin text announces Nero's performance:

> CIVES ROMANI
> Ne obliviscere certamen musicum
> magnum hortibus Neronis Imperatoris
> caterva actorum optimorum
> palmam secundam petent petet
> Nero Imperator palmam primam

Those in the audience with the benefit of a classical education will notice several amusing mistakes here. The sign dissolves to a translation, provided for all others:

> CITIZENS OF ROME
> Don't forget the big Concert
> in the Gardens of the Emperor
> Nero. An all star cast will compete
> for the 2nd Prize \ Emperor Nero
> will compete for the 1st Prize

In Nero's palace a swing band is playing a ditty for athletic dancing girls. An elegantly clad and rather chubby Nero is surrounded by a bevy of beauties. But he is bored: "I'm tired of looking at beautiful women."

His *maître de plaisir* informs him that "we have a new batch of victims to throw to the lions." No good. Poison may offer a bigger thrill. Then Nero tells Eve: "Thou art about to hear Rome's greatest entertainer." Who could it be? "*I* am going to sing. Everybody hang on to thy togas." The archaic language makes fun of the pretensions of historical drama; the wrong grammar need not be intentional. Nero's fiddle is a violin. He begins:

> I always play my Stradivarius when I'm feeling low.
> And if my fiddling is fair to middling
> I put some rhythm in my bow.

Nero's favorite is the G-string. A male quartet then joins in, singing into a microphone of radio station SPQR. Chorines begin to tap their sandaled feet as if they were on Broadway. Finally Adam and Eve arrive in – where else? – Hollywood.

The centerpiece of Mel Brooks's episodic farce *History of the World: Part I* (1981) was "The Roman Empire." Even if its emperor is called only Caesar, this must be Nero. (He is so identified in the final credits.) When he complains "It's so lonely at the top of Olympus," he echoes Ustinov's Nero: "It's lonely to be an emperor." "The Muse is upon me," Caesar announces and commands: "Bring me a small lyre!" The lyre turns out to be a vociferous near-midget who exclaims: "I didn't do it! I didn't do it!" (Lyre, liar!) Nero is a porcine gourmand. When he takes a "treasure bath," we know that he is also a material boy. His wife is called Empress Nympho. There is a reason for this.

Nero has been a regular in animated humor as well. Here is just one example. Friz Freleng's *Roman Legion-Hare* (1955), one of the best *Loonie Tunes*, has an unusual fate in store for Nero. A text card tells us that it we are in "ROME 54 A.D." A Colosseum, however, has already been built. "Emperor Nero has kindly consented," the imperial games' announcer informs us, "to throw out the first victim." But none is available. Nero charges Yosemite Sam, captain of the guards, with procuring suitable lion fodder, or else! "Ooooohhh, what a grouch," Sam complains, racing off. He and his men encounter a certain carrot muncher. As always, Bugs turns the *mensae* on his pursuer in ingenious ways and unleashes a horde of lions on hapless Sam. "O, woe is me!" Bugs exclaims insincerely before finding himself in the middle of the arena. "There's your victim, Your Neroship," Sam tells his boss. "Release the lions," Nero commands. The ferocious felines storm in, race past Bugs, and climb straight up to Nero and Sam in the imperial box. The two hightail it up a column. Bugs crowns himself with a gold wreath: "Well, like the Romans always say: *e pluribus uranium.*" The lions begin to dislodge the column's drums one by one. Nero suddenly has his fiddle to play Taps as he and Sam sink out of the frame. A growl on the soundtrack indicates a feline feeding frenzy. This Nero's resemblance to Charles Laughton is wholly intentional.

20.6 FIDDLER ON THE ROOF, OR, HIS INFAMOUS VARIETY

Fort Delivery in the Arizona Territory is "a hundred miles from nowhere." The U.S. cavalry stationed there is a sorry bunch, whose discipline is conspicuous by its absence. So the new lieutenant from West Point has his task cut out for him. One night he is helplessly watching from a rooftop as his men are cavorting with "good whiskey and bad women." His lady love is at hand to ask him a probing question: "Burning while Rome fiddles?"

The moment occurs in Raoul Walsh's epic Western *A Distant Trumpet* (1964), loosely adapted from the 1951 novel by Paul Horgan. In both novel and film, a cavalry general generously quotes maxims from Cicero, Caesar, Virgil, and Tacitus, all in Latin, but the allusion to Nero occurs only in the film. The lieutenant has no answer to the young lady's observation; none is necessary. At that time as perhaps not today, audiences could be expected to appreciate the witty reversal of what was a familiar topos. Nero's fiddling was a staple of popular culture even when not a single Roman was anywhere to be seen. "Ever heard of Nero?" an ineffectual deputy sheriff whose town is being threatened by outlaws is asked in Andre de Toth's Western *Riding Shotgun* (1954). "He fiddled while his town burned up." The lawman has never heard of such a thing. He is obviously in the minority.

In the glossy M-G-M extravaganza *Ziegfeld Girl* (1941), an old-time father-daughter vaudeville act is performing a number called "Laugh? I Thought I'd Split My Sides." It contains these lines: "Nero played with his fiddle while Rome was burning bright. / He played *There'll Be a Hot Time in the Old Town Tonight.*" The fact that we hear a young Judy Garland, who had herself started out in vaudeville, singing this makes the instance memorable. An earlier film tells us about popular culture's huge debt to Nero. In *Some Like It Hot* (1939), a Bob Hope vehicle featuring Gene Krupa and his orchestra, the latter perform the title song, whose second verse includes these lines:

Later on, fiddle, Mr. Nero;
Down in Rome, he was quite a hero.
Ever since, thanks to Mr. Nero,
Some like it hot!

The introductory text of Howard Hawks's classic screwball comedy *Ball of Fire* (1941) tells us about eight wise men who were writing an encyclopedia: "They were so wise they knew everything," including "what tune Nero fiddled while Rome was burning." The one thing they did not know sets the semantic-romantic plot in motion. Director Hawks had begun as DeMille's property man. Decades later, he characterized DeMille like this: "On the set, he was a Nero."[5]

Flighty Holly Golightly in Blake Edwards's 1961 film of Truman Capote's *Breakfast at Tiffany's* is waxing eloquent about her Brazilian fiancé, José, but: "Now, if I could choose from anybody alive, I wouldn't pick José. Nero, maybe, or Albert Schweitzer ... or Leonard Bernstein." Rarely has Nero been in such distinguished humanitarian and musical (!) company. But there is more – lots more. Brutus and Nero are Madame Medusa's pet crocodiles in Walt Disney's animated feature *The Rescuers* (1977). In the Coen brothers' *Intolerable Cruelty* (2003), a cheap diner is called *Nero's*. And so it goes. As late as 2012 Woody Allen had a different title in mind for his romantic comedy *To Rome with Love*. He explained that his first choice, an allusion to Boccaccio's *Decameron*, had been rejected: "So I changed it to *Nero Fiddles*, and half the countries in the world said, 'we don't know what that means, we don't have the expression.' So finally I settled on a generic title like *To Rome with Love* so everybody would get it."[6] Allen did not much like this title.

"Is this then the end of Nero?" The line given to Ustinov's Nero moments before he commits suicide is a conscious echo of one given to another famous antihero in a film by director LeRoy. Facing death, the titular gangster of his classic *Little Caesar* (1930) muses: "Mother of mercy, is this the end of Rico?" Rico dies without a merciful mother, but LeRoy's Nero has his faithful Acte for assisted suicide. If we apply Nero's question to the future of our visual media, only one answer seems possible: *Of course not*. Since the cinema took its first baby steps, the screen's earliest super-villain has provided thrilling spectacle and elevating melodrama galore. He even was reincarnated as futuristic (and nonhuman) space baddie Captain Nero in J. J. Abrams's *Star Trek*

[5] Quoted from Brownlow 1975: 187.
[6] Quoted from "Woody Allen Dislikes Own Films, But Won't Retire."

(2009). This Nero even threatens the survival of planet Earth. Mr. Spock knows what that means: "Nero's very presence has altered the flow of history." So did the real Nero's. The Nero of *Star Trek* is capable of time travel and creates, in the words of Officer Uhura, "an alternate reality."

All fictional incarnations of Nero create alternate realities. What, then, does it all boil down – or burn up – to? This: *Vice cannot wither him, nor movies stale / his infamous variety.*

Further Reading

On Nero's evil image in and since antiquity: Gwyn 1991, McGinn 1994, Gumerlock 2006, Malik 2012, Maier 2013: 388–94. On the *quinquennium Neronis*: Lepper 1957, Levick 1983a. On Nero's building program: Elsner 1994, Knell 2004 114–24. On fiddling: Gyles 1947. The following are fundamental for Nero on screen: Wyke 1997 110–46; Junkelmann 2004, passim; Lindner 2007, passim; Scodel and Bettenworth 2009. Dumont 2009: 478–506 provides extensive information, rare illustrations, and brief critical evaluations concerning virtually all Nero films. On DeMille's *The Sign of the Cross*: Eyman 2010: 289–97. On Nero as precursor of Adolf Hitler: Winkler 2001: 55–62, 2009: 141–9. On prologues to epic films: Winkler 2008.

Part VI

After the Last Laugh

21: The Neronian "Symptom"

Erik Gunderson

> He spared neither the people nor the walls of his fatherland. Once a man said in conversation [the tragic line] "When I am dead let the world be swallowed in flame." "No," said Nero, "while I yet live." And that's just what he brought to pass.
>
> (Suetonius, *Nero* 38)

This chapter offers a prologue to a reading of the Flavian and Antonine ages, the ages that, not coincidentally, give to us much of what we know – or at least think we know – about Nero. So one might fruitfully turn to the relevant primary and secondary materials of these eras while asking the question, "Who needs Nero to be what?" That is, how does Nero "yet live" within the imagination of successive generations as someone who is both "good to think with" as well as "unthinkable"? And of what use is "our" Nero for us to think with?

21.1 The Neronian "Symptom"

If we say that Nero and his age are somehow decadent, what do we really mean by "decadent"? That is not clear. Consider a definitive definition, the entry in the *Oxford English Dictionary*: "a. The process of falling away or declining (from a prior state of excellence, vitality, prosperity, etc.); decay; impaired or deteriorated condition."[1] The truth of the word is perfectly etymological and it bears its meaning on its face: *de* (away) + *cadere* (to fall). Consider, though, another definitive definition, the entry from Oxford Dictionaries online: "Moral or cultural decline as characterized by excessive indulgence

[1] www.oed.com.myaccess.library.utoronto.ca/view/Entry/47973?redirectedFrom=decadence#eid.

in pleasure or luxury."[2] Behind the mask of mere decay, the truth: wanton decay. This specifically ethical version of "to fall away" overwhelms the neutral, generic sense of the term. This slippage is symptomatic.[3] And, importantly, this is a symptom of our own neurosis, not Nero's.[4]

Nero's is the mask that one sets on the face of the politics of this pleasure.[5] In fact, one insists that he wear this mask. Indeed, the "true history" of a given set of years matters less than the "decadent history" of this fallen age. The label "decadent" enables an appraisal that is simultaneously aesthetic, ethical, class-biased, and nostalgic for a certain configuration of power. And yet the political and sociological commitments folded within the very gesture of making such an appraisal are occluded. The real scandal is that the Neronian reign itself is not necessarily illegitimate, nor, for that matter, is Nero's pleasure necessarily base and vulgar. It has merely been declared unsound by a certain kind of elitist political subject who has wagered everything on a fundamentally "decent" proposal: his or her own ethical orientation is antithetical to a species of thought that has been denounced as unthinkable and obscene. Neronian monstrosity as a construct – even if there are historical reasons to consider him guilty of a number of monstrous acts – works as a fantasmatic elaboration on a socio-politico theme, an elaboration that has been given ethical force.[6]

21.2 *Arcanum imperi*

Neronian decadence seduces as an appraisal. A certain community gathers around the spectacle that this label organizes for its disapproving eyes. This is the community of the not-decadent, those who like to think of themselves as anything but fallen and anything but hedonists. And not only are they themselves ethically superior, they are also at a decided epistemological advantage. They both know and judge. They

[2] www.oxforddictionaries.com/definition/english/decadence?q=decadence.

[3] Žižek 1989: 21: "[T]he 'symptom' is, strictly speaking, a particular element which subverts its own universal foundation, a species subverting its own genus."

[4] See again Žižek 1989: 21 on the symptom: "[A] formation whose very consistency implies a certain non-knowledge on the part of the subject: the subject can 'enjoy his symptom' only in so far as its logic escapes him."

[5] Nero is not the only name, though: the tyrant and his obscenity are very old and familiar figures of Greek political thought. See Wohl 2002: 215–69.

[6] See Ferri 2003: 9–11 for the emergence of Nero the monster. In 68–9 CE, people were still making claims for political legitimacy based on being "the next Nero." Similarly, the notion of Nero the crazed and tyrannical builder also seems to have a retrospective cast to it. See Elsner 1994.

know power and judge power. And they specifically know that a key element of power's power comes from its veiled quality.

Tacitus' *Histories* tells the story of the aftermath of the death of Nero, a confused moment when a number of new emperors arise and swiftly fall. Tacitus uses a famous phrase near the opening that explains, in effect, the chaos. In the wake of Nero's death and amidst the varied reactions to it, "the secret of empire (*imperi arcano*) had been divulged: emperors could be created elsewhere than at Rome."[7]

Tacitus and his reader pride themselves on probing mysteries.[8] The narrative structure of Tacitus' historical works routinely invests in a profound interconnection between power and the mysterious. The choice of *arcana*, a word closely tied to religious mysteries, only highlights the (purported) profundity of the relationship.[9] Behind some opaque surface resides the truth. Power holds that truth in reserve. The author and his reader can move from one side of that barrier to the other.[10]

The historian returns to the past. The inscrutable object has its mysteries probed. The historian acquires a knowledge-of-power that is structurally convergent with knowledge-as-power.[11] There is something triumphal about this return to the inner sanctum of power on the part of a historian, even if it is painful to see what one finds. In fact, even meaninglessness becomes meaningful by this means: the real point is the very ability to move behind the curtain, not the direct enjoyment of what one finds on the other side. This yields the oblique pleasure of being "in the know" rather than naïve and deceived by the surface of the world.[12]

But the mysteries of the cynics are mysteries to the cynics. The piercing gaze backward fetishizes a retrograde relationship to power even – if not especially – where power is being criticized. Looking back at Nero and looking around at the world Nero left in his wake, Tacitus sees a morality play staged in Roman dress: the dignity of the dignitaries is reviewed with a jaundiced eye. And in seeing such a decadent play,

7 Tacitus, *Histories* 1.4: "evulgato imperii arcano posse principem alibi quam Romae fieri."

8 See O'Gorman 2000: 10 on Tacitean unmasking, disclosure, and decoding. See *arcana* and power at Tacitus, *Annals* 1.6, 2.36, 2.59, and 6.21.

9 See Tacitus, *Germania* 18 and 40; both of them are ethnographic passages about religious rites.

10 Henderson 1989: 193: "Tacitus trains his readers, to be(come) 'insiders.'"

11 See the introduction of O'Gorman 2000 for the politics of literary form in Tacitus as well as the way in which Tacitus' Latin forces complicity upon the reader. See also her concluding chapter (176–83) for more on politics and form.

12 See Ronell 2002: 10 on the manner in which reserve, depth, and intelligence array themselves against stupidity. And yet stupidity is never quite so stupid as to be merely stupid and merely some simple other to canniness.

Tacitus – a prominent member of the new order that emerges in the wake of the history contained in the *Histories* themselves – also reveals a hesitation to describe the real revolution and the real secret: the imperial system needs *someone* to play the role of emperor, and it is indeed a role.

That system does not really care about the man behind the mask of power so long as someone wears it. Someone has to play the part of Caesar, and one demands of him that he perform his role earnestly rather than wantonly falling away from the stern original. And yet it was Nero himself who seems to have appreciated this "secret of the secret" and to have compromised in advance any and all efforts at any would-be unmasking of Roman power on the part of analysts. He himself explores – or is presented as exploring, and it makes no difference how much of this story is "really real" – the theatricality of power in its most radical sense: it is all just an act; there is really nothing "behind it all."[13] This is acting that parades itself as acting (because that's all there is). And certainly nothing "back there" can be designated as pristine, original, chaste, and legitimate. Says the grinning mask of this actor, only the leer does not lie.[14]

The initial pages of Tacitus' *Histories* are suffused with ethical language. And this language also serves as a class-based critique of the historical moment. Upon Nero's death, everyone is stirred up (*con civerat*, 1.4), but they are stirred differently as their social (and "hence" ethical) position would dictate. Good people hated Nero; bad people loved him. And here Tacitus leans on the socio-semantic blur between ethics and money, *boni* and *bona*. The "sordid plebs" miss Nero as do the "worst of the slaves" and so too those who had consumed their own property (*bona*) amidst their debauchery.[15] All of these were Nero's nurslings, and they miss his beneficence toward their depraved sort. As an exercise in obviousness, the "sordidness" of the sordid commons is to be connected to their "habituation" to the theatrical world of Nero's Rome (*et circo ac theatris sueta*). The illusion habit is hard to kick. People feed on lies and love it. This is part of a general habituation to vice

[13] Compare Rimell 2007: 112–13 on the obsession with "getting inside it all" in Petronius. But exploring the *arcanum* is traumatic and disconcerting and only destabilizes the knower him- or herself.

[14] See Suetonius, *Nero* 29: "ex nonnullis comperi persuasissimum habuisse eum neminem hominem pudicum aut ulla corporis parte purum esse, uerum plerosque dissimulare uitium et callide optegere; ideoque professis apud se obscaenitatem cetera quoque concessisse delicta."

[15] Tacitus, *Histories* 1.4: "plebs sordida et circo ac theatris sueta, simul deterrimi servorum, aut qui adesis bonis per dedecus Neronis alebantur, maesti et rumorum avidi." See also *adsuetis* and *ut est mos vulgi* at *Histories* 1.7. The circus-and-theater association returns at *Histories* 1.72, where it is also associated with "vulgar license."

that infected all as the contagion of decadence spread ever outward: once the urban soldiers loved the virtues of their rulers; now they have gotten used to loving their vices.[16]

Nero perverts Rome because he turns Romans into perverts. Instead of feeling a reverence for the secret behind the mask of power, everyone relishes masks and shows. Instead of virtue in and as "reserved" (morally restrained + held back from sight + made a precious and scarce commodity), we have an everyday love of the mask *qua* mask. One enjoys directly here and now. A sick love of license suffuses these people.[17]

The authorial voice sets itself up as the site of resistance to all of this. When we first meet the narrator on the opening page of the *Histories*, he is telling us about his objectivity. After a baroque fugue on the troubled relationship between power and veracity, an emphatic "but in my case" transitions us to our assurances that the convoluted perversions of praise and blame that have just been described do not apply to this text: "But as for me, Galba, Otho, and Vitellius showed me neither kindness nor affront. My political career (*dignitas*) began thanks to Vespasian, was furthered by Titus, and significantly advanced by Domitian. I will not deny that. But . . ."[18]

Our relationship to the *Histories* requires a slippage between *dignitas* as "political career" and *dignitas* as "moral dignity." The trajectory of this word and its two senses moves both in tandem with and in the opposite direction from the course that charts the paired meanings of decadence as fall and decadence as pleasurable fall. The Flavian arrival puts a stop to Neronianism.[19] If Book One opens with a praise of the narrator's qualifications to speak, note that Book Two opens with a praise of Vespasian's qualifications to lead.[20] And the *dignitatam incohatam* of 1.1 is echoed by the beginning-of-dignity and dignified beginning of the second book.

A gratuitous episode comes very early in the second book. It tells us nothing about the revolutions of 69 CE, but it nevertheless tells us

[16] Tacitus, *Histories* 1.5: "ita quattuordecim annis a Nerone adsuefactos ut haud minus vitia principum amarent quam olim virtutes verebantur."

[17] Compare Tacitus, *Histories* 1.25: "quos memoria Neronis ac desiderium prioris licentiae accenderet."

[18] Tacitus, *Histories* 1.1: "mihi Galba Otho Vitellius nec beneficio nec iniuria cogniti. dignitatem nostram a Vespasiano inchoatam, a Tito auctam, a Domitiano longius provectam non abnuerim: set incorruptam fidem . . ." Symei, 1958: 146: read this straight. Fabia 1901: 68–70: it's specious, and the name Domitian alerts us to this. Compare O'Gorman 2000: 178 on Tacitus, Domitian, Nerva, and Trajan.

[19] See Ando 2000: 34–5 on the Flavian efforts to negotiate a transfer of charismatic imperial authority over into their family.

[20] For an overview of Tacitus' Vespasian, see Ash 1999: 127–46.

something important about one of the revolutionaries. The pleasures of Vespasian are excused in 2.2 – a permissiveness that we have never seen before in the *Histories*. If sensualism is the truth of Nero, Tacitus flags a different sort of desire on Vespasian's part: a *cupido visendi*. Both narrator and Vespasian turn aside to take a look at Aphrodite's temple at Paphos. Knowledge-of-desire supplants carnal knowledge. Though the word is not present, we are indeed being shown the *arcana* of the goddess of pleasure. And yet there is nothing dirty to see, and what Vespasian comes to know is not obscene: the statue is not anthropomorphic. It is instead an abstract conical figure.

Juxtaposed to these "dignified" openings of both the first and the second books, openings that accredit both the narrator and the Flavian emperor, is a collection of "mockeries," a set of travesties of narrative as well as political form: the Pseudo-Nerones. A single Pseudo-Nero is mentioned as an item on the long list of the contents of the *opus* at 1.2: *falsi Neronis ludibrio*. But at the opening of Book Two, one of our first orders of business is a discussion of one of several false Nerones. They have multiplied since Book One. Others are to be spoken of "in their proper narrative place" (*in contextu operis*, 2.8).[21] At this moment we take a look at but one of many: a slave from Pontus, or was he a freedman from Italy? Not only are the fake Nerones proliferating, they are even doubling within themselves. The man was a talented singer and cithara player who bore a certain resemblance to Nero. The scoundrel gathered to himself a collection of rogues: deserters enticed by promises and slaves given arms. They took to robbery to support themselves. But the horror of persons and deeds is obvious only to the narrator and his readers. In fact, the enterprise enticed others: the name Nero arouses in them a lust for revolution amidst their loathing for the status quo.[22] Or so we are told.

21.3 Cynical (Un)reason

Tacitus depicts a mixed, motley, and heterogeneous mob of average citizens, rebelling soldiers, and criminals. Nero's name – and not even his substance – offers a point of convergence for them. They hate the present. They itch pruriently for something new. And yet the very phrase "new things" (*res novae*) is never to be translated literally, but

[21] See Suetonius, *Nero* 57 for yet another pseudo-Nero who crops up almost twenty years later. Chilver 1979: 50 offers a tidy review of the known false Nerones.

[22] Tacitus, *Histories* 2.8: "multi ad celebritatem nominis erecti rerum novarum cupidine et odio praesentium."

instead here and elsewhere it should be rendered as "revolution." A punitive exercise of not just political power but so too hermeneutic power is justified by (the positing of) such a situation. The power/knowledge apparatus of objective history intervenes in a campaign against a figure of power who represents pleasure/power, that is pleasure pursued via power, power begetting pleasure, pleasure in the exercise of power, and an endless looping between terms as means and ends oscillate.[23] False Neronianism – something no different, it would seem, from authentic Neronianism – is the name one gives to this forbidden political pleasure where everything is immediate and out in the open and nothing is deferred or arcane.

Conversely Flavian post-Neronianism is presented as legitimate, and as a justified reaction against a specious species of pleasure. Legitimate power is deep, it is profound, it is reserved. The cynical eye of the historian is itself invested in this figuration of power. Indeed, it has conjured it for us. While not necessarily advocating, of course, the policies of any given emperor, Tacitus nevertheless invests in the profundity of the profound: power should have a depth to it; and the historian is the one who plumbs those depths. The symptom of this symbiosis between profound historian and history as deep can be observed in the Tacitean narrative voice, which is notorious for its clipped syntax and pregnant expressions. And as a style its devices remind us most of Tacitus' own monster, the inscrutable Tiberius.[24] Nero's clownishness of power repulses: it is vulgar, superficial, immediate, and lewd. To even speak of such things is itself dangerously undignified. Nevertheless, let us not tumble into the game of depth: Tacitean cynicism is itself nothing but the mask worn by a revolutionary modernity that has given itself a retrograde disguise, the dignified *dignitas* of authorized power and legitimate knowledge.[25]

"Nero also sang tragic arias wearing the masks of heroes and gods, and so too of heroines and goddesses. The masks were fashioned to look like his own face and that of the woman he loved at the moment."[26]

[23] On the revulsion that historicists evince toward *jouissance*, see Copjec 1994: 157. See Frederick 2003 and Gunderson 2003a on the Foucauldian fusion of power and knowledge in the architecture of Flavian Rome.

[24] And Tacitus even lets us imagine a literal resemblance between his own prose style and that of Tiberius. See Syme 1958: 429 on *Annales* 13.2.3.

[25] Mellor 2003: the Flavians foster an aristocratic class recruited from a wide geographic span and skilled in the imperial system itself; the Julio-Claudians had been tied to a more local and family-based sense of aristocracy. Syme 1970: 140: "Tacitus speaks for the new imperial aristocracy of the western provinces, for Trajan and Hadrian as for Agricola – and himself."

[26] Suetonius, *Nero* 21: "tragoedias quoque cantauit personatus heroum deorumque, item heroidum ac dearum, personis effectis ad similitudinem oris sui et feminae, prout quamque diligeret."

Suetonius' Nero relishes doing violence to the borders between real and fake. This can be seen whether he is/is playing a thief (26), a pimp (27), a bride (28), or a (sexual) animal (29). Acting gives the key to the whole mockery of the reality effect:[27] even when Nero "is" an actor, he is always also merely pretending to be an actor.[28]

In his speech urging a Gaulish revolt, Dio's Vindex argues that the horror of histrionics constitutes a political crisis. He has seen Nero acting out a variety of vile parts. "Will anyone call a man like this Caesar, emperor, and Augustus?"[29] Vindex insists that Nero has turned into a character from one of his own beloved tragedies: he has outraged these sacred imperial titles (τὰ ἱερὰ ἐκεῖνα ὀνόματα), and should instead be called Thyestes and Oedipus and Orestes since these are the names he seeks for himself (63.22.6). This argument forms the climax of Vindex's oration, and Dio says that his audience all agreed with him. Nero stopped playing Caesar and started playing a player, and in so doing he lost one set of names and gained another. Although one doubts that such is his aim, Dio, an author from the third century CE, allows for the deconstruction of Caesarism as an essence: a good emperor aspires to be worthy of the role he plays, namely, emperor. Unlike Nero, a man born to his titles, upstart men like Vespasian earnestly seek to be called Caesar and emperor and Augustus. And a sort of miracle of power occurs when everyone, including cynical critics, agrees not so much merely to call him Caesar, but instead to believe that he really is Caesar, and not just a man playing Caesar.

However, if Nero's theatrical mask were a simple mask, and if it concealed familiar motives there would be less to dread: Neronian terror would be of the banal sort. Nero would merely be Thyestes. The fantasy of a cruel emperor masking his hatred saves one from the horror of the truly mad one.[30] The hypothesis of a cynical Neronian mask would serve the cynic's own efforts at explaining decadence: the pleasure of the fall into Neronianism becomes legible because it offers a (masked) version of masterful mastery.[31]

27 See Barthes 1986 on the reality effect. And see also Freudenburg, Chapter 7 in this volume.

28 See Bartsch 1994: 46–50 on Nero playing himself.

29 Dio, *Roman Histories* 63.22.5.

30 Seneca's *Thyestes*, for example, is a masterful play about masterly plotting. Seneca, the author of the play, and Thyestes, the author of the criminal play within the play, are both figures of authority, power, and control. See Schiesaro 2003.

31 See Sloterdijk 1987 on the Weimar moment when "knowledge is power" and everyone expresses this by unmasking everyone else (Sloterdijk 1987: 89–90). Compare as well the comfort offered to cynics by the specter of the impostors: they offer a reassurance that simplifies the question of contemporary complexity (Sloterdijk 1987: 484).

In the *Annals* Tacitus stages a scene. In it Nero plays a tyrant, not a mad man. Seneca wants to withdraw from public life, and so Seneca himself puts on a little show wherein he delivers a monolog on the topic of why he ought to be allowed to retire. Nero replies by sadistically thanking Seneca for teaching him how to make a clever, dissembling reply (14.55). Nero avers that it would be a shame to lose such a trusted advisor. "And after this he adds an embrace and kisses: not only was he naturally inclined to cast a veil over his loathing with deceitful blandishments, but he had practiced the habit as well. Seneca – and such is the way all conversations with a master end – offers his thanks."[32] Nothing is lost on anyone here, certainly not on the narrator or the reader. Reasons the cynic: "Perhaps if Seneca had himself been more cynical and been so at the right moment he could have evaded his predicament." One more investment in hermeneutics is all we need to get behind the scenes and so to get ahead.[33] Interviews with the emperor are – or at least should be – dialogs between the canny holder of power and the clever reader of power. Both parties speak the same language and share core beliefs. This conclusion is cold, but nevertheless comforting.

But this is not the only way to look at Nero. In the anonymous play *Octavia*, Seneca and Nero have a similar interview to the one we see in Tacitus' *Annals*. Follow Augustus' merciful path, urges the stage Seneca, and you will be revered as a god. The Nero of the *Octavia* replies by saying how he relishes the terror that compels false praises. The exercise of power is itself obscenely pleasurable: no canniness will ever be able to hold a dialog with let alone outthink someone who wallows in pleasure/power. In fact, cynical canniness only feeds the monster's delight: he knows that you know, that you can "see through it all," but all of this cunning only ensures that you can see your own subjection all the more clearly. When pitted against pleasure/power, knowledge becomes powerlessness to the nth power.

And then this Nero offers a reading of Roman history: Augustus was a blood-soaked victor, and the lesson he taught his successors was to slay and to hold power. This is the sure path to the stars.[34] I assume that the audience of the *Octavia* was supposed to shudder at this. Nevertheless, this Nero-in-a-tragedy is saying something important about the historical

[32] Tacitus, *Annals* 14.56: "his adicit complexum et oscula, factus natura et consuetudine exercitus velare odium fallacibus blanditiis. Seneca, qui finis omnium cum dominante sermonum, grates agit."

[33] Henderson 1989: 194: "The *Annals* make citizen-historians of us all. . . . Do *we* rise above the tide of *seruitium*? Do *we* read Super-Power any better than those senators and princes?" [original emphasis].

[34] See [Seneca], *Octavia* 472–532.

figure Nero. Nero is not the decadent falling away from the principles of the principate; he is its jubilant apotheosis.[35]

The "mockery" of the false Nerones gives the truth of the true Nero: it's all an act. The emperor is a con man. And nobody seems especially inclined to do anything with this bit of knowledge. Some are fooled outright, but only some. Others are happy to assume a no-questions-asked relationship to whatever it is that is going on: they are getting what they want, and the matter can end there. And the clever have throughout been working the system for their own cynical reasons.[36]

Nero names a cancerous configuration of power and the subject. The plenitude of politics has vanished and in its place is a fallen illusion that gives pleasure. The dignified who have repudiated decadence sit back and sneer with a cold self-satisfaction: "I know better, and they do worse." But this too is an illusion and one that gives pleasure. The dignified slake their aristocratic nostalgia for another version of Caesarism, the Augustan fantasy. One snatches at imperial order-and-dignity. The dignified make a show of stopping up their ears to disorderly vulgarity. And in so doing they also play dumb. For Augustus himself had been instrumental in the killing of the man who had once upon a time himself nostalgically praised "engagement without peril and dignified leisure."[37]

21.4 Metastatic Neronianism

The present moment in Anglo-American society is hardly one that would be characterized as especially scholarly and historically minded. Unsurprisingly the historical figure of Nero is little known and difficult to find in the here and now. And yet the fable of Neronean decadence does live on: it subsists within a specific perspective that constitutes itself by sitting in judgment of (stupid) power and (vulgar) pleasure. But while one fiddles about sitting in judgment, the emperor's palace itself never burns.

[35] Boyle 1997: 90: "[W]hat Nero succeeded in doing was to recycle the tyranny of his predecessors (including that of Augustus) together with the political, social, religious and legal forms of the Roman world emptied of their substance."

[36] 'Twas ever thus. See Syme 1983: 15 on Roman political life *tout court*: "The Roman constitution was a screen and a sham." Compare Syme 1983: 335 on the timely support of Augustus' new regime by old Republicans.

[37] See Cicero, *De Oratore* 1.1: "qui in optima re publica, cum et honoribus et rerum gestarum gloria florerent, eum vitae cursum tenere potuerunt, ut vel in negotio sine periculo vel in otio cum dignitate esse possent."

Various moments from Suetonius' *Life* are resonant with contemporary life without, of course, being connected with the present via lines of direct transmission or even allusion. Profligate Nero bankrupts an empire, but his spending never abates, especially after he becomes enflamed with the idea of finding Dido's treasure in Africa.[38] What could sound more modern than greedy, wastrel elites spending beyond their already lavish means while betting on some sort of speculative money-for-and-from-nothing? Whether it is Iraqi oil wealth or pyramid schemes like bitcoin or securities backed by underwater mortgages, the cynical (because powerless) academic elite are all able to play Tacitus and to decry the obscenity of wealth and its hollow charades. And yet such denunciations do absolutely nothing to slow the quasi-autonomous movement of global capital that circulates under the misleading albeit decadent label of vulgar money-lust. The profound economic connection between the universities that house the cynics and the economic and political elite remains singularly unaffected amidst all of the sighing and eye-rolling.[39]

In Suetonius and other Roman accounts Nero's Golden House is metonym for his excess. The house swallows both the public space and the imperial purse. Nero's financial collapse is strongly associated with this specific building program in Suetonius' life of the emperor. Meanwhile we have our own fascination with the houses of the rich and famous. They act as symptoms of social maladies, but also sites of ambivalent projection for the critic. Between 1984 and 1994 one could tune in to *Lifestyles of the Rich and Famous* and tour various golden houses. Born amidst the febrile trickle-down economic dreams of Reaganomics, the show was decried by the intelligentsia for its vulgarity. Big, expensive, and tasteless homes were paraded in front of the eyes of a vulgar audience who lapped up the vulgarity. Or so said the cynics.[40] And the show's logical successor is little better: MTV's *Cribs* (2000–11) offered a similar spectacle of tacky expenditure more or less tailor-made for the derision of the better sort: "What have we come to?" But the whole question of better-and-

[38] See Suetonius, *Nero* 32.

[39] See Bourdieu 1988: 222 on the professoriate as "a sort of upper petty bourgeoisie committed to an *ethical and intellectual aristocratism*" [original emphasis]. And yet the academic is not so much outside the dominant and dominating structures of society as he or she is a partially dominated member of the most dominant social fraction.

[40] Criticism of displays of wealth on the part of *arrivistes* as well as the interpretation of such displays would be well advised to concern itself with terms such as "reflexive sociology" and "dominated aesthetic." See Bourdieu and Wacquant 1992 and Bourdieu 1984. Specifically members of the dominated social factions know full well that they are looked at, judged, and found wanting by the established cultural aristocracy (aka, the "dignified" in both social rank and aesthetic taste). And this knowledge leaves traces in all of their interactions with the cultural field.

worse or taste and tastelessness is itself a species of misdirection. What matters is only that the shows get ratings. Ironic, overeducated viewers and hostile critics cannot possibly do harm to the corporate interests that are served by the promulgation of spectacles of Golden House-ism. Indeed, criticism frequently serves only to give a show buzz and to improve ratings. Accordingly, canny producers can be counted on to incite a certain brand of criticism.

Caesar's Palace: yes, but which Caesar? The answer is, "obviously" Nero. Nero's Golden House is the best fit: glitzy, faux-glamorous, and full of pleasures and shows. But it is also clear that one cannot say Nero's Palace either. A corporate entity has declared the name to be Caesar's Palace and not Nero's Palace. Moreover the name argues for the uncomfortable truth from the *Octavia*: all Caesars are indistinguishable in their decadence. The nostalgic might long for a glamorous Old Vegas filled with colorful mobsters and they-don't-make-'em-like-that-anymore celebrities, but even that Las Vegas was all about the bottom line and the shattered lives that fed it.

Caesar's Palace manifestly sells a lie: beneath the mask – why, the same thing all over again. It offers real-but-fake glamor by radically democratizing access to luxury: all you need is a big enough pile of colorful chips. The Palace houses while instantiating a decadent fever-dream. And amidst the lurid shapes that hover before the dreamer's eyes is a lewd figure beckoning us to commit – either earnestly or ignorantly or ironically or cynically: it does not matter, so long as you play – to the idea of voluptuous Decline-and-Fall™. Meanwhile Caesar's Palace is palatial but not a palace. It is Caesar's, but not owned by Caesar. Indeed Caesar's Palace is not even really distinct as a corporate entity from a number of other "competing" establishments. The casino is one of a number of gaming properties owned by an umbrella corporation that is itself an element within still larger enterprises. All of these corporate relationships are relatively fluid and subject to a variety of mergers and acquisitions. Nevertheless the specific-and-generic name inscribed on the Palace itself never changes.[41] And the (Golden) House always wins. It wins because, mathematically, it must. And it wins more than just money inasmuch as everyone who loses knows in advance that the house always wins and yet they gamble anyway, even the hipsters and

[41] Caesar's Entertainment Properties owns a variety of "Casino Brands" including Ballys,' Caesar's, Harrah's, and Horseshoe. Presently Caesar's Entertainment itself is described as "a public company, with a joint venture of Apollo Global Management and Texas Pacific Group owning a large portion of the stock and Blackstone Group also holding a significant stake." [https://en.wikipedia.org/wiki/Caesars_Entertainment_Corporation]

the cynics who are "too good" for the vulgar lot of it and only play because they "happen" to be in town for a wedding or for work.

21.5 Wit and Its Relationship to the Political Unconscious

Neronian decadence can be described as a sort of obscenity that is impervious to unmasking. Something is leering at us, and behind the leer is another leer that defies our efforts to interpret away the horror in the name of some return to dignity. There can no longer be a nostalgic return to the orderly order of things. There can only be a cynical, compromised pretense of a return to order. Even as we struggle to establish our own *dignitas*/dignity by making this gesture, we nevertheless find ourselves stained and unable to escape from the orbit of the dialectic of decadence, a dialectic that can always make a next and disconcerting move after we posit the thesis of our own rectitude. The antithetical mockery of the decadent captures a fundamental secret of the logic of the original, an *arcanum* that is arcane only to the so-called critic.[42] And hence the final synthesis is redolent of the *Octavia* and not the chaste and sublime shrine Vespasian visited on Paphos.

I would like to offer one last, long take on "Reception and Nero" as per earlier. None of this is even Nero, and it's not even reception, but . . . But one could compare the ghost story of communism that haunted Europe, a story that was understood as a mere ghost story – or at least a tale consisting of a rogue's gallery of Pontic imposters and disaffected ne'er-do-wells – that the millennia-spanning tale of class struggle might be the harder to apprehend.[43] And today even Marx himself has become spectral, or at least so we are told by Derrida's ghost.[44] And yet some "essential" work gets done precisely by ghosts, monsters, and men wearing masks even as more level heads aver that nothing at all could really be happening: there is no such thing as "hauntology" because only ontology knows what the meaning of is is, and it knows as well that there are no such things as ghosts.[45] Anachrony is impossible, says the historicist who has no time for stagey Danish princes, because, of course, time is ever well articulated, and perfectly joined – where else? – at the joints.[46] And yet the Neronian *revenant* insists on returning because, until one figures out how

[42] See Bourdieu 1988: 207 for professors as "mystified mystifiers" who are blind to the social dimension of their objective judgments.

[43] The specter that power hopes to exorcise: Marx and Engels 1978: 481. The story of class that lies behind the ghost story: Marx and Engels 1978: 482.

[44] The full meditation is at Derrida 1994.

[45] Hauntology: Derrida 1994: 10.

[46] Anachrony: throughout, but see Derrida 1994: 7 for an early appearance.

to break the back-to-where-we-started cycle of cynical return and its conservative political economy, there will always be another man in a Nero mask who himself arrives to intone again certain uncanny home truths about the cynic himself, truths Nero once histrionically uttered as he wore his Nero mask.

Christopher Nolan's 2008 film *The Dark Knight* is a sequel to his reboot of the Batman franchise. Like Caesar's Palace, Batman is both a fantasy and a commercial entity. The film cost $185 million to make and it grossed more than $1 billion. The Batman franchise relies on the notion that it is set in some sort of parallel America overrun by criminals. And this America needs a reclusive billionaire to save the law-abiding citizens from rampant lawlessness in the face of police corruption and impotence. Bruce Wayne will, with his own resources raise a personal army: himself.

The veiled allusion to the Augustus of the *Res Gestae* is not a casual one. *The Dark Knight* appreciates that it is addressing the question of Caesarism and the problem of the man who is both above and beyond the law and yet who also acts in the name of the law. The republic is restored when such a man successfully intervenes. Or, rather, the principate begins with a tickertape parade and banners celebrating restoration: *Nunc est bibendum*, said Horace when Cleopatra died.[47] The mad queen is dead. But the threat to the Capitoline arose from neither the queen nor her alleged madness. Indeed, no matter who won that war, the Capitol as head of government would lose.

When over dinner district attorney Harvey Dent defends Batman against a charge of vigilantism, Dent says, "When their enemies were at the gates, the Romans would suspend democracy and appoint one man to protect the city. It wasn't considered an honor, it was considered a public service."[48] His date Rachel – who is also the woman Bruce Wayne had to give up in the name of his heroism – responds: "Harvey, the last man they appointed to protect the republic was named *Caesar*, and he never gave up his power."[49] And to this Dent replies, "OK, fine. You either die a hero or you live long enough to see yourself become the villain."[50] It's

[47] See Horace, *Carmina* 1.37. [48] At 20:35 and following.

[49] Which Caesar does she really have in mind? Does it matter? See Henderson 2014: 93–4 on Julius as prequel to Suetonius' other Caesars, especially Augustus. And see Gunderson 2014 on Augustus' exemplary Caesarism. But one suspects Rachel herself would point to Augustus' *Res Gestae* 5 where he specifically highlights the fact that he refused to be named dictator though the title was offered to him.

[50] Dent's line about living to become a villain is vital to the whole of the film given that it can be heard again in the final scene. This time it is Bruce Wayne as Batman who can be heard delivering the lines in a voice-over.

a cynical message delivered by the law itself: power has an innate decadence to it; it is destined to fall, no matter how noble its intentions. But even decadent law is better than lawlessness. A masked man (Batman) or a two-faced man (Dent) acting in the name of order is better than a homicidal clown (Joker). Who, did he possess but an ounce of dignity, would pick Nero over Augustus, or even Tiberius?

The film is preoccupied with good and evil as well as man and overman. The movie's villain is the symmetrical double of our hero Batman. Joker too is beyond ordinary mortals. Joker rewrites Nietzsche at the end of his first killing spree, "I believe whatever does not kill you simply makes you stranger."[51] He tells Batman, "I am not a monster, I am just ahead of the curve."[52] The movie is not just interested in the good, the evil, and their beyond, but also in masks. The beneficent billionaire Wayne is hidden behind the mask of Batman. And even Wayne's life as a dissolute playboy is a façade that prevents people from suspecting that he is in fact a hero. Dent becomes the monstrous Two-Face, but this only makes manifest preexisting two-faced aspects of his character.

The whole Western tradition of reading power, including and especially imperial power, is quite comfortable with the idea of masks like these. Tacitus, Suetonius, and others are all happy to detect the hero or dissembling villain behind the public persona. But, like an extreme version of Nero playing Nero, Joker is always effectively wearing his Joker mask: he constantly wears makeup, and it barely disguises a horribly scarred face. In fact, his makeup only makes the hideousness of his scars more present and more real.

A Joker or a Nero unnerves cynics precisely by being so much less cynical than they are. These monsters embody something that subverts any investment in hermeneutics and the privileged position of those who can see more because they see deeper. No, they insist, we defy you to deal with a world where everything is immediate and only skin deep, a world where a random cithara player who may or may not be from Pontus can promise you the world and be every bit as "really real" as some other guy who played the cithara while the world burned. The secret of this sort of power is that Nerones can create themselves anywhere and everywhere, even and especially far outside of the allegedly dignified circuits that regulate the holding of offices lesser and greater within the grand imperial machine. The year of four emperors is a tawdry drama starring consulars, governors, and generals at the heads

[51] At 5:40. [52] At 1:29:00.

of armies. But even bathetic tragedy is more dignified than mere farce. The cynic ciphers the Neronian/Pseudo-Neronian democratization of the will to power as vulgar anarchism. But this is because the cynic wills not power itself, but only knowledge-of-power, an arcanely dignified power to which the cynic is ultimately self-subjected.

The film multiply stages desires to get behind literal and metaphorical masks: Batman's as well as Joker's.[53] When we first see Joker, he is a member of a gang of thieves all of whom are wearing Joker masks. As the scene ends the last surviving gang member removes his mask and, we see Joker's Neronian flair: underneath a Joker mask was Joker himself. Just before killing a man Joker gives a long etiology, "Wanna know how I got these scars?"[54] He knows that we want to know what arcane truth animates him. Joker narrates a gruesome tale. But when he asks the same question later in the film to another victim, he tells an entirely different story of origins.[55]

Even as Joker is always wearing a true mask or a non-mask, he is obsessed with unmasking others. The world is full of schemers, he says, and his job is to expose them for who they are. One is reminded of Nero's thesis of universal depravity and his desire that people admit as much.[56] Joker's chief terroristic demand is that Batman unmask himself. And Joker tells a policeman who is holding him prisoner that only in the moment of death can you really see who a person is. Joker is a radical agent of truth and in his radicalness he escapes even wise old Alfred who only gets him half right. Alfred says, "Some men aren't looking for anything logical like money. They can't be bought, bullied, reasoned or negotiated with. Some men just want to watch the world burn."[57] One wonders if Alfred has read Suetonius' tales of the Great Fire at Rome.

Joker himself is in fact a critic of the link between logic and money: money is for schemers; it is an end that requires various shifty means. Joker burns a veritable mountain of money and declares, "You see, I am a guy of simple tastes. I enjoy dynamite and gunpowder and gasoline."[58] And that's our Joker, a fiddler watching the hypocritical money-mad world of schemers burn. "I like this job," he says, "I like it."[59] And there are a number of exuberant shots of his face that mark the many scenes of mayhem. And even though he is always outsmarting his

[53] The film even has pseudo-Batmen and non-Jokers wearing Joker masks. Also, disturbingly, the movie seems to have inspired "real" pseudo-Jokers. James Holmes's murders in 2012 were multiply connected to the Batman franchise. And Joker remains a potent symbol in extremist circles in the United States. Notice as well the poster of Barack Obama as a socialist Joker that would crop up at right-wing protests.

[54] At 30:05. [55] At 50:55. [56] See again Suetonius, *Nero* 29. [57] At 55:00.

[58] At 1:42:45. [59] At 1:18:40.

foes and several steps ahead of them, Joker adamantly refuses to declare that there is any grand scheme behind it all: "Do I really look like a guy with a plan?" "I just DO things." But all of this is a prelude to his denunciation of the orderly order of things, the big corrupt scheme that is legitimate society: "You know what I've noticed? Nobody panics when things go according to plan, even if the plan is horrifying."[60]

Joker offers a commentary on Arendt and the Banality of Evil. And yet his alternative to fascism is mere anarchy in its most chaotic form. Viewed from the perspective of power, Joker-as-symptom posits a false antithesis that leaves us with only one legitimate – albeit cynical – option: "Either you live in a corrupt, authoritarian world ... Or you die a baroque death in a crazed, lawless one." Even if the world itself is fallen and dishonest, one is nevertheless told to refuse specifically Neronian decadence, a decadence that wears its depravity as its ghastly face.

Joker tells Batman, "You complete me."[61] It is a lewd suggestion in every sense of the word given that that phrase is more or less exclusively reserved for lovers speaking to one another. Joker tells the truth in inverted form: what would the rule do without the crisis provoked by the madman? As Joker notes, the plan is free to be horrifying once we step outside of the rules of civilized humanity "of necessity."[62] And one is reminded of the many (cynical) necessities of the (il)logic of the war on terror and all of the other unwinnable wars on abstractions whose concrete effects entail a transformation of our own society along authoritarian lines: "Of course we have to carry out extrajudicial killings in the name of preventing crazy people from killing us and therewith destroying our world of law and order." Whether Augustus restores the Republic or Vespasian is Augustus reborn, Roman imperial power is constantly saving the Romans from – imperial power. Republican *libertas* is not on offer from any quarter.

Batman utterly refuses to see any truth in what Joker says about his obscene intimacy with the monster. Instead Batman identifies with the words of two-faced Harvey Dent precisely at the moment when he grounds his own ethical fidelity to saving Gotham by pretending to be a villain. What Batman cannot see is the logic of nostalgic decadence folded into his own gesture, a gesture doomed to reproduce a polarized and victimized Gotham forever in need of saving by vigilante-heroes such as himself. This retrograde futurity can and will enable innumerable

60 At 1:49.50.

61 At 1:28:10. From the same scene: "I don't want to kill you; what would I do without you?" at 1:28:00.

62 Compare Agamben 2005 on *homo sacer*.

sequels wherein the billionaire Wayne makes billions for various Hollywood production companies, but it blocks access to the radical critique of good and evil proffered by Joker. As many Caesars as you want and for as long as you want, but only Caesars, some good, some middling, some bad.

The schemer insists that beneath the mask of Nero one can find the truth of power, some sort of plan in accordance to which things happen. But Nero jubilantly insists there is no plan at all, only a glorious masquerade. The phrase "Neronian decadence" asserts that Nero was the aberration and that past and future require cauterizing the wound and circuiting around it. The likes of Tacitus will maintain this even though they know that both Augustus and Nero have already happened again (and again). Moreover, even Augustus was a lot more like Nero than one cares to admit. The so-called solution only consolidates the structural problem. Conversely Neronian *jouissance* short-circuits past, present, and future by insisting in the most painful way possible that Nero offers power's own truth emergent at last. This leer makes manifest what had been latent in the schema that links of power, plenitude, fall, and pleasure. The easy way out is to pretend that the madman's ravings are alien and aberrant rather than a structuring element part of our own fantasies about power. It is only when we have thought our way through this unfunny joke that we can move forward into a future where, *inter alia*, the political empowerment and gratification of the common man is not decried as vulgar and illegitimate and marked out as an unambiguous symptom of some sort of fall away from power's putative original dignity.[63]

Decadent or ahead of the curve? Nero most assuredly marks a turning-point if not a limit-point. And when we ourselves get there, do we loop back or jump ahead? Even when stuck within the circuit of the old palindromic run-around of power-and-knowledge we can at least fantasize about what might come after the world-engulfing flames: *In girum imus nocte et consumimur ignI.*

Further Reading/Viewing

On Flavian Rome, see A. J. Boyle and W. J. Dominik, eds., *Flavian Rome: Culture, Image, Text* and A. Zissos, ed., *A Companion to the Flavian*

[63] For Romans, costumes, masks, power, and retrograde bourgeois revolutions, see Marx 1978. Louis Bonaparte's farce stands in stark contrast to the structure of a proletarian revolution (Marx 1978: 106–7).

Age of Imperial Rome. One could also turn to V. Pagán, ed., *A Companion to Tacitus* as well as T. Power and R. Gibson, eds., *Suetonius the Biographer: Studies in Roman Lives*.

Žižek has excellent things to say about power, the unthought, and the unthinkable in *The Sublime Object of Ideology*. For the more lateral-minded, Halberstam's *The Queer Art of Failure* makes for a good primer on how to productively misread popular culture. And there are plenty of film recommendations one could make. The Hollywood noir – a genre to which *The Dark Knight* is very much indebted – frequently ends with cynical recognition: the clever hero comes to appreciate the depth of the depravity of the postwar boom. Revisit Eisenstein's pointedly incomplete trilogy about Ivan the Terrible, especially the orgiastic sequences shot with captured color stock film. Stalin will not let Ivan's story be told because, obviously – or at least this is obvious if you are a Stalinist censor – the story is not just Ivan's, images are never mere images, and this ugly past is not merely the prologue to our glorious present but instead both a denunciation of the present as well as a call to a certain future.

Appendix: Nero's Image: The Four Portrait Types

(notes by Eugenio La Rocca)

The first two portrait types feature a bowl-like "cap" of hair with straight bangs in front, a style derived from earlier iconographic schemes of the Julio-Claudian family, as on portrait busts of Germanicus, the Younger Drusus, and his son, Tiberius Gemellus. On the relief sculpture from the Sabasteion at Aphrodisias, Nero and Britannicus, both very young, have a similar look and sport the same hairstyle, but Nero holds a small globe in his left hand and an *aplustre* in his right to symbolize his power over land and sea. The symbols send a clear signal that rule would soon be assigned to Nero, not to Britannicus, despite the apparent compromise implied by their matching physical features. In another relief sculpture from the Sebasteion, the *princeps*, having just been named emperor, is fashioned at a more advanced age, wearing an anatomically shaped cuirass, but he wears the same "helmet" of hair as he is crowned by his mother, Agrippina, who, as Tyche/Fortuna, holds a cornucopia in her left arm, a symbol of abundance. This implies that it was to his mother that the young prince owed his imperial seat. It is possible – though the idea deserves a study of its own – that between the first two portrait types one might add an intermediary type (evidenced by portrait heads of the Ennetwies Gallery in Zurich and the Fondazione Sorgente in Rome) on which the head of the *princeps* has a style of hair similar to the first type but facial features that are not yet mature.

Only the last two portrait types accentuate the characterizing elements of the face, by rounding and fattening it with a pronounced chin and neck (his neck was "obese," according to Suet. 51.1). These portraits show a degree of iconographic independence from the past that indicates Nero's desire, now that he was fully autonomous, to break free from the schemes of representation adopted up to that time, and to construct a personal image of his own that featured a new style of hair with a row of crescent-curls serving as bangs across the front. The new style is in keeping with two different typologies. One recognizes in it the *coma in gradus formata* (literally "hair formed into steps") that Suetonius

A.1 Type 1 portrait of Nero from the Basilica of Velleia (Museo Nazionale di Antichità, Parma). The statue dates to 50 CE, when the thirteen-year-old Nero was adopted by Claudius, thus to become the presumptive heir to the throne on a par with Britannicus, Claudius' son by Valeria Messalina. For a similar portrait of the same type, cf. Louvre Inv. No. MR 337 (Ma 1210; N 1580).

A.2 Type 2 portrait of Nero (Museo Archeologico Nazionale, Cagliari), from the cast in the Museo della Civiltà Romana, Rome. The portrait dates to 44 CE, when Nero was proclaimed emperor at the age of sixteen.

A.3 Type 3 portrait of Nero (Museo delle Terme, Rome). The portrait dates to 59/60 CE, when the *princeps*, now more than twenty years old and freed of his demanding mother, celebrated the fifth anniversary of his reign.

A.4 Type 4 portrait of Nero (Munich, Glyptothek). The portrait dates to 63 CE, or shortly thereafter, in the aftermath of the celebrations of the Parthian peace accord, an event Romans hailed as the arrival of a new age of peace and prosperity.

found "embarrassing": the crescent-row bangs were made with a curling iron, and in types 3 and 4, they form a "stairway" running sideways across the brow. Some have seen in this hairstyle a reference to the Hellenistic tradition, or to the theater costumes of the Hellenistic age. Nothing of the sort! The crescent-row bangs were a rising fashion in Nero's own day, and by wearing them he wanted to break free from the past and assert his complete autonomy.

Among the most significant portraits of the second type, and again in types 3 and 4, the face is fixed and looks toward the viewer. The intensity of his gaze is underscored by the eyes being set more deeply in larger sockets, and by the fleshy swelling along the outside of the raised brows. By raising his brow so prominently, the emperor appears to "scrutinize" his onlooker. In addition, long sideburns and a light down of facial hair or a scant but actual beard, represented sometimes by raised features on the marble surface, sometimes apparently by paint applied to the surface, cover the sides of his cheeks and the area between his chin and neck.

Such is the image that Nero wanted to present to the world. But what aspects of his representation in the figurative arts are specific to Nero? In essence, apart from the hairstyles that belong to the period (and that thus provide evidence for iconographic changes, but not for the emergence of a personally crafted "style") one finds no innovative peculiarities in the portraits of the period. The forms are in keeping with the Julio-Claudian tradition. A certain accentuation of *chiaroscuro*, especially in portrait sculptures, cannot be considered on its own an authentic revolution of form. In painting and architecture as well, when set against the principate of Claudius, formal innovations are hard to spot. As a result, many monuments cannot be dated with precision.

General Bibliography

AFP Relaxnews. (2015) "Woody Allen Dislikes Own Films, But Won't Retire" (June 25, 2012); www.timeslive.co.za/entertainment/movies/2012/06/25/woody-allen-dislikes-own-films-but-won-t-retire.

Agamben, G. (2005) *State of Exception*. Chicago, IL.

Ahl, F. (1971) "Lucan's *De incendio urbis, Epistulae ex Campania* and Nero's Ban," *Transactions and Proceedings of the American Philological Association* 102: 1–27.

Ahl, F. (1976) *Lucan: An Introduction*. Ithaca, NY, and London.

Albertson, F. (2001) "Zenodorus' Colossus of Nero," *Memoirs of the American Academy in Rome* 46: 95–118.

Alföldy, A. and E. Alföldy. (1976–90) *Die Kontorniat-Medaillons*. Berlin.

Alföldy, G. (1995) "Eine Bauinschrift aus dem Colosseum," *Zeitschrift für Papyrologie* 109: 195–226.

Ambrogi, A. (2011) "Sugli occultamenti antichi di statue. Le testimonianze archeologiche a Roma," *RM* 117: 511–66.

Ameling, W. (2010) "Pliny: The Piety of a Persecutor," in *Myths, Martyrs, and Modernity: Studies in the History of Religions in Honour of Jan N. Bremmer*, eds. J. Dijkstra, J. Kroesen, and Y. Kuiper. Numen Book Series 127, 271–99. Leiden.

Andel, G. K. van (1976) *The Christian Concept of History in the Chronicle of Sulpicius Severus*. Amsterdam.

Anderson, W. S. (1960) "Part versus the Whole in Persius' Fifth Satire," *Philological Quarterly* 39: 66–81.

Anderson, W. S. (1982) *Essays in Roman Satire*. Princeton, NJ.

Ando, C. (2000) *Imperial Ideology and Provincial Loyalty in the Roman Empire*. Berkeley, CA.

André, J.-M. (1987) "Les écoles philosophiques aux deux premiers siècles de l'Empire," *ANRW* II.36.1: 5–77.

Andrew, E. (2004) "The Senecan Moment: Patronage and Philosophy in the Eighteenth Century," *Journal of the History of Ideas* 65.2: 277–99.

Aquinas, T. (1964–1981) *Summa Theologiae*, eds. T. Gilby and T.C. O'Brien. London.

Arminsen-Marchetti (2008) "Imagination and Meditation in Seneca: The Example of *Praemeditatio*," in *Oxford Readings in Classical Studies: Seneca*, ed. J. G. Fitch, 102–23. Oxford.

Armstrong, D. (2011) "Epicurean Virtues, Epicurean Friendship: Cicero vs. the Herculaneum Papyri," in *Epicurus and the Epicurean Tradition*, eds. J. Fish and K. Sanders,105–28. Cambridge.

Armstrong, E. (1954) *Robert Estienne, Royal Printer: An Historical Study of the Elder Stephanus*. Cambridge.

Arnaud-Lindet, M.-P. ed. (1991) *Histoires (Contra les Païens)/Orose.* Collection des Universités de France, latine 297. Vol. III. Paris.

Asbell, W. J., Jr. (1990) "The date of Nero's persecution of the Christians." PhD diss., Vanderbilt University. Nashville, TN.

Ash, R. (1999) *Ordering Anarchy: Armies and Leaders in Tacitus' Histories.* London, Duckworth.

Asmis, E. (2015) "Seneca's Originality," in Bartsch and Schiesaro, *Seneca and the Self,* 224–38.

Asso, P. (2010) Lucan, De Bello Civili, Book IV, edition of the Latin text, English translation, and commentary. Texte und Kommentare, vol. 33. Berlin and New York.

Asso, P. ed. (2011) *Brill's Companion to Lucan.* Leiden and Boston.

Auerbach, E. (1953) *Mimesis.* Princeton, NJ.

Aune, D. E. (1991) "Romans as a *logos protreptikos* in the Context of Ancient Religious and Philosophical Propaganda," in *Paulus und das antike Judentum*, eds. M. Hengel and U. Heckel. WUNT 58, 91–124. Tübingen.

Aygon, J.-P. (2004) *Pictor in fabula. L'ecphrasis-descriptio dans les tragédies de Sénèque.* Brussels.

Baglio, M. (2000) "Seneca e le 'ingannese lusinghe' di Nerone: Zanobi da Strada e la fortuna latina e volgare di Tacito, *Annale. A.* "s XIV 52–56," *Studi Petrarcheschi* n.s. 13: 81–149.

Baglio, M. et al. (1999) "Montecassino e gli umanisti," in *Libro, scrittura, documento della civiltà monastica e conventuale nel Basso Medioevo (secoli XIII–XV)*, eds. G. Avarucci et al., 183–240. Spoleto.

Bakirtzis, C. and H. Koester, eds. (1998) *Philippi at the Time of Paul and after His Death.* Harrisburg, PA.

Baldwin, B. (2005) "Nero the Poet," in *Studies in Latin Literature and Roman History* XII, ed. C. Deroux, 307–18. Brussels.

Ball, L. F. (2003) *The Domus Aurea and the Roman Architectural Revolution.* Cambridge.

Baltussen, H. (2002) "Matricide Revisited: Dramatic and Rhetorical Allusion in Tacitus, Suetonius and Cassius Dio," *Antichthon* 36: 30–40.

Baraz, D. (1998) "Seneca, Ethics and the Body: The Treatment of Cruelty in Medieval Thought," *Journal of the History of Ideas* 59.2: 195–215.

Barchiesi, A. (2001) *Speaking Volumes: Narrative and Intertext in Ovid and Other Latin Poets.* London.

Barchiesi, A. ed. (2005) *Ovidio Metamorfosi*, vol. 1. Milan.

Barchiesi, A. (2008) "Le Cirque du Soleil," in *Le cirque romain et son image*, eds. J. Nelis-Clément and J.-M. Roddaz, 521–37. Bordeaux.

Barchiesi, A. and A. Cucchiarelli (2005) "Satire and the Poet: The Body as Self-Referential Symbol," in *The Cambridge Companion to Roman Satire*, ed. K. Freudenburg, 207–23. Cambridge.

Barclay, J. M. G. (2008) "Is It Good News that God Is Impartial: A Response to Robert Jewett, *Romans: A Commentary*," *JSNT* 31 (2008): 89–111.

Barker, D. (1996) "'The Golden Age Is Proclaimed?': The *Carmen saeculare* and the Renascence of the Golden Race," *Classical Quarterly* 46: 434–46.

Barnes, T. D. (1968) "Legislation against the Christians," *JRS* 58: 32–50.

Barnes, T. D. (1985) *Tertullian: A Historical and Literary Study.* Rev. ed. Oxford.

Barnes, T. D. (2010) *Early Christian Hagiography and Roman History.* Tübingen.

Barr, W. and G. Lee (1987) *The Satires of Persius*. Liverpool.

Barrenechea, F. (2010) "Didactic Aggressions in the Nile Excursus of Lucan's *Bellum Ciuile*," *American Journal of Philology* 131.2: 259–84.

Barrett, A. A. (1996) *Agrippina: Sex, Power, and Politics in the Early Empire*. New Haven, CT.

Barrett, A. A. (2002) *Livia: First Lady of Imperial Rome*. New Haven, CT.

Barthes, R. (1968) "L'effet de réel," *Communications* II: 84–9.

Barthes, R. (1986) "The Reality Effect," in *The Rustle of Language*. 141–8. Oxford.

Bartman, E. (1999) *Portraits of Livia: Imaging the Imperial Woman in Augustan Rome*. Cambridge.

Barton, C. (1993) *The Sorrows of the Ancient Romans*. Princeton, NJ.

Barton, T. (1994) "The *Invention* of Nero: Suetonius," in *Reflections of Nero*, eds. J. Elsner and J. Masters, 48–63. London.

Bartsch, S. (1994) *Actors in the Audience: Theatricality and Doublespeak from Nero to Hadrian*. Cambridge, MA.

Bartsch, S. (1997) *Ideology in Cold Blood. A Reading of Lucan's* Civil War. Cambridge, MA.

Bartsch, S. (2005) "Lucan," in Foley 2005: 492–502.

Bartsch, S. (2006) *The Mirror of the Self: Sexuality, Self-Knowledge, and the Gaze in the Early Roman Empire*. Chicago, IL.

Bartsch, S. (2009) "Senecan Metaphor and Stoic Self-Instruction," in Bartsch and Wray *Seneca and the Self*, 188–217.

Bartsch, S. (2012) "Persius, Juvenal, and Stoicism," in Braund and Osgood 2012: 217–38.

Bartsch, S. (2015a) "Philosophers in Politics." Review essay on J. Romm, *Dying Every Day: Seneca at the Court of Nero*, and Emily Wilson, *The Greatest Empire: A Life of Seneca*, in the *London Review of Books*.

Bartsch, S. (2015b) "Senecan Selves," in *The Cambridge Companion to Seneca*, eds. Bartsch and Schiesaro, 187–98. Cambridge.

Bartsch, S. (2015c) *Persius: A Study in Food, Philosophy, and the Figural*. Chicago, IL.

Bartsch, S. and D. Wray, eds. (2009) *Seneca and the Self*. Cambridge.

Bartsch, S. and A. Schiesaro, eds. (2015) *The Cambridge Companion to Seneca*. Cambridge.

Bastet, F. L. (1971) "Domus Transitoria I," *BABesch* 46: 144–72.

Bastet, F. L. (1972) "Domus Transitoria II," *BABesch* 47: 61–87.

Bastomsky, S. J. (1992) "Tacitus, Annals 14, 64: Octavia's Pathetic Plea," *Latomus* 51: 606–10.

Beard, M. (2008) *Pompeii: The Life of the Roman Town*. London.

Beard, M. (2014a) *Laughter in Ancient Rome: On Joking, Tickling, and Cracking Up*. Berkeley, CA.

Beard. M. (2014b) "How Stoical Was Seneca?" *The New York Review of Books*, October 9 at www.nybooks.com/articles/archives/2014/oct/09/how-stoical-was-seneca/.

Beard, M., J. North, and S. Price (1998) *Religions of Rome I–II: A History*. Cambridge.

Beaujeu, J. (1960) *L'incendie de Rome en 64 et les Chrétiens*. Collection Latomus 49. Brussels.

Beck, R. (1979) "Eumolpus *poeta*, Eumolpus *fabulator*: A Study of Characterization in the *Satyricon*," *Phoenix* 33.3: 239–53.

Benferhat, Y. (2005) *Cives epicurei: les épicuriens et l'idée de monarchie à Rome et en Italie de Sylla à Octave*. Brussels.

Benke, L and T. Grüll (2011) "A Hebrew/Aramaic Graffito and Poppaea's Alleged Jewish Sympathy," *JJS* 62: 37–55.
Benko, S. (1984) *Pagan Rome and the Early Christians*. Bloomington, IN.
Berg, C. S. van den (2014) *The World of Tacitus'* Dialogus de Oratoribus. Cambridge.
Bergmann, M. (1994) *Der Koloss Neros, die Domus Aurea und die Mentalitätswandel im Rom der fruhen Kaiserzeit, 13. Trierer Winckelmannsprogramm 1993*. Mainz am Rhein.
Bergmann, M. (1998) *Die Strahlen der Herrscher. Theomorphes Herrscherbild und politische Symbolik im Hellenismus und in der römischen Kaiserzeit*. Mainz am Rhein.
Bergmann, M. (2013) "Portraits of an Emperor: Nero, the Sun, and Roman *Otium*," in *A Companion to the Neronian Age*, eds. Buckley and Dinter, 332–62.
Bergmann, M. and P. Zanker (1981) "Damnatio memoriae. Umgearbeitete Nero- und Domitiansporträts. Zur Ikonographie der flavischen Kaiser und des Nerva," *JdI* 96: 317–412.
Berno, F. R., ed. (2006) *Seneca Lettere a Lucilio, libro VI, le lettere 53–57*. Bologna.
Beste, H.-J. (2011a) "La Domus Transitoria: un' ipotesi di collocazione," in *Nerone*, eds. M. Tomei and R. Rea, 152–5. Milan.
Beste, H.-J. (2011b) "Domus Aurea, il padiglione dell'Oppio," in *Nerone*, eds. M. Tomei and R. Rea, 170–5. Milan.
Beste, H.-J. and H. von Hesberg (2013) "Buildings of an Emperor – How Nero Transformed Rome," in *A Companion to the Neronian Age*, eds. Buckley and Dinter, 314–31.
Betz, H. D. (2013) *Der Apostel Paulus in Rom*. Berlin.
Betz, H. D. (2015) *Studies in Paul's Letter to the Philippians*. WUNT 343. Tubingen.
Billanovich, G. (1996) *Petrarca e il primo umanesimo*. Padua.
Bingham, S. (2013) *The Praetorian Guard: A History of Rome's Elite Special Forces*. London.
Bloom, H. (1973) *The Anxiety of Influence*. Oxford.
Bloomer, M. (1997) *Latinity and Literary Society at Rome*. Philadelphia, PA.
Boatwright, M. T. (2008) "Tacitus and the Final Rites of Agrippina: Annals 14,9," *Latomus* 14: 375–93.
Bobbio, A. (1941) "Seneca e la formazione spirituale e culturale del Petrarca," *La Bibliofilia* 43 (1941): 224–92.
Bodel, J. (1994) "Trimalchio's Underworld," in *The Search for the Ancient Novel*, ed. J. Tatum. 237–59. Baltimore, MD.
Bodel, J. (1997) "Monumental Villas and Villa Monuments," *Journal of Roman Archaeology* 10: 5–35.
Bodin, J. (1962) *The Six Bookes of a Commonweale*, ed. K. McRae, tr. R. Knolles [1606]. Cambridge, MA.
Boethius, A. and J. B. Ward Perkins (1970) *Etruscan and Roman Architecture*. Harmondsworth and Baltimore, MD.
Boman, J. (2011) "*Inpulsore Cherestro?* Suetonius' *Divus Claudius* 25.4 in Sources and Manuscripts," *Liber Annuus* 61: 355–76.
Bonner, S. F. (1966) "Lucan and the Declamation Schools," *American Journal of Philology* 87.3: 257–89. Reprinted in Tesoriero 2010: 69–106.
Bonneville, D. A. (1966) *Diderot's* Vie de Sénèque: *A Swan Song Revised*. Gainesville, FL.
Born, H. and K. Stemmer (1996) *Sammlung Axel Guttmann, 5. Damnatio memoriae. Das Berliner Nero-Porträt*. Mainz am Rhein.

Bourdieu, P. (1977) *Outline of a Theory of Practice*. Cambridge.

Bourdieu, P. (1984) *Distinction: A Social Critique of the Judgement of Taste*. Cambridge, MA.

Bourdieu, P. (1988) *Homo Academicus*. Stanford, CA.

Bourdieu, P. and L. J. D. Wacquant (1992) *An Invitation to Reflexive Sociology*. Chicago, IL.

Boyle, A. J., ed. (1983) *Seneca Tragicus: Ramus Essays on Senecan Drama*. Berwick.

Boyle, A. J. ed. (1988) *The Imperial Muse: Ramus Essays on Roman Literature of the Empire. To Juvenal through Ovid*. Berwick.

Boyle, A. J. (1994) *Seneca's Troades*. Leeds.

Boyle, A. J. ed. (1995) *Roman Literature and Ideology: Ramus Essays for J. P Sullivan*. Victoria, Australia.

Boyle, A. J. (1997) *Tragic Seneca: An Essay in the Theatrical Tradition*. New York.

Boyle, A. J. (2014) *Medea/Seneca*. Oxford.

Braden, G. (1985) *Renaissance Tragedy and the Senecan Tradition: Anger's Privilege*. New Haven, CT.

Bradley, K. R. (1978) *Suetonius' Life of Nero: An Historical Commentary*. Collections Latomus 157. Brussels.

Bradley, K. R. (1998) "Introduction," in *Suetonius*, vol. I., tr. J. C. Rolf. LCL. Cambridge, MA: 1–34.

Bradley, M. (2011) "Obesity, Corpulence and Emaciation in Roman Art," *Papers of the British School at Rome* 79: 1–41.

Bragantini, I. (2011) "La pittura di età neroniana," in *Nerone*, eds. M. Tomei and R. Rea, 190–201. Milan.

Bramble, J. C. (1974) *Persius and the Programmatic Satire*. Cambridge.

Bramble, J. C. (1982a) "Minor Figures," in Kenney and Clausen 1982: 467–94.

Bramble, J. C. (1982b) "Lucan," in Kenney and Clausen 1982: 533–57.

Brändle, R. and E. W. Stegemann (1998) "The Formation of the First 'Christian Congregations' at Rome in the Context of the Jewish Congregations," in Donfried and Richardson 1998: 117–27.

Braund, D. (2013) "Apollo in Arms: Nero at the Frontier," in *A Companion to the Neronian Age*, eds. Buckley and Dinter, 83–101.

Braund, S. (1992) *Lucan, Civil War*. Oxford.

Braund, S. (2006) "A Tale of Two Cities: Statius, Thebes and Rome," *Phoenix* 60: 259–73.

Braund, S. ed. (2009) *Seneca: de Clementia*. Oxford.

Braund, S. (2013) "Haunted by Horror: The Ghost of Seneca in Renaissance Drama," in *A Companion to the Neronian Age*, eds. Buckley and Dinter, 425–43.

Braund, S. and J. Osgood (2012) *A Companion to Persius and Juvenal*. Chichester.

Bravi, A. (2009) "Immagini adeguate: opere d'arte greche nel *Templum Pacis*," in *Divus Vespasianus. Il biemillenario dei Flavi*, ed. F. Coarelli, 176–83. Milan.

Bridger, C. and K. Kraus (2000) "Römische Gräber in Xanten, Viktorstrasse 21," *Bonner Jahrbücher* 200: 25–81.

Brink, C. O. (1989) "Quintilian's *De Causis Corruptae Eloquentiae* and Tacitus' *Dialogus De Oratoribus*," *Classical Quarterly* 39: 472–503.

Brown, F. E. (1958) "Roman Architecture," *College Art Journal*, 17: 105–14.

Brownlow, K. (1975) *The Parade's Gone By* .... Corrected rpt. Berkeley.

Bruni, L. (1968) *Laudatio Florentinae Urbis in From Petrarch to Leonardo Bruni*, ed. H. Baron, 232–63. Chicago.

Bruni, L. (1999) *Constitutionum Regni Siciliarum libri III*, vol. I. Ed. A. Romano. Catanzaro.

Bruni, L. (2001) *History of the Florentine People*, 3 vols., tr. J. Hankins. Cambridge, MA.

Brunt, P. A. (1975) "Stoicism and the Principate." *Papers of the British School at Rome* 43: 7–35

Brunt, P. A. (1990, first ed. 1961) *Roman Imperial Themes*. Oxford.

Bryan, J. (2013) "Neronian Philosophy," in *A Companion to the Neronian Age*, eds. Buckley and Dinter,134–48.

Buckley, E. (2013a) "Senecan Tragedy," in *A Companion to the Neronian Age*, eds. Buckley and Dinter,204–24.

Buckley, E. (2013b) "Nero *Insitiuus*: Constructing Neronian Identity in the Pseudo-Senecan Octavia," in *The Julio-Claudian Succession: Reality and Perception of the Augustan Model*, ed. A. G. G. Gibson, 133–54. Leiden.

Buckley, E. and M. T. Dinter (2013) *A Companion to the Neronian Age. Chichester*, Malden, and Oxford.

Buren, A. W. van (1953) "Pompeii-Nero-Poppaea," in G. E. Mylonas and D. Raymond, *Studies Presented to D. M. Robinson on His Seventieth Birthday*. St Louis: II. 970–4.

Burke, P. (1991) "Tacitism, Scepticism and Reason of State," in *The Cambridge History of Political Thought, 1450–1700*, ed. J. H. Burns with M. Goldie, 479–98. Cambridge.

Burke, P. (1992) *The Fabrication of Louis XIV*. New Haven, CT.

Burrow, C. (2013) *Shakespeare and Classical Antiquity*. Oxford.

Cadario, M. (2011) "Nerone e il 'potere delle immagini,'" in *Nerone*, eds. M. Tomei and R. Rea, 176–89.

Cadbury, H. J. (1933) "Roman Law and the Trial of Paul," in *The Beginnings of Christianity; Part I: The Acts of the Apostles*, eds. F. J. Foakes-Jackson and K. Lake; Vol. V: *Additional Notes to the Commentary*, eds. K. Lake and H. J. Cadbury, 297–338. London.

Carandini, A. (2010) *Le case del potere nell'antica Roma*. Rome.

Carandini, A. and E. Papi eds. (1999) *Palatium e Sacra Via II. L'età tardo-repubblicana e la prima età imperiale (fine III secolo a.C–64 d.C.)*. Rome.

Carandini, A., D. Bruno, and F. Fraioli (2011) "Gli atri odiosi di un re crudele," *in Nerone*, eds. M. Tomei and R. Rea, 136–51. Milan.

Cardano, G. (1663) *Encomium Neronis* in Cardano, *Opera omnia*, ed. C. Spon. 10 vols. I:179–220. Lyons.

Cardano, G. (1994) *Cardanos Encomium Neronis*, ed. N. Eberl. Frankfurt.

Cardano, G. (1998) *Elogio di Nerone*, ed. P. Cigada. Milan.

Cardano, G. (2008) *Elogio di Nerone*, ed. M. di Branco. Rome.

Carey, S. (2002) "A Tradition of Adventures in the Imperial Grotto," *Greece and Rome* 49: 44–61.

Carey, S. (2004) *Pliny's Catalogue of Culture. Art and Empire in the Natural History*. Oxford.

Carradice, I. A. and T. V. Buttrey (2007) *The Roman Imperial Coinage*. Volume II, part 1. Second fully revised edition. London.

Carré, R. (1999) "Othon et Vitellius, deux nouveaux Néron?" in *Neronia V. Néron: histoire et légende (Collection Latomus 247)*, eds. J. M. Corisille, R. Martin, and Y. Perrin, 152–81. Brussels.

Caruso, G. (1999) "Thermae Titi, Titianae," in *Lexicon Topographicum Urbis Romae* 5 ed. E. M. Steinby, 66–7. Rome.

Casali, S. (2011) "The *Bellum Civile* as an Anti-*Aeneid*," in Asso 2011: 81–110.

Champlin, E. (1998) "God and Man in the Golden House," in *Horti romani. Atti del convegno internazionale, Roma 4–6 maggio 1995*, eds. M. Cima and E. La Rocca, 333–44. Rome.

Champlin, E. (2003a) *Nero*. Cambridge, MA.

Champlin, E. (2003b) "Nero, Apollo, and the Poets," *Phoenix* 57: 276–83.

Chilver, G. E. F. (1979) *A Historical Commentary on Tacitus' Histories I and II*. Oxford.

Citti, F. (2015) "Seneca and the Moderns," in *The Cambridge Companion to Seneca*, eds. S. Bartsch and A. Schiesaro. 303–17. Cambridge.

Cizek, E. (1972) *L'Époque de Néron et ses controverses idéologiques*. Paris.

Cizek, E. (1977) Structure et Idéologie dans *Les Vies des douze* Césars de Suétone. Paris.

Clarke, G. W. (1996) "The Origins and Spread of Christianity," in *CAH*[2], 848–72.

Clarke, J. R. (1991) *The Houses of Roman Italy, 100 B.C.–A.D. 250: Ritual, Space, and Decoration*. Berkeley and Oxford.

Clay, C. L. (1982) "Die Münzprägung des Kaisers Nero in Rom und Lugdunum 1. Die Edelmetallprägung der Jahre 54–64 n. Chr.," *Numismatische Zeitschrift* 96: 7–52.

Coarelli, F. (1999) "*Pax, Templum*," in *Lexicon Topographicum Urbis Romae* 4, ed. E. M. Steinby, 67–70. Rome.

Coarelli, F. (2009) *Divus Vespasianus. Il bimillenario dei Flavi*. Milan.

Colebrook, C. (2004) *Irony (the New Critical Idiom)*. London.

Coleman, K. M. (1990) "Fatal Charades: Roman Executions Staged as Mythological Enactments," *The Journal of Roman Studies* 80: 44–73.

Coleman, K. M. (2006) *M. Valerii Martialis Liber Spectaculorum*. Oxford.

Colini, A. M. (1975–6) "La tomba di Nerone," *Colloqui del Sodalizio tra Studiosi dell'Arte* 5: 35–40.

Collins, A. Y. (1976) *The Combat Myth in the Book of Revelation*. HDR 9. Missoula, MT.

Collins, J. J. (1974) *The Sibylline Oracles of Egyptian Judaism (Society of Biblical Literature Dissertation Series 13), 80–87*. Missoula, MT.

Collins, J. J. (1998) *The Apocalyptic Imagination: An Introduction to Jewish Apocalyptic Literature*. 2nd ed. Grand Rapids, MI.

Connor, P. (1988) "The Satires of Persius: A Stretch of the Imagination," in Boyle 1988: 55–77.

Connors, C. (1998) *Petronius the Poet. Verse and Literary Tradition in the Satyricon*. Cambridge.

Conroy, W. T., Jr. (1975) *Diderot's* Essai sur Sénèque. Banbury.

Conte, G. B. (1996) *The Hidden Author: An Interpretation of Petronius' Satyricon*. Berkeley, CA.

Copjec, J. (1994) *Read My Desire: Lacan Against the Historicists*. Cambridge, MA.

Corsaro, A. (2014) "La decorazione scultorea e pittorica del *templum Pacis*," in *La Biblioteca Infinita. I luoghi del sapere nel mondo antico*, eds. R. Meneghini and R. Rea, 317–26. Milan.

Cottier, M. et al. eds. (2008) *The Customs Law of Asia*. Oxford.

Courtney, E. ed. (1993) *The Fragmentary Latin Poets*. Oxford.

Courtney, E. (2001) *A Companion to Petronius*. Oxford.

Coxe, A. C. (1993) *Latin Christianity: Its Founder, Tertullian*. The Ante-Nicene Fathers. Vol. III. Grand Rapids, MI.

Creed, J. L (ed. and tr.) (1984) *De Mortibus Persecutorum/Lactantius*. Oxford.

Critchley, S. (2002) *On Humor*. London and New York.

Croisille, J.-M. (1982) *Poésie et art figuré de Néron aux Flaviens. Recherches sur l'iconographie et la correspondance des arts à l'époque impériale.* Brussels.
Croisille, J.-M. (1994) *Néron a tué Agrippine.* Brussels.
Cucchiarelli, A. (1999) "Mimo e mimesi culinaria nella *Cena di Trimalchione* (con un'esegesi di *Satyr.* 70)," *Rheinisches Museum* 142: 176–88.
Cucchiarelli, A. (2005) "Speaking from Silence: The Stoic Paradoxes of Persius," in *The Cambridge Companion to Roman Satire,* ed. K. Freudenburg, 62–80.
Cugusi, P. (2008) "Poesia 'ufficiale' e poesia 'epigrafica' nei graffiti dei centri vesuviani. In appendice alcuni nuovi carmi epigrafici pompeiani," *Studia Philologica Valentina* 11: 43–102.
Curtius, L. (1963) "Der geschichtliche Charakter Roms," in L. Curtius and A. Nawrath, *Das antike Rom.* 3rd ed. rev. by E. Nash, 7–32. Originally 1944. Rpt. 1970. Vienna and Munich.
D'Alessandro, F. (2007) *Petrarca e i moderni da Machiavelli a Carducci.* Florence.
D'Alessandro Behr, F. (2007) *Feeling History: Lucan, Stoicism, and the Poetics of Passion.* Columbus, OH.
Dacos, N. (1968) "Fabullus et l'autre peintre de la Domus Aurea," *DdA* 2: 210–26.
Dacos, N. (1969) *La découverte de la Domus Aurea et la formation des grotesques à la Renaissance.* London.
Damschen, G. and A. Heil eds. (2014) *Brill's Companion to Seneca, Philosopher and Dramatist.* Leiden.
Dando-Collins, S. (2010) *The Great Fire of Nero: The Fall of the Emperor Nero and His City.* Philadelphia, PA.
Darwall-Smith, R. H. (1996) *Emperors and Architecture.* Brussels.
Das, A. A. (2003) *Paul and the Jews.* Peabody, MA.
Das, A. A. (2007) *Solving the Romans Debate.* Minneapolis, MN.
Davies, P. J. E. (2000) "'What Worse than Nero, What Better than His Baths?' *Damnatio memoriae* and Roman Architecture," in *From Caligula to Constantine: Tyranny and Transformation in Roman Portraiture,* ed. E. R. Varner, 27–44. Emory, GA.
Davis, G. (1991) *Polyhymnia: The Rhetoric of Horatian Lyric Discourse.* Berkeley, CA.
Dawson, A. (1968) "Whatever Happened to Lady Agrippina?" *Classical Journal* 64: 253–67.
Dawson, D. (1992) *Cities of the Gods: Communist Utopias in Greek Thought.* Oxford and New York.
Day, H. J. M. (2013) *Lucan and the Sublime: Power, Representation and Aesthetic Experience.* Cambridge.
De Caro, S. (1996) "Le ville residenziali," in *Pompei: Abitare sotto il Vesuvio,* eds. M. Boriello, A. d'Ambrosio, S. de Caro, and P. G. Guzo, 20–27. Ferrara.
De Jong, J. and O. Hekster (2008) "Damnation, Deification, Commemoration," in *Un Discours en Images de la Condamnation de la Mémoire. Centre Régional Universitaire Lorrain D'Histoire Site de Metz,* eds. S. Benoist and A. Daguet-Gagey, 79–96. Metz.
De Ruyt, C. (1983) *Macellum: Marché alimentaire des Romains.* Luvain.
Degl'Innocenti Pierini, R. (2008) *Il parto dell'orsa. Studi su Virgilio, Ovidio e Seneca.* Bologna.
Della Corte, F. (1967) *Suetonio eques Romanus.* Florence.
Derrida, J. (1994) *Specters of Marx: The State of the Debt, the Work of Mourning, and the New International.* New York.

Dessen, C. (1968/1996) *Iunctura Callidus Acri: A Study of Persius' Satires*. Illinois Studies in Language and Literature 59. London. 2nd ed., 1996, Bristol.

Devilliers, O. (1999) "Le conjuration de Pison dans les Annales de Tacite (XV, 48–75): quelques aspects," in *Neronia V*, eds. J.-M. Croisille, R. Martin, and Y. Perrin, 45–65. Brussels.

Devilliers, O. (2007) "Néron et les spectacles d'après les *Annales* de Tacite," in *Neronia VII*, ed. Y. Perrin, 271–84. Brussels.

Di Branco, M. (1996) "L'eroe greco e il paradigma del tiranno. Alle radici del mito di Nerone," *Metis* 11: 101–22.

Dick, B. F. (1967) "*Fatum* and *fortuna* in Lucan's *Bellum Ciuile*," *Classical Philology* 62.4: 235–42.

Diderot, D. (1989) *Satire Première*, "Sur les caractères." Diderot, *Œuvres complètes* [Édition critique et annotée publiée sous la direction de Herbert Dieckmann, Jean Fabre et Jacques Proust; avec les soins de Jean Varloot], 1975–. Vol. 12. Paris.

Diderot, D. (1994) *Essai sur les règnes de Claude et de Néron* in Diderot, *Oeuvres*, edited by Laurent Versini, 1994–7, Vol. 1 (Philosophie). Paris.

Diderot, D. (1995a) *Mélanges pour Catherine II*, in Diderot, ed. Versini, *Oeuvres*, vol. 3 (Politique).

Diderot, D. (1995b) *Observations sur le Nakaz*, in Diderot, ed. Versini, *Oeuvres*, vol. 3 (Politique).

Diderot, D. (1995c) *Ruines et paysages. Salon de 1767*, ed. Else Marie Bukdahl et al. Paris.

Diderot, D. (1997) *Correspondance*, in Diderot, *Oeuvres*, 5 vols., edited by Laurent Versini, 1994–7, Vol. 5 (*Correspondance*). Paris.

Diderot, D. (2011) *Pensées détachées, ou: Fragments politiques échappés du portefeuille d'un philosophe*, ed. Gianluigi Goggi. Paris.

Diller, A. (1961) "The Greek Codices of Palla Strozzi and Guarino Veronese," *Journal of the Warburg and Courtauld Institutes* 24: 313–21.

Diller, A. (1963) "The Library of Francesco and Ermolao Barbaro," *Italia medioevale e umanistica* 6: 253–62.

Dinter, M. T. (2012a) *Anatomizing Civil War: Studies in Lucan's Epic Technique*. Ann Arbor, MI.

Dinter, M. T. (2012b) "The Life and Times of Persius: The Neronian Literary Renaissance," in *A Companion to Juvenal and Persius*, eds. Braund and Osgood, 41–58.

Dinter, M. T. (2013) "Introduction: The Neronian (Literary) 'Renaissance,'" in *A Companion to the Neronian Age*, eds. E. Buckley and M. T. Dinter, 1–16. Chichester.

Dominik, W. J., J. Garthwaite, and P. A. Roche (2009) *Writing Politics in Imperial Rome*. Leiden.

Donfried, K. P. (1991) *The Romans Debate*. Rev. ed. Peabody, MA.

Donfried, K. R. and P. Richardson eds. (1998) *Judaism and Christianity in First-Century Rome*. Grand Rapids, MI.

Doody, A. (2007) "Virgil the Farmer? Critiques of the *Georgics* in Columella and Pliny," *Classical Philology* 102: 180–97.

Dotti, U. (2006) *Petrarca a Parma*. Reggio Emilia.

Dowling, M. B. (2006) *Clemency and Cruelty in the Roman World*. Ann Arbor, MI.

Drexler, H. (1939) *Tacitus. Grundzüge einer politischen Pathologie*. Frankfurt.

Drinkwater, J. (2013) "Nero Caesar and the Half-Baked Principate," in *The Julio-Claudian Succession: Reality and Perception of the "Augustan Model,"* ed. A. Gibson, 155–73. Leiden.

Ducos, M. (2006) "Pouvoir et cruauté dans les Annales de Tacite," in *Aere perennius. Hommages à Hubert Zehnacker*, eds. J. Champeaux and M. Chassignet. Paris: 395–415.

Dulac, G. (1986) "Le discours politique de Pétersbourg," *Recherches sur Diderot et sur l'Encyclopédie* 1, Oct: 32–58.

Dulac, G. (1991) "Politique, littérature, mystification: échec à Rulhière," *Dix-huitième siècle* 23: 213–22.

Dumont, H. (2009) *L'antiquité au cinéma: Vérités, légendes et manipulations.* Paris and Lausanne.

Dunbabin, K. M. D. (1999) *Mosaics of the Greek and Roman World.* Cambridge.

Duncan, A. (2006) *Performance and Identity in the Classical World.* Cambridge.

Duncan-Jones, R. P. (1994) *Money and Government in the Roman Empire.* Cambridge.

Dunkle, J. R. (1971) "The Rhetorical Tyrant in Roman Historiography: Sallust, Livy, and Tacitus," *CW* 65: 12–19.

Dunn, J. D. G. (1988) *Romans.* 2 vols. Word Biblical Commentary 38a–b. Dallas, TX.

Dupont, F. (1986) *L'Acteur roi.* Paris.

Duret, L. (1983) "Dans l'ombre des plus grands: I. Poètes et prosateurs mal connus de l'époque augustéenne," *Aufstieg und Niedergang der römischen Welt II*.30.3: 1447–1560.

Dyson S. (2010) *Rome: A Living Portrait of an Ancient City.* Baltimore, MD.

Eastman, P. (2011) *Paul the Martyr: The Cult of the Apostle in the Latin West. SBL Writings from the Greco-Roman World, Suppl. Ser. 4.* Atlanta, GA.

Eberl, N. (1999) "Cardan's *Encomium Neronis,*" in *Neronia V: Néron: histoire et légende*, eds. J. Croisille, R. Martin, and Y. Perrin, 227–38. Brussels.

Eck, W. (1991) "La riforma dei gruppi dirigenti: L'ordine senatore e l'ordine equestre," in *Storia di Roma Vol. 2.II: I principi e il mondo*, eds. G. Clemente, F. Coarelli, and E. Gabba, 73–118. Torino.

Eck, W. (1993) *Agrippina, die Stadtgründerin Kölns: Eine Frau in der frühkaiserzeitlichen Politik.* Cologne.

Eck, W. (1995) "Domus: Africanus," in *Lexicon Topographicum Urbis Romae* 2, ed. E. M. Steinby, 27. Rome.

Eck, W. (2000) "Government and Civil Administration," in *The Cambridge Ancient History*, eds. A. K. Bowman et al.195–292. Cambridge.

Eck, W. (2002) "Die Vernichtung der memoria Neros: Inschriften der neronischen Zeit aus Rom," in *Neronia VI. Rome à l'époque néronienne: institutions et vie politique, économie et société, vie intellectuelle, artistique et spirituelle (Collection Latomus 268)*, eds. J. M. Croisille and Y. Perrin, 285–95. Brussels.

Edelstein, D. (2009) *The Terror of Natural Right: Republicanism, the Cult of Nature, and the French Revolution.* Chicago, IL.

Edwards, C. (1993) *The Politics of Immorality in Ancient Rome.* Cambridge.

Edwards, C. (1994) "Beware of Imitations: Theatre and the Subversion of Imperial Identity," in *Reflections of Nero*, eds. J. Elsner and J. Masters, 83–97.

Edwards, C. (1997a) "Self-Scrutiny and Self-Transformation in Seneca's Letters," *G&R* 44: 23–38.

Edwards, C. (1997b) "Unspeakable Professions: Public Performance and Prostitution in Ancient Rome," in *Roman Sexualities*, eds. J. P. Hallett and M. B. Skinner, 66–98.

Edwards, C. (2007) *Death in Ancient Rome*. New Haven, CT.

Edwards, C. (2008) "Self-Scrutiny and Self-Transformation in Seneca's Letters," in Fitch ed. 84–101 [first published *in Greece & Rome* 44 (1997): 23–38]

Edwards, C. Forthcoming. "On not Being in Rome: Exile and Displacement in Seneca's Prose," in *The Production of Space in Latin Literature*, eds. W. Fitzgerald and E. Spentzou. Oxford.

Ehrman, B. D. (2016) *The New Testament: A Historical Introduction to the Early Christian Writings*. 6th ed. New York.

Ehrman, B. D. (2013) *Forgery and Counterforgery: The Use of Literary Deceit in Early Christian Polemics*. New York.

Elbern, S. (2011) "Täterin oder Opfer?: Agrippina minor," *AW* 1: 19–23.

Elliott, J. K. (1993) *The Apocryphal New Testament*. Oxford.

Elsner, J. (1994) "Constructing Decadence: The Representation of Nero as Imperial Builder," in *Reflections of Nero: Culture, History, & Representation*, eds. Elsner and Masters, 112–27.

Elsner, J. (2004) "Review of E. W. Leach, *The Social Life of Painting in Ancient Rome and on the Bay of Naples, Cambridge* 2004," *BMCR* 2004.12.33: 1–5.

Elsner, J. and J. Masters eds. (1994) *Reflections of Nero: Culture, History, and Representation*. Cambridge and Chapel Hill, NC.

Engberg, J. (2007) *Impulsore Chresto: Opposition to Christianity in the Roman Empire c. 50–250 AD*. Frankfurt am Main.

Ensoli, S. (2000) "I colossi di bronzo a Roma in età tardoantica. Dal colosso di Nerone al colosso di Costantino. A proposito dei tre frammenti bronzei dei Musei Capitolini," in *Aurea Roma. Dalla città pagana alla città cristiana*, eds. S. Ensoli and E. La Rocca, 66–90. Rome.

Erasmo, M. (2004) *Roman Tragedy: Theatre to Theatricality*. Austin, TX.

Erler, M. (2009) "Epicureanism in the Roman Empire," in *The Cambridge Companion to Epicureanism*, ed. J. Warren,46–64. Cambridge.

Eyman, S. (2010) *Empire of Dreams: The Epic Life of Cecil B. DeMille*. New York. Rpt. 2013.

Fabbrini, L. (1983) "Domus Aurea. Una nuova lettura planimetrica del palazzo sul colle Oppio," in *Città e architettura nella Roma imperiale, Atti del seminario del 27 ottobre 1981 nel 25° anniversario dell'Accademia di Danimarca, Anal. Rom. Inst. Dan. Suppl. X*, ed. K. De Fine Licht, 169–85. Odense.

Fabia, P. (1901) "La Préface des *Histoires* de Tacite," *Revue des Études Anciennes* 3, 41–76.

Fantham, E. (1982) *Seneca's* Troades: *A Literary Commentary*. Princeton, NJ.

Fantham, E. ed. (1992) *Lucan: De Bello Ciuili, Book II*. Cambridge Greek and Latin Classics. Cambridge.

Fantham, E. (1996) *Roman Literary Culture*. London.

Fantham, E. (1998–1989) "Mime: The Missing Link in Roman Literary History," *CW* 82: 153–63.

Fantham, E. et al., eds. (1995) *Women in the Classical World*. Oxford.

Fantham, E. (2011) "A Controversial Life," in Asso 2011: 3–31.

Fantham, E. (2013) "The Performing Prince," in *A Companion to the Neronian Age*, eds. Buckley and Dinter, 17–28.

Farrell, J. and D. P. Nelis eds. (2013) *Augustan Poetry and the Roman Republic*. Oxford.

Favro, D. G. (1996) *The Urban Image of Augustan Rome*. Cambridge.

Fear, A. T. (tr.) (2010) *Seven Books of History against the Pagans / Orosius*, with tr. and notes. Vol. III. Liverpool.

Feeney, D. C. (1986) "*Stat magni nominis umbra*: Lucan on the Greatness of Pompeius Magnus," *Classical Quarterly* 36.1: 239–43. Reprinted in Tesoriero 2010: 346–54.

Feeney, D. C. (1991) *The Gods in Epic: Poets and Critics of the Classical Tradition*. Oxford.

Feeney, D. C. (2012) "Representation and the Materiality of the Book in Catullus's Polymetrics," in *Catullus: Poems, Books, Readers*, eds. I. M. le M. Du Quesnay and T. Woodman, 29–47. Cambridge.

Feldherr, A. (2010) *Playing Gods: Ovid's Metamorphoses and the Politics of Fiction*. Princeton, NJ.

Ferri, R. (2003) *Octavia: A Play Attributed to Seneca*. Cambridge.

Ferroni, A. M. (2000) "L'Arco di Adriano nel contesto urbano," *in Adriano. Architettura e Progetto* Milan: 149–56.

Filippi, F. (2010) "Le indagini in Campo Marzio Occidentale. Nuovi dati sulla topografia antica il ginnasio di Nerone e 'l'Euripus,'" in *Archeologiua e infrastrutture. Il tracciato fondamentale della linea C della metropolitana di Roma: prime indagini archeologiche* (BArte Special Volume), eds. R. Egidi, F. Filippi, and S. Martone, 39–53. Florence.

Fitch, J. G. (1981) "Sense, Pauses and Relative Dating in Seneca, Sophocles and Shakespeare," *AJPh* 102: 289–307.

Fitch, J. G., ed. (2008) *Oxford Readings in Classical Studies: Seneca*. Oxford.

Fittschen K. and P. Zanker (1985) *Katalog der römischen Porträts in den Capitolinischen Museen und den anderen kommunalen Sammlungen der Stadt Rom* 1. Mainz.

Fittschen K. and P. Zanker (2014) *Katalog der römischen Porträts in den Capitolinischen Museen und den anderen kommunalen Sammlungen der Stadt Rom* 4. Berlin and New York.

Fitzgerald, W. (2007) "The Letter's the Thing (in Pliny, Book 7)," in *Ancient Letters: Classical and Late Antique Epistolography*, eds. R. Morello and A. Morrison, 191–210. Oxford.

Fitzmyer, J. A. (1992) *Romans: A New Translation with Introduction and Commentary*. Anchor Yale Bible Commentaries 33. New Haven, CT.

Fitzmyer, J. A. (1998) *The Acts of the Apostles: A New Translation with Introduction and Commentary*. Anchor Yale Bible Commentaries 31. New Haven, CT.

Flower, H. I. (1996) *Ancestor Masks and Aristocratic Power in Roman Culture*. Oxford.

Flower, H. I. (2006) *The Art of Forgetting. Disgrace and Oblivion in Roman Political*

Foley, J. M. ed. (2005) *A Companion to Ancient Epic*. Malden, MA, and Oxford.

Fowler, D. (1989) "Lucretius and Politics," in *Philosophia Togata I: Essays on Philosophy and Roman Society*, eds. M. Griffin and J. Barnes, 120–50. Oxford.

Fredrick, D. (2003) "Architecture and Surveillance in Flavian Rome," in *Flavian Rome. Culture, Image, Text*, eds. A. J. Boyle and W. J. Dominik, 199–227. Leiden.

Freudenburg, K. (2001) *Satires of Rome: Threatening Poses from Lucilius to Juvenal*. Cambridge.

Freudenburg, K. (2005) *Roman Satire*. Cambridge.

Friedrich, J., W. Pöhlmann, and P. Stuhlmacher (1976) "Zur historischen Situation und Intention von Röm 13, 1–7," *ZTK* 73: 131–66.

Friedrich, W. H. (1938) "Cato, Caesar und Fortuna bei Lucan," *Hermes* 73.4: 391–423. Reprinted as "Cato, Caesar, and Fortune in Lucan," in Tesoriero 2010: 369–410.

Friggeri, R., M. M. Cianetti, and. C. Caruso, eds. (2014) *Terme di Diocleziano. Il chiostro piccolo della certosa di Santa Maria degli Angeli*. Milan.

Frost, W. (1968) "The English Persius: The Golden Age," *Eighteenth Century Studies* 2: 77–101.

Furneaux, H. ed. (1907) *Cornelii Taciti Annalium ab excessu divi Augusti libri* (The *Annals* of Tacitus, with Introduction and Notes) vol. II: Books XI–XVI, 2nd ed. Oxford.

Fürst, A. ed. (2006) *Der apokryphe Briefwechsel zwischen Seneca und Paulus.* Sapere 11. Tübingen.

Fyfe, H. (1983) "An Analysis of Seneca's *Medea*," in *Seneca Tragicus: Ramus Essays on Senecan Drama*, ed. A. J. Boyle, 77–93. Berwick.

Galimberti Biffino, G. (1999) "Le personnage de Néron dans l'*Ottavia* d'Alfieri," *in Neronia V: Néron: histoire et légende*, eds. J. Croisille, R. Martin, and Y. Perrin. Brussels: 253–66.

Galimberti Biffino, G. (2003) "Il *Neronis Encomium* di Cardano: tra apologia e panegirico comparato," in *Gerolamo Cardano nel suo tempo: atti del Convegno, 16–17 novembre 2001, Castello Visconti di San Vito, Somma Lombardo, Varese*, 177–91. Pavia.

Gallivan, P. A. (1974) "Confusion Concerning the Age of Octavia," *Latomus* 33: 116–17.

Galtier, F. (1999) "Néron, personnage tragique," in *Neronia V*, eds. J.-M. Croisille, R. Martin, and Y. Perrin, 66–74. Brussels.

Gamble, H., Jr. (1977) *The Textual History of the Letter to the Romans: A Study in Textual and Literary Criticism.* Studies and Documents 42. Grand Rapids, MI.

Garthwaite, J. and B. Martin (2009) "Visions of Gold: Hopes for the New Age in Calpurnius Siculus' Eclogues," in Dominik, Garthwaite, and Roche, 307–22.

Gascou, J. (1984) *Suétone historien.* Bibliothèque des Écoles françaises d'Athènes et de Rome, 255, Rome.

Gasparri, C. ed. (2009) *Le Sculture Farnese. I ritratti.* Milan.

Gasparri, C. and R. Paris, eds. (2013) *Palazzo Massimo alle Terme. Le Collezioni.* Milan.

Gasparri, C. and M. A. Tomei, eds. (2014) *Museo Palatino. Le Collezioni.* Milan.

Geominy, W. (1997) *Der goldene Nero. Ein Bildnis der Sammlung Axel Guttmann. Begleitheft zur Ausstellung, 6. September bis 7. November 1997. Akademisches Kunstmuseum Antikensammlung der Universität.* Bonn.

George, P. A. (1974) "Petronius and Lucan *De bello ciuili*," *Classical Quarterly* 24.1: 119–33.

Gerald of Wales (2000). *The Topography of Ireland*, tr. T. Forester. Cambridge, Ont.

Ghini, G. (1995) "Gymnasium Neronis," in *Lexicon Topographicum Urbis Romae*, 2nd ed. E. M. Steinby, 374. Rome.

Giardina, A. (2007) "18 luglio 64 d.C. L'incendio di Roma," in *I giorni di Roma [Nove grandi storici raccontano nove giornate cruciali per la storia di Roma e del mondo]*, eds. A. Carandini, L. Canfora, et al., 55–86. Rome.

Giardina, A. (2011) "Nerone o dell'impossibile," in *Nerone*, eds. M. Tomei and R. Rea, 10–25. Milan.

Gibson, R. K. and R. Morello (2012) *Reading the Letters of Pliny the Younger: An Introduction.* Cambridge.

Gill, C. (1988) "Personhood and Personality: The Four-Personae Theory in Cicero's *De Officiis I*," *Oxford Studies in Ancient Philosophy* 6: 169–99.

Gill, C. (2003) "The School in the Roman Imperial Period," in *The Cambridge Companion to the Stoics*, ed. B. Inwood, 33–58. Cambridge.

Gill, C. (2009) "Seneca and Selfhood: Integration and Disintegration," in *Seneca and the Self*, eds. Bartsch and Wray, 65–83. Cambridge.

Ginsburg, J. (2005) *Representing Agrippina: Constructions of Female Power in the Early Roman Empire.* Oxford and Philadelphia, PA.

Giuliano, A. ed. (1979) *Museo Nazionale Romano. Le Sculture* 1.1. Rome.

Giuliano, A. ed. (1989) *I Cammei della Collezione Medicea del Museo Archeologico di Firenze.* Rome.

Goldberg, S. (1996) "The Fall and Rise of Roman Tragedy," *Transactions of the American Philological Association* 126: 265–86.

Goodman, M. (1987) *The Ruling Class of Judaea: The Origins of the Jewish Revolt against Rome A.D. 66–70.* Cambridge.

Goodman, M. (2007) *Rome and Jerusalem: The Clash of Ancient Civilizations.* London.

Gowers, E. (1993) *The Loaded Table: Representations of Food in Latin Literature.* Oxford.

Gowers, E. (1994) "Persius and the Decoction of Nero," in *Reflections of Nero: Culture, History and Representation*, 131–50.

Gowing, A. M. (2005) *Empire and Memory: The Representation of the Roman Republic in Imperial Culture.* Cambridge.

Grafton, A. (1999) *Cardano's Cosmos.* Cambridge, MA.

Grant, M. (1970) *Nero.* London.

Graver, M. (1998) "The Manhandling of Maecenas: Senecan Abstractions of Masculinity," *American Journal of Philology* 119: 607–32.

Graver, M. (2014) "Honeybee Reading and Self-Scripting: *Epistulae Morales* 84," in *Seneca Philosophus: Trends in Classics* 27, eds. Colish and Wildberger, 269–93. Berlin.

Graver, M. and A. A. Long (2015) *Seneca: Letters on Ethics.* Chicago, IL.

Gray-Fow, M. J. G. (1998) "Why the Christians? Nero and the Great Fire," *Latomus* 57: 595–616.

Green, C. M. C. (1991) "*Stimulos dedit aemula uirtus*: Lucan and Homer Reconsidered," *Phoenix* 45.3: 230–54. Reprinted in Tesoriero 2010: 149–83.

Green, L. (1993) "The Image of Tyranny in Early Fourteenth-Century Italian Historical Writing," *Renaissance Studies* 7.4: 335–51.

Greenblatt, S. (1980) *Renaissance Self-Fashioning: From More to Shakespeare.* Chicago.

Griffin, M. T. (2000, 1st ed. 1976) *Seneca: A Philosopher in Politics.* Oxford.

Griffin, M. T. (1984) *Nero. The End of a Dynasty.* London and New Haven, CT.

Griffin, M. T. (1986) "Philosophy, Cato, and Roman Suicide," *G&R* 33: 64–77, 192–202.

Griffin, M. T. (1989) "Philosophy, Politics, and Politicians," in *Philosophia Togata*, eds. M. Griffin and J. Barnes, 1–37. Oxford.

Griffin, M. T. (1999) "Pliny and Tacitus," *Scripta Classica Israelica* 18: 139–58.

Griffin, M. T. (2002) *Néron ou la fin d'une dynastie.* Dijon.

Griffin, M. T. (2008) "Imago Vitae Suae," in *Oxford Readings in Seneca*, ed. J. G. Fitch, 23–58. Oxford.

Griffin, M. T. (2013) *Seneca on Society: A Guide to* De Beneficiis. Oxford.

Gros, P. (1999) "La transfiguration du modèle de la domus dans les palais néroniens de Rome. L'exemple de la suite du nymphée de la Domus Aurea," in *Neronia 6: Rome à l'époque néronienne. Institutions et vie politique, économie et société, vie intellectuelle, artistique et spirituelle, Actes du VIe Colloque international de la Société internationale d'études néroniennes (Rome 19–23 mai 1999)*, 54–73. Brussels.

Groß, D. (2013) *Plenus Litteris Lucanus: Zur Rezeption der horazischen Oden und Epoden in Lucans Bellum Civile.* Rahden/Westf.

Gruen, E. S. (1998) *Heritage and Hellenism.* Berkeley, CA.

Gruen, E. S. (2002) *Diaspora: Jews amidst Greeks and Romans*. Cambridge, MA.

Gruen, E. S. (2011) *Rethinking the Other in Antiquity*. Princeton, NJ.

Grund, G. ed. (2011) *Humanist Tragedies*. Cambridge, MA.

Gualdo, R. (1990) "Sul volgarizzamento della Storia Romana di Dione Cassio di N. Leoniceno," *Studi linguistici italiani*, 16: 223–46.

Gumerlock, F. X. (2006) "Nero Antichrist: Patristic Evidence for the Use of Nero's Naming in Calculating the Number of the Beast (Rev 13:18)," *The Westminster Theological Journal*, 68: 347–60.

Gunderson, E. (2003a) "The Flavian Amphitheatre: All the World as Stage," in *Flavian Rome Culture, Image, Text*, eds. A. J. Boyle and W. J. Dominik, 637–58. Leiden, Brill.

Gunderson, E. (2003b) *Declamation, Paternity, and Roman History: Authority and the Rhetorical Self*. Cambridge.

Gunderson, E. (2014) "E.G. Augustus: *Exemplum* in the *Augustus* and *Tiberius*," in *Suetonius the Biographer: Studies in Roman Lives*, eds. T. Power and R. K. Gibson, 130–45. Oxford.

Gunderson, E. (2015) *The Sublime Seneca: Ethics, Literature, Metaphysics*. Cambridge.

Guze, J. (2008) *Zloty Dom Nerona. Wystawa w 200-lecie smierci Franciszka Smuglewicza, Muzeum Narodowe w Warszawie*. Warsaw.

Gwyn, W. B. (1991) "Cruel Nero: The Concept of the Tyrant and the Image of Nero in Western Political Thought," *History of Political Thought*, 12: 421–55.

Gyles, M. F. (1947) "Nero Fiddled While Rome Burned," *CJ*, 42: 211–17.

Habinek, T. (2000) "Seneca's Renown: *Gloria, claritudo* and the Replication of the Roman Elite," *Classical Antiquity* 19: 264–303.

Habinek, T. (2014) "*Imago suae vitae* Seneca's Life and Career," in Damschen and Heil, eds., 3–31.

Haffter, H. (1957) "Dem schwanken Zünglein lauschend wachte Cäsar dort," *Museum Helveticum* 14.2: 118–26.

Hales, S. (2003) *The Roman House and Social Identity*. Cambridge.

Hanslik, R. (1963) "Der Erzählungskomplex vom Brand Roms und der Christenverfolgung bei Tacitus," *WS* 76: 92–108.

Hardie, P. R. (1990) "Ovid's Theban History: The First Anti-*Aeneid?*," *Classical Quarterly* 40: 224–35.

Hardie, P. R. (1992) "Augustan Poets and the *Mutability of Rome*," in *Roman Poetry and Propaganda in the Age of Augustus*, ed. A. Powell, 59–82. London.

Hardie, P. R. (1993) *The Epic Successors of Virgil: A Study in the Dynamics of a Tradition*. Cambridge.

Hardie, P. R. (2012) *Rumour and Renown: Representations of* Fama *in Western Literature*. Oxford.

Hardie, P. R. (2013) "Lucan's *Bellum Ciuile*," in Buckley and Dinter 2013: 225–40.

Harpham, G. G. (1982) *On the Grotesque: Strategies of Contradiction in Art and Literature*. Princeton, NJ.

Harrill, J. A. (2011) "Paul and Empire: Studying Roman Identity after the Cultural Turn," *Early Christianity* 2: 281–311.

Harrill, J. A. (2012) *Paul the Apostle: His Life and Legacy in Their Roman Context*. Cambridge.

Harrison, J. R. (2011) *Paul and the Imperial Authorities at Thessalonica and Rome: A Study in the Conflict of Ideology*. WUNT 273. Tübingen.

Harvey, R. A (1981) *A Commentary on Persius*. Leiden.

Hasegawa, K. (2005) *The* Familia Urbana *during the Early Empire: A Study of Columbaria Inscriptions*. BAR International Series 1440. Oxford.

Haselberger, L. (2007) *Urbem adornare – Die Stadt Rom und ihre Gestaltumwandlung unter Augustus/Rome's Urban Metamorphosis under Augustus*. Portsmouth.

Häuber, C. (2013) *The Eastern Part of the Mons Oppius in Rome: the Sanctuary of Isis et Serapis in Regio III, the Temples of Minerva Medica, Fortuna Virgo and Dea Syria, and the Horti of Maecenas* (BCAR Suppl. 22). Rome.

Hedrick, C. W. (2000) *History and Silence. The Purge and Rehabilitation of Memory in Late Antiquity*. Austin, TX.

Heinz, K. (1948) "Das Bild Kaiser Neros bei Seneca, Tacitus, Sueton und Cassius Dio: Historisch-philologische Synopsis." Phil. Diss. Bern.

Hekster, O. (2015) *Emperors and Ancestors. Roman Rulers and the Constraints of Tradition*. Oxford.

Hemer, C. J. (1989) *The Book of Acts in the Setting of Hellenistic History*. Ed. C. H. Gempf. WUNT 49. Tübingen.

Henderson, J. (1987) "Lucan/the World at War," *Ramus* 16: 122–64. Reprinted in Tesoriero 2010: 433–91.

Henderson, J. (1989) "Tacitus/the World in Pieces," *Ramus* 18, 167–210.

Henderson, J. (1999) "Learning Persius' Didactic Satire: Teacher as Pupil," in *Writing Down Rome: Satire, Comedy, and other Offences in Latin Poetry*. Oxford.

Henderson, J. (2003) "*Par Operi Sedes*: Mrs. Arthur Strong and Flavian Style: The Arch of Titus and the Cancelleria Reliefs," in *Flavian Rome. Culture, Image, Text*, eds. A. J. Boyle and W. J. Dominik, 229–54. Leiden.

Henderson, J. (2004) *Morals and Villas in Seneca's Letters: Places to Dwell*. Cambridge.

Henderson, J (2014) "Was Suetonius' *Julius* a Caesar?" in *Suetonius the Biographer: Studies in Roman Lives*, eds. Power and Gibson, 81–110.

Henrichs, A. (1970) "Pagan Ritual and the Alleged Crimes of the Early Christians: A Reconsideration," in *Kyriakon. Festschrift Johannes Quasten*, vol. I, eds. P. Granfield and J. A. Jungmann, 18–35. Münster.

Hermary, A. (1986) "Dioskouroi," in *Lexicon Iconographicum Mythologiae Classicae*. 567–93. Zurich and Munich.

Hershkowitz, D. (1998) *The Madness of Epic*. Oxford.

Hesberg, H. v. (2011) "L'attività edilizia a Roma all'epoca di Nerone," in *Nerone*, eds. M, Tomei and R. Rea, 108–17.

Hexter, R. and D. Selden eds. (1992) *Innovations of Antiquity*. New York and London.

Hiesinger, U. W. (1975) "The Portraits of Nero," *American Journal of Archaeology* 79: 113–24.

Highet, G. (1941) "Petronius the Moralist," *TAPA* 72: 176–94.

Hinds, S. (1998) *Allusion and Intertext: Dynamics of Appropriation in Roman Poetry*. Cambridge.

Hinds, S. (2011) "Seneca's Ovidian *Loci*," *Studi Italiani di Filologia Classica* 9: 5–63.

Hine, H. (2006) "Rome, the Cosmos and the Emperor in Seneca's *Natural Questions*," *JRS* 96: 42–72.

Hollis, A. S. ed. (2007) *Fragments of Roman Poetry c. 60 BC–AD 20*. Oxford.

Holztrattner, F. (1995) *Neronis potens, Die Gestalt der Poppaea Sabina in den Nerobüchern des Tacitus. Mit einem Anhang zu Claudia Acte* (Grazer Beiträge: Supplementband 6). Horn.

Hommel, H. (1984) "Tacitus und die Christen," in idem, *Sebasmata: Studien zur antiken Religionsgeschichte und zum frühen Christentum*. WUNT 32, 174–99. Tübingen.

Hooley, Daniel (1997) *The Knotted Thong: Structures of Mimesis in Persius*. Ann Arbor, MI.

Hooley, Daniel (2004) "Persius in the Middle," in Kyriakidis and De Martino, 217–43.

Hooley, Daniel (2007) *Roman Satire*. Malden, MA, and Oxford.

Hopkins, K. (1983) *Death and Renewal*. Cambridge.

Hopkins, K. (1999) *A World Full of Gods: The Strange Triumph of Christianity*. New York.

Hopkins, K. (2009) "The Political Economy of the Roman Empire," in *The Dynamics of Ancient Empires*, eds. I. Morris and W. Scheidel, 178–204. Oxford.

Horsfall, N. (1999) *Virgil, Aeneid 7: A Commentary*. Leiden.

Hosius, C. ed. (1913) *M. Annaei Lucani Belli Ciuilis libri decem*. 3rd ed. Leipzig.

Høtje, J. (2005) *Roman Imperial Statue Bases, from Augustus to Commodus*. Aarhus.

Hume, D. (1983) *The History of England from the Invasion of Julius Caesar to the Revolution in 1688*, vol. 5. Foreword by William B. Todd, 6 vols. Indianapolis, IN.

Iacopi, I. (1999) *Domus Aurea*. Milan.

Inwood, B. (1995) "Politics and Paradox in Seneca's *De beneficiis*," in *Justice and Generosity*, eds. A. Laks and M. Schofield, 241–65. Cambridge.

Inwood, B. (2005) *Reading Seneca: Stoic Philosophy at Rome*. Oxford.

Janssen, L. F. (1979) "Superstition and the Persecution of the Christians," *Vigiliae Christianae* 33: 131–59.

Jenkinson, J. R. (1980) *Persius: The Satires*. Warminster.

Jenks, G. C. (1991) *The Origins and Early Development of the Antichrist Myth*. BZNW 59. Berlin.

Jewett, R. (2007) *Romans: A Commentary*. Ed. E. J. Epp. Hermeneia Commentary Series. Minneapolis, MN.

Johnson, P. (2008) *Ovid before Exile: Art and Punishment in the Metamorphoses*. Madison, WI.

Johnson, W. R. (1987) *Momentary Monsters: Lucan and His Heroes*. Ithaca, NY, and London.

Johnstone, S. (1992) "On the Uses of Arson in Classical Rome," in *Studies in Latin Literature and Roman History VI*, ed. C. Deroux. Collection Latomus 217, 41–69. Brussels.

Jolivet, J.-C. (2013) "Caesar, Lucan, and the Massilian *Marathonomachia*," in *Farrell and Nelis* 2013: 146–60.

Jones, C. P. (2017) "The Historicity of the Neronian Persecution : A Response to Brent Shaw," *New Testament Studies* 63: 146–52.

Jucker, H. (1981) "Iulisch-Claudische Kaiser- und Prinzenporträts als 'Palimseste,'" *Jahrbuch des Deutschen Archäologischen Instituts* 96: 236–316.

Junkelmann, M. (2004) *Hollywoods Traum von Rom: "Gladiator" und die Tradition des Monumentalfilms*. Mainz am Rhein.

Kallendorf, C. W. ed. (2002) *Humanist Educational Treatises*. Cambridge, MA.

Karris, R. J. (1991) "Romans 14:1–15:13 and the Occasion of Romans," in Donfried 1991: 65–84.

Käsemann, E. (1961) "Principles of Interpretation of Romans 13," tr. in Meeks and Fitzgerald 2003: 573–86.

Keane, Catherine. (2012) "Life in the Text: The Corpus of Persius' Satires," in Braund and Osgood 2012: 79–96.

Keegan, P. (2004) "Boudica, Cartimandua, Messalina and Agrippina the Younger: Independent Women of Power and the Gendered Rhetoric of Roman History," *AH* 34: 99–148.

Keegan, P. (2007) "'She is a mass of riddles': Julia Augusta Agrippina and the Sources," *AH* 37: 158–76.

Keitel, E. E. (2010) "'Is Dying so very Terrible?' The Neronian *Annals*," in *The Cambridge Companion to Tacitus*, ed. A. J. Woodman, 127–43.

Keith, A. (2011) "Ovid in Lucan," in Asso: 111–32.

Kelly, H. A. (1979) "Tragedy and the Performance of Tragedy in Late Roman Antiquity," *Traditio* 35: 21–44.

Kennell, N. M. (1988) "ΝΕΡΩΝ ΠΕΡΙΟΔΟΝΙΚΗΣ," *American Journal of Philology* 109: 239–51.

Kenney, E. J. (1970) "*Doctus Lucretius*," *Mnemosyne* 4: 23: 373–80.

Kenney, E. J. and W. V. Clausen eds. (1982) *The Cambridge History of Classical Literature II: Latin Literature*. Cambridge.

Keppie, L. (2011) "'Guess Who's Coming to Dinner': The Murder of Nero's Mother Agrippina in Its Topographical Setting," *G&R* 258: 33–47.

Ker, J. (2006) "Seneca, Man of Many Genres?" in *Seeing Seneca Whole*, eds. Volk and Williams: 19–42.

Ker, J. (2009) *The Deaths of Seneca*. Oxford.

Ker, J. (2015) "Seneca and Augustan Culture," in *The Cambridge Companion to Seneca*, eds. Bartsch and Schiesaro, 109–21. Cambridge.

Keresztes, P. (1984) "Nero, the Christians and the Jews in Tacitus and Clement of Rome," *Latomus* 43: 404–13.

Kissel, T. (2006) "Nero. Ein Künstler auf dem Kaiserthron," *AbenteuerA* Nr. 2: 22–6.

Kissel, W. (1990) *Aules Persius Flaccus Satiren*. Heidelberg.

Klauck, H. J. (2001) "Do They Never Come Back? Nero Redivivus and the Apocalypse of John," *The Catholic Biblical Quarterly* 63.4: 683–98.

Klauck, H. J. (2003) "Do They Come Back? Nero *redivivus* and the Apocalypse of John," in *idem, Religion und Gesellschaft in frühen Christentum: Neutestamentliche Studien*. WUNT 152, 268–89. Tübingen.

Kleiner, D. (1992) *Roman Sculpture*. New Haven, CT.

Kleiner, F. S. (1985) *The Arch of Nero in Rome: A Study of the Roman Honorary Arch Before and Under Nero*. Rome.

Knell, H. (2004) *Bauprogramme römischer Kaiser*. Mainz am Rhein.

Knox, J. (1987) *Chapters in a Life of Paul*. Rev. ed. Macon, GA.

Koch, G. (1995) "Ein römischer Kaiser in Dyrrachium," *RM* 102: 321–6.

Kragelund, P. (2000) "Nero's *luxuria*, in Tacitus and in the *Octavia*," *CQ* 50: 494–515.

Kragelund, P. (2010) "The Temple and Birthplace of Diva Poppaea," *CQ* 60: 559–68.

Krauter, S. (2009) *Studien zu Röm 13,1–7: Paulus und der politische Diskurs der neronischen Zeit*. WUNT 243. Tübingen.

Kreikenbom, D. (1992) *Griechische und römische Kolossal porträts bis zum späten ersten Jahrhunderts nach Christus (JdI-EH)*. Berlin.

Kristensen, T. M. (2013) *Making and Breaking the Gods: Christian Responses to Pagan Sculpture in Late Antiquity (Aarhus Studies in Mediterranean Antiquity)*. Aarhus.

Kümmel, E. G. (1975) *Introduction to the New Testament*. 17th ed. Tr. H. C. Kee. Nashville, TN.

Kyle, D. (1998) *Spectacles of Death in Ancient Rome*. Routledge.

Kyriakidis, S. and F. De Martino eds. (2004) *Middles in Latin Poetry*. Bari.

L'Orange, H. P. (1973) *Likeness and Icon. Selected Studies in Classical and Early Medieval Art*. Odense.

La Rocca, E. (1992) "'Disiecta membra neroniana.' L'arco partico di Nerone sul Campidoglio," in *Kotinos. Festschrift für Erika Simon*, eds. E. Simon, H. Froning, T. Hölscher, and H. Mielsch, 400–14. Mainz am Rhein.

La Rocca, E. (2001) "La Nuova immagine dei Fori Imperiali," *Rämische Mitteilungen* 108: 171–213.

La Rocca, E. (2013) *Augusto*. Milan.

Lamberty, G. (1724–40) *Mémoires pour servir à l'histoire du XVIIIe siècle*, La Haye, 14 vols.; Ferney catalogue B1638, BV1889 (see also http://dictionnaire-journalistes.gazettes18e.fr/journaliste/447-guillaume-de-lamberty).

Lampe, P. (2003) *From Paul to Valentinus: The Christians at Rome in the First Two Centuries*. Tr. M. Steinhauser. Ed. M. D. Johnson. Minneapolis, MN.

Lane, W. L. (1998) "Social Perspectives on Roman Christianity during the Formative Years from Nero to Nerva, Romans, Hebrews, *1 Clement*," in Donfried and Richardson 1998: 196–244.

Lapidge, M. (1979) "Lucan's Imagery of Cosmic Dissolution," *Hermes* 107.3: 344–70. Reprinted in Tesoriero 2010: 289–323.

Larner, J. (1980) *Italy in the Age of Dante and Petrarch*. London.

Lavagne, H. (1970) "Le nymphée au Polypheme de la Domus Aurea," *Mélanges de l'école française de Rome* 82: 673–721.

Lavan, M. (2013) "The Empire in the Age of Nero," in *A Companion to the Neronian Age*, eds. Buckley and Dinter, 65–82. Malden, MA.

Leach, E. W. (2004) *The Social Life of Painting in Ancient Rome and on the Bay of Naples*. Cambridge.

Leach, E. W. (2008) "The Implied Reader and the Political Argument in Seneca's *Apocolocyntosis* and *de Clementia*," in *Seneca*, ed. J. G. Fitch, 264–98. Oxford. First published in *Arethusa* 22 (1989) 197–230.

Leigh, M. (1997) *Lucan: Spectacle and Engagement*. Oxford.

Lepper, F. A. (1957) "Some Reflections on the 'Quinquennium Neronis,'" *JRS* 47: 95–103.

Levick, B. (1983a) "Nero's Quinquennium," in *Studies in Latin Literature and Roman History*, vol. 3; ed. C. Deroux, 211–25. Brussels.

Levick, B. (1983b) "The *Senatus consultum* from Larinum," *JRS* 73: 97–115.

Levick, B. (1990) *Claudius*. New Haven, CT.

Levinskaya, I. (1996) *The Book of Acts in Its Diaspora Setting*. The Book of Acts in Its First Century Setting 5. Grand Rapids, MI.

Lichtenberger, H. (1996) "Jews and Christians in Rome in the time of Nero: Josephus and Paul in Rome," *ANRW* II: 26.3: 2142–76.

Lieberman, W.-L. (2014) "*Medea*," in *Brill's Companion to Seneca: Philosopher and Dramatist. Brill's Companions in Classical Studies*, eds. G. Damschen and A. Heil, 459–74. Boston, MA.

Lietaert Peerbolte, L. T. (1996) *The Antecedents of the Antichrist: A Traditio-historical Study of the Earliest Christian Views on Eschatological Opponents*. Supplements to the *Journal for the Study of Judaism* 49. Leiden.

Lindner, M. (2007) *Rom und seine Kaiser im Historienfilm*. Frankfurt am Main.

Ling, R. (1991) *Roman Painting*. Cambridge.

Ling, R. (2014) "Roman Painting of the Middle and Late Empire," in *The Cambridge History of Painting in the Classical World*, 370–422. Cambridge.

Lintott, A. W. (1971) "Lucan and the History of the Civil War," *Classical Quarterly* 21.2: 488–505. Reprinted in Tesoriero 2010: 239–68.

Lipsius, R. A. ed. (1959) *Acta apostolorum apocrypha*. Vol. I. Darmstadt.

Littlewood, C. A. J. (2002) "Integer Ipse: Self-Knowledge and Self-Representation in Persius Satires 4," *Phoenix* 56: 56–83.

Littlewood, C. A. J. (2015) "Theater and Theatricality in Seneca's World," in *The Cambridge Companion to Seneca*, eds. Bartsch and Schiesaro, 161–73.

Lo Cascio, E. (1981) "State and Coinage in the Late Republic and Early Empire," *Journal of Roman Studies* 71: 76–86.

Lo Monaco, A. (2008) "Il culto di Nerone in Grecia. Immagini e cerimoniale della festa," in *Pathways to Power. Civic Elites in the Eastern Part of the Roman Empire*, in *Proceedings of the International Workshop held at Athens, Scuola archeologica italiana di Atene, 19 December 2005*, eds. A. Rizakis and F. Camia, 43–71. Athens.

Locati, S. (2006) *La rinascita del genere tragico nel medioevo: l'Ecerinis di Albertino Mussato*. Florence.

Locchi, A. (2012) "La vicenda della sepoltura di Nerone: coordinate storiche e risvolti leggendari," in *"Tomba di Nerone": Toponimo, comprensorio e zona urbanistica di Roma Capitale. Scritti tematici in memoria di Gaetano Messineo*, ed. F. Vistoli, 103–22. Rome.

Long, A. A. (2002) *Epictetus. A Stoic and Socratic Guide to Life*. Oxford.

Long, A. (2007) "Lucan and Moral Luck," *Classical Quarterly* 57: 183–97.

Lorenz, K. (2007) "The Ear of the Beholder: Spectator Figures and Narrative Structure in Pompeian Painting," *Art History* 30: 665–82.

Lorenz, K. (2013) "Neronian Wall-Painting: A Matter of Perspective," in *A Companion to the Neronian Age*, eds. Buckley and Dinter, 363–81.

Luck, G. (1972) "On Petronius' *Bellum Ciuile*," *American Journal of Philology* 93: 133–41.

Luedemann, G. (1984) *Paul: Apostle to the Gentiles. Studies in Chronology*. Tr. F. S. Jones. Philadelphia, PA.

Luedemann, G. (1989) *Early Christianity According to Acts: A Commentary*. Tr. J. Bowden. Minneapolis, MN.

Luque-Moreno, J. (1997) "Seneca musicus," in *Séneca dos mil años después, Actas del Congreso Internacional Conmemorativo del Bimilenario de su Nacimiento (Córdoba, 24 a 27 de septiembre de 1996)*, ed. M. Rodriguez Pantoja, 77–115. Córdoba.

Maccoby, H. (1986) *The Mythmaker: Paul and the Invention of Christianity*. San Francisco, CA.

MacDowall, D. W. (1979) *The Western Coinages of Nero*. New York.

Machiavelli, N. (1988) *The Prince*, eds. Q. Skinner and R. Price. Cambridge.

MacMullen, R. (1966) *Enemies of the Roman Order: Treason, Unrest, and Alienation in the Empire*. Cambridge, MA.

MacMullen, R. (1984) *Christianizing the Roman Empire A.D. 100–400*. New Haven, CT.

Maderna, C. (2010) "Die Bildhauerkunst während der Regierungszeit des Nero (54–68 n.Chr.)," in *Die Geschicte der antiken Bildhauerkunst 4. Plastik der römischen Kaiserzeit bis zum Tode Kaiser Hadrians*, eds. D. Kreikenbom, C. Maderna, J. Raeder, P. Schollmeyer, F. Sinn, and M. Söldner, 101–33. Mainz am Rhein.

Madsen, J. M. (2009) *Eager to Be Roman: Greek Response to Roman Rule in Pontus and Bithynia*. London.

Maes, Y. (2005) "Starting Something Huge: Pharsalia I 83–193 and the Virgilian Intertext," in *Lucan im 21. Jahrhundert*, ed. C. Walde, 1–25. Leipzig.

Maes, Y. (2013) "*Haec monstra edidit.* Translating Lucan in the Early Seventeenth Century," in *A Companion to the Neronian Age*, eds. Buckley and Dinter, 405–24.

Maggi, S. (1986) "Il ritratto giovanile di Nerone. Un esempio a Mantova," *RdA* 10: 47–51.

Maier, H. O. (2013) "Nero in Jewish and Christian Tradition from the First Century to the Reformation," in *A Companion to the Neronian Age*, eds. Buckley and Dinter, 385–404.

Malamud, M. (1995) "Happy Birthday, Dead Lucan: (P)raising the Dead in *Siluae* 2.7," *Ramus* 24: 1–30.

Malamud, M. (2009) "Primitive Politics: Lucan and Petronius," in Dominik, Garthwaite, and Roche, 273–306.

Malaspina, E. (2003) "Pensiero politico ed. esperienza storica nelle tragedie di Seneca," in *Sénèque le tragique. Entretiens sur l'Antiquité Classique*, eds. M. Billerbeck and E. A. Schmidt, 67–320. Vandoeuvres-Genève.

Malik, S. (2012) "Ultimate Corruption Manifest: Nero as the Antichrist in Late Antiquity," in *Acta Classica: Proceedings of the Classical Association of South Africa, suppl. 4: Corruption and Integrity in Ancient Greece and Rome*, ed. Philip Bosman, 169–86. Pretoria.

Malitz, J. (2004) "Nero. Der Herrscher als Künstler," in *Mythen Europas. Schlüsselfiguren der Imagination*, eds. A. Hartmann and M. Neumann, 145–64. Regensburg.

Manning, C. E. (1975) "Acting and Nero's Conception of the Principate," *Greece and Rome* 22: 164–75.

Manolaraki, E. (2011) "*Noscendi Nilum Cupido*: The Nile Digression in Book 10," in Asso 2011: 153–82.

Manolaraki, E. (2013) *Noscendi Nilum Cupido: Imagining Egypt from Lucan to Philostratus*. Berlin and Boston, MA.

Manuwald, G. (2013) *Nero in Opera: Librettos as Transformations of Ancient Sources*. Berlin.

Marchesi, I. (2008) *The Arts of Pliny's Letters: A Poetics of Allusion in the Private Correspondence*. Cambridge.

Marigliani, C. (2012) *Caligola e Nerone. Vicende e opere dei due imperatori di Anzio*. Rome.

Marin, E. (2001) "The Temple of the Imperial Cult (Augusteum) at Narona and Its Statues: Interim Report," *Journal of Roman Archaeology* 14: 81–112.

Marincola, J. (1997) *Authority and Tradition in Ancient Historiography*. Cambridge.

Marlowe, E. (2006) "Framing the Sun: The Arch of Constantine and the Roman Cityscape," *The Art Bulletin* 88: 223–42.

Marshall, C. W. (2014) "The Works of Seneca the Younger and Their Dates," in *Brill's Companion to Seneca: Philosopher and Dramatist*, eds. G. Damschen and A. Heil, 33–44. Leiden.

Martellotti, G. (1972) "La questione dei due Seneca da Petrarca a Benvenuto da Imola," *Italia medioevale e umanistica* 15: 149–69.

Marti, B. M. (1945) "The Meaning of the *Pharsalia*," *American Journal of Philology* 66.4: 352–76.

Martin, J. M. K (1939) "Persius – Poet of the Stoics," *G&R* 8.24: 172–82.

Martin, R. (1999) "Les récits tacitéens des crimes de Néron sont-ils fiables?" in *Neronia V*, eds. J.-M. Croisille, R. Martin, and Y. Perrin, 75–85. Brussels.

Martin, R. F. (1991) *Les Douze Césars*. Paris.

Martindale, C. (1993) *Redeeming the Text: Latin Poetry and the Hermeneutics of Reception*. Cambridge.

Marx, K. (1978) "The Eighteenth Brumaire of Louis Bonaparte," in *Collected Works. Volume 11. Marx and Engels: 1851–53*. New York, International Publishers, 103–97.

Marx, K. and F. Engels (1978) "Manifesto of the Communist Party," in *Collected Works. Volume 6. Marx and Engels: 1845–48*. New York, International Publishers, 477–517.

Marxsen, W. (1968) *Introduction to the New Testament*. Tr. G. Buswell. Philadelphia, PA.

Maso, S. (1999) *Lo sguardo della Verità. Cinque studi su Seneca*. Padua.

Masters, J. (1992) *Poetry and Civil War in Lucan's* Bellum Ciuile. Cambridge.

Masters, J. (1999) Review of Bartsch 1997. *Classical Review* 49.2:401–2.

Mastroroberto, M. (2003) "Una visita di Nerone a Pompei: le deversoriae tabernae di Moregine," in *Storie da un'eruzione: Pompei, Ercolano, Oplontis*, eds. A. d'Ambrosio, P. G. Guzzo, and M. Mastroroberto, 479–523. Pompeii and Milan.

Mastroroberto, M. (2007) "L'aurea aetas neronia sulle pareti dipinte di Moregine a Pompei," in *Rosso Pompeiano: la decorazione pittorica nelle collezioni del Museo di Napoli e a Pompei*, eds. M. L. Nava, R. Paris, and R. Friggeri, 60–73. Naples.

Mattingly, D. J. (2007) *An Imperial Possession: Britain in the Roman Empire*. London.

Mattingly. H. (1923) *Coins of the Roman Empire in the British Museum, vol. 1: Augustus to Vitellius*. London.

Mattusch, C. C. (2008) *Pompeii and the Roman Villa: Art and Culture around the Bay of Naples*. Washington, DC, and London.

Matz, A. (2010) *Satire in and Age of Realism*. Cambridge.

Mayer, F. A. (1982) "What Caused Poppaea's Death?" *Historia* 31: 248–9.

Mayer, R. (1981) *Lucan: Civil War VIII* (Aris & Phillips Classical Texts) (Bk.8) (Latin Edition).

Mayer, R. (1982) "Neronian Classicism," *American Journal of Philology* 103: 305–18.

Mayer, R. (1994) "Personata Stoa: Neostoicism and Senecan Tragedy," *Journal of the Warburg and Courtauld Institutes* 57: 151–74.

Mayer, R. (2006) "Latin Pastoral after Virgil," in *Brill's Companion to Greek and Latin Pastoral*, eds. M. Fantuzzi and T. Papanghelis, 451–66. Leiden.

Mazzoli, G. (1970) *Seneca e la poesia*. Milan.

Mazzoli, G. (2014) "The Chorus: Seneca as Lyric Poet," in *Brill's Companion to Seneca: Philosopher and Dramatist*, eds. G. Damschen and A. Heil, 561–74. Leiden.

McAlindon, D. (1956) "Senatorial Opposition to Claudius and Nero." *The American Journal of Philology* 77: 113–32.

McGinn, B. (2000) *Antichrist: Two Thousand Years of the Human Fascination with Evil*. New York. Originally 1994.

McGowan, A. (1994) "Eating People: Accusations of Cannibalism," in *Journal of Early Christian Studies* 2: 413–42.

McNelis C. (2012) "Persius, Juvenal, and Literary History after Horace," 239–61 in Braund and Osgood.

Meeks, W. A. (1983) *The First Urban Christians: The Social World of the Apostle Paul*. New Haven, CT.

Meeks, W. A. (2002) "Judgment and the Brother (Romans 14:1–15:13)," in *idem, In Search of the Early Christians*, eds. A. R. Hilton and H. G. Snyder, 153–66. New Haven, CT.

Meeks, W. A. (2003) *The First Urban Christians: The Social World of the Apostle Paul*. 2nd ed. New Haven, CT.

Meeks, W. A. (2013) "From Jerusalem to Illyricum, Rome to Spain: The World of Paul's Missionary Imagination," in *The Rise and Expansion of Christianity in the First*

Three Centuries of the Common Era, eds. C. K. Rothschild and J. Schröter. WUNT 301, 167–81. Tübingen.

Meeks, W. A. and J. T. Fitzgerald eds. (2007) *The Writings of St. Paul: Annotated Texts, Reception and Criticism*. 2nd ed. Norton Critical Editions. New York.

Megow, W. R. (1987) *Kameen von Augustus bis Alexander Severus (Antiken Münzen und Geschnittene Steine 11.)* Berlin.

Megow, W. R. (1993) "Zum Florentiner Tituskameo," *Archäologisches Anzeiger*: 401–8.

Megow, W. R. (2011) "Spätantike Herrscherkameen. Beobachtung zum konstantinischen "Klassizismus," *Jahreshefte des österreichisschen archäologischen Institutes in Wien* 80: 167–241.

Meier, M. (2008) "Qualis artifex pereo. Neros letzte Reise," *HZ* 286: 561–608.

Mellor, R. (2003) "The New Aristocracy of Power," in *Flavian Rome Culture, Image, Text*, eds. A. J. Boyle and W. J. Dominik, 69–101. Leiden, Brill.

Meneghini, R., A. Corsaro, and B. Pinna Caboni (2009) "Il Templum Pacis alla luce dei recenti scavi," *in Divus Vespasianus. Il biemillenario dei Flavi*, ed. F. Coarelli, 190–201. Milan.

Méthy, N. (2000) "Néron: mage ou monstre? Sur un passage de Pline l'Ancien (NH30, 14–17)," *RhM* 143.3–4:381–99.

Meyboom, P. G. P. (1984) "Fabullus démasqué," in *Om de tuin geleid. Feestbundel Prof. Dr. W.J.T. Peters*, 31–9. Nijmegen.

Meyboom, P. G. P. (1995) "Famulus and the Painters' Workshops of the Domus Aurea," *Mededelingen van het Nederlands Instituut te Rome* 54: 229–44.

Meyboom, P. G. P. and E. M. Moormann (2013) *Le decorazioni dipinte e marmoree della domus aurea di Nerone a Roma (2 vols.)*. Leuven and Paris.

Miles, M. (2008) *Art as Plunder. The Ancient Origins of Debate about Cultural Property*. Cambridge.

Miola, R. (1992) *Shakespeare and Classical Tragedy: The Influence of Seneca*. Oxford.

Mitchell, M. M. (2002) *The Heavenly Trumpet: John Chrysostom and the Art of Pauline Interpretation*. Louisville, KY.

Mitthof, F. ed. (2002) *Griechische Texte XVI: Neue Dokumente aus römischen und spätantiken Ägypten zu Verwaltung und Reichsgeschichte*. CPR 23. Vienna.

Moles, J. (1990) "The Kingship Orations of Dio Chrysostom," *Papers of the Leeds Latin Seminar* 6: 297–375.

Moltesen, M. and A. M. Nielsen (2007) *Agrippina Minor. Life and Afterlife*. Copenhagen.

Momigliano, A. (1934) "Nero," in *Cambridge Ancient History* X, eds. S. A. Cook, F. E. Adcock, and M. P. Charlesworth, 702–42. Cambridge.

Montaigne, M. de (1991) *The Complete Essays*, tr. M. A. Screech. London.

Monteleone, C. (1991) *Il Thyestes di Seneca. Sentieri ermeneutici*. Fasano.

Monti, C. M. (2003) "Seneca 'preceptor morum incomparabilis'? La posizione di Petrarca," in *Motivi e forme delle Familiari di Francesco Petrarca*, ed. C. Berra, 189–228. Milan.

Moormann, E. M. (1995) "Domus Aurea; Domus Tiberiana," in *Lisippo: l'arte e la fortuna*, ed. P. Moreno, 308–9. Milan.

Moreno, P. and A. Viacava (2003) *Galleria Borghese. Le Sculture Antiche*. Rome.

Morford, M. (1967) *The Poet Lucan: Studies in Rhetorical Epic*. Oxford.

Morford, M. (1984) *Persius*. Boston, MA.

Morgan, G. (2000) "Clodius Macer and Calvia Crispinilla," *Historia* 49: 467–87.

Morgan, L. (1999) *Patterns of Redemption in Virgil's "Georgics."* Cambridge.

Moss, C. R. (2012) *Ancient Christian Martyrdom: Diverse Practices, Theologies, and Traditions*. New Haven, CT.

Moss, C. R. (2013) *The Myth of Persecution: How Early Christians Invented a Story of Martyrdom*. New York.

Most, G. W. (1992) "*Disiecti membra poetae*: The Rhetoric of Dismemberment in Neronian Poetry," in Hexter and Selden 1992: 391–419.

Mowbray, C. (2012) "Captive Audience? The Aesthetics of *Nefas* in Senecan Drama," in *Aesthetic Value in Classical Antiquity*, eds. I. Sluiter and R. Rosen, 393–420. Leiden.

Mucha, R. (2014) "Ein flavischer Nero: Zur Domitian-Darstellung und Datierund der Johannesoffenbarung," *New Testament Studies* 60: 83–105.

Narducci, E. (1979) *La provvidenza crudele. Lucano e la distruzione dei miti augustei*. Pisa.

Narducci, E. (2002) *Lucano: un'epica contro l'impero: interpretazione della Pharsalia*. Rome.

Neudecker, R. (2015) "Collecting Culture: Statues and Fragments in Roman Gardens," in *Museum Archetypes and Collecting in the Ancient World* (*Monumenta Graeca et Romana* 21), eds. M. Wellington Gahtan and D. Pergazzano, 129–36. Leiden.

Newlands, C. E. ed. (2011a) *Statius: Siluae, Book II*. Cambridge Greek and Latin Classics. Cambridge.

Newlands, C. E. (2011b) "The First Biography of Lucan: Statius' *Siluae* 2.7," in Asso 2011: 435–51.

Newman, R. J. (2008) "In *umbra virtutis. Gloria* in the Thought of Seneca the Philosopher," in Fitch ed., 316–34 [first published in *Eranos* 86 (1988): 145–59].

Nichols, M. F. (2013) "Persius," in Buckley and Dinter 2013: 258–74.

Nisbet, R. G. M. (2008) "The Dating of Seneca's Tragedies with Special Reference to the *Thyestes*," in Fitch, ed. 348–71 [first published in *Papers of the Leeds International Latin Seminar 6* (1990): 95–114].

Noreña, C. (2003) "Medium and Message in Vespasian's *Templum Pacis*," *Memoirs of the American Academy in Rome* 48: 25–43.

Noreña, C. (2007) "The Social Economy of Pliny's Correspondence with Trajan," *AJP* 128: 239–77.

North, J. (2000) *Roman Religion (Greece and Rome: New Surveys in the Classics 30)*. Oxford.

Nuffelen, P. van (2012) *Orosius and the Rhetoric of History*. Oxford.

Nussbaum, M. (1994) *The Therapy of Desire: Theory and Practice in Hellenistic Ethics*. Princeton, NJ.

O'Gorman, E. (2000) *Irony and Misreading in the Annals of Tacitus*. Cambridge.

O'Higgins, D. (1988) "Lucan as 'Vates,'" *Classical Antiquity* 7: 208–26.

Oliensis, E. (1998) *Horace and the Rhetoric of Authority*. Cambridge.

Osgood, J. (2011) *Claudius Caesar: Image and Power in the Early Roman Empire*. Cambridge.

Owen, M. and I. Gildenhard (2013) *Tacitus, Annals, 15.20–23, 33–45*. Cambridge. http://dx.doi.org/10.11647/OBP.0035.

Packer, J. (2003) "*Plurima et Amplissima Opera*: Parsing Flavian Rome," in *Flavian Rome. Culture, Image, Text*, eds. A. J. Boyle and W. J. Dominik, 167–98. Leiden.

Pagan, V. (2004) *Conspiracy Narratives in Roman History*. Austin, TX.

Pagels, E. (2012) *Revelations: Visions, Prophecy, and Politics in the Book of Revelations*. New York.

Palombini, D. (1993) "Amphitheatrum Neronis," in *Lexicon Topographicum Urbis Romae*, ed. M. Steinby, 36. Rome.

Panayotakis, C. (1995) *Theatrum Arbitri: Theatrical Elements in the Satyrica of Petronius*. Leiden.

Panella, C. (2011a) "La Domus Aurea nella valle del Colosseo e sulle pendici della Velia e del Palatino," in *Nerone*, eds. M. Tomei and R. Rea, 160–9. Milan.

Panella, C. (2011b) "Nerone e il grande incendio del 64 d.C.," in *Nerone*, eds. Tomei and Rea, 76–91.

Panella, C. and F. Ferrandes (2013) "Gli Interventi Flavi tra trasformazione e continuità," in *Scavare nel Centro. Sorie Uomini Paesaggi*, ed. C. Panella, 115–24. Rome.

Panoussi, V. (2009) *Greek Tragedy in Vergil's "Aeneid."* Cambridge.

Pappalardo, U. (2009) *The Splendor of Roman Wall Painting*. Los Angeles, CA.

Parke, H. W. (1988) *Sibyls and Sibylline Prophecy in Classical Antiquity*. London.

Paschalis, M. (1982) "Two Horatian Reminiscences in the Proem of Lucan," *Mnemosyne* 35: 342–6.

Peirano, I. (2013) "*Non subripiendi causa sed palam mutuandi*: Intertextuality and Literary Deviancy between Law, Rhetoric, and Literature in Roman Imperial Culture," *American Journal of Philology* 134: 83–100.

Penwill, J. (2003) "Expelling the Mind: Politics and Philosophy in Flavian Rome," in *Flavian Rome: Culture, Image, Text*, eds. A. J. Boyle and W. Dominik, 345–68. Leiden.

Perrin, Y. (1982) "Être mythiques, fantastiques et grotesques dans la Domus Aurea," *Dialogues d'Histoire Ancienne* 8: 303–38.

Perrin, Y. (1987) "La Domus Aurea et l'idéologie néronienne," in *Le système palatial en Orient, en Grèce et à Rome. Actes du colloque de Strasbourg 19–22 juin 1985*, ed. E. Lévy 359–91. Leiden.

Perrin, Y. (2002) "IVe style, culture et société à Rome. Propositions pour une lecture historique de la peinture murale d'époque néronienne," in *Neronia VI. Rome à l'époque néronienne. Institutions et vie politique, économie et société, vie intellectuelle, artistique et spirituelle. Actes di Vie colloque international de la SIEN (Rome, 19–23 mai 1999)*, eds. J. M. Croisille and Y. Perrin, 384–404. Brussels.

Perutelli, A. (2000) *La poesia epica latina: dalle origini all'età dei Flavi*. Rome.

Pervo, R. I. (2009) *Acts: A Commentary*. Hermeneia Commentary Series. Minneapolis, MN.

Pervo, R. I. (2010) *The Making of Paul: Constructions of the Apostle in Early Christianity*. Minneapolis, MN.

Peters, F. E. (1994) *Muhammad and the Origins of Islam*. Albany, NY.

Petrarca, F. (1910) *Petrarch's Letters to Classical Authors*, tr. M. Cosenza. Chicago, IL.

Petrarca, F. (1933–42) *Le familiari*, ed. V. Rossi, 4 vols. Florence.

Petrarca, F. (1975–85) *Letters on Familiar Matters*, tr. A. S. Bernardo, 3 vols., Albany, NY.

Petrarca, F. (2003) *Invectives*, tr. D. Marsh. Cambridge, MA.

Petrone, G. (1986–7) "Paesaggio dei morti e paesaggio del male in Seneca tragico," *Quaderni di Cultura e di Tradizione Classica* 4–5: 131–43.

Picard, G. C. (1962) *Auguste et Néron. Le secret de l'empire*. Paris.

Piecha, R. (2003) "Wenn Frauen baden gehen...: Agrippinas Ende bei Tac. ann. 14, 1–13," in *"Altera Ratio": Klassische Philologie zwischen Subjektivität und Wissenschaft*, ed. M. Von Schauer, 120–35. Stuttgart.

Platz-Horster, G. (2001) "Agrippina Minor, die obsolete Mutter," *Bonner Jahrbücher* 201: 53–68.

Plavinskaia, Nadejda: (1988) "Catherine II ébauche le *Nakaz*. Premières notes de lecture de *L'Esprit des lois*," *Revue Montesquieu* 2: 67–88.

Plaza, Maria (2008) *The Function of Humour in Roman Verse Satire*. Oxford.

Plaza, Maria (2009) *Persius and Juvenal*. Oxford.

Pollard, E. A. (2009) "Pliny's Natural History and the Flavian Templum Pacis: Botanical Imperialism in First Century C.E. Rome," *Journal of World History* 20: 309–38.

Pollini, J. (1984) "Damnatio Memoriae in Stone: Two Portraits of Nero Recut to Vespasian in American Museums," *AJA* 88: 547–55.

Pollini, J. (2007) "Christian Desecration and Mutilation of the Parthenon," *MDAI(A)* 122: 207–28.

Pollini, J. (2008) "Gods and Emperors in the East: Images of Power and the Power of Intolerance," in *The Sculptural Environment of the Roman Near East: Reflections on Culture, Ideology, and Power (Interdisciplinary Studies in Ancient Culture and Religion)*, eds. E. A. Friedland, S.C. Herbert, and Y. Z. Eliav, 165–96. Leuven.

Pollini, J. (2012) *From Republic to Empire: Rhetoric, Religion, and Power in the Visual Culture of Ancient Rome*. Norman, OK.

Pollini, J. (2013) "The Archaeology of Destruction: Christians, Images of Classical Antiquity, and Some Problems of Interpretation," in *The Archaeology of Violence: Interdisciplinary Approaches*, ed. S. Ralph, 241–65. Albany, NY.

Pollini, J. (forthcoming) *Christian Destruction and Desecration of Images of Classical Antiquity*.

Potter, D. and R. Talbert eds. (2011) "Classical Courts and Courtiers," *AJP* 132.1 (special issue).

Power, T. (2010) "Pliny, *Letters* 5.10 and the Literary Career of Suetonius," *JRS* 100: 140–62.

Power, T. (2014) "Suetonius' Tacitus," *JRS* 104: 205–25.

Power, T. and R. K. Gibson eds. (2014) *Suetonius the Biographer. Studies in Roman Lives*. Oxford.

Prag, J. and I. Repath eds. (2009) *Petronius: A Handbook*. Chichester.

Prusac, M. (2011a) *From Face to Face. Recarving of Roman Portraits and the Late-Antique Portrait Arts (Monuenta Graeca et Romana 18)*. Leiden.

Prusac, M. (2011b) "The Missing Portraits from the Augusteum at Narona," *Zbornik Katčć Acta Provinciae SS. Redemptoris Ordinis Fratrum Minorum in Croatia, Miscellanea Emilio Marin Sexagenario Dicata*, vols. 41–3, ed. I. Jurišić G.H., 509–34. Split.

Pucci, G. (2011) "Nerone Superstar," in *Nerone*, eds. M. Tomei and R. Rea, 62–75. Milan.

Purcell, N. (1987) "Town in Country and Country in Town," in *Ancient Roman Villa Gardens*, ed. E. B. MacDougall, 185–203. Washington, DC.

Putnam, M. C. J. (1995) "Virgil's Tragic Future: Senecan Drama and the *Aeneid*," in *Vergil's Aeneid: Interpretation and Influence*, 246–85. London.

Quint, D. (1993) *Epic and Empire: Politics and Generic Form from Virgil to Milton*. Princeton, NJ.

Ranieri Panetta, M. (2011) "Fine di una dinastia. La morte di Nerone," in *Nerone*, eds. M. Tomei and R. Rea, 26–35. Milan.

Rapske, B. (1994) *The Book of Acts and Paul in Roman Custody*. The Book of Acts in Its First Century Setting 3. Grand Rapids, MI.

Rathbone, D. (1996) "The Imperial Finances," in *The Cambridge Ancient History* vol. 10, eds. A. K. Bowman et al., 309–23. Cambridge.

Rathbone, D. (2008) "Nero's Reforms of *Vectigalia* and the Inscription of the *Lex Portorii Asiae*," in *The Customs Law of Asia*, eds. M. Cottier et al., 251–78. Oxford.

Rea, R. (2011) "Nerone, le arti e i ludi," in *Nerone*, eds. M. Tomei and R. Rea, 202–17. Milan.

Reasoner, M. (1999) *The Strong and the Weak: Romans 14:1–15:13 in Context*. SNTSMS 103. Cambridge.

Reckford, K. (1962) "Studies in Persius," *Hermes* 90: 476–504.

Reckford, K. (1998) "Reading the Sick Body: Decomposition and Morality in Persius' Third Satire," *Arethusa* 31.3: 337–54.

Reckford, K. (2009) *Recognizing Persius*. Princeton, NJ.

Relihan, J. (1989) "The Confessions of Persius," *Illinois Classical Studies* 14: 145–67.

Reumann, J. (2008) *Philippians: A New Translation with Introduction and Commentary*. Anchor Yale Bible Commentary Series 38b. New Haven, CT.

Richardson, L., Jr. 1992. *A New Topographical Dictionary of Ancient Rome*. Baltimore, MD.

Riemer, A. F. (2007) "The Description of Palace in Seneca Thy, 641–682 and the Literary Unit of the Play," *Mnemosyne* 60: 427–42.

Riesner, R. (1998) *Paul's Early Period: Chronology, Mission Strategy*, Theology. Tr. D. Stott. Grand Rapids, MI.

Rimell, V. (2002) *Petronius and the Anatomy of Fiction*. Cambridge.

Rimell, V. (2007) "Petronius' Lessons in Learning – The Hard Way," in *Ordering Knowledge in the Roman Empire*, eds. J. König and T. Whitmarsh, 108–32. Cambridge.

Rimell, V. (2012) "The Labour of Empire: Womb and World in Seneca's *Medea*," *Studi Italiani di Filologia Classica* 10: 211–38.

Ripat, P. (2011) "Expelling Misconceptions: *Astrologers at Rome*," *CP* 106: 115–54.

Ripoll, F. (1999) "Aspects et functions de Néron dans la propagande flavienne," in *Neronia V. Néron: histoire et légende (Collection Latomus 247)*, eds. J. M. Corisille, R. Martin, and Y. Perrin, 137–51. Brussels.

Roby, C. A. (2014) "Seneca's Scientific Fictions: Models as Fictions in the *Natural Questions*," *JRS* 104: 155–80.

Roche, P. ed. (2009) *Lucan: De Bello Ciuili, Book I*. Oxford.

Rodríguez-Almeida, E. (1994) "Marziale in Marmo," *MEFRA* 106: 197–217.

Roetzel, C. J. (1998) *Paul: The Man and the Myth*. Columbia, SC.

Roetzel, C. J. (2009) *The Letters of Paul: Conversations in Context*. 5th ed. Louisville, KY.

Roller, R. (2001) *Constructing Autocracy: Aristocrats and Emperors in Julio-Claudian Rome*. Princeton, NJ.

Roman, L. (2014) *Poetic Autonomy in Ancient Rome*. Oxford.

Romm, Jamie. (2014) *Dying Every Day: Seneca at the Court of Nero*. New York.

Ronell, A. (2002) *Stupidity*. Urbana, IL.

Rordorf, W. W. (1993) "Die neronische Christenverfolgung im Spiegel der apokryphen Paulusakten," in idem, *Lex orandi, lex credendi: Gesammelte Aufsätze zum 60. Geburtstag*, eds. D. Van Damme and O. Wermelinger. Paradosis 36, 368–77. Freiburg.

Rosati, G. (1999) "Trimalchio on Stage," in *Oxford Readings in the Roman Novel*, ed. S. J. Harrison, 85–104. Oxford.

Rosati, G. (2002) "La scena del potere. Retorica del paesaggio nel teatro di Seneca," in *Hispania terris omnibus felicior*, ed. G. Urso, 225–39. Cividale del Friuli.

Rose, C. B. (1997) *Dynastic Commemoration and Imperial Portraiture in the Julio-Claudian Period*. Cambridge.

Rose, K. (1971) *The Date and Author of the Satyricon*. Leiden.

Rose, K. F. C. (1966) "Problems of Chronology in Lucan's Career," *Transactions and Proceedings of the American Philological Association* 97: 379–96.

Rosner-Siegel, J. A. (1983) "The Oak and the Lightning: Lucan, *Bellum Ciuile* 1. 135–157," *Athenaeum* 61: 165–77. Reprinted in Tesoriero 2010: 184–200.

Rosso, E. (2008) "Le destins mutiples de la *Domus Aurea*. L'exploitation de la condamnation de Néron dans l'idéologie flavienne," in *Un Discours en Images de la Condamnation de la Mémoire. Centre Régional Universitaire Lorrain D'Histoire Site de Metz*, eds. S. Benoist and A. Daguet-Gagey, 43–78. Metz.

Rubiés, J.-P. (1994) "Nero in Tacitus and Nero in Tacitism: The Historian's Craft," in *Reflections of Nero*, eds. Elsner and Masters, 29–47. Chapel Hill, NC, and London.

Rubinstein, N. (1958) "Political Ideas in Sienese Art: The Frescoes by Ambrogio Lorenzetti and Taddeo di Bartolo in the Palazzo Pubblico," *Journal of the Warburg and Courtauld Institutes* 21: 179–207.

Rudd, Niall (1976) "Association of Ideas in Persius," in *Lines of Inquiry*. Cambridge.

Rudd, Niall (1993, first ed. 1973), tr. *The Satires of Horace and Persius*. Harmondsworth.

Rudich, V. (1993) *Political Dissidence under Nero: The Price of Dissimulation*. London and New York.

Rudich, V. (1997) *Dissidence and Literature under Nero*. Routledge.

Rulhières, C. C. de. (1797) *Histoire ou Anecdotes sur la Révolution de Russie en l'année 1762*, Paris.

Rutgers, L. V. (1998) "Roman Policy Toward the Jews: Expulsions from the City of Rome during the First Century C.E.," in Donfried and Richardson 1998: 93–116.

Rutledge, S. (2001) *Imperial Inquisitions: Prosecutors and Informants from Tiberius to Domitian*. New York.

Rutledge, S. (2012) *Ancient Rome as a Museum. Power, Identity, and Culture of Collecting*. Oxford.

Sabbadini, R (1898) *"Dione Cassio nel secolo XV," in Studi italiani di filologia classica* 6: 397–406.

Saint-Just, L.-A. de. (1984) *Œuvres complètes*; ed. M. Duval. Paris.

Salmon, J. H. M. (1991) "Seneca and Tacitus in Jacobean England," in *The Mental World of the Jacobean Court*, ed. L. Peck, 169–88. Cambridge.

Sampley, J. P. (1995) "The Weak and the Strong: Paul's Careful and Crafty Rhetorical Strategy in Romans 14:1–15:13," in *The Social World of the First Christians: Essays in Honor of Wayne A. Meeks*, eds. L. M. White and O. L. Yarbrough, 40–52. Minneapolis, MN.

Sande, S. (1996) "*Qualis artifex*. Theatrical Influences on Neronic Fashions," *SymbOslo* 71: 135–46.

Sanford, E. M. (1931) "Lucan and His Roman Critics," *Classical Philology* 26.3: 233–57.

Sansone, D. (1986) "Atticus, Suetonius and Nero's Ancestors," in *Studies in Latin Literature and Roman History* vol. IV, ed. C. Deroux, 269–77. Brussels.

Santangeli Valenzani, R. and R. Volpe (1986) "Ambienti tra Via Nova e Clivo Palatino," *BCAR* 91: 411–23.

Sauer, E. (2003) *The Archaeology of Religious Hatred in the Roman and Early Medieval World.* Gloucestershire.

Scheithauer, A. (2000) *Kaiserliche Bautätigkeit in Rom. Das Echo in der antiken Literatur. (Heidelberger Althistorishe Beiträge und Epigraphische Studien 32).* Stuttgart.

Schellhase, K. C. (1976) *Tacitus in Renaissance Political Thought.* Chicago.

Scherer, P. (2008) "Agrippina minor als Concordia?: Bemerkungen zu den imperialen Reliefs am Sebasteion in Aphrodisias," in *Thiasos: Festschrift für Erwin Pochmarski zum 65. Geburtstag*, ed. C. von Franek, 873–84. Vienna.

Schiesaro, A. (2003) *The Passions in Play: Thyestes and the Dynamics of Senecan Drama.* Cambridge.

Schiesaro, A. (2006) "A Dream Shattered? Pastoral Anxieties in Senecan Drama," in *Brill's Companion to Greek and Latin Pastoral*, eds. M. Fantuzzi and T. Papanghelis, 427–49. Leiden.

Schlegel, C. (2000) "Horace and His Fathers: Satires 1.4 and 1.6," *American Journal of Philology* 121: 93–119.

Schmeling, G. (2003) "No One Listens: Narrative and Background Noise in the *Satyrica*," in *Petroniana: Gedenkschrift für Hubert Petersmann*, eds. J. Herman and R. Rosen, 183–92. Heidelberg.

Schmeling, G. (2011) *A Commentary on the Satyrica of Petronius.* Oxford.

Schmidt, E. A. (2014) "Space and Time in Senecan Drama," in *Brill's Companion to Seneca: Philosopher and Dramatist*, eds. G. Damschen and A. Heil, 531–46. Leiden.

Schneider, R. M. (2002) "Gegenbilder im römischen Kaiserporträt. Die neuen Gesichter Neros und Vespasians," in *Das Porträt vor der Erfindung des Porträts. Beiträge des Internationalen Kolloquiums des Kunstgeschichtlichen Instituts der Universität Frankfurt, Frankfurt 4.–6. Juni 1999*, eds. M. Büchsel and P. Schmidt, 59–76. Mainz am Rhein.

Schofield, M. (1991) *The Stoic Idea of the City.* Cambridge.

Schofield, M. (1999) *Saving the City. Philosopher-Kings and Other Classical Paradigms.* London.

Schofield, M. (2015) "Seneca on Monarchy and the Political Life: *De Clementia, De Tranquillitate Animi, De Otio*," in *The Cambridge Companion to Seneca*, eds. S. Bartsch and A. Schiesaro, 68–81. Cambridge.

Schollmeyer, P. (2005) *Römische Plastik. Eine Einführung.* Darmstadt.

Schönegg, B. (1999) *Senecas epistulae morales als philosophisches Kunstwerk.* Bern.

Schubert, C. (1998) *Studien zum Nerobild in der lateinischen Dictung der Antike.* Beiträge zur Altertumskunde 116. Stuttgart and Leipzig.

Scodel, R. and A. Bettenworth (2009) *Whither* Quo Vadis? *Sienkiewicz's Novel in Film and Television.* Oxford.

Scullard, H. H. (1982) *From the Gracchi to Nero: A History of Rome 133 BC to AD 68.* London.

Segal, C. P. (1959) "Ὕψος and the Problem of Cultural Decline in the *De Sublimitate*," *Harvard Studies in Classical Philology* 64: 121–46.

Segal, C. P. (1986) *Language and Desire in Seneca's Phaedra*. Princeton, NJ.
Seneca, Lucius Annaeus. (1778–9) *Les Oeuvres de Sénèque le Philosophe*, 7 vols., tr. N. Lagrange and J.-A. Naigeon, Paris.
Seneca, Lucius Annaeus. (1995) *Moral and Political Essays*, eds. and tr. J. M. Cooper and J. F. Procopé. Cambridge.
Seneca, Lucius Annaeus [pseudo]. (1581) *Octavia, in Seneca: His Tenne Tragedies Translated into Englysh by Thomas Marshe*, London, 1581. Cambridge.
Senneville-Grave, G. de, ed. and tr. (1999) Severus, Sulpicius, *Chroniques*. Introduction, texte critique, traduction et commentaire. Paris.
Seo, J. M. (2011) "Lucan's Cato and the Poetics of Exemplarity," in Asso 2011: 199–221.
Seo, J. M. (2013) *Exemplary Traits: Reading Characterization in Roman Poetry*. Oxford.
Serbat, G. (1986) "Pline l'Ancien: état présent des études sur sa vie, son œuvre et son influence," in *ANRW*, II, 32, 4, eds. W. Hasse and H. Temporini. Berlin.
Setaioli, A. (2000) *Facundus Seneca: aspetti della lingua e dell'ideologia senecana*. Bologna.
Setaioli, A. (2011) *Arbitri Nugae: Petronius' Short Poems in the Satyrica*. Peter Lang.
Setaioli, A. (2015) "Seneca and the Ancient World," in *The Cambridge Companion to Seneca*, eds. S. Bartsch and A. Schiesaro, 255–65. Cambridge.
Severy-Hoven, B. (2012) "Master Narratives and the Wall Painting of the House of the Vettii, Pompeii," *Gender & History* 24.3: 540–80.
Shaw, B. D. (2015) "The Myth of the Neronian Persecution," *JRS* 105: 73–100.
Sherard, R. H. (1916) *The Real Oscar Wilde*. London.
Sherwin-White, A. N. (1966) *The Letters of Pliny: A Historical and Social Commentary*. Oxford.
Shoemaker, S. J. (2016) "The Afterlife of the Apocalypse of John in Byzantium," in *The New Testament in Byzantium*, eds. D. Krueger and R. S. Nelson, 301–6 Washington, DC.
Shumate, N. (1997) "Compulsory Pretense and the 'Theatricalization of Experience' in Tacitus," in *Studies in Latin Literature and Roman History* vol. VIII, ed. C. Deroux. Brussels.
Skinner, Q. (1978) *The Foundations of Modern Political Thought*, 2 vols. Cambridge.
Skinner, Q. (2002). *Visions of Politics*, 3 vols. Cambridge.
Sklenář, R. (1999) "Nihilistic Cosmology and Catonian Ethics in Lucan's *Bellum Ciuile*," *American Journal of Philology* 120.2: 281–96.
Slater, N. W. (1994) "Calpurnius and the Anxiety of Vergilian Influence: *Eclogue* I," *Syllecta Classica* 5: 71–8.
Slingerland, H. D. (1997) *Claudian Policymaking and the Early Imperial Repression of Judaism at Rome*. South Florida Studies in the History of Judaism 160. Atlanta, GA.
Sloterdijk, P. (1987) *Critique of Cynical Reason*. Minneapolis, MN.
Smallwood, E. M. (1959) "The Alleged Jewish Sympathies of Poppaea," *Journal of Theological Studies* 10: 329–35.
Smallwood, E. M. (1967) *Documents Illustrating the Reigns of Tiberius, Gaius and Nero*. Cambridge.
Smallwood, E. M. (1981) *The Jews under Roman Rule from Pompey to Diocletian: A Study in Political Relations*. Leiden.
Smith, J. (2003) "Flavian Drama: Looking Back with Octavia," in *Flavian Rome. Culture, Image, Text*, eds. A. J. Boyle and W. J. Dominik, 391–430. Leiden.
Smith, M. (1978) *Jesus the Magician: Charlatan or Son of God?* New York.

Smith, R. R. R. (1987) "The Imperial Reliefs from the Sebasteion at Aphrodisias," *JRS* 77: 88–138.

Smith, R. R. R. (2000) "Nero and the Sun-God: Divine Accessories and Political Symbols in Roman Imperial Images," *Journal of Roman Archaeology* 13: 532–42.

Smolenaars, J. J. L. (1996) "The Literary Tradition of the *locus horridus* in Seneca's *Thyestes*," in *Studies of Greek and Roman Literature*, ed. J. Styka, 89–108. Krakow.

Smolenaars, J. J. L. (1998) "The Virgilian Background of Seneca's *Thyestes* 641–682," *Vergilius* 44: 51–65.

Snyder, G. E. (2013) *Acts of Paul: The Formation of a Pauline Corpus*. WUNT 2/352. Tübingen.

Spaeth, B. S. (1996) *The Roman Goddess Ceres*. Austin, TX.

Späth, T. (2000) "Skrupellose Herrscherin?: das Bild der Agrippina minor bei Tacitus," in *Frauenwelten in der Antike: Geschlechterordnung und weibliche Lebenspraxis*, eds, T. Späth and B. Wagner-Hasel, 262–81. Stuttgart.

Spencer, D. (2009) "Roman Alexanders: Epistemology and Identity," in *Alexander the Great: A New History*, eds. W. Heckel and L. Tritle, 251–74. Chichester.

Sperti, L. (1990) *Nerone e la "submissio" di Tiridate in un bronzetto da Opitergium (Rivista d'Arte Suppl. 8)*. Rome.

Spier, J. (2010) *Treasures of the Ferrel Collection*. Wiesbaden.

Spinola, G. (1996) *Guide Cataloghi Musei Vaticani 3. Il Museo Pio Clementino 1*. Rome.

Squire, M. (2013) "'Fantasies so Varied and Bizzare': The *Domus Aurea*, the Renaissance and the 'Grotesque,'" in *A Companion to the Neronian Age*, eds. Buckley and. Dinter, 444–64.

Stacey, P. (2007) *Roman Monarchy and the Renaissance Prince*. Cambridge.

Stacey, P. (2013) "Free and Unfree States in Machiavelli's Political Philosophy," in *Freedom and the Construction of Europe*, 2 vols., eds. Q. Skinner and M. van Gelderen, I:176–94. Cambridge.

Stacey, P. (2014) "The Princely Republic," *Journal of Roman Studies* 104: 133–54.

Stacey, P. (2015) "Senecan Political Thought from the Middle Ages to Early Modernity," in *The Cambridge Companion to Seneca*, eds. S. Bartsch and A. Schiesaro, 289–302.

Staley, G. (2002) "Seneca and Socrates," in *Noctes Atticae: 34. Articles on Graeco-Roman Antiquity and Its Nachleben: Studies Presented to J. Meyer on His Sixtieth Birthday*, ed. B. Amden, 281–5. Copenhagen.

Stark, R. (1996) *The Rise of Christianity: A Sociologist Reconsiders History*. Princeton.

Star, C. (2012) *The Empire of the Self. Self-Command and Political Speech in Seneca and Petronius*. Baltimore, MD.

Stemmer, K. (1978) *Untersuchungen zur Typologie, Chronologie und Ikonographie der Panzerstatuen (Antike Forschungen 4)*. Berlin.

Sternberg, R. H. (2006) *Tragedy Offstage: Suffering and Sympathy in Ancient Athens*. Austin, TX.

Stevens, G. L. (2014) *Revelation: The Past and Future of John's Apocalypse*. Eugene, OR.

Stinson, P. (2011) "Perspective Systems in Roman Second Style Wall Painting," *American Journal of Archaeology* 115.3: 403–26.

Stover, T. (2008) "Cato and the Intended Scope of Lucan's *Bellum Ciuile*," *Classical Quarterly* 58.2: 571–80.

Stowers, S. K. (1981) *The Diatribe and Paul's Letter to the Romans*. SBL Dissertation Series 57. Chico, CA.

Stowers, S. K. (1994) *A Rereading of Romans: Justice, Jews, and Gentiles*. New Haven, CT.

Strocka, V. M. (1994) "Neubeginn und Steigerung des Prinzipats. Zu den Ursachen des claudischen Stilwandels," in *Die Regierungszeit des Kaisers Claudius (41–54 n. Chr.). Umbruch oder Episode? Int. Symp. Freiburg i. Br. 1991*, ed. V. M. Strocka, 191–220. Mainz am Rhein.

Strocka, V. M. (2002) "Neros Statuenraub für die *Domus Aurea*. Zeitgenössische Reflexe," in *Neronia VI. Rome à l'époque néronienne: institutions et vie politique, économie et société, vie intetllectuelle, artistique et spirituelle. Actes du VIe Colloque international de la SIEN (Rome 19–23 mai 1999). CollLat 268*, eds. J. M. Croisille and Y. Perrin, 35–45. Brussels.

Strocka, V. M. (2007) "Domestic Decoration: Painting and the 'Four Styles,'" in *The World of Pompeii*, eds. J. H. Dobbins and P. Foss, 302–22. Andover.

Strocka, V. M. (2010) *Die Gefangenenfassade an der Agora von Korinth. Ihr Ort in der romischen Kunstgeschichte*. Regensburg.

Strugnell, A. (1973) *Diderot's Politics*. The Hague.

Sullivan, J. P. (1968) *The Satyricon of Petronius: A Literary Study*. London.

Sullivan, J. P. (1972) "In Defense of Persius," *Ramus* 1: 48–62.

Sullivan, J. P. (1978) "Ass's Ears and Attises," *AJP* 99: 159–70.

Sullivan, J. P. (1985) *Literature and Politics in the Age of Nero*. Ithaca, NY, and London.

Sutherland, C. H. V. (1984) *The Roman Imperial Coinage 1, from 31 BC to AD 69*. London.

Sydenham, E. A. (1920) *The Coinage of Nero*. London.

Syme, R. (1956) "The Senator as Historian," in *Histoire et historiens dans l'Antiquité*, eds., Vandoeuvres, foundation Hardt, entretiens sur l'Antiquité classique, IV: 185–201.

Syme, R. (1958) *Tacitus* Vol. I. Oxford.

Syme, R. (1970) "The Political Opinions of Tacitus," in *Ten Studies in Tacitus*, 119–40. Oxford.

Syme, R. (1983) *The Roman Revolution*. Oxford.

Syme, R. (1984) *Roman Papers*. Ed. A. R. Birley. Vol. III. Oxford.

Syme, R. (1986) *The Augustan Aristocracy*. Oxford.

Tacitus. (1965) *Annals*, ed. H. Furneaux, 2nd ed. Oxford.

Tacitus. (2009) *Annals, Histories, Agricola, Germania*, tr. A. J. Church and W. J. Brodribb, with an introduction by R. L. Fox. New York.

Talbert, R. J. A. (1984) *The Senate of Imperial Rome*. Chapel Hill, NC.

Talbert, R. J. A. (1996) "The Senate and Senatorial and Equestrian Posts," in *The Cambridge Ancient History* (2nd ed.) Vol. 10, eds. A. K. Bowman, E. Champlin, and A. Lintott, 324–43. Cambridge.

Tamm, B. (1970) *Neros Gymnasium in Rom. (Stockholm Studies in Classical Archaeology 7)*. Stockholm.

Tarrant, R. J. ed. (1985) *Seneca's Thyestes*. Atlanta, GA.

Tarrant, R. J. (1995) "Greek and Roman in Seneca's Tragedies," *Harvard Studies in Classical Philology* 97: 215–30.

Tesoriero, C. ed. (2010) *Oxford Readings in Classical Studies: Lucan*. Oxford.

Thomas, R. F. (2001) *Virgil and the Augustan Reception*. Cambridge.

Thompson, L., and R. T. Bruère (1968) "Lucan's Use of Virgilian Reminiscence," *Classical Philology* 63.1: 1–21. Reprinted in Tesoriero 2010: 107–48.

Thornton, M. K. and R. L. Thornton (1989) *Julio-Claudian Building Programs: A Quantitative Study in Political Management*. Wauconda, IL.

Thorsteinsson, R. M. (2003) *Paul's Interlocutor in Romans 2: Function and Identity in the Context of Ancient Epistolography*. Coniectanea Biblica NT Series 40. Stockholm.

Tipping, B. (2011) "Terrible Manliness?: Lucan's Cato," in Asso 2011: 223–36.

Tomei, A. M. and E. R. Rea eds. (2011) *Nerone. Catalogo della Mostra* (Roma, Colosseo, Curia Iulia e tempio di Romolo al Foro Romano, Criptoportico neroniano, "Domus Tiberiana," Museo Palatino, Vigna Barberini, Coenatio Rotunda, 12 aprile–18 settembre 2011). Milan.

Tomei, M. and R. Rea eds. (2011) *Nerone*. Milan.

Tomei, M. A. (1997) *Museo Palatino*. Rome.

Tomei, M. A. (1999) *Scavi Francesi sul Palatino. Le Indagini di Pietro Roas per Napoleone III (1861–1870)*. Rome

Tomei, M. A. (2011) "Nerone sul Palatino," in eds. Tomei and Rea, *Nerone*, 118–35.

Torelli, M. (2003) "Conclusioni," *Ostraka* 12: 285–90 = (2005) "Conclusioni," in *Moregine: Suburbio 'portuale' di Pompei*, ed. V. S. Ussani, 107–36. Naples.

Tortorici, E. (1993) "La Terrazza domizianea, l'*Aqua Marcia*, ed il taglio della sella tra Campidoglio e Quirinale," *Bolletino della Commissione Archeologica Communale in Roma* 95: 7–24.

Tracy, J. (2011) "Internal Evidence for the Completeness of the *Bellum Ciuile*," in Asso 2011: 33–53.

Tracy, J. (2014) *Lucan's Egyptian Civil War*. Cambridge.

Traina, A. (1987) *Lo stilo "drammatico" del filosofo Seneca*. Bologna.

Trebilco, P. (2012) *Self-Designations and Group Identity in the New Testament*. Cambridge.

Treggiari, S. (1973) "Domestic Staff at Rome in the Julio-Claudian Period, 27 B.C. to A.D. 68," *Social History/Histoire sociale* 12: 241–55.

Trillmich, W. (2007) "Typologie der Bildnisse der Iulia Agrippina," in *Agrippina Minor. Life and Afterlife*, eds. M. Moltesen and A. M. Nielsen, 45–66. Copenhagen.

Trinacty, C. V. (2014) *Senecan Tragedy and the Reception of Augustan Poetry*. Oxford.

Turpin, W. (2008) "Tacitus, Stoic exempla, and the *praecipuum munus annalium*," *Classical Antiquity* 27: 359–404.

Ulery, R. W., Jr. (1986) "Cornelius Tacitus," in *Catalogus Translationum et Commentariorum: Mediaeval and Renaissance Latin Translations and Commentaries: Annotated Lists and Guides*, vol. VI, ed. F. E. Cranz, 87–174. Washington, DC.

Valenti, M. (2005) "Tra storia e politica: l'Elogio di Nerone di Cardano," *Colloquium philosophicum* 8–9: 57–64.

Van Essen, C. C. (1954) "La topographie de la Domus Aurea Neronis," *Mededelingen der Koninklijke Nederlandse, Akademie van Wetenschappen, Afd. Letterkunde, Nieuwe Reeks*, 17, no. 12: 371–98.

Varner, E. R. (2000) "Grotesque vision: Seneca's Tragedies and Neronian art," in *Seneca in Performance*, ed. G. W. M. Harrison, 119–36. Duckworth.

Varner, E. R. (2004) *Mutilation and Transformation. Damnatio Memoriae and Roman Imperial Portraiture*. Leiden.

Varner, E. R. (2015) "Fluidity and Fluctuation: The Shifting Dynamics of Condemnation in Roman Imperial Portraits," in *Bodies in Transition. Dissolving the*

Boundaries of Embodied Knowledge. Morphomata 23, eds. D. Boschung, A. Shapiro, and F. Wascheck, 33–88. Cologne.

Vernant, J.-P. (1991, first published in French 1982) "A 'Beautiful Death' and the Disfigured Corpse in Homeric Epic," tr. A. Szegedy-Maszak, in *Mortals and Immortals: Collected Essays*, ed. F. I. Zeitlin, 50–74. Princeton, NJ.

Vernant, J.-P. (forthcoming) "Lucan, Statius and the Piercing Eroticism of War," in *A Companion to Latin Epic, 14–96 CE.*, eds. L. Fratantuono and C. Stark, Chichester.

Vervaet, F. J. (2002) "Domitius Corbulo and the Senatorial Opposition to the Reign of Nero," *Anc. Soc.* 32: 135–93.

Veyne, P. (2003) *Seneca: The Life of a Stoic*, tr. D. Sullivan. London.

Villedieu, F. (2011) "Une construction néronienne mise au jour sur le site de la Vigna Barberini: la cenatio rotunda de la Domus Aurea?" *Neronia Electronica* 1: 37–52.

Viscogliosi, A. (2011a) "'Qualis artifex pereo.' L'architettura neroniana," in *Nerone*, eds. M. Tomei and R. Rea, 92–107. Milan.

Viscogliosi, A. (2011b) "La Domus Aurea," in *Nerone*, eds. M. Tomei and R. Rea, 156–9. Milan.

Volk, K. and G. Williams eds. (2006) *Seeing Seneca Whole: Perspectives on Philosophy, Poetry and Politics.* Leiden.

Vollenweider, M. L. and M. Avisseau-Broustet (2003) *Camées et Intailles. Tome II. Les portraits romains du Cabinet des Médailles. Catalogue raisonné.* Paris.

Volpe, R. and A. Parisi (2009) "Alla ricerca di una coperta: Felice de Fredis e il luogo di ritrovamento del Laocoonte," *Bulletino Cmm* 110: 81–109.

Voltaire. (1968–77) *Correspondence and related documents.* Ed. Theodore Besterman. 51 vol. *Les Œuvres complètes de Voltaire.* Geneva, Banbury & Oxford: Institut et Musée Voltaire & Voltaire Foundation, 1968–77. *The Electronic Enlightenment Project.*

Voltaire. (1968–) *Notebooks*, in *Oeuvres complètes de Voltaire / Complete works of Voltaire*, eds. Ulla Kölving et al., Voltaire Foundation, vol. 82, 1968. Genève, Banbury, Oxford.

Voltaire. (1996) *Histoire de Charles XII* (*Preface of* 1748), *Oeuvres complètes de Voltaire / Complete works of Voltaire*, vol. 4.

Voltaire. (1999) *Histoire de l'empire de Russie*, (1763), *Oeuvres complètes de Voltaire / Complete works of Voltaire*, vol. 47.

Voltaire. (2007) *Le Pyrrhonisme de l'histoire* (1768), *in Oeuvres complètes de Voltaire / Complete works of Voltaire*, vol. 67.

von Albrecht, M. (1999) *Roman Epic: An Interpretative Introduction.* Leiden, Boston and Köln.

Vout, C. (2008) "The Art of *Damnatio Memoriae*," in*Un discours en images de la condemnation de mémoire. Centre régional Universitaire Lorrain d'histoire*, eds. S. Benoist and A. Daguet-Gagey, 153–72, Metz.

Vout, C. (2009) "The *Satyrica* and Neronian Culture," in eds. Prag and Redpath 2009: 101–13.

Vout, C. (2013) "Face to Face with Fiction: Portraiture and the Biographical Tradition," in *Fictions of Art History*, ed. M. Ledbury, 71–86. Williamstown, MA.

Walde, C. (2006) "Muses," *Brill's Encyclopaedia of the Ancient World: New Pauly*, 322–5. Leiden.

Wallace-Hadrill, A. (1982) "*Civilis princeps*: Between Citizen and King," *JRS* 72: 32–48.

Walsh, P. G. (1970) *The Roman Novel*. Cambridge.

Walsh, P. G. (tr.) (1996) *The Satyricon*. Oxford.

Walter, G. (1957) *Nero*. London.

Walters, J. C. (1993) *Ethnic Issues in Paul's Letter to the Romans: Changing Self-Definitions in Earliest Roman Christianity*. Valley Forge, PA.

Warmington, B. H. (1969) *Nero: Reality and Legend*. London.

Warmington, B. H. ed. (1999) *Suetonius/Nero*. 2nd ed. Bristol.

Wedderburn, A. J. M. (1988) *The Reasons for Romans*. Ed. J. Riches. Studies of the New Testament and Its World. Edinburgh.

Wehrle, William (1992) *The Satiric Voice: Program, Form, and Meaning in Persius and Juvenal*. Altertumswissenschaftliche Texte und Studien 23. Hildesheim.

Welch, K. (2002) "Nerone e i Flavi: dialoghi fra la *Domus Aurea* ed il Colosseo, il rtratto di Nerone di quarto tipo e l'immagine di Vespasiano," *Neronia VI. Rome à l'époque néroniennn: institutions et vie politique, économie et société, vie intetllectuelle, artistique et spirituelle Actes du VIe Colloque international de la SIEN (Rome 19–23 mai 1999) (CollLat 268)*, eds. J. M. Croisille and Y. Perrin, 123–40. Rome and Brussels.

West, D. (1990) *Virgil, The Aeneid*. Oxford.

Wheeler, S. (2002) "Lucan's Reception of Ovid's *Metamorphoses*," *Arethusa* 35: 361–80.

White, L. M. (1988) "Shifting Sectarian Boundaries in Early Christianity," *Bulletin of the John Rylands University Library of Manchester* 70: 7–24.

White, P. (2010) *Cicero in Letters: Epistolary Relations in the Late Republic*. Oxford.

Whitmarsh, T. (1999) "Greek and Roman in Dialogue: The Pseudo-Lucianic *Nero*," *JHS* 119: 142–60.

Whitton, C. (2012) "'Let us tread our path together': Tacitus and the Younger Pliny," in *A Companion to Tacitus*, ed. V. E. Pagán. Blackwell Companions to the Ancient World, 345–68. Malden, MA.

Whitton, C. (2013) "Seneca, *Apocolocyntosis*," in *A Companion to the Neronian Age*, eds. Buckley and Dinter, 151–69.

Wiedemann, T. E. J. (1996) "Tiberius to Nero," in *CAH*², 198–255.

Wiefel, W. (1991) "The Jewish Community in Ancient Rome and the Origins of Roman Christianity," in Donfried 1991: 85–101.

Wilken, R. L. (1984, 2nd ed. 2003) *The Christians as the Romans Saw Them*. New Haven, CT.

Wilkins, E. H. (1958) *Petrarch's Eight Years in Milan*. Cambridge, MA.

Wilkins, E. H. (1963) "Petrarch's *Exul ab Italia*," *Speculum* 38.3: 453–60.

Wille, G. (1967) *Musica romana: die Bedeutung der Musik im Leben der Römer*. Amsterdam.

Williams, G., ed. (2003) *Seneca De otio, de brevitate vitae*. Cambridge.

Williams, G. (2012) *The Cosmic Viewpoint: A Study of Seneca's "Natural Questions."* Oxford.

Williams, G. (2014) "Double-Vision and Cross-Reading in Seneca's *Epistulae morales* and *Naturales Quaestiones*," in *Seneca Philosophus*, eds. Colish and Wildberger, 135–66.

Williams, M. H. (1988) "Θεοσεβὴς γὰρ ἦν. The Jewish Tendencies of Poppaea Sabina," *JThS* 39: 97–111.

Williamson, G. A (tr.) (1989) *The History of the Church from Christ to Constantine/Eusebius*. Rev. A. Louth. London.

Wilson, A. N. (1997) *Paul: The Mind of the Apostle*. London.

Wilson, E. (2014) *The Greatest Empire: A Life of Seneca*. Oxford.

Wilson, M. (2001) "Seneca's Epistles Reclassified," in *Texts, Ideas and Classical Literature*, ed. S. J. Harrison, 164–88. Oxford.

Wildberger, J. and M. Colish. (2014) *Seneca philosophus*. Berlin.

Winkler, M. M. (2001) "The Roman Empire in American Cinema after 1945," in *Imperial Projections: Ancient Rome in Modern Popular Culture*, eds. S. R. Joshel, M. Malamud, and D. T. McGuire Jr., 50–76. Baltimore, MD.

Winkler, M. M. (2008) "Hollywood Presents the Roman Empire, 1951–1964: The Rhetoric of Cinematic Prologues," *CML* 28.1: 53–80.

Winkler, M. M. (2009) *The Roman Salute: Cinema, History, Ideology*. Columbus.

Winterling, A. (2009) *Politics and Society in Imperial Rome*. Malden, MA.

Wirszubski, C. (1950) *Libertas as a Political Idea at Rome during the Late Republic and Early Principate*. Cambridge.

Wiseman, T. P. (1982) "Calpurnius Siculus and the Claudian Civil War," *Journal of Roman Studies* 72: 57–67.

Wohl, V. (2002) *Love among the Ruins: The Erotics of Democracy in Classical Athens*. Princeton, NJ.

Wood, J. (2004) *The Irresponsible Self: On Laughter and the Novel*. New York.

Wood, S. (1999) *Imperial Women: A Study in Public Images, 40 B.C.–A.D. 68*. Leiden.

Woodman, A. J. (1992) "Nero's Alien Capital: Tacitus as Paradoxographer (Annals, 15, 36–7)," in *Author and Audience in Latin Literature*, eds. J. Powell and T. Woodman, 173–88. Cambridge.

Woodman, A. J. (1998) *Tacitus Reviewed*. Oxford.

Woodman, A. J. (2004) *Tacitus: The Annals*. Indianapolis, IN.

Woodman, A. J. (2009a) "Tacitus and the Contemporary Scene," in *The Cambridge Companion to Tacitus*, 31–44.

Woodman, A. J. ed. (2009b) *The Cambridge Companion to Tacitus*. Cambridge.

Wyke, M. (1997) *Projecting the Past: Ancient Rome, Cinema and History*. New York.

Zanker, P. (1979) "Galba, Nero, Nerva. Drei barocke Charakterstudien," in *Studies in Classical Art and Archaeology. A Tribute to Peter Heinrich von Blanckenhagen*, eds. M. B. Moore and G. Kopcke, 305–14. Locust Valley, NJ.

Zanker, P. (1988) *The Power of Images in the Age of Augustus*. Ann Arbor, MI.

Zanobi, A. (2008) *Seneca's Tragedies and the Aesthetics of Pantomime*. Durham University, Durham E-Theses Online: http://etheses.dur.ac.uk/2158/.

Zeitlin, F. I. (1971) "Petronius as Paradox: Anarchy and Artistic Integrity," *Transactions and Proceedings of the American Philological Association* 102: 631–84.

Zeitlin, F. I. (1990) "Thebes: Theater of Self and Society in Athenian Drama," in *Nothing to Do with Dionysos? Athenian Drama in Its Social Context*, eds. J. J. Winkler and F. I. Zeitlin, 130–67. Princeton, NJ.

Zissos, A. (2009) "Shades of Virgil: Seneca's *Troades*," *Materiali e Discussioni per l'analisi dei Testi Classici* 61: 191–210.

Zissos, A. (2016) *A Companion to the Flavian Age of Imperial Rome*. Malden, MA.

Žižek, S. (1989) *The Sublime Object of Ideology*. London.

Zwierlein, O. (1986) "Lucans Caesar in Troia," *Hermes* 114.4: 460–78. Reprinted as "Lucan's Caesar at Troy," in Tesoriero 2010: 411–32.

Zwierlein, O. (2009) *Petrus in Rom: Die literarischen Zeugnisse*. Untersuchungen zur antiken Literatur und Geschichte 96. Berlin.

Index